Ford
Probe
Automotive
Repair
Manual

by Mike Stubblefield
and John H Haynes
Member of the Guild of Motoring Writers

Models covered:

All Ford Probe models
1989 through 1990

ABCDE
FGHIJ
KLMNO
PQRST

Haynes Publishing Group
Sparkford Nr Yeovil
Somerset BA22 7JJ England

Haynes Publications, Inc
861 Lawrence Drive
Newbury Park
California 91320 USA

Acknowledgements

We are grateful for the help and cooperation of the Ford Motor Company for assistance with technical information and certain illustrations, and the Champion Spark Plug Company, who supplied the illustrations of various spark plug conditions. Technical writers who contributed to this project include Ken Freund.

A book in the **Haynes Automotive Repair Manual Series**

Printed by J.H. Haynes & Co., Ltd. Sparkford Nr. Yeovil, Somerset BA22 7JJ, England

ISBN 1 85010 670 3

Library of Congress Catalog Card Number 90-83972

Contents

1989 Ford Probe GT

About this manual

Its purpose

The purpose of this manual is to help you get the best value from your vehicle. It can do so in several ways. It can help you decide what work must be done, even if you choose to have it done by a dealer service department or a repair shop; it provides information and procedures for routine maintenance and servicing; and it offers diagnostic and repair procedures to follow when trouble occurs.

We hope you use the manual to tackle the work yourself. For many simpler jobs, doing it yourself may be quicker than arranging an appointment to get the vehicle into a shop and making the trips to leave it and pick it up. More importantly, a lot of money can be saved by avoiding the expense the shop must pass on to you to cover its labor and overhead costs. An added benefit is the sense of satisfaction and accomplishment that you feel after doing the job yourself.

Using the manual

The manual is divided into Chapters. Each Chapter is divided into numbered Sections, which are headed in bold type between horizontal lines. Each Section consists of consecutively numbered paragraphs.

At the beginning of each numbered section you will be referred to any illustrations which apply to the procedures in that section. The reference numbers used in illustration captions pinpoint the pertinent Section and the Step within that section. That is, illustration 3.2 means the illustration refers to Section 3 and Step (or paragraph) 2 within that Section.

Procedures, once described in the text, are not normally repeated. When it's necessary to refer to another Chapter, the reference will be given as Chapter and Section number. Cross references given without use of the word "Chapter" apply to Sections and/or paragraphs in the same Chapter. For example, "see Section 8" means in the same Chapter.

References to the left or right side of the vehicle assume you are sitting in the driver's seat, facing forward.

Even though we have prepared this manual with extreme care, neither the publisher nor the author can accept responsibility for any errors in, or omissions from, the information given.

NOTE

A **Note** provides information necessary to properly complete a procedure or information which will make the procedure easier to understand.

CAUTION

A **Caution** provides a special procedure or special steps which must be taken while completing the procedure where the **Caution** is found. Not heeding a **Caution** can result in damage to the assembly being worked on.

WARNING

A **Warning** provides a special procedure or special steps which must be taken while completing the procedure where the **Warning** is found. Not heeding a **Warning** can result in personal injury.

Introduction to the Ford Probe

All Ford Probes have two-door liftback body styles.

The transversely mounted inline four-cylinder and V6 engines used in these models are equipped with electronic fuel injection.

The engine drives the front wheels through either a five-speed manual or four-speed automatic transaxle via independent driveaxles.

Independent suspension, featuring coil springs and struts, is used on all four wheels. The power assisted rack and pinion steering unit is mounted behind the engine.

The brakes are disc at the front with either drums or discs at the rear, depending on model, with power assist standard.

Vehicle identification numbers

Modifications are a continuing and unpublicized process in vehicle manufacturing. Since spare parts manuals and lists are compiled on a numerical basis, the individual vehicle numbers are essential to correctly identify the component required.

Vehicle Identification Number (VIN)

This very important identification number is stamped on a plate attached to the dashboard inside the windshield on the driver's side of the vehicle **(see illustration)**. The VIN also appears on the Vehicle Certificate of Title and Registration. It contains information such as where and when the vehicle was manufactured, the model year and the body style.

Vehicle Certification Label

The Vehicle Certification Label is attached to the driver's side door pillar. Information on this label includes the name of the manufacturer, the month and year of production, the Gross Vehicle Weight Rating (GVWR), the Gross Axle Weight Rating (GAWR) and the certification statement.

Engine number

The engine number is stamped into a machined pad on the external surface of the engine block. On four-cylinder engines, it's located below the number one spark plug.

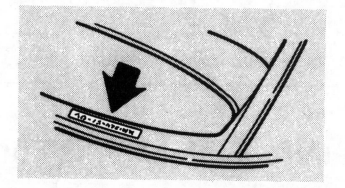

The Vehicle Identification Number (VIN) is visible from outside the vehicle through the driver's side of the windshield

Buying parts

Replacement parts are available from many sources, which generally fall into one of two categories – authorized dealer parts departments and independent retail auto parts stores. Our advice concerning these parts is as follows:

Retail auto parts stores: Good auto parts stores will stock frequently needed components which wear out relatively fast, such as clutch components, exhaust systems, brake parts, tune-up parts, etc. These stores often supply new or reconditioned parts on an exchange basis, which can save a considerable amount of money. Discount auto parts stores are often very good places to buy materials and parts needed for general vehicle maintenance such as oil, grease, filters, spark plugs, belts, touch-up paint, bulbs, etc. They also usually sell tools and general accessories, have con-venient hours, charge lower prices and can often be found not far from home.

Authorized dealer parts department: This is the best source for parts which are unique to the vehicle and not generally available else-where (such as major engine parts, transmission parts, trim pieces, etc.).

Warranty information: If the vehicle is still covered under warranty, be sure that any replacement parts purchased – regardless of the source – do not invalidate the warranty!

To be sure of obtaining the correct parts, have engine and chassis numbers available and, if possible, take the old parts along for positive identification.

Maintenance techniques, tools and working facilities

Maintenance techniques

There are a number of techniques involved in maintenance and repair that will be referred to throughout this manual. Application of these tech-niques will enable the home mechanic to be more efficient, better orga-nized and capable of performing the various tasks properly, which will ensure that the repair job is thorough and complete.

Fasteners

Fasteners are nuts, bolts, studs and screws used to hold two or more parts together. There are a few things to keep in mind when working with fasteners. Almost all of them use a locking device of some type, either a lockwasher, locknut, locking tab or thread adhesive. All threaded fasten-ers should be clean and straight, with undamaged threads and undam-aged corners on the hex head where the wrench fits. Develop the habit of replacing all damaged nuts and bolts with new ones. Special locknuts with nylon or fiber inserts can only be used once. If they are removed, they lose their locking ability and must be replaced with new ones.

Rusted nuts and bolts should be treated with a penetrating fluid to ease removal and prevent breakage. Some mechanics use turpentine in a spout-type oil can, which works quite well. After applying the rust pene-trant, let it work for a few minutes before trying to loosen the nut or bolt. Badly rusted fasteners may have to be chiseled or sawed off or removed with a special nut breaker, available at tool stores.

If a bolt or stud breaks off in an assembly, it can be drilled and removed with a special tool commonly available for this purpose. Most automotive machine shops can perform this task, as well as other repair procedures, such as the repair of threaded holes that have been stripped out.

Flat washers and lockwashers, when removed from an assembly, should always be replaced exactly as removed. Replace any damaged washers with new ones. Never use a lockwasher on any soft metal surface (such as aluminum), thin sheet metal or plastic.

Fastener sizes

For a number of reasons, automobile manufacturers are making wider and wider use of metric fasteners. Therefore, it is important to be able to tell the difference between standard (sometimes called U.S. or SAE) and metric hardware, since they cannot be interchanged.

All bolts, whether standard or metric, are sized according to diameter, thread pitch and length. For example, a standard 1/2 – 13 x 1 bolt is 1/2 inch in diameter, has 13 threads per inch and is 1 inch long. An M12 – 1.75 x 25 metric bolt is 12 mm in diameter, has a thread pitch of 1.75 mm (the distance between threads) and is 25 mm long. The two bolts are nearly identical, and easily confused, but they are not interchangeable.

In addition to the differences in diameter, thread pitch and length, metric and standard bolts can also be distinguished by examining the bolt heads. To begin with, the distance across the flats on a standard bolt head is measured in inches, while the same dimension on a metric bolt is sized in millimeters (the same is true for nuts). As a result, a standard wrench should not be used on a metric bolt and a metric wrench should not be

used on a standard bolt. Also, most standard bolts have slashes radiating out from the center of the head to denote the grade or strength of the bolt, which is an indication of the amount of torque that can be applied to it. The greater the number of slashes, the greater the strength of the bolt. Grades 0 through 5 are commonly used on automobiles. Metric bolts have a property class (grade) number, rather than a slash, molded into their heads to indicate bolt strength. In this case, the higher the number, the stronger the bolt. Property class numbers 8.8, 9.8 and 10.9 are commonly used on automobiles.

Strength markings can also be used to distinguish standard hex nuts from metric hex nuts. Many standard nuts have dots stamped into one side, while metric nuts are marked with a number. The greater the number of dots, or the higher the number, the greater the strength of the nut.

Metric studs are also marked on their ends according to property class (grade). Larger studs are numbered (the same as metric bolts), while smaller studs carry a geometric code to denote grade.

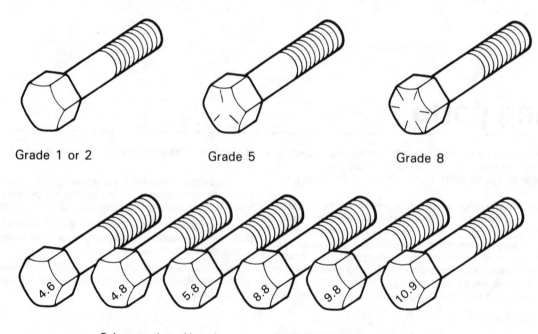

Grade 1 or 2   Grade 5   Grade 8

Bolt strength markings (top — standard/SAE/USS; bottom — metric)

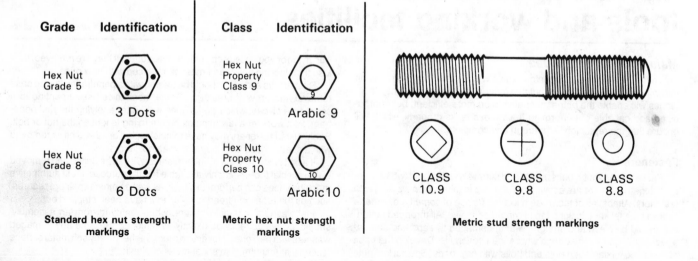

Grade	Identification	Class	Identification
Hex Nut Grade 5	3 Dots	Hex Nut Property Class 9	Arabic 9
Hex Nut Grade 8	6 Dots	Hex Nut Property Class 10	Arabic 10

Standard hex nut strength markings

Metric hex nut strength markings

CLASS 10.9   CLASS 9.8   CLASS 8.8

Metric stud strength markings

It should be noted that many fasteners, especially Grades 0 through 2, have no distinguishing marks on them. When such is the case, the only way to determine whether it is standard or metric is to measure the thread pitch or compare it to a known fastener of the same size.

Standard fasteners are often referred to as SAE, as opposed to metric. However, it should be noted that SAE technically refers to a non-metric *fine thread* fastener only. Coarse thread non-metric fasteners are referred to as USS sizes.

Since fasteners of the same size (both standard and metric) may have different strength ratings, be sure to reinstall any bolts, studs or nuts removed from your vehicle in their original locations. Also, when replacing a fastener with a new one, make sure that the new one has a strength rating equal to or greater than the original.

Tightening sequences and procedures

Most threaded fasteners should be tightened to a specific torque value (torque is the twisting force applied to a threaded component such as a nut or bolt). Overtightening the fastener can weaken it and cause it to break, while undertightening can cause it to eventually come loose. Bolts, screws and studs, depending on the material they are made of and their thread diameters, have specific torque values, many of which are noted in the Specifications at the beginning of each Chapter. Be sure to follow the torque recommendations closely. For fasteners not assigned a specific torque, a general torque value chart is presented here as a guide. These torque values are for dry (unlubricated) fasteners threaded into steel or cast iron (not aluminum). As was previously mentioned, the size and grade of a fastener determine the amount of torque that can safely be

	Ft-lbs	Nm
Metric thread sizes		
M-6	6 to 9	9 to 12
M-8	14 to 21	19 to 28
M-10	28 to 40	38 to 54
M-12	50 to 71	68 to 96
M-14	80 to 140	109 to 154
Pipe thread sizes		
1/8	5 to 8	7 to 10
1/4	12 to 18	17 to 24
3/8	22 to 33	30 to 44
1/2	25 to 35	34 to 47
U.S. thread sizes		
1/4 – 20	6 to 9	9 to 12
5/16 – 18	12 to 18	17 to 24
5/16 – 24	14 to 20	19 to 27
3/8 – 16	22 to 32	30 to 43
3/8 – 24	27 to 38	37 to 51
7/16 – 14	40 to 55	55 to 74
7/16 – 20	40 to 60	55 to 81
1/2 – 13	55 to 80	75 to 108

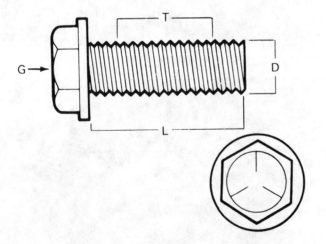

Standard (SAE and USS) bolt dimensions/grade marks

G   Grade marks (bolt length)
L   Length (in inches)
T   Thread pitch (number of threads per inch)
D   Nominal diameter (in inches)

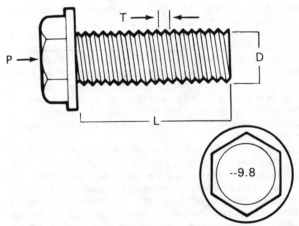

Metric bolt dimensions/grade marks

P   Property class (bolt strength)
L   Length (in millimeters)
T   Thread pitch (distance between threads in millimeters)
D   Diameter

applied to it. The figures listed here are approximate for Grade 2 and Grade 3 fasteners. Higher grades can tolerate higher torque values.

Fasteners laid out in a pattern, such as cylinder head bolts, oil pan bolts, differential cover bolts, etc., must be loosened or tightened in sequence to avoid warping the component. This sequence will normally be shown in the appropriate Chapter. If a specific pattern is not given, the following procedures can be used to prevent warping.

Initially, the bolts or nuts should be assembled finger-tight only. Next, they should be tightened one full turn each, in a criss-cross or diagonal pattern. After each one has been tightened one full turn, return to the first one and tighten them all one-half turn, following the same pattern. Finally, tighten each of them one-quarter turn at a time until each fastener has been tightened to the proper torque. To loosen and remove the fasteners, the procedure would be reversed.

Component disassembly

Component disassembly should be done with care and purpose to help ensure that the parts go back together properly. Always keep track of the sequence in which parts are removed. Make note of special characteristics or marks on parts that can be installed more than one way, such as a grooved thrust washer on a shaft. It is a good idea to lay the disassembled parts out on a clean surface in the order that they were removed. It may also be helpful to make sketches or take instant photos of components before removal.

When removing fasteners from a component, keep track of their locations. Sometimes threading a bolt back in a part, or putting the washers and nut back on a stud, can prevent mix-ups later. If nuts and bolts cannot be returned to their original locations, they should be kept in a compartmented box or a series of small boxes. A cupcake or muffin tin is ideal for this purpose, since each cavity can hold the bolts and nuts from a particular area (i.e. oil pan bolts, valve cover bolts, engine mount bolts, etc.). A pan of this type is especially helpful when working on assemblies with very small parts, such as the carburetor, alternator, valve train or interior dash and trim pieces. The cavities can be marked with paint or tape to identify the contents.

Whenever wiring looms, harnesses or connectors are separated, it is a good idea to identify the two halves with numbered pieces of masking tape so they can be easily reconnected.

Gasket sealing surfaces

Throughout any vehicle, gaskets are used to seal the mating surfaces between two parts and keep lubricants, fluids, vacuum or pressure contained in an assembly.

Many times these gaskets are coated with a liquid or paste-type gasket sealing compound before assembly. Age, heat and pressure can sometimes cause the two parts to stick together so tightly that they are very difficult to separate. Often, the assembly can be loosened by striking it with a soft-face hammer near the mating surfaces. A regular hammer can be used if a block of wood is placed between the hammer and the part. Do not hammer on cast parts or parts that could be easily damaged. With any particularly stubborn part, always recheck to make sure that every fastener has been removed.

Avoid using a screwdriver or bar to pry apart an assembly, as they can easily mar the gasket sealing surfaces of the parts, which must remain smooth. If prying is absolutely necessary, use an old broom handle, but keep in mind that extra clean up will be necessary if the wood splinters.

After the parts are separated, the old gasket must be carefully scraped off and the gasket surfaces cleaned. Stubborn gasket material can be soaked with rust penetrant or treated with a special chemical to soften it so it can be easily scraped off. A scraper can be fashioned from a piece of copper tubing by flattening and sharpening one end. Copper is recommended because it is usually softer than the surfaces to be scraped, which reduces the chance of gouging the part. Some gaskets can be removed with a wire brush, but regardless of the method used, the mating surfaces must be left clean and smooth. If for some reason the gasket surface is gouged, then a gasket sealer thick enough to fill scratches will have to be used during reassembly of the components. For most applications, a non-drying (or semi-drying) gasket sealer should be used.

Hose removal tips

Warning: *If the vehicle is equipped with air conditioning, do not disconnect any of the A/C hoses without first having the system depressurized by a dealer service department or a service station.*

Hose removal precautions closely parallel gasket removal precautions. Avoid scratching or gouging the surface that the hose mates against or the connection may leak. This is especially true for radiator hoses. Because of various chemical reactions, the rubber in hoses can bond itself to the metal spigot that the hose fits over. To remove a hose, first loosen the hose clamps that secure it to the spigot. Then, with slip-joint pliers, grab the hose at the clamp and rotate it around the spigot. Work it back and forth until it is completely free, then pull it off. Silicone or other lubricants will ease removal if they can be applied between the hose and the outside of the spigot. Apply the same lubricant to the inside of the hose and the outside of the spigot to simplify installation.

As a last resort (and if the hose is to be replaced with a new one anyway), the rubber can be slit with a knife and the hose peeled from the spigot. If this must be done, be careful that the metal connection is not damaged.

If a hose clamp is broken or damaged, do not reuse it. Wire-type clamps usually weaken with age, so it is a good idea to replace them with screw-type clamps whenever a hose is removed.

Tools

A selection of good tools is a basic requirement for anyone who plans to maintain and repair his or her own vehicle. For the owner who has few tools, the initial investment might seem high, but when compared to the spiraling costs of professional auto maintenance and repair, it is a wise one.

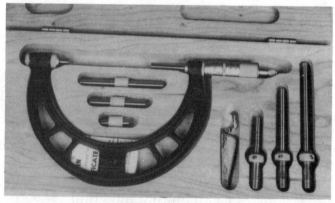

Micrometer set

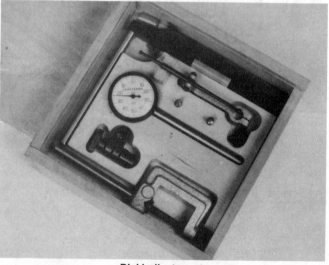

Dial indicator set

Dial caliper

Hand-operated vacuum pump

Timing light

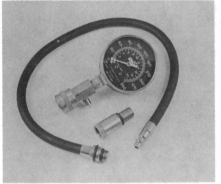
Compression gauge with spark plug hole adapter

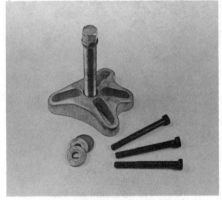
Damper/steering wheel puller

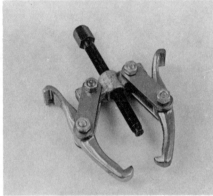
General purpose puller

Hydraulic lifter removal tool

Valve spring compressor

Valve spring compressor

Ridge reamer

Piston ring groove cleaning tool

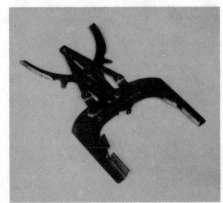
Ring removal/installation tool

Ring compressor

Cylinder hone

Brake hold-down spring tool

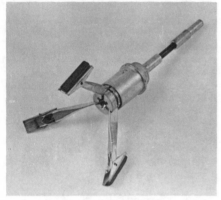

Brake cylinder hone

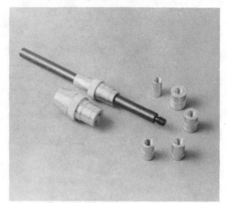

Clutch plate alignment tool

Tap and die set

To help the owner decide which tools are needed to perform the tasks detailed in this manual, the following tool lists are offered: *Maintenance and minor repair, Repair/overhaul* and *Special*.

The newcomer to practical mechanics should start off with the maintenance and minor repair tool kit, which is adequate for the simpler jobs performed on a vehicle. Then, as confidence and experience grow, the owner can tackle more difficult tasks, buying additional tools as they are needed. Eventually the basic kit will be expanded into the repair and overhaul tool set. Over a period of time, the experienced do-it-yourselfer will assemble a tool set complete enough for most repair and overhaul procedures and will add tools from the special category when it is felt that the expense is justified by the frequency of use.

Maintenance and minor repair tool kit

The tools in this list should be considered the minimum required for performance of routine maintenance, servicing and minor repair work. We recommend the purchase of combination wrenches (box-end and open-end combined in one wrench). While more expensive than open end wrenches, they offer the advantages of both types of wrench.

Combination wrench set (1/4-inch to 1 inch or 6 mm to 19 mm)
Adjustable wrench, 8 inch
Spark plug wrench with rubber insert
Spark plug gap adjusting tool
Feeler gauge set
Brake bleeder wrench
Standard screwdriver (5/16-inch x 6 inch)
Phillips screwdriver (No. 2 x 6 inch)
Combination pliers – 6 inch
Hacksaw and assortment of blades
Tire pressure gauge
Grease gun
Oil can
Fine emery cloth
Wire brush

Battery post and cable cleaning tool
Oil filter wrench
Funnel (medium size)
Safety goggles
Jackstands(2)
Drain pan

Note: *If basic tune-ups are going to be part of routine maintenance, it will be necessary to purchase a good quality stroboscopic timing light and combination tachometer/dwell meter. Although they are included in the list of special tools, it is mentioned here because they are absolutely necessary for tuning most vehicles properly.*

Repair and overhaul tool set

These tools are essential for anyone who plans to perform major repairs and are in addition to those in the maintenance and minor repair tool kit. Included is a comprehensive set of sockets which, though expensive, are invaluable because of their versatility, especially when various extensions and drives are available. We recommend the 1/2-inch drive over the 3/8-inch drive. Although the larger drive is bulky and more expensive, it has the capacity of accepting a very wide range of large sockets. Ideally, however, the mechanic should have a 3/8-inch drive set and a 1/2-inch drive set.

Socket set(s)
Reversible ratchet
Extension – 10 inch
Universal joint
Torque wrench (same size drive as sockets)
Ball peen hammer – 8 ounce
Soft-face hammer (plastic/rubber)
Standard screwdriver (1/4-inch x 6 inch)
Standard screwdriver (stubby – 5/16-inch)
Phillips screwdriver (No. 3 x 8 inch)
Phillips screwdriver (stubby – No. 2)

Pliers – vise grip
Pliers – lineman's
Pliers – needle nose
Pliers – snap-ring (internal and external)
Cold chisel – 1/2-inch
Scribe
Scraper (made from flattened copper tubing)
Centerpunch
Pin punches (1/16, 1/8, 3/16-inch)
Steel rule/straightedge – 12 inch
Allen wrench set (1/8 to 3/8-inch or 4 mm to 10 mm)
A selection of files
Wire brush (large)
Jackstands (second set)
Jack (scissor or hydraulic type)

Note: Another tool which is often useful is an electric drill with a chuck capacity of 3/8-inch and a set of good quality drill bits.

Special tools

The tools in this list include those which are not used regularly, are expensive to buy, or which need to be used in accordance with their manufacturer's instructions. Unless these tools will be used frequently, it is not very economical to purchase many of them. A consideration would be to split the cost and use between yourself and a friend or friends. In addition, most of these tools can be obtained from a tool rental shop on a temporary basis.

This list primarily contains only those tools and instruments widely available to the public, and not those special tools produced by the vehicle manufacturer for distribution to dealer service departments. Occasionally, references to the manufacturer's special tools are included in the text of this manual. Generally, an alternative method of doing the job without the special tool is offered. However, sometimes there is no alternative to their use. Where this is the case, and the tool cannot be purchased or borrowed, the work should be turned over to the dealer service department or an automotive repair shop.

Valve spring compressor
Piston ring groove cleaning tool
Piston ring compressor
Piston ring installation tool
Cylinder compression gauge
Cylinder ridge reamer
Cylinder surfacing hone
Cylinder bore gauge
Micrometers and/or dial calipers
Hydraulic lifter removal tool
Balljoint separator
Universal-type puller
Impact screwdriver
Dial indicator set
Stroboscopic timing light (inductive pick-up)
Hand operated vacuum/pressure pump
Tachometer/dwell meter
Universal electrical multimeter
Cable hoist
Brake spring removal and installation tools
Floor jack

Buying tools

For the do-it-yourselfer who is just starting to get involved in vehicle maintenance and repair, there are a number of options available when purchasing tools. If maintenance and minor repair is the extent of the work to be done, the purchase of individual tools is satisfactory. If, on the other hand, extensive work is planned, it would be a good idea to purchase a modest tool set from one of the large retail chain stores. A set can usually be bought at a substantial savings over the individual tool prices, and they often come with a tool box. As additional tools are needed, add-on sets, individual tools and a larger tool box can be purchased to expand the tool selection. Building a tool set gradually allows the cost of the tools to be spread over a longer period of time and gives the mechanic the freedom to choose only those tools that will actually be used.

Tool stores will often be the only source of some of the special tools that are needed, but regardless of where tools are bought, try to avoid cheap ones, especially when buying screwdrivers and sockets, because they won't last very long. The expense involved in replacing cheap tools will eventually be greater than the initial cost of quality tools.

Care and maintenance of tools

Good tools are expensive, so it makes sense to treat them with respect. Keep them clean and in usable condition and store them properly when not in use. Always wipe off any dirt, grease or metal chips before putting them away. Never leave tools lying around in the work area. Upon completion of a job, always check closely under the hood for tools that may have been left there so they won't get lost during a test drive.

Some tools, such as screwdrivers, pliers, wrenches and sockets, can be hung on a panel mounted on the garage or workshop wall, while others should be kept in a tool box or tray. Measuring instruments, gauges, meters, etc. must be carefully stored where they cannot be damaged by weather or impact from other tools.

When tools are used with care and stored properly, they will last a very long time. Even with the best of care, though, tools will wear out if used frequently. When a tool is damaged or worn out, replace it. Subsequent jobs will be safer and more enjoyable if you do.

Working facilities

Not to be overlooked when discussing tools is the workshop. If anything more than routine maintenance is to be carried out, some sort of suitable work area is essential.

It is understood, and appreciated, that many home mechanics do not have a good workshop or garage available, and end up removing an engine or doing major repairs outside. It is recommended, however, that the overhaul or repair be completed under the cover of a roof.

A clean, flat workbench or table of comfortable working height is an absolute necessity. The workbench should be equipped with a vise that has a jaw opening of at least four inches.

As mentioned previously, some clean, dry storage space is also required for tools, as well as the lubricants, fluids, cleaning solvents, etc. which soon become necessary.

Sometimes waste oil and fluids, drained from the engine or cooling system during normal maintenance or repairs, present a disposal problem. To avoid pouring them on the ground or into a sewage system, pour the used fluids into large containers, seal them with caps and take them to an authorized disposal site or recycling center. Plastic jugs, such as old antifreeze containers, are ideal for this purpose.

Always keep a supply of old newspapers and clean rags available. Old towels are excellent for mopping up spills. Many mechanics use rolls of paper towels for most work because they are readily available and disposable. To help keep the area under the vehicle clean, a large cardboard box can be cut open and flattened to protect the garage or shop floor.

Whenever working over a painted surface, such as when leaning over a fender to service something under the hood, always cover it with an old blanket or bedspread to protect the finish. Vinyl covered pads, made especially for this purpose, are available at auto parts stores.

Booster battery (jump) starting

Observe these precautions when using a booster battery to start a vehicle:

a) Before connecting the booster battery, make sure the ignition switch is in the Off position.

b) Turn off the lights, heater and other electrical loads.

c) Your eyes should be shielded. Safety goggles are a good idea.

d) Make sure the booster battery is the same voltage as the dead one in the vehicle.

e) The two vehicles MUST NOT TOUCH each other!

f) Make sure the transmission is in Neutral (manual) or Park (automatic).

g) If the booster battery is not a maintenance-free type, remove the vent caps and lay a cloth over the vent holes.

Connect the red jumper cable to the positive (+) terminals of each battery.

Connect one end of the black jumper cable to the negative (–) terminal of the booster battery. The other end of this cable should be connected to a good ground on the vehicle to be started, such as a bolt or bracket on the engine block **(see illustration)**. Make sure the cable will not come into contact with the fan, drivebelts or other moving parts of the engine.

Start the engine using the booster battery, then, with the engine running at idle speed, disconnect the jumper cables in the reverse order of connection.

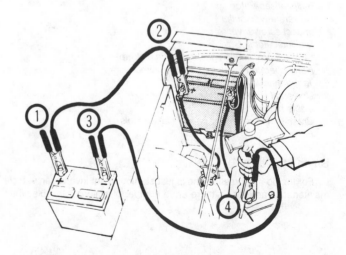

Make the booster battery cable connections in the numerical order shown (note that the negative cable of the booster battery is NOT attached to the negative terminal of the dead battery)

Jacking and towing

Jacking

The jack supplied with the vehicle should only be used for raising the vehicle when changing a tire or placing jackstands under the frame. **Warning:** *Never work under the vehicle or start the engine while this jack is being used as the only means of support.*

The vehicle should be on level ground with the wheels blocked and the transaxle in Park (automatic) or Neutral (manual). If a tire is being changed, loosen the lug nuts one-half turn and leave them in place until the wheel is raised off the ground. Make sure no one is in the vehicle as it's being raised off the ground.

Place the jack under the side of the vehicle and adjust the jack height until it fits between the notches in the vertical rocker panel flange nearest the wheel to be changed **(see illustration)**. Operate the jack with a slow, smooth motion until the wheel is raised off the ground. Remove the lug nuts, pull off the wheel, install the spare and thread the lug nuts back on with the bevelled sides facing in. Tighten them snugly, but wait until the vehicle is lowered to tighten them completely.

Lower the vehicle, remove the jack and tighten the lug nuts (if loosened or removed) in a criss-cross pattern. If possible, tighten them with a torque wrench (see Chapter 1 for the torque figures). If you don't have access to a torque wrench, have the nuts checked by a service station or repair shop as soon as possible.

If the vehicle is equipped with a temporary spare tire, remember that it's intended only for temporary use until the regular tire can be repaired. Do not exceed 50 mph while using the temporary spare.

Towing

To prevent transaxle damage, the vehicle must be towed with the front (drive) wheels off the ground. If they can't be raised, place them on a dolly. The ignition key must be in the ACC position, since the steering lock mechanism isn't strong enough to hold the front wheels straight while towing.

While towing, don't exceed 50 mph (35 mph on rough roads). Release the parking brake, put the transaxle in Neutral and place the ignition key in the ACC position.

Equipment specifically designed for towing should be used. It should be attached to the main structural members of the vehicle, not the bumpers or brackets.

Safety is a major consideration when towing and all applicable state and local laws must be obeyed. A safety chain system must be used at all times. Remember that power steering and power brakes will not work with the engine off.

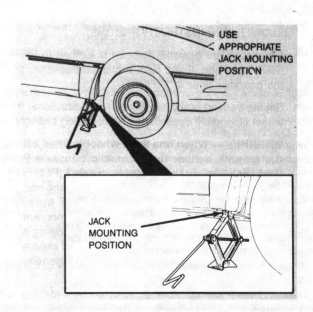

USE APPROPRIATE JACK MOUNTING POSITION

JACK MOUNTING POSITION

Front jacking point (the rear jacking point is just in front of the rear wheel)

Automotive chemicals and lubricants

A number of automotive chemicals and lubricants are available for use during vehicle maintenance and repair. They include a wide variety of products ranging from cleaning solvents and degreasers to lubricants and protective sprays for rubber, plastic and vinyl.

Cleaners

Carburetor cleaner and choke cleaner is a strong solvent for gum, varnish and carbon. Most carburetor cleaners leave a dry-type lubricant film which will not harden or gum up. Because of this film it is not recommended for use on electrical components.

Brake system cleaner is used to remove grease and brake fluid from the brake system, where clean surfaces are absolutely necessary. It leaves no residue and often eliminates brake squeal caused by contaminants.

Electrical cleaner removes oxidation, corrosion and carbon deposits from electrical contacts, restoring full current flow. It can also be used to clean spark plugs, carburetor jets, voltage regulators and other parts where an oil-free surface is desired.

Demoisturants remove water and moisture from electrical components such as alternators, voltage regulators, electrical connectors and fuse blocks. They are non-conductive, non-corrosive and non-flammable.

Degreasers are heavy-duty solvents used to remove grease from the outside of the engine and from chassis components. They can be sprayed or brushed on and, depending on the type, are rinsed off either with water or solvent.

Lubricants

Motor oil is the lubricant formulated for use in engines. It normally contains a wide variety of additives to prevent corrosion and reduce foaming and wear. Motor oil comes in various weights (viscosity ratings) from 5 to 80. The recommended weight of the oil depends on the season, temperature and the demands on the engine. Light oil is used in cold climates and under light load conditions. Heavy oil is used in hot climates and where high loads are encountered. Multi-viscosity oils are designed to have characteristics of both light and heavy oils and are available in a number of weights from 5W-20 to 20W-50.

Gear oil is designed to be used in differentials, manual transmissions and other areas where high-temperature lubrication is required.

Chassis and wheel bearing grease is a heavy grease used where increased loads and friction are encountered, such as for wheel bearings, balljoints, tie-rod ends and universal joints.

High-temperature wheel bearing grease is designed to withstand the extreme temperatures encountered by wheel bearings in disc brake equipped vehicles. It usually contains molybdenum disulfide (moly), which is a dry-type lubricant.

White grease is a heavy grease for metal-to-metal applications where water is a problem. White grease stays soft under both low and high temperatures (usually from −100 to +190-degrees F), and will not wash off or dilute in the presence of water.

Assembly lube is a special extreme pressure lubricant, usually containing moly, used to lubricate high-load parts (such as main and rod bearings and cam lobes) for initial start-up of a new engine. The assembly lube lubricates the parts without being squeezed out or washed away until the engine oiling system begins to function.

Silicone lubricants are used to protect rubber, plastic, vinyl and nylon parts.

Graphite lubricants are used where oils cannot be used due to contamination problems, such as in locks. The dry graphite will lubricate metal parts while remaining uncontaminated by dirt, water, oil or acids. It is electrically conductive and will not foul electrical contacts in locks such as the ignition switch.

Moly penetrants loosen and lubricate frozen, rusted and corroded fasteners and prevent future rusting or freezing.

Heat-sink grease is a special electrically non-conductive grease that is used for mounting electronic ignition modules where it is essential that heat is transferred away from the module.

Sealants

RTV sealant is one of the most widely used gasket compounds. Made from silicone, RTV is air curing, it seals, bonds, waterproofs, fills surface irregularities, remains flexible, doesn't shrink, is relatively easy to remove, and is used as a supplementary sealer with almost all low and medium temperature gaskets.

Anaerobic sealant is much like RTV in that it can be used either to seal gaskets or to form gaskets by itself. It remains flexible, is solvent resistant and fills surface imperfections. The difference between an anaerobic sealant and an RTV-type sealant is in the curing. RTV cures when exposed to air, while an anaerobic sealant cures only in the absence of air. This means that an anaerobic sealant cures only after the assembly of parts, sealing them together.

Thread and pipe sealant is used for sealing hydraulic and pneumatic fittings and vacuum lines. It is usually made from a teflon compound, and comes in a spray, a paint-on liquid and as a wrap-around tape.

Chemicals

Anti–seize compound prevents seizing, galling, cold welding, rust and corrosion in fasteners. High-temperature anti-seize, usually made with copper and graphite lubricants, is used for exhaust system and exhaust manifold bolts.

Anaerobic locking compounds are used to keep fasteners from vibrating or working loose and cure only after installation, in the absence of air. Medium strength locking compound is used for small nuts, bolts and screws that may be removed later. High-strength locking compound is for large nuts, bolts and studs which aren't removed on a regular basis.

Oil additives range from viscosity index improvers to chemical treatments that claim to reduce internal engine friction. It should be noted that most oil manufacturers caution against using additives with their oils.

Gas additives perform several functions, depending on their chemical makeup. They usually contain solvents that help dissolve gum and varnish that build up on carburetor, fuel injection and intake parts. They also serve to break down carbon deposits that form on the inside surfaces of the combustion chambers. Some additives contain upper cylinder lubricants for valves and piston rings, and others contain chemicals to remove condensation from the gas tank.

Miscellaneous

Brake fluid is specially formulated hydraulic fluid that can withstand the heat and pressure encountered in brake systems. Care must be taken so this fluid does not come in contact with painted surfaces or plastics. An opened container should always be resealed to prevent contamination by water or dirt.

Weatherstrip adhesive is used to bond weatherstripping around doors, windows and trunk lids. It is sometimes used to attach trim pieces.

Undercoating is a petroleum-based, tar-like substance that is designed to protect metal surfaces on the underside of the vehicle from corrosion. It also acts as a sound-deadening agent by insulating the bottom of the vehicle.

Waxes and polishes are used to help protect painted and plated surfaces from the weather. Different types of paint may require the use of different types of wax and polish. Some polishes utilize a chemical or abrasive cleaner to help remove the top layer of oxidized (dull) paint on older vehicles. In recent years many non-wax polishes that contain a wide variety of chemicals such as polymers and silicones have been introduced. These non-wax polishes are usually easier to apply and last longer than conventional waxes and polishes.

Safety first!

Regardless of how enthusiastic you may be about getting on with the job at hand, take the time to ensure that your safety is not jeopardized. A moment's lack of attention can result in an accident, as can failure to observe certain simple safety precautions. The possibility of an accident will always exist, and the following points should not be considered a comprehensive list of all dangers. Rather, they are intended to make you aware of the risks and to encourage a safety conscious approach to all work you carry out on your vehicle.

Essential DOs and DON'Ts

DON'T rely on a jack when working under the vehicle. Always use approved jackstands to support the weight of the vehicle and place them under the recommended lift or support points.

DON'T attempt to loosen extremely tight fasteners (i.e. wheel lug nuts) while the vehicle is on a jack – it may fall.

DON'T start the engine without first making sure that the transmission is in Neutral (or Park where applicable) and the parking brake is set.

DON'T remove the radiator cap from a hot cooling system – let it cool or cover it with a cloth and release the pressure gradually.

DON'T attempt to drain the engine oil until you are sure it has cooled to the point that it will not burn you.

DON'T touch any part of the engine or exhaust system until it has cooled sufficiently to avoid burns.

DON'T siphon toxic liquids such as gasoline, antifreeze and brake fluid by mouth, or allow them to remain on your skin.

DON'T inhale brake lining dust – it is potentially hazardous (see Asbestos below)

DON'T allow spilled oil or grease to remain on the floor – wipe it up before someone slips on it.

DON'T use loose fitting wrenches or other tools which may slip and cause injury.

DON'T push on wrenches when loosening or tightening nuts or bolts. Always try to pull the wrench toward you. If the situation calls for pushing the wrench away, push with an open hand to avoid scraped knuckles if the wrench should slip.

DON'T attempt to lift a heavy component alone – get someone to help you.

DON'T rush or take unsafe shortcuts to finish a job.

DON'T allow children or animals in or around the vehicle while you are working on it.

DO wear eye protection when using power tools such as a drill, sander, bench grinder, etc. and when working under a vehicle.

DO keep loose clothing and long hair well out of the way of moving parts.

DO make sure that any hoist used has a safe working load rating adequate for the job.

DO get someone to check on you periodically when working alone on a vehicle.

DO carry out work in a logical sequence and make sure that everything is correctly assembled and tightened.

DO keep chemicals and fluids tightly capped and out of the reach of children and pets.

DO remember that your vehicle's safety affects that of yourself and others. If in doubt on any point, get professional advice.

Asbestos

Certain friction, insulating, sealing, and other products – such as brake linings, brake bands, clutch linings, torque converters, gaskets, etc. – contain asbestos. *Extreme care must be taken to avoid inhalation of dust from such products since it is hazardous to health*. If in doubt, assume that they *do* contain asbestos.

Fire

Remember at all times that gasoline is highly flammable. Never smoke or have any kind of open flame around when working on a vehicle. But the risk does not end there. A spark caused by an electrical short circuit, by two metal surfaces contacting each other, or even by static electricity built up in your body under certain conditions, can ignite gasoline vapors, which in a confined space are highly explosive. Do not, under any circumstances, use gasoline for cleaning parts. Use an approved safety solvent.

Always disconnect the battery ground (–) cable *at the battery* before working on any part of the fuel system or electrical system. Never risk spilling fuel on a hot engine or exhaust component.

It is strongly recommended that a fire extinguisher suitable for use on fuel and electrical fires be kept handy in the garage or workshop at all times. Never try to extinguish a fuel or electrical fire with water.

Fumes

Certain fumes are highly toxic and can quickly cause unconsciousness and even death if inhaled to any extent. Gasoline vapor falls into this category, as do the vapors from some cleaning solvents. Any draining or pouring of such volatile fluids should be done in a well ventilated area.

When using cleaning fluids and solvents, read the instructions on the container carefully. Never use materials from unmarked containers.

Never run the engine in an enclosed space, such as a garage. Exhaust fumes contain carbon monoxide, which is extremely poisonous. If you need to run the engine, always do so in the open air, or at least have the rear of the vehicle outside the work area.

If you are fortunate enough to have the use of an inspection pit, never drain or pour gasoline and never run the engine while the vehicle is over the pit. The fumes, being heavier than air, will concentrate in the pit with possibly lethal results.

The battery

Never create a spark or allow a bare light bulb near a battery. They normally give off a certain amount of hydrogen gas, which is highly explosive.

Always disconnect the battery ground (–) cable *at the battery* before working on the fuel or electrical systems.

If possible, loosen the filler caps or cover when charging the battery from an external source (this does not apply to sealed or maintenancefree batteries). Do not charge at an excessive rate or the battery may burst.

Take care when adding water to a non maintenance–free battery and when carrying a battery. The electrolyte, even when diluted, is very corrosive and should not be allowed to contact clothing or skin.

Always wear eye protection when cleaning the battery to prevent the caustic deposits from entering your eyes.

Household current

When using an electric power tool, inspection light, etc., which operates on household current, always make sure that the tool is correctly connected to its plug and that, where necessary, it is properly grounded. Do not use such items in damp conditions and, again, do not create a spark or apply excessive heat in the vicinity of fuel or fuel vapor.

Secondary ignition system voltage

A severe electric shock can result from touching certain parts of the ignition system (such as the spark plug wires) when the engine is running or being cranked, particularly if components are damp or the insulation is defective. In the case of an electronic ignition system, the secondary system voltage is much higher and could prove fatal.

Conversion factors

Length (distance)

Inches (in)	X 25.4	= Millimetres (mm)	X 0.0394	= Inches (in)
Feet (ft)	X 0.305	= Metres (m)	X 3.281	= Feet (ft)
Miles	X 1.609	= Kilometres (km)	X 0.621	= Miles

Volume (capacity)

Cubic inches (cu in; in^3)	X 16.387	= Cubic centimetres (cc; cm^3)	X 0.061	= Cubic inches (cu in; in^3)
Imperial pints (Imp pt)	X 0.568	= Litres (l)	X 1.76	= Imperial pints (Imp pt)
Imperial quarts (Imp qt)	X 1.137	= Litres (l)	X 0.88	= Imperial quarts (Imp qt)
Imperial quarts (Imp qt)	X 1.201	= US quarts (US qt)	X 0.833	= Imperial quarts (Imp qt)
US quarts (US qt)	X 0.946	= Litres (l)	X 1.057	= US quarts (US qt)
Imperial gallons (Imp gal)	X 4.546	= Litres (l)	X 0.22	= Imperial gallons (Imp gal)
Imperial gallons (Imp gal)	X 1.201	= US gallons (US gal)	X 0.833	= Imperial gallons (Imp gal)
US gallons (US gal)	X 3.785	= Litres (l)	X 0.264	= US gallons (US gal)

Mass (weight)

Ounces (oz)	X 28.35	= Grams (g)	X 0.035	= Ounces (oz)
Pounds (lb)	X 0.454	= Kilograms (kg)	X 2.205	= Pounds (lb)

Force

Ounces-force (ozf; oz)	X 0.278	= Newtons (N)	X 3.6	= Ounces-force (ozf; oz)
Pounds-force (lbf; lb)	X 4.448	= Newtons (N)	X 0.225	= Pounds-force (lbf; lb)
Newtons (N)	X 0.1	= Kilograms-force (kgf; kg)	X 9.81	= Newtons (N)

Pressure

Pounds-force per square inch (psi; lbf/in^2; lb/in^2)	X 0.070	= Kilograms-force per square centimetre (kgf/cm^2; kg/cm^2)	X 14.223	= Pounds-force per square inch (psi; lbf/in^2; lb/in^2)
Pounds-force per square inch (psi; lbf/in^2; lb/in^2)	X 0.068	= Atmospheres (atm)	X 14.696	= Pounds-force per square inch (psi; lbf/in^2; lb/in^2)
Pounds-force per square inch (psi; lbf/in^2; lb/in^2)	X 0.069	= Bars	X 14.5	= Pounds-force per square inch (psi; lbf/in^2; lb/in^2)
Pounds-force per square inch (psi; lbf/in^2; lb/in^2)	X 6.895	= Kilopascals (kPa)	X 0.145	= Pounds-force per square inch (psi; lbf/in^2; lb/in^2)
Kilopascals (kPa)	X 0.01	= Kilograms-force per square centimetre (kgf/cm^2; kg/cm^2)	X 98.1	= Kilopascals (kPa)

Torque (moment of force)

Pounds-force inches (lbf in; lb in)	X 1.152	= Kilograms-force centimetre (kgf cm; kg cm)	X 0.868	= Pounds-force inches (lbf in; lb in)
Pounds-force inches (lbf in; lb in)	X 0.113	= Newton metres (Nm)	X 8.85	= Pounds-force inches (lbf in; lb in)
Pounds-force inches (lbf in; lb in)	X 0.083	= Pounds-force feet (lbf ft; lb ft)	X 12	= Pounds-force inches (lbf in; lb in)
Pounds-force feet (lbf ft; lb ft)	X 0.138	= Kilograms-force metres (kgf m; kg m)	X 7.233	= Pounds-force feet (lbf ft; lb ft)
Pounds-force feet (lbf ft; lb ft)	X 1.356	= Newton metres (Nm)	X 0.738	= Pounds-force feet (lbf ft; lb ft)
Newton metres (Nm)	X 0.102	= Kilograms-force metres (kgf m; kg m)	X 9.804	= Newton metres (Nm)

Power

Horsepower (hp)	X 745.7	= Watts (W)	X 0.0013	= Horsepower (hp)

Velocity (speed)

Miles per hour (miles/hr; mph)	X 1.609	= Kilometres per hour (km/hr; kph)	X 0.621	= Miles per hour (miles/hr; mph)

Fuel consumption*

Miles per gallon, Imperial (mpg)	X 0.354	= Kilometres per litre (km/l)	X 2.825	= Miles per gallon, Imperial (mpg)
Miles per gallon, US (mpg)	X 0.425	= Kilometres per litre (km/l)	X 2.352	= Miles per gallon, US (mpg)

Temperature

Degrees Fahrenheit = (°C x 1.8) + 32   Degrees Celsius (Degrees Centigrade; °C) = (°F - 32) x 0.56

*It is common practice to convert from miles per gallon (mpg) to litres/100 kilometres (l/100km), where mpg (Imperial) x l/100 km = 282 and mpg (US) x l/100 km = 235

Troubleshooting

Contents

This Section provides an easy reference guide to the more common problems which may occur during operation of the vehicle. These problems and their possible causes are grouped under headings denoting various components or systems, such as Engine, Cooling system, etc. They also refer you to the Chapter and/or Section which deals with the problem.

Remember that successful troubleshooting is not a mysterious black art practiced only by professional mechanics. It is simply the result of the right knowledge combined with an intelligent, systematic approach to the problem. Always work by a process of elimination, starting with the simplest solution and working through to the most complex – and never overlook the obvious. Anyone can run the gas tank dry or leave the lights on overnight, so don't assume that you are exempt from such oversights.

Finally, always establish a clear idea of why a problem has occurred and take steps to ensure that it doesn't happen again. If the electrical system fails because of a poor connection, check the other connections in the system to make sure that they don't fail as well. If a particular fuse continues to blow, find out why – don't just replace one fuse after another. Remember, failure of a small component can often be indicative of potential failure or incorrect functioning of a more important component or system.

Engine

1   Engine will not rotate when attempting to start

1   Battery terminal connections loose or corroded (see Chapter 1).
2   Battery discharged or faulty (see Chapter 1).
3   Automatic transaxle not completely engaged in Park or clutch not completely depressed.
4   Broken, loose or disconnected wiring in the starting circuit (see Chapters 5 and 12).
5   Starter motor pinion jammed in flywheel ring gear (see Chapter 5).
6   Starter solenoid faulty (see Chapter 5).
7   Starter motor faulty (see Chapter 5).
8   Ignition switch faulty (see Chapter 12).
9   Starter pinion or flywheel teeth worn or broken (see Chapter 5).

2   Engine rotates but will not start

1   Fuel tank empty.
2   Battery discharged (engine rotates slowly) (see Chapter 5).
3   Battery terminal connections loose or corroded (see Chapter 1).
4   Leaking fuel injector(s), faulty cold start valve, fuel pump, pressure regulator, etc. (see Chapter 4).
5   Fuel not reaching fuel rail (see Chapter 4).
6   Ignition components damp or damaged (see Chapter 5).
7   Worn, faulty or incorrectly gapped spark plugs (see Chapter 1).
8   Broken, loose or disconnected wiring in the starting circuit (see Chapter 5).
9   Loose distributor is changing ignition timing (see Chapter 5).
10 Broken, loose or disconnected wires at the ignition coil or faulty coil (see Chapter 5).

3   Engine hard to start when cold

1   Battery discharged or low (see Chapter 1).
2   Malfunctioning fuel system (see Chapter 4).
3   Faulty cold start injector (see Chapter 4).
4   Injector(s) leaking (see Chapter 4).
5   Distributor rotor carbon tracked (see Chapter 5).

4   Engine hard to start when hot

1   Air filter clogged (see Chapter 1).
2   Fuel not reaching the fuel injection system (see Chapter 4).
3   Corroded battery connections, especially ground (see Chapter 1).

5   Starter motor noisy or excessively rough in engagement

1   Pinion or flywheel gear teeth worn or broken (see Chapter 5).
2   Starter motor mounting bolts loose or missing (see Chapter 5).

6   Engine starts but stops immediately

1   Loose or faulty electrical connections at distributor, coil or alternator (see Chapter 5).
2   Insufficient fuel reaching the fuel injector(s) (see Chapters 1 and 4).
3   Vacuum leak at the gasket between the intake manifold/plenum and throttle body (see Chapters 1 and 4).

7   Oil puddle under engine

1   Oil pan gasket and/or oil pan drain bolt washer leaking (see Chapter 2).
2   Oil pressure sending unit leaking (see Chapter 2).
3   Cylinder head covers leaking (see Chapter 2).
4   Engine oil seals leaking (see Chapter 2).
5   Oil pump housing leaking (see Chapter 2).

8   Engine lopes while idling or idles erratically

1   Vacuum leakage (see Chapters 2 and 4).
2   Leaking EGR valve (see Chapter 6).
3   Air filter clogged (see Chapter 1).
4   Fuel pump not delivering sufficient fuel to the fuel injection system (see Chapter 4).
5   Leaking head gasket (see Chapter 2).
6   Timing belt and/or pulleys worn (see Chapter 2).
7   Camshaft lobes worn (see Chapter 2).

9   Engine misses at idle speed

1   Spark plugs worn or not gapped properly (see Chapter 1).
2   Faulty spark plug wires (see Chapter 1).
3   Vacuum leaks (see Chapter 1).
4   Incorrect ignition timing (see Chapter 1).
5   Uneven or low compression (see Chapter 2).

10   Engine misses throughout driving speed range

1   Fuel filter clogged and/or impurities in the fuel system (see Chapter 1).
2   Low fuel output at the injector(s) (see Chapter 4).
3   Faulty or incorrectly gapped spark plugs (see Chapter 1).
4   Incorrect ignition timing (see Chapter 5).
5   Cracked distributor cap, disconnected distributor wires or damaged distributor components (see Chapters 1 and 5).
6   Leaking spark plug wires (see Chapters 1 or 5).
7   Faulty emission system components (see Chapter 6).
8   Low or uneven cylinder compression pressures (see Chapter 2).
9   Weak or faulty ignition system (see Chapter 5).

10 Vacuum leak in fuel injection system, intake manifold, air control valve or vacuum hoses (see Chapter 4).

11   Engine stumbles on acceleration

1   Ignition timing incorrect (see Chapter 5).
2   Spark plugs fouled (see Chapter 1).
3   Fuel injection system needs adjustment or repair (see Chapter 4).
4   Fuel filter clogged (see Chapters 1 and 4).
5   Intake manifold air leak (see Chapters 2 and 4).

12   Engine surges while holding accelerator steady

1   Intake air leak (see Chapter 4).
2   Fuel pump faulty (see Chapter 4).
3   Loose fuel injector wire harness connectors (see Chapter 4).
4   Defective ECU (see Chapter 6).

13   Engine stalls

1   Fuel filter clogged and/or water and impurities in the fuel system (see Chapters 1 and 4).
2   Distributor components damp or damaged (see Chapter 5).
3   Faulty emissions system components (see Chapter 6).
4   Faulty or incorrectly gapped spark plugs (see Chapter 1).
5   Faulty spark plug wires (see Chapter 1).
6   Vacuum leak in the fuel injection system, intake manifold or vacuum hoses (see Chapters 2 and 4).

14   Engine lacks power

1   Ignition timing incorrect (see Chapter 5).
2   Excessive play in distributor shaft (see Chapter 5).
3   Worn rotor, distributor cap or wires (see Chapters 1 and 5).
4   Faulty or incorrectly gapped spark plugs (see Chapter 1).
5   Fuel injection system out of adjustment or excessively worn (see Chapter 4).
6   Faulty coil (see Chapter 5).
7   Brakes binding (see Chapter 9).
8   Automatic transaxle fluid level incorrect (see Chapter 1).
9   Clutch slipping (see Chapter 8).
10 Fuel filter clogged and/or impurities in the fuel system (see Chapters 1 and 4).
11 Emission control system not functioning properly (see Chapter 6).
12 Low or uneven cylinder compression pressures (see Chapter 2).

15   Engine backfires

1   Emission control system not functioning properly (see Chapter 6).
2   Ignition timing incorrect (see Chapter 5).
3   Faulty secondary ignition system (cracked spark plug insulator, faulty plug wires, distributor cap and/or rotor) (see Chapters 1 and 5).
4   Fuel injection system in need of adjustment or worn excessively (see Chapter 4).
5   Vacuum leak at fuel injector(s), intake manifold, air control valve or vacuum hoses (see Chapters 2 and 4).

16   Pinging or knocking engine sounds during acceleration or uphill

1   Incorrect grade of fuel.
2   Ignition timing incorrect (see Chapter 5).
3   Fuel injection system in need of adjustment (see Chapter 4).
4   Improper or damaged spark plugs or wires (see Chapter 1).
5   Worn or damaged distributor components (see Chapter 5).
6   Faulty emission system (see Chapter 6).
7   Vacuum leak (see Chapters 2 and 4).

17   Engine runs with oil pressure light on

1   Low oil level (see Chapter 1).
2   Idle rpm below specification (see Chapter 1).
3   Short in wiring circuit (see Chapter 12).
4   Faulty oil pressure sender (see Chapter 2).
5   Worn engine bearings and/or oil pump (see Chapter 2).

18   Engine diesels (continues to run) after switching off

1   Problem with the fuel injection system (see Chapter 4)
2   Excessive engine operating temperature (see Chapter 3).

Engine electrical system

19   Battery will not hold a charge

1   Alternator drivebelt defective or not adjusted properly (see Chapter 1).
2   Battery electrolyte level low (see Chapter 1).
3   Battery terminals loose or corroded (see Chapter 1).
4   Alternator not charging properly (see Chapter 5).
5   Loose, broken or faulty wiring in the charging circuit (see Chapter 5).
6   Short in vehicle wiring (see Chapter 12).
7   Internally defective battery (see Chapters 1 and 5).

20   Alternator light fails to go out

1   Faulty alternator or charging circuit (see Chapter 5).
2   Alternator drivebelt defective or out of adjustment (see Chapter 1).
3   Alternator voltage regulator inoperative (see Chapter 5).

21   Alternator light fails to come on when key is turned on

1   Warning light bulb defective (see Chapter 12).
2   Fault in the printed circuit, dash wiring or bulb holder (see Chapter 12).

Fuel system

22   Excessive fuel consumption

1   Dirty or clogged air filter element (see Chapter 1).
2   Incorrectly set ignition timing (see Chapter 5).
3   Emissions system not functioning properly (see Chapter 6).
4   Fuel injection internal parts excessively worn or damaged (see Chapter 4).
5   Low tire pressure or incorrect tire size (see Chapter 1).

23   Fuel leakage and/or fuel odor

1   Leaking fuel feed or return line (see Chapters 1 and 4).
2   Tank overfilled.
3   Evaporative canister filter clogged (see Chapters 1 and 6).
4   Fuel injector internal parts excessively worn (see Chapter 4).

Cooling system

24   Overheating

1   Insufficient coolant in system (see Chapter 1).
2   Water pump drivebelt defective or out of adjustment (see Chapter 1).
3   Radiator core blocked or grille restricted (see Chapter 3).
4   Thermostat faulty (see Chapter 3).
5   Electric coolant fan blades broken or cracked (see Chapter 3).
6   Radiator cap not maintaining proper pressure (see Chapter 3).
7   Ignition timing incorrect (see Chapter 5).

25   Overcooling

1   Faulty thermostat (see Chapter 3).
2   Inaccurate temperature gauge sending unit (see Chapter 3)

26   External coolant leakage

1   Deteriorated/damaged hoses; loose clamps (see Chapters 1 and 3).
2   Water pump seal defective (see Chapter 3).
3   Leakage from radiator core or coolant reservoir bottle (see Chapter 3).
4   Engine drain or water jacket core plugs leaking (see Chapter 2).

27   Internal coolant leakage

1   Leaking cylinder head gasket (see Chapter 2).
2   Cracked cylinder bore or cylinder head (see Chapter 2).

28   Coolant loss

1   Too much coolant in system (see Chapter 1).
2   Coolant boiling away because of overheating (see Chapter 3).
3   Internal or external leakage (see Chapter 3).
4   Faulty radiator cap (see Chapter 3).

29   Poor coolant circulation

1   Inoperative water pump (see Chapter 3).
2   Restriction in cooling system (see Chapters 1 and 3).
3   Water pump drivebelt defective/out of adjustment (see Chapter 1).
4   Thermostat sticking (see Chapter 3).

Clutch

30   Pedal travels to floor – no pressure or very little resistance

1   Master or release cylinder faulty (see Chapter 8).
2   Hose/pipe burst or leaking (see Chapter 8).

3   Connections leaking (see Chapter 8).
4   No fluid in reservoir (see Chapter 8).
5   If fluid level in reservoir rises as pedal is depressed, master cylinder center valve seal is faulty (see Chapter 8).
6   If there is fluid on dust seal at master cylinder, piston primary seal is leaking (see Chapter 8).
7   Broken release bearing or fork (see Chapter 8).

31   Fluid in area of master cylinder dust cover and on pedal

Rear seal failure in master cylinder (see Chapter 8).

32   Fluid on release cylinder

Release cylinder plunger seal faulty (see Chapter 8).

33   Pedal feels spongy when depressed

Air in system (see Chapter 8).

34   Unable to select gears

1   Faulty transaxle (see Chapter 7).
2   Faulty clutch disc (see Chapter 8).
3   Fork and bearing not assembled properly (see Chapter 8).
4   Faulty pressure plate (see Chapter 8).
5   Pressure plate-to-flywheel bolts loose (see Chapter 8).

35   Clutch slips (engine speed increases with no increase in vehicle speed)

1   Clutch plate worn (see Chapter 8).
2   Clutch plate is oil soaked by leaking rear main seal (see Chapter 8).
3   Clutch plate not seated. It may take 30 or 40 normal starts for a new one to seat.
4   Warped pressure plate or flywheel (see Chapter 8).
5   Weak diaphragm spring (see Chapter 8).
6   Clutch plate overheated. Allow to cool.

36   Grabbing (chattering) as clutch is engaged

1   Oil on clutch plate lining, burned or glazed facings (see Chapter 8).
2   Worn or loose engine or transaxle mounts (see Chapters 2 and 7).
3   Worn splines on clutch plate hub (see Chapter 8).
4   Warped pressure plate or flywheel (see Chapter 8).
5   Burned or smeared resin on flywheel or pressure plate (see Chapter 8).

37   Transaxle rattling (clicking)

1   Release fork loose (see Chapter 8).
2   Clutch plate damper spring failure (see Chapter 8).
3   Low engine idle speed (see Chapter 1).

38 Noise in clutch area

1 Fork shaft improperly installed (see Chapter 8).
2 Faulty release bearing (see Chapter 8).

39 Clutch pedal stays on floor

1 Piston binding in bore (see Chapter 8).
2 Broken release bearing or fork (see Chapter 8).

40 High pedal effort

1 Piston binding in bore (see Chapter 8).
2 Pressure plate faulty (see Chapter 8).
3 Incorrect size master or release cylinder (see Chapter 8).

Manual transaxle

41 Knocking noise at low speeds

1 Worn driveaxle constant velocity (CV) joints (see Chapter 8).
2 Worn side gear shaft counterbore in differential case (see Chapter 7A)*.

42 Noise most pronounced when turning

Differential gear noise (see Chapter 7A).*

43 Clunk on acceleration or deceleration

1 Loose engine or transaxle mounts (see Chapters 2 and 7A).
2 Worn differential pinion shaft in case.*
3 Worn side gear shaft counterbore in differential case (see Chapter 7A).*
4 Worn or damaged driveaxle inner CV joints (see Chapter 8).

44 Clicking noise in turns

Worn or damaged outer CV joint (see Chapter 8).

45 Vibration

1 Rough wheel bearing (see Chapters 1 and 10).
2 Damaged driveaxle (see Chapter 8).
3 Out of round tires (see Chapter 1).
4 Tire out of balance (see Chapters 1 and 10).
5 Worn CV joint (see Chapter 8).

46 Noisy in neutral with engine running

1 Damaged input gear bearing (see Chapter 7A).*
2 Damaged clutch release bearing (see Chapter 8).

47 Noisy in one particular gear

1 Damaged or worn constant mesh gears (see Chapter 7A).*
2 Damaged or worn synchronizers (see Chapter 7A).*
3 Bent reverse fork (see Chapter 7A).*
4 Damaged fourth speed gear or output gear (see Chapter 7A).*
5 Worn or damaged reverse idler gear or idler bushing (see Chapter 7A).*

48 Noisy in all gears

1 Insufficient lubricant (see Chapter 7A).
2 Damaged or worn bearings (see Chapter 7A).*
3 Worn or damaged input gear shaft and/or output gear shaft (see Chapter 7A).*

49 Slips out of gear

1 Worn or improperly adjusted linkage (see Chapter 7A).
2 Transaxle loose on engine (see Chapter 7A).
3 Shift linkage does not work freely, binds (see Chapter 7A).
4 Input gear bearing retainer broken or loose (see Chapter 7A).*
5 Dirt between clutch cover and engine housing (see Chapter 7A).
6 Worn shift fork (see Chapter 7A).*

50 Leaks lubricant

1 Side gear shaft seals worn (see Chapter 8).
2 Excessive amount of lubricant in transaxle (see Chapters 1 and 7A).
3 Loose or broken input gear shaft bearing retainer (see Chapter 7A).*
4 Input gear bearing retainer O-ring and/or lip seal damaged (see Chapter 7A).*

51 Difficulty in engaging gears

1 Clutch not releasing completely (see Chapter 8).
2 Loose, damaged or out-of-adjustment shift linkage. Make a thorough inspection, replacing parts as necessary (see Chapter 7).

* Although the corrective action necessary to remedy the symptoms described is beyond the scope of the home mechanic, the above information should be helpful in isolating the cause of the condition so that the owner can communicate clearly with a professional mechanic.

Automatic transaxle

Note: *Due to the complexity of the automatic transaxle, it is difficult for the home mechanic to properly diagnose and service this component. For problems other than the following, the vehicle should be taken to a dealer service department or transmission shop.*

52 Fluid leakage

1 Automatic transmission fluid is a deep red color. Fluid leaks should not be confused with engine oil, which can easily be blown onto the transaxle by air flow.
2 To pinpoint a leak, first remove all built-up dirt and grime from the transaxle housing with degreasing agents and/or steam cleaning. Then drive the vehicle at low speeds so air flow will not blow the leak far from its source. Raise the vehicle and determine where the leak is coming from. Common areas of leakage are:
   a) Pan (see Chapters 1 and 7)

b) Dipstick tube (see Chapters 1 and 7)
c) Transaxle oil lines (see Chapter 7)
d) Speed sensor (see Chapter 7)

53   Transaxle fluid brown or has a burned smell

Transaxle fluid burned (see Chapter 1).

54   General shift mechanism problems

1   Chapter 7, Part B, deals with checking and adjusting the shift linkage on automatic transaxles. Common problems which may be attributed to poorly adjusted linkage are:
a) Engine starting in gears other than Park or Neutral.
b) Indicator on shifter pointing to a gear other than the one actually being used.
c) Vehicle moves when in Park.
2   Refer to Chapter 7B for the shift linkage adjustment procedure.

55   Transaxle will not downshift with accelerator pedal pressed to the floor

Throttle valve cable out of adjustment (see Chapter 7B).

56   Engine will start in gears other than Park or Neutral

Neutral start switch malfunctioning (see Chapter 7B).

57   Transaxle slips, shifts roughly, is noisy or has no drive in forward or reverse gears

There are many probable causes for the above problems, but the home mechanic should be concerned with only one possibility – fluid level. Before taking the vehicle to a repair shop, check the level and condition of the fluid as described in Chapter 1. Correct the fluid level as necessary or change the fluid and filter if needed. If the problem persists, have a professional diagnose the cause.

Driveaxles

58   Clicking noise in turns

Worn or damaged outer CV joint (see Chapter 8).

59   Shudder or vibration during acceleration

1   Excessive toe-in (see Chapter 10).
2   Incorrect spring heights (see Chapter 10).
3   Worn or damaged inner or outer CV joints (see Chapter 8).
4   Sticking inner CV joint assembly (see Chapter 8).

60   Vibration at highway speeds

1   Out of balance front wheels and/or tires (see Chapters 1 and 10).
2   Out of round front tires (see Chapters 1 and 10).
3   Worn CV joint(s) (see Chapter 8).

Brakes

Note: *Before assuming that a brake problem exists, make sure that:*
a) The tires are in good condition and properly inflated (see Chapter 1).
b) The front end alignment is correct (see Chapter 10).
c) The vehicle is not loaded with weight in an unequal manner.

61   Vehicle pulls to one side during braking

1   Incorrect tire pressures (see Chapter 1).
2   Front end out of line (have the front end aligned).
3   Front or rear tires not matched to one another.
4   Restricted brake lines or hoses (see Chapter 9).
5   Malfunctioning drum brake or caliper assembly (see Chapter 9).
6   Loose suspension parts (see Chapter 10).
7   Loose calipers (see Chapter 9).
8   Excessive wear of brake shoe or pad material or disc/drum on one side.

62   Noise (high-pitched squeal when the brakes are applied)

Front and/or rear disc brake pads worn out. The noise comes from the wear sensor rubbing against the disc (does not apply to all vehicles). Replace pads with new ones immediately (see Chapter 9).

63   Brake roughness or chatter (pedal pulsates)

1   Excessive lateral runout (see Chapter 9).
2   Uneven pad wear (see Chapter 9).
3   Defective rotor (see Chapter 9).

64   Excessive brake pedal effort required to stop vehicle

1   Malfunctioning power brake booster (see Chapter 9).
2   Partial system failure (see Chapter 9).
3   Excessively worn pads or shoes (see Chapter 9).
4   Piston in caliper or wheel cylinder stuck or sluggish (see Chapter 9).
5   Brake pads or shoes contaminated with oil or grease (see Chapter 9).
6   New pads or shoes installed and not yet seated. It will take a while for the new material to seat against the rotor or drum.

65   Excessive brake pedal travel

1   Partial brake system failure (see Chapter 9).
2   Insufficient fluid in master cylinder (see Chapters 1 and 9).
3   Air trapped in system (see Chapters 1 and 9).

66   Dragging brakes

1   Incorrect adjustment of brake light switch (see Chapter 9).
2   Master cylinder pistons not returning correctly (see Chapter 9).
3   Restricted brakes lines or hoses (see Chapters 1 and 9).
4   Incorrect parking brake adjustment (see Chapter 9).

67   Grabbing or uneven braking action

1   Malfunction of proportioning valve (see Chapter 9).
2   Malfunction of power brake booster unit (see Chapter 9).
3   Binding brake pedal mechanism (see Chapter 9).

68   Brake pedal feels spongy when depressed

1   Air in hydraulic lines (see Chapter 9).

2 Master cylinder mounting bolts loose (see Chapter 9).
3 Master cylinder defective (see Chapter 9).

69   Brake pedal travels to the floor with little resistance

1 Little or no fluid in the master cylinder reservoir caused by leaking caliper piston(s) (see Chapter 9).
2 Loose, damaged or disconnected brake lines (see Chapter 9).

70   Parking brake does not hold

Parking brake linkage improperly adjusted (see Chapters 1 and 9).

Suspension and steering systems

Note: *Before attempting to diagnose the suspension and steering systems, perform the following preliminary checks:*
   a) Tires for wrong pressure and uneven wear.
   b) Steering universal joints from the column to the rack and pinion for loose connectors or wear.
   c) Front and rear suspension and the rack and pinion assembly for loose or damaged parts.
   d) Out-of-round or out-of-balance tires, bent rims and loose and/or rough wheel bearings.

71   Vehicle pulls to one side

1 Mismatched or uneven tires (see Chapter 10).
2 Broken or sagging springs (see Chapter 10).
3 Wheel alignment (see Chapter 10).
4 Front brake dragging (see Chapter 9).

72   Abnormal or excessive tire wear

1 Wheel alignment (see Chapter 10).
2 Sagging or broken springs (see Chapter 10).
3 Tire out of balance (see Chapter 10).
4 Worn strut damper (see Chapter 10).
5 Overloaded vehicle.
6 Tires not rotated regularly.

73   Wheel makes a thumping noise

1 Blister or bump on tire (see Chapter 10).
2 Improper strut damper action (see Chapter 10).

74   Shimmy, shake or vibration

1 Tire or wheel out-of-balance or out-of-round (see Chapter 10).
2 Loose or worn wheel bearings (see Chapters 1, 8 and 10).
3 Worn tie-rod ends (see Chapter 10).
4 Worn lower balljoints (see Chapters 1 and 10).
5 Excessive wheel runout (see Chapter 10).
6 Blister or bump on tire (see Chapter 10).

75   Hard steering

1 Lack of lubrication at balljoints, tie-rod ends and rack and pinion assembly (see Chapter 10).
2 Front wheel alignment (see Chapter 10).
3 Low tire pressure(s) (see Chapters 1 and 10).

76   Poor returnability of steering to center

1 Lack of lubrication at balljoints and tie-rod ends (see Chapter 10).
2 Binding in balljoints (see Chapter 10).
3 Binding in steering column (see Chapter 10).
4 Lack of lubricant in rack and pinion assembly (see Chapter 10).
5 Front wheel alignment (see Chapter 10).

77   Abnormal noise at the front end

1 Lack of lubrication at balljoints and tie-rod ends (see Chapters 1 and 10).
2 Damaged strut mounting (see Chapter 10).
3 Worn control arm bushings or tie-rod ends (see Chapter 10).
4 Loose stabilizer bar (see Chapter 10).
5 Loose wheel nuts (see Chapters 1 and 10).
6 Loose suspension bolts (see Chapter 10).

78   Wander or poor steering stability

1 Mismatched or uneven tires (see Chapter 10).
2 Lack of lubrication at balljoints and tie-rod ends (see Chapters 1 and 10).
3 Worn strut assemblies (see Chapter 10).
4 Loose stabilizer bar (see Chapter 10).
5 Broken or sagging springs (see Chapter 10).
6 Wheel alignment (see Chapter 10).

79   Erratic steering when braking

1 Wheel bearings worn (see Chapter 10).
2 Broken or sagging springs (see Chapter 10).
3 Leaking wheel cylinder or caliper (see Chapter 10).
4 Warped rotors or drums (see Chapter 10).

80   Excessive pitching and/or rolling around corners or during braking

1 Loose stabilizer bar (see Chapter 10).
2 Worn strut dampers or mountings (see Chapter 10).
3 Broken or sagging springs (see Chapter 10).
4 Overloaded vehicle.

81   Suspension bottoms

1 Overloaded vehicle.
2 Worn strut dampers (see Chapter 10).
3 Incorrect, broken or sagging springs (see Chapter 10).

82   Cupped tires

1 Front wheel or rear wheel alignment (see Chapter 10).

2 Worn strut dampers (see Chapter 10).
3 Wheel bearings worn (see Chapter 10).
4 Excessive tire or wheel runout (see Chapter 10).
5 Worn balljoints (see Chapter 10).

83 Excessive tire wear on outside edge

1 Inflation pressures incorrect (see Chapter 1).
2 Excessive speed in turns.
3 Front end alignment incorrect (excessive toe-in). Have professionally aligned.
4 Control arm bent or twisted (see Chapter 10).

84 Excessive tire wear on inside edge

1 Inflation pressures incorrect (see Chapter 1).
2 Front end alignment incorrect (toe-out). Have professionally aligned.
3 Loose or damaged steering components (see Chapter 10).

85 Tire tread worn in one place

1 Tires out of balance.
2 Damaged or buckled wheel. Inspect and replace if necessary.
3 Defective tire (see Chapter 1).

86 Excessive play or looseness in steering system

1 Wheel bearing(s) worn (see Chapter 10).
2 Tie-rod end loose (see Chapter 10).
3 Rack and pinion loose (see Chapter 10).
4 Worn or loose steering intermediate shaft (see Chapter 10).

87 Rattling or clicking noise in rack and pinion

1 Insufficient or improper lubricant in rack and pinion assembly (see Chapter 10).
2 Rack and pinion attachment loose (see Chapter 10).

Chapter 1 Tune-up and routine maintenance

Contents

Specifications

Recommended lubricants and fluids

Engine oil
  Type .... API grade SG, SG/CC or SG/CD multigrade and fuel efficient oil
  Viscosity .... See accompanying chart
  Capacity
    1989
      With filter change .... 4.9 qts
      Without filter change .... 4.5 qts

---

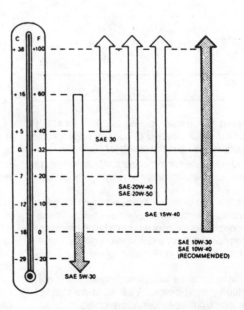

A ENGINE OIL VISCOSITY CHART

For best fuel economy and cold starting, select the lowest SAE viscosity grade oil for the expected temperature range

Recommended lubricants and fluids (continued)

1990
    Non-turbo four-cylinder and V6 engines
With filter change	4.5 qts
Without filter change	4.0 qts

    Turbo four-cylinder engine
With filter change	4.9 qts
Without filter change	4.5 qts
Brake fluid type	DOT 3 heavy-duty brake fluid
Power steering fluid type	Motorcraft MERCON automatic transmission fluid (part no. XT-2-QDX)
Automatic transaxle fluid type	Motorcraft MERCON automatic transmission fluid (part no. XT-2-QDX)

Manual transaxle lubricant
Type	Motorcraft MERCON automatic transmission fluid (part no. XT-2-QDX)

  Capacity (approximate)
Non-turbo	7.2 pts
Turbo	7.8 pts
Coolant type	A 50/50 mixture of ethylene glycol-based antifreeze and water
Cooling system capacity (approximate)	7.9 qts

Drivebelt tension (measured with special gauge)

Power steering/air conditioning compressor
New belt	154 to 198 lbs
Used belt	132 to 176 lbs

Alternator
New belt	132 to 176 lbs
Used belt	110 to 154 lbs

Brakes

Disc brake pad lining thickness (minimum)	1/8 in
Drum brake shoe lining thickness (minimum)	1/16 in

Ignition system

Spark plug type	Refer to the Vehicle Emission Control Information label
Spark plug gap	Refer to the Vehicle Emission Control Information label

Clutch pedal

Height	8 1/2 to 8 3/4 in
Freeplay	1/4 to 1/2 in

Torque specifications

Ft-lbs (unless otherwise indicated)

Wheel lug nuts	65 to 87

Spark plugs
Four-cylinder engine	11 to 17
V6 engine	7 to 15

Oil pan drain plug
1989	26 to 35
1990	10
Automatic transaxle pan bolts	69 to 95 in-lbs

---

1   Introduction

Warning: *The electric cooling fan on these models can activate at any time, even when the ignition is in the Off position. Disconnect the fan motor or negative battery cable when working in the vicinity of the fan.*

This Chapter is designed to help the home mechanic maintain the Ford Probe with the goals of maximum performance, economy, safety and reliability in mind.

On the following pages is a master maintenance schedule, followed by procedures dealing specifically with each item on the schedule. Visual checks, adjustments, component replacement and other helpful items are included. Refer to the accompanying illustrations of the engine compartment and the underside of the vehicle for the locations of various components.

Servicing your vehicle in accordance with the mileage/time maintenance schedule and the step-by-step procedures will result in a planned maintenance program that should produce a long and reliable service life.

Keep in mind that it is a comprehensive plan, so maintaining some items but not others at the specified intervals will not produce the same results.

As you service your vehicle, you will discover that many of the procedures can – and should – be grouped together because of the nature of the particular procedure you're performing or because of the close proximity of two otherwise unrelated components to one another.

For example, if the vehicle is raised for chassis lubrication, you should inspect the exhaust, suspension, steering and fuel systems while you're under the vehicle. When you're rotating the tires, it makes good sense to check the brakes since the wheels are already removed. Finally, let's suppose you have to borrow or rent a torque wrench. Even if you only need it to tighten the spark plugs, you might as well check the torque of as many critical fasteners as time allows.

The first step in this maintenance program is to prepare yourself before the actual work begins. Read through all the procedures you're planning to do, then gather up all the parts and tools needed. If it looks as if you might run into problems during a particular job, seek advice from a mechanic or an experienced do-it-yourselfer.

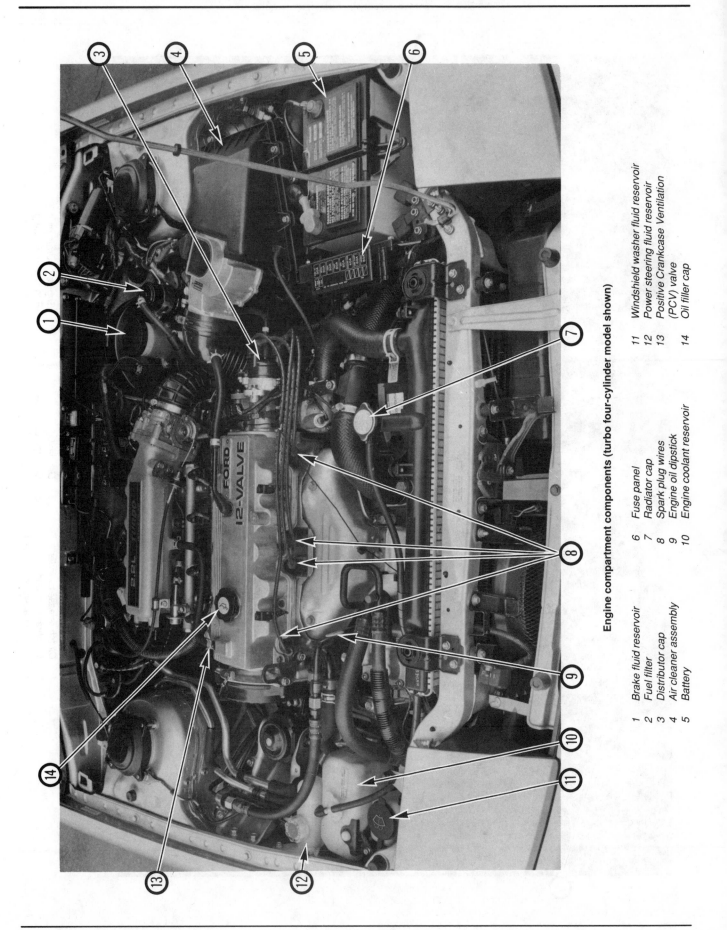

Engine compartment components (turbo four-cylinder model shown)

1   Brake fluid reservoir
2   Fuel filter
3   Distributor cap
4   Air cleaner assembly
5   Battery

6   Fuse panel
7   Radiator cap
8   Spark plug wires
9   Engine oil dipstick
10 Engine coolant reservoir

11 Windshield washer fluid reservoir
12 Power steering fluid reservoir
13 Positive Crankcase Ventilation
    (PCV) valve
14 Oil filler cap

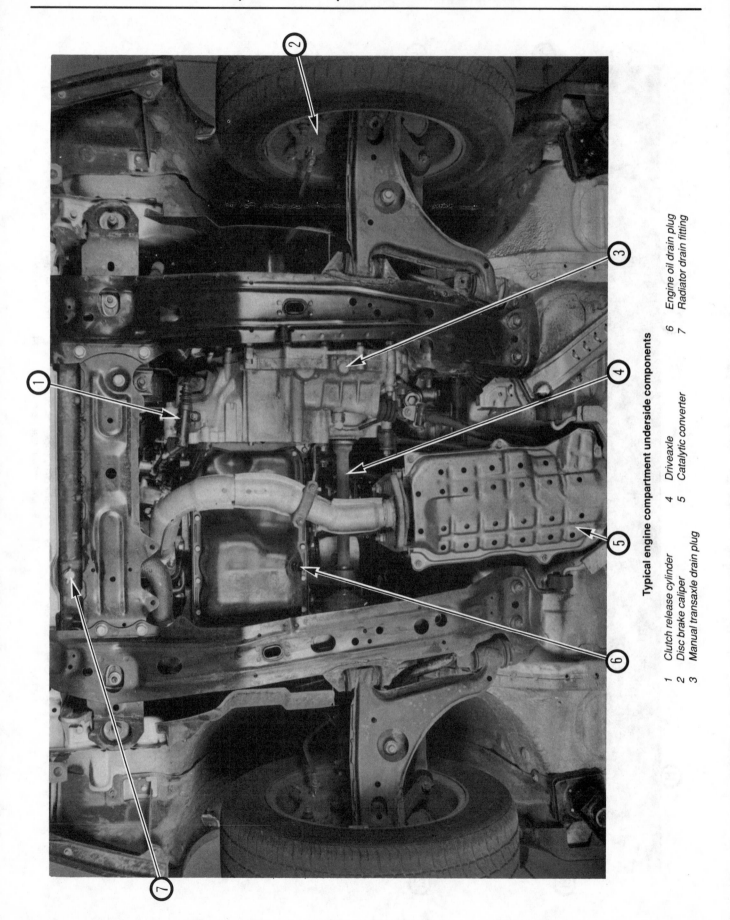

Typical engine compartment underside components

1   Clutch release cylinder
2   Disc brake caliper
3   Manual transaxle drain plug
4   Driveaxle
5   Catalytic converter
6   Engine oil drain plug
7   Radiator drain fitting

Typical vehicle rear underside components

1	Rear lateral link	4	Stabilizer bar
2	Parking brake cable	5	Fuel filler neck
3	Front lateral link	6	Exhaust system hanger
		7	Muffler

2 Ford Probe Maintenance schedule

The following maintenance intervals are based on the assumption that the vehicle owner will be doing the maintenance or service work, as opposed to having a dealer service department do the work. Although the time/mileage intervals are loosely based on factory recommendations, most have been shortened to ensure, for example, that such items as lubricants and fluids are checked/changed at intervals that promote maximum engine/driveline service life. Also, subject to the preference of the individual owner interested in keeping his or her vehicle in peak condition at all times, and with the vehicle's ultimate resale in mind, many of the maintenance procedures may be performed more often than recommended in the following schedule. We encourage such owner initiative.

When the vehicle is new it should be serviced initially by a factory authorized dealer service department to protect the factory warranty. In many cases the initial maintenance check is done at no cost to the owner.

Every 250 miles or weekly, whichever comes first

Check the engine oil level (see Section 4)
Check the engine coolant level (see Section 4)
Check the windshield washer fluid level (see Section 4)
Check the brake fluid level (see Section 4)
Check the tires and tire pressures (see Section 5)

Every 3000 miles or 3 months, whichever comes first

All items listed above plus . . .
Check the power steering fluid level (see Section 6)
Check the automatic transaxle fluid level (see Section 7)
Change the engine oil and oil filter (see Section 8)

Every 6000 miles or 6 months, whichever comes first

All items listed above plus . . .
Adjust the clutch pedal (see Section 9)
Inspect/replace the underhood hoses (see Section 10)
Check/adjust the drivebelts (see Section 11)
Check/service the battery (see Section 12)

Every 12,000 miles or 12 months, whichever comes first

All items listed above plus . . .
Inspect/replace the windshield wiper blades (see Section 13)
Replace the air filter (see Section 14)
Check the PCV valve (see Section 15)
Check the fuel system (see Section 16)
Replace the fuel filter (see Section 17)
Inspect the cooling system (see Section 18)
Inspect the exhaust system (see Section 19)
Rotate the tires (see Section 20)
Inspect the steering and suspension components (see Section 21)*
Inspect the brake system (see Section 22)
Lubricate the parking brake cable (see Section 22)
Check/replenish the manual transaxle lubricant (see Section 23)

Every 30,000 miles or 30 months, whichever comes first

Replace the spark plugs (see Section 24)
Check/replace the spark plug wires, distributor cap and rotor (see Section 25)*
Service the cooling system (drain, flush and refill) (see Section 26)
Change the automatic transaxle fluid and filter (see Section 27)**

* This item is affected by "severe" operating conditions as described below. If the vehicle in question is operated under "severe" conditions, perform all maintenance indicated with an asterisk (*) at 6000-mile/six-month intervals. Consider the conditions "severe" if most driving is done . . .
in dusty areas
when towing a trailer
at low speeds or with extended periods of engine idling
when outside temperatures remain below freezing and most trips are less than four miles.

** If most driving is done under one or more of the following conditions, change the automatic transaxle fluid every 12,000 miles:
In heavy city traffic where the outside temperature regularly reaches 90-degrees F (32-degrees C) or higher
In hilly or mountainous terrain
Frequent trailer pulling

3   Tune-up general information

The term tune-up is used in this manual to represent a combination of individual operations rather than one specific procedure.

If, from the time the vehicle is new, the routine maintenance schedule is followed closely and frequent checks are made of fluid levels and high wear items, as suggested throughout this manual, the engine will be kept in relatively good running condition and the need for additional work will be minimized.

More likely than not, however, there will be times when the engine is running poorly. This is even more likely if a used vehicle, which has not received regular and frequent maintenance checks, is purchased. In such cases, an engine tune-up will be needed outside of the regular routine maintenance intervals.

The first step in any tune-up or diagnostic procedure to help correct a poor running engine is a cylinder compression check. A compression check (see Chapter 2 Part C) will help determine the condition of internal engine components and should be used as a guide for tune-up and repair procedures. If, for instance, a compression check indicates serious internal engine wear, a conventional tune-up will not improve the performance of the engine and would be a waste of time and money. Because of its importance, the compression check should be done by someone with the right equipment and the knowledge to use it properly.

The following procedures are those most often needed to bring a generally poor running engine back into a proper state of tune.

Minor tune-up

Clean, inspect and test the battery (see Section 12)
Check all engine related fluids (see Section 4)
Check and adjust the drivebelts (see Section 11)
Replace the spark plugs (see Section 24)
Inspect the distributor cap and rotor (see Section 25)
Inspect the spark plug and coil wires (see Section 25)
Check the PCV valve (see Section 15)
Check the air filter (see Section 14)
Check the cooling system (see Section 18)
Check all underhood hoses (see Section 10)

Major tune-up

All items listed under Minor tune-up, plus . . .
Check the EGR system (see Chapter 6)
Check the ignition system (see Chapter 5)
Check the charging system (see Chapter 5)
Check the fuel system (see Chapter 4)
Replace the air and crankcase ventilator filters (see Sections 14 and 15)
Replace the distributor cap and rotor (see Section 25)
Replace the spark plug wires (see Section 25)

4   Fluid level checks

1   Fluids are an essential part of the lubrication, cooling, brake and windshield washer systems. Because the fluids gradually become depleted and/or contaminated during normal operation of the vehicle, they must be periodically replenished. See Recommended lubricants, fluids and capacities at the beginning of this Chapter before adding fluid to any of the following components. **Note:** *The vehicle must be on level ground when fluid levels are checked.*

Engine oil

Refer to illustrations 4.2, 4.4 and 4.6

2   The oil level is checked with a dipstick, which is located on the front of

4.2   The engine oil dipstick is located on the front (radiator) side of the engine (four-cylinder model shown)

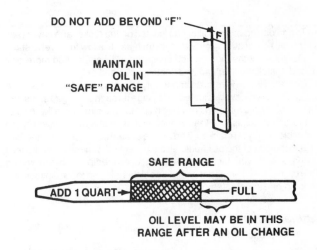

4.4   The oil level should be in the Safe range – if it's below the L or ADD mark, add enough oil to bring it up to or near the F or FULL mark

the engine **(see illustration)**. The dipstick extends through a metal tube down into the oil pan.

3   The oil level should be checked before the vehicle has been driven, or about 15 minutes after the engine has been shut off. If the oil is checked immediately after driving the vehicle, some of the oil will remain in the upper part of the engine, resulting in an inaccurate reading on the dipstick.

4   Pull the dipstick from the tube and wipe all the oil from the end with a clean rag or paper towel. Insert the clean dipstick all the way back into the tube and pull it out again. Note the oil at the end of the dipstick. At its highest point, the level should be above the L or ADD mark, in the SAFE range **(see illustration)**.

5   It takes one quart of oil to raise the level from the L or ADD mark to the F or FULL mark. Do not allow the level to drop below the L or ADD mark, or oil starvation may cause engine damage. Conversely, overfilling the engine (adding oil above the F or FULL mark) may cause oil fouled spark plugs, oil leaks or oil seal failures.

4.6   Turn the oil filler cap counterclockwise to remove it – always make sure the area around the opening is clean before unscrewing the cap (to prevent dirt from contaminating the engine)

4.8   The coolant reservoir is clearly marked with LOW and FULL marks – make sure the level is slightly above the LOW mark when the engine is cold and at or near the FULL mark when the engine is warmed up

6   To add oil, remove the filler cap located on the rocker arm cover **(see illustration)**. After adding oil, wait a few minutes to allow the level to stabilize, then pull out the dipstick and check the level again. Add more oil if required. Install the filler cap and tighten it by hand only.

7   Checking the oil level is an important preventive maintenance step. A consistently low oil level indicates oil leakage through damaged seals, defective gaskets or worn rings or valve guides. If the oil looks milky in color or has water droplets in it, the cylinder head gasket may be blown or the head or block may be cracked. The engine should be checked immediately. The condition of the oil should also be checked. Whenever you check the oil level, slide your thumb and index finger up the dipstick before wiping off the oil. If you see small dirt or metal particles clinging to the dipstick, the oil should be changed (see Section 8).

Engine coolant

Refer to illustration 4.8

Warning: *Do not allow antifreeze to come in contact with your skin or painted surfaces of the vehicle. Flush contaminated areas immediately with plenty of water. Do not store new coolant or leave old coolant lying around where it's accessible to children or pets – they are attracted by its sweet taste. Ingestion of even a small amount of coolant can be fatal! Wipe up garage floor and drip pan coolant spills immediately. Keep antifreeze containers covered and repair leaks in your cooling system immediately.*

8   All vehicles covered by this manual are equipped with a pressurized coolant recovery system. A white plastic coolant reservoir located in the right front corner of the engine compartment is connected by a hose to the radiator filler neck. The coolant and windshield washer reservoirs are very close to each other, so always be sure to add only the correct fluids to each; the filler caps are clearly marked **(see illustration)**. If the engine overheats, coolant escapes through a valve in the radiator cap and travels through the hose into the reservoir. As the engine cools, the coolant is automatically drawn back into the cooling system to maintain the correct level.

9   The coolant level in the reservoir should be checked regularly. **Warning:** *Do not remove the radiator cap to check the coolant level when the engine is warm.* The level in the reservoir varies with the temperature of the engine. When the engine is cold, the coolant level should be at or slightly above the ADD mark on the reservoir. Once the engine has warmed up, the level should be at or near the FULL mark. If it isn't, allow the engine to cool, then remove the cap from the reservoir and add a 50/50 mixture of ethylene glycol based antifreeze and water.

10   Drive the vehicle and recheck the coolant level. Do not use rust inhibi-

tors or additives. If only a small amount of coolant is required to bring the system up to the proper level, water can be used. However, repeated additions of water will dilute the antifreeze and water solution. In order to maintain the proper ratio of antifreeze and water, always top up the coolant level with the correct mixture. An empty plastic milk jug or bleach bottle makes an excellent container for mixing coolant.

11   If the coolant level drops consistently, there may be a leak in the system. Inspect the radiator, hoses, filler cap, drain plugs and water pump (see Section 18). If no leaks are noted, have the radiator cap pressure tested by a service station.

12   If you have to remove the radiator cap, wait until the engine has cooled completely, then wrap a thick cloth around the cap and turn it to the first stop. If coolant or steam escapes, let the engine cool down longer, then remove the cap.

13   Check the condition of the coolant as well. It should be relatively clear. If it is brown or rust colored, the system should be drained, flushed and refilled. Even if the coolant appears to be normal, the corrosion inhibitors wear out, so it must be replaced at the specified intervals.

Brake fluid

Refer to illustration 4.15

14   The brake fluid level is checked by looking through the plastic reservoir mounted on the master cylinder. The master cylinder is mounted on the front of the power booster unit in the left rear corner of the engine compartment.

15   The fluid level should be between the MAX and MIN lines on the side of the reservoir **(see illustration)**.

16   If the fluid level is low, wipe the top of the reservoir and the cap with a clean rag to prevent contamination of the system as the cap is unscrewed.

17   Add only the specified brake fluid to the reservoir (see *Recommended lubricants and fluids* at the front of this Chapter or your owner's manual). Mixing different types of brake fluid can damage the system. Fill the reservoir to the MAX line. **Warning:** *Brake fluid can harm your eyes and damage painted surfaces, so use extreme caution when handling or pouring it. Do not use brake fluid that has been standing open or is more than one year old. Brake fluid absorbs moisture from the air. Excess moisture can cause damage to the braking system.*

18   While the reservoir cap is off, check the master cylinder reservoir for contamination. If rust deposits, dirt particles or water droplets are present, the system should be drained and refilled by a dealer service department or repair shop.

19   After filling the reservoir to the proper level, make sure the cap is seated to prevent fluid leakage and/or contamination.

4.15   The brake fluid level should be kept between the MIN and MAX lines on the translucent plastic reservoir – unscrew the cap to add fluid

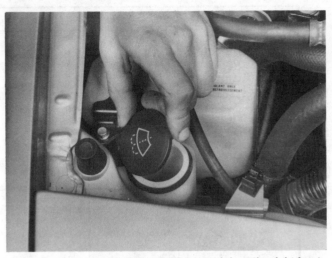

4.22   The windshield washer fluid reservoir is at the right front corner of the engine compartment – be careful not to confuse it with the coolant reservoir

20   The fluid level in the master cylinder will drop slightly as the brake shoes or pads at each wheel wear down during normal operation. If the brake fluid level drops significantly, check the entire system for leaks immediately. Examine all brake lines, hoses and connections, along with the calipers, wheel cylinders and master cylinder (see Section 22).

21   When checking the fluid level, if you discover one or both reservoirs empty or nearly empty, the brake system should be bled (see Chapter 9).

Windshield washer fluid

Refer to illustration 4.22

22   The windshield washer fluid reservoir **(see illustration)** is mounted on the right side of the engine compartment, right in front of the coolant reservoir.

23   In milder climates, plain water can be used in the reservoir, but it should be kept no more than 2/3 full to allow for expansion if the water freezes. In colder climates, use windshield washer system antifreeze, available at any auto parts store, to lower the freezing point of the fluid. Mix the antifreeze with water in accordance with the manufacturer's directions on the container. **Caution:** *Do not use cooling system antifreeze – it will damage the vehicle's paint.*

Hydraulic clutch fluid

Refer to illustration 4.24

24   With the engine off, locate the clutch fluid reservoir near the brake master cylinder on the firewall **(see illustration)**.

4.24   Keep the clutch fluid reservoir filled to the seam on the side – to add fluid, remove the cap (arrow)

25   Wipe off any accumulated dirt from the translucent reservoir and note the fluid level. If it's at or above the step in the reservoir body, the level is okay. **Caution:** *The fluid level in the reservoir slowly increases as the clutch wears, so raising the level above the step may cause the fluid to overflow.*

26   To add fluid to the reservoir, remove the cap by rotating it counter-clockwise and remove the diaphragm. Use only the fluid specified at the beginning of this Chapter. Don't fill the reservoir above the step in the reservoir body.

27   Install the diaphragm and cap immediately after you've added fluid to prevent moisture from contaminating the fluid.

5   Tire and tire pressure checks

Refer to illustrations 5.2, 5.3, 5.4a, 5.4b and 5.8

1   Periodic inspection of the tires may spare you the inconvenience of being stranded with a flat tire. It can also provide you with vital information regarding possible problems in the steering and suspension systems before major damage occurs.

2   The original tires on this vehicle are equipped with 1/2-inch side bands that will appear when tread depth reaches 1/16-inch, but they don't appear until the tires are worn out. Tread wear can be monitored with a simple, inexpensive device known as a tread depth indicator **(see illustration)**.

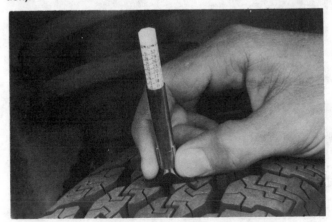

5.2   A tread depth indicator should be used to monitor tire wear – they are available at auto parts stores and service stations and cost very little

Condition	Probable cause	Corrective action	Condition	Probable cause	Corrective action
Shoulder wear	• Underinflation (both sides wear) • Incorrect wheel camber (one side wear) • Hard cornering • Lack of rotation	• Measure and adjust pressure. • Repair or replace axle and suspension parts. • Reduce speed. • Rotate tires.	Feathered edge **Toe wear**	• Incorrect toe	• Adjust toe-in.
Center wear	• Overinflation • Lack of rotation	• Measure and adjust pressure. • Rotate tires.	**Uneven wear**	• Incorrect camber or caster • Malfunctioning suspension • Unbalanced wheel • Out-of-round brake drum • Lack of rotation	• Repair or replace axle and suspension parts. • Repair or replace suspension parts. • Balance or replace. • Turn or replace. • Rotate tires.

5.3   This chart will help you determine the condition of your tires, the probable cause(s) of abnormal wear and the corrective action necessary

3   Note any abnormal tread wear **(see illustration)**. Tread pattern irregularities such as cupping, flat spots and more wear on one side than the other are indications of front end alignment and/or balance problems. If any of these conditions are noted, take the vehicle to a tire shop or service station to correct the problem.
4   Look closely for cuts, punctures and embedded nails or tacks. Sometimes a tire will hold air pressure for a short time or leak down very slowly after a nail has embedded itself in the tread. If a slow leak persists, check the valve stem core to make sure it is tight **(see illustration)**. Examine the tread for an object that may have embedded itself in the tire or for a "plug" that may have begun to leak (radial tire punctures are repaired with a plug that is installed in the puncture). If a puncture is suspected, it can be easily verified by spraying a solution of soapy water onto the puncture area **(see illustration)**. The soapy solution will bubble if there is a leak. Unless the puncture is unusually large, a tire shop or service station can normally repair the tire.
5   Carefully inspect the inner sidewall of each tire for evidence of brake fluid leakage. If you see any, inspect the brakes immediately.
6   Correct air pressure adds miles to the lifespan of the tires, improves mileage and enhances overall ride quality. Tire pressure cannot be accurately estimated by looking at a tire, especially if it's a radial. A tire pressure gauge is essential. Keep an accurate gauge in the glovebox. The pressure gauges attached to the nozzles of air hoses at gas stations are often inaccurate.

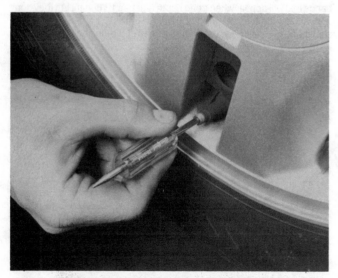

5.4a   If a tire loses air on a steady basis, check the valve core first to make sure it's snug (special inexpensive wrenches are commonly available at auto parts stores)

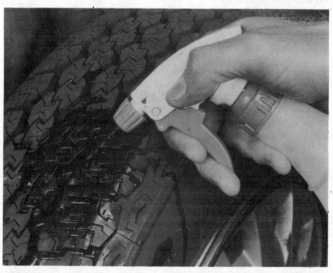

5.4b   If the valve core is tight, raise the corner of the vehicle with the low tire and spray a soapy water solution onto the tread as the tire is turned slowly – slow leaks will cause bubbles to appear

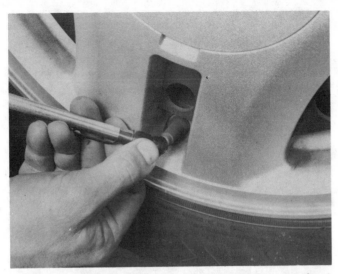

5.8   To extend the life of the tires, check the air pressure at least once a week with an accurate gauge (don't forget the spare!)

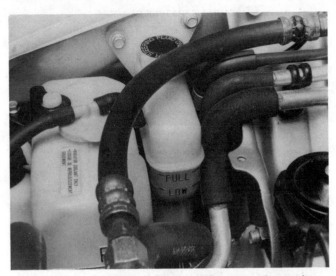

6.2   The fluid level in the power steering reservoir must be between the LOW and FULL marks

7   Always check tire pressure when the tires are cold. Cold, in this case, means the vehicle has not been driven over a mile in the three hours preceding a tire pressure check. A pressure rise of four to eight pounds is not uncommon once the tires are warm.

8   Unscrew the valve cap protruding from the wheel or hubcap and push the gauge firmly onto the valve stem **(see illustration)**. Note the reading on the gauge and compare the figure to the recommended tire pressure shown on the tire placard on the driver's side door. Be sure to reinstall the valve cap to keep dirt and moisture out of the valve stem mechanism. Check all four tires and, if necessary, add enough air to bring them up to the recommended pressure.

9   Don't forget to keep the spare tire inflated to the specified pressure (see your owner's manual or the tire sidewall). Note that the pressure recommended for the compact spare is higher than for the tires on the vehicle.

6   Power steering fluid level check

Refer to illustration 6.2

1   Check the power steering fluid level periodically to avoid steering system problems, such as damage to the pump. **Caution:** *DO NOT hold the steering wheel against either stop (extreme left or right turn) for more than five seconds. If you do, the power steering pump could be damaged.*

2   The power steering reservoir, located at the right front corner of the engine, has LOW and FULL fluid level marks on the side **(see illustration)**.

3   Park the vehicle on level ground and apply the parking brake.

4   Run the engine until it has reached normal operating temperature. With the engine at idle, turn the steering wheel back and forth about 10 times to get any air out of the steering system. Shut the engine off with the wheels in the straight ahead position.

5   Note the fluid level. It must be between the LOW and FULL marks.

6   Add small amounts of fluid until the level is correct. **Caution:** *Do not overfill the reservoir. If too much fluid is added, remove the excess with a clean syringe or suction pump.*

7   Check the power steering hoses and connections for leaks and wear (see Section 10).

8   Check the condition and tension of the power steering pump drivebelt (see Section 11).

7   Automatic transaxle fluid level check

Refer to illustrations 7.4 and 7.6

1   The automatic transaxle fluid level should be carefully maintained.

Low fluid level can lead to slipping or loss of drive, while overfilling can cause foaming and loss of fluid. Either condition can cause transaxle damage.

2   Since transmission fluid expands as it heats up, the fluid level should only be checked when the transaxle is warm (at normal operating temperature). If the vehicle has just been driven over 20 miles (32 km), the transaxle can be considered warm. **Caution:** *If the vehicle has just been driven for a long time at high speed or in city traffic in hot weather, or if it has been pulling a trailer, an accurate fluid level reading cannot be obtained. Allow the transaxle to cool down for about 30 minutes.* You can also check the transaxle fluid level when the transaxle is cold. If the vehicle has not been driven for over five hours and the fluid is about room temperature (70 to 95-degrees F), the transaxle is cold. However, the fluid level is normally checked with the transaxle warm to ensure accurate results.

3   Immediately after driving the vehicle, park it on a level surface, set the parking brake and start the engine. While the engine is idling, depress the brake pedal and move the selector lever through all the gear ranges, beginning and ending in Park.

4   Locate the automatic transaxle dipstick tube near the air filter housing **(see illustration)**.

5   With the engine still idling, pull the dipstick from the tube, wipe it off with a clean rag, push it all the way back into the tube and withdraw it again, then note the fluid level.

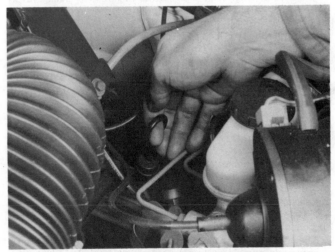

7.4   The automatic transaxle dipstick is located in a tube at the rear of the engine compartment

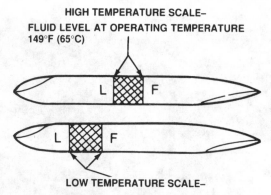

HIGH TEMPERATURE SCALE–
FLUID LEVEL AT OPERATING TEMPERATURE
149°F (65°C)

LOW TEMPERATURE SCALE–

FLUID LEVEL AT ROOM TEMPERATURE
68°F (20°C)

SCALES ARE ON EITHER SIDE OF DIPSTICK

7.6   If the fluid in the transaxle is cold, the level should be between the L and F marks of the low temperature scale; if the fluid is hot, it should be between the L and F marks of the high temperature scale

6   If the transaxle is cold, the indicated level should be between the L and F marks of the low temperature scale; if the transaxle is hot, the fluid level should be between the L and F marks of the high temperature scale **(see illustration)**. If the level is low, add the specified automatic transmission fluid through the dipstick tube. Use a funnel to prevent spills.

7   Add just enough of the recommended fluid to fill the transaxle to the proper level. It takes about one pint to raise the level from the L mark to the F mark when the fluid is hot, so add the fluid a little at a time and keep checking the level until it's correct.

8   The condition of the fluid should also be checked along with the level. If the fluid is black or a dark reddish-brown color, or if it smells burned, it should be changed (see Section 28). If you are in doubt about its condition, purchase some new fluid and compare the two for color and smell.

8   Engine oil and filter change

Refer to illustrations 8.2, 8.7, 8.12 and 8.16

1   Frequent oil changes are among the most important preventive maintenance procedures that can be done by the home mechanic. As engine oil ages, it becomes diluted and contaminated, which leads to premature engine wear. Although some sources recommend oil filter changes every other oil change, a new filter should be installed every time the oil is changed.

2   Make sure that you have all the necessary tools before you begin this procedure **(see illustration)**. You should also have plenty of rags or newspapers handy for mopping up oil spills.

3   Access to the oil drain plug and filter will be improved if the vehicle can be lifted on a hoist, driven onto ramps or supported by jackstands. **Warning:** *Do not work under a vehicle supported only by a bumper, hydraulic or scissors-type jack – always use jackstands!*

4   If you haven't changed the oil on this vehicle before, get under it and locate the oil drain plug and the oil filter. The exhaust components will be warm as you work, so note how they are routed to avoid touching them when you are under the vehicle.

5   Start the engine and allow it to reach normal operating temperature – oil and sludge will flow out more easily when warm. Park on a level surface and shut off the engine when it's warmed up. Remove the oil filler cap.

6   Raise the vehicle and support it on jackstands. Make sure it is safely supported!

7   Being careful not to touch the hot exhaust components, position a drain pan under the plug in the bottom of the engine oil pan **(see illustration)**, then remove the plug. It's a good idea to wear an old glove while unscrewing the plug the final few turns to avoid being scalded by hot oil.

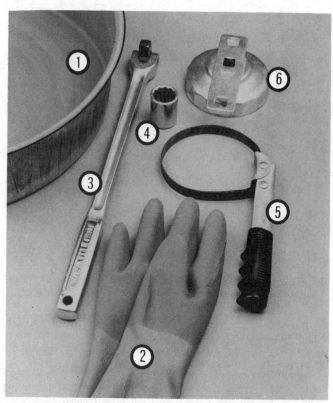

8.2   These tools are required when changing the engine oil and filter

1   *Drain pan – It should be fairly shallow in depth, but wide to prevent spills*
2   *Rubber gloves – When removing the drain plug and filter, you will get oil on your hands (the gloves will prevent burns)*
3   *Breaker bar – Sometimes the oil drain plug is tight and a long breaker bar is needed to loosen it*
4   *Socket – To be used with the breaker bar or a ratchet (must be the correct size to fit the drain plug – 6-point preferred)*
5   *Filter wrench – This is a metal band-type wrench, which requires clearance around the filter to be effective*
6   *Filter wrench – This type fits on the bottom of the filter and can be turned with a ratchet or breaker bar (different size wrenches are available for different types of filters)*

8.7   Use a box-end wrench or six-point socket to remove the oil drain plug without rounding it off

8.12 The oil filter is usually on very tight and will require a special wrench for removal – DO NOT use the wrench to tighten the new filter!

8.16 Lubricate the gasket with clean oil before installing the filter on the engine

8   It may be necessary to move the drain pan slightly as oil flow slows to a trickle. Inspect the old oil for the presence of metal particles.

9   After all the oil has drained, wipe off the drain plug with a clean rag. Any small metal particles clinging to the plug would immediately contaminate the new oil.

10   Clean the area around the drain plug opening, reinstall the plug and tighten it securely, being careful not to strip the threads.

11   Move the drain pan into position under the oil filter, located on the front (radiator side) of the engine.

12   Loosen the oil filter by turning it counterclockwise with a filter wrench (see illustration). Any standard filter wrench will work.

13   Sometimes the oil filter is screwed on so tightly that it cannot be loosened. If it is, punch a metal bar or long screwdriver directly through it, as close to the engine as possible, and use it as a lever to turn the filter. Be prepared for oil to spurt out of the canister as it is punctured.

14   Once the filter is loose, use your hands to unscrew it from the block. Just as the filter is detached from the block, immediately tilt the open end up to prevent the oil inside the filter from spilling out. **Warning:** *The engine exhaust manifold may still be hot, so be careful.*

15   Using a clean rag, wipe off the mounting surface on the block. Make sure the old gasket does not remain stuck to the mounting surface.

16   Compare the old filter with the new one to make sure they are the same type. Smear some engine oil on the rubber gasket of the new filter and screw it into place (see illustration). Overtightening the filter will damage the gasket, so don't use a filter wrench. Most filter manufacturers recommend tightening the filter by hand only. Normally they should be tightened 3/4-turn after the gasket contacts the block, but be sure to follow the directions on the filter or container.

17   Remove all tools and materials from under the vehicle, being careful not to spill the oil in the drain pan, then lower the vehicle.

18   Add four quarts of new oil to the engine (see Section 4 if necessary). Use a funnel to prevent oil from spilling onto the top of the engine. Wait a few minutes to allow the oil to drain into the pan, then check the level on the dipstick. If the oil level is in the SAFE range, install the filler cap.

19   Start the engine and run it for about a minute. While the engine is running, look under the vehicle and check for leaks at the oil pan drain plug and around the oil filter. If either one is leaking, stop the engine and tighten the plug or filter slightly.

20   Stop the engine, wait a few minutes, then recheck the level on the dipstick. Add oil as necessary to bring the level into the SAFE range.

21   During the first few trips after an oil change, make it a point to check frequently for leaks and proper oil level.

22   The old oil drained from the engine cannot be reused in its present state and should be discarded. Oil reclamation centers, auto repair shops and gas stations will normally accept the oil, which can be recycled. After

the oil has cooled, it can be drained into a container (plastic jugs, bottles, milk cartons, etc.) for transport to a disposal site.

9   Clutch pedal adjustment

Pedal height

Refer to illustration 9.1

1   To determine whether the pedal height is correct, measure the distance from the bulkhead to the upper center of the pedal pad (see illustration). Compare the measurement with this Chapter's Specifications.

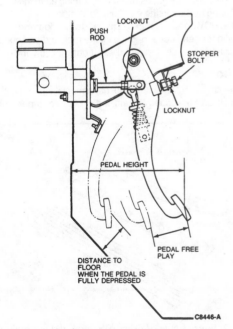

9.1 Clutch pedal height and freeplay adjustment details

2   If adjustment is necessary, remove the lower dash panel (see Chapter 11) and air ducts.
3   Loosen the locknut and turn the stopper bolt until the pedal height is within specification.

Pedal freeplay

4   Freeplay is the distance the clutch pedal moves freely before clutch resistance is felt. To determine whether the pedal freeplay is correct, measure it as shown (**see illustration 9.1**) and compare your measurement to this Chapter's Specifications.
5   If an adjustment is required, remove the lower dash panel and air ducts (see Chapter 11).
6   Loosen the locknut and turn the pushrod until the pedal freeplay is with specification.
7   Tighten the locknut.
8   Install the air ducts and lower dash panel (see Chapter 11).

---

10   Underhood hose check and replacement

Warning: *Replacement of air conditioning hoses must be left to a dealer service department or air conditioning shop that has the equipment to depressurize the system safely. Never remove air conditioning components or hoses until the system has been depressurized.*

General

1   High temperatures under the hood can cause the deterioration of the rubber and plastic hoses used for engine, accessory and emission systems operation. Inspect the hoses periodically for cracks, loose clamps, material hardening and leaks.
2   Information specific to the cooling system hoses can be found in Section 18.
3   Most (but not all) hoses are secured to the fittings with clamps. Where clamps are used, check to be sure they haven't lost their tension, allowing the hose to leak. If clamps aren't used, make sure the hose has not expanded and/or hardened where it slips over the fitting, allowing it to leak.

PCV system hose

4   To reduce hydrocarbon emissions, crankcase blow-by gas is vented through the PCV valve in the rocker arm cover to the intake manifold via a rubber hose. The blow-by gases mix with incoming air in the intake manifold before being burned in the combustion chambers.
5   Check the PCV hose for cracks, leaks and other damage. Disconnect it from the cylinder head cover and the intake manifold and check the inside for obstructions. If it's clogged, clean it out with solvent.

Vacuum hoses

6   It is quite common for vacuum hoses, especially those in the emissions system, to be color coded or identified by colored stripes molded into each hose. Various systems require hoses with different wall thicknesses, collapse resistance and temperature resistance. When replacing hoses, be sure the new ones are made of the same material.
7   Often the only effective way to check a hose is to remove it completely from the vehicle. If more than one hose is removed, be sure to label the hoses and fittings to ensure correct installation.
8   When checking vacuum hoses, be sure to include any plastic T-fittings in the check. Inspect the fittings for cracks and the hose where it fits over each fitting for distortion, which could cause leakage.
9   A small piece of vacuum hose (1/4-inch inside diameter) can be used as a stethoscope to detect vacuum leaks. Hold one end of the hose to your ear and probe around vacuum hoses and fittings, listening for the "hissing" sound characteristic of a vacuum leak. **Warning:** *When probing with the vacuum hose stethoscope, be careful not to allow your body or the hose to come into contact with moving engine components such as drivebelts, the cooling fan, etc.*

Fuel hose

Warning: *Gasoline is extremely flammable, so take extra precautions when you work on any part of the fuel system. Don't smoke or allow open flames or bare light bulbs near the work area, and don't work in a garage where a natural gas-type appliance (such as a water heater or clothes dryer) with a pilot light is present. If you spill any fuel on your skin, rinse it off immediately with soap and water. When you perform any kind of work on the fuel tank, wear safety glasses and have a Class B type fire extinguisher on hand. The fuel system is under pressure. You must relieve this pressure before servicing the fuel lines. Refer to Chapter 4 for the fuel pressure relief procedure.*

10   Check all rubber fuel lines for deterioration and chafing. Check especially for cracks in areas where the hose bends and just before fittings, such as where a hose attaches to the fuel tank, fuel filter or a fuel injection component.
11   If any fuel lines show damage, deterioration or wear, they should be replaced (see Chapter 4). Be sure to use fuel line that is designed for use in fuel injection systems and is an exact duplicate of the original.
12   Spring-type clamps are commonly used on fuel lines. These clamps often lose their tension over a period of time, and can be "sprung" during the removal process. As a result, it is recommended that all spring-type clamps be replaced with screw clamps whenever a hose is replaced.

Metal lines

13   Sections of metal line are often used for fuel line between the fuel pump and fuel injection unit. Check carefully to be sure the line has not been bent and crimped and that cracks have not started in the line, particularly where bends occur.
14   If a section of metal fuel line must be replaced, use seamless steel tubing only, since copper and aluminum tubing do not have the strength necessary to withstand vibration caused by the engine.

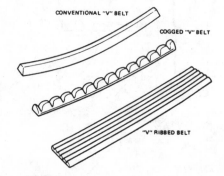

11.2   Different types of drivebelts are used to power the various accessories mounted on the engine

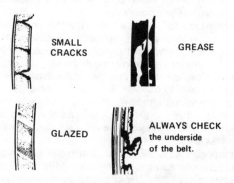

11.3   Here are some of the common problems associated with drivebelts (check the belts very carefully to prevent an untimely breakdown)

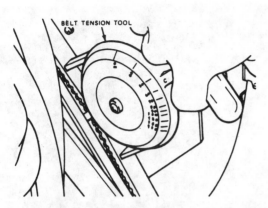

11.4   A drivebelt tension gauge is recommended for checking the belts on four-cylinder engines

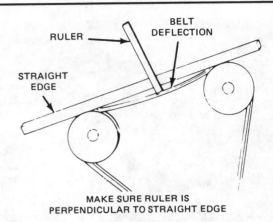

11.5   Measuring drivebelt deflection with a straightedge and ruler

11.6a   Loosen the alternator pivot bolt (arrow) from underneath the vehicle . . .

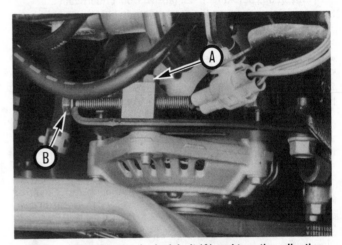

11.6b   . . . then loosen the lock bolt (A) and turn the adjusting screw (B) until the tension is correct

Warning: *The fuel system pressure must be relieved before any fuel lines can be replaced (see Chapter 4).*

15   Check the metal brake lines where they enter the master cylinder and brake proportioning unit (if used) for cracks in the lines and loose fittings. Any sign of brake fluid leakage calls for an immediate thorough inspection of the brake system.

11   Drivebelt check, adjustment and replacement

1   The accessory drivebelts, also referred to as V-belts or simply fan belts, are located at the right end of the engine. The condition and tension of the drivebelts are critical to the operation of the engine and accessories. Excessive tension causes bearing wear, while insufficient tension produces slippage, noise, component vibration and belt failure. Because of their composition and the high stresses to which they are subjected, drivebelts stretch and deteriorate as they get older. As a result, they must be periodically checked and adjusted.

Check

Refer to illustrations 11.2, 11.3, 11.4 and 11.5

2   The number and type of belts used on a particular vehicle depends on the accessories installed **(see illustration)**. Only the four-cylinder engine drivebelts require adjustment, as the V6 engine is equipped with automatic drivebelt tensioners.

3   With the engine off, open the hood and locate the drivebelts at the right end of the engine. With a flashlight, check each belt for separation of the rubber plies from each side of the core, a severed core, separation of the ribs from the rubber, cracks, torn or worn ribs and cracks in the inner

ridges of the ribs. Also check for fraying and glazing, which give belts a shiny appearance **(see illustration)**. Both sides of each belt should be inspected, which means you'll have to twist them to check the undersides. Use your fingers to feel a belt where you can't see it. If any of the above conditions are evident, replace the belt as described below.

4   To check the tension of each belt in accordance with factory recommendations, install a drivebelt tension gauge (special tool no. T63L-8620-A or equivalent) **(see illustration)**. Measure the tension in accordance with the tension gauge instructions and compare your measurement to the figure listed in this Chapter's Specifications for a used belt. **Note:** *A "new" belt is defined as any belt which has not been run; a "used" belt is one that has been run for more than ten minutes.*

5   The special gauge is the most accurate way to check belt tension. However, if you don't have a gauge, and cannot borrow one, the following "rule-of-thumb" method is recommended as an alternative. Lay a straightedge across the longest free span (the distance between two pulleys) of the belt. Push down firmly on the belt at a point half way between the pulleys and see how much the belt moves (deflects). Measure the deflection with a ruler **(see illustration)**. The belt should deflect 1/8 to 1/4-inch if the distance from pulley center-to-pulley center is less than 12 inches; it should deflect from 1/8 to 3/8-inch if the distance from pulley center-to-pulley center is over 12-inches.

Adjustment

Refer to illustrations 11.6a, 11.6b and 11.7

6   If the alternator drivebelt must be adjusted, first loosen the pivot bolt, then loosen the lock bolt that secures the alternator to the slotted bracket. Turn the adjusting screw to adjust the drivebelt tension and retighten the pivot and lock bolts **(see illustrations)**. Recheck the belt tension using

11.7   To adjust the power steering/air conditioning drivebelt, loosen this adjustment nut (arrow) from underneath the vehicle, push up on the compressor to tighten the belt (or pull down to loosen it) and tighten the bolt

one of the above methods. Repeat this Step until the alternator drivebelt tension is correct.

7   If the power steering/air conditioner compressor drivebelt must be adjusted, raise the vehicle and place it securely on jackstands. From underneath the vehicle, locate the adjustment bolt on the air conditioning compressor bracket at the front of the block **(see illustration)**. Loosen the adjustment bolt slightly and push up on the compressor to tighten the belt (or pull down on the compressor to loosen it). Tighten the adjustment bolt. Check the belt tension as described earlier in this Section.

8   If the vehicle is equipped with an air pump, loosen the pivot and adjustment bolts, then move the pump up or down as required to change the belt tension. The air pump has a cast-in lug designed to accept an open end wrench, which can be used as a lever to tension the belt. Be sure to tighten the bolts when the belt tension is correct.

Replacement

9   To replace a belt, follow the above procedures for drivebelt adjustment, but slip the belt off the pulleys and remove it. On tensioner equipped models, use a ratchet or breaker bar to lift the tensioner and remove the drivebelt. Since belts tend to wear out more or less at the same time, it's a good idea to replace all of them at the same time. Mark each belt and the corresponding pulley grooves so the replacement belts can be installed properly.

10   Take the old belts with you when purchasing new ones in order to make a direct comparison for length, width and design.

11   When replacing a V-ribbed drivebelt (the wide one used to drive the power steering pump and air conditioning compressor), make sure that it fits properly into the pulley grooves – it must be completely engaged and ride in the center of each pulley.

12   Adjust the belts as described earlier in this Section.

---

12   Battery check and maintenance

Refer to illustrations 12.1, 12.8a, 12.8b, 12.8c and 12.8d

Warning: *Certain precautions must be followed when checking and servicing the battery. Hydrogen gas, which is highly flammable, is always present in the battery cells, so keep lighted tobacco and all other open flames and sparks away from the battery. The electrolyte inside the battery is actually dilute sulfuric acid, which will cause injury if splashed on your skin or in your eyes. It will also ruin clothes and painted surfaces. When removing the battery cables, always detach the negative cable first and hook it up last!*

1   Battery maintenance is an important procedure which will help ensure that you are not stranded because of a dead battery. Several tools are required for this procedure **(see illustration)**.

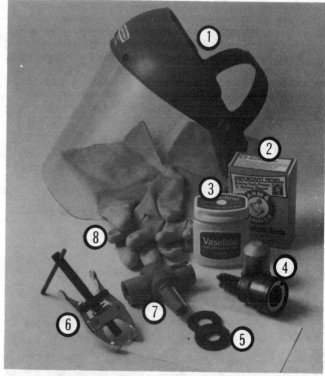

12.1   Tools and materials required for battery maintenance

1   *Face shield/safety goggles – When removing corrosion with a brush, the acidic particles can easily fly up into your eyes*

2   *Baking soda – A solution of baking soda and water can be used to neutralize corrosion*

3   *Petroleum jelly – A layer of this on the battery posts will help prevent corrosion*

4   *Battery post/cable cleaner – This wire brush cleaning tool will remove all traces of corrosion from the battery posts and cable clamps*

5   *Treated felt washers – Placing one of these on each post, directly under the cable clamps, will help prevent corrosion*

6   *Puller – Sometimes the cable clamps are very difficult to pull off the posts, even after the nut/bolt has been completely loosened. This tool pulls the clamp straight up and off the post without damage.*

7   *Battery post/cable cleaner – Here is another cleaning tool which is a slightly different version of number 4 above, but it does the same thing*

8   *Rubber gloves – Another safety item to consider when servicing the battery; remember that's acid inside the battery!*

2   Before servicing the battery, always turn the engine and all accessories off and disconnect the cable from the negative terminal of the battery.

3   A sealed (sometimes called maintenance-free) battery is standard equipment on the these models. The cell caps cannot be removed, no electrolyte checks are required and water cannot be added to the cells. However, if an aftermarket battery has been installed and it is a type that requires regular maintenance, the following procedure can be used.

4   Check the electrolyte level in each of the battery cells. It must be above the plates. There's usually a split-ring indicator in each cell to indicate the correct level. If the level is low, add distilled water only, then install the cell caps. **Caution:** *Overfilling the cells may cause electrolyte to spill over during periods of heavy charging, causing corrosion and damage to nearby components.*

5   If the positive terminal and cable clamp on your vehicle's battery is equipped with a rubber protector, make sure that it's not torn or damaged. It should completely cover the terminal.

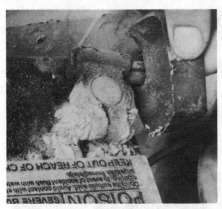

12.8a   Battery terminal corrosion usually appears as a light, fluffy powder

12.8b   Removing a cable from the battery post with a wrench – sometimes special battery pliers are required for this procedure if corrosion has caused deterioration of the nut hex (always remove the ground cable first and hook it up last!)

12.8c   Regardless of the type of tool used to clean the battery post, a clean, shiny surface should be the result

6   The external condition of the battery should be checked periodically. Look for damage such as a cracked case.

7   Check the tightness of the battery cable clamps to ensure good electrical connections and inspect the entire length of each cable, looking for cracked or abraded insulation and frayed conductors.

8   If corrosion (visible as white, fluffy deposits) is evident, remove the cables from the terminals, clean them with a battery brush and reinstall them **(see illustrations)**. Corrosion can be kept to a minimum by installing specially treated washers available at auto parts stores or by applying a layer of petroleum jelly or grease to the terminals and cable clamps after they are assembled.

9   Make sure that the battery carrier is in good condition and that the hold-down clamp bolt is tight. If the battery is removed (see Chapter 5 for the removal and installation procedure), make sure that no parts remain in the bottom of the carrier when it's reinstalled. When reinstalling the hold-down clamp, don't overtighten the bolt.

10   Corrosion on the carrier, battery case and surrounding areas can be removed with a solution of water and baking soda. Apply the mixture with a small brush, let it work, then rinse it off with plenty of clean water.

11   Any metal parts of the vehicle damaged by corrosion should be coated with a zinc-based primer, then painted.

12   Additional information on the battery, charging and jump starting can be found in Chapter 5 and at the front of this manual.

13   Windshield wiper blade check and replacement

1   Road film can build up on the wiper blades and affect their efficiency, so they should be washed regularly with a mild detergent solution.

Check

2   The windshield wiper and blade assembly should be inspected periodically for damage, loose components and cracked or worn blade elements. The action of the wiping mechanism can loosen bolts, nuts and fasteners, so they should be checked and tightened, as necessary, at the same time the wiper blades are checked.

3   If the wiper blade elements are cracked, worn or warped, or no longer clean adequately, they should be replaced with new ones.

Replacement

Refer to illustration 13.5

4   Place the wiper switch in the Low position and turn the ignition switch to ACC. When the wiper blades are pointing straight up, turn off the ignition key.

5   Grasp the wiper blade assembly firmly with one hand, pinch the tabs at the end of the element with the other hand and slide the element out **(see illustration)**.

12.8d   When cleaning the cable clamps, all corrosion must be removed (the inside of the clamp is tapered to match the taper on the post, so don't remove too much material)

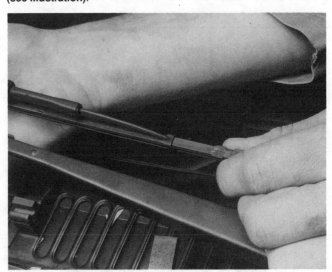

13.5   To remove the wiper blade element, pinch the tabs at the end and pull it straight out of the wiper frame

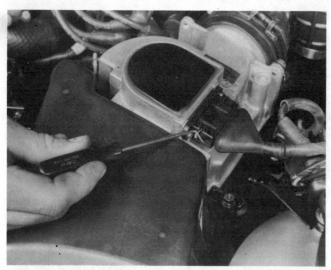

14.1   If the vehicle has a four-cylinder engine, unplug the vane
        airflow (VAF) meter electrical connector

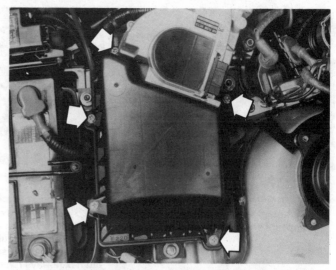

14.2a   Remove the air filter housing screws (turbo four-cylinder
        model shown, other four-cylinder models similar)

6   To install a new blade element, insert one end of the element's backing strip into the wiper frame's first claw, then slide it through each frame
claw. Make sure the element backing strip is installed through all the frame
claws and the length of the element extending beyond the frame claw at
each end is equal.

14   Air filter replacement

Refer to illustrations 14.1, 14.2a, 14.2b and 14.3
Note: *The air filter cannot be cleaned. If it's dirty, replace it.*
1   If the vehicle has a four-cylinder engine, unplug the vane airflow
(VAF) meter electrical connector **(see illustration)**. Loosen the air duct
clamp and detach the air duct from the VAF meter assembly.
2   Remove the air filter housing cover screws and lift the cover off **(see
illustrations)**.
3   Remove the filter. Note the direction it faces **(see illustration)**.
4   Check the inner sealing surface of the cover for evidence of leakage
past the air filter. Place a light on the inside (clean side) of the filter and look
through the filter at the light. If the light cannot be seen or if there are holes
in the element, no matter how small, replace it with a new one.

5   Clean the inner sealing surface between the air filter housing and cover.
6   Before installing the new air filter, check it for deformed seals and
holes in the paper. If the filter is marked TOP, be sure the marked side
faces up.
7   Position the cover on the housing and make sure it is seated all the
way around, then install and tighten the cover screws.
8   Reconnect the air duct to the VAF meter and tighten the hose clamp
securely. Plug in the VAF meter electrical connector.

15   Positive Crankcase Ventilation (PCV) valve check
      and replacement

Refer to illustration 15.2
Note: *To maintain efficient operation of the PCV system, clean the hoses
and check the PCV valve and crankcase ventilation filter at the intervals
recommended in the maintenance schedule. For additional information on
the PCV system, see Chapter 6.*
1   Locate the PCV valve on the rocker arm cover.

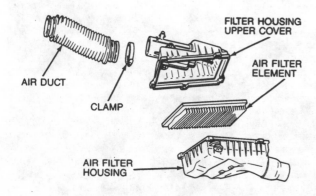

14.2b   An exploded view of the air filter housing
        assembly on a V6 model

14.3   The sealing lip on the filter faces up – be sure you put the
        new filter in the same way or it won't fit

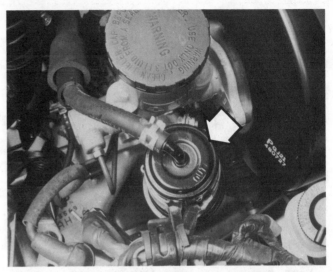

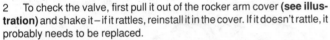

15.2   Pull the PCV valve out and shake it – a rattling sound indicates it is not clogged

17.2   To replace the fuel filter (arrow) on four-cylinder models, relieve the fuel pressure, remove the hose clamps from both ends of the filter, loosen the filter pinch clamp and slide the filter out

2   To check the valve, first pull it out of the rocker arm cover **(see illustration)** and shake it – if it rattles, reinstall it in the cover. If it doesn't rattle, it probably needs to be replaced.
3   Start the engine and allow it to idle, then disconnect the PCV hose from the air filter housing and feel for suction at the hose. If you feel suction, the PCV valve/system is working properly.
4   If you don't feel suction, the oil filler cap, hoses or rocker arm cover gasket may be leaking or the PCV valve may be bad. Check for vacuum leaks at the valve, filler cap, filter assembly (if used) and all hoses.
5   If you still don't feel suction, again remove the PCV valve. Check the rubber grommet in the rocker arm cover for cracks and distortion. If it's damaged, replace it.
6   Replace the valve if it's clogged with deposits. If it's clogged, the hoses are also probably clogged. Remove the hose between the valve and the intake manifold and the hose between the engine and the air filter housing and clean them with solvent.
7   After cleaning the hoses, inspect them for damage, wear and deterioration. Make sure the hoses fit snugly on the fittings.
8   If necessary, install a new PCV valve. **Note:** *The elbow, if used, is not part of the PCV valve. A new valve will not include the elbow. The original must be transferred to the new valve. If a new elbow is purchased, it may be necessary to soak it in warm water for up to an hour to slip it onto the new valve. Do not attempt to force the elbow onto the valve or it will break.*
9   Install the clean PCV system hoses. Make sure that the PCV valve and hoses are secure.

16   Fuel system check

Warning: *Gasoline is extremely flammable, so take extra precautions when you work on any part of the fuel system. Don't smoke or allow open flames or bare light bulbs near the work area, and don't work in a garage where a natural gas-type appliance (such as a water heater or clothes dryer) with a pilot light is present. If you spill any fuel on your skin, rinse it off immediately with soap and water. When you perform any kind of work on the fuel tank, wear safety glasses and have a Class B type fire extinguisher on hand.*

1   If you smell gasoline while driving or after the vehicle has been sitting in the sun, inspect the fuel system immediately.
2   Remove the gas filler cap and inspect if for damage and corrosion. The gasket should have an unbroken sealing imprint. If the gasket is damaged or corroded, install a new cap.

3   Inspect the fuel feed and return lines for cracks. Make sure that the connections between the fuel lines and fuel injection system and between the fuel lines and the in-line fuel filter are tight. **Warning:** *You must relieve fuel system pressure before servicing fuel system components. The fuel system pressure relief procedure is outlined in Chapter 4.*
4   Since some components of the fuel system – the fuel tank and part of the fuel feed and return lines, for example – are underneath the vehicle, they can be inspected more easily with the vehicle raised on a hoist. If a hoist is unavailable, raise the vehicle and support it on jackstands.
5   With the vehicle raised and safely supported, inspect the gas tank and filler neck for punctures, cracks and other damage. The connection between the filler neck and the tank is particularly critical. Sometimes a rubber filler neck will leak because of loose clamps or deteriorated rubber. Inspect all fuel tank mounting brackets and straps to be sure that the tank is securely attached to the vehicle. **Warning:** *Do not, under any circumstances, try to repair a fuel tank (except rubber components). A welding torch or any open flame can easily cause fuel vapors inside the tank to explode.*
6   Carefully check all rubber hoses and metal lines leading away from the fuel tank. Check for loose connections, deteriorated hoses, crimped lines and other damage. Repair or replace damaged sections as necessary (see Chapter 4).

17   Fuel filter replacement

Refer to illustrations 17.2 and 17.3
Warning: *Gasoline is extremely flammable, so take extra precautions when you work on any part of the fuel system. Don't smoke or allow open flames or bare light bulbs near the work area, and don't work in a garage where a natural gas-type appliance (such as a water heater or clothes dryer) with a pilot light is present. If you spill any fuel on your skin, rinse it off immediately with soap and water. When you perform any kind of work on the fuel tank, wear safety glasses and have a Class B type fire extinguisher on hand. Before removing the fuel filter, the fuel system pressure must be relieved (See Chapter 4).*

1   Relieve the fuel system pressure (see Chapter 4).
2   Locate the fuel filter on the firewall, next to the brake fluid reservoir **(see illustration)**. Inspect the hose fittings at both ends of the filter to see if they're clean. If more than a light coating of dust is present, clean the fittings before proceeding.

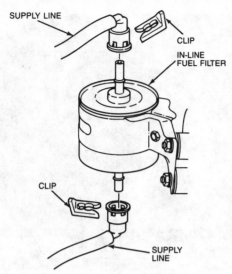

17.3   Exploded view of the fuel filter used on V6 models

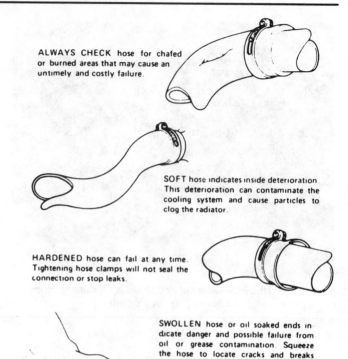

18.4   Hoses, like drivebelts, have a habit of failing at the worst possible time – to prevent the inconvenience of a blown radiator or heater hose, inspect them carefully, as shown here

3   Loosen the hose clamps (four-cylinder engine) or remove the hairpin clips (V6 engine). To disengage a hairpin clip **(see illustration)** from a fitting, spread the two clip legs apart about 1/8-inch and simultaneously push on them. Once the clip is halfway off, grasp the other end of the clip and pull it off. **Caution:** *Don't use any tools to remove the hairpin clips. Tools may damage the clips, and you may have to re-use them (particularly if there aren't any new ones with the new filter).*
4   Once both hose clamps are loose, or the hairpin clips are removed, grasp the fuel hoses, one at a time, and pull them off the filter. Plug both hoses to prevent leakage and contamination.
5   On models with a V6 engine, check the hairpin clips for damage and distortion. If they were damaged in any way during removal, new ones must be used when the hoses are reattached to the new filter (if new clips are packaged with the filter, be sure to use them in place of the originals).
6   Note which way the arrow on the filter is pointing – the new filter must be installed the same way. Loosen the clamp screw and detach the filter from the bracket.
7   Install the new filter in the bracket with the arrow pointing in the right direction. Tighten the clamp screw securely.
8   Unplug each hose, then carefully push it onto the filter until it's seated against the collar on the fitting. Slip the hose clamps back into place and tighten them securely, or install the hairpin clips. **Warning:** *Make sure the clips are securely attached to the hose fittings – if they come off, the hoses could back off the filter and a fire could result!*
9   Start the engine and check for fuel leaks.

18   Cooling system check

Refer to illustration 18.4
1   Many major engine failures can be attributed to a faulty cooling system. If the vehicle is equipped with an automatic transaxle, the cooling system also plays an important role in prolonging transaxle life because it cools the transmission fluid.
2   The engine should be cold for the cooling system check, so perform the following procedure before the vehicle is driven for the day or after it has been shut off for at least three hours.
3   Remove the radiator cap and clean it thoroughly, inside and out, with clean water. Also clean the filler neck on the radiator. The presence of rust or corrosion in the filler neck means the coolant should be changed (see Section 27). The coolant inside the radiator should be relatively clean and transparent. If it's rust colored, drain the system and refill it with new coolant.
4   Carefully check the radiator hoses and the smaller diameter heater hoses **(see illustration)**. Inspect each coolant hose along its entire

length, replacing any hose which is cracked, swollen or deteriorated. Cracks will show up better if the hose is squeezed. Pay close attention to hose clamps that secure the hoses to cooling system components. Hose clamps can pinch and puncture hoses, resulting in coolant leaks.
5   Make sure that all hose connections are tight. A leak in the cooling system will usually show up as white or rust colored deposits on the area adjoining the leak. If wire-type clamps are used on the hoses, it may be a good idea to replace them with screw-type clamps.
6   Clean the front of the radiator and air conditioning condenser with compressed air, if available, or a soft brush. Remove all bugs, leaves, etc. embedded in the radiator fins. Be extremely careful not to damage the cooling fins or cut your fingers on them.
7   If the coolant level has been dropping consistently and no leaks are detectable, have the radiator cap and cooling system pressure checked at a service station.

19   Exhaust system check

1   With the engine cold (at least three hours after the vehicle has been driven), check the complete exhaust system from the engine to the end of the tailpipe. Ideally, the inspection should be done with the vehicle on a hoist to permit unrestricted access. If a hoist is not available, raise the vehicle and support it securely on jackstands.
2   Check the exhaust pipes and connections for evidence of leaks, severe corrosion and damage. Make sure that all brackets and hangers are in good condition and tight.
3   At the same time, inspect the underside of the body for holes, corrosion, open seams, etc. which may allow exhaust gases to enter the passenger compartment. Seal all body openings with silicone sealant or body putty.

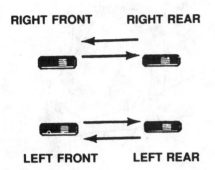

20.2   The recommended rotation pattern for radial tires

4   Rattles and other noises can often be traced to the exhaust system, especially the mounts and hangers. Try to move the pipes, muffler and catalytic converter. If the components can come in contact with the body or suspension parts, secure the exhaust system with new mounts.
5   Check the running condition of the engine by inspecting inside the end of the tailpipe. The exhaust deposits here are an indication of engine state-of-tune. If the pipe is black and sooty or coated with white deposits, the engine is in need of a tune-up, including a thorough fuel system inspection and adjustment.

20   Tire rotation

Refer to illustration 20.2
1   The tires should be rotated at the specified intervals and whenever uneven wear is noticed. Since the vehicle will be raised and the tires removed anyway, check the brakes also (see Section 22).
2   Radial tires must be rotated in a specific pattern **(see illustration)**.
3   Refer to the information in Jacking and towing at the front of this manual for the proper procedure to follow when raising the vehicle and changing a tire. If the brakes are to be checked, do not apply the parking brake, as stated.
4   The vehicle must be raised on a hoist or supported on jackstands to get two wheels at a time off the ground. Make sure the vehicle is safely supported!
5   After the rotation procedure is finished, check and adjust the tire pressures as necessary and be sure to check the lug nut tightness.

21   Suspension and steering check

Note: *The steering linkage and suspension components should be checked periodically. Worn or damaged suspension and steering linkage components can result in excessive and abnormal tire wear, poor ride quality and vehicle handling and reduced fuel economy. For detailed illustrations of the steering and suspension components, refer to Chapter 10.*

Strut check

1   Park the vehicle on level ground, turn the engine off and set the parking brake. Check the tire pressures.
2   Push down at one corner of the vehicle, then release it while noting the movement of the body. It should stop moving and come to rest in a level position within one or two bounces.
3   If the vehicle continues to move up and down or if it fails to return to its original position, a worn or weak strut is probably the reason.

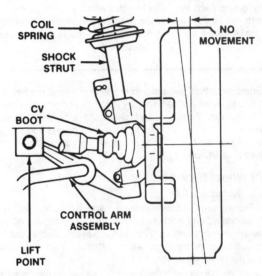

21.10   To check the balljoints, try to move the lower edge of each front wheel in and out while watching or feeling for movement at the top of the tire and balljoint

4   Repeat the above check at each of the three remaining corners of the vehicle.
5   Raise the vehicle and support it on jackstands.
6   Check the shock struts for evidence of fluid leakage. A light film of fluid on the shaft is no cause for concern. Make sure that any fluid noted is from the shocks and not from some other source. If leakage is noted, replace both struts at that end of the vehicle (front or rear).
7   Check the struts to be sure that they are securely mounted and undamaged. Check the upper mounts for damage and wear. If damage or wear is noted, replace both struts on that end of the vehicle.
8   If struts must be replaced, refer to Chapter 10 for the procedure.

Front suspension and steering check

Refer to illustrations 21.10 and 21.11
9   Visually inspect the steering system components for damage and distortion. Look for leaks and damaged seals, boots and fittings.
10   Wipe off the lower end of the steering knuckle and control arm assembly. Have an assistant grasp the lower edge of the tire and move the wheel in and out **(see illustration)** while you look for movement at the steering knuckle-to-control arm joint. If there is any movement, the balljoints must be replaced (see Chapter 10).

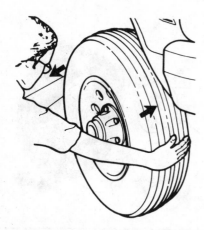

21.11   To check the steering gear mounts and tie-rod ends for play, grasp each front tire like this and try to move it back and forth – if play is noted, check the steering gear mounts and make sure they're tight; if either tie-rod is worn or bent, replace it

11   Grasp each front tire at the front and rear edges, push in at the rear, pull out at the front and feel for play in the steering system components **(see illustration)**. If any freeplay is noted, check the steering gear mounts and the tie-rod ends for looseness. If the steering gear mounts are loose, tighten them. If the tie-rod ends are loose, they will probably need to be replaced (see Chapter 10).

Front wheel bearing check

Refer to illustration 21.12
Note: *The front wheel bearings are a "cartridge" design and are permanently lubricated and sealed at the factory. They require no scheduled maintenance or adjustment. They can, however, be checked for excessive play. If the following check indicates that either of the front bearings is faulty, replace both bearings.*

12   Grasp each front tire at the front and rear edges, then push in and out on the wheel and feel for play **(see illustration)**. There should be no noticeable movement. Turn the wheel and listen for noise from the bearings. If either of these conditions is noted, refer to Chapter 10 for the bearing replacement procedure.

Driveaxle Constant Velocity (CV) joint boot check

Refer to illustration 21.14
13   If the driveaxle rubber boots are damaged or deteriorated, serious and costly damage can occur to the CV joints.
14   It is very important that the boots be kept clean, so wipe them off before inspection. Check the four boots (two on each driveaxle) for cracks, tears, holes, deteriorated rubber and loose or missing clamps. Pushing on the boot surface can reveal cracks not ordinarily visible **(see illustration)**.
15   If damage or deterioration is evident, check the CV joints for damage (see Chapter 8) and replace the boot(s) with new ones.

---

22   Brake check

Note: *In addition to the specified intervals, the brake system should be inspected each time the wheels are removed or a malfunction is indicated. Because of the obvious safety considerations, the following brake system checks are some of the most important maintenance procedures you can perform on your vehicle.*

Symptoms of brake system problems

1   The disc brake pads have built-in wear indicators which should make a high-pitched squealing or scraping noise when they are worn to the re-

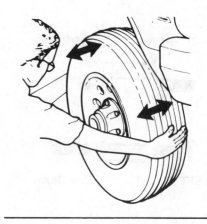
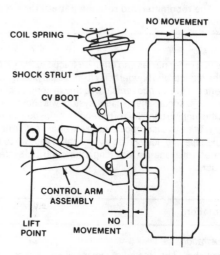

21.12   To check the wheel bearings, try to move the tire in and out – if any play is noted, or if the bearings feel rough or sound noisy when the tire is rotated, the bearings need to be replaced

placement point. When you hear this noise, replace the pads immediately or expensive damage to the rotors could result.
2   Any of the following symptoms could indicate a brake system defect: the vehicle pulls to one side when the brake pedal is depressed, the brakes make squealing or dragging noises when applied, brake pedal travel is excessive, the pedal pulsates or brake fluid leaks are noted (usually on the inner side of the tire or wheel). If any of these conditions are noted, inspect the brake system immediately.

Brake lines and hoses

Note: *Steel tubing is used throughout the brake system, with the exception of flexible, reinforced hoses at the front and rear wheels. Periodic inspection of these lines is very important.*

3   Park the vehicle on level ground and turn the engine off.
4   Remove the wheel covers. Loosen, but do not remove, the lug nuts.
5   Raise the vehicle and support it securely on jackstands.
6   Remove the wheels (see Jacking and towing at the front of this manual, or refer to your owner's manual, if necessary).
7   Check all brake hoses and lines for cracks, chafing of the outer cover, leaks, blisters and distortion. Check all threaded fittings for leaks and make sure the brake hose mounting bolts and clips are secure.
8   If leaks or damage are discovered, they must be fixed immediately. Refer to Chapter 9 for detailed information on brake system repair procedures.

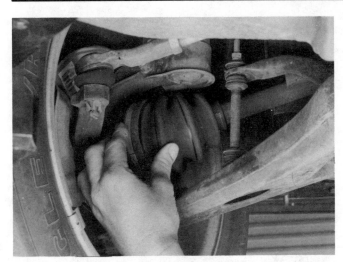

21.14 Flex the driveaxle boots by hand to check for cracks and leaking grease

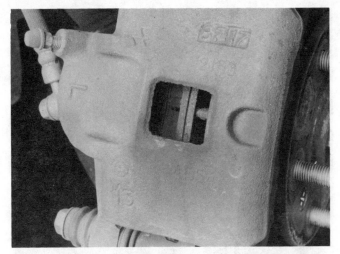

22.11 The disc brake pad thickness can be checked through the caliper inspection hole

Disc brakes

Refer to illustration 22.11

9   If it hasn't already been done, raise the front (or rear) of the vehicle and support it securely on jackstands. Apply the parking brake and remove the front wheels.

10   The disc brake calipers, which contain the pads, are now visible. Each caliper has an outer and an inner pad – all pads should be checked.

11   Note the pad thickness by looking through the inspection hole in the caliper **(see illustration)**. If the lining material is 1/8-inch thick or less, or if it is tapered from end to end, the pads should be replaced (see Chapter 9). Keep in mind that the lining material is riveted or bonded to a metal plate or shoe – the metal portion is not included in this measurement.

12   Check the condition of the brake disc. Look for score marks, deep scratches and overheated areas (they will appear blue or discolored). If damage or wear is noted, the disc can be removed and resurfaced by an automotive machine shop or replaced with a new one. Refer to Chapter 9 for more detailed inspection and repair procedures.

Rear drum brakes

Refer to illustration 22.15

13   Refer to Chapter 9 and remove the rear brake drums.

14   Warning: Brake dust produced by lining wear and deposited on brake components may contain asbestos, which is hazardous to your health. DO NOT blow it out with compressed air and DO NOT inhale it! DO NOT use gasoline or solvents to remove the dust. Brake system cleaner should be used to flush the dust into a drain pan. After the brake components are wiped clean with a damp rag, dispose of the contaminated rag(s) and solvent in a covered and labelled container.

15   Note the thickness of the lining material on the rear brake shoes **(see illustration)** and look for signs of contamination by brake fluid and grease.

If the lining material is within 1/16-inch of the recessed rivets or met shoes, replace the brake shoes with new ones. The shoes should also be replaced if they are cracked, glazed (shiny lining surfaces) or contaminated with brake fluid or grease. See Chapter 9 for the replacement procedure.

16   Check the shoe return and hold-down springs and the adjusting mechanism to make sure they are installed correctly and in good condition. Deteriorated or distorted springs, if not replaced, could allow the linings to drag and wear prematurely.

17   Check the wheel cylinders for leakage by carefully peeling back the rubber boots. If brake fluid is noted behind the boots, the wheel cylinders must be replaced (see Chapter 9).

18   Check the drums for cracks, score marks, deep scratches and hard spots, which will appear as small discolored areas. If imperfections cannot be removed with emery cloth, the drums must be resurfaced by an automotive machine shop (see Chapter 9 for more detailed information).

19   Refer to Chapter 9 and install the brake drums.

20   Install the wheels, but do not lower the vehicle yet.

Parking brake lubrication and check

Refer to illustration 22.22

Note: *The parking brake cable and linkage should be periodically checked and lubricated. This maintenance procedure helps prevent the parking brake cable adjuster or the linkage from binding and adversely affecting the operation or adjustment of the parking brake.*

Lubrication

21   Set the parking brake.

22   Apply multi-purpose grease to the parking brake linkage, adjuster assembly, connectors and the areas of the parking brake cables that come in contact with the other parts of the vehicle **(see illustration)**.

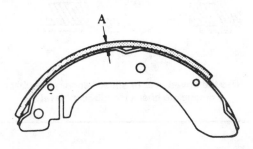

22.15 The rear brake shoe lining thickness (A) is measured from the outer surface of the lining to the metal shoe

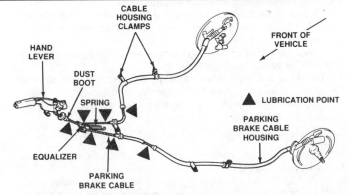

22.22 Lubricate the parking brake cables at the points indicated

23.1a   If the vehicle has analog instruments, locate the speedometer driven gear assembly – to remove the assembly, disconnect the speedometer cable and remove the hold-down bolt (arrow)

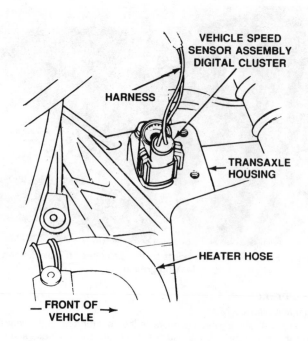

23.1b   If the vehicle has digital instruments, locate the vehicle speed sensor assembly – to remove the assembly, disconnect the harness and remove the hold-down bolt

23   Release the parking brake and repeat the lubrication procedure.
24   Remove the jackstands and lower the vehicle.
25   Tighten the wheel lug nuts to the torque listed in this Chapter's Specifications and install the wheel covers.

Check

26   The easiest, and perhaps most obvious, method of checking the parking brake is to park the vehicle on a steep hill with the parking brake set and the transaxle in Neutral. If the parking brake cannot prevent the vehicle from rolling, refer to Chapter 9 and adjust it.

---

23   Manual transaxle lubricant level check

Refer to illustrations 23.1a, 23.1b and 23.7

Note: *The transaxle lubricant should not deteriorate under normal driving conditions. However, it is recommended that you check the level occasionally. The most convenient time is when the vehicle is raised for another reason, such as an engine oil change.*

1   Park the vehicle on a level surface. Turn the engine off, apply the parking brake and block the wheels. Open the hood and locate the speedometer driven gear assembly (analog instruments) or vehicle speed sensor assembly (digital instruments) **(see illustrations)**.
2   To protect the transaxle from contamination, wipe off any dirt or grease in the area around the speed sensor or speedometer driven gear assembly.
3   On vehicles equipped with digital instruments, unplug the electrical lead from the vehicle speed sensor.
4   On vehicles equipped with analog instruments, disconnect the speedometer cable from the speedometer driven gear assembly.
5   Remove the retaining bolt and remove the speedometer driven gear assembly or vehicle speed sensor.
6   Wipe the driven gear or speed sensor clean, then fully reinsert it into the transaxle.
7   Remove the driven gear or speed sensor and check the lubricant level as shown **(see illustration)**.
8   If the lubricant level is below the driven gear, add the specified lubricant through the opening until the level is even with the top of the gear. If you add too much, remove the excess with a syringe.

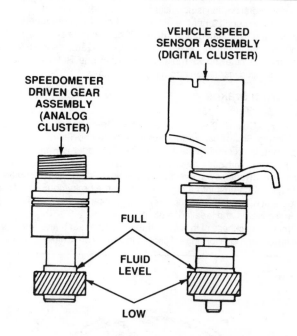

23.7   Use the driven gear or speed sensor assembly as a dipstick to check the lubricant level

---

9   Install the driven gear or speed sensor. Install the retaining bolt and tighten it securely.
10   Connect the speedometer cable or plug in the speed sensor electrical lead.

CARBON DEPOSITS

Symptoms: Dry sooty deposits indicate a rich mixture or weak ignition. Causes misfiring, hard starting and hesitation.

Recommendation: Check for a clogged air cleaner, high float level, sticky choke and worn ignition points. Use a spark plug with a longer core nose for greater anti-fouling protection.

OIL DEPOSITS

Symptoms: Oily coating caused by poor oil control. Oil is leaking past worn valve guides or piston rings into the combustion chamber. Causes hard starting, misfiring and hesition.

Recommendation: Correct the mechanical condition with necessary repairs and install new plugs.

TOO HOT

Symptoms: Blistered, white insulator, eroded electrode and absence of deposits. Results in shortened plug life.

Recommendation: Check for the correct plug heat range, over-advanced ignition timing, lean fuel mixture, intake manifold vacuum leaks and sticking valves. Check the coolant level and make sure the radiator is not clogged.

PREIGNITION

Symptoms: Melted electrodes. Insulators are white, but may be dirty due to misfiring or flying debris in the combustion chamber. Can lead to engine damage.

Recommendation: Check for the correct plug heat range, over-advanced ignition timing, lean fuel mixture, clogged cooling system and lack of lubrication.

HIGH SPEED GLAZING

Symptoms: Insulator has yellowish, glazed appearance. Indicates that combustion chamber temperatures have risen suddenly during hard acceleration. Normal deposits melt to form a conductive coating. Causes misfiring at high speeds.

Recommendation: Install new plugs. Consider using a colder plug if driving habits warrant.

GAP BRIDGING

Symptoms: Combustion deposits lodge between the electrodes. Heavy deposits accumulate and bridge the electrode gap. The plug ceases to fire, resulting in a dead cylinder.

Recommendation: Locate the faulty plug and remove the deposits from between the electrodes.

NORMAL

Symptoms: Brown to grayish-tan color and slight electrode wear. Correct heat range for engine and operating conditions.

Recommendation: When new spark plugs are installed, replace with plugs of the same heat range.

ASH DEPOSITS

Symptoms: Light brown deposits encrusted on the side or center electrodes or both. Derived from oil and/or fuel additives. Excessive amounts may mask the spark, causing misfiring and hesitation during acceleration.

Recommendation: If excessive deposits accumulate over a short time or low mileage, install new valve guide seals to prevent seepage of oil into the combustion chambers. Also try changing gasoline brands.

WORN

Symptoms: Rounded electrodes with a small amount of deposits on the firing end. Normal color. Causes hard starting in damp or cold weather and poor fuel economy.

Recommendation: Replace with new plugs of the same heat range.

DETONATION

Symptoms: Insulators may be cracked or chipped. Improper gap setting techniques can also result in a fractured insulator tip. Can lead to piston damage.

Recommendation: Make sure the fuel anti-knock values meet engine requirements. Use care when setting the gaps on new plugs. Avoid lugging the engine.

SPLASHED DEPOSITS

Symptoms: After long periods of misfiring, deposits can loosen when normal combustion temperature is restored by an overdue tune-up. At high speeds, deposits flake off the piston and are thrown against the hot insulator, causing misfiring.

Recommendation: Replace the plugs with new ones or clean and reinstall the originals.

MECHANICAL DAMAGE

Symptoms: May be caused by a foreign object in the combustion chamber or the piston striking an incorrect reach (too long) plug. Causes a dead cylinder and could result in piston damage.

Recommendation: Remove the foreign object from the engine and/or install the correct reach plug.

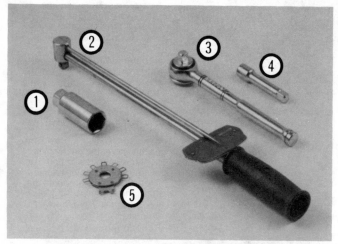

24.2   Tools required for changing spark plugs

1   **Spark plug socket** – This will have special padding inside
    to protect the spark plug's porcelain insulator
2   **Torque wrench** – Although not mandatory, using this tool is
    the best way to ensure the plugs are tightened properly
3   **Ratchet** – Standard hand tool to fit the spark plug socket
4   **Extension** – Depending on model and accessories, you may
    need special extensions and universal joints to reach one or
    more of the plugs
5   **Spark plug gap gauge** – This gauge for checking the gap
    comes in a variety of styles. Make sure the gap for your
    engine is included.

24   Spark plug replacement

Refer to illustrations 24.2, 24.5a, 24.5b, 24.6 and 24.10

1   The spark plugs are located on the front (radiator) side of the engine
on four-cylinder models and on both sides on V6 models.
2   In most cases, the tools necessary for spark plug replacement include
a spark plug socket which fits onto a ratchet (spark plug sockets are
padded inside to prevent damage to the porcelain insulators on the new
plugs), various extensions and a gap gauge to check and adjust the gaps
on the new plugs **(see illustration)**. A special plug wire removal tool is
available for separating the wire boots from the spark plugs, but it isn't absolutely necessary. A torque wrench should be used to tighten the new
plugs.
3   The best approach when replacing the spark plugs is to purchase the
new ones in advance, adjust them to the proper gap and replace the plugs
one at a time. When buying the new spark plugs, be sure to obtain the correct plug type for your particular engine. This information can be found on
the Vehicle Emission Control Information label located under the hood and
in the factory owner's manual. If differences exist between the plug specified on the emissions label and in the owner's manual, assume that the
emissions label is correct.
4   Allow the engine to cool completely before attempting to remove any
of the plugs. While you are waiting for the engine to cool, check the new
plugs for defects and adjust the gaps.
5   The gap is checked by inserting the proper thickness gauge between
the electrodes at the tip of the plug **(see illustration)**. The gap between
the electrodes should be the same as the one specified on the Vehicle
Emissions Control Information label. The wire should just slide between
the electrodes with a slight amount of drag. If the gap is incorrect, use the
adjuster on the gauge body to bend the curved side electrode slightly until
the proper gap is obtained **(see illustration)**. If the side electrode is not
exactly over the center electrode, bend it with the adjuster until it is. Check
for cracks in the porcelain insulator (if any are found, the plug should not be
used).

**24.5a   Spark plug manufacturers recommend using a wire-type
gauge when checking the gap – if the wire does not slide between
the electrodes with a slight drag, adjustment is required**

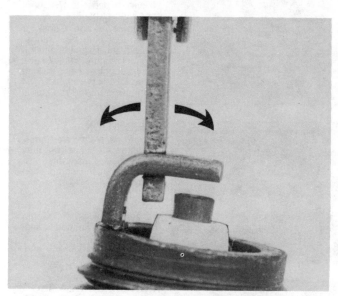

**24.5b   To change the gap, bend the side electrode only, as
indicated by the arrows, and be very careful not to crack or chip
the porcelain insulator surrounding the center electrode**

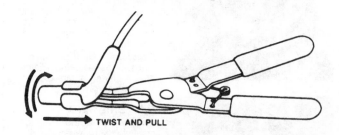

TWIST AND PULL

**24.6   When removing the spark plug wires, pull only on the
boot and use a twisting/pulling motion**

6   With the engine cool, remove the spark plug wire from one spark plug.
Pull only on the boot at the end of the wire – do not pull on the wire. A plug
wire removal tool should be used if available **(see illustration)**.

24.10   A length of 3/16-inch ID rubber hose will save time and prevent damaged threads when installing the spark plugs

7   If compressed air is available, use it to blow any dirt or foreign material away from the spark plug hole. A common bicycle pump will also work. The idea here is to eliminate the possibility of debris falling into the cylinder as the spark plug is removed.

8   Place the spark plug socket over the plug and remove it from the engine by turning it in a counterclockwise direction.

9   Compare the spark plug to those shown in the accompanying color photos to get an indication of the general running condition of the engine.

10   Thread one of the new plugs into the hole until you can no longer turn it with your fingers, then tighten it with a torque wrench (if available) or the ratchet. It might be a good idea to slip a short length of rubber hose over the end of the plug to use as a tool to thread it into place **(see illustration)**. The hose will grip the plug well enough to turn it, but will start to slip if the plug begins to cross-thread in the hole – this will prevent damaged threads and the accompanying repair costs.

11   Before pushing the spark plug wire onto the end of the plug, inspect it following the procedures outlined in Section 25.

12   Attach the plug wire to the new spark plug, again using a twisting motion on the boot until it is seated on the spark plug.

13   Repeat the procedure for the remaining spark plugs, replacing them one at a time to prevent mixing up the spark plug wires.

---

25   Spark plug wire, distributor cap and rotor check and replacement

---

Spark plug wires

1   The spark plug wires should be checked and, if necessary, replaced at the same time new spark plugs are installed.

2   The easiest way to identify bad wires is to make a visual check while the engine is running. In a dark, well-ventilated garage, start the engine and look at each plug wire. Be careful not to come into contact with any moving engine parts. If there is a break in the wire, you will see arcing or a small spark at the damaged area. If arcing is noticed, make a note to obtain new wires.

3   The spark plug wires should be inspected one at a time, beginning with the spark plug for the number one cylinder (the one nearest the right end of the engine), to prevent confusion. Clearly label each original plug wire with a piece of tape marked with the correct number. The plug wires must be reinstalled in the correct order to ensure proper engine operation.

4   Disconnect the plug wire from the first spark plug. A removal tool can be used **(see illustration 24.6)**, or you can grab the wire boot, twist it slightly and pull the wire free. Do not pull on the wire itself, only on the rubber boot.

5   Push the wire and boot back onto the end of the spark plug. It should fit snugly. If it doesn't, detach the wire and boot once more and use a pair of pliers to carefully crimp the metal connector inside the wire boot until it does.

6   Using a clean rag that's damp with solvent, wipe the entire length of the wire to remove built-up dirt and grease.

7   Once the wire is clean, check for burns, cracks and other damage. Do not bend the wire sharply or you might break the conductor.

8   Disconnect the wire from the distributor. Again, pull only on the rubber boot. Check for corrosion and a tight fit. Reinstall the wire in the distributor.

9   Inspect each of the remaining spark plug wires, making sure that each one is securely fastened at the distributor and spark plug when the check is complete.

10   If new spark plug wires are required, purchase a set for your specific engine model. Pre-cut wire sets with the boots already installed are available. Remove and replace the wires one at a time to avoid mix-ups in the firing order.

Distributor cap and rotor

Refer to illustrations 25.11, 25.12a, 25.12b and 25.13

Note: *It is common practice to install a new distributor cap and rotor each time new spark plug wires are installed. If you're planning to install new wires, install a new cap and rotor also. But if you are planning to reuse the existing wires, be sure to inspect the cap and rotor to make sure that they are in good condition.*

11   Remove the mounting screws and detach the cap from the distributor. Check it for cracks, carbon tracks and worn, burned or loose terminals **(see illustration)**

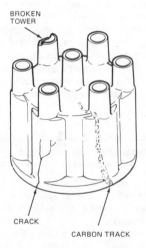

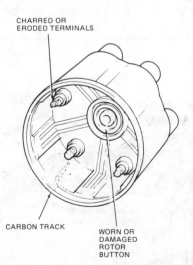

25.11   Shown here are some of the common defects to look for when inspecting the distributor cap (if in doubt about its condition, install a new one)

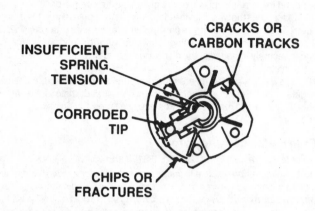

25.12a   On four-cylinder models, check the rotor for damage and corrosion as indicated – if you're in doubt about its condition, replace it

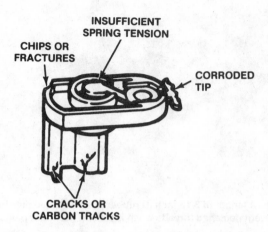

25.12b   On V6 models, check the rotor for damage and corrosion as indicated – if in doubt, replace it

12   Check the rotor for cracks and carbon tracks. Make sure the center terminal spring tension is adequate and look for corrosion and wear on the rotor tip **(see illustrations)**.

13   Replace the cap and rotor if damage or defects are found. Note that the rotor is indexed so it can only be installed one way. Before installing the cap, apply silicone dielectric compound to the rotor tip **(see illustration)**.

14   When installing a new cap, remove the wires from the old cap one at a time and attach them to the new cap in the exact same location – do not simultaneously remove all the wires from the old cap or firing order mix-ups may occur.

26   Cooling system servicing (draining, flushing and refilling)

Warning: *Do not allow antifreeze to come in contact with your skin or painted surfaces of the vehicle. Rinse off spills immediately with plenty of water. Antifreeze is highly toxic if ingested. Never leave antifreeze lying around in an open container or in puddles on the floor; children and pets are attracted by it's sweet smell and may drink it. Check with local authorities about disposing of used antifreeze. Many communities have collection centers which will see that antifreeze is disposed of safely.*

1   Periodically, the cooling system should be drained, flushed and re-filled to replenish the antifreeze mixture and prevent formation of rust and corrosion, which can impair the performance of the cooling system and cause engine damage. When the cooling system is serviced, all hoses and the radiator cap should be checked and replaced if necessary.

Draining

Refer to illustration 26.4

2   Apply the parking brake and block the wheels. If the vehicle has just been driven, wait several hours to allow the engine to cool down before beginning this procedure.

3   Once the engine is completely cool, remove the radiator cap to vent the cooling system.

4   Move a large container under the radiator to catch the coolant and open the drain fitting **(see illustration)**.

5   After the coolant stops flowing out of the radiator, move the container under the engine block drain plug(s). Remove the plug(s) and allow the coolant in the block to drain. **Note:** *Four-cylinder engines have one block drain plug, normally on the front side of the engine. V6 engines have two plugs: one on each side of the engine.*

6   While the coolant is draining, check the condition of the radiator hoses, heater hoses and clamps (see Section 18 if necessary).

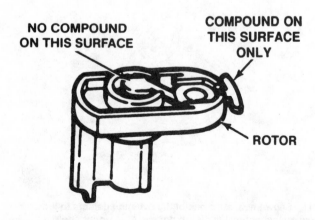

25.13   Apply silicone dielectric compound to the rotor, as shown, before installing the distributor cap (V6 rotor shown)

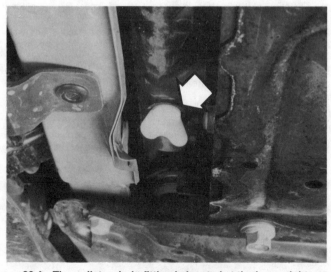

26.4   The radiator drain fitting is located at the lower right corner of the radiator

27.5   Remove all the pan bolts except two of the rear ones, then carefully pry the pan loose from the transaxle case – be careful; too much force could damage the flange and cause leaks

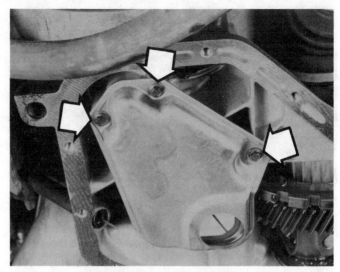

27.8a   On some transaxles, the filter is held in place by bolts (arrows), . . .

7   Replace any damaged clamps or hoses (see Chapter 3 for detailed replacement procedures).

Flushing

8   Once the system is completely drained, flush the radiator with fresh water from a garden hose until water runs clear at the drain. The flushing action of the water will remove sediments from the radiator but will not remove rust and scale from the engine and cooling tube surfaces.
9   These deposits can be removed by the chemical action of a cleaner such as Ford Cooling System Fast Flush. Follow the procedure outlined in the manufacturer's instructions. If the radiator is severely corroded, damaged or leaking, it should be removed (see Chapter 3) and taken to a radiator repair shop.
10   Remove the overflow hose from the coolant recovery reservoir. Drain the reservoir and flush it with clean water, then reconnect the hose.

Refilling

11   Close and tighten the radiator drain. Install and tighten the block drain plug(s).
12   Place the heater temperature control in the maximum heat position.
13   Slowly add new coolant (a 50/50 mixture of water and antifreeze) to the radiator until it is full. Add coolant to the reservoir up to the lower mark.
14   Leave the radiator cap off and run the engine in a well-ventilated area until the thermostat opens (coolant will begin flowing through the radiator and the upper radiator hose will become hot).
15   Turn the engine off and let it cool. Add more coolant mixture to bring the level back up to the lip on the radiator filler neck.
16   Squeeze the upper radiator hose to expel air, then add more coolant mixture if necessary. Replace the radiator cap.
17   Start the engine, allow it to reach normal operating temperature and check for leaks.

---

27   Automatic transaxle fluid and filter change

Refer to illustrations 27.5, 27.8a, 27.8b, 27.9a, 27.9b and 27.11

1   Before beginning work, purchase the specified transmission fluid (see Recommended lubricants and fluids at the beginning of this Chapter) and a new filter. The filter will come with a new pan gasket and O-ring.
2   The fluid should be drained immediately after the vehicle has been driven. More sediment and contaminants will be removed with the fluid if

27.8b   . . . while others have a clip (arrow) which is pulled down to release the filter

it's hot. **Caution:** *Fluid temperature can exceed 350-degrees F in a hot transaxle, so wear gloves when draining the fluid.*
3   After the vehicle has been driven to warm up the fluid, raise it and support it on jackstands.
4   Position a drain pan capable of holding four quarts under the transaxle. Be careful not to touch any of the hot exhaust components.
5   Remove all of the pan bolts except for the two at the rear corners **(see illustration)**. Unscrew the two remaining bolts two turns, but leave them in place to support the pan.
6   Carefully separate the pan from the transaxle case and allow the fluid to drain out. Try not to splash fluid as the gasket seal is broken and the pan is detached. Once the fluid has drained, remove the two bolts and detach the pan.
7   Scrape all traces of the old gasket from the pan and the transaxle case, then clean the pan with solvent and dry it with compressed air – DO NOT use a rag to wipe out the pan (lint from the rag could contaminate the transaxle).
8   Remove the filter bolts or clip and detach the filter **(see illustrations)**. Discard the filter and the O-ring.

27.9a   Some transaxles have an O-ring which fits in a recess in the filter housing, . . .

9   Attach the new O-ring(s) to the new filter **(see illustrations)**, then bolt or clip the filter to the transaxle.
10   Position the new gasket on the pan, then hold the pan against the transaxle case and install the bolts or clip.
11   Tighten the pan bolts to the torque listed in this Chapter's Specifications in a criss-cross pattern **(see illustration)**. Work up to the final torque in three steps. **Caution:** *Don't overtighten the bolts or the pan flange could be distorted and leaks could result.*
12   Lower the vehicle. With the engine off, fill the transaxle with fluid (see Section 7 if necessary). Use a funnel to prevent spills. It is best to add a little fluid at a time, continually checking the level with the dipstick. Allow the fluid time to drain into the pan.
13   Start the engine and shift the selector into all positions from Park through Low, then shift into Park and apply the parking brake.
14   With the engine idling, check the fluid level. Lower the vehicle, drive it for several miles, then recheck the fluid level and look for leaks at the transaxle pan.

27.9b   . . . while others have two O-rings which fit on the filter tube

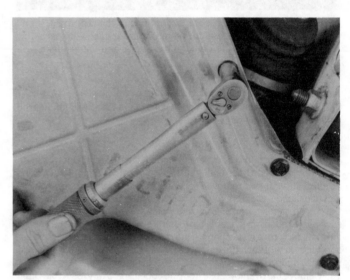

27.11   Tighten the transaxle pan bolts with a torque wrench – follow a criss-cross pattern and work up to the final torque in three steps to avoid warping the pan flange

Chapter 2 Part A   Four-cylinder engine

Contents

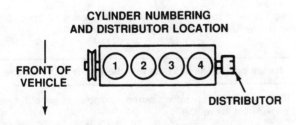

CYLINDER NUMBERING
AND DISTRIBUTOR LOCATION

FRONT OF
VEHICLE

DISTRIBUTOR

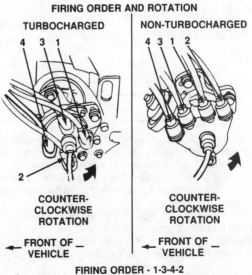

FIRING ORDER AND ROTATION

TURBOCHARGED

NON-TURBOCHARGED

COUNTER-
CLOCKWISE
ROTATION

COUNTER-
CLOCKWISE
ROTATION

FRONT OF
VEHICLE

FRONT OF
VEHICLE

FIRING ORDER - 1-3-4-2
2.2L ENGINE

Specifications

General
Rocker arm-to-shaft clearance (maximum) . . . .   0.004 in (0.10 mm)
Timing belt deflection . . . .   0.030 to 0.33 in (7.5 to 8.5 mm) at 22 lb (98 Nm)

Camshaft
Endplay service limit . . . .   0.003 to 0.008 in (0.08 to 0.016 mm)
Bearing journal diameter
  Front and rear . . . .   1.2575 to 1.2585 in (31.940 to 31.965 in
  Center three . . . .   1.2563 to 1.2573 in (31.910 to 31.935 mm)
Bearing oil clearance
  Front and rear . . . .   0.0014 to 0.0033 in (0.035 to 0.085 mm)
  Center three . . . .   0.0026 to 0.0045 in (0.065 to 0.115 mm)
  Service limit (all) . . . .   0.0059 in (0.15 mm)
Lobe lift
  Intake
    Standard . . . .   1.626 to 1.630 in (41.29 mm)
    Service limit . . . .   1.620 in (41.14 mm)
  Exhaust
    Standard . . . .   1.646 to 1.650 in (41.80 to 41.90 mm)
    Service limit . . . .   1.640 in (41.65 mm)

Oil pump
Outer gear tooth-to-crescent clearance limit . . . .   0.013 in (0.33 mm)
Inner gear tooth-to-crescent clearance limit . . . .   0.016 in (0.41 mm)
Outer gear-to-pump body clearance . . . .   0.008 in (0.20 mm)
Gear-to-pump cover clearance . . . .   0.008 in (0.20 mm)

Torque specifications
Ft-lbs (unless otherwise indicated)

Camshaft sprocket bolt . . . .   35 to 48
Rocker arm cover bolts . . . .   52 to 69 in-lbs
Camshaft/rocker arm bolts . . . .   13 to 20
Crankshaft pulley bolts . . . .   109 to 152 in-lbs
Crankshaft rear oil seal retainer bolts . . . .   6 to 9
Crankshaft sprocket bolt . . . .   108 to 116
Cylinder head bolts . . . .   59 to 64
Exhaust manifold nuts . . . .   16 to 21
Flywheel/driveplate bolts . . . .   71 to 76
Front housing-to-cylinder head bolts/nuts . . . .   14 to 19
Intake manifold bolts . . . .   14 to 22
Oil pan bolts . . . .   69 to 104 in-lbs
Oil pump-to-block bolts
Through O-ring . . . .   14 to 19
All others . . . .   27 to 38
Rear housing-to-cylinder head bolts/nuts . . . .   14 to 19
Rocker arm assembly bolts . . . .   13 to 20
Timing belt cover bolts . . . .   61 to 87 in-lbs
Timing belt tensioner lockbolt . . . .   27 to 38

---

1 General information

This Part of Chapter 2 covers in-vehicle repairs to the four-cylinder engine. The repair procedures included in this part are based on the assumption that the engine is still installed in the vehicle. Therefore, if this information is being used during a complete engine overhaul, with the engine already out of the vehicle and on a stand, many of the steps included here will not apply.

Information concerning engine block and cylinder head servicing can be found in Part C of this Chapter.

The engine block is made of cast iron and the cylinder head is cast aluminum. The camshaft is located in the cylinder head and actuates the valves via shaft-mounted rocker arms.

The specifications included in this part of Chapter 2 apply only to the procedures found here. Part C of Chapter 2 contains the specifications necessary for engine block and cylinder head rebuilding.

---

2 Repair operations possible with the engine in the vehicle

Many major repair operations can be accomplished without removing the engine from the vehicle.

Clean the engine compartment and the exterior of the engine with some type of degreaser before any work is done. It'll make the job easier and help keep dirt out of the internal areas of the engine.

Depending on the components involved, it may be helpful to remove the hood to improve access to the engine as repairs are performed (refer to Chapter 11 if necessary). Cover the fenders to prevent damage to the paint. Special pads are available, but an old bedspread or blanket will also work.

If vacuum, exhaust, oil or coolant leaks develop, indicating a need for gasket or seal replacement, the repairs can generally be made with the engine in the vehicle. The intake and exhaust manifold gaskets, oil pan gasket, crankshaft oil seals and cylinder head gasket are all accessible with the engine in place.

Exterior engine components, such as the intake and exhaust manifolds, the oil pan, oil pump, water pump, starter motor, alternator and the fuel system components can be removed for repair with the engine in place.

Since the cylinder head can be removed without pulling the engine, valve component servicing can also be accomplished with the engine in the vehicle. Replacement of the timing belt and sprockets is also possible with the engine in the vehicle.

In extreme cases caused by a lack of necessary equipment, repair or replacement of piston rings, pistons, connecting rods and rod bearings is possible with the engine in the vehicle. However, this practice is not recommended because of the cleaning and preparation work that must be done to the components involved.

3 Rocker arm cover – removal and installation

Refer to illustrations 3.1, 3.3, 3.5a and 3.5b.

Removal

1   Remove the breather tube and PCV valve (see illustration).
2   Remove the spark plug wire clips.
3   Remove the retaining bolts and separate the cover from the engine. It may be necessary to break the gasket seal by tapping the cover with a soft-face hammer, lifting it with a prying tool (see illustration) or inserting a very thin blade scraper or screwdriver at the corner. Be extremely careful not to gouge, break or distort the mating surfaces.
4   Clean all traces of gasket material from the rocker arm cover gasket mating surfaces. Be careful not to nick or gouge the soft aluminum.

Installation

5   Install a new gasket in the rocker arm cover (see illustration). Apply RTV sealant (Ford ESE-M4G195-A, or equivalent) to the corners of the cylinder head (see illustration) and place the cover in position on the head.
6   Install the attaching bolts and tighten them to the torque listed in this Chapter's specifications.
7   Install the PCV valve and hoses and reattach the spark plug wire clips.

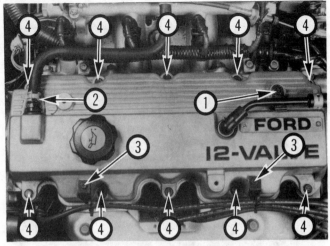

3.1 Rocker arm cover details

1   Breather tube bolt   3   Spark plug wire clip
2   PCV valve and tube   4   Camshaft cover retaining bolts

3.3 Lift up on the rocker arm cover

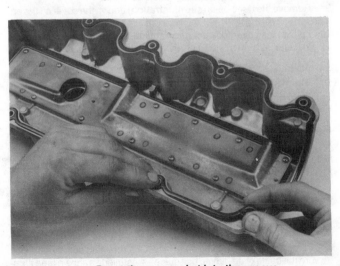

3.5a Press the new gasket into the groove

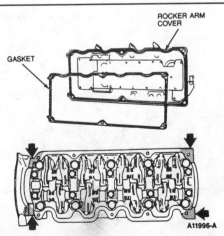

3.5b Apply RTV sealant to the shaded areas in the corners (arrows)

4.2   Remove the upper timing belt cover bolts (arrows)

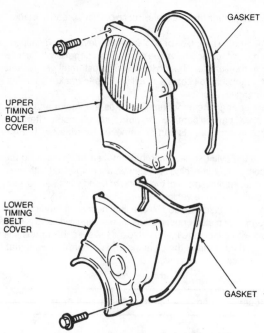

4.9   Timing belt covers – exploded view

5.3   Loosen the six bolts (arrows)

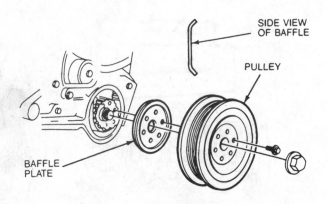

5.6   Crankshaft pulley components – exploded view

4   Timing belt covers – removal and installation

Refer to illustrations 4.2 and 4.9
1   Disconnect the negative cable from the battery.

Upper cover

2   Remove the four cover bolts **(see illustration)** and lift the cover from the engine.
3   Inspect the cover and gasket for wear and damage and replace as necessary.
4   Install the cover and tighten the bolts securely.

Lower cover

5   Remove the upper cover first (see above).
6   Loosen the lug nuts on the right front wheel. Raise the front of the vehicle, support it securely on jackstands and remove the right front wheel and splash guard.
7   Remove the drivebelts (see Chapter 1).
8   Remove the crankshaft pulley (see Section 5).
9   Remove the three bolts **(see illustration)** and lift the cover off the engine.
10   Inspect the cover for wear and damage and replace as necessary.
11   Installation is the reverse of removal.

5   Crankshaft pulley – removal and installation

Refer to illustrations 5.3 and 5.6

Removal

1   Loosen the lug nuts on the right front wheel. Raise the front of the vehicle and support it securely on jackstands.
2   Remove the right front wheel and inner fender splash guards
3   Loosen the crankshaft pulley retaining bolts **(see illustration)**.
4   Remove the drivebelts (see Chapter 1).
5   Remove the bolts and lift the crankshaft pulley from the engine.

Installation

6   Place the pulley in position and install the retaining bolts finger tight. Be sure the baffle plate (timing belt guide) is installed as shown **(see illustration)**.

6.5a   Align the mark on the crankshaft pulley (arrow) with the "T"
or "0" mark on the lower timing belt cover

6.5b   Align the arrow on the camshaft sprocket with the mark on
the front housing (arrows)

7   Tighten the bolts to the torque listed in this Chapter's Specifications.

8   Install the remaining components in the reverse order of removal.

---

6   Timing belt – removal, installation and adjustment

Note: *If the timing belt broke during engine operation, the valves and/or pistons may be damaged.*

Removal

Refer to illustrations 6.5a, 6.5b, 6.5c, 6.6, 6.7, 6.8, 6.9, 6.10a, 6.10b, 6.11 and 6.12

1   Disconnect the negative cable from the battery.

2   Remove the spark plugs (see Chapter 1).

3   Remove the upper timing belt cover (see Section 4).

4   Loosen the lug nuts on the right (passenger's side) front wheel. Raise the front of the vehicle and support it securely on jackstands. Remove the right front wheel and inner fender splash guard.

5   Use a wrench on the crankshaft center bolt to rotate the crankshaft clockwise until the timing mark on the crankshaft pulley is aligned with the "T" or "0" mark on the lower timing belt cover and the arrow on the camshaft sprocket (adjacent to the "1" mark) lines up with the mark on the front housing as shown **(see illustrations)**. **Note:** *If you intend to reuse the timing belt, mark an arrow on it to indicate the direction of rotation* **(see illustration).**

6   Remove the crankshaft pulley, lower timing belt cover and belt guide (baffle plate). Refer to Sections 4 and 5 as necessary. Be sure the timing marks for the crankshaft sprocket are aligned **(see illustration)**.

6.5c   If you intend to reuse the timing belt, mark an arrow on it to
indicate direction of rotation

6.6   Make sure the crankshaft sprocket timing mark is aligned
with the mark on the oil pump (arrows)

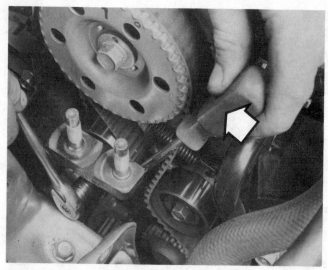

6.7   Loosen the tensioner lock bolt, push the idler pulley toward
the rear and tighten the bolt (engine mount removed for clarity)

6.8   Work the belt off the sprockets

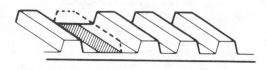

6.9   Check the timing belt for cracked and missing teeth

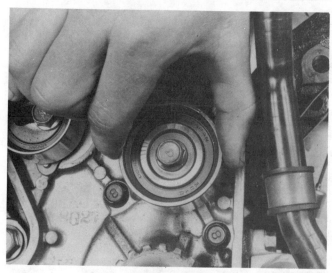

6.10a   Turn the idler pulley . . .

6.10b   . . . and tensioner pulley, checking for roughness and play

6.11   If the belt is cracked or worn, check the pulleys for
nicks and burrs

6.12   Wear on one side of the belt indicates pulley
misalignment problems

6.14a The timing belt should be installed as shown (engine removed for clarity)

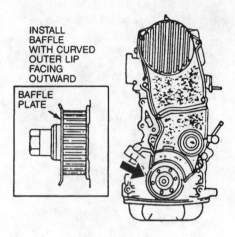

INSTALL BAFFLE WITH CURVED OUTER LIP FACING OUTWARD

BAFFLE PLATE

6.14b   Be sure the baffle plate is installed as shown

7   Loosen the timing belt tensioner lock bolt, push the idler rearward (against spring tension) and tighten the bolt **(see illustration)**.
8   Work the belt off the sprockets and remove it from the engine **(see illustration)**. **Caution:** *Do not bend, twist or turn the belt inside out. Do not allow it to come in contact with oil, coolant, or fuel. Do not utilize timing belt tension to keep the camshaft or crankshaft from turning when installing the sprocket bolt(s). Do not turn the crankshaft or camshaft more than a few degrees (necessary for tooth alignment) while the timing belt is removed.*
9   Inspect the belt for damage, peeling, wear, cracks, hardening, crimping or signs of oil **(see illustration)**. The belt should be replaced with a new one if any of these conditions exist.
10   Turn the idler and tensioner pulleys by hand, checking the bearings for smooth operation and excessive play **(see illustrations)**. Inspect the return spring for damage.
11   If there is noticeable wear or cracks in the belt, check the sprockets for nicks or burrs **(see illustration)**.
12   If the wear or damage is only on one side of the belt, check the alignment of the idler, tensioner and sprockets **(see illustration)**.

Installation

Refer to illustrations 6.14a and 6.14b

13   Make sure the crankshaft and camshaft sprocket timing marks are aligned (see illustrations 6.5b and 6.6).
14   Install the timing belt over the sprockets **(see illustration)**. Work the belt onto the camshaft and crankshaft sprockets from the side opposite the tensioner. If the old belt is being reinstalled, make sure the arrow is pointing in the proper direction. Install the belt guide (baffle plate) with the curved lip out **(see illustration)**.

Adjustment

Refer to illustration 6.19

15   With the spring attached to the tensioner, loosen the tensioner bolt to tension the belt and then tighten the lock bolt to hold the tensioner in place.
16   Loosen the tensioner lock bolt so that the spring is applying pressure to the belt.
17   Using a socket and breaker bar on the crankshaft pulley bolt, turn the crankshaft clockwise two full revolutions so that equal tension is applied to both sides of the timing belt. **Caution:** *If you feel resistance while rotating the engine by hand, do not use force. The valves may be contacting the pistons due to incorrect valve timing. Tighten the lock bolt.*
18   Recheck the timing marks. If the marks aren't aligned exactly, repeat the belt installation procedure. **Caution:** *DO NOT start the engine until you're absolutely certain the timing belt is installed correctly!*
19   Check the deflection of the belt midway between the camshaft sprocket and idler pulley to make sure it is within the range listed in this

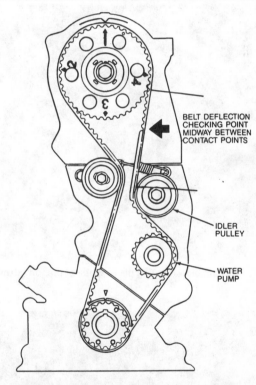

BELT DEFLECTION CHECKING POINT MIDWAY BETWEEN CONTACT POINTS

IDLER PULLEY

WATER PUMP

6.19   Measure belt deflection at the indicated point

Chapter's specifications **(see illustration)**. If the tension is not correct, repeat the adjustment operation described in Steps 15 through 18.
20   Reinstall the remaining parts in the reverse order of removal.
21   Run the engine and check for proper operation.

7   Camshaft sprocket – removal and installation

Refer to illustrations 7.3, 7.4 and 7.5

Removal

1   Remove the timing belt covers (see Section 4)
2   Remove the timing belt (see Section 6).

7.3   Keep the sprocket from turning by inserting a screwdriver or other tool through a hole

7.4   Mark the sprocket adjacent to the locating pin (arrows)

7.5   The camshaft locating pin must be at the top (arrow)

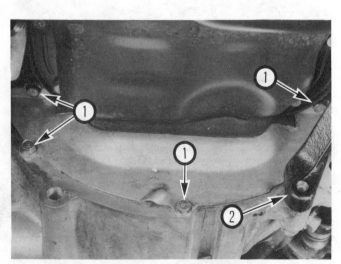

8.4a   Remove the lower bellhousing bolts and brace

1   Bolts   2   Brace

3   Hold the sprocket in position so it cannot turn, using a lever slipped through the sprocket and held against the front housing **(see illustration)**. Remove the sprocket bolt.

4   Make a mark on the sprocket adjacent to the camshaft locating pin **(see illustration)**. Remove the sprocket.

Installation

5   Place the sprocket in position on the camshaft with the locating pin at the top **(see illustration)**.

6   Hold the camshaft sprocket from turning as described above and install the washer and bolt. Tighten the bolt to the torque listed in this Chapter's specifications.

7   Install the timing belt, covers and all other components which were removed.

---

8   Crankshaft sprocket – removal and installation

Refer to illustrations 8.4a, 8.4b, 8.5, 8.6, 8.7a and 8.7b

Removal

1   Remove the crankshaft pulley (see Section 5).

2   Remove the timing belt (see Section 6).

3   Raise the vehicle and support it securely on jackstands.

4   Remove the lower cover from the transaxle bellhousing. Insert a large screwdriver through the access hole into the teeth of the starter ring gear so the crankshaft cannot turn **(see illustrations)**.

5   With an assistant holding the screwdriver so the crankshaft is locked, remove the center bolt from the crankshaft **(see illustration)**.

6   Attach a bolt-type puller to the crankshaft sprocket **(see illustration)** and remove the sprocket.

Installation

7   Inspect the sprocket for wear and damage. Align the keyway with the crankshaft key **(see illustrations)**. Slip the sprocket onto the crankshaft and install the crankshaft sprocket mounting bolt finger tight.

8   Hold the crankshaft from turning as described above and tighten the bolt to the torque listed in this Chapter's Specifications.

9   Install the remaining parts in the reverse order of removal.

8.4b   Hold a large screwdriver against the ring gear teeth as shown here

8.5   Crankshaft sprocket details

1   *Center bolt*   2   *Timing marks*

8.6   Remove the sprocket with a bolt-type puller as shown here

8.7a   The keyway (arrow) must align with key in the crankshaft

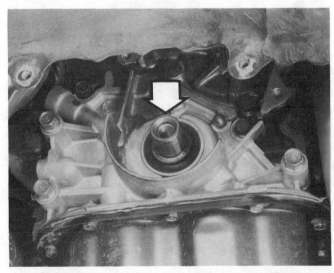

8.7b   The crankshaft key should be at the top (arrow)

9.2   Carefully pry the old seal out with a screwdriver

9.4   Gently tap the new seal into place with a hammer and socket

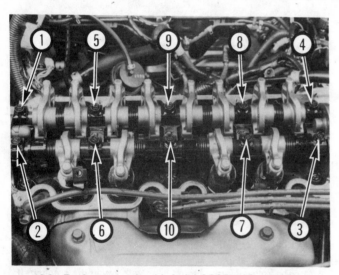

10.3   Rocker arm assembly bolt LOOSENING sequence

10.5   Lift the rocker arm assembly off as a unit – the bolts will hold it together

9   Crankshaft front oil seal – replacement

Refer to illustrations 9.2 and 9.4

Removal

1   Remove the crankshaft sprocket (see Section 8).
2   Pry the oil seal out with a screwdriver **(see illustration)**. Take care to avoid damaging the crankshaft and seal bore.

Installation

3   Lubricate the inner diameter of the seal with engine oil and place the seal in position.
4   Tap the seal evenly and fully into the bore using a hammer and socket with a diameter slightly smaller than the outside diameter of the seal **(see illustration)**.
5   Reinstall the remaining parts in the reverse order of removal.
6   Run the engine and check for oil leaks.

10   Rocker arm assembly – removal, inspection and installation

Refer to illustrations 10.3 and 10.5

Removal

1   Disconnect the negative battery cable.
2   Remove the rocker arm cover (see Section 3).
3   Loosen the rocker arm assembly retaining bolts, a little at a time, in the sequence shown **(see illustration)**.
4   Once the bolts are loose, leave them in place to hold the rocker assembly together as it is lifted off the engine.
5   Lift the rocker arm assembly from the engine **(see illustration)**.

Inspection

Refer to illustrations 10.7, 10.8a and 10.8b

6   If you wish to disassemble and inspect the rocker arm assemblies (a good idea as long as you have them off), remove the retaining bolts and slip the rocker arms and springs off the shafts. Keep the parts in order so you can reassemble them in the same positions.
7   Carefully clean and inspect all components for wear and damage, including the contact areas of the rocker arm assembly and the lash adjuster tips. Also check to make sure the oil holes in the shaft are not plugged. The lash adjusters may be pulled out with pliers for replacement **(see illustration)**.

10.7   The lash adjusters can be pulled out with pliers for replacement

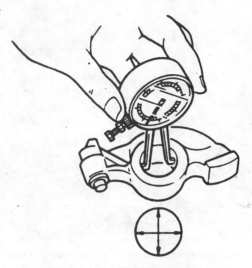

10.8a Measure the inside diameter of the rocker arm bores

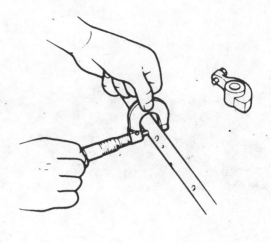

10.8b Measure the diameter of the rocker arm shaft where the rocker arm rides

8   Measure and record the inside diameter of each rocker arm and the outside diameter of the rocker shaft where it rides **(see illustrations)**.

9   Subtract the shaft diameter from the rocker arm inside diameter to determine the oil clearance. Compare the results with the clearance listed in this Chapter's Specifications. Replace any parts that are damaged or excessively worn.

Installation

Refer to illustration 10.12

10   If the rocker arms have been removed from the shafts, lubricate them liberally with clean engine oil prior to assembly.

11   Lower the rocker arm assembly into place and install the bolts finger tight.

12   Tighten the bolts a little at a time, in the sequence shown **(see illustration)** to the torque listed in this Chapter's Specifications.

13   Install the rocker arm cover and connect the negative battery cable.

11   Camshaft – removal, inspection and installation

Removal

Refer to illustration 11.7

1   Remove the timing belt covers, timing belt and camshaft sprocket (see Sections 4, 6 and 7).

2   Remove the rocker arm cover (see Section 3).

3   Remove the distributor (see Chapter 5).

4   Remove the rear housing (see Section 12).

5   Remove the front housing (see Section 18).

6   Remove the rocker arm and shaft assemblies (see Section 10).

7   Note the markings on the bearing caps **(see illustration)**. Remove the camshaft bearing caps and lift the camshaft from the engine.

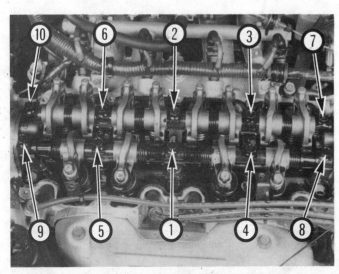

10.12   Rocker arm assembly bolt TIGHTENING sequence

11.7   The second cap has a number 2 stamped in it (arrow), the middle cap has an oil slot and the fourth cap is unmarked

11.8a   Check the cam lobes for pitting, wear and score marks – if scoring is excessive, as is the case here, replace the camshaft

11.8b   Inspect the camshaft bearing surfaces for excessive scuffing and wear

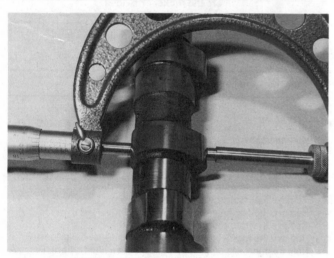

11.9   Measure the height of each lobe with a micrometer

11.10a   Lay a strip of Plastigauge on each camshaft journal

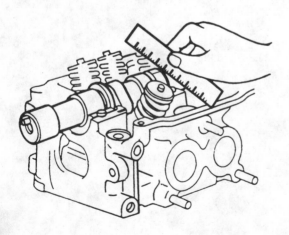

11.10b   Compare the width of the crushed Plastigauge to the scale on the envelope to determine the oil clearance

Inspection

Refer to illustrations 11.8a, 11.8b, 11.9, 11.10a, 11.10b and 11.11

8   Visually inspect the cam lobes, bearing journals and bearing surfaces **(see illustrations)** for score marks, pitting, galling and evidence of over-heating (blue, discolored areas). Look for flaking away of the hardened surface layer of each lobe.

9   Using a micrometer, measure the height of each camshaft lobe **(see illustration)** and the diameter of each journal. If the measurements are less than specified, replace the camshaft.

10   Check the oil clearance for each camshaft journal as follows:

    a) Clean the bearings and camshaft journals with lacquer thinner or acetone and a clean cloth.

    b) Carefully lay the camshaft in place in the cylinder head. Don't use any lubrication. **Caution:** *Do not turn the camshaft during this procedure.*

    c) Lay a strip of Plastigage on each journal **(see illustration)**.

    d) Temporarily install the bearing caps and rocker arm assemblies (see Section 10), tightening the bolts to the torques listed in this Chapter's Specifications.

    e) Remove the rocker arm assemblies and bearing caps. Compare the width of the crushed Plastigage (at it's widest point) to the scale on the Plastigage envelope **(see illustration)**.

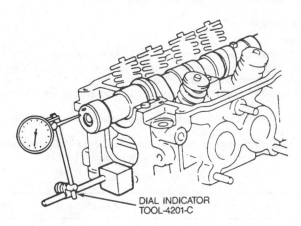

11.11 Measure camshaft endplay with a dial indicator

11.12 The camshaft locating pin (arrow) must be at the top

11.13 The bearing caps must be in their original positions and the arrows must point towards the timing belt

12.5 Before the housing can be detached, all the bolts/nuts must be removed (arrows)

f) If the clearance is greater than specified and the camshaft journal diameters are within specifications, replace the cylinder head.

g) Scrape off the Plastigage with your fingernail or the edge of a credit card – don't nick or scratch the journals or bearing caps.

11 Mount a dial indicator on the end of the cylinder head and check camshaft endplay **(see illustration)**. Compare the reading to the endplay clearance listed in this Chapter's specifications.

Installation

Refer to illustrations 11.12 and 11.13

12 Lubricate the camshaft lobes and journals with engine assembly lube or moly-based grease. Place the camshaft in position with the locating pin (dowel) at the top **(see illustration)**.

13 Install the bearing caps **(see illustration)**, then the rocker arm and shaft assemblies.

14 Install the front housing.

15 Install the camshaft sprocket, making sure the sprocket and front housing marks are aligned.

16 Install the rear housing and distributor.

17 Install the rocker arm cover, timing belt and cover.

18 Run the engine and check for proper operation and oil leaks.

12 Rear housing – removal and installation

Refer to illustrations 12.5 and 12.6

Removal

1 Drain the cooling system (see Chapter 1).

2 Detach the upper radiator hose and electrical connectors from the thermostat housing.

3 Place a rag under the housing to catch the oil when the housing is removed.

4 Remove the distributor (see Chapter 5).

5 Remove the engine lifting eye/throttle body brace and rear housing bolts and nuts **(see illustration)**.

12.6   Slide the rear housing off the studs

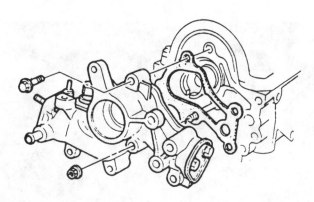

12.9   Rear housing mounting details – exploded view

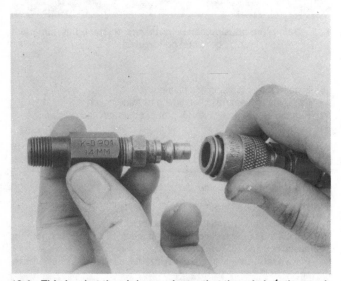

13.4   This is what the air hose adapter that threads into the spark plug hole looks like – they're commonly available from auto parts stores

6   Use a soft-face hammer to separate the housing from the engine, then slide it off the studs **(see illustration)**.

Installation

Refer to illustration 12.9

7   Thoroughly clean the contact surfaces of the housing and cylinder head of old gasket material. If you use a scraper, be very careful not to gouge the delicate aluminum surfaces.

8   Coat the new gasket with sealant and place it in position on the housing.

9   Install the housing on the cylinder head **(see illustration)** and finger tighten the nuts and bolts.

10   Tighten the bolts to the torque listed in this Chapter's Specifications.

11   Install the remaining parts in the reverse order of removal.

---

13   Valve springs, retainers and seals – replacement

Refer to illustrations 13.4, 13.9 and 13.17

Note: *Broken valve springs and defective valve stem seals can be replaced without removing the cylinder head. Two special tools and a compressed air source are normally required to perform this operation, so read through this Section carefully and rent or buy the tools before beginning the job. If compressed air isn't available, a length of nylon rope can be used to keep the valves from falling into the cylinder during this procedure.*

1   Remove the rocker arm cover and rocker arm assembly (see Sections 3 and 10).

2   Remove the spark plug from the cylinder which has the defective component. If all of the valve stem seals are being replaced, all of the spark plugs should be removed.

3   If you're replacing all of the valve stem seals, begin with cylinder number one and work from front to rear.

4   Thread an adapter into the spark plug hole **(see illustration)** and connect an air hose from a compressed air source to it. Most auto parts stores can supply the air hose adapter. **Note:** *Many cylinder compression gauges utilize a screw-in fitting that may work with your air hose quick-disconnect fitting.*

5   Apply compressed air to the cylinder. **Warning:** *The piston may be forced down by compressed air, causing the crankshaft to turn suddenly. If a wrench is attached to the bolt in the crankshaft nose, it could cause damage or injury when the crankshaft moves.*

6   The valves should be held in place by the air pressure. If the valve faces or seats are in poor condition, leaks may prevent air pressure from retaining the valves – refer to the alternative procedure below.

7   If you don't have access to compressed air, an alternative method can be used. Position the piston at a point just before it reaches the top, then feed a long piece of nylon rope through the spark plug hole until it fills the combustion chamber. Be sure to leave the end of the rope hanging out of the engine so it can be removed easily.

8   Use a large ratchet and socket to rotate the crankshaft in the normal clockwise direction of rotation, until slight resistance is felt.

9   Stuff shop rags into the oil return holes adjacent to the valves to prevent parts and tools from falling into the engine, then use a valve spring compressor to compress the spring. Remove the keepers with small needle-nose pliers or a magnet **(see illustration)**. **Note:** *A couple of different types of tools are available for compressing the valve springs with the head in place. One type grips the lower spring coils and presses on the retainer as the knob is turned, while the other type utilizes a hook and lever. When using the hook and lever type, remove the rocker arms and springs from the shafts and temporarily install the shafts as fulcrums.*

10   Remove the spring retainer and valve spring, then remove the stem oil seal. **Note:** *If air pressure fails to hold the valve in the closed position during this operation, the valve face and/or seat is probably damaged. If so the cylinder head will have to be removed for additional repair operations.*

11   Wrap a rubber band or tape around the top of the valve stem so the valve won't fall into the combustion chamber, then release the air pressure. **Note:** *If a rope was used instead of air pressure, turn the crankshaft slightly in the direction opposite normal rotation.*

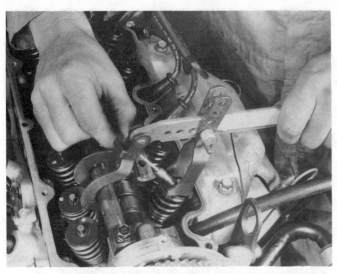

13.9   Compress the valve spring and remove the keepers

13.17   Apply a small dab of grease to each keeper before installation to hold them in place on the valve stem until the spring is released

12   Inspect the valve stem for damage. Rotate the valve in the guide and check the end for eccentric movement, which would indicate that the valve is bent.
13   Move the valve up-and-down in the guide and make sure it doesn't bind. If the valve stem binds, either the valve is bent or the guide is damaged. In either case, the head will have to be removed for repair.
14   Reapply air pressure to the cylinder to retain the valve in the closed position, then remove the tape or rubber band from the valve stem. If a rope was used instead of air pressure, rotate the crankshaft in the normal direction of rotation until slight resistance is felt.
15   Lubricate the valve stem with engine oil and install a new oil seal.
16   Install the spring in position over the valve. Be sure the closely wound coils are next to the head.
17   Install the valve spring retainer. Compress the valve spring and carefully position the keepers in the groove. Apply a small dab of grease to the inside of each keeper to hold it in place if necessary (see illustration).
18   Remove the pressure from the spring tool and make sure the keepers are seated.
19   Disconnect the air hose and remove the adapter from the spark plug hole. If a rope was used in place of air pressure, pull it out of the cylinder.

20   Refer to Sections 3 and 10 and install the rocker assembly and rocker arm cover.
21   Install the spark plug(s) and hook up the wire(s).
22   Start and run the engine, then check for oil leaks and unusual sounds coming from the rocker arm cover area.

14   Camshaft oil seal – replacement

Refer to illustrations 14.3 and 14.5
1   Remove the timing belt (see Section 5).
2   Remove the camshaft sprocket (see Section 6).
3   Pry the old oil seal out with a screwdriver, taking care not to damage the sealing surface (see illustration).
4   Apply a thin coat of engine oil to the outer diameter of the new seal.
5   Place the seal squarely in position in the bore and use a socket and hammer to gently tap it into place (see illustration).
6   Install the sprocket, timing belt and cover.
7   Run the engine and check for oil leaks.

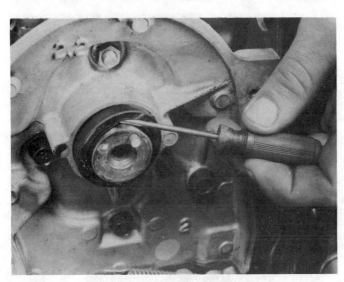

14.3   Carefully pry out the old seal

14.5   Using a hammer and socket, tap the new seal squarely into place

15.3a   Detach the brackets from the intake plenum (arrows)

15.3b   Remove the throttle body, hoses, cables, brackets and nuts (arrows) from the intake plenum (turbo model shown, non-turbo models similar)

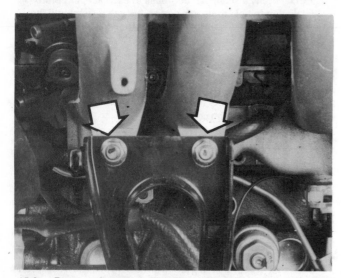

15.6a   Remove the nuts (arrows) and detach the brace from the underside of the intake manifold

15   Intake manifold – removal and installation

Refer to illustrations 15.3a, 15.3b, 15.6a, 15.6b, 15.7, 15.8 and 15.9

Removal

1   Relieve fuel pressure (see Chapter 4) and disconnect the negative cable from the battery.
2   Drain the coolant (see Chapter 1).
3   Remove the wires, cables, brackets, hoses and throttle body from the intake plenum (see Chapter 4). Unbolt the intake plenum **(see illustrations)**.
4   Disconnect and plug the fuel lines and detach the fuel rail and fuel injectors (see Chapter 4).
5   Mark any remaining wiring, hoses and connections which will interfere with manifold removal with numbered pieces of tape and disconnect them.
6   Remove the lower brace from the manifold **(see illustration)**. Remove the manifold mounting nuts and slide the intake manifold off the studs, separating it from the cylinder head **(see illustration)**.

Installation

7   Clean all traces of gasket and other foreign material from the manifold, plenum and cylinder head mating surfaces, taking care not to gouge

15.6b   This view of the intake manifold with the plenum removed shows the locations of the fuel line brackets and manifold mounting nuts (arrows)

15.7   Scrape off all traces of old gasket material – be very careful not to nick or gouge the delicate aluminum mating surfaces

15.8   Install a new gasket over the studs (arrows)

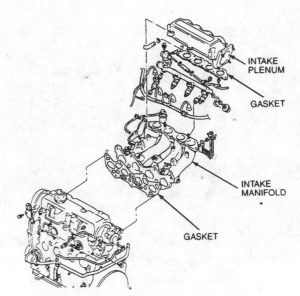

**15.9   Non-turbo intake manifold components –
exploded view (turbo components similar)**

the soft aluminum surface **(see illustration)**.

8   Install a new gasket **(see illustration)**, place the manifold in position on the studs and install the mounting nuts. Tighten the nuts to the torque listed in this Chapter's Specifications. Work from the center of the manifold out, in a criss-cross pattern.

9   Install the components which were removed to gain access to the intake manifold **(see illustration)**.

16   Exhaust manifold – removal and installation

Refer to illustration 16.2

Warning: *Allow the engine to cool completely before following this procedure.*

Note: *This procedure applies to non-turbo models only. On turbocharged models, the exhaust manifold and turbocharger are removed as an assembly and separated off the vehicle (see Chapter 4).*

Removal

1   Disconnect the negative cable from the battery.

2   Remove the oxygen sensor and detach the heat shield **(see illustration)**.

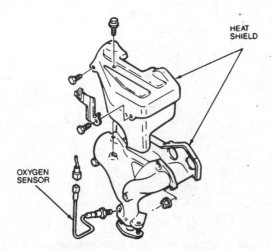

**16.2   Non-turbo exhaust manifold components –
exploded view**

3   Engage the parking brake and block the rear wheels. Raise the front of the vehicle and support it securely on jackstands.

4   Apply penetrating oil to the cylinder head and exhaust pipe retaining stud threads and allow it to soak for ten minutes.

5   Remove the nuts retaining the exhaust pipe and detach it from the manifold.

6   Remove the nuts retaining the manifold to the cylinder head.

7   Grasp the manifold, separate it from the cylinder head and lift it from the engine compartment.

Installation

8   Remove all traces of gasket material from the manifold and cylinder head with a gasket scraper. Take care not to nick or gouge the soft aluminum of the head.

9   Place the manifold in position on the cylinder head, using a new gasket, and install the retaining nuts to hold it in place. Install the nuts retaining the manifold to the exhaust pipe. Tighten the manifold nuts to the torque listed in this Chapter's Specifications. Work from the center of the manifold out, in a criss-cross pattern.

10   Reinstall the remaining components in the reverse order of removal.

17   Cylinder head – removal and installation

Note: *The engine must be cold whenever the cylinder head bolts are loosened or removed.*

Removal

Refer to illustrations 17.8 and 17.10

1   Relieve the fuel pressure (see Chapter 4) and disconnect the negative cable from the battery.

2   Remove the spark plugs and drain the coolant from the engine block and radiator (see Chapter 1).

3   Remove the rocker arm cover, rocker arm assemblies and camshaft (see Sections 3, 10 and 11).

4   Remove the distributor (see Chapter 5) and rear housing (see Section 12).

5   Remove the intake manifold (see Section 15).

6   Check the cylinder head. Label and remove any remaining items, such as coolant fittings, tubes, cables, hoses or wires.

7   Remove the exhaust manifold (see Section 16) or turbocharger assembly (see Chapter 4).

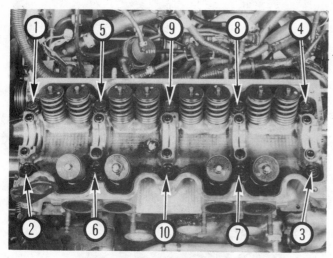

17.8   Cylinder head bolt LOOSENING sequence

17.10   Carefully pry up on a cylinder head protrusion

17.12   Remove all traces of old gasket material

8   Loosen the cylinder head bolts, a few turns at a time, in the sequence shown **(see illustration)**.
9   After they are all loose, remove the cylinder head bolts.
10   If the cylinder head cannot be lifted off easily, break the gasket seal using a pry bar inserted between the cylinder head protrusion and the block **(see illustration)**.
11   Separate the cylinder head from the engine and remove the gasket.

Installation

Refer to illustrations 17.12, 17.13 and 17.14

12   Remove all traces of gasket material from the engine block and cylinder head **(see illustration)**. Make sure the cylinder head bolt threads and the threaded holes in the block are clean, as this could affect torque readings during installation.
13   Place the new gasket **(see illustration)** and the cylinder head in position.
14   Install the cylinder head bolts and tighten them to the torque listed in this Chapter's specifications in the sequence shown **(see illustration)**.
15   The remainder of the installation procedure is the reverse of removal.
16   Add coolant and change the oil and filter (see Chapter 1).

17.13   Position the new gasket over the dowels (arrows)

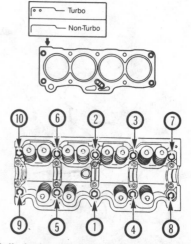

17.14   Cylinder head bolt TIGHTENING sequence – note the different markings on turbo and non-turbo gaskets

18.3   Remove the nut and three bolts (arrows)

19.6   Remove the exhaust pipe bracket bolts (arrows)

---

18   Front housing cover – removal and installation

Refer to illustration 18.3

Removal

1   Remove the timing belt covers (see Section 4) and timing belt (see Section 6).
2   Remove the camshaft sprocket (see Section 7).
3   Remove the nut and bolts **(see illustration)** and carefully separate the cover from the cylinder head, using a screwdriver placed under a casting protrusion to break the gasket seal.

Installation

4   Carefully clean the mating surfaces of gasket material.
5   Place the housing cover in position using a new gasket and install the retaining nut and bolts. Tighten the fasteners to the torque listed in this Chapter's specifications.
6   The remainder of installation is the reverse of removal.

19   Oil pan – removal and installation

Refer to illustrations 19.6, 19.9, 19.10, 19.13a, 19.13b and 19.13c

Removal

1   Disconnect the battery negative cable.
2   Loosen the lug nuts on the front wheel on the passenger's side.
3   Block the rear wheels and engage the parking brake. Raise the front of the vehicle and support it securely on jackstands.
4   Remove the right front wheel and the inner fender splash guard.
5   Drain the engine oil and replace the filter (see Chapter 1).
6   Disconnect and lower the front exhaust pipe and remove the bracket **(see illustration)**.
7   Remove the engine-to-bellhousing brace.
8   Remove the bellhousing access cover (see illustration 8.4a).
9   Remove the oil pan bolts **(see illustration)**.
10   Connect an engine hoist and support the engine weight. Unbolt the mount (see Section 24) and lift the engine enough for the oil pan to clear the crossmember **(see illustration)**.

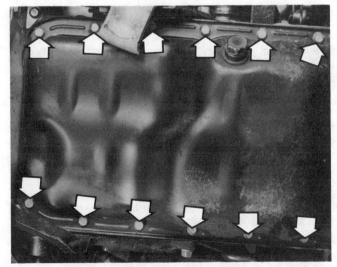

19.9   Remove the bolts (arrows) around the perimeter of the oil pan (viewed from below)

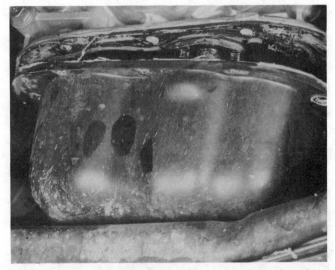

19.10   The oil pan may not clear the crossmember unless the engine is lifted

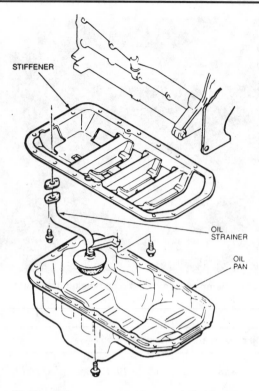

19.13a   Oil pan components – exploded view

19.13b   Remove the oil strainer bolts (arrows)

19.13c   Remove the two bolts (arrows) to detach the
stiffener (baffle)

11   Break the oil pan gasket seal by tapping the pan with a soft-face hammer. If this doesn't work, carefully insert a putty knife between the pan and the block. Be very careful not to damage the gasket mating surfaces or distort the pan mounting flange.
12   Remove the oil pan from the engine.
13   Unbolt the oil strainer and stiffener **(see illustrations)**.
14   Remove all traces of old gasket material. Wash the parts thoroughly in solvent and inspect for damage. Carefully inspect the oil pan mating flange for distortion. You can straighten distorted flanges by supporting the bottom of the flange with a wood block while you tap on the top of the flange with a hammer.

Installation

15   Apply a 1/4-inch bead of RTV-type sealant to the contact surfaces of the oil pan and stiffener (baffle).
16   Place the oil pan, stiffener, oil strainer and gasket into position and install the retaining bolts. Tighten the oil pan bolts to the torque listed in this Chapter's specifications. Tighten the other bolts securely.
17   The remainder of installation is the reverse of removal.
18   After installation fill the engine with the specified amount and grade of oil, start the engine and check for leaks.

20   Oil pump – removal and installation

Refer to illustrations 20.5 and 20.6

Removal

1   Remove the timing belt covers, timing belt and crankshaft sprocket (see Sections 4, 6 and 8).
2   Remove the oil pan, stiffener and the oil strainer assembly (see Section 19).
3   Carefully insert a screwdriver between the oil pump and engine block from beneath. Pry gently to break the gasket seal and remove the pump.

Caution: *Do not pry at the gasket mating surfaces. You can easily damage the surfaces, causing a leak.*
4   Clean the mating surfaces of the block and oil pump to remove all traces of old gasket material. Be very careful not to scratch or gouge the delicate aluminum.

Installation

5   Coat a new O-ring with petroleum jelly and insert it into the pump. Lightly coat the pump-to-block surface with RTV sealant **(see illustration)**. **Note:** *If your vehicle was equipped with an oil pump-to-block gasket, use a new one during assembly.*
6   Apply clean engine oil to the lip of the oil seal. Now would be a very good time to install a new seal (see Section 9). Place the pump (and gasket, where applicable) in position and install the bolts **(see illustration)**. Tighten the bolts to the torque listed in this Chapter's Specifications.
7   Using a new gasket, install the oil strainer assembly. Tighten the bolts to the torque listed in this Chapter's Specifications.
8   Install the oil pan, a new oil filter and add oil.
9   Install the remaining components in the reverse order of removal. Run the engine and check for oil pressure and leaks.

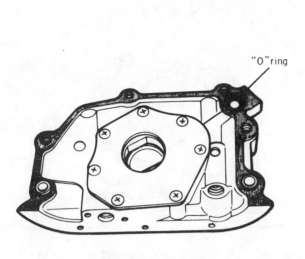

20.5   Apply RTV sealant to the shaded areas

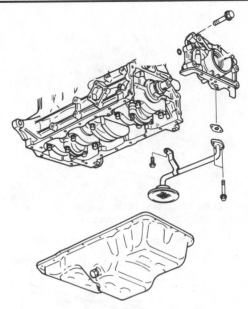

20.6   Oil pump mounting details – exploded view

21   Oil pump – disassembly, inspection and reassembly

Disassembly

Refer to illustrations 21.1 and 21.3

1   Remove the retaining screws and cover from the rear of the pump **(see illustration)**.
2   Remove the gears from the pump body. It may be necessary to turn the body over to remove the gears by allowing them to fall out.
3   Mount the pump body in a soft-jawed vise and remove the snap-ring and plunger assembly **(see illustration)**.

Inspection

Refer to illustrations 21.6a, 21.6b and 21.6c

4   Wash the oil pump parts in solvent.
5   Inspect the components for wear, cracks or other damage.
6   Check the inner gear tooth-to-crescent clearance, the outer gear tooth-to-crescent clearance, the outer gear-to-pump body clearance and the gear-to-cover clearance **(see illustrations)**.

Reassembly

7   Install the plunger assembly and snap-ring.
8   Install the gears, noting that the outer gear is identified by a mark. This mark must face the cover.
9   Pack the gear cavity with petroleum jelly. Install the pump cover and tighten the screws securely.

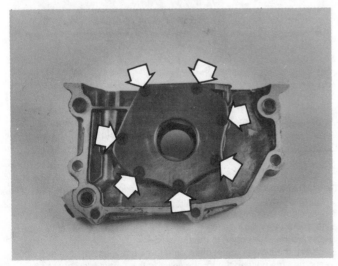

21.1   Remove the cover retaining screws (arrows)

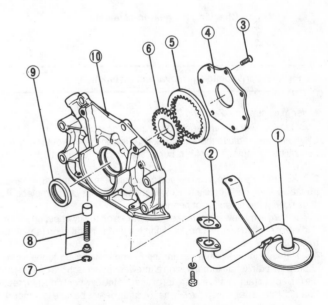

21.3   Oil pump components – exploded view

1	Oil strainer	6	Inner gear
2	Gasket	7	Snap-ring
3	Screw	8	Plunger assembly
4	Pump cover	9	Oil seal
5	Outer gear	10	Pump body

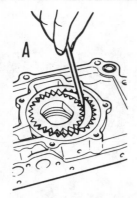

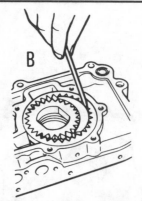

21.6a   Checking the inner gear
tooth-to-crescent clearance

21.6b   Checking the outer gear
tooth-to-crescent clearance

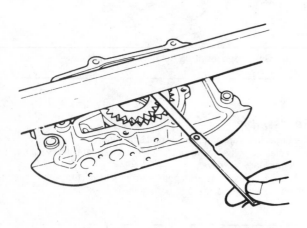

21.6c   Checking the gear-to-cover clearance

22.3   Mark the relative position of the flywheel/driveplate to the
crankshaft (arrow) before removing the bolts

22 Flywheel/driveplate – removal and installation

Refer to illustrations 22.3 and 22.5

1   Raise the vehicle and support it securely on jackstands, then refer to Chapter 7 and remove the transaxle. If it's leaking, now would be a very good time to replace the front pump seal/O-ring (automatic transaxle only).

2   Remove the pressure plate and clutch disc (see Chapter 8 – manual transaxle equipped vehicles). Now is a good time to check/replace the clutch components and pilot bearing.

3   If there is no dowel pin, make some marks on the flywheel/driveplate and crankshaft to ensure correct alignment during installation **(see illustration)**.

4   Remove the bolts that secure the flywheel/driveplate to the crankshaft. If the crankshaft turns, wedge a screwdriver through the openings in the driveplate (automatic transaxle) or against the flywheel ring gear teeth (manual transaxle). Since the flywheel is fairly heavy, be sure to support it while removing the last bolt.

5   Remove the flywheel/driveplate from the crankshaft. On automatic transaxle models, there are spacer plates on both sides of the driveplate **(see illustration)**.

6   Clean the flywheel to remove grease and oil. Inspect the friction surface for cracks, rivet grooves, burned areas and score marks. Light scoring can be removed with emery cloth. Check for cracked and broken ring gear teeth. Lay the flywheel on a flat surface and use a straightedge to check for warpage.

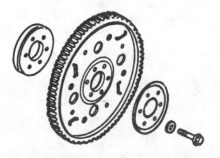

22.5   On automatic transaxle models, there are spacer
plates on both sides of the driveplate

7   Clean and inspect the mating surfaces of the flywheel/driveplate and the crankshaft. If the crankshaft rear seal is leaking, replace it before reinstalling the flywheel/driveplate (see Section 23).

8   Position the flywheel/driveplate against the crankshaft. Be sure to align the marks made during removal. Before installing the bolts, apply thread locking compound to the threads.

9   Keep the flywheel/driveplate from turning as described above while you tighten the bolts to the torque listed in this Chapter's Specifications.

10   The remainder of installation is the reverse of the removal procedure.

23.2 Work from the inside of the seal when prying it out to lessen the chance of damaging the bore surface

23.4 If the special installation tool is not available, tap lightly around the seal outer circumference with a hammer and blunt punch until the seal is fully seated in the bore

24.8 Engine mount details

1 *Mount-to-block bracket nuts*
2 *Through-bolt nut*

23 Crankshaft rear oil seal – replacement

Refer to illustrations 23.2 and 23.4

1 Remove the flywheel/driveplate (see Section 22).
2 Using a thin screwdriver or seal removal tool, carefully remove the oil seal from the engine block **(see illustration)**. Be very careful not to damage the crankshaft surface while prying the seal out.
3 Clean the bore in the block and the seal contact surface on the crankshaft. Check the seal contact surface on the crankshaft for scratches and nicks that could damage the new seal lip and cause oil leaks – if the crankshaft is damaged, the only alternative is a new or different crankshaft. Inspect the seal bore for nicks and scratches. Carefully smooth it with a fine file if necessary, but don't nick the crankshaft in the process.
4 A special tool is recommended to install the new oil seal. Lubricate the oil seal lips. Slide the seal onto the mandril of the tool until the dust lip bottoms squarely against the collar of the tool. **Note:** *If the special tool isn't available, carefully work the seal lip over the crankshaft and tap it into place with a hammer and punch* **(see illustration)**.
5 Align the dowel pin on the tool with the dowel pin hole in the crankshaft and attach the tool to the crankshaft by hand-tightening the bolts.
6 Turn the tool handle until the collar bottoms against the case, seating the seal.
7 Loosen the tool handle and remove the bolts. Remove the tool.
8 Check the seal and make sure it's seated squarely in the bore.
9 Install the flywheel/driveplate (see Section 22).
10 Install the transaxle (and clutch, on manual transaxle models).

24 Engine mount – check and replacement

1 The engine mount seldom requires attention, but a broken or deteriorated mount should be replaced immediately or the added strain placed on the driveline components may cause damage or wear.

Check

2 During the check, the engine must be raised slightly to remove the weight from the mount.
3 Raise the vehicle and support it securely on jackstands, then position a jack under the engine oil pan. Place a large block of wood between the jack head and the oil pan, then carefully raise the engine just enough to take the weight off the mount. **Warning:** *DO NOT place any part of your body under the engine when it's supported only by a jack!*

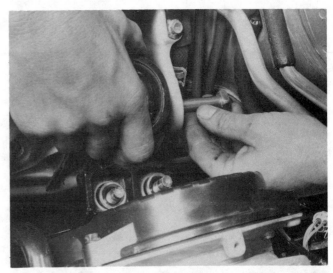

24.9 After removing the nut, pull the through-bolt out of the frame bracket

4 Check the mount to see if the rubber is cracked, hardened or separated from the metal plates. Sometimes the rubber will split right down the center.
5 Check for relative movement between the mount plates and the engine or frame (use a large screwdriver or prybar to attempt to move the mounts). If movement is noted, lower the engine and tighten the mount fasteners.
6 Rubber preservative should be applied to the mount to slow deterioration.

Replacement

Refer to illustrations 24.8 and 24.9

7 Disconnect the negative battery cable from the battery, then raise the vehicle and support it securely on jackstands (if not already done).
8 Raise the engine slightly with a jack or hoist. Remove the mount-to-block bracket nuts **(see illustration)**.
9 Remove the nut and detach the mount through-bolt from the frame bracket **(see illustration)**. Remove the mount.
10 Installation is the reverse of removal. Use thread locking compound on the threads and be sure to tighten all fasteners securely.

Chapter 2 Part B V6 engine

Contents

Specifications

General

Cylinder numbering (drivebelt end-to-transaxle end)
  Rear bank 1-2-3
  Front bank 4-5-6

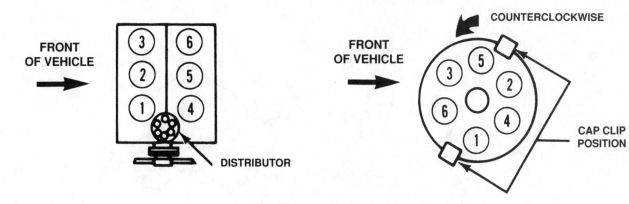

Cylinder numbers and firing order

Firing order	1-4-2-5-3-6
Timing chain deflection	6-degrees (see text)
Collapsed tappet gap (nominal)	0.085 to 0.185 in

Torque specifications

	Ft-lbs
Camshaft sprocket bolt	40 to 51
Cylinder head bolts	
Step one	33 to 41
Step two	63 to 73
Exhaust manifold bolts	15 to 22
Flywheel/driveplate bolts	54 to 64
Intake manifold bolts	
Step one	11
Step two	21
Oil pump mounting bolt	30 to 40
Oil pan bolts	7 to 10
Oil filter adapter-to-timing chain cover bolt	18 to 22
Rocker arm fulcrum bolts	
Step one	5 to 11
Step two	20 to 28
Rocker arm cover bolts/studs	7 to 10
Timing chain cover bolts	
6 mm	6 to 8
8 mm	15 to 22
Vibration damper-to-crankshaft bolt	92 to 122

1   General information

This Part of Chapter 2 is devoted to in-vehicle repair procedures for the V6 engine. All information concerning engine removal and installation, repairs which require engine removal and engine block and cylinder head overhaul can be found in Part C of this Chapter.

The following repair procedures are based on the assumption that the engine is installed in the vehicle. If the engine has been removed from the vehicle and mounted on a stand, many of the steps outlined in this Part of Chapter 2 will not apply.

The specifications included in this Part of Chapter 2 apply only to the procedures contained in this Part. Part C of Chapter 2 contains the specifications necessary for cylinder head and engine block rebuilding.

2   Repair operations possible with the engine in the vehicle

Many major repair operations can be accomplished without removing the engine from the vehicle.

Clean the engine compartment and the exterior of the engine with some type of pressure washer before any work is done. A clean engine will make the job easier and will help keep dirt out of the internal areas of the engine.

Depending on the components involved, it may be a good idea to remove the hood to improve access to the engine as repairs are performed (refer to Chapter 11 if necessary).

If vacuum, exhaust, oil or coolant leaks develop, indicating a need for gasket or seal replacement, the repairs can generally be made with the

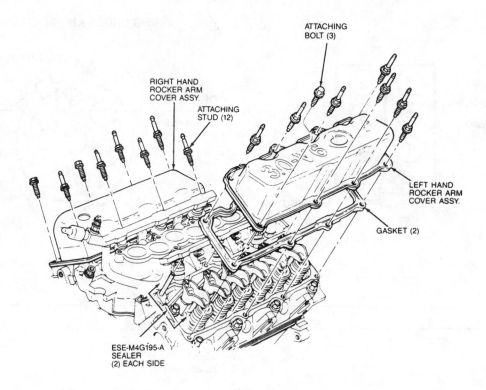

3.3   Rocker arm cover mounting details – exploded view

engine in the vehicle. The intake and exhaust manifold gaskets, oil pan gasket and cylinder head gaskets are all accessible with the engine in place.

Exterior engine components such as the intake and exhaust manifolds, the oil pan (and the oil pump), the water pump, the starter motor, the alternator, the distributor and the fuel injection system components can be removed for repair with the engine in place.

Since the cylinder heads can be removed without pulling the engine, valve component servicing can also be accomplished with the engine in the vehicle.

In extreme cases caused by a lack of necessary equipment, repair or replacement of piston rings, pistons, connecting rods and rod bearings is possible with the engine in the vehicle. However, this practice is not recommended because of the cleaning and preparation work that must be done to the components involved.

3   Rocker arm covers – removal and installation

Refer to illustrations 3.3 and 3.4

1   Disconnect the negative cable from the battery.

2   Disconnect the ignition wires from the spark plugs on the side(s) you are disassembling. If they are not numbered, tag them so they won't get mixed up on reassembly.

3   Note the location of the wire routing clips and studs **(see illustration)** and pull the clips off the studs.

4   If the front cover is being removed, disconnect the crankcase breather hose and move the wiring harnesses aside **(see illustration)**.

5   If the rear cover is being removed, remove the PCV valve (see Chapter 1) and the upper intake manifold (plenum) as described in Chapter 4.

6   Remove the rocker arm cover attaching bolts and studs. Use a deep socket to remove the studs.

7   Carefully remove the cover. If the cover is stuck, tap it with a soft-face hammer to break it loose.

8   Using a gasket scraper or putty knife, remove all traces of gasket ma-

terial from the cylinder head and rocker arm cover. Clean off any oil or dirt with acetone or lacquer thinner and a cloth.

9   Lightly oil all bolt and stud threads prior to installation.

10   Apply a bead of RTV sealant at the cylinder head-to-intake manifold rail step (two places per rail).

11   Position a new gasket and install the rocker arm cover.

12   Tighten the bolts to the torque listed in this Chapter's Specifications, working around the cover in several steps.

13   Reinstall the parts removed for access. Be sure to add coolant if it was drained.

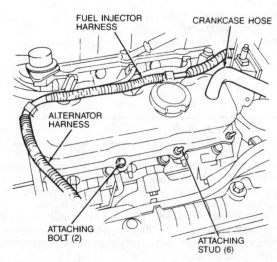

3.4   Remove the wiring harnesses and crankcase breather hose from the front rocker arm cover

4.2 Loosen the bolt (arrow) and pivot the rocker arm to the side to remove the pushrod

4.3 A perforated cardboard box can be used to store the pushrods to ensure installation in their original locations

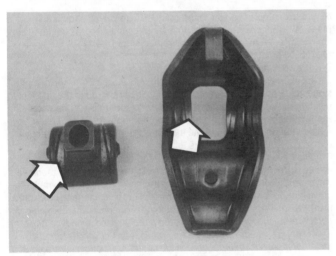

4.5 Check the rocker arm and fulcrum for wear and galling (arrows)

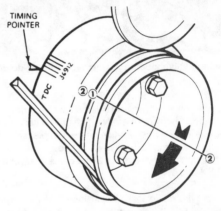

TIMING POINTER

POSITION 1 –
NO. 1 AT TDC, AT
END OF COMPRESSION
STROKE

POSITION 2 –
ROTATE CRANKSHAFT 360°
(ONE REVOLUTION) CLOCKWISE
FROM POSITION 1

4.11 Positioning the crankshaft for the valve clearance check

---

4   Rocker arms and pushrods – removal, inspection, installation and adjustment

Removal, inspection and installation

Refer to illustrations 4.2, 4.3 and 4.5

1   Remove the rocker arm cover(s) (see Section 3).
2   Loosen the rocker arm fulcrum bolt until you can pivot the rocker arm to one side and pull the pushrod out of the valve lifter **(see illustration)**.
3   If you are removing more than one pushrod, store them in a holder made from a cardboard box **(see illustration)** so they can be returned to their original locations.
4   If you are going to remove all of the rocker arms, mark them so they can be returned to their original locations – don't mix them up!
5   Clean and examine all components for wear and damage. Pushrods may be rolled over a flat surface such as a piece of glass to check for straightness. Check the fulcrums and rockers for galling and wear. Wear frequently occurs at the points where the pushrods contact the rockers **(see illustration)**. Replace any parts showing evidence of wear.
6   Prior to installation, apply moly-base grease or engine assembly lube to the fulcrums and the ends of the rocker arms.
7   Check to be sure that the valve lifter is all the way down before install-

ing the pushrod. Turn the crankshaft with a wrench until the lifter is down, if needed.
8   Tighten the rocker arm bolt to the torque listed in this Chapter's Specifications.
9   If any parts have been replaced, check the valve adjustment, as described below.
10   Reinstall the rocker arm cover(s) (see Section 3).

Adjustment

Refer to illustrations 4.11 and 4.13

Note: *Adjustment is only needed when valve train parts have been replaced or valves and/or seats have been ground a considerable amount.*

11   Set the number one piston at Top Dead Center (TDC) on the compression stroke (see Chapter 2C). This is position 1 **(see illustration)**.
12   In this position you can check the following valves:
      Intake – 1, 3 and 6
      Exhaust – 1, 2 and 4

Note: *The arrangement of intake (I) and exhaust (E) valves, starting at the front (drivebelt) end of the engine, is as follows:*
Front cylinder bank
      I-E-I-E-I-E
Rear cylinder bank
      E-I-E-I-E-I

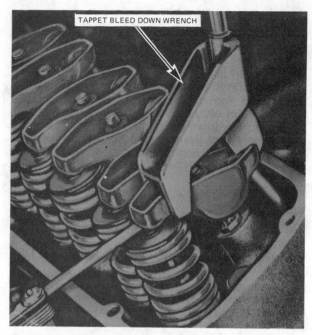

4.13   Checking valve clearance with a lifter bleed-down tool and a feeler gauge

13   Using Ford lifter bleed-down tool T70P-6513-A or equivalent **(see illustration)**, press on the rocker arm until the lifter leaks down completely. Check the clearance between the valve stem and rocker arm with a feeler gauge. Compare it to the Specifications in this Chapter and write it down. Repeat this procedure for each valve listed above.

14   Rotate the crankshaft to position 2 and check the following valves:
   Intake – 2, 4 and 5
   Exhaust – 3, 5 and 6
If the clearances are within specification, install the rocker arm covers.

15   If there is not enough clearance, use a shorter pushrod; too much clearance, use a longer one (available from your dealer).

---

5   Valve springs, retainers and seals – replacement

Refer to illustrations 5.8, 5.9, 5.14 and 5.15
Note: *Broken valve springs and defective valve stem seals can be replaced without removing the cylinder head. Two special tools and a com-*

pressed air source are normally required to perform this operation, so read through this Section carefully and rent or buy the tools before beginning the job. If compressed air is not available, a length of nylon rope can be used to keep the valves from falling into the cylinder during this procedure.

1   Refer to Section 3 and remove the rocker arm cover from the affected cylinder head. If all of the valve stem seals are being replaced, remove both rocker arm covers.

2   Remove the spark plug from the cylinder which has the defective component. If all of the valve stem seals are being replaced, all of the spark plugs should be removed.

3   Turn the crankshaft until the piston in the affected cylinder is at top dead center on the compression stroke (refer to Chapter 2 part C for instructions). If you are replacing all of the valve stem seals, begin with cylinder number one and work on the valves for one cylinder at a time. Move from cylinder-to-cylinder following the firing order sequence (1-4-2-5-3-6).

4   Thread an adapter into the spark plug hole and connect an air hose from a compressed air source to it. Most auto parts stores can supply the air hose adapter. **Note:** *Many cylinder compression gauges utilize a screw-in fitting that may work with your air hose quick-disconnect fitting.*

5   Remove the bolt, fulcrum and rocker arm for the valve with the defective part and pull out the pushrod. If all of the valve stem seals are being replaced, all of the rocker arms and pushrods should be removed (refer to Section 4).

6   Apply compressed air to the cylinder. The valves should be held in place by the air pressure. If the valve faces or seats are in poor condition, leaks may prevent the air pressure from retaining the valves – refer to the alternative procedure below.

7   If you do not have access to compressed air, an alternative method can be used. Position the piston at a point just before TDC on the compression stroke, then feed a long piece of nylon rope through the spark plug hole until it fills the combustion chamber. Be sure to leave the end of the rope hanging out of the engine so it can be removed easily. Use a large breaker bar and socket to rotate the crankshaft in the normal direction of rotation until slight resistance is felt.

8   Stuff shop rags into the cylinder head holes above and below the valves to prevent parts and tools from falling into the engine, then use a valve spring compressor to compress the spring/damper assembly. Remove the keepers with small needle-nose pliers or a magnet **(see illustration)**. **Note:** *A couple of different types of tools are available for compressing the valve springs with the head in place. One type grips the lower spring coils and presses on the retainer as the knob is turned, while the other type, shown here, utilizes the rocker arm bolt for leverage. Both types work very well, although the lever type is usually less expensive.*

9   Remove the spring retainer shield and valve spring assembly, then remove the valve stem seal **(see illustration)**. **Note:** *If air pressure fails to hold the valve in the closed position during this operation, the valve face or seat is probably damaged. If so, the cylinder head will have to be removed for additional repair operations.*

5.8   Compress the spring and remove the keepers with a magnet or needle-nose pliers

5.9   Once the valve spring assembly is removed, the seal (arrow) can be pulled off the valve guide boss

10   Wrap a rubber band around the top of the valve stem so the valve will not fall into the combustion chamber, then release the air pressure. **Note:** *If a rope was used instead of air pressure, turn the crankshaft slightly in the direction opposite normal rotation.*

11   Inspect the valve stem for damage. Rotate the valve in the guide and check the end for eccentric movement, which would indicate that the valve is bent.

12   Move the valve up-and-down in the guide and make sure it doesn't bind. If the valve stem binds, either the valve is bent or the guide is damaged. In either case, the head will have to be removed for repair.

13   Reapply air pressure to the cylinder to retain the valve in the closed position, then remove the tape or rubber band from the valve stem. If a rope was used instead of air pressure, rotate the crankshaft in the normal direction of rotation until slight resistance is felt.

14   Lubricate the valve stem with engine oil and install a new seal **(see illustration)**. The intake seals have a silver band while the exhaust seals have a red band.

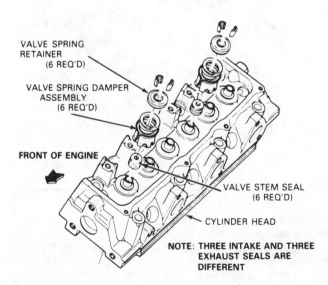

5.14   Carefully seat the valve seal using a deep socket and a hammer

15   Install the spring assembly and spring seat (where applicable) in position over the valve **(see illustration)**.

16   Install the valve spring retainer. Compress the valve spring assembly.

17   Position the keepers in the grooves. Apply a small dab of grease to the inside of each keeper to hold it in place if necessary. Remove the pressure from the spring tool and make sure the keepers are seated.

18   Disconnect the air hose and remove the adapter from the spark plug hole. If a rope was used in place of air pressure, pull it out of the cylinder.

19   Refer to Section 4 and install the rocker arm(s) and pushrod(s).

20   Install the spark plug(s) and hook up the wire(s).

21   Refer to Section 3 and install the rocker arm cover(s).

22   Start and run the engine, then check for oil leaks and unusual sounds coming from the rocker arm cover area.

---

6   Intake manifold – removal and installation

Refer to illustrations 6.8, 6.10, 6.11a, 6.11b and 6.13

Warning: *Relieve the fuel system pressure before following this procedure (see Chapter 4).*

1   Drain the coolant and disconnect the negative cable from the battery (see Chapter 1).

2   Disconnect the EGR tube nut from the EGR valve (if equipped). Loosen the tube nut and rotate the tube away from the valve. Remove the upper intake manifold (plenum) and throttle body (see Chapter 4).

3   Label and disconnect all wiring, vacuum and coolant hoses from the intake manifold.

4   Disconnect the fuel rails and lines and cap the fittings (see Chapter 4). **Note:** *The injectors and fuel rails may be removed with the intake manifold as an assembly.*

5   Remove the distributor and coil with the bracket as described in Chapter 5 and remove the pushrods (see Section 4).

6   Remove the intake manifold mounting bolts/studs (this requires a Torx T-50 driver bit), noting the locations of the studs for reinstallation.

7   Remove the intake manifold. It may be necessary to pry on the transaxle end of the manifold with a screwdriver to break the RTV seal. Use care to avoid damaging the machined surfaces.

8   Clean away all traces of old gasket material **(see illustration)**. Remove oil and dirt with a cloth and solvent, such as acetone or lacquer thinner.

9   Lightly oil all bolts and studs prior to assembly.

VALVE SPRING
RETAINER
(6 REQ'D)

VALVE SPRING DAMPER
ASSEMBLY
(6 REQ'D)

FRONT OF ENGINE

VALVE STEM SEAL
(6 REQ'D)

CYLINDER HEAD

NOTE: THREE INTAKE AND THREE
EXHAUST SEALS ARE
DIFFERENT

5.15   An exploded view of the valve spring components

6.8   Use a scraper to remove the intake manifold gaskets

6.10   Put extra sealant in the four corners before installing the
new gaskets

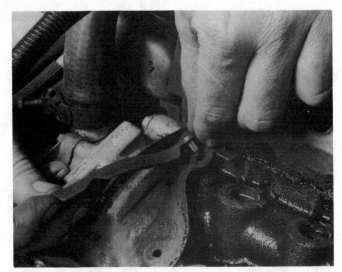

6.11a   The end seals have locating pins which must be pressed
into place

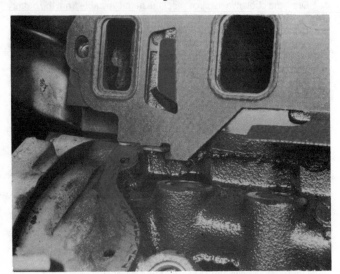

6.11b   Be sure the locking tabs on the gaskets are engaged

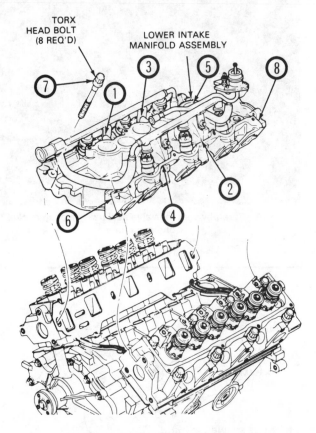

6.13   Intake manifold bolt tightening sequence

10   Apply a 1/8-inch bead of RTV sealant (Ford D6AZ-19562 or equivalent) at each corner where the head joins the engine block **(see illustration)**.
11   Position the new gaskets and end seals on the engine with adhesive (Ford D7AZ-19B508-A or equivalent). Be sure the locating pins/tabs fit properly **(see illustrations)**. **Note:** *Assembly must be completed within several minutes. Don't allow the RTV sealant to dry.*
12   Carefully set the lower manifold into place. Be sure the gaskets don't shift out of place. Install the bolts and studs in their original locations.
13   Tighten the bolts/studs in numerical sequence **(see illustration)**, reaching the torque listed in this Chapter's Specifications in two steps.
14   Reinstall all parts removed for access in the reverse order of removal.
15   Refill the cooling system and run the engine. Check the ignition timing.
16   Run the engine and check for fuel, vacuum and coolant leaks.

7   Exhaust manifolds – removal and installation

Warning: *Allow the engine to cool completely before following this procedure.*

Removal

Refer to illustrations 7.4, 7.5, 7.7 and 7.8

1   Raise the vehicle and support it securely on jackstands. Disconnect the exhaust pipe(s) from the manifold(s) being removed. **Note:** *To ease removal of the manifold-to-pipe nuts, apply penetrating oil to the threads and allow it to soak in about 10 minutes.*
2   Remove the spark plugs from the side(s) being removed (see Chapter 1).

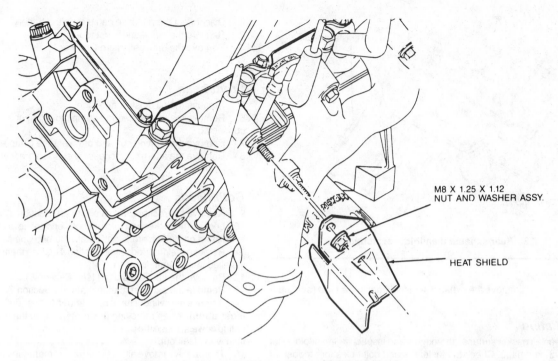

7.4 Front exhaust manifold heat shield – exploded view

M8 X 1.25 X 1.12
NUT AND WASHER ASSY.

HEAT SHIELD

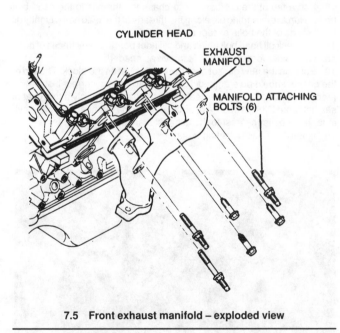

CYLINDER HEAD

EXHAUST MANIFOLD

MANIFOLD ATTACHING BOLTS (6)

7.5 Front exhaust manifold – exploded view

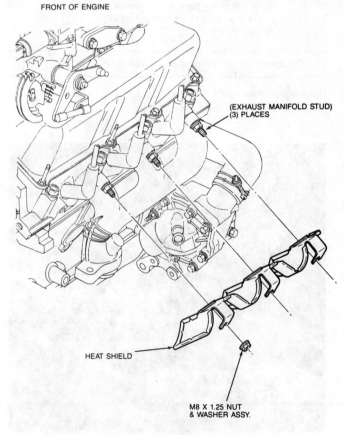

FRONT OF ENGINE

(EXHAUST MANIFOLD STUD) (3) PLACES

HEAT SHIELD

M8 X 1.25 NUT & WASHER ASSY.

7.7 Heat shield mounting details – exploded view (rear manifold shown)

Front manifold

3　Unbolt the oil dipstick tube and bracket.
4　Remove the heat shield retaining nuts **(see illustration)**. Penetrating oil will make the nuts easier to remove.
5　Unbolt and remove the exhaust manifold from the vehicle **(see illustration)**.

Rear manifold

6　Disconnect the EGR tube from the manifold (see Chapter 6). Be sure to use a back-up wrench on the lower fitting adapter.
7　Remove the heat shield retaining nuts **(see illustration)**.

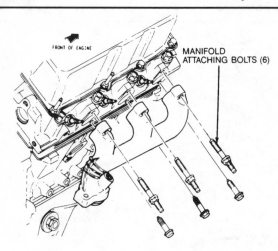

7.8   Rear exhaust manifold – exploded view

8   Unbolt and remove the exhaust manifold from the vehicle **(see illustration)**.

Installation

9   Clean all gasket surfaces thoroughly and inspect the manifold(s) for cracks and damage. Check the fasteners and bolt holes for stripped or damaged threads.
10   Lightly oil all bolts prior to installation.
11   Position a new gasket and the manifold in place on the cylinder head.
12   Install the bolts and studs finger tight in their correct locations, then tighten them to the torque listed in this Chapter's Specifications.
13   Reinstall the remaining parts in the reverse order of removal.
14   Run the engine and check for exhaust leaks.

8   Cylinder heads – removal and installation

Refer to illustrations 8.14, 8.18 and 8.20
1   Drain the cooling system (see Chapter 1).

2   Disconnect the negative cable from the battery.
3   Remove the air cleaner duct tube.
4   Remove the drivebelts (see Chapter 1).

Front head

5   Remove the oil dipstick and tube.
6   Remove the power steering pump mounting nuts, leaving the hoses connected.
7   Remove the ignition coil and bracket (see Chapter 5).
8   Remove the alternator/accessory support bracket.

Both heads

9   Remove the rocker arm cover(s) (see Section 3).
10   Loosen the rocker arm fulcrum bolts enough to allow the rocker arms to be lifted off the pushrods and rotate them to one side.
11   Remove the pushrods (see Section 4). Store them so they can be re-installed in the same location.
12   Remove the intake manifold (see Section 6).
13   Remove the exhaust manifold(s) (see Section 7).
14   Remove the cylinder head bolts and lift the head(s) off the engine **(see illustration)**. When removing the front head, lift the head clear of the locating dowels. Place the power steering pump aside in such a way that the fluid won't leak out.
15   Thoroughly remove all traces of gasket material with a gasket scraper and clean all parts with solvent. Use a rag and acetone or lacquer thinner to remove any traces of oil. See Chapter 2 Part C for cylinder head inspection procedures.
16   Use a tap of the correct size to chase the threads in the head bolt holes. Run a rethreading die along the threads of the head bolts. Lightly oil the threads of the bolts except as noted below.
17   Recheck all head bolt holes and cylinder bores for any traces of coolant, oil or other foreign matter. Remove as needed.
18   Position the new gasket over the dowel pins on the block. The top of the gasket should be stamped TOP or UP to ensure correct installation **(see illustration)**. Don't use sealant on the gaskets. Apply a thin coat of sealant (Ford D8AZ-19554-A or equivalent) to the threads of the short cylinder head bolts (nearest to the exhaust manifold).
19   Install the head bolts finger tight.

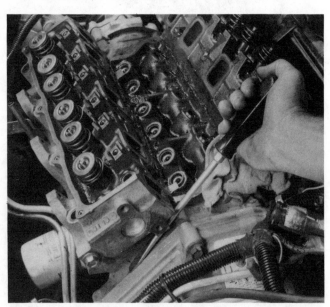

8.14   Once the bolts are removed, pry the head loose at a point where the gasket surfaces won't be damaged

8.18   Position the new gasket over the dowels – make sure the UP (shown) or TOP mark is visible

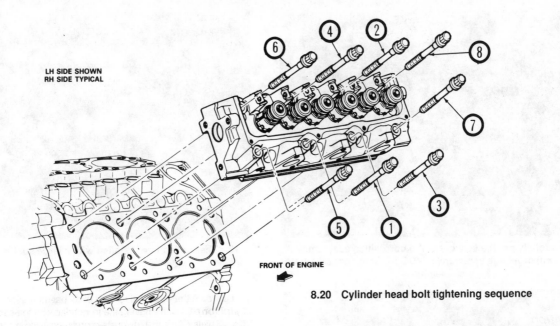

8.20   Cylinder head bolt tightening sequence

LH SIDE SHOWN
RH SIDE TYPICAL

FRONT OF ENGINE

20   Following the sequence shown (see illustration), tighten the head bolts in two steps to the torque listed in this Chapter's Specifications. **Note:** *When cylinder head bolts have been tightened using the above procedure, it is not necessary to retighten bolts after extended engine operation. However, bolts may be rechecked for tightness if desired.*
21   Reinstall the parts removed in the reverse order of removal. Lubricate the rocker arm components with oil conditioner (Ford D9AZ-19579-C or equivalent) or high-viscosity engine oil.
22   Install the pushrods in their original locations. For each valve, rotate the crankshaft until the valve lifter is at its lowest position. Install the rocker arms, fulcrums and bolts. Tighten them to the torque listed in this Chapter's Specifications.
23   Refill the cooling system, change the oil and filter (see Chapter 1) and run the engine. Check the ignition timing and inspect for any leaks.
24   If a component has been replaced or the valves ground, check valve clearance as described in Section 4.

9   Crankshaft front oil seal – replacement

Refer to illustrations 9.8, 9.9, 9.10, 9.13 and 9.14
1   Disconnect the negative cable from the battery and remove the water pump drivebelt (see Chapter 1).
2   Raise the front of the vehicle and support it securely on jackstands. Remove the right front wheel. Remove the inner fender splash guard (see Chapter 11).
3   Support the engine with a floor jack under the oil pan. Protect the oil pan with a block of wood placed between the jack and pan.
4   Remove the right (passenger's side) engine mount (manual transaxle models – see Section 15) or spacer from the water pump bracket (automatic transaxle models).
5   Remove the three nuts that hold the right upper engine mount to the timing cover.
6   Lower the floor jack carefully to allow the engine to rest on the remaining mounts.
7   Remove the bolt and washer attaching the crankshaft damper to the crankshaft.
8   Remove the crankshaft damper with a puller (Ford T58P-6316-D and T82L-6316-B or equivalent). **Caution:** *Don't use a gear puller as it will damage the damper. Use a puller with bolts that thread into the hub* (see illustration).
9   Remove the three nuts and one bolt that attach the right (passenger's) side of the subframe to the body. Pull the subframe down slightly to provide clearance for damper removal (see illustration).

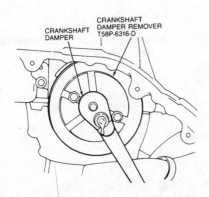

9.8   Ford recommends this special tool to remove the crankshaft damper – a standard bolt-type puller (available at most auto parts stores) may also work – do not use a jaw-type puller!

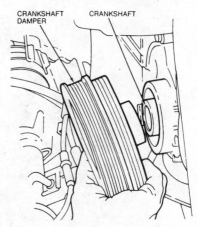

9.9   Pull the subframe down to allow clearance for damper removal

9.10   Carefully pry the seal out of the bore with a seal removal tool (shown) or a large screwdriver – DO NOT nick or scratch the crankshaft

9.13   The seal can be installed with a large socket and hammer

9.14   Press the crankshaft damper into place with an installation tool

10   Carefully pry out the old seal with a screwdriver or seal puller **(see illustration)**.
11   Clean and inspect the seal bore and crankshaft surfaces for damage, nicks, burrs or other roughness which may cause a new seal to fail. Correct as necessary.

12   Lubricate the new seal lip with moly-based grease and the outside edge of the seal with engine oil and install it with the special tools (Ford T82L-6316-A T70P-6B070-A) or equivalents.
13   If special tools are unavailable, carefully tap the seal into place using a large socket and a hammer **(see illustration)**.
14   Apply RTV sealant to the keyway in the damper and position the damper on the crankshaft. Be sure the keyway is aligned with the crankshaft key. Install the damper using an installation tool (Ford T82L-6316-A) or equivalent **(see illustration)**. If unavailable, start the damper on with a soft-faced hammer and finish installation using the damper retaining bolt. Tighten the bolt to the torque listed in this Chapter's Specifications.
15   Reinstall the remaining parts in the reverse order of removal.
16   Run the engine and check for oil leaks.

10   Timing chain cover – removal and installation

Refer to illustrations 10.3, 10.7, 10.10 and 10.12

Removal
1   Disconnect the negative cable from the battery.
2   Raise the vehicle and support it securely on jackstands. Drain the oil and coolant and remove the drivebelts (see Chapter 1).
3   Disconnect the coolant hoses from the timing chain cover/water pump **(see illustration)**.
4   Support the engine from above and remove the right (passenger's side) engine mount (see Section 15).

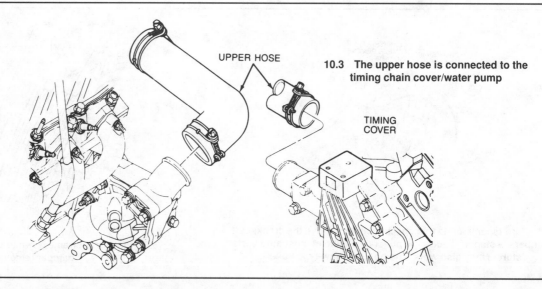

UPPER HOSE

10.3   The upper hose is connected to the timing chain cover/water pump

TIMING COVER

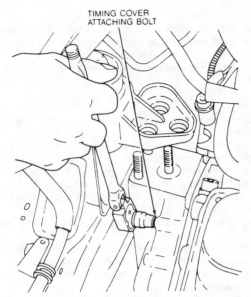

10.7 Remove the timing chain cover attaching bolts

10.10 Scrape away all gasket material, then clean the mating surfaces with lacquer thinner or acetone

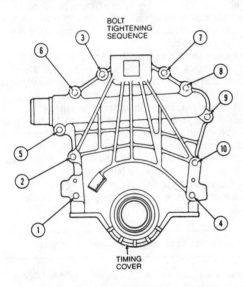

10.12 Timing chain cover bolt tightening sequence

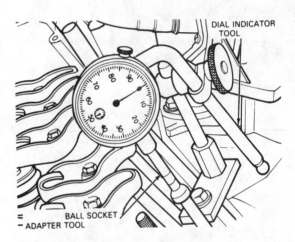

11.4 Mount a dial indicator on the pushrod to check valve lifter movement

listed in this Chapter's Specifications in the sequence shown (see illustration).
13 Reinstall the remaining parts in the reverse order of removal.
14 Add oil and coolant as needed, run the engine and check for leaks.

11 Timing chain and sprockets – check, removal and installation

Refer to illustrations 11.4, 11.7, 11.11, 11.12, 11.15 and 11.18

Check

Note: *Timing chain deflection increases due to wear. If deflection becomes excessive, the timing chain and sprockets must be replaced. The following check is a method of measuring wear without disassembling the engine.*

1   Disconnect the negative cable from the battery.
2   Remove the front rocker arm cover (see Section 3).
3   Loosen the number five (center) cylinder exhaust rocker arm bolt. This is the fourth rocker arm from the drivebelt end of the engine. Rotate the rocker arm aside.
4   Install a dial indicator on the end of the pushrod (see illustration).
5   Turn the crankshaft clockwise until TDC is reached (see Chapter 2C). This will take up the slack on the right side of the chain.

5   Remove the crankshaft damper (see Section 9).
6   Remove the oil pan (see Section 13).
7   Remove the ten timing chain cover attaching bolts (see illustration).
8   Tap the cover loose with a soft-face hammer or carefully pry it loose with a flat-bladed screwdriver and remove it from the engine. **Caution:** *Do not use excessive force or you may crack the cover. If the cover is difficult to remove, recheck for remaining bolts.*
9   Lower the cover from the engine compartment.
10   Thoroughly clean and inspect all parts and remove all traces of gasket material (see illustration). Remove oil film with a solvent such as lacquer thinner or acetone.

Installation

11   Install the new gasket on the engine over the dowels. Use contact adhesive (Ford D7AZ-19B508-A or equivalent) to hold it in place. Position the cover on the engine.
12   Apply pipe sealant (Ford D6AZ-19558-A or equivalent) to the threads of bolts 2 and 5 in the tightening sequence. Tighten the bolts to the torque

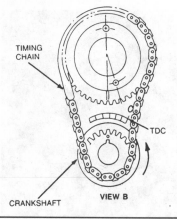

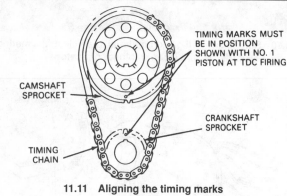

11.7   Turn the crankshaft counterclockwise until the dial indicator registers movement

11.11   Aligning the timing marks

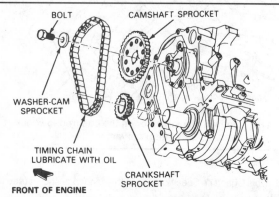

11.12   An exploded view of the timing chain components

6   Zero the dial indicator.

7   Slowly turn the crankshaft counterclockwise until the first movement is seen on the dial indicator (**see illustration**). Stop and observe the timing marks to determine the number of degrees from TDC.

8   If the reading exceeds six-degrees, replace the timing chain and sprockets.

Removal

9   Position the number one piston at Top Dead Center (see Chapter 2C).

10   Remove the timing chain cover (see Section 10). Do not turn the crankshaft during damper removal.

11   Check that the upper and lower timing chain sprocket marks are aligned (**see illustration**). If they are not, temporarily install the crankshaft damper bolt and use it to turn the crankshaft clockwise until the two marks are adjacent to each other.

12   Remove the camshaft sprocket retaining bolt and washer (**see illustration**).

13   Pull the camshaft sprocket away from the engine and move it down slightly to release the chain from the crankshaft sprocket.

14   If the crankshaft sprocket won't come off by hand, carefully pry it off with two screwdrivers.

Installation

15   Reinstall the crankshaft sprocket (**see illustration**), making sure the keyway and timing mark are at the top (12 o'clock position).

16   If the sprocket is difficult to install, slip a length of pipe over the crankshaft and tap the sprocket into place with a small hammer. Make sure the key does not slip out of place.

17   Place the chain around the camshaft sprocket with the timing mark facing down (six o'clock position). Slip the chain over the crankshaft sprocket and position the camshaft sprocket on the camshaft. Tighten the bolt to the torque listed in this Chapter's Specifications.

18   At this point, the timing marks should be adjacent (camshaft sprocket mark at six o'clock and crankshaft sprocket mark at 12 o'clock) (**see illustration**). **Caution:** *Severe engine damage could result from improper timing. Rotate the engine very slowly clockwise, through two revolutions, using a wrench on the crankshaft bolt. If anything hits, do not force the engine to turn; back up and recheck the timing procedure.*

19   Reinstall the remaining parts in the reverse order of removal.

20   Add coolant and oil as needed, run the engine and check for leaks.

---

12   Valve lifters – removal, inspection and installation

Refer to illustrations 12.3a, 12.3b, 12.4a, 12.4b, 12.6a, 12.6b and 12.6c

1   Remove the rocker arms and pushrods (see Section 4).

11.15   The crankshaft sprocket should have the keyway at the top (12 o'clock)

11.18   The timing marks (arrows) should be directly across from each other

12.3a   Stuck lifters can be removed with a special tool

12.3b   You may be able to remove the lifters with a magnet

12.4a   Be sure to store the lifters in an organized manner so they
can be reinstalled in their original locations

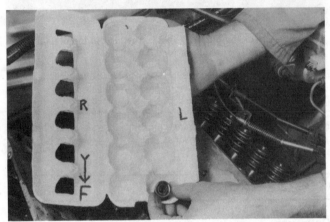

12.4b   Old egg cartons work well for lifter storage

2   Remove the intake manifold (see Section 6).
3   There are several ways to extract the lifters from the bores. Special tools designed to grip and remove lifters (Ford T70L-6500-A or equivalent) are manufactured by several tool companies and are widely available **(see illustration)**, but may not be needed in every case. On newer engines without a lot of varnish buildup, the lifters can often be removed with a small magnet **(see illustration)** or even with your fingers. A machinist's scribe with a bent end can be used to pull the lifters out by positioning the point under the retainer ring in the top of each lifter. **Caution:** *Do not use pliers to remove the lifters unless you intend to replace them with new ones (along with the camshaft). The pliers may damage the precision machined and hardened lifters, rendering them useless. On engines with*

considerable gum and varnish, work the lifters up and down, using carburetor cleaner spray to loosen the deposits.
4   Before removing the lifters, arrange to store them in a clearly labelled box to ensure that they are reinstalled in their original locations. Remove the lifters and store them where they will not get dirty **(see illustrations)**.
5   Clean the lifters with solvent and dry them thoroughly while still keeping them in order.
6   Check each lifter wall, pushrod seat and foot for scuffing, score marks and uneven wear. Each lifter foot (the surface that rides on the cam lobe) must be slightly convex, although this can be difficult to determine by eye. If the foot of the lifter is concave **(see illustrations)**, the lifters and camshaft must be replaced. If the lifter walls are damaged or worn (which is not

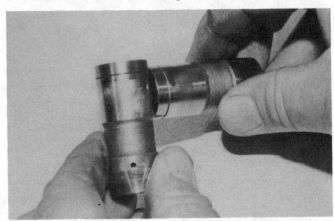

12.6a   The foot of each lifter should be slightly convex – the side
of another lifter can be used as a straightedge to check it; if it
appears flat, it is worn and must not be reused

12.6b   If the foot of any lifter is concave, scratched or galled,
replace the entire set with new lifters

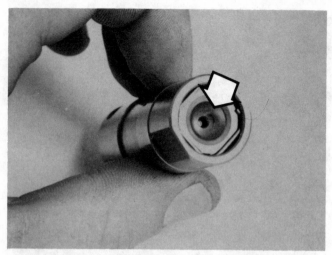

12.6c   Check the pushrod seat (arrow) in the top of each lifter for wear

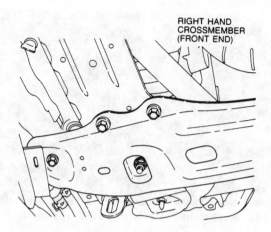

13.8   Remove the mounting bolts and nuts from the front end of the crossmember

very likely), inspect the lifter bores in the engine block as well. If the push-rod seats **(see illustration)** are worn, check the pushrod ends.

7   If new lifters are being installed, a new camshaft must also be in-stalled. If a new camshaft is installed, then use new lifters as well. Never install used lifters unless the original camshaft is used and the lifters can be installed in their original locations.

13   Oil pan – removal and installation

Removal

Refer to illustrations 13.8, 13.9 and 13.10

1   Disconnect the negative cable from the battery.
2   Remove the oil dipstick.
3   Raise the vehicle and support it securely on jackstands. Drain the coolant and oil and remove the oil filter (see Chapter 1).
4   Remove the retainer clip from the oil pan sensor and unplug the elec-trical connector from the sensor.

5   Remove the front exhaust pipe assembly (see Chapter 4).
6   Remove the starter motor (see Chapter 5).
7   Remove the water pump, mounting bracket and idler pulley tensioner (see Chapter 3).
8   Remove the mounting bolts and nut from the front end of the right (passenger's side) crossmember **(see illustration)**.
9   Loosen but don't remove the bolts and nut from the rear end of the right (passenger's side) crossmember. Allow the crossmember to drop as low as possible to permit removal of the oil pan. **Caution:** *If any attempt is made to remove the oil pan without lowering the crossmember, damage to the baffle may occur* **(see illustration)**.
10   Unbolt the oil pan and remove it from the vehicle **(see illustration)**. If the pan is difficult to break loose, tap on it with a rubber mallet.

Installation

Refer to illustration 13.12

11   Remove all traces of old gasket material from the mating surfaces and clean the oil pan with solvent. Clean the block and pan mating surfaces with acetone or lacquer thinner to remove any traces of oil.

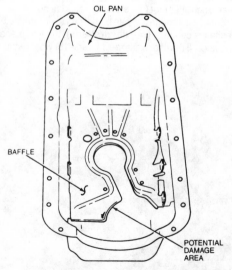

13.9   The oil pan must be pulled straight down without turning or prying or the baffle may be damaged near the oil pump

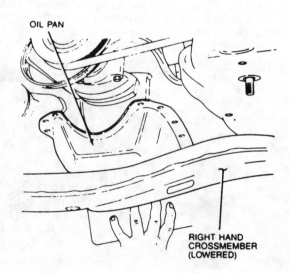

13.10   Lower the oil pan and slip it over the crossmember

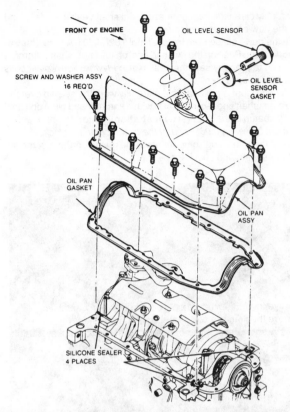

13.12   An exploded view of the oil pan components

14.2   Oil pump mounting bolt and locating dowel locations (arrows)

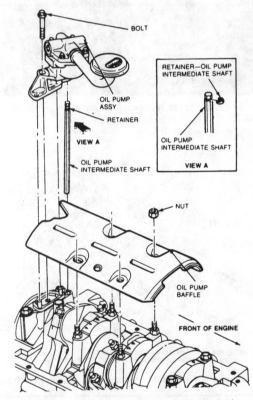

14.5   An exploded view of the oil pump components

12   Install a new gasket on the oil pan **(see illustration)** using contact adhesive (Ford D7AZ-19B508-A or equivalent).

13   Apply a 1/4-inch bead of RTV sealant (Ford D6AZ-19562-A or equivalent) to the junctions of the block and rear main bearing cap and also the timing chain cover for a total of four places. **Note:** *Follow the gasket manufacturer's instructions. Don't allow the sealant to dry before installing the pan.*

14   Position the oil pan on the engine block and install the bolts, tightening them to the torque listed in this Chapter's Specifications.

15   Reinstall the remaining parts in the reverse order of removal.

16   Install a new oil filter, add coolant and oil. Run the engine and check for oil and coolant leaks.

14   Oil pump and pickup – removal and installation

Removal

Refer to illustration 14.2

1   Remove the oil pan (see Section 13).

2   Remove the oil pump mounting bolt **(see illustration)**.

3   Lower the oil pump assembly from the block.

Installation

Refer to illustration 14.5

4   Prime the pump by pouring oil into the oil pickup and turning the pump shaft by hand.

5   Fit the oil pump intermediate shaft into the pump **(see illustration)**, taking care that the shaft seats completely in the pump. Do not try to force it. If it does not align, turn the pump slightly and try again.

6   Install the oil pump assembly, taking care to position the locating dowel and tighten the bolt to the torque listed in this Chapter's Specifications.

7   Reinstall the oil pan (see Section 13), add oil and a new filter. Run the engine and check for leaks.

15   Engine mount – check and replacement

Refer to Chapter 2, Part A, Section 24 for this procedure.

16   Flywheel/driveplate – removal and installation

Refer to Chapter 2, Part A, Section 22 for this procedure, but be sure to use the torque Specification in this Part of Chapter 2.

17 Crankshaft rear oil seal – replacement

Refer to illustrations 17.3, 17.5, 17.7 and 17.8

1   Remove the transaxle (see Chapter 7).

2   Remove the flywheel/driveplate (see Section 16).

3   Using a sharp awl, carefully punch one hole into the seal between the lip and the engine block **(see illustration)**.

4   Screw in the threaded end of Ford tool T77L-9533-B or equivalent. Use the tool to remove the seal.

5   If the special tool is unavailable, you may be able to pry the seal out with a screwdriver **(see illustration)**.

6   Thoroughly clean the seal bore and crankshaft sealing surface and lubricate the new seal with engine oil.

7   Place the new seal on Ford installer tool T82L-6701-A **(see illustration)** or equivalent. Position the tool and seal on the crankshaft. Alternate bolt tightening to properly seat the seal. **Note:** *Flywheel/driveplate bolts may be used if necessary.*

8   If the special tool is not available, carefully work the seal lip over the end of the crankshaft and tap the seal in with a hammer and blunt drift until it's properly seated in the bore **(see illustration)**. **Note:** *The rear face of this seal must be within 0.005-inch of the rear face of the block.*

9   Reinstall the remaining components in the reverse order of removal.

10   Start the engine and check for oil leaks.

17.3   Do not scratch the crankshaft when punching a hole in the seal

17.5   You may be able to gently pry the seal out, but don't scratch the sealing surfaces

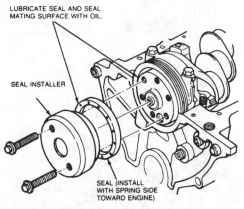

LUBRICATE SEAL AND SEAL MATING SURFACE WITH OIL.

SEAL INSTALLER

SEAL (INSTALL WITH SPRING SIDE TOWARD ENGINE)

NOTE: REAR FACE OF SEAL MUST BE WITHIN 0.127mm (0.005-INCH) OF THE REAR FACE OF THE BLOCK

17.7   A special Ford tool is recommended to install the seal

17.8   If the special tool is not available, tap around the seal, slowly working it into position

Chapter 2 Part C
General engine overhaul procedures

Contents

Specifications

Four-cylinder engine

General

Displacement	2.2 liters
Compression pressure	101 psi minimum (see text)
Oil pressure (hot at 3000 rpm)	57 psi

Valves and related components

Valve face angle	45-degrees
Valve seat angle	45-degrees
Valve head thickness (margin)	not available
Valve stem diameter	
Intake	0.2744 to 0.2750 in (6.970 to 6.985 mm)
Exhaust	0.2742 to 0.2748 in (6.965 to 6.980 mm)
Valve stem-to-guide clearance (limit)	0.008 in (0.020 mm)
Valve seat width	0.047 to 0.063 in (1.2 to 1.6 mm)
Valve spring angle (limit)	0.067 in (1.7 mm)
Valve spring installed height	1.58 in (40.08 mm)
Valve spring free length	
Intake	
Standard	1.949 in (49.5 mm)
Service limit	1.744 in (44.3 mm)
Exhaust	
Standard	1.984 in (50.4 mm)
Service limit	1.937 in (49.2 mm)

Crankshaft and connecting rods

Main bearing oil clearance
  No. 1, 2, 4 and 5 .... 0.0010 to 0.0017 in (0.025 to 0.043 mm)
  No. 3 .... 0.012 to 0.0019 in (0.031 to 0.049 mm)
Connecting rod
  Endplay (side clearance)
    Standard .... 0.004 to 0.010 in (0.110 to 0.262 mm)
    Service limit .... 0.012 in (0.30 mm)
  Bearing oil clearance .... 0.0011 to 0.0026 in (0.027 to 0.067 mm)
  Small end bore diameter .... 0.8640 to 0.8645 in (21.943 to 21.980 mm)
Crankshaft
  Endplay
    Standard .... 0.0031 to 0.0071 in (0.08 to 0.18 mm)
    Service limit .... 0.012 in (0.30 mm)
  Main bearing journal diameter .... 2.3597 to 2.3604 in (59.937 to 59.955 mm)
  Connecting rod bearing journal diameter
    Standard .... 2.0055 to 2.0061 in (50.940 to 50.955 mm)
    Service limit .... 2.004 in (50.89 mm)
  Journal taper/out-of-round limit .... 0.0020 in (0.05 mm)
  Runout limit .... 0.0012 in (0.03 mm)

Engine block

Cylinder bore
  Diameter
    Standard .... 3.3858 to 3.3866 in (86.000 to 86.019 mm)
    Service limit .... 3.4063 in (86.519 mm)
  Taper/out-of-round limit .... 0.0007 in (0.019 mm)
Deck warpage limit .... 0.006 in (0.15 mm)

Cylinder head warpage limit .... 0.006 in

Pistons and rings

Piston diameter .... 3.3836 to 3.3844 in (85.944 to 85.964 mm)
Piston-to-bore clearance .... 0.0014 to 0.0030 in (0.036 to 0.075 mm)
Piston side clearance (top and second rings only) .... 0.001 to 0.003 in (0.03 to 0.07 mm)
Piston ring end gap
  Top .... 0.008 to 0.014 in (0.20 to 0.35 mm)
  Second .... 0.006 to 0.012 in (0.15 to 0.30 mm)
  Oil
    Turbo .... 0.006 to 0.014 in (0.2 to 0.7 mm)
    Non-turbo .... 0.012 to 0.035 in (0.3 to 0.9 mm)
  Service limit (all models) .... 0.039 in (1.0 mm)
Piston pin diameter .... 0.8651 to 0.8654 in (21.974 to 21.980 mm)

Torque specifications   **Ft-lbs**

Main bearing cap bolts .... 61 to 65
Connecting rod nuts .... 48 to 51

V6 engine

General

Cylinder compression pressure .... 101 psi minimum (see text)
Oil pressure (hot at 3000 rpm) .... 43 to 57 psi

Cylinder head and valves

Cylinder head warpage limit .... 0.003 inch in any 6 inches(0.006 overall)
Minimum valve margin .... 1/32 in
Valve seat angle 45-degrees
Valve stem diameter (standard)
  Intake .... 0.3134 to 0.3126 in
  Exhaust .... 0.3129 to 0.3121 in
Valve stem-to-guide clearance
  Intake .... 0.0010 to 0.0028 in
  Exhaust .... 0.0015 to 0.0033 in
Valve spring
  Free length .... 1.84 in
  Installed height .... 1.58 in
Valve lifter diameter .... 0.874 in
Lifter-to-bore clearance
  Standard .... 0.0007 to 0.0027 in
  Service limit .... 0.005 in

Crankshaft and connecting rods

Connecting rod journal	
Diameter	2.1253 to 2.1261 in
Out-of-round limit	0.0003 in
Taper limit	0.0003 in per inch
Connecting rod bearing oil clearance	
Desired	0.0010 to 0.0014 in
Allowable	0.0008 to 0.0027 in
Connecting rod side clearance (endplay)	0.006 to 0.014 in
Main bearing journal	
Diameter	2.5190 to 2.5198 in
Out-of-round limit	0.0003 in
Taper limit	0.0006 in
Runout limit	0.002 in
Main bearing oil clearance	
Desired	0.0001 to 0.0014 in
Allowable	0.0005 to 0.0023 in
Crankshaft endplay	0.004 to 0.008 in

Cylinder bore

Diameter (service limit)	3.4063 in
Taper/out-of-round limit	0.0007 in

Pistons and rings

Piston diameter	
Coded red	3.5024 to 3.5031 in
Coded blue	3.5035 to 3.5041 in
Coded yellow	3.5045 to 3.5051 in
Piston-to-bore clearance	
Standard	0.0014 to 0.0022 in
Service limit	0.0032 in
Piston ring	
End gap	0.010 to 0.020 in
Side clearance	0.0012 to 0.0031 in

Camshaft

Lobe lift	0.260 in
Allowable lobe lift loss	0.005 in
Theoretical valve lift at zero lash	0.419 in
Endplay	0.001 to 0.005 in
Journal-to-bearing (oil) clearance	0.001 to 0.003 in
Journal diameter (all)	2.0074 to 2.0084 in
Bearing inside diameter	2.0094 to 2.0104 in
Bearing out-of-round limit	0.004 in
Bearing inside diameter	
Nos. 1 and 4	2.1531 to 2.1541 in
Nos. 2 and 3	2.1334 to 2.1344 in

Torque specifications

	Ft-lbs
Camshaft thrust plate bolts	7
Connecting rod cap nuts	26
Main bearing cap bolts	65 to 81

1   General information

Included in this portion of Chapter 2 are the general overhaul procedures for the cylinder head(s) and internal engine components.

The information ranges from advice concerning preparation for an overhaul and the purchase of replacement parts to detailed, step-by-step procedures covering removal and installation of internal engine components and the inspection of parts.

The following Sections have been written based on the assumption the engine has been removed from the vehicle. For information concerning in-vehicle engine repair, as well as removal and installation of the external components necessary for the overhaul, see Part A or B of this Chapter and Section 8 of this Part.

The Specifications included in this Part are only those necessary for the inspection and overhaul procedures which follow. Refer to Parts A or B for additional Specifications.

2   Engine overhaul – general information

Refer to illustrations 2.4a and 2.4b

It's not always easy to determine when, or if, an engine should be completely overhauled, as a number of factors must be considered.

High mileage isn't necessarily an indication an overhaul is needed, while low mileage doesn't preclude the need for an overhaul. Frequency of servicing is probably the most important consideration. An engine that's had regular and frequent oil and filter changes, as well as other required maintenance, will most likely give many thousands of miles of reliable service. Conversely, a neglected engine may require an overhaul very early in its life.

Excessive oil consumption is an indication that piston rings, valve seals and/or valve guides are in need of attention. Make sure oil leaks aren't responsible before deciding the rings and/or guides are bad. Perform a cylinder compression check to determine the extent of the work re-

2.4a   Remove the oil pressure sending unit (arrow – four-cylinder model shown) . . .

2.4b   . . . and temporarily install a mechanical pressure gauge in its place

quired (see Section 3).

Remove the oil pressure sending unit and check the oil pressure with a gauge installed in its place **(see illustrations)**. The sending unit is located above the oil filter on four-cylinder engines and adjacent to the distributor on V6 engines. Compare the results to this Chapter's Specifications. As a general rule, engines should have about ten psi oil pressure for every 1,000 rpm. If the pressure is extremely low, the bearings and/or oil pump are probably worn out.

Loss of power, rough running, knocking or metallic engine noises, excessive valve train noise and high fuel consumption rates may also point to the need for an overhaul, especially if they're all present at the same time. If a complete tune-up doesn't remedy the situation, major mechanical work is the only solution.

An engine overhaul involves restoring the internal parts to the specifications of a new engine. During an overhaul, the piston rings are replaced and the cylinder walls are reconditioned (rebored and/or honed). If a rebore is done by an automotive machine shop, new oversize pistons will also be installed. The main bearings, connecting rod bearings and camshaft bearings are generally replaced with new ones and, if necessary, the crankshaft may be reground to restore the journals. Generally, the valves are serviced as well, since they're usually in less-than-perfect condition at this point. While the engine is being overhauled, other components, such as the starter and alternator, can be rebuilt as well. The end result should be a like-new engine that will give many trouble free miles. **Note:** *Critical cooling system components such as the hoses, drivebelts, thermostat and water pump MUST be replaced with new parts when an engine is overhauled. The radiator should be checked carefully to ensure it isn't clogged or leaking (see Chapter 3). Also, we don't recommend overhauling the oil pump – always install a new one when an engine is rebuilt.*

Before beginning the engine overhaul, read through the entire procedure to familiarize yourself with the scope and requirements of the job. Overhauling an engine isn't particularly difficult, if you follow all of the instructions carefully, have the necessary tools and equipment and pay close attention to all specifications; however, it can be time consuming. Plan on the vehicle being tied up for a minimum of two weeks, especially if parts must be taken to an automotive machine shop for repair or reconditioning. Check on availability of parts and make sure any necessary special tools and equipment are obtained in advance. Most work can be done with typical hand tools, although a number of precision measuring tools are required for inspecting parts to determine if they must be replaced. Often an automotive machine shop will handle the inspection of parts and offer advice concerning reconditioning and replacement. **Note:** *Always wait until the engine has been completely disassembled and all components, especially the engine block, have been inspected before deciding what service and repair operations must be performed by an automotive machine shop.* Since the block's condition will be the major factor to consider when determining whether to overhaul the original engine or buy a rebuilt one, never purchase parts or have machine work done on other

components until the block has been thoroughly inspected. As a general rule, time is the primary cost of an overhaul, so it doesn't pay to install worn or substandard parts.

As a final note, to ensure maximum life and minimum trouble from a rebuilt engine, everything must be assembled with care in a spotlessly clean environment.

3   Compression check

Refer to illustrations 3.6 and 3.8

1   A compression check will tell you what mechanical condition the upper end (pistons, rings, valves, head gaskets) of the engine is in. Specifically, it can tell you if the compression is down due to leakage caused by worn piston rings, defective valves and seats or a blown head gasket. **Note:** *The engine must be at normal operating temperature and the battery must be fully charged for this check.*

2   Begin by cleaning the area around the spark plugs before you remove them. Compressed air should be used, if available, otherwise a small brush or even a bicycle tire pump will work. The idea is to prevent dirt from getting into the cylinders as the compression check is being done.

3   Remove all of the spark plugs from the engine (see Chapter 1).

4   Block the throttle wide open.

5   Disable the fuel system by removing the "engine" fuse (see Chapter 12).

6   Install the compression gauge in the number one spark plug hole **(see illustration)**.

7   Crank the engine over at least seven compression strokes and watch the gauge. The compression should build up quickly in a healthy engine. Low compression on the first stroke, followed by gradually increasing pressure on successive strokes, indicates worn piston rings. A low compression reading on the first stroke, which doesn't build up during successive strokes, indicates leaking valves or a blown head gasket (a cracked head could also

be the cause). Deposits on the undersides of the valve heads can also cause low compression. Record the highest gauge reading obtained.

8   Repeat the procedure for the remaining cylinders and compare the results to this Chapter's Specifications and the accompanying chart **(see illustration)**.

9   If the readings are below normal, add some engine oil (about three squirts from a plunger-type oil can) to each cylinder, through the spark plug hole, and repeat the test.

10   If the compression increases after the oil is added, the piston rings are definitely worn. If the compression doesn't increase significantly, the leakage is occurring at the valves or head gasket. Leakage past the valves may be caused by burned valve seats and/or faces or warped, cracked or bent valves.

Maximum PSI	Minimum PSI	Maximum PSI	Minimum PSI
134	101	164	123
136	102	166	124
138	104	168	126
140	105	170	127
142	107	172	129
144	108	174	131
146	110	176	132
148	111	178	133
150	113	180	135
152	114	182	136
154	115	184	138
156	117	186	140
158	118	188	141
160	120	190	142
162	121	192	144

3.6 A compression gauge with a threaded fitting for the spark plug hole is preferred over the type that requires hand pressure to maintain the seal

3.8 The difference between the highest and lowest readings should not exceed those shown on this chart

11   If two adjacent cylinders have equally low compression, there's a strong possibility the head gasket between them is blown. The appearance of coolant in the combustion chambers or the crankcase would verify this condition.

12   If one cylinder is about 20-percent lower than the others, and the engine has a slightly rough idle, a worn lobe on the camshaft could be the cause.

13   If the compression is unusually high, the combustion chambers are probably coated with carbon deposits. If that's the case, the cylinder head(s) should be removed and decarbonized.

14   If compression is way down or varies greatly between cylinders, it would be a good idea to have a leak-down test performed by an automotive repair shop. This test will pinpoint exactly where the leakage is occurring and how severe it is.

15   Install the "engine" fuse.

4   Top Dead Center (TDC) for number one piston – locating

1   Top Dead Center (TDC) is the highest point in the cylinder each piston reaches as it travels up-and-down when the crankshaft turns. Each piston reaches TDC on the compression stroke and again on the exhaust stroke, but TDC generally refers to piston position on the compression stroke.

2   Positioning the piston(s) at TDC is an essential part of certain procedures such as camshaft removal and timing belt/sprocket removal.

3   Before beginning this procedure, be sure to place the transaxle in Neutral (or Park on automatic transaxle models), apply the parking brake and block the rear wheels.

4   Remove the spark plugs (see Chapter 1).

5   When looking at the drivebelt end of the engine, normal crankshaft rotation is clockwise. In order to bring any piston to TDC, the crankshaft must be turned with a socket and ratchet attached to the bolt threaded into the center of the lower drivebelt pulley on the crankshaft.

6   Have an assistant turn the crankshaft with a socket and ratchet as described above while you hold a finger over the number one spark plug hole. **Note:** See the Specifications in Chapter 2A or 2B for the number one cylinder location.

7   When the piston approaches TDC, pressure will be felt at the spark plug hole. Have your assistant stop turning the crankshaft when the ignition timing marks are aligned **(see illustration 6.5a in Chapter 2A)**.

8   If the timing marks are bypassed, turn the crankshaft two complete revolutions clockwise until the timing marks are properly aligned.

9   After the number one piston has been positioned at TDC on the compression stroke, TDC for any of the remaining pistons can be located by turning the crankshaft one-half turn (180-degrees) on four-cylinder engines or one-third turn (120-degrees) on V6 engines to get to TDC for the next cylinder in the firing order.

5   Engine removal – methods and precautions

If you've decided the engine must be removed for overhaul or major repair work, several preliminary steps should be taken.

Locating a suitable place to work is extremely important. Adequate work space, along with storage space for the vehicle, will be needed. If a shop or garage isn't available, at the very least a flat, level, clean work surface made of concrete or asphalt is required.

Cleaning the engine compartment and engine before beginning the removal procedure will help keep tools clean and organized.

An engine hoist or A-frame will also be necessary. Make sure the equipment is rated in excess of the combined weight of the engine and transaxle. Safety is of primary importance, considering the potential hazards involved in lifting the engine out of the vehicle.

If the engine is being removed by a novice, a helper should be available. Advice and aid from someone more experienced would also be helpful. There are many instances when one person cannot simultaneously perform all of the operations required when lifting the engine out of the vehicle.

Plan the operation ahead of time. Arrange for or obtain all of the tools and equipment you'll need prior to beginning the job. Some of the equipment necessary to perform engine removal and installation safely and with relative ease are (in addition to an engine hoist) a heavy-duty floor jack, complete sets of wrenches and sockets as described in the front of this manual, wooden blocks and plenty of rags and cleaning solvent for mopping up

spilled oil, coolant and gasoline. If the hoist must be rented, be sure to arrange for it in advance and perform all of the operations possible without it beforehand. This will save you money and time.

Plan for the vehicle to be out of use for quite a while. A machine shop will be required to perform some of the work which the home mechanic can't accomplish without special equipment. These shops often have a busy schedule, so it would be a good idea to consult them before removing the engine in order to accurately estimate the amount of time required to rebuild or repair components that may need work.

Always be extremely careful when removing and installing the engine. Serious injury can result from careless actions. Plan ahead, take your time and a job of this nature, although major, can be accomplished successfully.

6.3   The fuse panel can be unbolted and moved aside

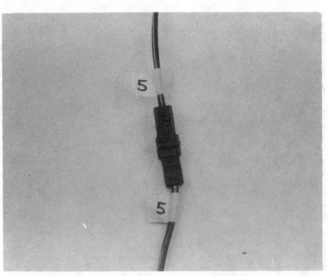

6.6   One way to ensure proper reattachment of wires and hoses is to fasten numbered pieces of masking tape to both sides of the connection, as shown here

6.14   If possible, unbolt the air conditioning compressor and set it aside without disconnecting the refrigerant lines

6.21   Connect a chain or sling to the lifting brackets and take up the slack

6   Engine – removal and installation

Refer to illustrations 6.3, 6.6, 6.14, 6.21, 6.23a, 6.23b, 6.26a, 6.26b and 6.27

Note: Read through the following steps carefully and familiarize yourself with the procedure before beginning work.

Warning: *Gasoline is extremely flammable, so take extra precautions when disconnecting any part of the fuel system. Don't smoke or allow open flames or bare light bulbs in or near the work area and don't work in a garage where a natural gas appliance (such as a clothes dryer or water heater) is installed. If you spill gasoline on your skin, rinse it off immediately. Have a fire extinguisher rated for gasoline fires handy and know how to use it! Also, the air conditioning system is under high pressure – have a dealer service department or service station discharge the system before disconnecting any of the hoses or fittings.*

Removal

1   On air-conditioned models, inspect the mounting position of the compressor to determine if it can be unbolted and set aside without disconnecting the refrigerant lines. If you have any doubts, have the air conditioning system discharged by a dealer service department or service station.

2   Refer to Chapter 4 and relieve the fuel system pressure.

3   Remove the battery and battery tray (see Chapter 5). The fuse panel and bracket can be detached as an assembly **(see illustration)**.

4   Cover the fenders and cowl and remove the hood (see Chapter 11). Special pads are available to protect the fenders, but an old bedspread or blanket will also work.

5   Remove the air cleaner assembly (see Chapter 4).

6   Label the vacuum lines, emissions system hoses, wiring connectors, ground straps and fuel lines to ensure correct reinstallation, then detach them. Pieces of masking tape with numbers or letters written on them work well **(see illustration)**. If there's any possibility of confusion, make a

6.23a   Remove the nuts (arrows) . . .

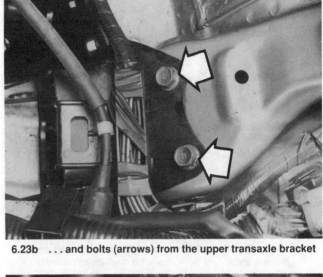

6.23b   . . . and bolts (arrows) from the upper transaxle bracket

6.26a   Guide the engine out of the vehicle to avoid damaging any components

6.26b   As the engine is raised, push the transaxle forward to provide clearance at the master cylinder (arrows)

sketch of the engine compartment and clearly label the lines, hoses and wires.

7   Raise the vehicle and support it securely on jackstands. Drain the cooling system (see Chapter 1).

8   Label and detach all coolant hoses from the engine.

9   Remove the coolant reservoir, cooling fan, shroud and radiator (see Chapter 3).

10   Remove the drivebelts (see Chapter 1).

11   Disconnect the fuel lines running from the engine to the chassis (see Chapter 4). Plug or cap all open fittings/lines.

12   Disconnect the throttle linkage (and TV linkage/speed control cable, if equipped) from the engine (see Chapters 4 and 7).

13   Disconnect the power steering hoses and cap the fittings (see Chapter 10).

14   Unbolt the air conditioning compressor (see Chapter 3) and set it aside, if possible **(see illustration)**. Otherwise, disconnect the lines and leave the compressor attached to the engine. On V6 models, disconnect the refrigerant lines from the condenser and chassis, leaving the lines attached to the compressor.

15   Drain the engine oil and remove the filter (see Chapter 1).

16   Remove the starter and the alternator (see Chapter 5).

17   Disconnect the exhaust system from the engine (see Chapter 4).

Note: *The engine and transaxle are removed from the vehicle as a unit.*

18   Disconnect all the components attaching the transaxle to the vehicle (including driveaxles, intermediate shaft, cables, wiring, linkage, etc. – see Chapter 7).

19   Support the transaxle with a jack. Position a block of wood on the jack head to prevent damage to the transaxle.

20   Attach an engine sling or a length of chain to the lifting brackets on the engine.

21   Roll the hoist into position and connect the sling to it. Take up the slack in the sling or chain, but don't lift the engine **(see illustration)**. **Warning:** *DO NOT place any part of your body under the engine when it's supported only by a hoist or other lifting device.*

22   If you're working on a vehicle with an automatic transaxle, refer to Chapter 7 and remove the torque converter-to-driveplate nuts.

23   Remove the transaxle-to-subframe mount through-bolts and pry the mounts out of the frame brackets. Remove the upper transaxle mounting bracket nuts/bolts **(see illustrations)**.

24   Remove the engine mount-to-chassis through bolt.

25   Recheck to be sure nothing is still connecting the engine to the vehicle or transaxle. Disconnect anything still remaining.

26   Raise the engine/transaxle assembly slightly to disengage the mounts. Slowly raise the engine out of the vehicle **(see illustration)**. Check carefully to make sure nothing is hanging up as the hoist is raised **(see illustration)**.

6.27   When the engine/transaxle is lifted clear of the vehicle, move it aside and set it down for transaxle removal

27   Once the engine/transaxle assembly is out of the vehicle (**see illustration**) and on the floor, remove the transaxle-to-engine block bolts. Carefully separate the engine from the transaxle. If you're working on a vehicle with an automatic transaxle, be sure the torque converter stays in place (clamp a pair of vise-grips to the housing to keep the converter from sliding out). If you're working on a vehicle with a manual transaxle, the input shaft must be completely disengaged from the clutch.
28   Remove the clutch and flywheel or driveplate and mount the engine on an engine stand.

Installation

29   Check the engine and transaxle mounts. If they're worn or damaged, replace them.
30   If you're working on a manual transaxle equipped vehicle, install the clutch and pressure plate (see Chapter 7). Now is a good time to install a new clutch. Apply a dab of high-temperature grease to the input shaft.
31   **Caution:** *DO NOT use the transaxle-to-engine bolts to force the transaxle and engine together. If you're working on an automatic transaxle equipped vehicle, take great care when installing the torque converter, following the procedure outlined in Chapter 7.*
32   Carefully lower the engine/transaxle into the engine compartment – make sure the mounts line up. Reinstall the remaining components in the reverse order of removal. Double-check to make sure everything is hooked up right.
33   Add coolant, oil, power steering and transmission fluid as needed.
34   Run the engine and check for leaks and proper operation of all accessories, then install the hood and test drive the vehicle.
35   If the air conditioning system was discharged, have it evacuated, recharged and leak tested by the shop that discharged it.

7   Engine rebuilding alternatives

The home mechanic is faced with a number of options when performing an engine overhaul. The decision to replace the engine block, piston/connecting rod assemblies and crankshaft depends on a number of factors, with the number one consideration being the condition of the block. Other considerations are cost, access to machine shop facilities, parts availability, time required to complete the project and the extent of prior mechanical experience.

Some of the rebuilding alternatives include:

Individual parts – If the inspection procedures reveal the engine block and most engine components are in reusable condition, purchasing indi-

vidual parts may be the most economical alternative. The block, crankshaft and piston/connecting rod assemblies should all be inspected carefully. Even if the block shows little wear, the cylinder bores should be surface honed.

Short block – A short block consists of an engine block with a crankshaft and piston/connecting rod assemblies already installed. All new bearings are incorporated and all clearances will be correct. The existing camshaft, valve train components, cylinder head(s) and external parts can be bolted to the short block with little or no machine shop work necessary.

Long block – A long block consists of a short block plus an oil pump, oil pan, cylinder head(s), camshaft/rocker arm cover(s), camshaft and valve train components, timing sprockets and belt/chain. All components are installed with new bearings, seals and gaskets incorporated throughout. The installation of manifolds and external parts is all that's necessary.

Give careful thought to which alternative is best for you and discuss the situation with local automotive machine shops, auto parts dealers and experienced rebuilders before ordering or purchasing replacement parts.

8   Engine overhaul – disassembly sequence

Refer to illustrations 8.3a, 8.3b, 8.3c and 8.3d

1   It's much easier to disassemble and work on the engine if it's mounted on a portable engine stand. A stand can often be rented quite cheaply from an equipment rental yard. Before it's mounted on a stand, the flywheel/driveplate should be removed from the engine.
2   If a stand isn't available, it's possible to disassemble the engine with it blocked up on the floor. Be extra careful not to tip or drop the engine when working without a stand.
3   If you're going to obtain a rebuilt engine, all external components (**see illustrations**) must come off first, to be transferred to the replacement engine, just as they will if you're doing a complete engine overhaul yourself. These include:

Alternator and brackets
Emissions control components
Distributor, spark plugs and spark plug wires
Thermostat and housing cover
Water pump
EFI components
Intake/exhaust manifolds
Oil filter
Engine mounts
Clutch and flywheel/driveplate
Engine rear plate (if equipped)

8.3a   Turbocharged four-cylinder engine – front view

Turbocharged Engine

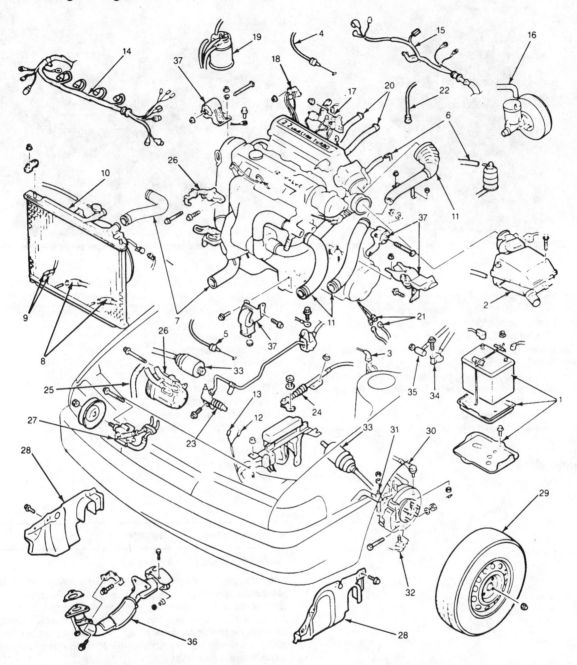

1. BATTERY AND BATTERY CARRIER
2. AIR CLEANER ASSEMBLY
3. HIGH TENSION LEAD
4. ACCELERATOR CABLE
5. THROTTLE CABLE (ATX)
6. FUEL HOSE
7. RADIATOR HOSE
8. ATF HOSE (ATX)
9. RADIATOR HARNESS
10. RADIATOR AND ELECTRIC FAN
11. INTERCOOLER PIPE AND HOSE (TURBO)
12. HEAT GAUGE UNIT CONNECTOR
13. WATER THERMO SWITCH CONNECTOR
14. EGI HARNESS
15. ENGINE HARNESS
16. BRAKE VACUUM HOSE
17. THREE-WAY SOLENOID ASSEMBLY
18. EGR SOLENOID ASSEMBLY (TURBO)
19. CANISTER HOSE
20. HEATER HOSE
21. TRANSAXLE HARNESS
22. SPEEDOMETER CABLE
23. CLUTCH RELEASE CYLINDER (MTX)
24. CONTROL CABLE (ATX)
25. DRIVE BELT
26. A/C COMPRESSOR AND BRACKET
27. P/S OIL PUMP
28. INNER FENDER SPLASH GUARDS
29. FRONT WHEEL
30. TIE ROD END
31. STABILIZER CONTROL ROD
32. LOWER ARM BUSHING
33. DRIVESHAFT
34. CHANGE ROD (MTX)
35. EXTENSION BAR (MTX)
36. EXHAUST PIPE
37. ENGINE MOUNT

8.3b Turbocharged engine components – exploded view (non-turbo four-cylinder engine similar)

8.3c   Turbocharged four-cylinder engine – timing belt end view

8.3d   Turbocharged four-cylinder engine – rear view

Note: *When removing the external components from the engine, pay close attention to details that may be helpful or important during installation. Note the installed position of gaskets, seals, spacers, pins, brackets, washers, bolts and other small items.*

4   If you're obtaining a short block, which consists of the engine block, crankshaft, pistons and connecting rods all assembled, then the cylinder head(s), oil pan and oil pump will have to be removed as well. See *Engine rebuilding alternatives* for additional information regarding the different possibilities to be considered.

5   If you're planning a complete overhaul, the engine must be disassembled and the internal components removed in the following general order:

Four-cylinder engine

Intake and exhaust manifolds
Camshaft cover
Timing belt cover
Timing belt and sprockets
Rocker arms
Camshaft
Cylinder head
Oil pan
Oil pump
Piston/connecting rod assemblies
Crankshaft rear oil seal housing
Crankshaft and main bearings

V6 engine

Rocker arm covers
Intake and exhaust manifolds
Rocker arms and pushrods
Valve lifters
Cylinder heads
Timing chain cover
Timing chain and sprockets
Camshaft
Oil pan
Oil pump
Piston/connecting rod assemblies
Crankshaft and main bearings

6   Before beginning the disassembly and overhaul procedures, make sure the following items are available. Also, refer to Engine overhaul – reassembly sequence for a list of tools and materials needed for engine reassembly.

Common hand tools
Small cardboard boxes or plastic bags for storing parts
Gasket scraper
Ridge reamer
Crankshaft damper puller
Micrometers
Telescoping gauges
Dial indicator set
Valve spring compressor
Cylinder surfacing hone
Piston ring groove cleaning tool
Electric drill motor
Tap and die set
Wire brushes
Oil gallery brushes
Cleaning solvent

---

9   Cylinder head – disassembly

Refer to illustrations 9.2, 9.3 and 9.4

Note: *New and rebuilt cylinder heads are commonly available for most engines at dealerships and auto parts stores. Due to the fact that some specialized tools are necessary for the disassembly and inspection procedures, and replacement parts aren't always readily available, it may be more practical and economical for the home mechanic to purchase replacement head(s) rather than taking the time to disassemble, inspect and recondition the original(s).*

1   Cylinder head disassembly involves removal of the intake and exhaust valves and related components. If you're working on a V6 engine, remove the rocker arms and fulcrums from the cylinder heads. Label the parts or store them separately so they can be reinstalled in their original locations.

2   Before the valves are removed, arrange to label and store them, along with their related components, so they can be kept separate and reinstalled in their original locations **(see illustration)**.

3   Compress the springs on the first valve with a spring compressor and remove the keepers **(see illustration)**. Carefully release the valve spring compressor and remove the retainer, the spring and the spring seat (if used).

4   Pull the valve out of the head, then remove the oil seal from the guide. If the valve binds in the guide (won't pull through), push it back into the head and deburr the area around the keeper groove with a fine file or whetstone **(see illustration)**.

9.2   Have several plastic bags ready (one for each valve) before you start disassembling the head – label each bag and put the entire contents of each valve assembly in one bag as shown

9.3   Use a valve spring compressor to compress the springs, then remove the keepers from the valve stem with a magnet or small needle-nose pliers

9.4   If you can't pull the valve through the guide, deburr the edge of the stem end and the area around the top of the keeper groove with a file or whetstone

5   Repeat the procedure for the remaining valves. Remember to keep all the parts for each valve together so they can be reinstalled in the same locations.

6   Once the valves and related components have been removed and stored in an organized manner, the head should be thoroughly cleaned and inspected. If a complete engine overhaul is being done, finish the engine disassembly procedures before beginning the cylinder head cleaning and inspection process.

---

10   Cylinder head – cleaning and inspection

---

1   Thorough cleaning of the cylinder head(s) and related valve train components, followed by a detailed inspection, will enable you to decide how much valve service work must be done during the engine overhaul. **Note:** *If the engine was severely overheated, the cylinder head is probably warped (see Step 12).*

Cleaning

2   Scrape all traces of old gasket material and sealant off the head gasket, intake manifold and exhaust manifold mating surfaces. Be very careful not to gouge the cylinder head. Special gasket removal solvents that soften gaskets and make removal much easier are available at auto parts stores.

3   Remove all built-up scale from the coolant passages.

4   Run a stiff wire brush through the various holes to remove deposits that may have formed in them.

5   Run an appropriate size tap into each of the threaded holes to remove corrosion and thread sealant that may be present. If compressed air is available, use it to clear the holes of debris produced by this operation. **Warning:** *Wear eye protection when using compressed air!*

6   Clean the rocker arm fulcrum bolt threads with a wire brush (V6 engine).

7   Clean the cylinder head with solvent and dry it thoroughly. Compressed air will speed the drying process and ensure that all holes and recessed areas are clean. **Note:** *Decarbonized chemicals are available and may prove very useful when cleaning cylinder heads and valve train components. They're very caustic and should be used with caution. Be sure to follow the instructions on the container.*

8   Clean the rocker arms, fulcrums, bolts and pushrods (as applicable) with solvent and dry them thoroughly (don't mix them up during the cleaning process). Compressed air will speed the drying process and can be used to clean out the oil passages. **Warning:** *Wear eye protection!*

9   Clean all the valve springs, spring seats, keepers and retainers with solvent and dry them thoroughly. Do the components from one valve at a time to avoid mixing up the parts.

10   Scrape off any heavy deposits that may have formed on the valves, then use a motorized wire brush to remove deposits from the valve heads and stems. Again, make sure the valves don't get mixed up.

Inspection

Refer to illustrations 10.12, 10.14, 10.15, 10.16, 10.17, and 10.18

Note: *Be sure to perform all of the following inspection procedures before concluding machine shop work is required. Make a list of the items that need attention.*

Cylinder head

11   Inspect the head very carefully for cracks, evidence of coolant leakage and other damage. If cracks are found, check with an automotive machine shop concerning repair. If repair isn't possible, a new cylinder head should be obtained.

10.12   Check the cylinder head gasket surface for warpage by trying to slip a feeler gauge under the straightedge (see this Chapter's Specifications for the maximum warpage allowed and use a feeler gauge of that thickness)

10.14   A dial indicator can be used to determine the valve stem-to-guide clearance (move the valve stem as indicated by the arrows)

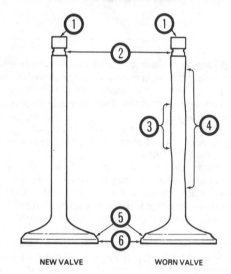

NEW VALVE   WORN VALVE

10.15   Check for valve wear at the points shown here

1	Valve tip	4	Stem (most worn areas)
2	Keeper groove	5	Valve face
3	Stem (least worn area)	6	Margin

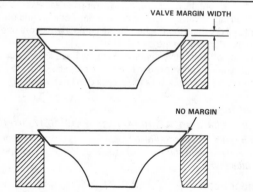

10.16   The margin width on each valve must be as listed in this Chapter's Specifications (if no margin exists, the valve cannot be reused)

12   Using a straightedge and feeler gauge, check the head gasket mating surface for warpage (see illustration). If the warpage exceeds the limit in this Chapter's Specifications, it can be resurfaced at an automotive machine shop. Note: If the V6 engine heads are resurfaced, the intake manifold flanges will also require machining.

13   Examine the valve seats in each of the combustion chambers. If they're pitted, cracked or burned, the head will require valve service that's beyond the scope of the home mechanic.

14   Check the valve stem-to-guide clearance by measuring the lateral movement of the valve stem with a dial indicator attached securely to the head (see illustration). The valve must be in the guide and approximately 1/16-inch off the seat. The total valve stem movement indicated by the gauge needle must be divided by two to obtain the actual clearance. After this is done, if there's still some doubt regarding the condition of the valve guides, they should be checked by an automotive machine shop (the cost should be minimal).

Valves

15   Carefully inspect each valve face for uneven wear, deformation, cracks, pits and burned areas. Check the valve stem for scuffing and galling and the neck for cracks. Rotate the valve and check for any obvious indication that it's bent. Look for pits and excessive wear on the end of the stem. The presence of any of these conditions (see illustration) indicates the need for valve service by an automotive machine shop.

16   Measure the margin width on each valve (see illustration). Any valve with a margin narrower than specified in this Chapter will have to be replaced with a new one.

Valve components

17   Check each valve spring for wear (on the ends) and pits. Measure the free length and compare it to this Chapter's Specifications (see illustration). Any springs that are shorter than specified have sagged and shouldn't be reused. The tension of all springs should be checked with a special fixture before deciding they're suitable for use in a rebuilt engine (take the springs to an automotive machine shop for this check).

18   Stand each spring on a flat surface and check it for squareness (see illustration). If any of the springs are distorted or sagged, replace all of them with new parts.

19   Check the spring retainers and keepers for obvious wear and cracks. Any questionable parts should be replaced with new ones, as extensive damage will occur if they fail during engine operation.

Rocker arm components (V6 engines only)

20   Check the rocker arm faces (the areas that contact the pushrod ends and valve stems) for pits, wear, galling, score marks and rough spots.

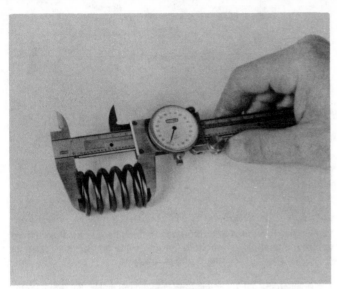

10.17   Measure the free length of each valve spring with a dial or vernier caliper

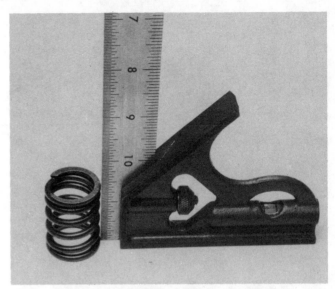

10.18   Check each valve spring for squareness

Check the rocker arm fulcrum contact areas and fulcrums as well. Look for cracks in each rocker arm and bolt.

21   Inspect the pushrod ends for scuffing and excessive wear. Roll each pushrod on a flat surface, like a piece of plate glass, to determine if it's bent.

22   Check the rocker arm bolts for damaged threads.

23   Any damaged or excessively worn parts must be replaced with new ones.

All components

24   If the inspection process indicates the valve components are in generally poor condition and worn beyond the limits specified, which is often the case in an engine that's being overhauled, reassemble the valves in the cylinder head and refer to Section 11 for valve servicing recommendations.

---

11   Valves – servicing

1   Because of the complex nature of the job and the special tools and equipment needed, servicing of the valves, the valve seats and the valve guides, commonly known as a valve job, should be done by a professional.

2   The home mechanic can remove and disassemble the head, do the initial cleaning and inspection, then reassemble and deliver it to a dealer service department or an automotive machine shop for the actual service work. Doing the inspection will enable you to see what condition the head and valvetrain components are in and will ensure that you know what work and new parts are required when dealing with an automotive machine shop.

3   The dealer service department, or automotive machine shop, will remove the valves and springs, recondition or replace the valves and valve seats, recondition the valve guides, check and replace the valve springs, spring retainers and keepers (as necessary), replace the valve seals with new ones, reassemble the valve components and make sure the installed spring height is correct. The cylinder head gasket surface will also be resurfaced if it's warped.

4   After the valve job has been performed by a professional, the head will be in like new condition. When the head is returned, be sure to clean it again before installation on the engine to remove any metal particles and abrasive grit that may still be present from the valve service or head resurfacing operations. Use compressed air, if available, to blow out all the oil holes and passages.

12   Cylinder head – reassembly

Refer to illustrations 12.4, 12.6a, 12.6b and 12.8

1   Regardless of whether or not the head was sent to an automotive repair shop for valve servicing, make sure it's clean before beginning reassembly.

2   If the head was sent out for valve servicing, the valves and related components will already be in place. Begin the reassembly procedure with Step 8.

3   Install the spring seats, if any, before the valve seals.

4   Install new seals on each of the valve guides. Using a hammer and a deep socket or seal installation tool, gently tap each seal into place until it's completely seated on the guide **(see illustration)**. Don't twist or cock the seals during installation or they won't seal properly on the valve stems.

5   Beginning at one end of the head, lubricate and install the first valve. Apply moly-base grease or clean engine oil to the valve stem.

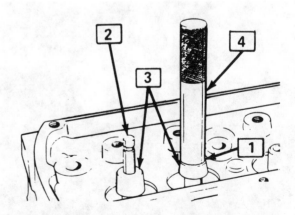

12.4   Make sure the new valve stem seals are seated against the tops of the valve guides

1	Valve seal seated in tool
2	Deburr the end of the valve stem before installing the seal
3	Seal
4	Valve seal installation tool

12.6a   V6 valve spring, shield and retainer

12.6b   Apply a small dab of grease to each keeper as shown here before installation – it will hold them in place on the valve stem as the spring is released

12.8   Be sure to check the valve spring installed height (the distance from the top of the seat/shims to the bottom of the retainer)

13.3   When checking the camshaft lobe lift, the dial indicator plunger must be positioned directly above and in line with the pushrod

6   Position the valve springs (and shields and shims, if used) over the valves (see illustration). Compress the springs with a valve spring compressor and carefully install the keepers in the groove, then slowly release the compressor and make sure the keepers seat properly. Apply a small dab of grease to each keeper to hold it in place if necessary (see illustration).

7   Repeat the procedure for the remaining valves. Be sure to return the components to their original locations – don't mix them up!

8   Check the installed valve spring height with a ruler graduated in 1/32-inch increments or a dial caliper (see illustration). If the head was sent out for service work, the installed height should be correct (but don't automatically assume it is). The measurement is taken from the top of each spring seat or top shim to the bottom of the retainer. If the height is greater than listed in this Chapter's Specifications, shims can be added under the springs to correct it. Caution: *Do not, under any circumstances, shim the springs to the point where the installed height is less than specified.*

9   Apply moly-base grease to the rocker arm faces and the fulcrums, then install the rocker arms on the cylinder heads (V6 only – see Part B).

10   If you're working on a four-cylinder engine, refer to Part A and install the camshaft and rocker arm assembly.

13   Camshaft and bearings – removal and inspection (V6 engine only)

Note: *This procedure applies to the V6 engines. Since there isn't enough room to remove the camshaft with the engine in the vehicle, the engine must be out of the vehicle and mounted on a stand for this procedure.*

Camshaft lobe lift check

With cylinder head installed
Refer to illustration 13.3

1   In order to determine the extent of cam lobe wear, the lobe lift should be checked prior to camshaft removal. Refer to Part B and remove the rocker arm covers.

2   Position the number one piston at TDC on the compression stroke (see Section 4).

3   Beginning with the number one cylinder valves, mount a dial indicator on the engine and position the plunger against the top surface of the first rocker arm. The plunger should be directly above and in line with the push-rod (see illustration).

4   Zero the dial indicator, then very slowly turn the crankshaft in the normal direction of rotation (clockwise) until the indicator needle stops and begins to move in the opposite direction. The point at which it stops indicates maximum cam lobe lift.

5   Record this figure for future reference, then reposition the piston at TDC on the compression stroke.

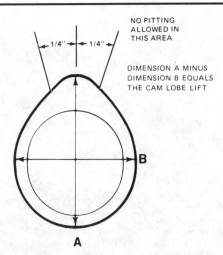

13.9 To verify camshaft lobe lift, measure the major (A) and minor (B) diameters of each lobe with a micrometer or vernier caliper – subtract the minor diameter from the major diameter to arrive at the lobe lift

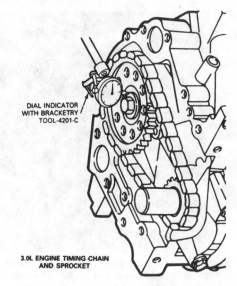

13.11 Camshaft endplay can be checked with a dial indicator

6   Move the dial indicator to the remaining number one cylinder rocker arm and repeat the check. Be sure to record the results for each valve.

7   Repeat the check for the remaining valves. Since each piston must be at TDC on the compression stroke for this procedure, work from cylinder-to-cylinder following the firing order sequence.

8   After the check is complete, compare the results to this Chapter's Specifications. If camshaft lobe lift is less than specified, cam lobe wear has occurred and a new camshaft should be installed.

With cylinder head removed

Refer to illustration 13.9

9   If the cylinder heads have already been removed, an alternate method of lobe measurement can be used. Remove the camshaft as described below. Using a micrometer, measure the lobe at its highest point. Then measure the base circle perpendicular (90-degrees) to the lobe **(see illustration)**. Do this for each lobe and record the results.

10   Subtract the base circle measurement from the lobe height. The difference is the lobe lift. See Step 8 above.

Removal

Refer to illustrations 13.11, 13.14 and 13.15

11   Mount a dial indicator as shown **(see illustration)**. Check the endplay: move the camshaft in and out and note the readings. Compare the endplay to the Specifications in this Chapter. Then, refer to the appropriate Sections in Part B and remove the timing chain and sprockets, lifters and pushrods.

12   Remove the oil pump (see Chapter 2B).

13   Remove the bolts and detach the camshaft thrust plate from the engine block. If camshaft endplay is excessive, replace the thrust plate.

14   Thread a bolt into the camshaft sprocket bolt hole to use as a handle when removing the camshaft from the block **(see illustration)**.

15   Carefully pull the camshaft out. Support the cam near the block so the lobes don't nick or gouge the bearings as it's withdrawn **(see illustration)**.

Inspection

Refer to illustration 13.17

16   After the camshaft has been removed from the engine, cleaned with solvent and dried, inspect the bearing journals for uneven wear, pitting and evidence of seizure. If the journals are damaged, the bearing inserts in the block are probably damaged as well. Both the camshaft and bearings will have to be replaced.

13.14 After removing the thrust plate, thread a bolt into the end of the camshaft to use as a handle during removal and installation

13.15 Support the camshaft near the block to avoid damaging the bearings

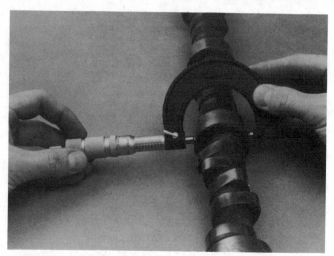

13.17   The camshaft bearing journal diameters are checked to pinpoint excessive wear and out-of-round conditions

14.1   A ridge reamer is required to remove the ridge from the top of each cylinder – do this before removing the pistons!

17   Measure the bearing journals with a micrometer **(see illustration)** to determine if they're excessively worn or out-of-round.
18   Check the camshaft lobes and distributor drive and driven gears for heat discoloration, score marks, chipped areas, pitting and uneven wear. If the lobes and gears are in good condition and if the lobe lift measurements are as specified, the components can be reused.
19   Check the bearings in the block for wear and damage. Look for galling, pitting and discolored areas.
20   The inside diameter of each bearing can be determined with a small hole gauge and outside micrometer or an inside micrometer. Subtract the camshaft bearing journal diameter(s) from the corresponding bearing inside diameter(s) to obtain the bearing oil clearance. If it's excessive, new bearings will be required regardless of the condition of the originals.
21   Camshaft bearing replacement requires special tools and expertise that place it outside the scope of the home mechanic. Take the block to an automotive machine shop to ensure the job is done correctly.

---

14   Pistons and connecting rods – removal

Refer to illustrations 14.1, 14.3 and 14.6

Note: *Prior to removing the piston/connecting rod assemblies, remove the cylinder head(s), the oil pan and the oil pump by referring to the appropriate Sections in Parts A or B of Chapter 2.*

1   Use your fingernail to feel if a ridge has formed at the upper limit of ring travel (about 1/4-inch down from the top of each cylinder). If carbon deposits or cylinder wear have produced ridges, they must be completely removed with a special tool **(see illustration)**. Follow the manufacturer's instructions provided with the tool. Failure to remove the ridges before attempting to remove the piston/connecting rod assemblies may result in piston breakage.
2   After the cylinder ridges have been removed, turn the engine upside-down so the crankshaft is facing up.
3   Before the connecting rods are removed, check the endplay with feeler gauges. Slide them between the first connecting rod and the crankshaft throw until the play is removed **(see illustration)**. The endplay is equal to the thickness of the feeler gauge(s). If the endplay exceeds the service limit, new connecting rods will be required. If new rods (or a new crankshaft) are installed, the endplay may fall under the minimum specified in this Chapter (if it does, the rods will have to be machined to restore it – consult an automotive machine shop for advice if necessary). Repeat the procedure for the remaining connecting rods.

14.3   Check the connecting rod side clearance (endplay) with a feeler gauge (V6 shown)

4   Check the connecting rods and caps for identification marks. If they aren't plainly marked, use a small center-punch to make the appropriate number of indentations on each rod and cap (1, 2, 3, etc., depending on the engine type and cylinder they're associated with).
5   Loosen each of the connecting rod cap nuts 1/2-turn at a time until they can be removed by hand. Remove the number one connecting rod cap and bearing insert. Don't drop the bearing insert out of the cap.
6   Slip a short length of plastic or rubber hose over each connecting rod cap bolt to protect the crankshaft journal and cylinder wall as the piston is removed **(see illustration)**.
7   Remove the bearing insert and push the connecting rod/piston assembly out through the top of the engine. Use a wooden or plastic hammer handle to push on the upper bearing surface in the connecting rod. If resistance is felt, double-check to make sure all of the ridge was removed from the cylinder.
8   Repeat the procedure for the remaining cylinders.
9   After removal, reassemble the connecting rod caps and bearing inserts in their respective connecting rods and install the cap nuts finger
10   Don't separate the pistons from the connecting rods (see Section 19 for additional information).

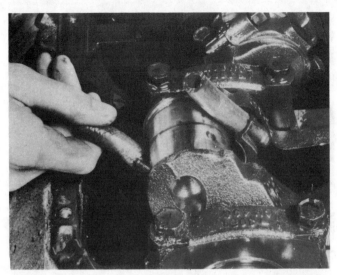

14.6 To prevent damage to the crankshaft journals and cylinder walls, slip sections of rubber hose over the rod bolts before removing the pistons

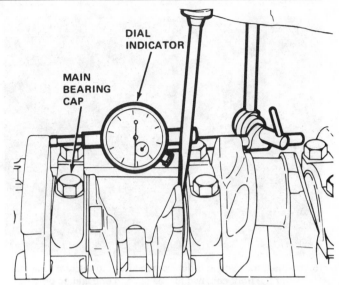

15.1 Check crankshaft endplay with a dial indicator . . .

15 Crankshaft – removal

Refer to illustrations 15.1, 15.3, 15.4a, 15.4b and 15.4c

Note: *The crankshaft can be removed only after the engine has been removed from the vehicle. It's assumed the flywheel or driveplate, crankshaft pulley, timing belt or chain, oil pan, oil pump and piston/connecting rod assemblies have already been removed. The rear oil seal housing (four-cylinder engines only) must be unbolted and separated from the block before proceeding with crankshaft removal.*

1   Before the crankshaft is removed, check the endplay. Mount a dial indicator with the stem in line with the crankshaft and just touching one of the crank throws **(see illustration)**.

2   Push the crankshaft all the way to the rear and zero the dial indicator. Next, pry the crankshaft to the front as far as possible and check the reading on the dial indicator. The distance it moves is the endplay. If it's greater than listed in this Chapter's Specifications, check the crankshaft thrust surfaces for wear. If no wear is evident, new main bearings should correct the endplay.

3   If a dial indicator isn't available, feeler gauges can be used. Gently pry or push the crankshaft all the way to the front of the engine. Slip feeler gauges between the crankshaft and the front face of the thrust main bearing to determine the clearance **(see illustration)**.

4   Check the main bearing caps to see if they're marked to indicate their locations. They should be numbered consecutively from the front of the engine to the rear. If they aren't, mark them with number stamping dies or a center-punch **(see illustrations)**. Main bearing caps generally have a cast-in arrow, which points to the front of the engine **(see illustration)**. Loosen the main bearing cap bolts 1/4-turn at a time each, until they can be removed by hand. Note if any stud bolts are used and make sure they're returned to their original locations when the crankshaft is reinstalled.

5   Gently tap the caps with a soft-face hammer, then separate them from the engine block. If necessary, use the bolts as levers to remove the caps. Try not to drop the bearing inserts if they come out with the caps.

6   Carefully lift the crankshaft out of the engine. It may be a good idea to have an assistant available, since the crankshaft is quite heavy. With the bearing inserts in place in the engine block and main bearing caps, return the caps to their respective locations on the engine block and tighten the bolts finger-tight.

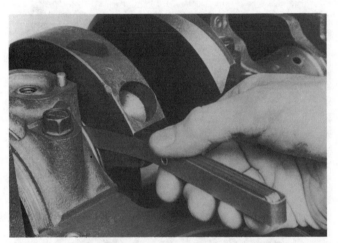

15.3 . . . or slip feeler gauges between the crankshaft and main bearing thrust surfaces – the endplay is equal to the feeler gauge thickness

15.4a Use a center-punch or number stamping dies to mark the main bearing caps to ensure installation in their original locations on the block – make the punch marks near one of the bolt heads

15.4b   Mark the caps in order from the front to the rear (one mark for the front cap, two for the second one and so on)

15.4c   The arrow on the main bearing cap indicates the front of the engine

16.4   Remove the core plugs with a puller – if they're driven into the block they may be difficult to retrieve

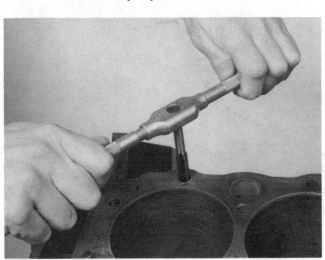

16.8   Clean and restore all threaded holes in the block – especially the main bearing cap and head bolt holes – with a tap (be sure to remove debris from the holes when you're done)

16   Engine block – cleaning

Refer to illustrations 16.4, 16.8 and 16.10

1   Remove the main bearing caps and separate the bearing inserts from the caps and the engine block. Tag the bearings, indicating which cylinder they were removed from and whether they were in the cap or the block, then set them aside.

2   Using a gasket scraper, remove all traces of gasket material from the engine block. Be very careful not to nick or gouge the gasket sealing surfaces.

3   Remove all of the covers and threaded oil gallery plugs from the block. The plugs are usually very tight – they may have to be drilled out and the holes retapped. Use new plugs when the engine is reassembled.

4   Drill a small hole in the center of each core plug and pull them out with an auto body type dent puller **(see illustration). Caution:** *The core plugs (also known as freeze or soft plugs) may be difficult or impossible to retrieve if they're driven into the block coolant passages.*

5   If the engine is extremely dirty, it should be taken to an automotive machine shop to be steam cleaned or hot tanked.

6   After the block is returned, clean all oil holes and oil galleries one more time. Brushes specifically designed for this purpose are available at most auto parts stores. Flush the passages with warm water until the water runs clear, dry the block thoroughly and wipe all machined surfaces with a light, rust preventive oil. If you have access to compressed air, use it to speed the drying process and blow out all the oil holes and galleries. **Warning:** *Wear eye protection when using compressed air!*

7   If the block isn't extremely dirty or sludged up, you can do an adequate cleaning job with hot soapy water and a stiff brush. Take plenty of time and do a thorough job. Regardless of the cleaning method used, be sure to clean all oil holes and galleries very thoroughly, dry the block completely and coat all machined surfaces with light oil.

8   The threaded holes in the block must be clean to ensure accurate torque readings during reassembly. Run the proper size tap into each of the holes to remove rust, corrosion, thread sealant or sludge and restore damaged threads **(see illustration).** If possible, use compressed air to clear the holes of debris produced by this operation. Now is a good time to clean the threads on the head bolts and the main bearing cap bolts as well.

9   Reinstall the main bearing caps and tighten the bolts finger tight.

10   After coating the sealing surfaces of the new core plugs with Permatex no. 2 sealant, install them in the engine block **(see illustration).** Make sure they're driven in straight and seated properly or leakage could result. Special tools are available for this purpose, but a large socket, with an outside diameter that will just slip into the core plug, a 1/2-inch drive extension and a hammer will work just as well.

16.10 A large socket on an extension can be used to drive the new core plugs into the bores

11 Apply non-hardening sealant (such as Permatex no. 2 or Teflon pipe sealant) to the new oil gallery plugs and thread them into the holes in the block. Make sure they're tightened securely.
12 If the engine isn't going to be reassembled right away, cover it with a large plastic trash bag to keep it clean.

17 Engine block – inspection

Refer to illustrations 17.4a, 17.4b and 17.4c
1 Before the block is inspected, it should be cleaned as described in Section 16.
2 Visually check the block for cracks, rust and corrosion. Look for stripped threads in the threaded holes. It's also a good idea to have the block checked for hidden cracks by an automotive machine shop that has the special equipment to do this type of work. If defects are found, have the block repaired, if possible, or replaced.
3 Check the cylinder bores for scuffing and scoring.
4 Measure the diameter of each cylinder at the top (just under the ridge area), center and bottom of the cylinder bore, parallel to the crankshaft axis **(see illustrations)**. **Note:** *These measurements should not be made with the bare block mounted on an engine stand – the cylinders will be distorted and the measurements will be inaccurate.*
5 Next, measure each cylinder's diameter at the same three locations across the crankshaft axis. Compare the results to this Chapter's Specifications.
6 If the required precision measuring tools aren't available, the piston-to-cylinder clearances can be obtained, though not quite as accurately, using feeler gauge stock. Feeler gauge stock comes in 12-inch lengths and various thicknesses and is generally available at auto parts stores.
7 To check the clearance, select a feeler gauge and slip it into the cylinder along with the matching piston. The piston must be positioned exactly as it normally would be. The feeler gauge must be between the piston and cylinder on one of the thrust faces (90-degrees to the piston pin bore).
8 The piston should slip through the cylinder (with the feeler gauge in place) with moderate pressure.
9 If it falls through or slides through easily, the clearance is excessive and a new piston will be required. If the piston binds at the lower end of the cylinder and is loose toward the top, the cylinder is tapered. If tight spots are encountered as the piston/feeler gauge is rotated in the cylinder, the cylinder is out-of-round.
10 Repeat the procedure for the remaining pistons and cylinders.
11 If the cylinder walls are badly scuffed or scored, or if they're out-of-round or tapered beyond the limits given in this Chapter's Specifications,

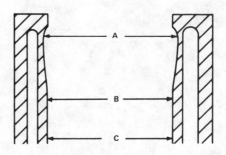

17.4a Measure the diameter of each cylinder just under the wear ridge (A), at the center (B) and at the bottom (C)

17.4b The ability to "feel" when the telescoping gauge is at the correct point will be developed over time, so work slowly and repeat the check until you are satisfied that the bore measurement is accurate

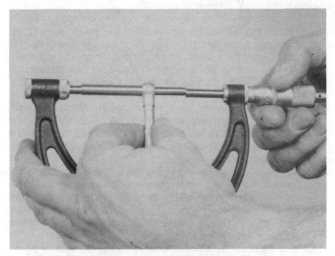

17.4c The gauge is then measured with a micrometer to determine the bore size

have the engine block rebored and honed at an automotive machine shop. If a rebore is done, oversize pistons and rings will be required.
12 If the cylinders are in reasonably good condition and not worn to the outside of the limits, and if the piston-to-cylinder clearances can be maintained properly, they don't have to be rebored. Honing is all that's necessary (see Section 18).

**18.3a   A "bottle brush" hone will produce better results if you
have never honed cylinders before**

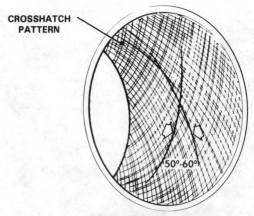

**18.3b   The cylinder hone should leave a smooth,
crosshatch pattern with the lines intersecting at
approximately a 60-degree angle**

18   Cylinder honing

Refer to illustrations 18.3a and 18.3b

1   Prior to engine reassembly, the cylinder bores must be honed so the new piston rings will seat correctly and provide the best possible combustion chamber seal. **Note:** *If you don't have the tools or don't want to tackle the honing operation, most automotive machine shops will do it for a reasonable fee.*

2   Before honing the cylinders, install the main bearing caps and tighten the bolts to the torque listed in this Chapter's Specifications.

3   Two types of cylinder hones are commonly available – the flex hone or "bottle brush" type and the more traditional surfacing hone with spring-loaded stones. Both will do the job, but for the less experienced mechanic the "bottle brush" hone will probably be easier to use. You'll also need some honing oil (kerosene will work if honing oil isn't available), rags and an electric drill motor. Proceed as follows:

   a) Mount the hone in the drill motor, compress the stones and slip it into the first cylinder **(see illustration)**. Be sure to wear safety goggles or a face shield!

   b) Lubricate the cylinder with plenty of honing oil, turn on the drill and move the hone up-and-down in the cylinder at a pace that will produce a fine crosshatch pattern on the cylinder walls. Ideally, the crosshatch lines should intersect at approximately a 60-degree angle **(see illustration)**. Be sure to use plenty of lubricant and don't take off any more material than is absolutely necessary to produce the desired finish. **Note:** *Piston ring manufacturers may specify a different crosshatch angle – read and follow any instructions included with the new rings.*

   c) Don't withdraw the hone from the cylinder while it's running. Instead, shut off the drill and continue moving the hone up-and-down in the cylinder until it comes to a complete stop, then compress the stones and withdraw the hone. If you're using a "bottle brush" type hone, stop the drill motor, then turn the chuck in the normal direction of rotation while withdrawing the hone from the cylinder.

   d) Wipe the oil out of the cylinder and repeat the procedure for the remaining cylinders.

4   After the honing job is complete, chamfer the top edges of the cylinder bores with a small file so the rings won't catch when the pistons are installed. Be very careful not to nick the cylinder walls with the end of the file.

5   The entire engine block must be washed again very thoroughly with warm, soapy water to remove all traces of the abrasive grit produced during the honing operation. **Note:** *The bores can be considered clean when a lint-free white cloth – dampened with clean engine oil – used to wipe them out doesn't pick up any more honing residue, which will show up as* gray areas on the cloth. Be sure to run a brush through all oil holes and galleries and flush them with running water.

6   After rinsing, dry the block and apply a coat of light rust preventive oil to all machined surfaces. Wrap the block in a plastic trash bag to keep it clean and set it aside until reassembly.

19   Pistons and connecting rods – inspection

Refer to illustrations 19.4a, 19,4b, 19.10 and 19.11

1   Before the inspection process can be carried out, the piston/connecting rod assemblies must be cleaned and the original piston rings removed from the pistons. **Note:** *Always use new piston rings when the engine is reassembled.*

2   Using a piston ring installation tool, carefully remove the rings from the pistons. Be careful not to nick or gouge the pistons in the process.

3   Scrape all traces of carbon from the top of the piston. A hand held wire brush or a piece of fine emery cloth can be used once the majority of the deposits have been scraped away. Do not, under any circumstances, use a wire brush mounted in a drill motor to remove deposits from the pistons. The piston material is soft and may be eroded away by the wire brush.

4   Use a piston ring groove cleaning tool to remove carbon deposits from the ring grooves. If a tool isn't available, a piece broken off the old ring will do the job. Be very careful to remove only the carbon deposits – don't remove any metal and do not nick or scratch the sides of the ring grooves **(see illustrations)**.

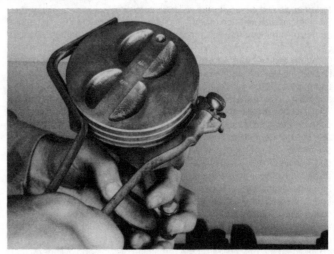

**19.4a   The piston ring grooves can be cleaned with a special
tool, as shown here, . . .**

19.4b ... or a piece of broken piston ring

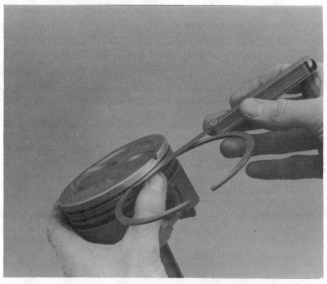

19.10 Check the ring side clearance with a feeler gauge at several points around the groove

5   Once the deposits have been removed, clean the piston/rod assemblies with solvent and dry them with compressed air (if available). **Warning:** *Wear eye protection. Make sure the oil return holes in the back sides of the ring grooves are clear.*

6   If the pistons and cylinder walls aren't damaged or worn excessively, and if the engine block isn't rebored, new pistons won't be necessary. Normal piston wear appears as even vertical
wear on the piston thrust surfaces and slight looseness of the top ring in its groove. New piston rings, however, should always be used when an engine is rebuilt.

7   Carefully inspect each piston for cracks around the skirt, at the pin bosses and at the ring lands.

8   Look for scoring and scuffing on the thrust faces of the skirt, holes in the piston crown and burned areas at the edge of the crown. If the skirt is scored or scuffed, the engine may have been suffering from overheating and/or abnormal combustion, which caused excessively high operating temperatures. The cooling and lubrication systems should be checked thoroughly. A hole in the piston crown is an indication that abnormal combustion (preignition) was occurring. Burned areas at the edge of the piston crown are usually evidence of spark knock (detonation). If any of the above problems exist, the causes must be corrected or the damage will occur again. The causes may include intake air leaks, incorrect fuel/air mixture, low octane fuel, ignition timing and EGR system malfunctions.

9   Corrosion of the piston, in the form of small pits, indicates coolant is leaking into the combustion chamber and/or the crankcase. Again, the cause must be corrected or the problem may persist in the rebuilt engine.

10   Measure the piston ring side clearance by laying a new piston ring in each ring groove and slipping a feeler gauge in beside it **(see illustration)**. Check the clearance at three or four locations around each groove. Be sure to use the correct ring for each groove – they are different. If the side clearance is greater than listed in this Chapter's Specifications, new pistons will have to be used.

11   Check the piston-to-bore clearance by measuring the bore (see Section 17) and the piston diameter. Make sure the pistons and bores are correctly matched. Measure the piston across the skirt, at a 90-degree angle to the piston pin **(see illustration)**. The measurement must be taken at a specific point, depending on the engine type, to be accurate.

    a) The piston diameter on four-cylinder engines is measured 18 mm (0.0709 in) below the oil ring groove.

    b) V6 engine pistons are measured at the level of the center of the piston pin hole.

12   Subtract the piston diameter from the bore diameter to obtain the clearance. If it's greater than specified, the block will have to be rebored and new pistons and rings installed.

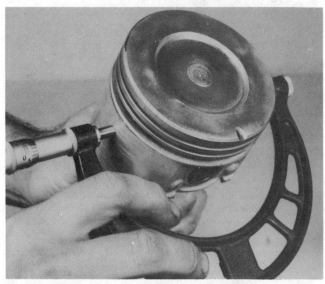

19.11 Measure the piston diameter at a 90-degree angle to the piston pin at the specified point on the skirt (see the text)

13   Check the piston-to-rod clearance by twisting the piston and rod in opposite directions. Any noticeable play indicates excessive wear, which must be corrected. The piston/connecting rod assemblies should be taken to an automotive machine shop to have the pistons and rods resized and new pins installed.

14   If the pistons must be removed from the connecting rods for any reason, they should be taken to an automotive machine shop. While they are there have the connecting rods checked for bend and twist, since automotive machine shops have special equipment for this purpose. **Note:** *Unless new pistons and/or connecting rods must be installed, do not disassemble the pistons and connecting rods.*

15   Check the connecting rods for cracks and other damage. Temporarily remove the rod caps, lift out the old bearing inserts, wipe the rod and cap bearing surfaces clean and inspect them for nicks, gouges and scratches. After checking the rods, replace the old bearings, slip the caps into place and tighten the nuts finger tight. **Note:** *If the engine is being rebuilt because of a connecting rod knock, be sure to install new rods.*

20 Crankshaft – inspection

Refer to illustrations 20.1, 20.3, 20.4 and 20.6

1   Clean the crankshaft with solvent and dry it with compressed air (if available). **Warning:** *Wear eye protection when using compressed air. Be sure to clean the oil holes with a stiff brush* **(see illustration)** *and flush them with solvent.*

2   Check the main and connecting rod bearing journals for uneven wear, scoring, pits and cracks.

3   Rub a penny across each journal several times **(see illustration)**. If a journal picks up copper from the penny, it's too rough and must be reground.

4   Remove all burrs from the crankshaft oil holes with a stone, file or scraper **(see illustration)**.

5   Check the rest of the crankshaft for cracks and other damage. It should be magnafluxed to reveal hidden cracks – an automotive machine shop will handle the procedure.

6   Using a micrometer, measure the diameter of the main and connecting rod journals and compare the results to this Chapter's Specifications **(see illustration)**. By measuring the diameter at a number of points around each journal's circumference, you'll be able to determine whether or not the journal is out-of-round. Take the measurement at each end of the journal, near the crank throws, to determine if the journal is tapered.

7   If the crankshaft journals are damaged, tapered, out-of-round or worn beyond the limits given in the Specifications, have the crankshaft reground by an automotive machine shop. Be sure to use the correct size bearing inserts if the crankshaft is reconditioned.

8   Check the oil seal journals at each end of the crankshaft for wear and damage. If the seal has worn a groove in the journal, or if it's nicked or scratched, the new seal may leak when the engine is reassembled. In some cases, an automotive machine shop may be able to repair the journal by pressing on a thin sleeve. If repair isn't feasible, a new or different crankshaft should be installed.

9   Refer to Section 21 and examine the main and rod bearing inserts.

20.1   Clean the crankshaft oil passages with a wire or stiff plastic bristle brush and flush them out with solvent

20.3   Rubbing a penny lengthwise on each journal will give you a quick idea of its condition – if copper rubs off the penny and adheres to the crankshaft, the journals should be reground

20.4   Chamfer the oil holes to remove sharp edges that might gouge or scratch the new bearings

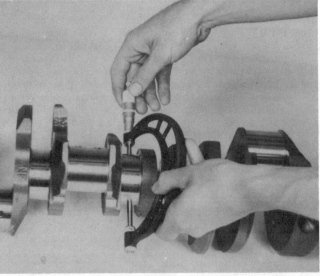

20.6   Measure the diameter of each crankshaft journal at several points to detect taper and out-of-round conditions

21   Main and connecting rod bearings – inspection

Refer to illustration 21.1

1   Even though the main and connecting rod bearings should be replaced with new ones during the engine overhaul, the old bearings should be retained for close examination, as they may reveal valuable information about the condition of the engine **(see illustration)**.

2   Bearing failure occurs because of lack of lubrication, the presence of dirt or other foreign particles, overloading the engine and corrosion. Regardless of the cause of bearing failure, it must be corrected before the engine is reassembled to prevent it from happening again.

3   When examining the bearings, remove them from the engine block, the main bearing caps, the connecting rods and the rod caps and lay them out on a clean surface in the same general position as their location in the engine. This will enable you to match any bearing problems with the corresponding crankshaft journal.

4   Dirt and other foreign particles get into the engine in a variety of ways. It may be left in the engine during assembly, or it may pass through filters or the PCV system. It may get into the oil, and from there into the bearings. Metal chips from machining operations and normal engine wear are often present. Abrasives are sometimes left in engine components after reconditioning, especially when parts aren't thoroughly cleaned using the proper cleaning methods. Whatever the source, these foreign objects often end up embedded in the soft bearing material and are easily recognized. Large particles won't embed in the bearing and will score or gouge the bearing and journal. The best prevention for this cause of bearing failure is to clean all parts thoroughly and keep everything spotlessly clean during engine assembly. Frequent and regular engine oil and filter changes are also recommended.

5   Lack of lubrication (or lubrication breakdown) has a number of interrelated causes. Excessive heat (which thins the oil), overloading (which squeezes the oil from the bearing face) and oil leakage or throw off (from excessive bearing clearances, worn oil pump or high engine speeds) all contribute to lubrication breakdown. Blocked oil passages, which usually are the result of misaligned oil holes in a bearing shell, will also oil starve a bearing and destroy it. When lack of lubrication is the cause of bearing failure, the bearing material is wiped or extruded from the steel backing of the bearing. Temperatures may increase to the point where the steel backing turns blue from overheating.

6   Driving habits can have a definite effect on bearing life. Full throttle, low speed operation (lugging the engine) puts very high loads on bearings, which tends to squeeze out the oil film. These loads cause the bearings to flex, which produces fine cracks in the bearing face (fatigue failure). Eventually the bearing material will loosen in pieces and tear away from the steel backing. Short trip driving leads to corrosion of bearings because insufficient engine heat is produced to drive off the condensed water and corrosive gases. These products collect in the engine oil, forming acid and sludge. As the oil is carried to the engine bearings, the acid attacks and corrodes the bearing material.

7   Incorrect bearing installation during engine assembly will lead to bearing failure as well. Tight fitting bearings leave insufficient oil clearance and will result in oil starvation. Dirt or foreign particles trapped behind a bearing insert result in high spots on the bearing which lead to failure.

22   Engine overhaul – reassembly sequence

1   Before beginning engine reassembly, make sure you have all the necessary new parts, gaskets and seals as well as the following items on hand:

Common hand tools
Torque wrench (1/2-inch drive)
Piston ring installation tool
Piston ring compressor
Crankshaft damper installation tool (V6 engines only)
Short lengths of rubber or plastic hose to fit over connecting rod bolts
Plastigage
Feeler gauges
Fine-tooth file
New engine oil
Engine assembly lube or moly-base grease
Gasket sealant
Thread locking compound

2   In order to save time and avoid problems, engine reassembly must be done in the following general order:

Four-cylinder engine

Crankshaft and main bearings
Crankshaft rear oil seal housing
Piston/connecting rod assemblies
Oil pump
Oil pan
Cylinder head
Camshaft and rocker assembly
Timing belt and sprockets
Intake and exhaust manifolds

V6 engine

Crankshaft and main bearings
Piston/connecting rod assemblies
Oil pump
Oil pan
Camshaft
Timing chain and sprockets
Timing chain cover
Cylinder heads
Valve lifters
Rocker arms and pushrods
Intake and exhaust manifolds
Rocker arm covers

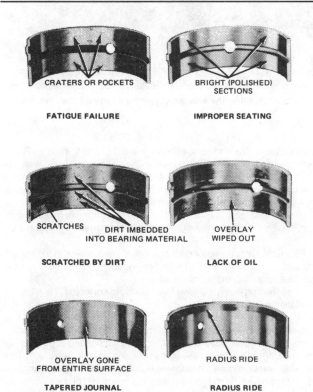

CRATERS OR POCKETS

FATIGUE FAILURE

BRIGHT (POLISHED) SECTIONS

IMPROPER SEATING

SCRATCHES   **DIRT IMBEDDED INTO BEARING MATERIAL**

SCRATCHED BY DIRT

OVERLAY WIPED OUT

LACK OF OIL

OVERLAY GONE FROM ENTIRE SURFACE

TAPERED JOURNAL

RADIUS RIDE

RADIUS RIDE

21.1   Typical bearing failures

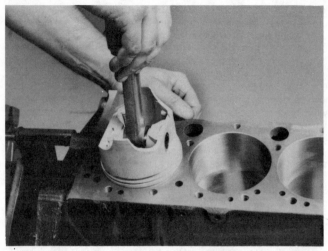

23.3   When checking piston ring end gap, the ring must be square in the cylinder bore (this is done by pushing the ring down with the top of a piston as shown)

23.4   With the ring square in the cylinder, measure the end gap with a feeler gauge

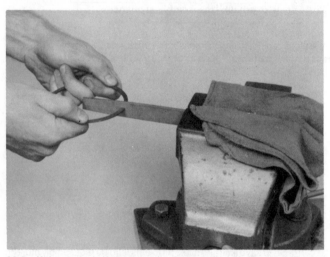

23.5   If the end gap is too small, clamp a file in a vise and file the ring ends (from the outside in only) to enlarge the gap slightly

23.9a   Installing the spacer/expander in the oil ring groove

23   Piston rings – installation

Refer to illustrations 23.3, 23.4, 23.5, 23.9a, 23.9b and 23.12

1   Before installing the new piston rings, the ring end gaps must be checked. It's assumed the piston ring side clearance has been checked and verified correct (see Section 19).

2   Lay out the piston/connecting rod assemblies and the new ring sets so the ring sets will be matched with the same piston and cylinder during the end gap measurement and engine assembly.

3   Insert the top (number one) ring into the first cylinder and square it up with the cylinder walls by pushing it in with the top of the piston **(see illustration)**. The ring should be near the bottom of the cylinder, at the lower limit of ring travel.

4   To measure the end gap, slip feeler gauges between the ends of the ring until a gauge equal to the gap width is found **(see illustration)**. The feeler gauge should slide between the ring ends with a slight amount of drag. Compare the measurement to this Chapter's Specifications. If the gap is larger or smaller than specified, double-check to make sure you have the correct rings before proceeding.

5   If the gap is too small, it must be enlarged or the ring ends may come in contact with each other during engine operation, which can cause serious engine damage. The end gap can be increased by filing the ring ends very carefully with a fine file. Mount the file in a vise equipped with soft jaws, slip the ring over the file with the ends contacting the file teeth and slowly move the ring to remove material from the ends. When performing this operation, file only from the outside in **(see illustration)**.

6   Excess end gap isn't critical unless it's greater than 0.040-inch. Again, double-check to make sure you have the correct rings for the engine.

7   Repeat the procedure for each ring that will be installed in the first cylinder and for each ring in the remaining cylinders. Remember to keep rings, pistons and cylinders matched up.

8   Once the ring end gaps have been checked/corrected, the rings can be installed on the pistons.

9   The oil control ring (lowest one on the piston) is usually installed first. It's composed of three separate components. Slip the spacer/expander into the groove **(see illustration)**. If an anti-rotation tang is used, make sure it's inserted into the drilled hole in the ring groove. Next, install the lower side rail. Don't use a piston ring installation tool on the oil ring side rails, as they may be damaged. Instead, place one end of the side rail into the groove between the spacer/expander and the ring land, hold it firmly in place and slide a finger around the piston while pushing the rail into the groove **(see illustration)**. Next, install the upper side rail in the same manner.

23.9b DO NOT use a piston ring installation tool when installing the oil ring side rails

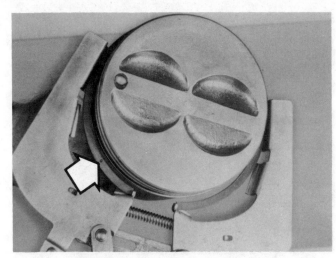

23.12 Installing the compression rings with a ring expander – the mark (arrow) must face up

10   After the three oil ring components have been installed, check to make sure both the upper and lower side rails can be turned smoothly in the ring groove.

11   The number two (middle) ring is installed next. It's usually stamped with a mark, which must face up, toward the top of the piston. **Note:** *Always follow the instructions printed on the ring package or box – different manufacturers may require different approaches. Don't mix up the top and middle rings, as they have different cross sections.*

12   Use a piston ring installation tool and make sure the identification mark is facing the top of the piston, then slip the ring into the middle groove on the piston **(see illustration)**. Don't expand the ring any more than necessary to slide it over the piston.

13   Install the number one (top) ring in the same manner. Make sure the mark is facing up. Be careful not to confuse the number one and number two rings.

14   Repeat the procedure for the remaining pistons and rings.

24   Crankshaft – installation and main bearing oil clearance check

Refer to illustrations 24.6, 24.11 and 24.15

1   Crankshaft installation is the first step in engine reassembly. It's assumed at this point that the engine block and crankshaft have been cleaned, inspected and repaired or reconditioned.

2   Position the engine with the bottom facing up.

3   Remove the main bearing cap bolts and lift out the caps. Lay them out in the proper order to ensure correct installation.

4   If they're still in place, remove the original bearing inserts from the block and the main bearing caps. Wipe the bearing surfaces of the block and caps with a clean, lint-free cloth. They must be kept spotlessly clean.

Main bearing oil clearance check

Note: *Don't touch the faces of the new bearing inserts with your fingers. Oil and acids from your skin can etch the bearings.*

5   Clean the back sides of the new main bearing inserts and lay one in each main bearing saddle in the block. If one of the bearing inserts from each set has a large groove in it, make sure the grooved insert is installed in the block. Lay the other bearing from each set in the corresponding main bearing cap. Make sure the tab on the bearing insert fits into the recess in the block or cap. **Caution:** *The oil holes in the block must line up with the oil holes in the bearing inserts. Do not hammer the bearing into place and don't nick or gouge the bearing faces. No lubrication should be used at this time.*

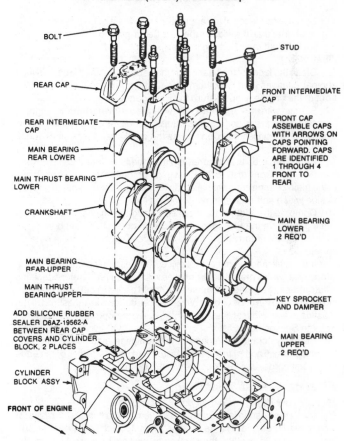

24.6 Crankshaft components – exploded view

6   The flanged thrust bearing **(see illustration)** must be installed in the number three cap and saddle (counting from the front of the engine).

7   Clean the faces of the bearings in the block and the crankshaft main bearing journals with a clean, lint-free cloth.

8   Check or clean the oil holes in the crankshaft, as any dirt here can go only one way – straight through the new bearings.

9   Once you're certain the crankshaft is clean, carefully lay it in position in the main bearings.

10   Before the crankshaft can be permanently installed, the main bearing oil clearance must be checked.

24.11   Lay the Plastigage strips (arrow) on the main bearing journals, parallel to the crankshaft centerline

11   Cut several pieces of the appropriate size Plastigage (they should be slightly shorter than the width of the main bearings) and place one piece on each crankshaft main bearing journal, parallel with the journal axis **(see illustration)**.

12   Clean the faces of the bearings in the caps and install the caps in their original locations (don't mix them up) with the arrows pointing toward the front of the engine. Don't disturb the Plastigage.

13   Starting with the center main and working out toward the ends, tighten the main bearing cap bolts, in three steps, to the torque figure listed in this Chapter's Specifications. Don't rotate the crankshaft at any time during this operation.

14   Remove the bolts and carefully lift off the main bearing caps. Keep them in order. Don't disturb the Plastigage or rotate the crankshaft. If any of the main bearing caps are difficult to remove, tap them gently from side-to-side with a soft-face hammer to loosen them.

15   Compare the width of the crushed Plastigage on each journal to the scale printed on the Plastigage envelope to obtain the main bearing oil clearance **(see illustration)**. Check the Specifications to make sure it's correct.

16   If the clearance is not as specified, the bearing inserts may be the wrong size (which means different ones will be required). Before deciding different inserts are needed, make sure no dirt or oil was between the bearing inserts and the caps or block when the clearance was measured. If the Plastigage was wider at one end than the other, the journal may be tapered (refer to Section 20).

17   Carefully scrape all traces of the Plastigage material off the main bearing journals and/or the bearing faces. Use your fingernail or the edge of a credit card – don't nick or scratch the bearing faces.

Final crankshaft installation

18   Carefully lift the crankshaft out of the engine.

19   Clean the bearing faces in the block, then apply a thin, uniform layer of moly-based grease or engine assembly lube to each of the bearing surfaces. Be sure to coat the thrust faces as well as the journal face of the thrust bearing.

20   Make sure the crankshaft journals are clean, then lay the crankshaft back in place in the block.

21   Clean the faces of the bearings in the caps, then apply lubricant to them.

22   Install the caps in their original locations with the arrows pointing toward the front of the engine. On V6 engines, apply silicone sealant (Ford D6AZ-19562-A or equivalent) in a 1/8-inch bead to the rear main bearing cap-to-cylinder block parting line **(see illustration 24.6)**.

23   Install the bolts.

24   Tighten all except the thrust bearing cap bolts to the torque specified in this Chapter (work from the center out and approach the final torque in three steps).

25   Tighten the thrust bearing cap bolts to 10-to-12 ft-lbs.

24.15   Compare the width of the crushed Plastigage to the scale on the container to determine the main bearing oil clearance (always take the measurement at the widest point of the Plastigage); be sure to use the correct scale – standard and metric scales are included

26   Tap the ends of the crankshaft forward and backward with a lead or brass hammer to line up the main bearing and crankshaft thrust surfaces.

27   Retighten all main bearing cap bolts to the torque specified in this Chapter, starting with the center main and working out toward the ends.

28   Rotate the crankshaft a number of times by hand to check for any obvious binding.

29   The final step is to check the crankshaft endplay with feeler gauges or a dial indicator as described in Section 15. The endplay should be correct if the crankshaft thrust faces aren't worn or damaged and new bearings have been installed.

30   Refer to Section 26 and install the new rear main oil seal.

25   Camshaft – installation (V6 engine only)

Refer to illustration 25.1

Note: *This procedure applies to V6 engines only.*

1   Lubricate the camshaft bearing journals and cam lobes with moly-based grease or engine assembly lube **(see illustration)**.

2   Slide the camshaft into the engine. Support the cam near the block and be careful not to scrape or nick the bearings. Install the thrust plate and tighten the bolts to the torque listed in this Chapter's Specifications.

3   Refer to Part B to complete the installation of the camshaft, lifters, timing chain and sprockets.

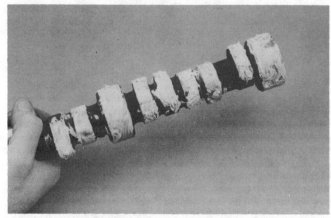

25.1   Be sure to apply moly-based grease or engine assembly lube to the cam lobes and bearing journals before installing the camshaft

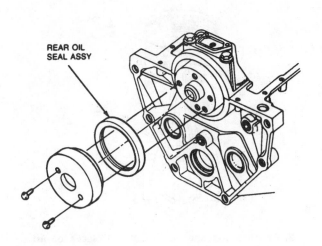

REAR OIL
SEAL ASSY

26.3   Press the seal into place with a special tool,
if available

26.6   After removing the housing assembly from the block,
support it on a couple of wood blocks and drive out the old seal
with a hammer and punch

26.7   Drive the new seal into the housing with a block of wood or
a section of pipe, if you have one large enough – make sure that
you don't cock the seal in the housing bore

26.9   Tighten the housing bolts (arrows) a little at a time until
they're all at the torque listed in the Part A Specifications

---

26   Crankshaft rear oil seal – installation

V6 engine

Refer to illustration 26.3

1   Clean the bore in the block/cap and the seal journal on the crankshaft. Check the crankshaft journal for scratches and nicks that could damage the new seal lip and cause oil leaks. If the crankshaft is damaged, the only alternative is a new or different crankshaft.

2   Apply a light coat of engine oil to the outer edge of the new seal and the seal lips.

3   Press the new seal into place with special tool T82L-6701-A (or equivalent) – if available **(see illustration)**. The seal lip must face toward the front of the engine. If the special tool isn't available, carefully work the seal lip over the end of the crankshaft and tap the seal in with a hammer and blunt punch until it's seated in the bore (see Chapter 2B).

Four-cylinder engine

Refer to illustrations 26.6, 26.7 and 26.9

4   This engine is equipped with a one-piece seal that fits into a housing attached to the block. The crankshaft must be installed first and the main

bearing caps bolted in place, then the new seal should be installed in the housing and the housing bolted to the block.

5   Before installing the crankshaft, check the seal journal very carefully for scratches and nicks that could damage the new seal lip and cause oil leaks. If the crankshaft is damaged, the only alternative is a new or different crankshaft.

6   The old seal can be removed from the housing with a hammer and punch by driving it out from the back side **(see illustration)**. Be sure to note how far it's recessed into the housing bore before removing it; the new seal will have to be recessed an equal amount. Be very careful not to scratch or otherwise damage the bore in the housing or oil leaks could develop.

7   Make sure the housing is clean, then apply a thin coat of engine oil to the outer edge of the new seal. The seal must be pressed squarely into the housing bore **(see illustration)**. Work slowly and make sure the seal enters the bore squarely.

8   The seal lips must be lubricated with moly-base grease or engine assembly lube before the seal/housing is slipped over the crankshaft and bolted to the block. Use a new gasket – no sealant is required – and make sure the dowel pins are in place before installing the housing.

9   Tighten the bolts **(see illustration)** a little at a time until they're all at the torque listed in the Part A Specifications.

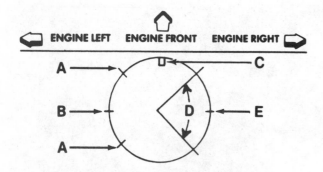

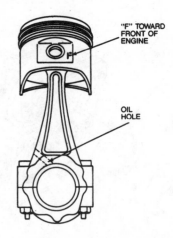

27.5   Position the piston ring gaps as shown before installing the piston/connecting rod assemblies in the engine

A *Oil ring rail gaps*
B *2nd compression ring gap*
C *Notch in piston (V6 engine)*

D *Oil ring spacer gap (tang in hole or slot with arc)*
E *Top compression ring gap*

27.9a   On four-cylinder models, the "F" faces toward the front (timing-belt end) of the engine

27.9b   On V6 engines, the notch in each piston must face the timing chain end of the engine as the pistons are installed

27.11   The piston can be driven (gently) into the cylinder bore with the end of a wooden hammer handle

27   Pistons and connecting rods – installation and rod bearing oil clearance check

Refer to illustrations 27.5, 27.9a, 27.9b, 27.11, 27.13 and 27.17

1   Before installing the piston/connecting rod assemblies, the cylinder walls must be perfectly clean, the top edge of each cylinder must be chamfered, and the crankshaft must be in place.

2   Remove the cap from the end of the number one connecting rod (check the marks made during removal). Remove the original bearing inserts and wipe the bearing surfaces of the connecting rod and cap with a clean, lint-free cloth. They must be kept spotlessly clean.

Connecting rod bearing oil clearance check

Note: *Don't touch the faces of the new bearing inserts with your fingers. Oil and acids from your skin can etch the bearings.*

3   Clean the back side of the new upper bearing insert, then lay it in place in the connecting rod. Make sure the tab on the bearing fits into the recess in the rod. Don't hammer the bearing insert into place and be very careful not to nick or gouge the bearing face. Don't lubricate the bearing at this time.

4   Clean the back side of the other bearing insert and install it in the rod cap. Again, make sure the tab on the bearing fits into the recess in the cap, and don't apply any lubricant. It's critically important that the mating surfaces of the bearing and connecting rod are perfectly clean and oil free when they're assembled.

5   Position the piston ring gaps in the correct locations around the piston **(see illustration)**.

6   Slip a section of plastic or rubber hose over each connecting rod cap bolt.

7   Lubricate the piston and rings with clean engine oil and attach a piston ring compressor to the piston. Leave the skirt protruding about 1/4-inch to guide the piston into the cylinder. The rings must be compressed until they're flush with the piston.

8   Rotate the crankshaft until the number one connecting rod journal is at BDC (bottom dead center) and apply a coat of engine oil to the cylinder walls.

9   With the "F" mark or notch on top of the piston facing the front of the engine **(see illustrations)**, gently insert the piston/connecting rod assembly into the number one cylinder bore and rest the bottom edge of the ring compressor on the engine block.

10   Tap the top edge of the ring compressor to make sure it's contacting the block around its entire circumference.

11   Gently tap on the top of the piston with the end of a wooden or plastic hammer handle **(see illustration)** while guiding the end of the connecting rod into place on the crankshaft journal. The piston rings may try to pop out

27.13   Lay the Plastigage strips on each rod bearing journal, parallel to the crankshaft centerline

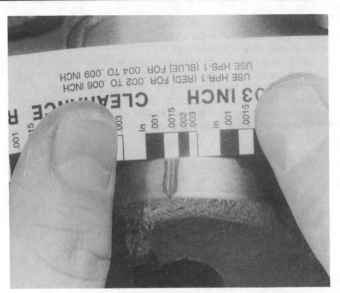

27.17   Measuring the width of the crushed Plastigage to determine the rod bearing oil clearance (be sure to use the correct scale – standard and metric scales are included)

of the ring compressor just before entering the cylinder bore, so keep some downward pressure on the ring compressor. Work slowly, and if any resistance is felt as the piston enters the cylinder, stop immediately. Find out what's hanging up and fix it before proceeding. Do not, for any reason, force the piston into the cylinder – you might break a ring and/or the piston.

12   Once the piston/connecting rod assembly is installed, the connecting rod bearing oil clearance must be checked before the rod cap is permanently bolted in place.

13   Cut a piece of the appropriate size Plastigage slightly shorter than the width of the connecting rod bearing and lay it in place on the number one connecting rod journal, parallel with the journal axis **(see illustration)**.

14   Clean the connecting rod cap bearing face, remove the protective hoses from the connecting rod bolts and install the rod cap. Make sure the mating mark on the cap is on the same side as the mark on the connecting rod.

15   Install the nuts and tighten them to the torque listed in this Chapter's Specifications. Work up to it in three steps. **Note:** *Use a thin-wall socket to avoid erroneous torque readings that can result if the socket is wedged between the rod cap and nut. If the socket tends to wedge itself between the nut and the cap, lift up on it slighty until it no longer contacts the cap. Do not rotate the crankshaft at any time during this operation.*

16   Remove the nuts and detach the rod cap, being very careful not to disturb the Plastigage.

17   Compare the width of the crushed Plastigage to the scale printed on the Plastigage envelope to obtain the oil clearance **(see illustration)**. Compare it to this Chapter's Specifications to make sure the clearance is correct.

18   If the clearance is not as specified, the bearing inserts may be the wrong size (which means different ones will be required). Before deciding different inserts are needed, make sure no dirt or oil was between the bearing inserts and the connecting rod or cap when the clearance was measured. Also, recheck the journal diameter. If the Plastigage was wider at one end than the other, the journal may be tapered (refer to Section 20).

Final connecting rod installation

19   Carefully scrape all traces of the Plastigage material off the rod journal and/or bearing face. Be very careful not to scratch the bearing – use your fingernail or the edge of a credit card.

20   Make sure the bearing faces are perfectly clean, then apply a uniform layer of clean moly-base grease or engine assembly lube to both of them. You'll have to push the piston into the cylinder to expose the face of the bearing insert in the connecting rod – be sure to slip the protective hoses over the rod bolts first.

21   Slide the connecting rod back into place on the journal, remove the

protective hoses from the rod cap bolts, install the rod cap and tighten the nuts to the torque specified in this Chapter. Again, work up to the torque in three steps.

22   Repeat the entire procedure for the remaining pistons/connecting rods.

23   The important points to remember are . . .

   a) Keep the back sides of the bearing inserts and the insides of the connecting rods and caps perfectly clean when assembling them.
   b) Make sure you have the correct piston/rod assembly for each cylinder.
   c) The arrow or mark on the piston must face the front (timing belt or chain end) of the engine.
   d) Lubricate the cylinder walls with clean oil.
   e) Lubricate the bearing faces when installing the rod caps after the oil clearance has been checked.

24   After all the piston/connecting rod assemblies have been properly installed, rotate the crankshaft a number of times by hand to check for any obvious binding.

25   As a final step, the connecting rod endplay must be checked. Refer to Section 14 for this procedure.

26   Compare the measured endplay to this Chapter's Specifications to make sure it's correct. If it was correct before disassembly and the original crankshaft and rods were reinstalled, it should still be right. If new rods or a new crankshaft were installed, the endplay may be inadequate. If so, the rods will have to be removed and taken to an automotive machine shop for resizing.

---

28   Initial start-up and break-in after overhaul

Warning: *Have a fire extinguisher handy when starting the engine for the first time.*

1   Once the engine has been installed in the vehicle, double-check the oil and coolant levels.

2   With the spark plugs out of the engine and the "engine" fuse removed, crank the engine until oil pressure registers on the gauge or the light goes out.

3   Install the spark plugs, hook up the plug wires and install the "engine" fuse.

4   Start the engine. It may take a few moments for the fuel system to build up pressure, but the engine should start without a great deal of effort. **Note:** *If the engine keeps backfiring, recheck the valve timing and spark plug wires.*

5   After the engine starts, it should be allowed to warm up to normal operating temperature. While the engine is warming up, make a thorough check for fuel, oil and coolant leaks.

6   Shut the engine off and recheck the engine oil and coolant levels.

7   Drive the vehicle to an area with minimum traffic, accelerate at full throttle from 30 to 50 mph, then allow the vehicle to slow to 30 mph with the throttle closed. Repeat the procedure 10 or 12 times. This will load the piston rings and cause them to seat properly against the cylinder walls. Check again for oil and coolant leaks.

8   Drive the vehicle gently for the first 500 miles (no sustained high speeds) and keep a constant check on the oil level. It's not unusual for an engine to use oil during the break-in period.

9   At approximately 500 to 600 miles, change the oil and filter.

10   For the next few hundred miles, drive the vehicle normally. Don't pamper it or abuse it.

11   After 2000 miles, change the oil and filter again and consider the engine broken in.

Chapter 3   Cooling, heating and air conditioning systems

Contents

Specifications

General

Drivebelt tension	See Chapter 1
Thermostat opening temperature (all models)	182 to 188-degrees F

Torque specifications

Ft-lbs

Thermostat cover	
Four-cylinder engine	14 to 22
V6 engine	8 to 10
Water pump mounting bolts	
Four-cylinder engine	14 to 19
V6 engine	15 to 22

1   General information

Engine cooling system

The Probe is equipped with a pressurized engine cooling system with an electric cooling fan that's controlled by an engine mounted coolant temperature switch.

The electric cooling fan system consists of a two-speed fan on all four-cylinder engines equipped with an automatic transaxle or a one-speed fan on all four-cylinder engines with a manual transaxle, and an electric motor attached to a fan shroud located behind the radiator. On V6 engines, the fan is controlled by the ECA. On air conditioned models, an additional fan is mounted ahead of the condenser.

A water pump, driven by the crankshaft through the timing belt on four-cylinder models and by a drivebelt on V6 engines, moves coolant through the engine. The coolant flows around each cylinder and toward the rear of the engine. Cast-in passages direct coolant around the intake and exhaust ports, the spark plug areas and the exhaust valve guides.

The thermostat is located in a housing at the transaxle-end of the engine. During warm-up, the closed thermostat prevents coolant from circulating through the radiator. As the engine nears normal operating temperature, the thermostat opens and allows coolant to travel through the radiator, where it's cooled before returning to the engine.

The radiator is a cross-flow type with vacuum brazed aluminum fins and tubes. The end tanks are made of nylon. Radiator and fan shroud mounting brackets are an integral part of the tank's design. Because of its construction, the radiator cannot be serviced by the home mechanic. If it's damaged, it must be taken to a radiator shop.

Heating system

The heating system consists of a blower fan and heater core located inside the dashboard, the heater hoses connecting the heater core to the engine cooling system and the heater/air conditioning control assembly on the dashboard.

Hot engine coolant is circulated through the heater core at all times. When the heater is activated, a flap door opens to expose the heater box to the passenger compartment. A fan switch on the control panel activates the blower motor, which forces air through the core, heating the air.

Air conditioning system

The air conditioning system consists of a condenser mounted in front of the radiator, an evaporator mounted inside the heater/air conditioner duct inside the dashboard, a compressor mounted on the engine, an engine compartment mounted accumulator (filter-drier), containing a high-pressure relief valve, and the plumbing connecting all the components.

The blower fan forces the warmer air of the passenger compartment through the evaporator core (sort of a radiator-in-reverse), transferring the heat from the air to the refrigerant. The liquid refrigerant boils off into low pressure vapor, taking the heat with it when it leaves the evaporator.

2   Antifreeze – general information

Warning: *Do not allow antifreeze to come in contact with your skin or painted surfaces of the vehicle. Rinse off spills immediately with plenty of water. Antifreeze is highly toxic if ingested. Never leave antifreeze lying around in an open container or in puddles on the floor; children and pets are attracted by it's sweet smell and may drink it. Check with local authorities about disposing of used antifreeze. Many communities have collection centers which will see that antifreeze is disposed of safely.*

The cooling system should be filled with a water/ethylene glycol based antifreeze solution which will prevent freezing down to at least -20 degrees F. It also provides protection against corrosion and increases the coolant boiling point.

The cooling system should be drained, flushed and refilled at least every other year (see Chapter 1). The use of antifreeze solutions for periods longer than two years could result in damage from the formation of rust and scale in the system.

Before adding coolant to the system, check all hose connections and fittings – antifreeze can leak through very minute openings.

The ideal mixture of antifreeze to water which you should use depends on the relative weather conditions. The mixture should contain at least 50-percent antifreeze, but never more than 70-percent antifreeze.

3   Thermostat – replacement

Refer to illustrations 3.3, 3.4, 3.6, 3.7 and 3.9

Removal

1   Disconnect the cable from the negative terminal of the battery.
2   Drain the cooling system (see Chapter 1). If the coolant is in good condition, save it for refilling the system.
3   If you're working on a four-cylinder engine, move the spark plug wires aside, then disconnect the wire from the temperature sensor located in the thermostat housing **(see illustration)**. In addition, on turbo models, remove the brace from the turbo outlet hose.
4   On V6 models, remove the nut which secures the wiring harness bracket, then the ground wire and bracket **(see illustration)**.
5   Loosen the hose clamp and disconnect the upper radiator hose from the thermostat housing.
6   Remove the mounting bolts/nuts **(see illustration)** and detach the thermostat housing. **Note:** *If the housing is difficult to remove, tap it gently with a soft-face hammer or a piece of wood. Don't try to pry the housing loose, or damage to the gasket sealing surfaces could occur and leaks may develop.*
7   If the thermostat is still in the V6 engine thermostat housing, rotate it counterclockwise to remove it **(see illustration)**. If it's stuck, carefully pry it loose with a small screwdriver.

Installation

8   Remove all gasket material and old sealant from the mating surfaces of the housing and cylinder head, then clean them with a cloth saturated with lacquer thinner or acetone.

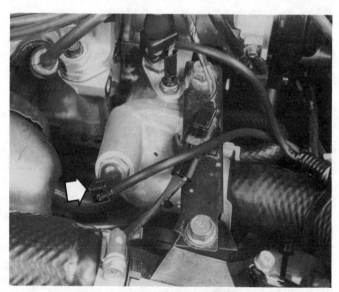

3.3   On four-cylinder engines, disconnect the wire from the temperature sensor

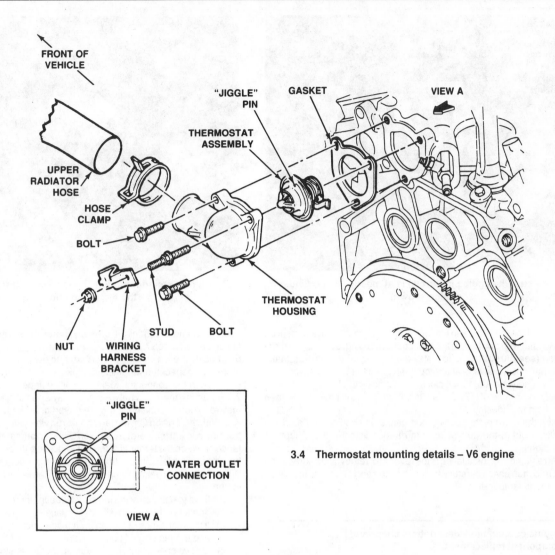

3.4 Thermostat mounting details – V6 engine

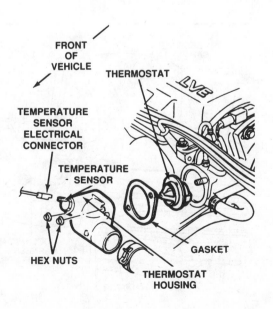

3.6 Thermostat mounting details – four-cylinder engine

3.7 To remove the thermostat from the V6 engine, turn it counterclockwise (place a shop rag over the frame to prevent cutting your fingers)

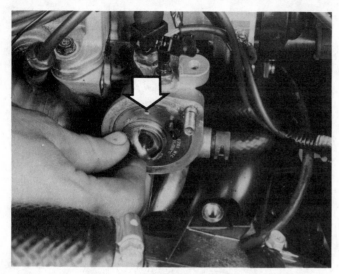

3.9   Be sure the jiggle pin (arrow) is at the top (four-cylinder engine shown)

4.2   On four-cylinder models the fan switch (arrow) is located in the thermostat housing

9   To install the thermostat in the four-cylinder engine, align the mark on the thermostat with the mark in the water outlet housing, so the jiggle pin is at the top **(see illustration)**. To install the V6 engine thermostat, make sure the ball check valve is at the top, then push the thermostat into the water outlet housing and turn it clockwise to lock it in place.

10   Apply a thin layer of RTV sealant to both sides of the new gasket, then position it on the housing.

11   Place the thermostat housing and gasket in position and start the nuts/bolts. Tighten the nuts/bolts to the torque listed in this Chapter's specifications.

12   The remainder of installation is the reverse of removal. Be sure to add coolant and then check carefully for leaks as the engine warms up to normal operating temperature.

---

4   Engine cooling fan – description, check and component replacement

Warning: *To avoid possible injury or damage, DO NOT operate the engine with the hood open until the fan has been examined for cracks or damage. Never attempt to repair a fan with damaged blades – replace it.*

Description

Refer to illustration 4.2

1   The cooling fan is wired so that it operates only when the ignition switch is in the Run position. It cannot operate after the ignition switch is turned to the Off position. **Warning:** *Disconnect the cable from the negative terminal of the battery prior to performing any work near the fan, since the fan could cycle if the ignition switch is left in the On position, even though the engine is not running.*

2   On four-cylinder models, a fan switch **(see illustration)** activates a cooling fan relay that turns the fan on when coolant temperature reaches 97-degrees C. It may also come on when the air conditioner is running. The high speed fan relay turns the fan on at high speed (automatic transaxle models only) if the engine temperature is higher than desirable and the fan has been operating at low speed.

3   On V6 models, the cooling fan is controlled during vehicle operation by the integrated relay control assembly and the EEC-IV module.

Check

Refer to illustrations 4.5 and 4.9

4   Because the V6 electric cooling fan motor circuit is under the control of the "integrated relay control assembly," which in turn is controlled by the EEC-IV system, a complete test of this system is beyond the scope of the

average home mechanic. However, there are several things you can check on all models.

5   Locate the fan motor electrical connectors **(see illustration)**. Unplug them and inspect the terminals to make sure they are free of corrosion.

6   Plug in the connector. Make sure it's plugged in securely.

7   Examine the wires between the relay and the fan to make sure that they're in good condition. If they're frayed or broken, repair them.

8   With the ignition On, the fan should run when the wire is disconnected from the coolant temperature sensor. Using an ohmmeter, check the resistance between the terminal of the fan switch (on V6 engines it's located by the thermostat housing, with a grey single pin connector) and ground. When the coolant gets hot, the resistance of the fan switch terminal should increase.

    a)   If the resistance of the fan switch doesn't increase when the coolant heats up, the switch is bad. Replace it.

    b)   If the resistance of the fan switch does increase, the switch is okay and the fan should come on.

    c)   On two speed fans, check the fan motor resistor (usually mounted on the fan shroud) for continuity and resistance. Replace it if it is open.

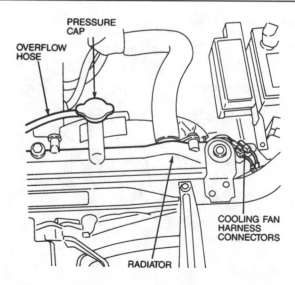

4.5   Unplug the fan motor electrical connectors

4.9   Run power directly from the battery to the fan with fused jumper wires

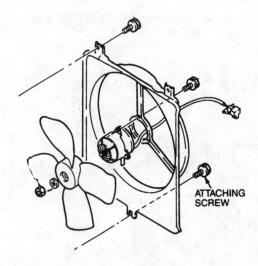

4.14   Engine cooling fan – exploded view

ATTACHING SCREW

9   If the fan motor still doesn't come on, the motor itself may be faulty. Unplug the motor electrical connectors and attach a pair of fused jumper wires between the fan motor terminals and the battery terminals **(see illustration)**. If the fan motor still doesn't work, replace it.

10   If the fan does come on when energized by the battery, two possibilities exist:

   a) There is an open in the circuit somewhere between the fan switch, the computer (V6 only), the control relays and the motor, in which case you can often troubleshoot the problem with a test light or continuity tester, using the wiring diagrams at the end of this book.

   b) If the circuits check out OK, there may a problem with either the integrated relay control assembly or with the computer itself (V6 only). Take the vehicle to a dealer service department and have the system diagnosed and repaired.

Component replacement

Refer to illustrations 4.14, 4.15 and 4.16

11   Detach the cable from the negative terminal of the battery.

12   If you haven't already done so, unplug the fan motor electrical connectors.

13   Drain the cooling system (see Chapter 1) and remove the upper radiator hose.

14   To detach the fan/shroud assembly from the radiator, remove the screws at the perimeter of the shroud **(see illustration)**, then lift the fan/shroud assembly from the radiator. **Note:** *It may be necessary to tilt the assembly slightly to clear assorted engine components when lifting it out.*

15   Place the fan/shroud assembly on a workbench with the fan facing up. Remove the retaining nut **(see illustration)** and remove the fan.

16   Remove the fan motor mounting screws and detach the motor from the shroud assembly **(see illustration)**.

17   Installation is the reverse of removal.

---

5   Radiator – removal and installation

Refer to illustrations 5.3, 5.5, 5.6a, 5.6b, 5.6c, 5.7a and 5.7b

Removal

1   Detach the cable from the negative terminal of the battery.

2   Drain the coolant from the radiator (see Chapter 1).

4.15   Remove the fan retaining nut (arrow)

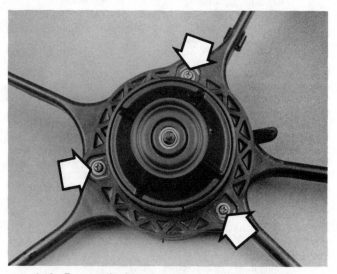

4.16   Remove the fan motor mounting screws (arrows)

5.3   Radiator attachments

1   *Upper hose*   3   *Electrical connector*
2   *Overflow hose*

5.5   Unplug the sensor wiring and detach the hose from the bottom of the radiator (arrows)

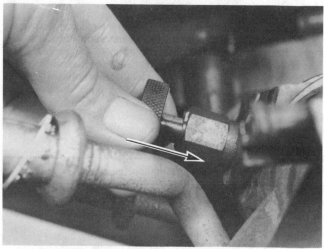

5.6a   Some transaxle cooler line fittings must be detached with Cooler Line Disconnect Tool T82L-9500-AH, or equivalvent – simply insert the tool as far as it will go into each fitting as shown . . .

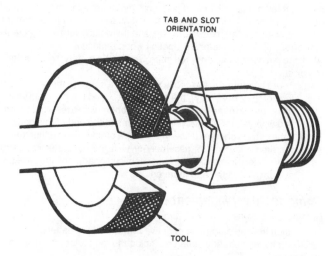

TAB AND SLOT
ORIENTATION

TOOL

5.6b   . . .with the slot on the knurled flange of the tool aligned with the tab on the edge of the fitting bore, . . .

3   Loosen the hose clamp and detach the upper hose from the radiator **(see illustration)**.
4   Detach the overflow hose from the radiator filler neck.
5   Unplug the sensor wiring **(see illustration)** and the fan wire harness and set it aside. Loosen the hose clamp and detach the lower hose from the radiator.
6   If your vehicle is equipped with an automatic transaxle, disconnect the transaxle cooler line fittings. **Note:** *Some vehicles are equipped with special oil cooler line fittings which must be detached with Cooler Line Disconnect Tool T82L-9500-AH* **(see illustrations)**. Cap the fittings and the lines to prevent leakage.
7   Remove the four nuts attaching the radiator hold-down brackets **(see illustrations)**. Lift the radiator and fan assembly from the vehicle as a unit.

Installation

8   Inspect the mounting bushings for damage. Replace if necessary.
9   Installation is the reverse of removal. Make sure the bottom of the radiator is seated properly.

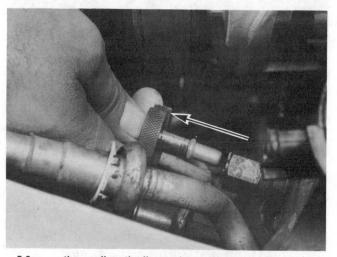

5.6c   . . .then pull on the line and separate it from the fitting

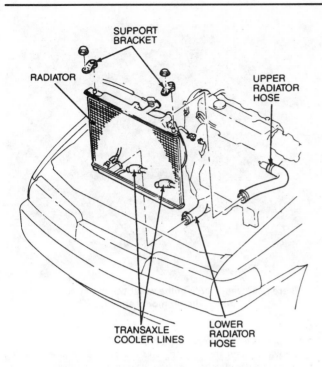

5.7b Remove the two nuts (arrows) from the hold-down bracket on each side of the radiator

5.7a Radiator mounting details – exploded view

10   When installation is complete, add coolant to the system (see Chapter 1).

6   Coolant temperature sending unit – replacement

Refer to illustrations 6.2a and 6.2b

Note: *Make sure the engine is completely cool before beginning this procedure. Also, refer to Chapter 1 and drain about 1 quart of coolant out of the radiator.*

1   Detach the cable from the negative terminal of the battery.
2   Locate the temperature sending unit on the left end (driver's side) of the intake manifold, by the thermostat housing (V6 engines), or adjacent to the thermostat housing on four-cylinder engines **(see illustrations)**.
3   Unplug the electrical connector from the sending unit.
4   Wrap the threads of the new sending unit with teflon tape to prevent leaks.
5   Remove the sending unit and quickly install the new one.
6   Tighten the sending unit securely and reconnect the wiring.

7   Coolant reservoir – removal and installation

Refer to illustration 7.2

1   Remove the coolant hose and cap assembly from the reservoir.

6.2a   On V6 engines, the coolant temperature sending unit is adjacent to the thermostat housing (arrow), at the left end of the intake manifold

6.2b   On four-cylinder engines, the coolant temperature sending unit is located adjacent to the thermostat housing (arrow)

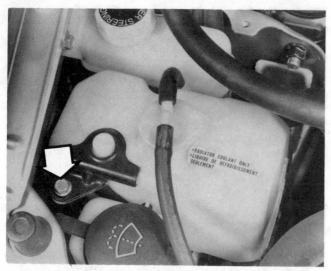

7.2   Remove the bolt (arrow) from the coolant reservoir hold-down bracket

8.3   There is a "weep" hole in the water pump housing (arrow) – four-cylinder model shown

2   Remove the mounting bolt **(see illustration)** and lift the reservoir from the engine compartment.

3   Temporarily pour the coolant into a properly labeled container. Clean the reservoir and inspect it for cracks and damage. Replace as necessary.

4   Installation is the reverse of removal.

8   Water pump – check

Refer to illustrations 8.3 and 8.4

1   A failure in the water pump can cause overheating and serious engine damage, because a defective pump will not circulate coolant through the engine.

2   There are two ways to check the operation of the water pump while it's in place on the engine. If either check indicates that the pump is defective, replace it with a new or rebuilt unit.

3   The water pump body has a "weep" hole in the side **(see illustration)**. If the pump seal fails, small amounts of coolant will leak out of the hole. You'll need to get underneath the water pump to see the hole, so raise the vehicle and place it securely on jackstands. Use a flashlight to help deter-

mine if coolant is leaking from the pump.

4   If the water pump shaft bearing fails it will usually make a howling sound (don't confuse drivebelt slippage, which makes a squealing sound, with water pump bearing failure). Even before the bearing actually fails, shaft wear can be detected by grasping the pulley firmly and moving it up and down **(see illustration)**. If excessive play is noted, the shaft and/or bearing are worn and the pump should be replaced.

9   Water pump – removal and installation

Four-cylinder engines

Refer to illustrations 9.4, 9.5 and 9.6

Removal

1   Detach the cable from the negative terminal of the battery.

2   Drain the engine coolant (see Chapter 1).

3   Remove the timing belt (see Chapter 2A).

4   Remove the water pump bolts **(see illustration)** and detach the pump.

8.4   With the timing belt (or drivebelt on V6 models) removed, the bearing can be checked for roughness and play

9.4   Remove the water pump mounting bolts (four-cylinder engine)

9.5   Scrape off all traces of old gasket material

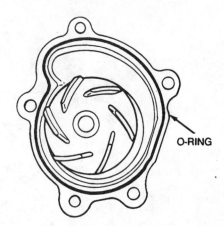

9.6   Some models use an O-ring to seal the pump to the block, others use a gasket

Installation
5   Make sure the mating surface of the engine block and the water pump are clean and free of gasket material (see illustration).
6   Position a new O-ring seal or gasket on the water pump (see illustration), then position the water pump assembly on the block.
7   Install the bolts and tighten them to the torque listed in this Chapter's specifications.
8   The remainder of installation is the reverse of removal.

V6 engines
Refer to illustrations 9.11, 9.15 and 9.16

Removal
9   Detach the cable from the negative terminal of the battery.
10   Drain the engine coolant (see Chapter 1).
11   Loosen the four water pump pulley bolts (see illustration). Note: *Be sure the water pump pulley bolts are loosened before the drivebelt is removed.*

12   Remove the drivebelt (see Chapter 1).
13   Loosen the hose clamps and disconnect the upper radiator and heater hoses from the water pump.
14   Detach the lower radiator hose from the water pump steel tube.
15   Remove the steel tube brace bolt from the water pump mounting bracket (see illustration).

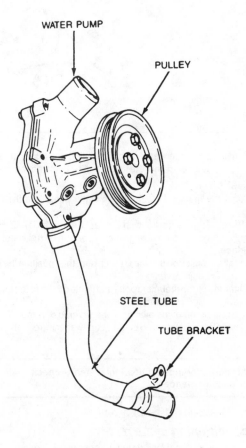

9.15   V6 water pump and steel tube

9.11   Be sure to loosen the water pump pulley bolts before removing the drivebelt – note that there is insufficient clearance to actually remove the pulley, which must remain in place until the water pump assembly is removed from the engine compartment

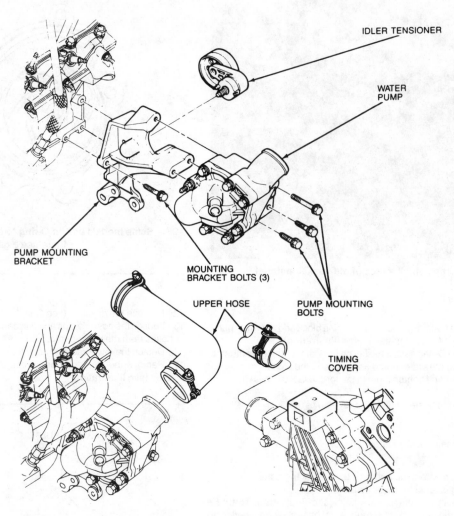

9.16   V6 water pump mounting details

16   Remove the three water pump mounting bolts **(see illustration)**.
17   Lift the water pump from the timing chain cover and remove the pulley.

Installation

18   Clean the mating surfaces of the water pump and the timing chain cover.
19   After coating the gasket with Contact Adhesive (D7AZ-19B508-A or the equivalent), place the new gasket in position on the water pump sealing surface.
20   Install the pulley on the water pump hub, then position the water pump on the timing chain cover.
21   Install the pump mounting bolts and tighten them to the torque listed in this Chapter's Specifications.
22   The remainder of installation is the reverse of removal.
23   Tighten the pulley-to-hub bolts securely after the drivebelt is installed.

---

10   Air conditioning and heating system – check and maintenance

---

Refer to illustrations 10.4, 10.7 and 10.11

Air conditioning system

Warning: *The air conditioning system is under high pressure. Do not loosen any hose fittings or remove any components until after the system has* *been discharged by a dealer service department or an automotive air conditioning shop. And always wear eye protection when disconnecting air conditioning system fittings.*

1   The following maintenance checks should be performed on a regular basis to ensure that the air conditioner continues to operate at peak efficiency.
   a) Inspect the tension and condition of the compressor drivebelt. If it is worn or deteriorated, replace it (see Chapter 1).
   b) Inspect the system hoses. Look for cracks, bubbles, hardening and deterioration. Inspect the hoses and all fittings for oil bubbles or seepage. If there is any evidence of wear, damage or leakage, replace the hose(s).
   c) Inspect the condenser fins for leaves, bugs and any other foreign material that may have embedded itself in the fins. Use a "fin comb" or compressed air to remove debris from the condenser.
   d) Make sure the system has the correct refrigerant charge.
2   It's a good idea to operate the system for about 10 minutes at least once a month. This is particularly important during the winter months because long term non-use can cause hardening, and subsequent failure, of the seals.
3   Because of the complexity of the air conditioning system and the special equipment necessary to service it, in depth troubleshooting and repairs are beyond the scope of this manual. However, simple checks and component replacement procedures are provided in this Chapter.

10.4   Measure the output air temperature at the center vent – it should be about 45-degrees F (slightly higher if the ambient air temperature and/or the relative humidity are higher)

10.7   Check for a temperature differential between the evaporator inlet and the accumulator housing

4   The most common cause of poor cooling is simply a low system refrigerant charge. If a noticeable drop in system cooling ability occurs **(see illustration)**, one of the following quick checks will help you determine whether the refrigerant level is low.

5   Warm up the engine to its normal operating temperature.

6   Place the air conditioning temperature selector at its coldest setting and put the blower at its highest setting. Open the doors (to make sure that the air conditioning system doesn't cycle off as soon as it cools the passenger compartment).

7   With the compressor engaged – the clutch will make an audible click and the center of the clutch will rotate – feel the evaporator inlet pipe between the orifice and the accumulator with one hand while placing your other hand on the surface of the accumulator housing **(see illustration)**.

8   If both surfaces feel about the same temperature and if both feel a little cooler than the surrounding air, the refrigerant level is probably okay. Further inspection of the system is beyond the scope of this manual (refer to the *Haynes Automotive Heating & Air Conditioning* manual).

9   If the inlet pipe has frost accumulation or feels cooler than the accumulator surface, the refrigerant charge is low. Add refrigerant as described below.

Adding refrigerant

10   Buy an automotive charging kit at an automotive parts store. A charging kit includes a 14-ounce can of refrigerant, a tap valve and a short section of hose which can be attached between the tap valve and the system low side service valve. Because one can of refrigerant may not be sufficient to bring the system charge up to its proper level, it's a good idea to buy a couple additional cans. Make sure the first can contains red refrigerant dye. If the system is leaking, the red dye will leak out with the refrigerant and help you pinpoint the location of the leak. Never add more than three cans.

11   Connect the charging kit by following the manufacturer's instructions **(see illustration). Warning:** *DO NOT connect the charging kit hose to the high side of the system. Wear eye protection.*

12   Warm up the engine and operate the system.

13   Add refrigerant to the low side of the system until both the accumulator surface and the evaporator inlet pipe feel about the same temperature. Allow stabilization time between each refrigerant addition. Once the accumulator surface and the evaporator inlet pipe feel about the same temperature, add the contents remaining in the can.

Heating system

14   If the air coming out of the dashboard heater vents isn't hot, the problem could stem from any of the following causes:

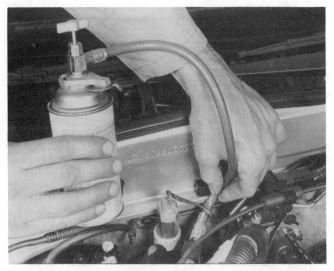

10.11   Connect the charging hose to the low side port near the firewall

a)   The thermostat is stuck open, preventing the engine coolant from warming up enough to carry heat to the heater core. Replace the thermostat (see Section 3).

b)   A heater hose is blocked, preventing the flow of coolant through the heater core. Feel both heater hoses at the firewall. They should be hot. If one of them is cold, there is an obstruction in one of the hoses or in the heater core itself, or the valve itself is shut. Detach the hoses and back flush it with a water hose.

c)   If the heater still fails to put out hot air, remove the heater core (see Section 13) and have it professionally back flushed. If flushing fails to remove the blockage from the heater core, the core must be replaced. Most radiator shops will not repair heater cores.

15   If the blower motor speed does not correspond to the setting selected on the blower switch, either the fuse is bad, the switch is bad, the blower motor resistor is burned out or the motor is bad.

a)   Before checking the blower motor or circuit, always check the fuse first.

b)   Check voltage at the blower motor.

11.2   Gently pry the trim plate off

11.3   Remove the mounting screws (arrows)

c) Pull the heating/air conditioning control assembly (see next Section) far enough from the dash to verify, with a test light or voltmeter, that current is reaching the blower switch on the control assembly. If the switch is not getting current, troubleshoot the circuit between the battery and the switch (see the wiring diagrams at the end of this manual).
d) Locate the blower motor resistor behind the glove box (see Section 12). Check the resistor to make sure that it is getting current from the blower switch.
   1) If the resistor is not getting current, check the wire.
   2) If the wire is good, replace the switch (see Section 11).
e) Using a test light or voltmeter, verify that the blower motor is getting current. If the blower motor is not getting current, test the resistor (see Section 12).

16   If there isn't any air coming out of the vents, place your ear at the heating/air conditioning vent nearest the blower motor, and listen. Most motors are audible. Can you hear the motor running?
   a) If you can't (and have already verified that the blower switch and the blower motor resistor are good), the blower motor itself is probably bad. Replace it (see Section 12). **Note:** *You can determine the motor's condition by connecting a fused jumper wire directly between the battery and the blower motor.*
   b) If you can hear the motor running, the vacuum operated doors may not be operating properly. If air comes different ducts when the engine is accelerated (lower intake vacuum), check the vacuum lines from the engine to the back side of the heating and air conditioning control assembly and from there to the servos to be sure that they're tightly attached. Further testing of the vacuum system for the doors is beyond the scope of this manual. Have the system diagnosed by a dealer service department.

17   If the carpet under the heater core is damp, or if antifreeze vapor or steam is coming through the vents, the heater core is leaking. Remove it (see Section 13) and install a new unit (most radiator shops will not repair a leaking heater core).

---

11   Heater and air conditioning control assembly – removal and installation

Note: *The following procedures apply only to vehicles with a heater (but no air conditioning) and to vehicles with a manual heating/air conditioning system. The functional tests for electronically controlled heating and air conditioning systems are beyond the scope of the average home mechanic.*

Control assembly
Refer to illustrations 11.2, 11.3, 11.4a, 11.4b, 11.5, 11.6, 11.7 and 11.9

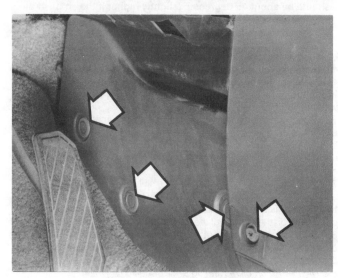

11.4a   Remove the screws (arrows) from the left console side panel

1   Detach the cable from the negative terminal of the battery.
2   Remove the trim plate **(see illustration)**.
3   Remove the four screws attaching the control assembly to the instrument panel **(see illustration)**.
4   Remove the console side panels **(see illustrations)**.
5   Remove the REC/FRESH control cable at the selector door assembly **(see illustration)**.
6   Disconnect the temperature control cable from the temperature blend door assembly at the right side of the heater case **(see illustration)**.
7   Remove the function selector cable from the function control door assembly at the left side of the heater case **(see illustration)**.
8   Pull the control assembly and cables from the instrument panel opening as a unit. Note the routing of the cables to ease reassembly.
9   Detach the electrical connectors from the back of the control assembly **(see illustration)**.
10   Installation is the reverse of removal. Check the operation of all controls before final installation.

Blower switch
Refer to illustrations 11.12, 11.13 and 11.15

11   Remove the control assembly as described above.
12   Remove the fan switch knob from the switch shaft by pulling it off the shaft **(see illustration)**.

11.4b Remove the screws (arrows) from the right console side panel

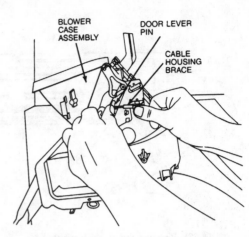

11.5 The REC/FRESH cable is on the right side of the console

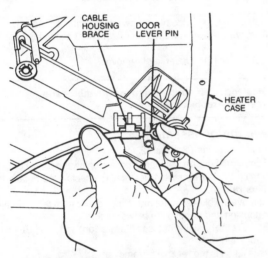

11.6 Disconnect the temperature control cable

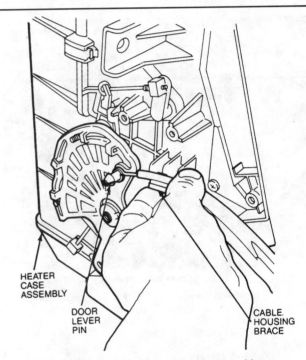

11.7 Detach the function selector cable

11.9 Pull the control assembly out of the dash as far as possible and detach the cables and wiring connectors (arrows)

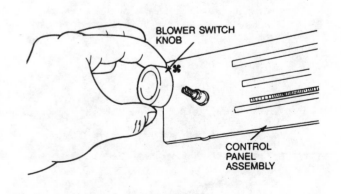

11.12 Pull off the knob

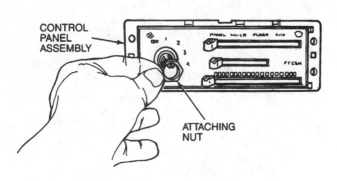

11.13   Remove the attaching nut

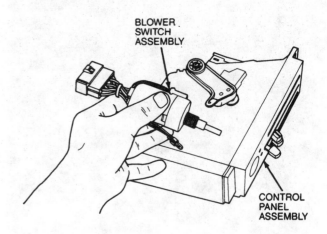

11.15   **Pull the switch out of the back of the control panel assembly**

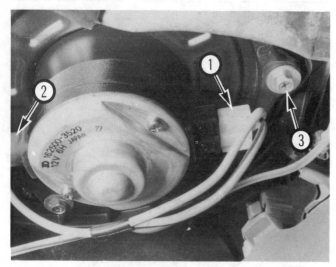

12.2   **Blower motor details**

1   Electrical connector   *3   Mounting screw*
2   Hose

13   Remove the attaching nut from the blower switch shaft **(see illustration)**.
14   Detach the male side blower switch electrical connector.
15   Remove the switch from the control panel assembly **(see illustration)**.
16   Installation is the reverse of removal.

12   Heater and air conditioning blower motor and resistor – replacement

Blower motor assembly
Refer to illustrations 12.2 and 12.4
1   Remove the under dash panel located below the glove compartment.
2   Unplug the blower motor electrical connector and detach the hose **(see illustration)**.
3   Remove the blower motor mounting screws from the perimeter of the motor housing and remove the blower motor.
4   Remove the retaining nut **(see illustration)** and pull the blower fan off the motor shaft.
5   Installation is the reverse of removal.

12.4   **Remove the retaining nut (arrow) and pull the blower fan off the motor shaft**

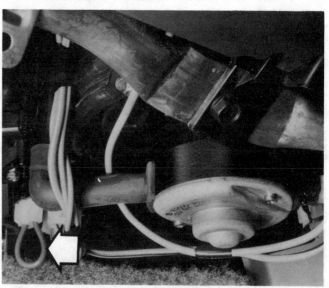

12.7   **The blower resistor (arrow) is located adjacent to the blower motor**

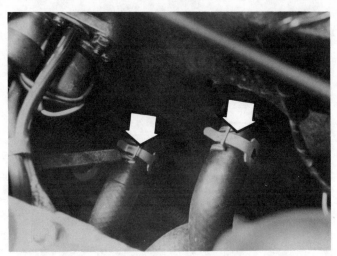

13.3 Detach the heater hoses (arrows) from the heater core at the firewall

Blower motor resistor

Refer to illustration 12.7

6   Detach the cable from the negative terminal of the battery.

7   To access the blower motor resistor and thermal limiter assembly, remove the underdash cover located below the glove compartment. The blower motor resistor and thermal limiter assembly **(see illustration)** is installed on the heater case, to the left of the blower.

8   Unplug the electrical connector from the resistor assembly and remove the resistor from the heater case.

9   Installation is the reverse of removal.

---

13   Heater core – replacement

Refer to illustrations 13.3, 13.5, 13.7, 13.8, 13.9a and 13.9b

Note: *If the vehicle is equipped with air conditioning, have the system dis-*

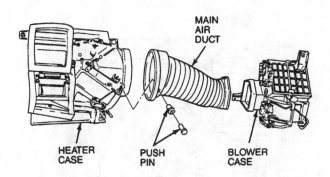

13.5   Remove the main air duct from the heater case

---

charged by a dealer service department or service station before beginning this procedure.

1   Detach the cable from the negative terminal of the battery.

2   Drain the engine coolant (see Chapter 1).

3   Working in the engine compartment, loosen the hose clamps and detach the heater hoses from the heater core at the firewall **(see illustration)**. Blow any coolant from the heater core with low-pressure air and plug the heater core tubes.

4   Remove the dash trim panels and instrument panel (see Chapter 11).

5   Remove the main air duct from the heater case **(see illustration)**.

Air conditioned models only

6   Remove the evaporative emissions canister for access (see Chapter 6), then disconnect and plug the refrigerant lines at the evaporator (see Chapter 4, Section 3 for spring lock coupling instructions). Disconnect the evaporator drain hose.

All models

7   Detach the ventilation ducts from the heater housing **(see illustration)**.

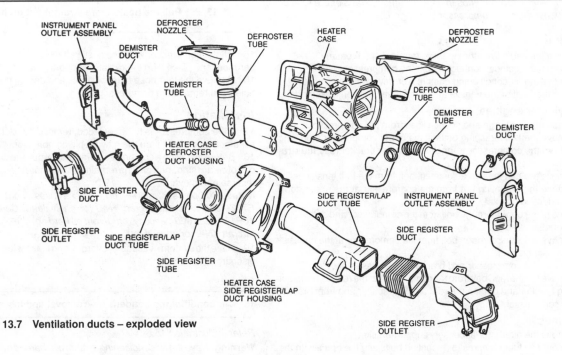

13.7   Ventilation ducts – exploded view

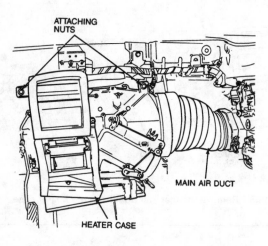

13.8   Remove the heater case attaching nuts

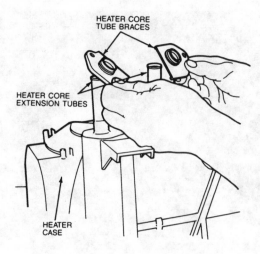

13.9a   Remove the heater core braces

8   Remove the heater case attaching nuts **(see illustration)**. Carefully pull the heater case away from the dash panel and remove it from the vehicle.

9   Remove the heater core tube braces and lift the heater core from the heater case **(see illustrations)**.

10   Installation is the reverse of removal. Check the operation of all levers and flaps prior to installation.

11   Add coolant and check the heating system for proper operation.

12   Have the air conditioning system evacuated, charged and leak tested by the shop that discharged it.

---

14   Air conditioning compressor – removal and installation

Refer to illustrations 14.6 and 14.14

Warning: *Have the air conditioning system discharged by a dealer service department or service station before beginning this procedure.*

Note: *The factory recommends that the accumulator and orifice tube be replaced whenever the compressor is changed.*

Removal

1   Detach the cable from the negative terminal of the battery.

2   Unplug the electrical connector from the compressor clutch.

3   Remove the air conditioning compressor drivebelt (see Chapter 1).

4   Raise the front of the vehicle and place it securely on jackstands.

Four cylinder engines

5   Detach the discharge and suction lines from the compressor.

6   Remove the two attaching bolts at the upper compressor mounting bracket from the compressor-to-engine mounting bracket **(see illustration)**.

7   Remove the belt tension adjustment bolt from the belt tensioner.

8   Remove the mounting nut from the compressor at the upper compressor mounting bracket.

9   Remove the upper through bolt from the compressor and detach the upper mounting bracket.

10   Remove the lower through bolt from the compressor at the chassis-to-compressor bracket.

11   Remove the compressor and brackets as an assembly.

12   Remove the through bolt from the compressor at the rear compressor mounting bracket and detach the rear bracket, spacer and front bracket from the compressor.

V6 engines

13   Remove the alternator/accessory support bracket.

14   Remove the four compressor mounting bolts and the brace with the two upper mounting bolts **(see illustration)**.

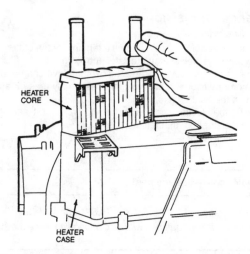

13.9b   Pull the heater core straight out of the case

15   Lift the compressor with hoses still attached out of the engine compartment and place it on the radiator support.

16   Remove the four hose manifold bolts and detach the lines. Plug the holes and remove the compressor.

Installation

17   If the compressor is to be replaced, remove the clutch and field coil assembly and install it on the new/rebuilt compressor.

18   Before installing a compressor, drain the oil out and add 100 ml (3.3 fl. oz.) of clean refrigerant oil. The remainder of compressor installation is the reverse of removal.

Note: *Compressor model no. 10P15 uses Ford refrigerant oil E73Z-19557-A or Motorcraft YN-9 (or equivalent). Compressor model 10P15A uses 500 viscosity refrigerant oil Ford no. C9AZ-19557-B or Motorcraft YN-2 (or equivalent).*

19   Have the system evacuated, charged and leak tested by the shop that discharged it.

---

15   Air conditioning condenser – removal and installation

Refer to illustration 15.6

Warning: *Have the air conditioning system discharged by a dealer service department or service station before beginning this procedure.*

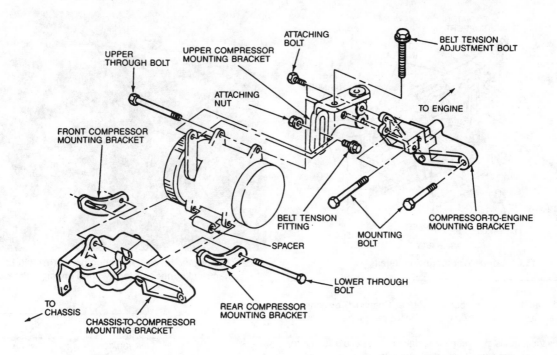

14.6 Air conditioning compressor mounting details – four-cylinder models

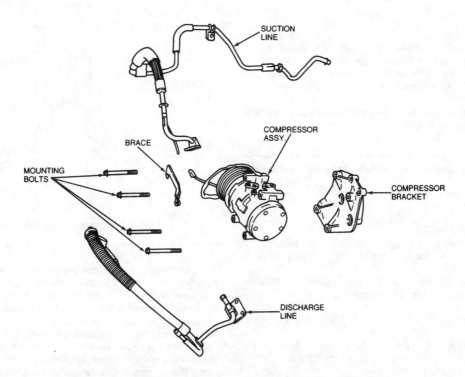

14.14 Air conditioning compressor mounting details – V6 models

Note: *The factory recommends that the accumulator be replaced whenever the condenser is changed. While you're at the dealer or repair shop, obtain a 1/2-inch spring lock coupling tool. This tool is inexpensive but absolutely essential because the system lines cannot be disconnected or reattached without it.*

Removal

1   Drain the cooling system (see Chapter 1).
2   Remove the electric cooling fan and shroud assembly (see Section 4).
3   Remove the radiator (see Section 5).

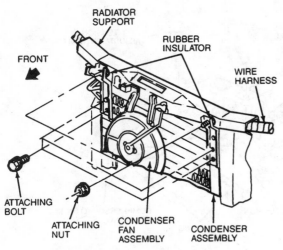

15.6 Condenser mounting details

16.2 To remove the clutch cycling pressure switch, unplug the electrical connector (arrow) and unscrew the switch

4   Using a 1/2-inch spring lock coupling tool (see Chapter 4), disconnect the two refrigerant lines from the condenser on the passenger side of the vehicle.

5   Unbolt the top mounts of the condenser fan (and intercooler, on turbo models) for access to the condenser mounting bolts.

6   Remove the bolts and nuts attaching the condenser to the radiator support **(see illustration)** and remove the condenser through the radiator opening.

Installation

7   Before installing the condenser, drain the oil out and add 30 ml (1.0 fl. oz.) of clean refrigerant oil. V6 models uses Ford refrigerant oil E73Z-19557-A or Motorcraft YN-9 (or equivalent). Four cylinder models use 500 viscosity refrigerant oil Ford no. C9AZ-19557-B or Motorcraft YN-2 (or equivalent). The remainder of installation is the reverse of removal.

8   The system must be evacuated, recharged and leak tested by a dealer service department or service station.

16 Air conditioning accumulator and pressure switch – removal and installation

Pressure switch

Refer to illustrations 16.2 and 16.3

1   Disconnect the cable from the negative terminal of the battery.

2   Unplug the electrical connector from the clutch cycling pressure switch **(see illustration)**.

3   Unscrew the pressure switch from the accumulator **(see illustration)**. **Note:** *It is not necessary to discharge the system to replace the switch.*

4   Lubricate the O-ring on the pressure switch fitting with clean refrigerant oil.

5   Screw the pressure switch onto the accumulator nipple. If the threaded fitting is plastic, tighten the switch finger tight. If the threaded fitting is metal, tighten the switch with a wrench.

6   Reattach the wire harness to the switch.

7   Verify proper operation of the switch (the compressor clutch should cycle on and off).

Accumulator

Warning: *Have the air conditioning refrigerant discharged by a dealer service department or service station before beginning this procedure. While you're at the dealer or repair shop, obtain a 1/2-inch spring lock coupling tool. This tool is inexpensive but absolutely essential because the system lines cannot be disconnected or reattached without it.*

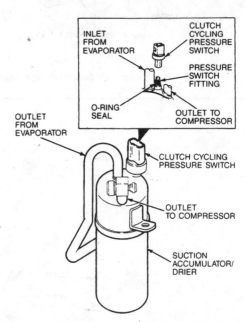

16.3 Clutch cycling pressure switch mounting details

8   Disconnect the cable from the negative terminal of the battery. Temporarily remove the evaporative emissions canister for accumulator access (see Chapter 6).

9   Unplug the electrical connector from the pressure switch on top of the accumulator **(see illustration 16.2)**.

10   Disconnect the refrigerant line at the top of the accumulator. Cap the ends to prevent contamination from dirt or moisture.

11   Using a spring lock coupling tool, disconnect the accumulator inlet tube at the evaporator. Cap the evaporator outlet and the accumulator inlet tube to prevent contamination from dirt or moisture.

12   Remove the mounting bolts and lift the accumulator from the engine compartment.

13   Installation is the reverse of removal. When replacing the accumulator, pour the oil out of it and add 30 ml (1 fl. oz.) of clean refrigerant oil. V6 models uses Ford refrigerant oil E73Z-19557-A or Motorcraft YN-9 (or equivalent). Four cylinder models use 500 viscosity refrigerant oil Ford no. C9AZ-19557-B or Motorcraft YN-2 (or equivalent). The remainder of installation is the reverse of removal. Have the system evacuated, recharged and leak tested by the shop that discharged it.

Chapter 4   Fuel and exhaust systems

Contents

Specifications

General
Fuel pressure (all) .... 34 to 40 psi

Torque specifications   **Ft-lbs** (unless otherwise indicated)
Fuel rail-to-intake manifold bolts
  Four-cylinder models .... 14 to 19
  V6 models .... 84 in-lbs
Intake plenum-to-intake manifold bolts (four-cylinder models) .... 14 to 19
Throttle body mounting nuts/bolts
  Four-cylinder models .... 14 to 19
  V6 models .... 15 to 22
Joint pipe-to-turbocharger bolts .... 27 to 46
Turbocharger-to-exhaust manifold bolts .... 20 to 29

---

1   General information

Fuel system

The fuel system consists of the fuel tank, the fuel pump, an air cleaner assembly, a fuel injection system and the various steel, plastic and/or nylon lines and fittings connecting everything together. The fuel pump is electric and is mounted inside the fuel tank.

Exhaust system

All vehicles are equipped with either a single exhaust manifold (four cylinder), or a pair of manifolds (V6), a catalytic converter, an exhaust pipe, a resonator and a muffler. The components of the exhaust system can be replaced separately. The three-way catalyst is mounted under the vehicle in the exhaust pipe (refer to Chapter 6 for further details regarding the catalytic converter).

Replacement exhaust systems may differ from the production system on your vehicle in the number of basic pieces used. The various components in the exhaust system bolt together at flanges.

---

2   Fuel pressure relief procedure

Refer to illustration 2.3

Warning: *Gasoline is extremely flammable, so take extra precautions when you work on any part of the fuel system. Don't smoke or allow open flames or bare light bulbs near the work area, and don't work in a garage where a natural gas-type appliance (such as a water heater or clothes dryer) with a pilot light is present. If you spill any fuel on your skin, rinse it off immediately with soap and water. When you perform any kind of work on the fuel tank, wear safety glasses and have a Class B type fire extinguisher on hand.*

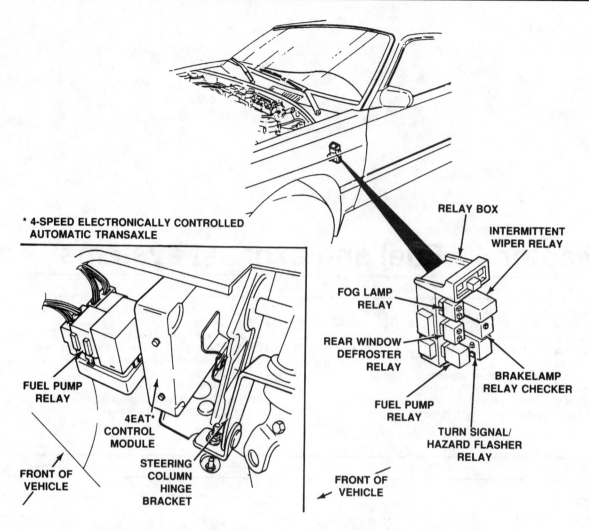

2.3   The fuel pump relay is located under the driver's side of the dashboard

1   The fuel pump relay affords a simple and convenient means by which fuel pressure can be relieved before servicing fuel injection components.
2   Start the engine and allow it to idle.
3   Disconnect the fuel pump relay **(see illustration)**.
4   After the engine stalls, turn the ignition switch OFF, then disconnect the cable from the negative terminal of the battery.
5   Wrap a rag around the fittings to protect yourself from fuel spray. See Section 3 for instructions on disconnecting fuel line fittings. **Warning:** *Wear eye protection!*
6   The fuel system pressure is now relieved. When finished working on the fuel system, simply plug the relay back in.
7   If your are willing to purchase, or have access to, Ford's Rotunda 014-0047 fuel pressure gauge (or equivalent) the fuel pressure on V6 models can be relieved through the Schrader valve on the fuel rail. **Warning:** *Never attempt to relieve the fuel pressure through the Schrader valve without the gauge attached – fuel will spray out under the high pressure and could cause serious injury or a fire!*

---

3   Fuel lines and fittings – repair and replacement

Warning: *The fuel system pressure must be relieved before disconnecting fuel lines and fittings (see Section 2). Gasoline is extremely flammable, so take extra precautions when you work on any part of the fuel system. Don't smoke or allow open flames or bare light bulbs near the work area,*

and don't work in a garage where a natural gas-type appliance (such as a water heater or clothes dryer) with a pilot light is present. If you spill any fuel on your skin, rinse it off immediately with soap and water. When you perform any kind of work on the fuel tank, wear safety glasses and have a Class B type fire extinguisher on hand.

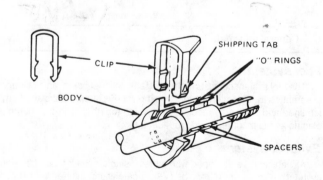

3.5   An exploded view of the hairpin clip type push connect fitting

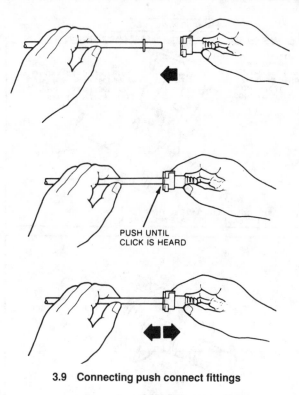

PUSH UNTIL
CLICK IS HEARD

3.9   Connecting push connect fittings

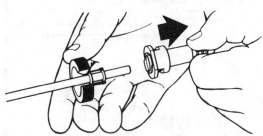

3.14   Pulling off the duck bill clip type push connect fitting

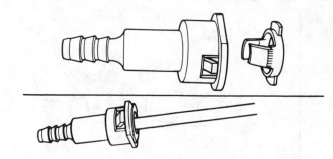

3.10   A push connect fitting with a duck bill clip

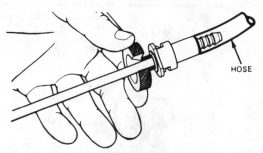

HOSE

3.13   Removing a duck bill clip fitting using the special Ford disassembly tool

Push connect fittings – disassembly and reassembly

Refer to illustrations 3.5, 3.9, 3.10, 3.13 and 3.14

1   Ford uses two different push connect fitting designs. Fittings used with 3/8- and 5/16-inch diameter lines have a "hairpin" type clip; fittings used with 1/4-inch diameter lines have a "duck bill" type clip. The procedure used for releasing each type of fitting is different. The clips should be replaced whenever a connector is disassembled.

2   Disconnect all push connect fittings from fuel system components such as the fuel filter, the fuel charging assembly, the fuel tank, etc. before removing the assembly.

3/8 and 5/16-inch fittings (hairpin clip)

3   Inspect the internal portion of the fitting for accumulations of dirt. If more than a light coating of dust is present, clean the fitting before disassembly.

4   Some adhesion between the seals in the fitting and the line will occur over a period of time. Twist the fitting on the line, then push and pull the fitting until it moves freely.

5   Remove the hairpin clip from the fitting by bending the shipping tab down until it clears the body **(see illustration)**. Then, using nothing but your hands, spread each leg about 1/8-inch to disengage the body and push the legs through the fitting. Finally, pull lightly on the triangular end of the clip and work it clear of the line and fitting. Remember, don't use any tools to perform this part of the procedure.

6   Grasp the fitting and hose and pull it straight off the line.

7   Do not reuse the original clip in the fitting. A new clip must be used.

8   Before reinstalling the fitting on the line, wipe the line end with a clean cloth. Inspect the inside of the fitting to ensure that it's free of dirt and/or obstructions.

9   To reinstall the fitting on the line, align them and push the fitting into place. When the fitting is engaged, a definite click will be heard. Pull on the fitting to ensure that it's completely engaged **(see illustration)**. To install the new clip, insert it into any two adjacent openings in the fitting with the triangular portion of the clip pointing away from the fitting opening. Using your index finger, push the clip in until the legs are locked on the outside of the fitting.

1/4-inch fittings (duck bill clip)

10   The duck bill clip type fitting consists of a body, spacers, O-rings and the retaining clip **(see illustration)**. The clip holds the fitting securely in place on the line. One of the two following methods must be used to disconnect this type of fitting.

11   Before attempting to disconnect the fitting, check the visible internal portion of the fitting for accumulations of dirt. If more than a light coating of dust is evident, clean the fitting before disassembly.

12   Some adhesion between the seals in the fitting and line will occur over a period of time. Twist the fitting on the line, then push and pull the fitting until it moves freely.

13   The preferred method used to disconnect the fitting requires a special tool. To disengage the line from the fitting, align the slot in the push connect disassembly tool (Ford Part No. T82L-9500-AH or equivalent tool) with either tab on the clip (90-degrees from the slots on the side of the fitting) and insert the tool **(see illustration)**. This disengages the duck bill from the line. **Note:** *Some fuel lines have a secondary bead which aligns with the outer surface of the clip. The bead can make tool insertion difficult. If necessary, use the alternative disassembly method described in Step 16.*

14   Holding the tool and the line with one hand, pull the fitting off **(see illustration)**. **Note:** *Only moderate effort is necessary if the clip is properly disengaged. The use of anything other than your hands should not be required.*

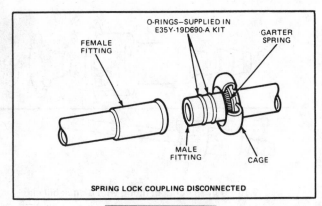

FEMALE FITTING

O-RINGS—SUPPLIED IN E35Y-19D690-A KIT

GARTER SPRING

MALE FITTING

CAGE

SPRING LOCK COUPLING DISCONNECTED

CAUTION—DISCHARGE SYSTEM BEFORE DISCONNECTING COUPLING

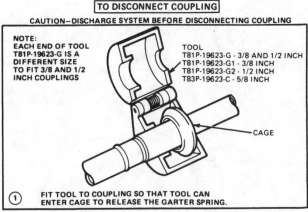

NOTE:
EACH END OF TOOL T81P-19623-G IS A DIFFERENT SIZE TO FIT 3/8 AND 1/2 INCH COUPLINGS

TOOL
T81P-19623-G - 3/8 AND 1/2 INCH
T81P-19623-G1 - 3/8 INCH
T81P-19623-G2 - 1/2 INCH
T83P-19623-C - 5/8 INCH

CAGE

① FIT TOOL TO COUPLING SO THAT TOOL CAN ENTER CAGE TO RELEASE THE GARTER SPRING.

TO CONNECT COUPLING

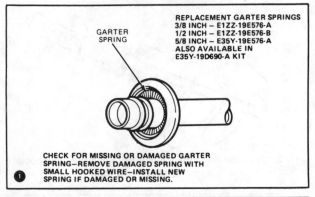

GARTER SPRING

REPLACEMENT GARTER SPRINGS
3/8 INCH — E1ZZ-19E576-A
1/2 INCH — E1ZZ-19E576-B
5/8 INCH — E35Y-19E576-A
ALSO AVAILABLE IN E35Y-19D690-A KIT

① CHECK FOR MISSING OR DAMAGED GARTER SPRING—REMOVE DAMAGED SPRING WITH SMALL HOOKED WIRE—INSTALL NEW SPRING IF DAMAGED OR MISSING.

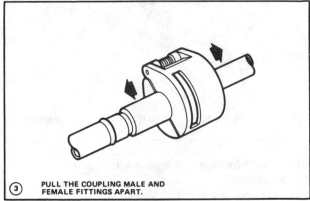

PUSH TOOL INTO CAGE

② PUSH THE TOOL INTO THE CAGE OPENING TO RELEASE THE FEMALE FITTING FROM THE GARTER SPRING.

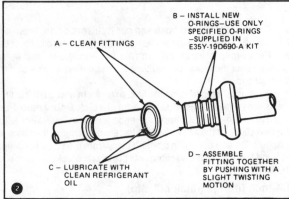

A – CLEAN FITTINGS

B – INSTALL NEW O-RINGS—USE ONLY SPECIFIED O-RINGS —SUPPLIED IN E35Y-19D690-A KIT

C – LUBRICATE WITH CLEAN REFRIGERANT OIL

D – ASSEMBLE FITTING TOGETHER BY PUSHING WITH A SLIGHT TWISTING MOTION

②

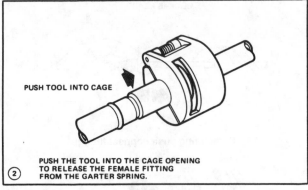

③ PULL THE COUPLING MALE AND FEMALE FITTINGS APART.

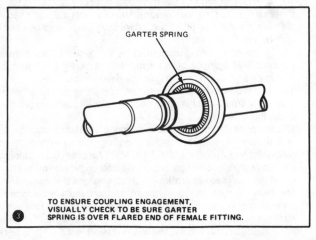

GARTER SPRING

③ TO ENSURE COUPLING ENGAGEMENT, VISUALLY CHECK TO BE SURE GARTER SPRING IS OVER FLARED END OF FEMALE FITTING.

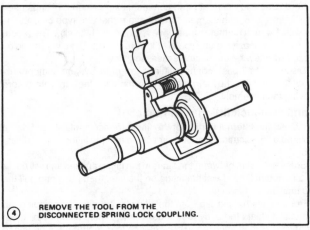

④ REMOVE THE TOOL FROM THE DISCONNECTED SPRING LOCK COUPLING.

3.24   **Connecting and disconnecting spring lock couplings**

3.28   If the spring lock couplings are equipped with safety clips, pry them off with a small screwdriver

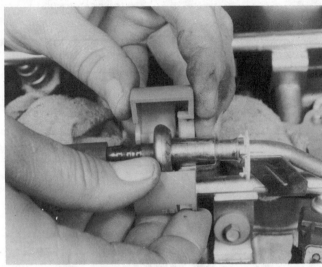

3.29   Open the spring-loaded halves of the spring lock coupling tool and place it in position around the coupling, then close it

15   After disassembly, inspect and clean the line sealing surface. Also inspect the inside of the fitting and the line for any internal parts that may have been dislodged from the fitting. Any loose internal parts should be immediately reinstalled (use the line to insert the parts).

16   The alternative disassembly procedure requires "water pump" type pliers. The pliers must have a jaw width of 3/16-inch or less.

17   Align the jaws of the pliers with the openings in the side of the fitting and compress the portion of the retaining clip that engages the body. This disengages the retaining clip from the body (often one side of the clip will disengage before the other – both sides must be disengaged).

18   Pull the fitting off the line. **Note:** *Only moderate effort is required if the retaining clip has been properly disengaged. Do not use any tools for this procedure.*

19   Once the fitting is removed from the line end, check the fitting and line for any internal parts that may have been dislodged from the fitting. Any loose internal parts should be immediately reinstalled (use the line to insert the parts).

20   The retaining clip will remain on the line. Disengage the clip from the line bead to remove it. Do not reuse the retaining clip – install a new one!

21   Before reinstalling the fitting, wipe the line end with a clean cloth. Check the inside of the fitting to make sure that it's free of dirt and/or obstructions.

22   To reinstall the fitting, align it with the line and push it into place. When the fitting is engaged, a definite click will be heard. Pull on the fitting to ensure that it's fully engaged.

23   Install the new replacement clip by inserting one of the serrated edges on the duck bill portion into one of the openings. Push on the other side until the clip snaps into place.

Spring lock couplings – disassembly and reassembly

Refer to illustrations 3.24, 3.28, 3.29, 3.30 and 3.37

24   The fuel supply and return lines used on some engines utilize spring lock couplings instead of plastic push connect fittings at the engine fuel rail end. The male end of the spring lock coupling, which is girded by two O-rings, is inserted into a female flared end engine fitting. The coupling is secured by a garter spring which prevents disengagement by gripping the flared end of the female fitting **(see illustration).**

25   The fuel feed and return line fittings are not the same diameter. To disconnect the 1/2-inch fuel feed line coupling, you will need to obtain a spring lock coupling tool D87L-9280-B or its equivalent; for the 3/8-inch return fitting, get tool D87L-9280-A or its equivalent (Ford dealers may not have

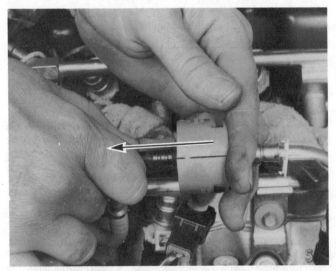

3.30   To disconnect the coupling, push the tool into the cage opening to expand the garter spring and release the female fitting, then pull the male and female fittings apart

these tools on hand, but they are readily available from manufacturers like Kent-Moore, Snap-on and Mac).

Disconnecting the coupling

26   Before detaching the spring lock coupling fittings, relieve the system fuel pressure (see Section 2).

27   Detach the cable from the negative terminal of the battery.

28   Pry the safety clip from each fitting with a small screwdriver **(see illustration).**

29   Place the appropriately-sized spring lock coupling disconnect tool in position **(see illustration).**

30   Close the tool and push it into the open side of the cage to expand the garter spring and release the female fitting **(see illustration). Note:** *The garter spring may not release if the tool is cocked while pushing it into the cage opening.*

31   Once the garter spring is expanded, pull the fittings apart.

32   Remove the tool.

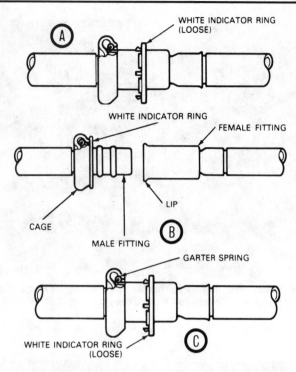

3.37   Spring lock coupling reconnection

4.3a   The fuel pump shutoff switch is located under this cover in the driver's side of the luggage compartment

Connecting the coupling

33   Make sure the garter spring is in the cage of the male fitting. If it's missing, install a new spring by pushing it into the cage opening. If the garter spring is damaged, remove it from the cage with a small wire hook (do not use a screwdriver) and install a new spring (**see illustration 3.24** for garter spring sizes).

34   Clean all dirt or foreign material from both pieces of the coupling. **Warning:** *Use only the specified O-rings – they are made of a special material and the use of any other O-ring may allow the connection to leak intermittently during vehicle operation.*

35   Lubricate the male fitting and O-rings and inside of the the female fitting with clean engine oil.

36   Install the plastic indicator ring into the cage opening if the indicator ring is to be used.

37   Fit the female fitting onto the male fitting and push them together until the garter spring snaps over the flared end of the female fitting. **Note:** *If the fitting is equipped with a plastic indicator ring, the ring will snap out of the cage opening when the coupling is connected to indicate engagement. If no indicator ring is used, make sure that the coupling is engaged by visual verification that the garter spring is over the flared end of the female fitting* (**see illustration**).

4.3b   Once the cover is removed, the switch mounting bolt is visible (arrow)

---

4   Fuel pump – check

Refer to illustrations 4.3a, 4.3b, 4.3c, 4.4a and 4.4b

Warning: *The fuel system pressure must be relieved before disconnecting fuel lines and fittings (see Section 2). Gasoline is extremely flammable, so take extra precautions when you work on any part of the fuel system. Don't smoke or allow open flames or bare light bulbs near the work area, and don't work in a garage where a natural gas-type appliance (such as a water heater or clothes dryer) with a pilot light is present. If you spill any fuel on your skin, rinse it off immediately with soap and water. When you perform any kind of work on the fuel tank, wear safety glasses and have a Class B type fire extinguisher on hand.*

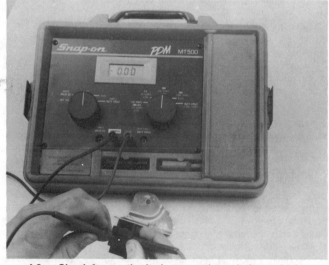

4.3c   Check for continuity between the switch terminals

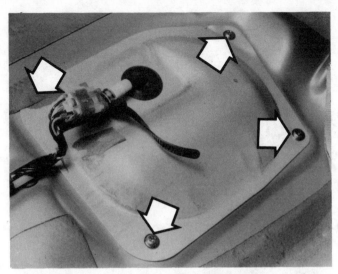

4.4a   Remove the cover plate screws from the corners of the cover (arrows)

4.4b   The ground wire is black and the positive wire is white or white with a red stripe

Note: *The electric fuel pump and circuit are an integral part of the EEC-IV system, so a complete diagnosis must determine whether the pump and the circuit are operating properly. Such a procedure is beyond the scope of the average home mechanic. However, a loss of fuel flow and/or pressure, usually indicated by a partial or complete loss of performance, is often a sign that the fuel pump has malfunctioned. Therefore, perform the following rudimentary check of the pump if the above symptoms occur. Further investigation of the fuel pump circuit, however, should be left to a qualified professional at a dealer service department or other repair shop.*

1   Always verify that there is fuel in the tank and that none of the lines and fittings are leaking fuel before starting this procedure.
2   The easiest way to determine whether the electric in-tank fuel pump is working is to have an assistant turn the ignition key to Start while you put your ear to the filler neck and listen for the telltale whirring sound that indicates the pump is operating. If the pump is silent, proceed to the next Step.
3   Locate the inertia (fuel pump shut-off) switch in the driver's side rear corner of the luggage compartment under the carpet **(see illustrations)**. Using a self-powered test light or ohmmeter, make sure that it is allowing current to reach the pump **(see illustration)**. If the switch has opened the circuit, reset it.
4   Remove the rear seat cushion and sending unit cover plate **(see illustration)**. Using a self-powered test light or ohmmeter, check the continuity of the pump positive and ground terminals **(see illustration)**.
5   If there is no continuity, the pump is defective. Replace it (see Section 7).
6   If there is continuity, bypass the pump circuit. Using a fused jumper wire, apply battery voltage to the positive terminal of the pump. Ground the negative terminal of the pump. It should operate.
7   If the pump operates, there is an open in the circuit somewhere between the battery and the pump terminal. Troubleshoot and repair it, referring to the Wiring Diagrams at the end of this book, if necessary.
8   If the pump doesn't operate, replace it (see Section 7).
9   Any further testing of the electric fuel pump, its relay or the circuit should be conducted by a dealer service department or other repair shop.

5   Fuel tank – removal and installation

Refer to illustrations 5.4, 5.5, 5.6, 5.7 and 5.9
Warning: *The fuel system pressure must be relieved before disconnecting fuel lines and fittings (see Section 2). Gasoline is extremely flammable,*

so take extra precautions when you work on any part of the fuel system. Don't smoke or allow open flames or bare light bulbs near the work area, and don't work in a garage where a natural gas-type appliance (such as a water heater or clothes dryer) with a pilot light is present. DO NOT siphon fuel by mouth. If you spill any fuel on your skin, rinse it off immediately with soap and water. When you perform any kind of work on the fuel tank, wear safety glasses and have a Class B type fire extinguisher on hand.
Note: *Don't begin this procedure until the gauge indicates that the tank is empty or nearly empty. If the tank must be removed when it's full, drain any remaining fuel from the tank into approved safety containers prior to tank removal.*

1   Relieve the fuel pressure (see Section 2).
2   Detach the cable from the negative terminal of the battery.
3   Raise the vehicle and support it securely on jackstands.
4   Unless the vehicle has been driven far enough to completely empty the tank, it's a good idea to drain the residual fuel into an approved storage container before removing the tank from the vehicle **(see illustration)**.

5.4   Remove the drain plug (arrow) located near the forward edge of the bottom of the tank, and allow the fuel to drain into an approved fuel container

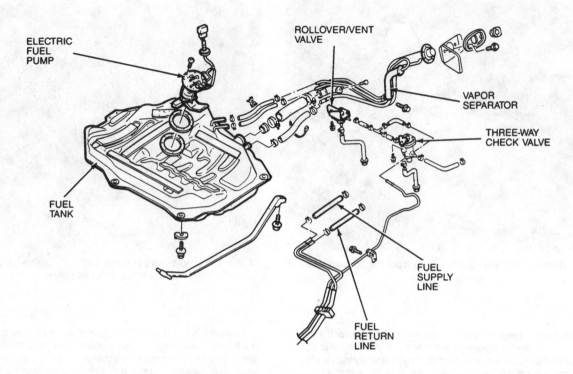

ELECTRIC FUEL PUMP

ROLLOVER/VENT VALVE

VAPOR SEPARATOR

THREE-WAY CHECK VALVE

FUEL TANK

FUEL SUPPLY LINE

FUEL RETURN LINE

5.5   Fuel tank mounting details – exploded view

5   Loosen the hose clamps securing the fuel filler neck hose and the breather hose to the fuel tank and detach the hoses **(see illustration)**.
6   Place a transmission jack or floor jack under the tank and position a block of wood between the jack pad and the tank. Raise the jack until it's supporting the tank **(see illustration)**.
7   Remove the bolts from the rear ends of the fuel tank straps **(see illustration)**. The straps are hinged at the front end so you can swing them forward and down, out of the way.
8   Unplug the electrical connector from the sending unit/fuel pump terminal, detach the fuel feed and return lines from the fuel tank (see Section 3), and detach the fuel vapor line from the vapor orifice. When all the connectors and fittings are disconnected, remove the tank from the vehicle.

9   Remove the bolts around the perimeter of the tank **(see illustration)**. Gently lower the tank, slightly tilting it to the right and sliding it toward the right to clear the exhaust pipe on the left. When the tank is low enough to allow access to the fuel lines, vapor hose and electrical connector, stop and disconnect the lines, hose and connector.

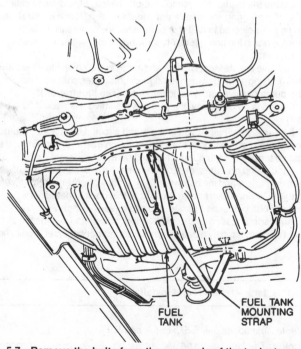

FUEL TANK

FUEL TANK MOUNTING STRAP

5.7   Remove the bolts from the rear ends of the tank straps

5.6   Support the tank with a jack – use wood blocks to protect the tank from damage

5.9   Remove the bolts around the perimeter of the tank (arrow)

7.3   Disconnect the fuel lines (arrows)

10   If you're replacing the tank, or having it cleaned or repaired, refer to Section 7 and remove the fuel pump/sending unit. For information regarding tank cleaning and repair, refer to Section 6.
11   Refer to Section 7 and install the fuel pump/sending unit.
12   Installation is the reverse of removal.

6   Fuel tank cleaning and repair – general information

1   Repairs to the fuel tank or filler neck should be performed by a professional with the proper training to carry out this critical and potentially dangerous work. Even after cleaning and flushing, explosive fumes can remain and could explode during repair of the tank.
2   If the fuel tank is removed from the vehicle, it should not be placed in an area where sparks or open flames could ignite the fumes coming out of the tank. Be especially careful inside garages where a natural gas appliance is located because the pilot light could cause an explosion.

7   Fuel pump – removal and installation

Refer to illustrations 7.3, 7.6 and 7.7
Warning: *The fuel system pressure must be relieved before disconnecting fuel lines and fittings (see Section 2). Gasoline is extremely flammable, so take extra precautions when you work on any part of the fuel system.*

Don't smoke or allow open flames or bare light bulbs near the work area, and don't work in a garage where a natural gas-type appliance (such as a water heater or clothes dryer) with a pilot light is present. If you spill any fuel on your skin, rinse it off immediately with soap and water. When you perform any kind of work on the fuel tank, wear safety glasses and have a Class B type fire extinguisher on hand.

1   Relieve the fuel system pressure (see Section 2).
2   Remove the rear seat cushion. Disconnect the electrical connector and unbolt the cover plate **(see illustration 4.4a).**
3   Remove any dirt that has accumulated around the fuel pump attaching flange so that it won't fall into the tank when the fuel pump/sending unit is pulled out. Disconnect the fuel supply and return hoses from the fuel pump/sending unit **(see illustration)**.
4   Remove the screws around the perimeter of the fuel pump/sending unit. Carefully pull the assembly from the tank.
5   Remove the old gasket and discard it.
6   If you intend to reinstall the original fuel pump/sending unit, remove the strainer, wash it in clean solvent, then push it back onto the bottom of the pump **(see illustration)**. If you're installing a new pump/sending unit, the assembly will include a new strainer.
7   If you intend to replace the fuel pump with a new one, remove the strap bolt, electrical connectors and hose **(see illustration)**.
8   Clean the fuel pump mounting flange and the tank mounting surface and gasket groove.

7.6   The strainer (arrow) is attached to the bottom of the fuel pump

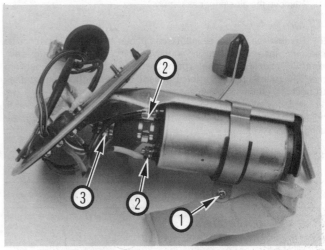

7.7   Remove the strap, electrical connectors and hose
1   Strap bolt   3   Hose clamp
2   Electrical connectors

8.2   Release the clip and unplug the electrical connector from the vane airflow meter

9   Installation is the reverse of removal. Apply a thin coat of heavy grease to the gasket to hold it in place during assembly.

8   Air cleaner assembly – removal and installation

Four-cylinder models

Refer to illustrations 8.2, 8.3a and 8.3b

1   Remove the cable from the negative terminal of the battery.
2   Disconnect the airflow meter electrical connector **(see illustration)**.
3   Remove the air duct clamp and duct from the airflow meter assembly **(see illustrations)**.
4   Remove the three air cleaner assembly hold-down nuts and one hold-down bolt.
5   Separate the air cleaner assembly from the resonance chamber(s) and lift it from the engine compartment.

V6 models

Refer to illustration 8.6

6   Loosen the clamp and detach the air duct from the upper cover of the filter housing **(see illustration)**.
7   Remove three air cleaner assembly hold-down nuts and hold-down bolt.
8   Remove the air cleaner assembly.

All models

9   Remove the air filter element (see Chapter 1). Clean and inspect the sealing surfaces on the housing and cover. If dirt leakage or damage is evident, verify the right element is being used and the housing fasteners are providing sufficient clamping force to keep the cover and housing together. Correct any problems as necessary.
10   Install a new element only after inspecting it for any damage – such as deformed seals or holes in the paper – that may have occurred during handling.
11   Installation is the reverse of removal.
12   Start the engine and check for air leaks. Correct as necessary.

9   Throttle cable – removal and installation

Four-cylinder models

Refer to illustrations 9.1, 9.2, 9.7 and 9.8

1   Remove the cable end from the throttle lever **(see illustration)**.
2   Remove the cable retaining brackets located near the throttle body on the intake plenum and the right end of the intake plenum **(see illustration)**.

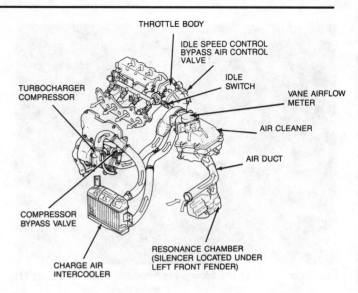

8.3a   Air cleaner details – turbo four-cylinder models

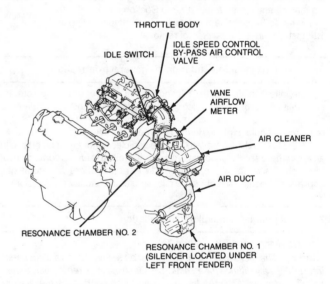

8.3b   Air cleaner details – non-turbo four-cylinder models

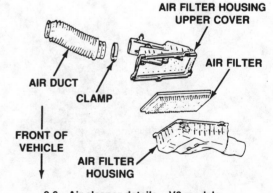

8.6   Air cleaner details – V6 models

3   If the vehicle is equipped with cruise control, remove the cruise control cable from the accelerator pedal.
4   Working under the dash, squeeze the lock tabs and remove the cable end from the pedal assembly.

9.1 Twist the throttle until the cable lines up with the slot (arrow) and pull the cable out sideways

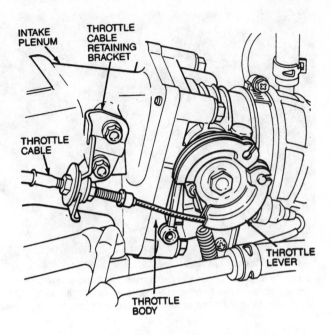

9.2 Detach the throttle cable at the retaining bracket

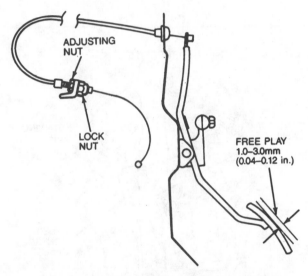

9.7 To adjust freeplay, loosen the locknut and turn the adjusting nut near the throttle body

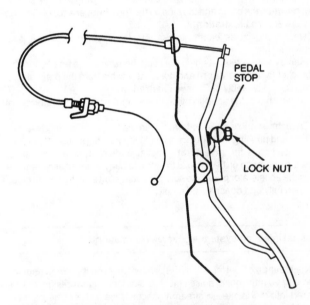

9.8 Loosen the locknut and adjust the pedal stop for wide open throttle

5   Squeeze the lock tabs together where the cable goes through the fire-wall and remove the cable.
6   Install the cable in the reverse order of removal. Snap the fasteners into place and reconnect the cable ends.
7   Measure the pedal freeplay (see illustration). Loosen the locknut, adjust the pedal freeplay as shown and retighten the locknut.
8   Have an assistant hold the accelerator pedal to the floor while you confirm that the throttle plates in the throttle body are in the wide open po-sition. If necessary, loosen the locknut (see illustration), adjust the pedal stop and retighten the locknut.

9.10 Remove the cover fasteners (arrows) for throttle cable access

9.11   To detach the throttle cable from the throttle lever, insert a small screwdriver between the cable end and the stud on the lever arm, then twist the screwdriver and the cable will pop loose

9.13a   To detach the cable from the cable bracket, remove the retainer bolt (arrow) and slide the cable from its slot in the bracket

V6 models

Refer to illustrations 9.10, 9.11, 9.13a and 9.13b

9   Disconnect the ground cable from the negative terminal of the battery.

10   Remove the cover from the throttle body **(see illustration)**.

11   Disconnect the throttle cable at the throttle lever by inserting a screwdriver between the cable and the stud on the throttle lever and twisting the screwdriver **(see illustration)**.

12   Detach the cruise control cable from the accelerator cable, if so equipped.

13   Remove the screw retaining the cable housing to the engine mounting bracket **(see illustration)** and detach the cable from the bracket slot. Lift the cable assembly clear **(see illustration)**.

14   Detach the cable snap-in nylon bushing from the accelerator pedal arm.

15   Detach the cable housing from the firewall by pinching the two tabs together and pushing them out from inside the passenger compartment.

16   Installation is the reverse of removal. Before starting the engine, check the operation of the cable at the throttle body while an assistant operates the accelerator pedal. Be sure the cable allows the throttle to close and open fully and doesn't bind or stick.

10   Fuel injection system – general information

The Electronic Fuel Injection (EFI) system used on the Probe engines is known as a multi-point, pulse time, mass airflow control design. Fuel is metered into the intake air stream in accordance with engine demand through injectors mounted on a tuned intake manifold. One fuel injector is supplied for each cylinder.

An on-board Electronic Engine Control version four (EEC-IV) computer accepts inputs from various engine sensors to compute the required fuel flow rate necessary to maintain a prescribed air/fuel ratio throughout the entire engine operational range. The computer then outputs a command to the fuel injectors to meter the approximate quantity of fuel.

The period of time that the injectors are energized (known as "on time" or "pulse width") is controlled by the EEC computer. Air entering the engine is sensed by speed, pressure and temperature sensors. The outputs of these sensors are processed by the EEC-IV computer. The computer determines the needed injector pulse width and outputs a command to the injector to meter the exact quantity of fuel.

The EEC-IV engine control system also compensates for changes in altitude.

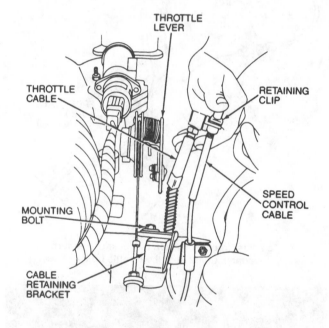

9.13b   After everything is detached, pull the cable assembly clear of the bracket

The fuel delivery systems for both designs are similar: An electric in-tank fuel pump forces pressurized fuel through a series of metal and plastic lines and an inline fuel filter/reservoir to the fuel charging manifold assembly.

The fuel charging manifold assembly incorporates electrically actuated fuel injectors directly above each intake port. When energized, the injectors spray a metered quantity of fuel into the intake air stream.

A constant fuel pressure drop is maintained across the injector nozzles by a pressure regulator. The regulator is connected in series with the fuel injectors and is positioned downstream from them. Excess fuel passes through the regulator and returns to the fuel tank through a fuel return line.

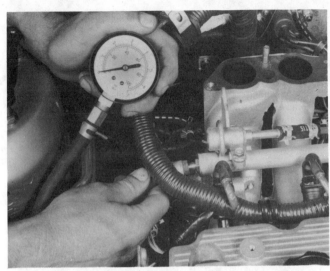

11.1   On four-cylinder models, the pressure gauge may be connected to the fuel rail adjacent to the pressure regulator

12.5   On turbo models, loosen the hose clamps (arrows) and remove the boot elbow

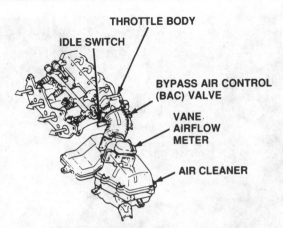

12.4   On four-cylinder non-turbo models, remove the duct between the throttle body and the vane airflow meter

11   Fuel injection system – pressure check

Refer to illustration 11.1

Warning: *The fuel system pressure must be relieved before disconnecting fuel lines and fittings (see Section 2). Gasoline is extremely flammable, so take extra precautions when you work on any part of the fuel system. Don't smoke or allow open flames or bare light bulbs near the work area, and don't work in a garage where a natural gas-type appliance (such as a water heater or clothes dryer) with a pilot light is present. If you spill any fuel on your skin, rinse it off immediately with soap and water. When you perform any kind of work on the fuel tank, wear safety glasses and have a Class B type fire extinguisher on hand.*

1   With a Ford Rotunda 014-0047 pressure gauge (or equivalent), the fuel pressure can be measured easily and quickly. On four-cylinder models, the fuel rail end plug may be removed and an adapter screwed into place **(see illustration)**. Most V6 models are equipped with Schrader valves; on these models it is not necessary to detach any fuel lines to read the fuel pressure.

2   The special Ford fuel pressure gauge/adapter assembly specified above is designed to relieve fuel pressure, as well as measure it. If you have this gauge, you can use this method as an alternative to the fuel pressure relief procedure outlined in Section 2. **Warning:** *Never attempt to relieve fuel pressure through the Schrader valve without this special setup.*

3   To attach the gauge to engines equipped with Schrader valves, simply remove the valve cap, screw on the adapter and attach the gauge to the adapter.

4   Start the engine and allow it to reach a steady idle. Note the indicated fuel pressure reading and compare it to the pressure listed in this Chapter's Specifications.

5   If the indicated fuel pressure is lower than specified, the problem is probably either a faulty pressure regulator, a leaking fuel line, a malfunctioning fuel pump or a leaking injector.

6   If the indicated pressure is higher than specified, the cause could be a blocked return line or a stuck fuel pressure regulator. Refer to the following Section for further information.

12   Electronic Fuel Injection (EFI) system – component replacement

Warning: *The fuel system pressure must be relieved before disconnecting fuel lines and fittings (see Section 2). Gasoline is extremely flammable, so take extra precautions when you work on any part of the fuel system. Don't smoke or allow open flames or bare light bulbs near the work area, and don't work in a garage where a natural gas-type appliance (such as a water heater or clothes dryer) with a pilot light is present. If you spill any fuel on your skin, rinse it off immediately with soap and water. When you perform any kind of work on the fuel tank, wear safety glasses and have a Class B type fire extinguisher on hand.*

Note: *It usually isn't necessary to disassemble the entire EFI system to replace most components. To determine what must be removed, carefully read the section which applies to the component(s) you wish to replace.*

Air intake/throttle body assembly

Four-cylinder models

Refer to illustrations 12.4, 12.5, 12.7 and 12.10

Note: *On four-cylinder models, if you are simply replacing the gasket between the air intake/throttle body assembly and the intake manifold, it isn't necessary to remove the various components attached to the throttle body. Simply remove the entire assembly as a unit in accordance with the following procedure.*

Removal

1   Remove the fuel filler cap to relieve fuel tank pressure.

2   Relieve the fuel system pressure (see Section 2).

3   Detach the cable from the negative terminal of the battery.

4   On non-turbo models, loosen the hose clamps and remove the air inlet duct **(see illustration)**.

5   On turbo models, remove the air intake boot elbow **(see illustration)**.

12.7   Disconnect all the hoses, electrical connections and brackets, then remove the mounting nuts (lower nuts hidden by throttle body housing)

1   *Hose*   3   *Mounting nuts*
2   *Electrical connectors*

6   Drain the cooling system (see Chapter 1). Label and disconnect the coolant hoses from the throttle body.
7   Label and then unplug the electrical connectors from the throttle body **(see illustration)**.

8   Detach the throttle cable from the throttle lever (see Section 9).
9   Clearly label, then detach, the vacuum lines from the throttle body components.
10   Remove the engine lifting bracket from the cylinder head adjacent to the transaxle. On non-turbo models, remove the EGR hose/coolant line retaining bracket **(see illustration)**.
11   Remove the four throttle body mounting nuts.
12   Remove the throttle body assembly. Temporarily stuff a rag into the intake manifold opening to prevent dirt intrusion.
13   Remove and discard the old gasket.

Installation

14   Clean and inspect the mounting faces of the throttle body assembly and the intake manifold. Both surfaces must be clean and flat.
15   Clean and oil the manifold stud threads.
16   Install a new gasket.
17   Position the throttle body assembly to the intake manifold.
18   Install the nuts and tighten them to the torque listed in this Chapter's Specifications.
19   The remainder of installation is the reverse of removal.

V6 models

Refer to illustrations 12.23, 12.28, 12.30a and 12.30b

Removal

20   Remove the fuel filler cap to relieve fuel tank pressure.
21   Relieve the fuel system pressure (see Section 2).
22   Detach the cable from the negative terminal of the battery.
23   Loosen the clamps and remove the air intake duct between the air cleaner housing and the throttle body **(see illustration)**.
24   Remove the plastic shield from the throttle body **(see illustration 9.10)**.

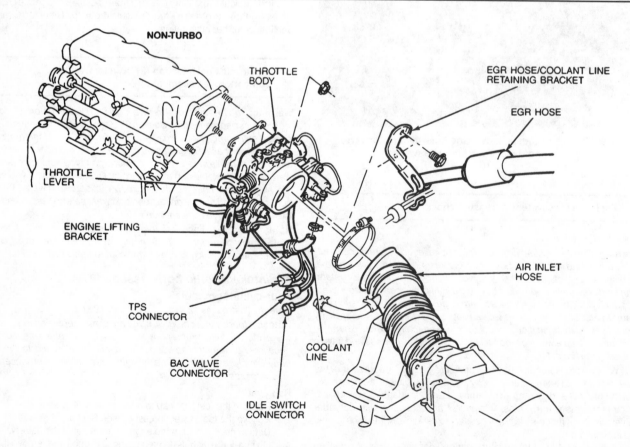

12.10   Four-cylinder throttle body installation details – exploded view

12.23 Loosen the clamps (arrows) and detach the air intake duct

12.28 Label and then disconnect all wires and hoses (arrows)

12.30a To remove the air intake/throttle body assembly, remove all six mounting bolts (arrows) – note that there are three different bolt lengths (two short, two medium and two long ones)

12.30b Lift the air intake/throttle body assembly out of the vehicle very carefully to prevent damage to the TPS, air bypass valve, EGR valve, etc.

25 Detach the EGR supply tube.

26 Label and then unplug the electrical connectors from the Throttle Position Sensor (TPS), the Idle Speed Control (ISC) servo and the Air Charge Temperature (ACT) sensor.

27 Remove the Manifold Absolute Pressure (MAP) sensor from the throttle body.

28 Clearly label, then disconnect all other wires and hoses from the throttle body (see illustration).

29 Detach the throttle cable (and throttle valve control cable on automatic transaxle models) from the throttle lever (see Section 9). Remove the fuel rail bracket bolt from the throttle body.

30 Remove the six air intake/throttle body mounting bolts and lift off the throttle body assembly (see illustrations).

Installation

31 Installation is the reverse of removal. Be sure to clean the mating surfaces of all gasket material, and use a new gasket. Tighten the throttle body-to-intake manifold bolts to the torque listed in this Chapter's Specifications.

Air bypass valve assembly

Refer to illustration 12.34

Removal

32 Unplug the electrical connector from the air bypass valve.

12.34 To detach the air bypass valve assembly from the air intake/throttle body assembly, remove the two screws (arrows)

12.40a   On four-cylinder models, scribe an alignment mark, unplug the electrical connector and remove the mounting screws

1   Wiring harness (follow it down   2   Mounting screws
*   to the electrical connector)*

12.40b On V6 models, to remove the Throttle Position Sensor (TPS), scribe an alignment mark on the sensor and the throttle body, unplug the electrical connector, then remove both mounting screws (arrows)

33   Remove the bolts and detach the plastic shield **(see illustration 9.10).**
34   Remove the two air bypass valve retaining screws **(see illustration).**
35   Remove the air bypass valve and gasket. Discard the old gasket.

Installation
36   Make sure that both the throttle body and the air bypass valve gasket surfaces are clean.
37   Install the gasket on the throttle body surface and place the air bypass valve assembly in position. Install the mounting screws and tighten them securely.
38   The remainder of installation is the reverse of removal.

Throttle Position Sensor (TPS)
Refer to illustrations 12.40a and 12.40b

Removal
39   Mark the relationship of the TPS to the throttle body to indicate the proper alignment during installation.
40   On four-cylinder models, follow the wiring harness from the TPS to the electrical connector, then unplug the connector **(see illustration)**. On V6 models, disconnect the electrical connector at the TPS **(see illustration)**.
41   Remove the two TPS retaining screws.
42   Remove the TPS.

Installation
43   Ensure that the rotary tangs on the sensor are in proper alignment and that the red seal is inside the connector housing. Slide the rotary tangs into position over the throttle shaft blade, then rotate the TPS clockwise to the installed position. **Caution:** *Failure to install the TPS in this manner may result in excessive idle speeds.*
44   Align the scribe marks on the throttle body and throttle position sensor. Secure the sensor to the throttle body assembly with the two retaining screws and tighten them securely.
45   The remainder of installation is the reverse of removal.

Fuel rail
Refer to illustrations 12.47a, 12.47b, 12.48a, 12.48b, 12.48c, 12.50a, 12.50b, 12.50c and 12.51

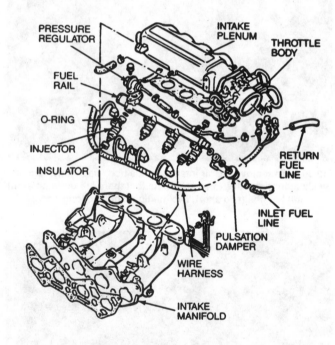

12.47a   Four-cylinder fuel injection components – exploded view

Removal
46   Remove the throttle body assembly (see above).
47   Detach the vacuum line from the fuel pressure regulator **(see illustrations)**.
48   Disconnect the injector wiring harness **(see illustrations)**. Using a small screwdriver, carefully unplug the electrical connectors from the fuel injectors **(see illustration)**.

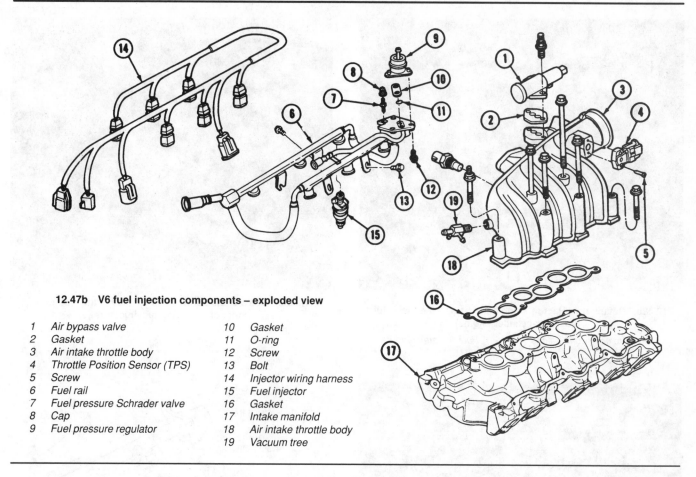

12.47b   V6 fuel injection components – exploded view

1	Air bypass valve	10	Gasket
2	Gasket	11	O-ring
3	Air intake throttle body	12	Screw
4	Throttle Position Sensor (TPS)	13	Bolt
5	Screw	14	Injector wiring harness
6	Fuel rail	15	Fuel injector
7	Fuel pressure Schrader valve	16	Gasket
8	Cap	17	Intake manifold
9	Fuel pressure regulator	18	Air intake throttle body
		19	Vacuum tree

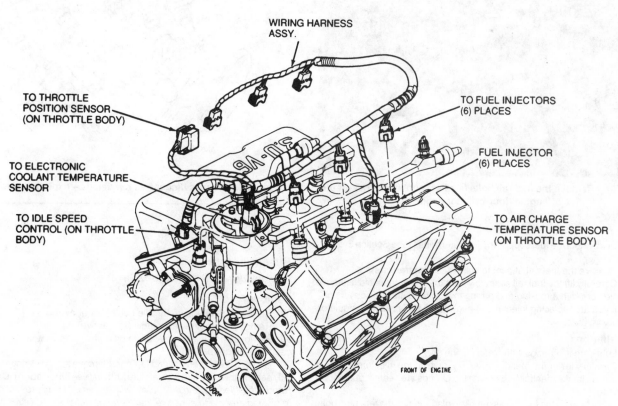

WIRING HARNESS ASSY.

TO THROTTLE POSITION SENSOR (ON THROTTLE BODY)

TO ELECTRONIC COOLANT TEMPERATURE SENSOR

TO IDLE SPEED CONTROL (ON THROTTLE BODY)

TO FUEL INJECTORS (6) PLACES

FUEL INJECTOR (6) PLACES

TO AIR CHARGE TEMPERATURE SENSOR (ON THROTTLE BODY)

FRONT OF ENGINE

12.48a   V6 injector wiring harness

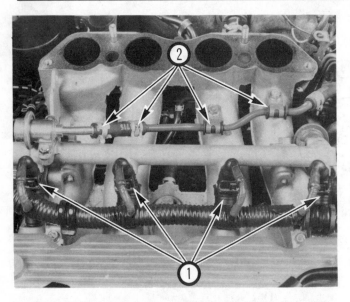

12.48b   Detach the injector wiring harness and the fuel return line (four-cylinder engine)

1   Injector connections   2   Fuel line attachments

12.48c   Use a small screwdriver to release the electrical connectors on the fuel injectors

12.50a   Remove the fuel rail bolts (arrows) and lift the rail off the engine (four-cylinder engine)

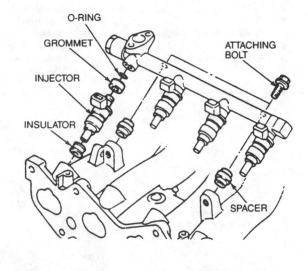

12.50b   Four-cylinder fuel rail details – exploded view

49   Disconnect the fuel supply and fuel return lines (see Section 3, if necessary).

50   Remove the fuel rail attaching bolts **(see illustrations)**.

51   Carefully lift the fuel rail assembly from the intake manifold. Remove the injectors with a rocking and pulling motion **(see illustration)**.

52   If you are replacing injectors, O-rings or the fuel pressure regulator, see below.

Installation

53   Lubricate all O-rings with clean engine oil.

54   Carefully lower the fuel rail assembly, guiding the injectors into their holes in the intake manifold. To ensure the O-rings are seated, push down on the fuel rail.

55   While holding the fuel rail assembly in place, install the retaining bolts finger tight, then tighten them securely.

56   The remainder of installation is the reverse of removal.

Fuel injectors

Refer to illustrations 12.60 and 12.62

Removal

57   Remove the air intake throttle body (see above).

58   Remove the fuel rail assembly (see above).

59   Remove each injector by pulling on it while simultaneously rocking it gently from side-to-side.

60   Replace the grommets and O-rings. Remove the old O-rings by carefully peeling them off with a small screwdriver **(see illustration). Caution:** *Handle the injectors and the fuel rail with extreme care to prevent damage to sealing areas and sensitive fuel metering orifices.*

61   Make sure that the injector caps are clean and free of contamination or damage.

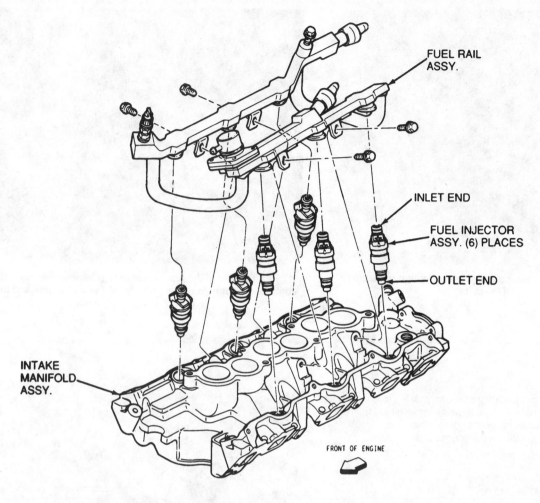

FUEL RAIL
ASSY.

INLET END

FUEL INJECTOR
ASSY. (6) PLACES

OUTLET END

INTAKE
MANIFOLD
ASSY.

FRONT OF ENGINE

12.50c   V6 fuel rail details – exploded view

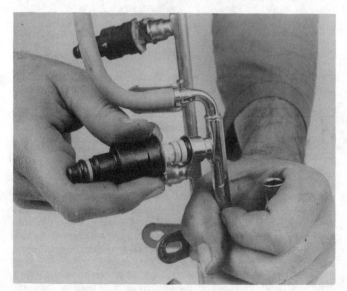

12.51   When pulling on an injector to remove it, use a gentle side-to-side rocking motion

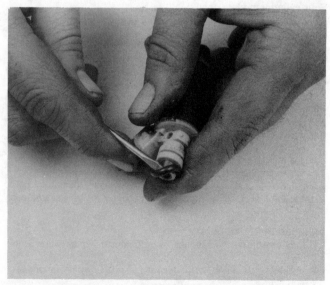

12.60   Use a small screwdriver to peel off the old O-rings from the ends of the injectors – be extremely careful not to damage the sealing areas or the sensitive fuel metering orifices

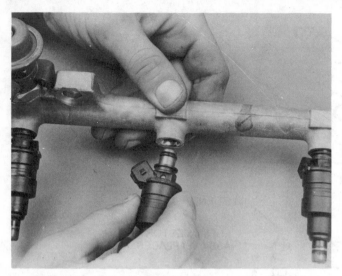

12.62   Use a light twisting and pushing motion to install the injectors

12.67   To remove the fuel pressure regulator on four-cylinder engines, disconnect the vacuum hose, fuel return line and then remove the mounting bolts

1	Vacuum hose	3	Mounting bolts
2	Fuel return line		

Installation

62   Install each injector by using a light twisting, pushing motion **(see illustration)**. **Note:** *Ford recommends applying motor oil to the injector holes in the manifold and fuel rail prior to installation.*
63   The remainder of installation is the reverse of removal.

Fuel pressure regulator
Refer to illustrations 12.67 and 12.70

Removal
64   Remove the fuel tank filler cap to relieve pressure in the fuel tank.
65   Relieve the system fuel pressure (see Section 2).
66   Detach the vacuum line from the pressure regulator.

Four-cylinder models only
67   Disconnect the fuel return line and remove the mounting bolts **(see illustration)**.
68   Remove all traces of old gasket material from the fuel rail and pressure regulator mating surfaces.
69   Using a new gasket, install the pressure regulator and reconnect the fuel return and vacuum lines.

V6 models only
70   Remove the three Allen screws from the underside of the pressure regulator mounting plate **(see illustration)**.
71   Remove the pressure regulator assembly, gasket and O-ring. Discard the old gasket and O-ring.
72   Make sure that the gasket surfaces of the fuel pressure regulator and fuel rail assembly are clean. If scraping is necessary, be careful not to damage the fuel pressure regulator or fuel supply line gasket surfaces.

Installation (all models)
73   Lubricate the pressure regulator O-ring with clean engine oil (V6 models only).
74   Install the new O-ring (V6 models) or gasket (four-cylinder models) on the regulator.
75   Install the fuel pressure regulator on the fuel rail assembly and tighten the retaining screws securely.
76   Complete the remaining steps in the reverse order of removal.

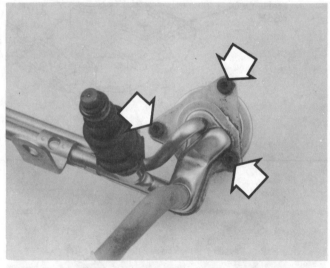

12.70   On V6 engines, remove the three Allen screws (arrows) to detach the fuel pressure regulator (fuel rail removed for clarity)

13   Turbocharger – check, removal and installation

Check
Refer to illustrations 13.1 and 13.5

1   The turbocharger increases engine power by using an exhaust gas driven turbine to pressurize the fuel/air mixture before it enters the combustion chambers, effectively forcing more fuel/air mixture into each cylinder than a naturally aspirated engine. The amount of boost (intake manifold pressure) is controlled by the wastegate (compressor bypass valve), which controls the maximum boost level by allowing some of the exhaust gas to bypass the turbine **(see illustration)**.
2   The turbocharger is a precision device which can be severely damaged by an interrupted oil or coolant supply or loose or damaged ducts. Due to the special techniques and equipment required, diagnosis of certain problems should be left to a dealer service department or repair shop. The home mechanic can, however, check the connections and linkages

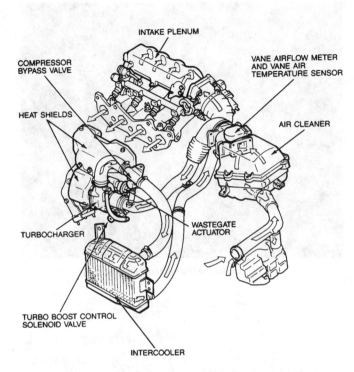

13.1   Turbocharger functional diagram

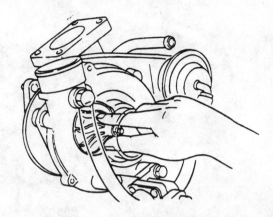

13.5   Check the turbine bearings for roughness and play

for damage and proper installation, check the turbine shaft for loose or seized bearings and remove and install the turbocharger to save the labor expense of replacing the turbo unit. Before replacing the turbo, check the owners manual for warranty information. Depending on the time in service, mileage and cause of failure, the turbo may be covered by extended or emission system warranties.

3   Because each turbocharger has its own distinctive sound, a change in the noise level can be a sign of potential problems. A high pitched whistling sound may indicate bearing failure or an intake or exhaust leak. If the turbocharger makes unusual sounds, have it checked by a dealer or repair shop.

4   Check the exhaust manifold and fittings periodically for leaks and cracks. Check for leaks in the coolant and oil lines. **Caution:** *Any time a*

major engine bearing such as a main, connecting rod or camshaft bearing is replaced, the turbocharger should be checked and flushed with clean engine oil.

5   To check the turbocharger for bearing failure, shut the engine off and allow it to cool completely. Remove the intake air duct. Turn and rock the turbine back and forth and in and out by hand **(see illustration)**. If the turbine rubs the housing, is seized or excessive bearing play or roughness is noted, replace the turbocharger.

Removal

Refer to illustrations 13.9a, 13.9b, 13.10, 13.11a, 13.11b, 13.12, 13.13, 13.14, 13.15, 13.19 and 13.20

6   If the vehicle is air conditioned, the factory recommends you have the refrigerant discharged by a dealer service department or automotive air conditioning shop. This allows removal of the air conditioning compressor refrigerant lines for clearance. However, we were able to remove the turbocharger assembly without detaching the refrigerant lines by removing the cooling fan assembly (see Chapter 3).

7   Disconnect the negative cable from the battery terminal.

8   Allow the engine to cool, then drain the coolant (see Chapter 1).

9   Remove the heat shields from the exhaust manifold and turbocharger assembly **(see illustrations)**. **Note:** *It may be necessary to disconnect the oxygen sensor and move the wiring away from the heat shield.*

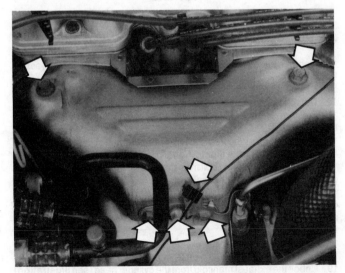

13.9a   Unclip the wire and unbolt the heat shields (arrows)

13.9b   The lower heat shield is secured by bolts (arrows)

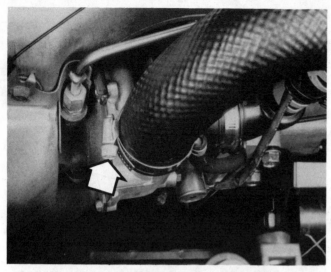

13.10   Loosen the hose clamp (arrow) and detach the air hose

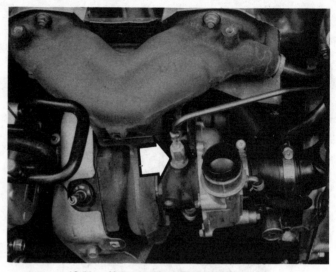

13.11a   Unscrew the oil feed line (arrow)

13.11b   Remove the oil return line bolts (arrows)

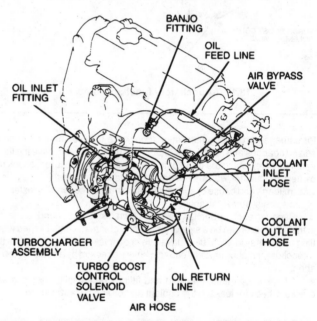

13.12   Turbocharger mounting details

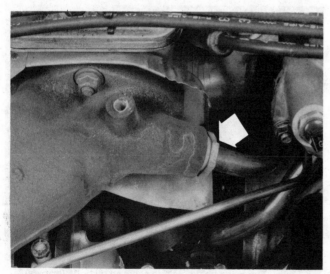

13.13   Disconnect the EGR tube (arrow)

10   Remove the air hoses from the turbocharger inlet and outlet (**see il-lustration**).

11   Disconnect the oil lines from the turbocharger (**see illustrations**).

12   Detach the coolant hoses from the turbocharger (**see illustration**).

13   Disconnect the EGR tube from the exhaust manifold (**see illustra-tion**).

14   Remove the air tube from the turbo boost control solenoid valve at the turbocharger outlet (**see illustration**).

15   Remove the mounting bolt from the retaining bracket under the turbo-charger assembly (**see illustration**).

16   On air conditioned models, detach the refrigerant line from the head of the air conditioning compressor to provide clearance for turbocharger removal (see Step 1). **Warning:** *The refrigerant must be discharged be-fore opening the system!*

17   Remove the exhaust gas oxygen sensor (see Chapter 6).

18   Unbolt the front exhaust pipe from the turbocharger joint pipe.

19   Unbolt the exhaust manifold from the cylinder head (**see illustration**) and lift the manifold/turbocharger from the engine compartment as an as-sembly.

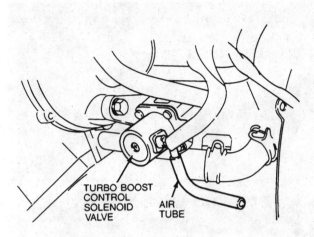

13.14 Remove the air tube from the turbo boost control solenoid valve

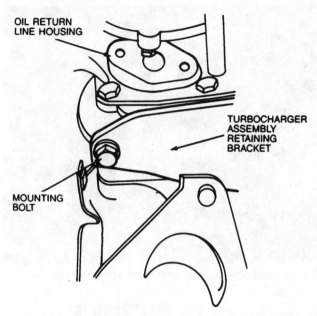

13.15 Remove the mounting bolt from the retaining bracket under the turbocharger assembly

13.19 Remove the six manifold-to-head nuts (arrows) – the lower ones are hidden by the manifold

13.20 Turbocharger components – exploded view

20 Remove the remaining heat shields and detach the manifold components from the turbocharger (see illustration).

Installation

Refer to illustration 13.21

21 Installation is basically the reverse of removal. Using new gaskets, install the joint pipe and heat shield assembly onto the turbocharger with the special mounting nuts and then install the exhaust manifold onto the turbocharger. Position the turbocharger/exhaust manifold assembly on the cylinder head with a new gasket (see illustration) and start the nuts by hand. Tighten the fasteners to the torque listed in this Chapter's Specifications. Note: *Be sure to add about one ounce of engine oil to the oil passage of the turbo before the oil feed line is installed.*

13.21 Place a new gasket/heat shield over the cylinder head studs

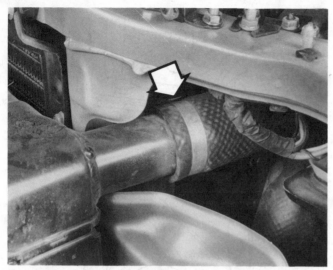

14.3   Loosen the hose clamps (arrow) from the upper and
lower hoses

14.4   Unbolt the bracket (arrows) for access

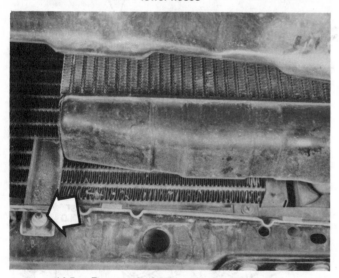

14.5a   Remove the lower mounting nut (arrow)

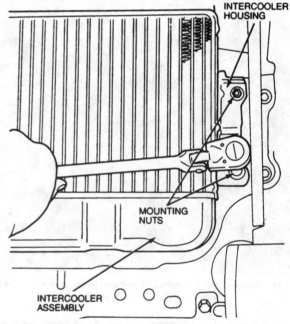

14.5b   Remove the mounting nuts on the lower side bracket

22   After installing the turbocharger, perform the following:
   a) Disconnect the electrical connector from the ignition coil
   b) Crank the engine for approximately 20 seconds
   c) Reconnect the ignition coil
23   If the air conditioning system was discharged, have it evacuated, recharged and leak tested by the shop that discharged it.

14   Intercooler – removal and installation

Refer to illustrations 14.3, 14.4, 14.5a, 14.5b and 14.5c

1   The intercooler lowers the temperature of the intake air on turbocharged engines.
2   Remove the grille and front bumper (see Chapter 11).
3   Loosen the hose clamps **(see illustration)**, then disconnect the air
hoses from the intercooler.
4   Remove the upper bracket for access **(see illustration)**.
5   Remove the mounting nuts **(see illustrations)** and lift the intercooler
from the vehicle.

14.5c   Remove the upper mounting nuts (arrows)

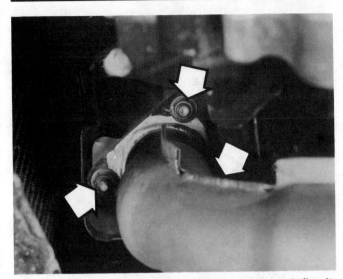

15.3 Apply penetrating oil to the fasteners (arrows) and allow it to soak in (rear nut hidden by pipe)

6   Inspect the intercooler for cracks and damage to the flanges, tubes and fins. Replace it if necessary.
7   Installation is the reverse of removal.

15   Exhaust system components – replacement

Warning: *Allow the exhaust system to cool completely before following this procedure. Wear eye protection when working on exhaust parts.*
Note: *See Chapter 6 for catalytic converter replacement.*

Front exhaust (converter inlet) pipe

Refer to illustrations 15.3, 15.4a and 15.4b

1   Detach the cable from the negative terminal of the battery.
2   Raise the vehicle and place it securely on jackstands.
3   Apply penetrating oil to the fasteners and allow it to soak in **(see illustration)**.
4   Remove the clamp on the heat shield, if equipped **(see illustrations)**. On V6 models, unplug the exhaust gas oxygen sensor.
5   Unbolt the front pipe from the manifold(s) at the front and the catalytic converter at the rear.
6   Push the catalytic converter back and lower the front exhaust pipe from the vehicle.
7   Inspect the flanges, gaskets and fasteners and replace as necessary.
8   Loosely assemble the pipe, gaskets and fasteners between the manifold(s) and catalytic converter. Ensure that the gaskets are properly seated and the parts aligned correctly. Tighten the fasteners securely from front to rear. Avoid placing stress on the exhaust manifold(s).
9   The remainder of installation is the reverse of removal.
10   Start the engine and check for exhaust leaks and rattles.

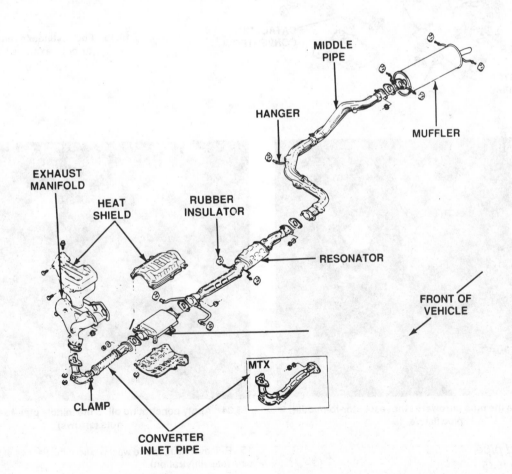

15.4a   Four-cylinder exhaust system (non-turbo) – exploded view

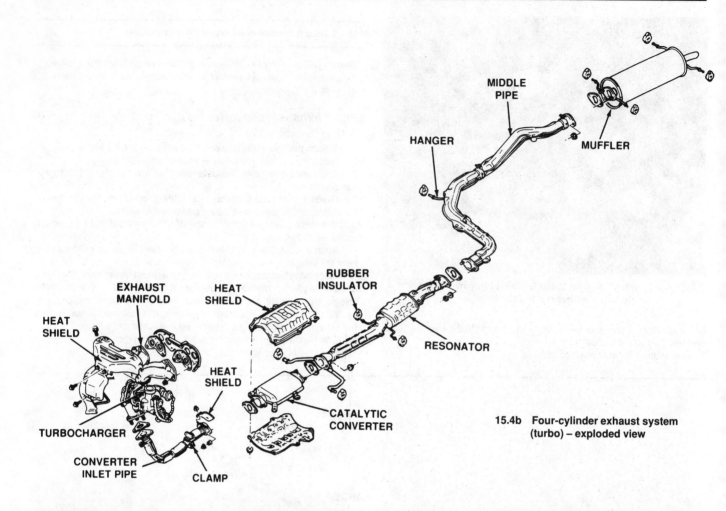

15.4b   Four-cylinder exhaust system
(turbo) – exploded view

15.15   Remove the nuts (arrows) at the resonator-to-middle
pipe flange

15.34   Apply penetrating oil to the middle pipe-to-muffler flange
nuts (arrows)

Resonator and pipe

Refer to illustration 15.15

11   Detach the cable from the negative terminal of the battery.
12   Raise the vehicle and place it securely on jackstands.
13   Support the exhaust system at the catalytic converter.
14   Apply penetrating oil to the fasteners and allow it to soak in.

15   Remove the nuts and washers from the flanges at both ends of the pipe (see illustration).
16   Remove the rubber hangers from the resonator pipe and middle pipe.
17   Push the resonator pipe back and separate it from the catalytic converter. Lower the pipe and pull it away from the middle pipe until it is free, then lower it from the vehicle.

18 Inspect the flanges, gaskets and fasteners and replace as necessary.
19 Loosely assemble the pipe, gaskets and fasteners between the catalytic converter and center pipe. Ensure that the gaskets are properly seated and the parts aligned correctly. Tighten the fasteners securely from front to rear.
20 The remainder of installation is the reverse of removal.
21 Start the engine and check for exhaust leaks and rattles.

Middle pipe

22 Detach the cable from the negative terminal of the battery.
23 Raise the vehicle and place it securely on jackstands.
24 Apply penetrating oil to the fasteners and allow it to soak in.
25 Remove the nuts and washers from the flanges at both ends of the middle pipe.
26 Remove the rubber hangers from the middle pipe and muffler.
27 Push the middle pipe back and separate it from the resonator pipe. Lower the pipe and pull it away from the muffler until it is free, then lower it from the vehicle.
28 Inspect the flanges, gaskets and fasteners and replace as necessary.
29 Loosely assemble the pipe, gaskets and fasteners between the resonator and muffler. Ensure that the gaskets are properly seated and the parts aligned correctly. Tighten the fasteners securely from front to rear.
30 The remainder of installation is the reverse of removal.
31 Start the engine and check for exhaust leaks and rattles.

Muffler

Refer to illustration 15.34

32 Detach the cable from the negative terminal of the battery.
33 Raise the vehicle and place it securely on jackstands.
34 Apply penetrating oil to the fasteners **(see illustration)** and allow it to soak in.
35 Remove the nuts and washers from the flange at the front of the muffler.
36 Remove the rubber hangers from the muffler.
37 Pull the muffler back and separate it from the middle pipe. Lower the muffler from the vehicle.
38 Inspect the flanges, gaskets and fasteners and replace as necessary.
39 Loosely assemble the muffler, gaskets and fasteners. Ensure that the gasket is properly seated and the parts aligned correctly. Tighten the fasteners securely.
40 The remainder of installation is the reverse of removal.
41 Start the engine and check for exhaust leaks and rattles.

Chapter 5   Engine electrical systems

Contents

Specifications

Drivebelt deflection .... See Chapter 1

Battery voltage

Engine off 12-volts
Engine running .... 14 to 15-volts

Ignition timing (BTDC)

Four cylinder turbo .... 9 degrees ± 1 degree
Four cylinder non-turbo .... 6 degrees ± 1 degree
V6 .... Refer to the VECI label under the hood

Spark plug wire resistance .... 5000 ohms per foot

Ignition coil resistance
Four-cylinder models
  Turbo
    Primary .... 0.72 to .88 ohms
    Secondary .... 10.3 to 13.9 K-ohms
    Case .... 10 M-ohms minimum
  Non-turbo
    Primary .... 1.04 to 1.27 ohms
    Secondary .... 7.1 to 9.7 K-ohms
    Case .... 10 M-ohms minimum
V6 models
  Primary .... 0.3 to 1.0 ohms
  Secondary .... 8.0 to 11.5 K-ohms

1   General information

The engine electrical systems include all ignition, charging and starting components. Because of their engine-related functions, these components are considered separately from chassis electrical devices such as the lights, instruments, etc.

Be very careful when working on the engine electrical components. They are easily damaged if checked, connected or handled improperly. The alternator is driven by an engine drivebelt which could cause serious injury if your hands, hair or clothes become entangled in it with the engine running. Both the starter and alternator are connected directly to the battery and could arc or even cause a fire if mishandled, overloaded or shorted out.

Never leave the ignition switch on for long periods of time with the engine off. Don't disconnect the battery cables while the engine is running. Correct polarity must be maintained when connecting battery cables from another source, such as another vehicle, during jump starting. Always disconnect the negative cable first and connect it last or the battery may be shorted by the tool being used to loosen the cable clamps.

Additional safety related information on the engine electrical systems can be found in Safety first near the front of this manual. It should be referred to before beginning any operation included in this Chapter.

2   Battery – removal and installation

1   Disconnect both cables from the battery terminals. **Caution:** *Always disconnect the negative cable first and hook it up last or the battery may be shorted by the tool being used to loosen the cable clamps.*
2   Locate the battery hold-down clamp between the battery and the air cleaner housing. Remove the bolt and the hold-down clamp.
3   Lift out the battery. Special straps that attach to the battery posts are available – lifting and moving the battery is much easier if you use one.
4   Installation is the reverse of removal.

3   Battery – emergency jump starting

Refer to the Booster battery (jump) starting procedure in the front part of this manual.

4   Battery cables – check and replacement

1   Periodically inspect the entire length of each battery cable for damage, cracked or burned insulation and corrosion. Poor battery cable connections can cause starting problems and decreased engine performance.
2   Check the cable-to-terminal connections at the ends of the cables for cracks, loose wire strands and corrosion. The presence of white, fluffy deposits under the insulation at the cable terminal connection is a sign that the cable is corroded and should be replaced. Check the terminals for distortion, missing mounting bolts and corrosion.
3   When replacing the cables, always disconnect the negative cable first and hook it up last, or the battery may be shorted by the tool used to loosen the cable clamps. Even if only the positive cable is being replaced, be sure to disconnect the negative cable from the battery first.
4   Disconnect and remove the cable. Make sure the replacement cable is the same length and diameter as the cable being replaced.
5   Clean the threads of the relay or ground connection with a wire brush to remove rust and corrosion. Apply a light coat of petroleum jelly to the threads to help prevent future corrosion.
6   Attach the cable to the relay or ground connection and tighten the mounting nut/bolt securely.
7   Before connecting the new cable to the battery, make sure that it reaches the battery post without having to be stretched.
8   Connect the positive cable first, followed by the negative cable.

5   Ignition system – general information

The ignition systems on the models covered by this manual are of a solid state electronic design consisting of an ignition module, coil, distributor, spark plug wires and spark plugs. Mechanically the systems are similar to a breaker point system, except that the distributor cam and ignition points are replaced by an armature and magnetic pickup unit. The coil primary circuit is controlled by an amplifier module.

On all models, when the ignition is switched on, the ignition primary circuit is energized. When the distributor armature "teeth" or "spokes" approach the magnetic coil assembly, a voltage is induced which signals the amplifier to turn off the coil primary current. A timing circuit in the amplifier module turns the coil current back on after the coil field has collapsed.

When it's on, current flows from the battery through the ignition switch, the coil primary winding, the amplifier module and then to ground. When the current is interrupted, the magnetic field in the ignition coil collapses, inducing a high voltage in the coil secondary windings. The voltage is conducted to the distributor where the rotor directs it to the appropriate spark plug. This process is repeated continuously.

All vehicles are equipped with a distributor which houses a "Hall Effect" switch. The distributors on four-cylinder non-turbo models have a centrifugal and vacuum advance. On V6 and turbocharged models, the ignition advance curve is controlled by the ECA.

V6 models use the Thick Film Integrated IV (TFI-IV) ignition module, which is housed in a plastic box mounted on the base of the distributor. On four-cylinder turbo models, the ignition module is mounted adjacent to the coil. On four-cylinder non-turbo models, the module is mounted inside the distributor.

6.2   To use a calibrated ignition tester (available at most auto parts stores), simply disconnect a spark plug wire, attach the wire to the tester, then clip the tester to a convenient ground – if there is enough power to fire the plug, sparks will be clearly visible between the electrode tip and the tester body as the engine is turned over

6   Ignition system – check

Refer to illustration 6.2

Warning: *Because of the very high secondary (spark plug) voltage generated by the ignition system, extreme care should be taken when this check is done.*

Calibrated ignition tester method

1   If the engine turns over but won't start, disconnect the spark plug lead from any spark plug and attach it to a calibrated ignition tester (available at most auto parts stores). Make sure the tester is designed for Ford ignition systems if a universal tester isn't available.

2   Connect the clip on the tester to a known good ground **(see illustration)**, crank the engine and watch the end of the tester to see if bright blue, well-defined sparks occur.

3   If sparks occur, sufficient voltage is reaching the plug to fire it (repeat the check at the remaining plug wires to verify that the distributor cap and rotor are OK). However, the plugs themselves may be fouled, so remove and check them as described in Chapter 1 or install new ones.

4   If no sparks or intermittent sparks occur, remove the distributor cap and check the cap and rotor as described in Chapter 1. If moisture is present, dry out the cap and rotor, then reinstall the cap and repeat the spark test.

5   If there's still no spark, detach the coil secondary wire from the distributor cap and connect it up to the tester (reattach the plug wire to the spark plug), then repeat the spark check.

6   If no sparks occur, check the primary (small) wire connections at the coil to make sure they're clean and tight. Refer to Section 7 and check the ignition coil supply voltage circuit. Make any necessary repairs, then repeat the check again.

7   If sparks now occur, the distributor cap, rotor, plug wire(s) or spark plug(s) (or all of them) may be defective.

8   If there's still no spark, the coil to the cap wire may be bad (check the resistance with an ohmmeter and compare it to the Specifications). If a known good wire doesn't make any difference in the test results, the ignition coil, module or other internal components may be defective.

Alternative method

Note: *If you're unable to obtain a calibrated ignition tester, the following method will allow you to determine if the ignition system has spark, but it*

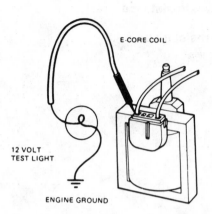

7.2   To check the ignition coil primary circuit, attach a 12-volt test light between the coil TACH terminal and a good engine ground

won't tell you if there's enough voltage produced to actually initiate combustion in the cylinders.

9   Remove the wire from one of the spark plugs. Using an insulated tool, hold the wire about 1/4-inch from a good ground and have an assistant crank the engine.

10   If bright blue, well-defined sparks occur, sufficient voltage is reaching the plug to fire it. However, the plug(s) may be fouled, so remove and check them as described in Chapter 1, or install new ones.

11   If there's no spark, check the remaining wires in the same manner. A few sparks followed by no spark is the same condition as no spark at all.

12   If no sparks occur, remove the distributor cap and check the cap and rotor as described in Chapter 1. If moisture is present, dry out the cap and rotor, then reinstall the cap and repeat the spark test.

13   If there's still no spark, disconnect the coil secondary wire from the distributor cap, hold it about 1/4-inch from a good engine ground and crank the engine again.

14   If no sparks occur, check the primary (small) wire connections at the coil to make sure they're clean and tight. Refer to Section 7 and check the ignition coil supply voltage circuit. Make any necessary repairs, then repeat the check again.

15   If sparks now occur, the distributor cap, rotor, plug wire(s) or spark plug(s) (or all of them) may be defective.

16   If there's still no spark, the coil-to-cap wire may be bad (check the resistance with an ohmmeter and compare it to the Specifications). If a known good wire doesn't make any difference in the test results, the ignition coil, module or other internal components may be defective.

7   Ignition coil, circuits and power relay – check and coil replacement

Check

Ignition coil primary circuit

Refer to illustration 7.2

1   Unplug the ignition wiring harness connectors and inspect them for dirt, corrosion and damage, then reconnect them.

2   Attach a 12-volt DC test light between the coil TACH terminal and a good engine ground **(see illustration)**.

3   Crank the engine.

4   If the light flashes, or comes on but doesn't flash, go to Step 7.

5   If the light stays off or is very dim, go to Step 16.

6   Remove the test light.

Ignition coil primary resistance

Refer to illustrations 7.9a, 7.9b and 7.9c

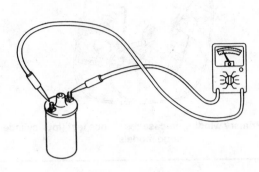

7.9a Coil primary resistance test (four-cylinder non-turbo models)

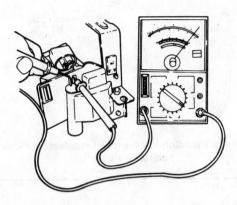

7.9b Coil primary resistance test (four-cylinder turbo models)

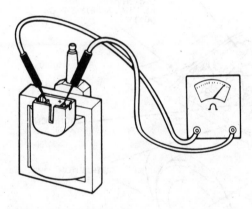

7.9c Measuring ignition coil primary resistance (V6 models)

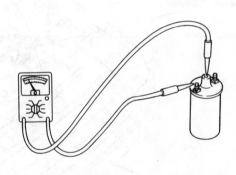

7.12a Measuring ignition coil secondary resistance (four-cylinder non-turbo models)

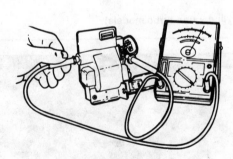

7.12b Measuring ignition coil secondary resistance (four-cylinder turbo models)

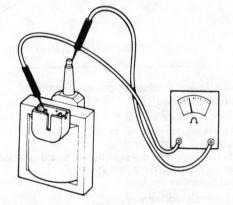

7.12c Measuring ignition coil secondary resistance (V6 models)

7 Turn the ignition switch to the Off position.

8 Unplug the ignition coil wire harness connector. Inspect it for dirt, corrosion and damage.

9 Using an ohmmeter, measure the resistance between the primary terminals of the ignition coil **(see illustrations)**.

10 If the indicated resistance is within the limits shown in this Chapter's Specifications, proceed to Step 12.

11 If the indicated resistance is less or more than specified, replace the ignition coil (Steps 26 through 29).

Ignition coil secondary resistance

Refer to illustrations 7.12a, 7.12b and 7.12c

12 Measure the resistance between the negative primary terminal and the secondary terminal of the ignition coil **(see illustrations)**.

13 If the indicated resistance is within the specification, proceed to Step 19.

14 If the indicated resistance is less or more than the specified resistance, replace the ignition coil (see Step 26).

15 Reconnect the ignition coil wires.

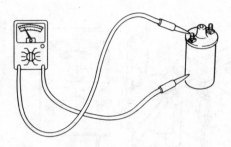

7.16a   Primary winding-to-case resistance test (four-cylinder non-turbo models)

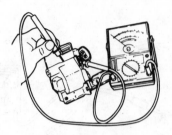

7.16b   Primary winding-to-case resistance test (four-cylinder turbo models)

NON-TURBO

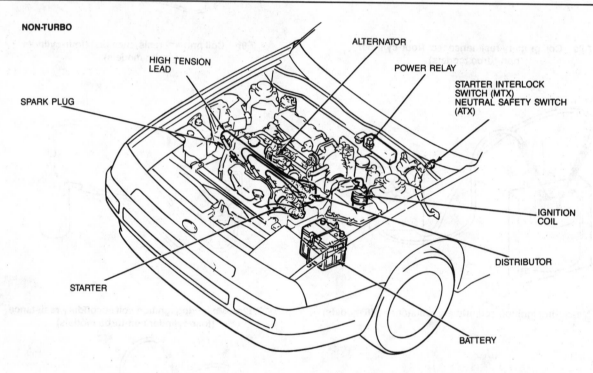

HIGH TENSION LEAD

ALTERNATOR

POWER RELAY

STARTER INTERLOCK SWITCH (MTX)
NEUTRAL SAFETY SWITCH (ATX)

SPARK PLUG

IGNITION COIL

DISTRIBUTOR

STARTER

BATTERY

7.30a   Ignition system component locations (four-cylinder non-turbo models)

Ignition coil primary winding-to-case resistance (four-cylinder engines)

Refer to illustrations 7.16a and 7.16b

16   Measure the resistance from the positive primary terminal to the case of the ignition coil (see illustrations).

17   If the indicated resistance is less or more than the specified resistance, replace the ignition coil (see Step 26).

18   Reconnect the ignition coil wires.

Ignition coil supply voltage

19   Unplug the ignition coil wire harness.

20   Attach the negative lead of a voltmeter to the distributor base.

21   Measure battery voltage.

22   Turn the ignition switch to the Run position.

23   Measure the voltage at the positive terminal of the ignition coil (see illustrations 7.2a, 7.2b and 7.2c).

24   If the indicated voltage is 90-percent of battery voltage, inspect the ignition coil connector and terminals for dirt, corrosion and damage. If both the connector and terminals are clean, replace the ignition coil.

25   If the indicated voltage is less than 90-percent of battery voltage, inspect and repair the circuit between the ignition coil and the ignition switch (refer to the wiring diagrams at the end of the book). Check the ignition switch for damage and wear.

7.30b   Power relay location (arrow) (four-cylinder turbo models)

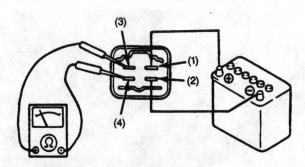

7.31   Checking power relay operation (four-cylinder models)

Ignition coil replacement

26   Detach the cable from the negative terminal of the battery.
27   Unplug the coil secondary lead, then detach the primary terminal connector from the coil **(see illustrations)**.
28   Remove the bracket bolts and detach the coil.
29   Installation is the reverse of removal.

Power relay check (four-cylinder models)

Refer to illustrations 7.30a, 7.30b and 7.31

30   A clicking sound should be heard at the relay when turning the ignition on and off **(see illustrations)**.
31   With an ohmmeter connected to terminals No. three and four of the relay, continuity should exist only when 12-volts is applied to terminal No. one and a ground is applied to terminal No. two **(see illustration)**.
32   Replace power relay if not as specified.

---

8   Distributor – removal and installation

Refer to illustration 8.5

Removal

1   Disconnect the primary wires from the coil.
2   Unplug the distributor primary electrical connector.
3   Remove the distributor cap.
4   Mark the relationship of the rotor to the distributor housing, directly below the tip of the rotor.
5   Mark the relationship of distributor to to the engine, if a mark doesn't already exist **(see illustration)**.
6   Remove the distributor hold down-bolt(s).
7   Pull the distributor straight out to remove it. If you are working on a V6 engine, be careful not to disturb the oil pump driveshaft.
Caution: *Do not turn the crankshaft while the distributor is removed, or the reference marks will be useless.*

Installation

If the crankshaft was not moved while the distributor was out

8   Using the reference marks made during removal, insert the distributor into the engine in exactly the same relationship to the engine when removed.
9   To mesh the camshaft and the distributor, it may be necessary to turn the rotor slightly back and forth.
10   On V6 models, if the distributor doesn't seat completely, the hex shaped recess in the lower end of the distributor shaft is not mating properly with the oil pump driveshaft.
11   On all models, recheck the alignment marks between the distributor and the engine to verify that the distributor is in the same position it was in before removal.
12   Check the rotor to see if it's aligned with the mark you made on the distributor. If it isn't, pull the distributor out, turn the rotor slightly and reinstall it. Install the distributor cap.
13   Install retaining bolt(s). Don't tighten them completely until the ignition timing has been checked and, if necessary, adjusted (see Section 9).

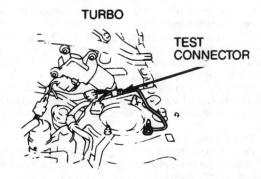

8.5   Mark the position of the distributor housing to the engine if marks don't already exist

9.4   Ground the STI connector (the single-wire connector near the left strut tower) to set the ignition timing (turbo models)

If the crankshaft was moved while the distributor was out

14   Locate Top Dead Center (TDC) for the number one piston by following the procedure in Chapter 2, Part C.
15   Insert the distributor so the rotor will be pointing to the number one spark plug wire terminal when the distributor cap is installed. Install the distributor cap.
16   Install the retaining bolt(s). Don't tighten them completely until the ignition timing has been checked and, if necessary, adjusted (see Section 9).

---

9   Ignition timing – check and adjustment

Refer to illustrations 9.4, 9.5a and 9.5b
Note: *If the information in this Section differs from the Vehicle Emission Control Information label in the engine compartment, the label should be considered correct.*

1   Apply the parking brake and block the wheels. Place the transmission in Park (automatic) or Neutral (manual). Turn off all accessories (heater, air conditioner, etc.).
2   Start the engine and warm it up. Once it has reached operating temperature, turn it off.
3   On non-turbo four cylinder models, disconnect and plug the vacuum lines at the distributor.
4   On turbo models, connect a jumper wire between the STI test connector and ground **(see illustration)**.

9.5a   The in-line spout connector (arrow) must be disconnected before the ignition timing is checked or adjusted

9.5b   To disconnect the in-line spout connector, simply pull the plastic plug out of the housing (don't lose the plug – you will not be able to operate the vehicle if you misplace it)

5   On V6 engines, unplug the in-line spout connector located near the distributor **(see illustrations)**.

6   Connect an inductive timing light and a tachometer in accordance with the manufacturer's instructions. **Caution:** *Make sure the timing light and tach wires don't hang anywhere near the drivebelt or electric cooling fan or they may become entangled.*

7   Locate the timing marks at the crankshaft pulley and timing cover **(see illustrations)**. **Note:** *You may have to clean the edge of the damper with a wire brush and solvent. Dabs of paint will make the marks more visible.*

8   Start the engine again.

9   Point the timing light at the timing marks on the crankshaft pulley and note whether the timing mark is aligned with the stationary pointer on the timing cover (see Section 9).

10   Tighten the distributor hold-down bolt securely when the timing is correct and recheck it to make sure it didn't change position when the bolt was tightened.

11   Turn off the engine.

12   On non-turbo four-cylinder models, reconnect the vacuum hoses.

13   On turbo models, remove the ground wire from the STI connector. On V6 models, plug in the spout connector.

14   On all models, turn off the engine and remove the timing light.

10   Ignition module – check and replacement

Caution: *The ignition module is a delicate and relatively expensive electronic component. The following tests must be done with the right equipment by someone who knows how to use it properly. Failure to follow the step-by-step procedures could result in damage to the module and/or other electronic devices, including the Electronic Control Assembly (ECA). Additionally, all devices under computer control are protected by a Federally mandated warranty. Check with your dealer before attempting to diagnose them yourself.*

Check (V6 models only)

Note: *The information for checking modules on four-cylinder models is not available.*

Refer to illustration 10.9

1   Unplug the wiring harness connector from the ignition module. Inspect it for dirt, corrosion and/or damage, then plug it back in.

2   Unplug the single wire connector located immediately above the ignition module connector.

3   Using a calibrated spark tester, check for spark (see Section 6).

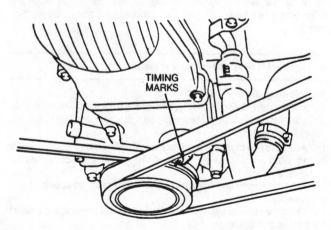

9.7a   Timing marks location (four-cylinder models)

9.7b   Timing marks location (V6 models)

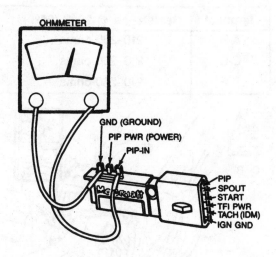

10.9   Ignition module terminal identification (V6 models)

10.16   To detach the TFI-IV ignition module from the distributor base, remove the two screws (arrows) (V6 models)

4   If there is no spark, proceed to Step 7.
5   If there is spark, the problem may be within the EEC-IV electronic control module (ECA). Diagnosis of such problems is beyond the scope of the home mechanic. Take the vehicle to a dealer service department.
6   Remove the spark tester and reconnect the single wire connector.
7   Remove the distributor from the engine.
8   Remove the module from the distributor.
9   Using an ohmmeter, ensure resistance between terminals GND and PIP IN is greater the 500 ohms **(see illustration)**.
10   Ensure resistance between terminals PIP PWR and PIP IN is less then 2000 ohms.
11   Ensure resistance between terminals PIP PWR and TFI PWR is less then 200 ohms.
12   Ensure resistance between terminals GND and IGN GND is less the 2 ohms.
13   Ensure resistance between terminals PIP IN and PIP is less than

200 ohms.
14   Replace the module if any of the readings are not as specified.

Replacement

Refer to illustrations 10.16, 10.17 and 10.18

15   Remove the distributor from the engine (refer to Section 8).
16   Remove the two module mounting screws with a 1/4-inch drive 7/32-inch deep socket **(see illustration)**.
17   Pull straight down on the module to disconnect the spade connectors from the stator connector **(see illustration)**.
18   Apply a film of silicone dielectric grease (usually included with new modules) to the back side of the module **(see illustration)**.
19   Installation is the reverse of removal. When plugging in the module, make sure the three terminals are inserted all the way into the stator connector.

10.17   Pull the module straight down to detach the spade terminals from the stator connector (V6 models)

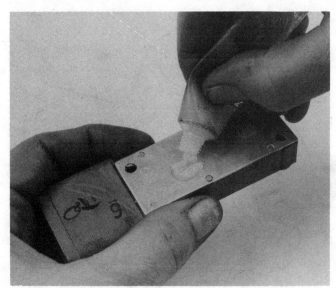

10.18   Be sure to wipe the back side of the module clean and apply a film of dielectric grease (essential for cool operation of the module) – DO NOT use any other type of grease (V6 models)

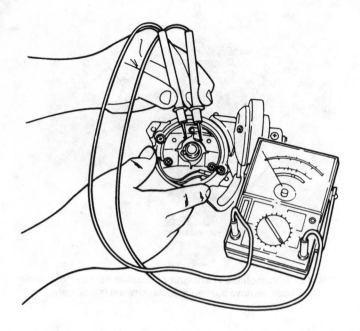

11.2   Checking the resistance of the distributor pickup coil (four-cylinder non-turbo models)

Terminal	Resistance @ 20°C (68°F)
A-B	210–260 ohms
C-D	210–260 ohms
E-F	210–260 ohms

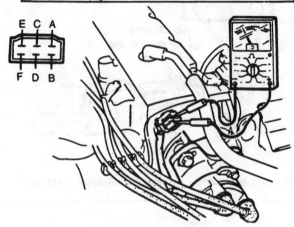

11.6   Checking the resistance of the distributor pickup coil (four-cylinder turbo models)

11   Distributor stator/pickup coil assembly – check (four-cylinder only) and replacement

Check

Four-cylinder non-turbo models

Refer to illustration 11.2

1   Remove the distributor cap, the rotor and the dust cover.
2   Using an ohmmeter, check the resistance between the pickup coil terminals **(see illustration)**.
3   If resistance is not 900 to 1200 ohms, it should be replaced.

Four-cylinder turbo models

Refer to illustration 11.6

4   Ensure the distributor electrical harness and connectors are okay.
5   Disconnect the distributor electrical connector.
6   Using an ohmmeter, check the resistance across terminals A and B, C and D, and E and F **(see illustration)**.
7   If any resistance is not within 210 to 260 ohms, the distributor should be replaced.

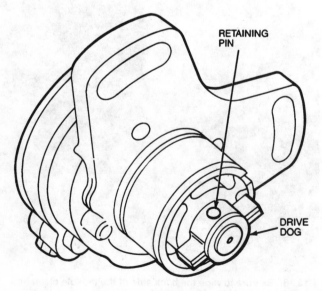

11.11   Remove the pin retaining the drive dog (four-cylinder non-turbo models)

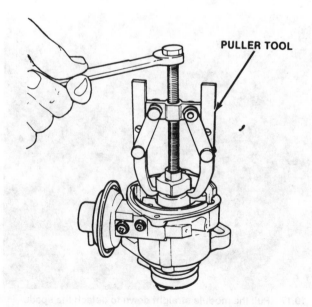

11.13   Before removing the signal rotor, note direction of arrow stamped on the rotor (four-cylinder non-turbo models)

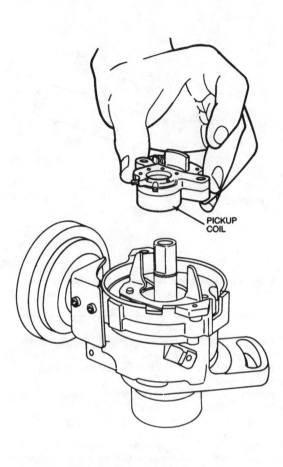

11.16   Removing the pickup coil (four cylinder
non-turbo models)

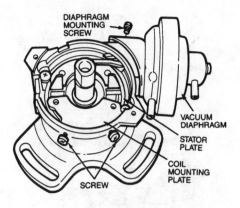

11.17   The pickup coil mounting plate is retained by two screws
(four-cylinder non-turbo models)

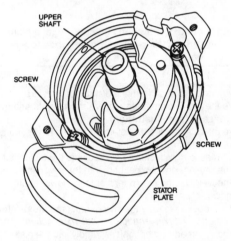

11.20   View of the stator plate and the upper shaft (four-cylinder
non-turbo models)

Replacement

Four-cylinder non-turbo models

Refer to illustrations 11.11, 11.13, 11.16, 11.17, 11.20, 11.22, 11.24, 11.31, 11.33, 11.34 and 11.43

8   Remove the rotor and the dust cover.
9   Remove the gasket from the cover.
10   Mark the relation of the drive dog to the lower shaft.
11   Using a punch and hammer, remove the retaining pin from the drive dog **(see illustration)**.
12   Remove the retaining screw from the center of the signal rotor.
13   Using a two jaw puller, pull the signal rotor and pin from the upper shaft. Note the direction of the arrow stamped into the rotor **(see illustration)**.
14   Label and disconnect the two wires from the pickup coil.
15   Remove the electrical harness from the distributor housing.
16   Remove the pickup coil **(see illustration)**.
17   Remove the two side mounting screws and the pickup coil mounting plate **(see illustration)**.
18   Remove the E-clip from the stator plate.
19   Remove the vacuum advance mounting screws, then remove the vacuum advance **(see illustration 11.17)**.
20   Remove the two screws retaining the stator plate. Remove the stator plate and the upper shaft **(see illustration)**.
21   Remove the stator from the upper shaft.
22   Since the distributor is dismantled this far, now is a good time to check

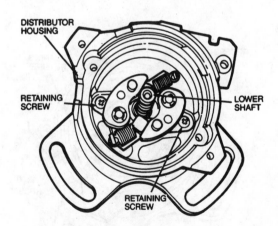

11.22   The lower shaft assembly is retained by two screws
(four-cylinder non-turbo models)

the lower shaft and centrifugal advance mechanism, as over time, the advance mechanism can become sticky and cease to function correctly. Remove the two screws retaining the lower shaft to the housing **(see illustration)**.

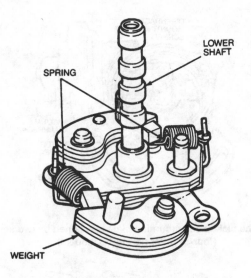

11.24   Details of the lower shaft and centrifugal advance weights and springs (four-cylinder non-turbo models)

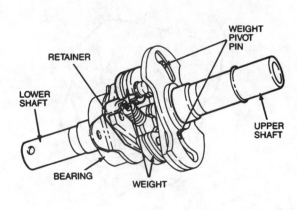

11.31   View of the lower and the upper shaft (four-cylinder non-turbo models)

23   Remove the lower shaft from the distributor housing.
24   Remove the two E-clips, then remove the weights and the springs from the lower shaft **(see illustration)**.
25   Remove the bearing and the retainer from the lower shaft.
26   Remove the seal from the distributor housing.
27   To begin reassembly, install a new seal into the distributor housing.
28   Install the retainer and the bearing onto the lower shaft.
29   Install the weights and the springs onto the lower shaft.
30   Install new E-clips.
31   Install the upper shaft onto the lower shaft **(see illustration)**. **Note:** *Ensure the weight pivot pins engage the advance mechanism.*
32   Install the upper and lower shaft assembly into the distributor housing.

33   Install two screws. Ensure the bearing retainer tabs align with the recesses in the housing **(see illustration)**.
34   Install the stator plate into the distributor **(see illustration)**.
35   Install the two retaining screws.
36   Install the vacuum advance, the E-clips and the two attaching screws.
37   Install the pickup coil mounting plate.
38   Install the pickup coil.
39   Install the pickup coil wiring harness.
40   Connect the pickup coil wires in the position noted during removal.
41   Using a deep socket and the palm of your hand, press the signal rotor and pin onto the upper shaft until it bottoms against the shoulder of the upper shaft. **Note:** *Ensure the direction of the of the arrow stamped onto the signal rotor is pointing in the same direction as before disassembly.*

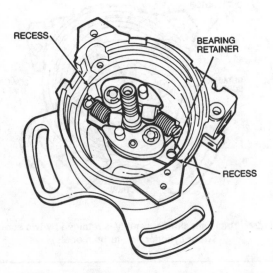

11.33   Be sure to align the tabs on the bearing retainer with the recesses in the housing (four-cylinder non-turbo models)

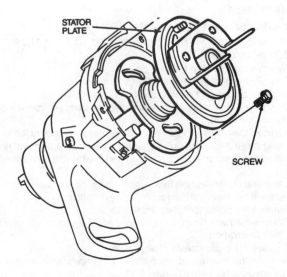

11.34   Installing the stator plate into the distributor (four-cylinder non-turbo models)

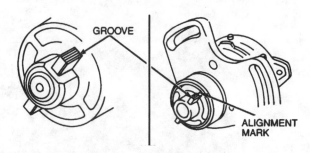

11.43   Align the groove in the drive dog with the mark on the distributor housing

42   Install the signal rotor retaining screw.
43   Align the groove in the drive dog with the alignment mark on the distributor housing **(see illustration)**.
44   Install the retaining pin.
45   Install the cover, gasket and rotor.

Four-cylinder turbo models
46   There is no replacement procedure for the stator/pickup coil on these distributors, because no parts are available. The entire distributor must be replaced (see Section 8).

V6 models
Refer to illustrations 11.54, 11.56, 11.57, 11.58, 11.59, 11.60, 11.64, 11.73a and 11.73b

47   Remove the distributor cap and position it out of the way with the wires attached.
48   Disconnect the TFI module from the wire harness.
49   Remove the distributor (see Section 8).
50   Remove the rotor (see Chapter 1 if necessary).
51   Although not absolutely necessary, it's a good idea to remove the ignition module (see Section 10) to prevent possible damage to the module while the distributor is being disassembled.

52   Clamp the lower end of the distributor housing in a vise. Place shop rags in the vise jaws to prevent damage to the distributor and don't over-tighten the vise.
53   Before removing the drive gear, note that the roll pin is slightly offset. When the distributor is reassembled, the roll pin cannot be reinstalled through the drive gear and distributor shaft holes unless the holes are perfectly lined up.
54   With an assistant holding the distributor steady in the vise, use a pin punch and hammer to drive the roll pin out of the shaft **(see illustration)**.
55   Loosen the vise and reposition the distributor with the drive gear facing up.
56   Remove the drive gear with a small puller **(see illustration)**.
57   Before removing the shaft from the distributor, check the shaft for burrs or built up residue, particularly around the drive gear roll pin hole **(see illustration)**. If burrs or residue are evident, polish the shaft with emery paper and wipe it clean to prevent damage to the lip seal and bushing in the distributor base.

11.54   With the distributor shaft housing locked securely in a vise lined with several shop rags to prevent damage to the housing, drive out the roll pin with a narrow pin punch

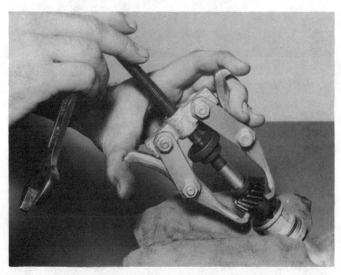

11.56   With the distributor shaft pointing up like this, use a small puller to separate the drive gear from the shaft

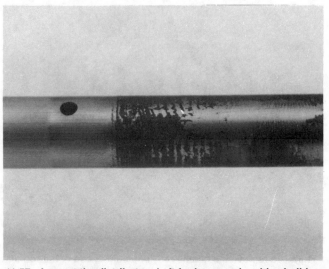

11.57   Inspect the distributor shaft for burrs and residue buildup in the vicinity of the hole for the drive gear roll pin (remove it with emery paper to prevent damage to the distributor shaft bushing when removing and installing the shaft)

11.58   As soon as you remove the distributor shaft, note how the washer is installed before removing it (it could easily fall out and get lost)

11.59   To detach the octane rod from the distributor, remove the retaining screw (arrow) – note the condition of the small square rubber grommet that seals the octane rod hole when you pull the rod out (it seals the interior of the distributor to prevent moisture from damaging the electronics)

58   After removing any burrs/residue, remove the shaft assembly by gently pulling on the plate. Note the relationship of the spacer washer to the distributor base before removing the washer **(see illustration)**.

59   Remove the octane rod retaining screw **(see illustration)**.

60   Lift the inner end of the rod off the stator retaining post **(see illustration)** and pull the octane rod from the distributor base. **Note:** *Don't lose the grommet installed in the octane rod hole. The grommet protects the electronic components of the distributor from moisture.*

61   Remove the two stator screws **(see illustration 11.60).**

62   Gently lift the stator straight up and remove it from the distributor.

63   Check the shaft bushing in the distributor base for wear or signs of excessive heat buildup. If signs of wear and/or damage are evident, replace the complete distributor assembly.

64   Inspect the O-ring at the base of the distributor. If it's damaged or worn, remove it and install a new one **(see illustration)**.

65   Inspect the base casting for cracks and wear. If any damage is evident, replace the distributor assembly.

66   Place the stator assembly in position over the shaft bushing and press it down onto the distributor base until it's completely seated on the posts.

67   Install the stator screws and tighten them securely.

68   Insert the octane rod through the hole in the distributor base and push the inner end of the rod onto the post. **Note:** *Make sure that the octane rod hole is properly sealed by the grommet.*

69   Reinstall the octane rod screw and tighten it securely.

70   Apply a light coat of engine oil to the distributor shaft and insert the shaft through the bushing.

11.60   To remove the octane rod, lift the inner end of the rod off the stator assembly post (arrow) – to remove the stator assembly, remove both mounting screws (arrows) and lift the stator straight up off the posts

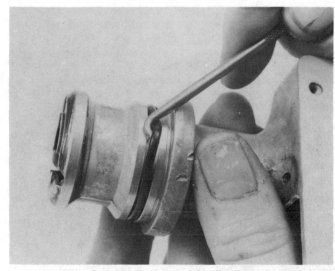

11.64   If the O-ring at the base of the distributor is worn or damaged, replace it with a new one

11.73a   After securing the distributor assembly upside down in a vise, note the roll pin holes in the drive gear and the shaft, then tap the drive gear onto the shaft with a deep socket and hammer

11.73b   If the drive gear and shaft roll pin holes are misaligned, the roll pin cannot be driven through the drive gear and shaft holes – this drive gear must now be pulled off the shaft and realigned

71   Mount the distributor in the vise with the lower end up. Be sure to line the vise jaws with a few clean shop rags to protect the distributor base. Place a block of wood under the distributor shaft to support it and prevent it from falling out while the drive gear is being installed.

72   Using the paint marks you made on the drive gear and the distributor shaft housing, turn the shaft until the drive gear hole (and paint mark), the shaft hole and the the paint mark on the distributor shaft housing are aligned.

73   Using a deep socket and hammer, carefully tap the drive gear back onto the distributor shaft (see illustration). Make sure the hole in the drive gear and the hole in the shaft are lined up. Because the holes were drilled off center by the factory, they must be perfectly aligned or the roll pin cannot be installed (see illustration).

74   Once the drive gear is seated and the holes are lined up, turn the distributor sideways in the vise and, with an assistant holding it steady, drive a new roll pin into the drive gear with a 5/32-inch pin punch. Make sure that neither end of the roll pin protrudes from the drive gear.

75   Check the distributor shaft for smooth rotation, then remove the distributor assembly from the vise.

76   Install the TFI-IV module (see Section 10).

77   Install the rotor (see Chapter 1 if necessary).

78   Install the distributor (see Section 8).

12   Charging system – general information and precautions

The charging system includes the alternator, an internal voltage regulator, a charge indicator or warning light, the battery, a fusible link and the wiring between all the components. The charging system supplies electrical power for the ignition system, the lights, the radio, etc. The alternator is driven by a drivebelt at the front (right end) of the engine.

The purpose of the voltage regulator is to limit the alternator's voltage to a preset value. This prevents power surges, circuit overloads, etc., during peak voltage output. A solid state regulator is housed inside a plastic module mounted on the alternator itself.

The charging system doesn't ordinarily require periodic maintenance. However, the drivebelt, battery and wires and connections should be inspected at the intervals outlined in Chapter 1.

Be very careful when making electrical circuit connections to a vehicle equipped with an alternator and note the following:
a)   When reconnecting wires to the alternator from the battery, be sure to note the polarity.
b)   Before using arc welding equipment to repair any part of the vehicle, disconnect the wires from the alternator and the battery terminals.
c)   Never start the engine with a battery charger connected.
d)   Always disconnect both battery leads before using a battery charger.

13   Charging system – check

1   If a malfunction occurs in the charging circuit, do not immediately assume that the alternator is causing the problem. First check the following items:
a)   The battery cables where they connect to the battery. Make sure the connections are clean and tight.
b)   The battery electrolyte specific gravity. If it is low, charge the battery.
c)   Check the external alternator wiring and connections.
d)   Check the drivebelt condition and tension (see Chapter 1).
e)   Check the alternator mounting bolts for tightness.
f)   Run the engine and check the alternator for abnormal noise.

2   Using a voltmeter, check the battery voltage with the engine off. It should be approximately 12 volts.

3   Start the engine and check the battery voltage again. It should now be approximately 14 to 15 volts.

4   If the indicated voltage reading is less or more than the specified charging voltage, replace the voltage regulator. If replacing the regulator fails to restore the voltage to the specified range, the alternator may be faulty.

5   Due to the special equipment necessary to test or service the alternator, is recommended that if a fault is suspected the vehicle be taken to a dealer or a shop with the proper equipment. Because of this the home mechanic should limit maintenance to checking connections and drive belt tension.

6   The ammeter (ALT) gauge or alternator warning light on the instrument panel indicates charge or discharge – current passing into or out of the battery. With the electrical equipment switched on and the engine idling, the gauge needle may show a discharge condition. At fast idle or at normal driving speeds the needle should stay on the charge side of the gauge, with the charged state of the battery determining just how much charging is needed.

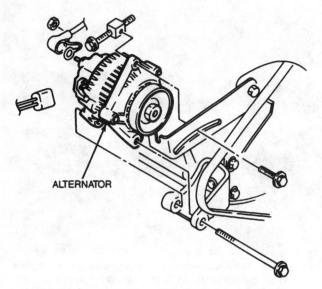

14.5 Alternator mounting details (four-cylinder models)

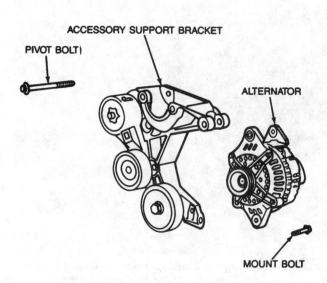

14.9 Alternator mounting details (V6 models)

7   If the gauge does not show a charge or the alternator light (if equipped) remains on, there is a problem in the system. Before replacing the alternator, the battery condition, belt tension and electrical cable connections should be checked.

14   Alternator – removal and installation

1   Detach the cable from the negative terminal of the battery.

Four-cylinder models

Refer to illustration 14.5

2   Raise the vehicle and support it securely on jackstands.
3   Detach the electrical connectors from the alternator.
4   Remove the catalytic converter (see Chapter 6).
5   Loosen the alternator adjustment and pivot bolts and detach the drivebelt **(see illustration)**.
6   Remove the adjustment and pivot bolts and separate the alternator from the engine. Remove the alternator by maneuvering it down, between the steering gear and the right driveaxle.

V6 models

Refer to illustration 14.9

7   Remove the windshield washer reservoir and set it aside (see Chapter 3).
8   Detach the power steering pressure and return hoses from the power steering pump (see Chapter 10).
9   Remove the upper and middle attaching bolts of the accessory support bracket **(see illustration)**.
10   Pull the idler tensioner back with a 1/2-inch drive breaker bar, then remove the lower attaching bolt of the accessory support bracket.
11   Remove the bolt from the side of the support bracket at the air conditioning compressor brace.
12   Lift the mounting bracket/alternator assembly up, then disconnect the electrical connectors from the alternator.
13   Remove the mounting bracket/alternator assembly from the engine. Remove the mounting bolts and separate the alternator from the bracket.

All models

14   Installation is the reverse of removal.
15   After the alternator is installed, adjust the drivebelt tension (see Chapter 1).

15   Voltage regulator/alternator brushes – replacement

Refer to illustrations 15.2, 15.4, 15.5, 15.6, 15.7, 15.8, 15.10, 15.11, 15.12, 15.14, 15.15 and 15.16

1   Remove the alternator (refer to Section 14) and set the alternator on a clean workbench.
2   Mark the alternator halves with a marking pen or a scribe to ensure proper reassembly **(see illustration)**.
3   Remove the through bolts. Don't attempt to pull the alternator apart until you have read the next Step.
4   The rotor bearing is pressed into the rear end frame. Place a 200-watt soldering iron on the rear end frame for two or three minutes **(see illustration)**. If you're using an iron with less output, keep it in contact a few minutes longer.
5   Pull the alternator halves apart. Pry them apart with a screwdriver if necessary, but don't use excessive force. Ensure not to lose the stopper spring around the rear bearing **(see illustration)**. **Caution:** *If the two*

15.2 Mark the relationship of the alternator halves

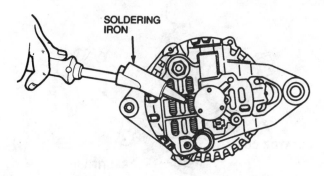

15.4 Heating the rear of the alternator housing to release the rear bearing

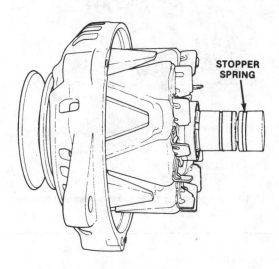

15.5 Be sure not to lose the stopper spring when separating the alternator halves

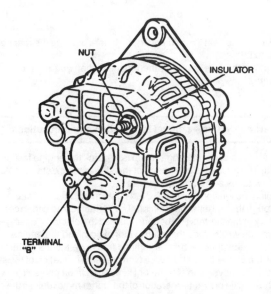

15.6 View of the rear of the alternator

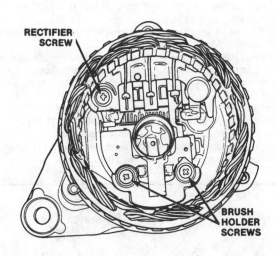

15.7 Rectifier and the brush holder mounting screw locations

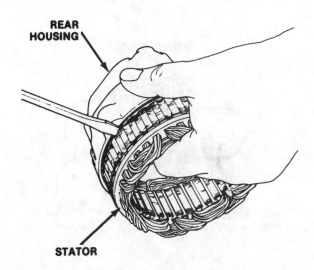

15.8 Removing the stator from the housing

halves don't come apart easily, the rotor bearing is still stuck in its bore. You will damage the bearing or the end frame housing if you use excessive force. Put the soldering iron back on the end frame for a few minutes.

6   Remove the B (battery) terminal nut and insulation brush **(see illustration)**.

7   Remove the mounting screws for the rectifier and brush holder **(see illustration)**.

8   Using a flat-blade screwdriver, separate the stator from the alternator rear housing **(see illustration)**.

9   From the rear of the alternator housing, remove the stator assembly (with the brush holder and rectifier attached).

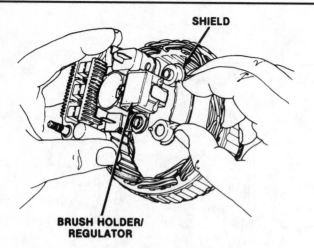

SHIELD

BRUSH HOLDER/
REGULATOR

**15.10   Remove the plastic shields from the brush
holder assembly**

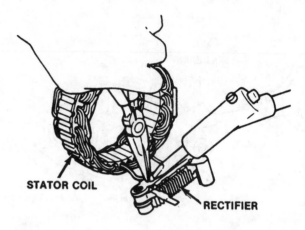

STATOR COIL

RECTIFIER

**15.11   When soldering or unsoldering electrical components,
it's a good idea to use needle-nose pliers as a heat sink**

10   Remove the two plastic shields from the brush holder/regulator assembly (see illustration).

11   Using a soldering iron, remove the solder from the rectifier and the stator lead (see illustration). Caution: *Don't use the soldering iron for more than five seconds at a time or the rectifier may be damaged if it is overheated.*

12   Using a soldering iron, remove the solder from the lead between the voltage regulator and the rectifier (see illustration).

13   Check the brushes while the alternator is disassembled and replace them if they are worn considerably.

14   To replace a brush, unsolder the pigtail (see illustration) and detach the brush from the holder.

15   Solder the pigtail for the new brush so the wear limit line of the brush projects out from the end of the brush holder (see illustration).

16   Reassembly is the reverse of disassembly except for the following procedures:

   a) When soldering components back in place, always use a pair of needle nose pliers for a heat sink (see illustration 15.11).

   b) Push the brushes into the brush holder and insert a rigid wire (a straightened paper clip will work) through the hole in the end frame to secure the brushes in position (see illustration).

   c) Be sure to heat the rear end frame before pushing the rear bearing into it.

17   Remove the wire retaining the brushes when you have completed reassembly.

16   Starting system – general information and precautions

The function of the starting system is to crank the engine fast enough to start it. The system is composed of the starter motor, starter solenoid, battery, switches and connecting wires.

Turning the ignition key to the Start position actuates the starter solenoid through the starter control circuit. The starter solenoid then connects the battery to the starter. The battery supplies the electrical energy to the starter motor, which does the actual work of cranking the engine.

Vehicles equipped with an automatic transaxle have a Neutral start switch in the starter control circuit, which prevents operation of the starter unless the shift lever is in Neutral or Park. The circuit on vehicles with a manual transaxle prevents operation of the starter motor unless the clutch pedal is depressed.

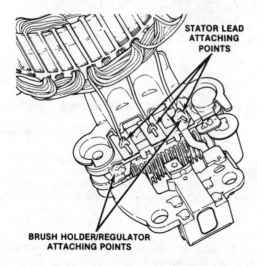

STATOR LEAD
ATTACHING
POINTS

BRUSH HOLDER/REGULATOR
ATTACHING POINTS

15.12   Soldered electrical component locations

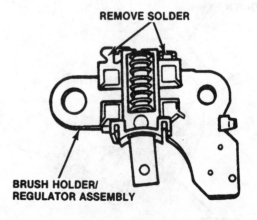

REMOVE SOLDER

BRUSH HOLDER/
REGULATOR ASSEMBLY

15.14   The brush soldered points

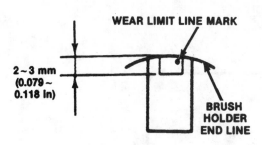

15.15   When replacing the brushes, ensure the wear limit mark projects from the brush holder

Never operate the starter motor for more than 15 seconds at a time without pausing to allow it to cool for at least two minutes. Excessive cranking can cause overheating, which can seriously damage the starter.

---

17   Starter motor and circuit – testing in vehicle

Note: *Before diagnosing starter problems, make sure the battery is fully charged.*

General check

1   If the starter motor doesn't turn at all when the switch is operated, make sure the shift lever is in Neutral or Park (automatic transaxle) or the clutch pedal is depressed (manual transaxle).
2   Make sure the battery is charged and that all cables at the battery and starter solenoid terminals are secure.
3   If the starter motor spins but the engine doesn't turn over, then the drive assembly in the starter motor is slipping and the starter motor must be replaced (see Section 18).

4   If, when the switch is actuated, the starter motor doesn't operate at all but the starter solenoid operates (clicks), then the problem lies with either the battery, the starter solenoid contacts or the starter motor connections.
5   If the starter solenoid doesn't click when the ignition switch is actuated, either the starter solenoid circuit is open or the solenoid itself is defective. Check the starter solenoid circuit (see the wiring diagrams at the end of this book) or replace the solenoid (see Section 19).
6   To check the starter solenoid circuit, remove the push-on connector from the solenoid wire. Make sure that the connection is clean and secure and the solenoid is grounded. If the connections are good, check the operation of the solenoid with a jumper wire. To do this, place the transaxle in Park (automatic) or Neutral (manual). Remove the push-on connector from the solenoid. Connect a jumper wire between the battery positive terminal and the exposed terminal on the solenoid. If the starter motor now operates, the starter solenoid is okay. The problem is in the ignition switch, Neutral start switch or in the starting circuit wiring (look for open or loose connections).
7   If the starter motor still doesn't operate, replace the starter solenoid (see Section 19).
8   If the starter motor cranks the engine at an abnormally slow speed, first make sure the battery is fully charged and all terminal connections are clean and tight. Also check the connections at the starter solenoid, the starter to engine and the battery to the engine ground. Eyelet terminals should not be easily rotated by hand. Also check for a short to ground. If the engine is partially seized, or has high viscosity oil in it during cold weather, it will crank slowly.

Starter cranking circuit test (four-cylinder models)
Refer to illustration 17.10
Note: *To determine the location of excessive resistance in the starter circuit, perform the following series of tests.*

9   Disconnect the coil wire from the distributor cap. Connect a remote starter switch between the starter solenoid terminal "S" and the positive battery post. **Note:** *Make all voltmeter connections at component terminals rather than the cable or the wire end.*

15.16   Retaining the brushes for reassembly

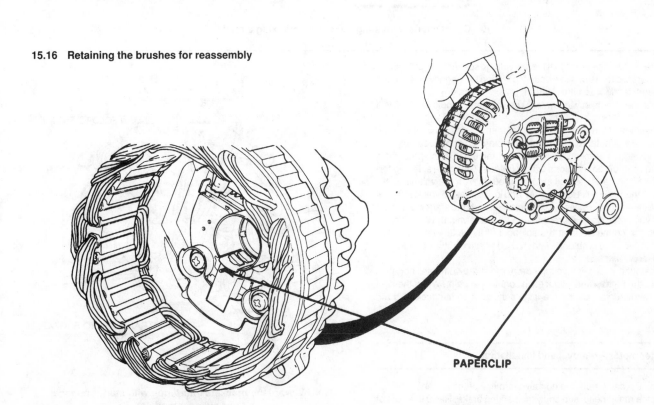

PAPERCLIP

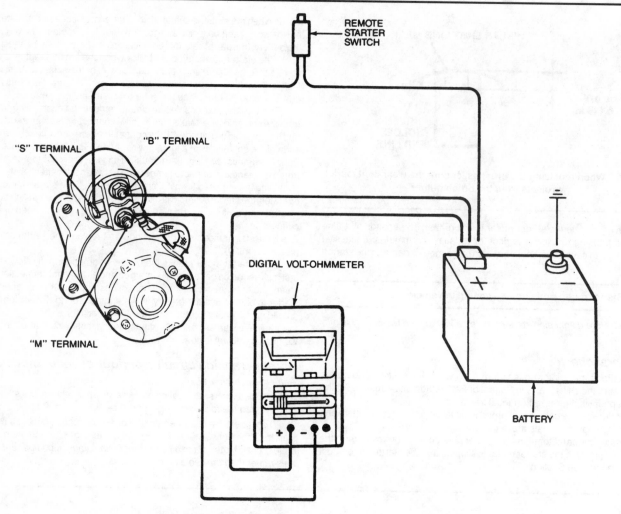

17.10   **Connections for testing the starter cranking circuit**

10   Using a digital voltmeter set at the low voltage scale, connect the positive voltmeter lead to the positive battery post and the negative lead to the solenoid terminal "M" **(see illustration)**.

11   Engage the remote starter switch. The voltmeter should read 0.5 volt or less.

12   If the voltage at terminal "M" is greater than 0.5 volt, move the negative lead of the voltmeter to the solenoid terminal "B" and repeat the test.

13   If the voltage at terminal "B" reads less than 0.5 volt, the problem is either in the solenoid connections or the contacts. Clean the solenoid terminals "B", "S" and "M". Repeat steps 9 through 12. If the voltmeter still reads higher than 0.5 volt at terminal "M" and lower than 0.5 volt at terminal "B", the problem is in the solenoid contacts. Remove the starter for repair.

14   If the voltmeter reads more than 0.5 volt at terminal "B", clean the cables and the connections at the solenoid. If the voltmeter still reads more than 0.5 volt, the problem is either a bad positive battery connection or cable. Repair as necessary.

15   To locate the excessive voltage drop, move the voltmeter negative lead toward the battery and check each connection point. When the high voltmeter reading disappears, the last connection point checked is the problem.

---

18   Starter motor – removal and installation

1   Detach the cable from the negative terminal of the battery.
2   Block the rear wheels and apply the parking brake. Raise the front of the vehicle and support it securely on jackstands.

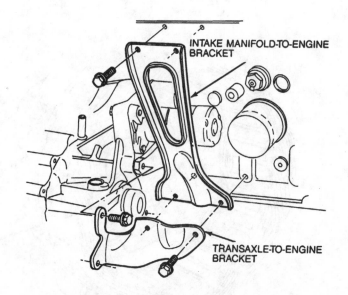

18.4   **View of the brackets interfering with starter removal (four-cylinder models)**

18.6   View of the upper and lower mounting bolts for the starter (four-cylinder model shown, V6 similar)

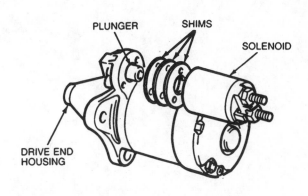

19.4   Starter solenoid details

3   Disconnect the wiring from the terminals on the starter solenoid.

Four-cylinder models only

Refer to illustration 18.4

4   Remove the transaxle-to-engine bracket and the intake manifold-to-engine bracket **(see illustration)**.
5   On vehicles equipped with manual transaxle, remove the exhaust pipe bracket.

All models

Refer to illustration 18.6

6   Remove the starter mounting bolts **(see illustration)**. Note that on some models a ground cable is attached to the upper starter bolt.

7   Remove the starter from the vehicle.
8   Installation is the reverse of removal.

---

19   Starter solenoid – removal and installation

Refer to illustration 19.4

1   Remove the starter motor (see Section 18).
2   Disconnect the strap from the solenoid to the starter motor terminal.
3   Remove the screws which secure the solenoid to the starter motor.
4   Pull the solenoid back, off the plunger **(see illustration)**. Take care not to lose the shims, if any are present.
5   Installation is the reverse of removal.

Chapter 6   Emissions control systems

Contents

1   General information

Refer to illustration 1.7

To prevent pollution of the atmosphere from incompletely burned and evaporating gases, and to maintain good driveability and fuel economy, a number of emission control systems are incorporated. They include the:

Electronic Engine Control (EEC-IV) system
Exhaust Gas Recirculation (EGR) system
Evaporative emissions control system
Positive Crankcase Ventilation (PCV) system
Catalytic converter

All of these systems are linked, directly or indirectly, to the Electronic Engine Control – version four (EEC-IV) system.

The Sections in this Chapter include general descriptions, checking procedures within the scope of the home mechanic and component replacement procedures (when possible) for each of the systems listed above.

Before assuming that an emissions control system is malfunctioning, check the fuel and ignition systems carefully. The diagnosis of some emission control devices requires specialized tools, equipment and training. If checking and servicing become too difficult or if a procedure is beyond your ability, consult a dealer service department.

This doesn't mean, however, that emission control systems are in general particularly difficult to maintain and repair. You can quickly and easily perform many checks and do most (if not all) of the regular maintenance at home with common tune-up and hand tools. **Note:** *The most frequent cause of emissions problems are simply loose or broken vacuum hoses or wires, dirty injectors and EGR valves, so always check these items first.*

Pay close attention to any special precautions outlined in this Chapter. It should be noted that the illustrations of the various systems may not exactly match the system installed on your vehicle because of changes made by the manufacturer during production or from year to year.

A Vehicle Emissions Control Information label is affixed to the underside of the hood **(see illustration)**. This label contains important emissions specifications and adjustment information, as well as a vacuum hose schematic with emissions components identified. When servicing the engine or emissions systems, the VECI label in your particular vehicle should always be checked for up-to-date information.

2   Electronic Engine Control (EEC-IV) system

Refer to illustrations 2.1, 2.2, 2.3, 2.5, 2.6, 2.7, 2.8a, 2.8b, 2.9, 2.11 and 2.12

General description

1   The Electronic Engine Control (EEC-IV) system consists of an on-board computer, known as the Electronic Control Assembly (ECA), and the information sensors, which monitor various functions of the engine and send data to the ECA **(see illustration)**. Based on the data and the information programmed into the computer's memory, the ECA generates output signals to control various engine functions.

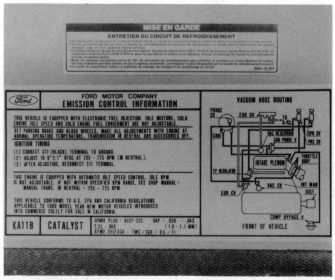

1.7   The Vehicle Emissions Control Information (VECI) label is affixed to the underside of the hood

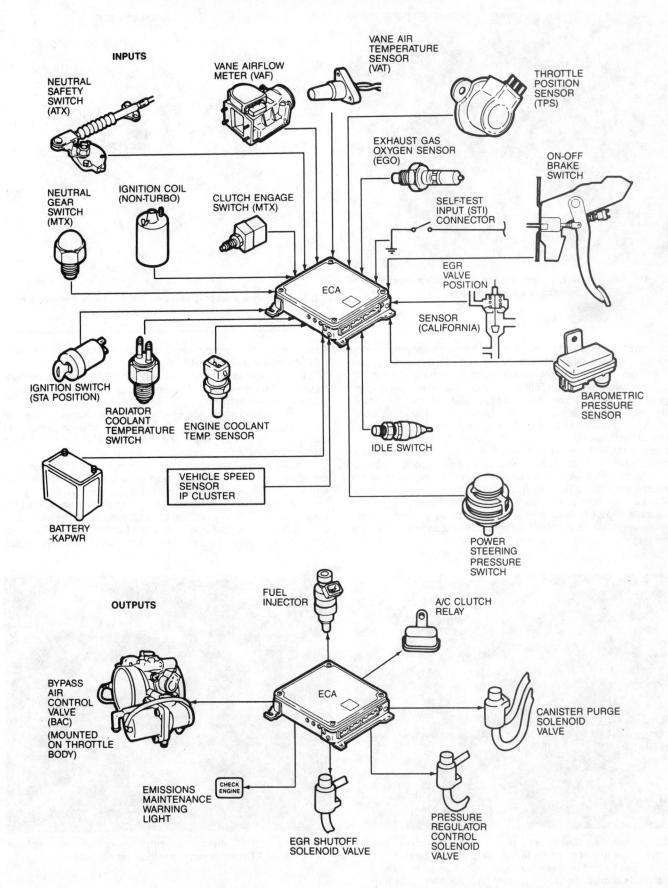

2.1   Schematic of the electronic engine control components (Four-cylinder shown, V6 similar)

2.2   The ECA (arrow) is mounted in the center console behind the passenger's side kick panel

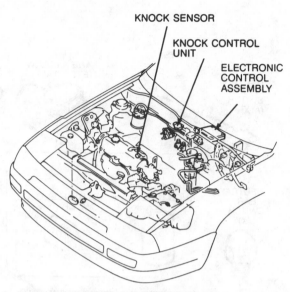

2.3   The knock sensor is screwed into the block above the oil filter (turbo models)

2   The ECA, located in the center console behind the passenger's side kick panel **(see illustration)**, is the "brain" of the EEC-IV system. It receives data from a number of sensors and other electronic components (switches, relays, etc.). Based on the information it receives, the ECA generates output signals to control various relays, solenoids and other actuators (see below). In addition, on four cylinder non-turbo models with automatic transaxles, the ECA contains the 4EAT microprocessor which is the control center for the four speed automatic transaxle. The ECA is specifically calibrated to optimize the emissions, fuel economy and driveability of your vehicle. **Note:** *It isn't a good idea to attempt diagnosis or replacement of the ECA at home because special testing equipment is required. In addition, a Federally-mandated extended warranty covers the ECA, the information sensors and all components under its control, and any damage to the ECA, the sensors and/or the control devices may void the warranty. Take your vehicle to a dealer service department if the ECA or a system component malfunctions.*

Information input sensors

3   Turbocharged engines are equipped with a knock sensor **(see illustration)** which signals the ECA when the engine "knocks," causing the ECA to alter ignition timing.
4   When battery voltage is applied to the air conditioner compressor clutch, a signal is sent to the ECA, which interprets the signal as an added load created by the compressor and increases engine idle speed at the bypass air control valve accordingly to compensate.
5   The Air Charge Temperature (ACT) sensor, threaded into a runner of the intake manifold on V6 models **(see illustration)**, provides the ECA with fuel/air mixture temperature information. On four-cylinder engines, the vane airflow meter includes a built-in air temperature sensor. The ECA uses this information to adjust fuel flow according to air temperature.
6   The EGR Valve Position Sensor (EVP), located on the EGR valve of turbocharged engines and California non-turbo four-cylinder engines **(see**

2.5   A typical Air Charge Temperature (ACT) sensor installed in the intake runner of a V6 – to replace it, unplug the electrical connector and unscrew the sensor – be sure to wrap the threads with Teflon tape to prevent air leaks when installing the new sensor

2.6   All turbo and California non-turbo four-cylinder engines have an EGR valve with a position sensor (arrow)

2.7   A V6 Engine Coolant Temperature (ECT) sensor (arrow) – to replace it, drain the engine coolant to a level below that of the water outlet connection housing, unplug the electrical connector and unscrew the sensor – be sure to wrap the threads with Teflon tape to prevent coolant leaks

2.8a   The MAP sensor (arrow) on four-cylinder models is mounted behind the engine on the firewall

illustration), tells the ECA the position of the EGR valve.

7   The Engine Coolant Temperature (ECT) sensor, which is located near the coolant thermostat **(see illustration)**, monitors engine coolant temperature. The ECT sends the ECA a constantly varying voltage signal which influences ECA control of the fuel mixture, ignition timing and EGR operation.

8   The Manifold Absolute Pressure (MAP) sensor, mounted on the firewall on four-cylinder models and on the engine in V6 models **(see illustrations)**, measures the absolute pressure of the air in the intake manifold and sends a signal to the ECA that is proportional to absolute pressure.

9   The Exhaust Gas Oxygen (EGO) sensor **(see illustration)**, which is threaded into the exhaust manifold on four-cylinder engines and into the front exhaust pipe on V6's, constantly monitors the oxygen content of the exhaust gases. A voltage signal which varies in accordance with the difference between the oxygen content of the exhaust gases and the surrounding atmosphere is sent to the ECA. The ECA translates this exhaust gas oxygen content signal to fuel/air ratio, then alters it to the ideal ratio for current engine operating conditions.

10   On V6 models, the Profile Ignition Pick-up (PIP), integral with the distributor, informs the ECA of crankshaft position and speed. The PIP assembly consists of an armature with windows and metal tabs that rotate past a stator assembly (the Hall Effect switch).

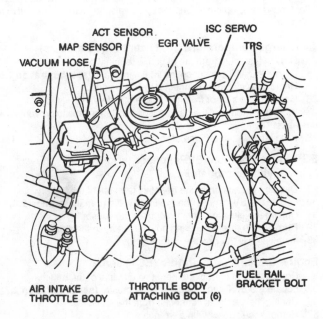

2.8b   On V6 models, the MAP sensor is mounted on the engine

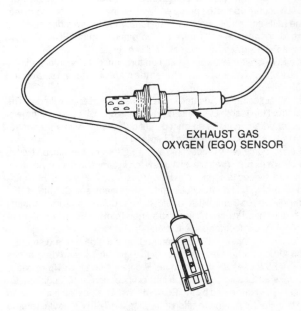

2.9   The EGO sensor screws into the exhaust pipe or manifold

2.11   The throttle position sensor (arrow) is mounted on the side of the throttle body

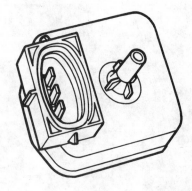

2.12   The PFE is used on V6 models to measure exhaust backpressure

11   The Throttle Position Sensor (TPS), which is mounted on the side of the throttle body **(see illustration)** and connected directly to the throttle shaft, senses throttle movement and position, then transmits an electrical signal to the ECA. This signal enables the ECA to determine when the throttle is closed, in its normal cruise condition or wide open.
12   On V6 models, the Pressure Feedback Electronic (PFE) EGR transducer **(see illustration)** converts a varying exhaust pressure signal into a proportional analog voltage which is digitized by the EEC-IV processor. The EEC-IV processor uses the signal from the PFE transducer to compute the optimum EGR flow.

Output devices

13   The integrated relay control module, which is operated by the ECA, provides an output signal which controls operation of the A/C compressor clutch, the engine cooling fan and the fuel pump.
14   The Canister purge solenoid (CANP), if equipped, switches manifold vacuum to operate the canister purge valve when a signal is received from the ECA. Vacuum opens the purge valve when the solenoid is energized.
15   The EGR control solenoid, used on turbo models, switches manifold vacuum to operate the EGR valve on command from the ECA. Vacuum opens the EGR valve when the solenoid is energized.
16   The EGR shut-off solenoid, used on turbo models, is an electrically operated vacuum valve located between the manifold vacuum source and the EGR valve.
17   The fuel injectors are located in the intake ports of each cylinder. The ECA controls the length of time each injector is open. The "open" time of the injector determines the amount of fuel delivered. For information regarding injector replacement, see Chapter 4.
18   The fuel pump relay is activated by the ECA when the ignition switch is in the On position. When the ignition switch is turned to the On position, the relay is activated to supply initial line pressure to the system. For information regarding fuel pump check and replacement, see Chapter 4.
19   The Idle Speed Control (ISC) motor (Idle Air Control on Turbo models) changes idle speed in accordance with signals from the ECA. For information regarding replacement, see Chapter 4.
20   The TFI-IV ignition module, mounted on the side of the distributor base on turbo and V6 models, triggers the ignition coil and determines dwell. The ECA uses a signal from the Profile Ignition Pick-Up to determine crankshaft position (except on four-cylinder non-turbo engines). Ignition timing is determined by the ECA, which then signals the module to fire the coil. For further information regarding the TFI-IV module, refer to the appropriate Section in Chapter 5.
21   The Wide Open Throttle (WOT) air conditioning cut-out circuit is energized by the ECA when a WOT condition is detected. During WOT, power

to the air conditioning compressor clutch is disconnected until sometime after partial throttle operation resumes. For further information regarding the WOT air conditioning cut-out, refer to Chapter 4.

Checking

22   Specialized test equipment is needed to check the sensors and output devices. Diagnosis of the components described above is well beyond the scope of the home mechanic. If engine driveability deteriorates, take the vehicle to a dealer service department to have the EEC-IV system checked.

Component replacement

Note: *Because of the Federally-mandated extended warranty (five years or 50,000 miles at the time this manual was written) which covers the ECA, the information sensors and the devices it controls, there's no point in replacing any of the following components yourself unless the warranty has expired. However, once the warranty has expired, you may wish to perform some of the following component replacement procedures yourself after having the problem diagnosed by a dealer service department or repair shop.*

Air Charge Temperature (ACT) sensor (V6 models)

23   Detach the cable from the negative terminal of the battery.
24   Locate the ACT sensor on the intake manifold **(see illustration 2.5)**.
25   Unplug the electrical connector from the sensor.
26   Unscrew the sensor from the intake manifold.
27   Wrap the threads of the new sensor with Teflon tape to prevent vacuum leaks.
28   Installation is the reverse of removal.

EGR Valve Position (EVP) sensor (some four-cylinder models)

29   Detach the cable from the negative terminal of the battery.
30   Locate the EVP sensor on the EGR valve **(see illustration 2.6)**.
31   Unplug the electrical connector from the sensor.
32   Remove the three mounting bolts and detach the sensor.
33   Installation is the reverse of removal.

Engine Coolant Temperature (ECT) sensor

34   Detach the cable from the negative terminal of the battery.
35   Locate the ECT sensor near the thermostat **(see illustration 2.7)**.
36   Unplug the electrical connector from the sensor.
37   Remove the sensor with a wrench.
38   Wrap the threads of the new sensor with Teflon tape to prevent coolant leakage.
39   Installation is the reverse of removal.

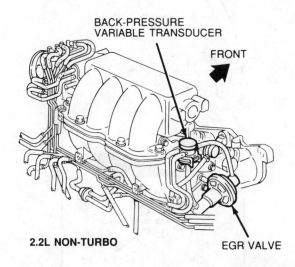

2.2L NON-TURBO

BACK-PRESSURE VARIABLE TRANSDUCER

FRONT

EGR VALVE

3.3a   The BVT is mounted adjacent to the EGR valve

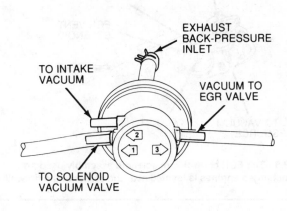

EXHAUST BACK-PRESSURE INLET

TO INTAKE VACUUM

VACUUM TO EGR VALVE

TO SOLENOID VACUUM VALVE

3.3b   The BVT is used on four-cylinder non-turbo engines

Manifold Absolute Pressure (MAP) sensor

40   Detach the cable from the negative terminal of the battery.
41   Locate the MAP sensor on the firewall or intake manifold **(see illustrations 2.8a and 2.8b)**.
42   Unplug the electrical connector from the sensor.
43   Detach the vacuum line from the sensor.
44   Remove the mounting bolts and detach the sensor.
45   Installation is the reverse of removal.

Exhaust Gas Oxygen (EGO) sensor

46   Refer to Section 6 for the oxygen sensor replacement procedure.

Throttle Position Sensor (TPS)

47   Don't attempt to replace the TPS before studying the replacement procedure for the switch on your vehicle (see Chapter 4). Specialized calibration equipment is often necessary to adjust the switch once it's installed, making adjustment beyond the scope of the home mechanic.

3   Exhaust Gas Recirculation (EGR) system

General description

1   The EGR system is designed to reintroduce small amounts of exhaust gas into the combustion cycle, thus reducing the generation of nitrous oxide emissions. The amount of exhaust gas reintroduced and the timing of the cycle is controlled by various factors such as engine speed, altitude, manifold vacuum, exhaust system backpressure, coolant temperature and throttle angle. All EGR valves are vacuum actuated and the vacuum diagram for your particular vehicle is shown on the Emissions Control Information label in the engine compartment.
2   Three types of EGR systems are used on the vehicles covered by this manual:
 a) Backpressure Variable Transducer (BVT) type, used on vehicles with a non-turbo four-cylinder engine
 b) Control/Vent Solenoid (CVT) type on turbo models
 c) Pressure Feedback Electronic (PFE) valve used on California V6's. **Note:** *Federal (49-state) V6 models have no EGR system.*

Backpressure Variable Transducer (non-turbo four-cylinder models)

Refer to illustrations 3.3a, 3.3b and 3.5

3   The EGR Backpressure Variable Transducer (BVT) **(see illustration)** translates engine vacuum and exhaust back pressure into a vacuum signal to operate the EGR valve. When the engine is cold and engine speed is less than 1500 rpm, the exhaust back pressure is low, the Transducer vacuum vent is open, ported vacuum is being vented off, and the EGR valve is closed. But when the engine is warmed up and engine load and vehicle speed are normal for road driving, the Transducer vacuum vent either closes or modulates near the closed position and shuts off or reduces the vacuum being vented, allowing ported vacuum to open the EGR valve **(see illustration)**.

Checking

4   Remove the Backpressure Variable Transducer.
5   Connect a hand operated vacuum pump to the no. 3 port **(see illustration)**.
6   Block the no. 1 port and blow into the exhaust port while applying vacuum to the no. 3 port.
7   The no. 3 port should hold vacuum until pressure is released from the exhaust port.

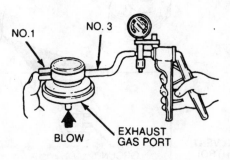

NO.1   NO. 3

BLOW   EXHAUST GAS PORT

3.5   Apply vacuum to the no. 3 port, block the no. 1 port and blow into the exhaust gas port – the no. 3 port should hold vacuum

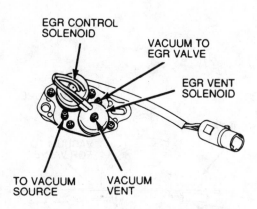

3.8   The EGR control/vent solenoid assembly used on turbocharged engines is located near the center of the firewall

Control/Vent Solenoid (four-cylinder turbo models)

Refer to illustrations 3.8, 3.10 and 3.13

8   On turbocharged engines, EGR flow is controlled by two different solenoids integrated into one assembly **(see illustration)**. The EGR control solenoid regulates vacuum to the EGR valve by a duty cycle signal received from the ECA. The vent solenoid, also controlled by the ECA, maintains the required EGR valve position by venting some or all of the vacuum applied to the EGR valve as necessary. Together, the EGR Control and Vent solenoids are capable of controlling the EGR flow to the engine more accurately throughout all modes of engine operation.

Checking

9   Label and disconnect the vacuum hoses and electrical wiring from the EGR control solenoid valve.
10   Verify that air can't be blown through port A **(see illustration)**.
11   Using fused jumper wires, apply 12 volts and ground to the connectors shown in illustration 3.10.
12   Blow air through the vacuum hose at port A **(see illustration 3.10)** and verify that air flows. Replace the solenoid if necessary.
13   Label and disconnect the vacuum hoses and electrical wiring from the EGR vent solenoid valve **(see illustration)**.

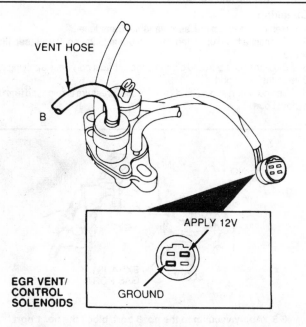

3.13   To test the EGR vent solenoid valve, connect jumper wires as shown here

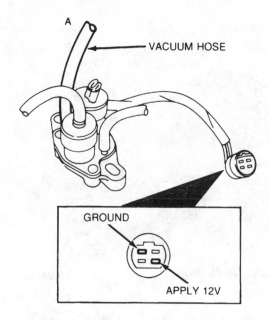

3.10   To test the EGR control solenoid, connect jumper wires as shown here

14   Verify that air can be blown through port B **(see illustration 3.13)**.
15   Apply 12 volts and ground to the connector shown in illustration 3.13.
16   Verify that air doesn't flow through the vent hose at port B. Replace the solenoid if necessary.

EGR valve check (all four-cylinder models)

Refer to illustration 3.17

17   Detach the vacuum hose **(see illustration)** from the EGR valve and connect a vacuum tester.
18   With the engine idling in Park or Neutral and the parking brake engaged, apply 1.6 to 2.4 in. Hg of vacuum to the EGR valve.
19   The diaphragm in the valve should move and the engine should begin to run rough or stall. The valve should hold vacuum and not leak down quickly.
20   If the diaphragm moves and holds vacuum but the engine doesn't run rough, check for carbon blocking the EGR passages.
21   If the diaphragm leaks or doesn't move, replace the EGR valve.

3.17   Detach the vacuum hose (arrow) and connect a vacuum tester to the fitting (turbo shown, non-turbo similar)

3.34   Use a wrench to unscrew the threaded fitting attaching the EGR pipe to the EGR valve – it's a good idea to use anti-seize compound on the threads when installing the new valve to prevent the threads from welding to the valve (V6 engine shown)

3.35   To detach the EGR valve from the throttle body/air intake of the V6, remove the mounting bolts

Pressure Feedback Electronic (PFE) EGR valve (V6 models)

Refer to illustrations 3.34 and 3.35

22   The PFE valve is a conventional ported EGR valve. The valve is used in conjunction with a pressure transducer which supplies pressure information to the EEC-IV processor. The EGR flow rate is proportional to the pressure drop across a remotely mounted, sharp-edged orifice.

Checking

23   Make sure that all vacuum hoses are correctly routed and securely attached. Replace cracked, crimped or broken hoses.
24   Make sure that there is no vacuum to the EGR valve at idle with the engine at normal operating temperature.
25   If the vehicle does not have a tachometer, temporarily connect a test tachometer in accordance with the manufacturer's instructions.
26   Detach the vacuum supply hose from the EGR transducer nipple and plug the hose. Do not disconnect the transducer from the EGR valve.
27   Place the transaxle in Neutral, start the engine, warm it up and allow it to idle. Note the engine's idle speed.
28   Attach a hand vacuum pump to the EGR transducer nipple and slowly apply five to ten inches Hg of vacuum.
29   Have an assistant hold a thick rag over the tailpipe, partly restricting flow.
30   If any of the following conditions occur when vacuum is applied to the EGR valve, replace the valve:
   a)   The engine does not stall.
   b)   The idle speed does not drop more than 100 rpm.
   c)   The idle speed does not return to normal (plus or minus 25 rpm) after the vacuum pump line is detached.
31   Unplug the vacuum pump and reattach the EGR vacuum supply line.

EGR valve replacement

32   Detach the cable from the negative terminal of the battery.
33   Unplug the electrical connector from the EGR valve position (EVP) sensor (see Section 2).
34   Using a wrench, unscrew the threaded fitting that attaches the EGR pipe to the EGR valve **(see illustration)**.
35   Remove the EGR valve mounting bolts **(see illustration)** and detach the valve and gasket from the intake manifold. Discard the old gasket.
36   If you are replacing the EGR valve but not the EVP sensor, remove the sensor from the old valve (see Section 2) and install it on the new valve.
37   Installation is otherwise the reverse of removal. Make sure that the gasket mating surfaces are clean and be sure to use a new EGR valve

gasket. **Note:** *It's a good idea to use anti-seize compound on the threads of the EGR pipe to prevent them from seizing to the EGR valve.*

---

4   Evaporative emissions control system

Refer to illustrations 4.2 and 4.4

General description

1   This system is designed to prevent hydrocarbons from being released into the atmosphere, by trapping and storing fuel vapor from the fuel tank and the fuel injection system.
2   The serviceable parts of the system include a charcoal filled evaporative emissions canister **(see illustration)** and the connecting lines between the fuel tank and the engine.
3   Vapor trapped in the gas tank is vented through a valve in the top of the tank. The vapor is routed to a evaporative emissions canister located on the right (passenger's side) of the the firewall, where it's stored until the next time the engine is started.

4.2   The evaporative emissions canister (arrow) is mounted on the firewall in the engine compartment

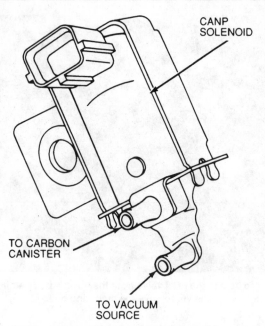

4.4   The canister purge solenoid, if equipped, is mounted near the center of the firewall

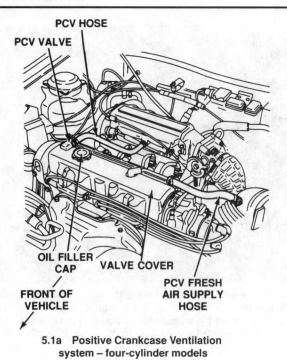

5.1a   Positive Crankcase Ventilation system – four-cylinder models

4   On some models, the canister outlet is connected to an electrically actuated canister purge (CANP) solenoid **(see illustration)** that is, in turn, connected to the engine. The canister purge solenoid valve is normally closed. When the engine is started, the solenoid is energized by a signal from the ECA and allows intake vacuum to open the line between the canister and the intake manifold, which draws vapor stored in the canister through the air cleaner and into the engine where it's burned.

Checking

Charcoal canister
5   There are no moving parts and nothing to wear in the canister. Check for loose, missing, cracked or broken fittings and inspect the canister for cracks and other damage. If the canister is damaged, replace it (refer to Step 9).

Canister purge solenoid
6   Remove the valve from the vehicle.
7   With the valve disconnected, attach a hose to the carbon canister port **(see illustration 4.4)** and attempt to blow through the hose. The valve should not pass air. If it does, replace the valve.
8   Using fused jumper wires, apply battery voltage to the terminals of the valve. The valve should open and pass air. If it doesn't, replace the valve.

Charcoal canister replacement
9   Locate the canister on the right (passenger's) side of the firewall in the engine compartment.
10   Label and then detach the hoses and remove the canister.
11   Lift up on the canister and release it from its mounting bracket.
12   Installation is the reverse of removal.

---

5   Positive Crankcase Ventilation (PCV) system

Refer to illustrations 5.1a and 5.1b

General description
1   The Positive Crankcase Ventilation (PCV) system **(see illustration)** cycles crankcase vapors back through the engine, where they are burned. The valve regulates the amount of ventilating air and blow-by gas to the intake manifold and prevents backfire from traveling into the crankcase.

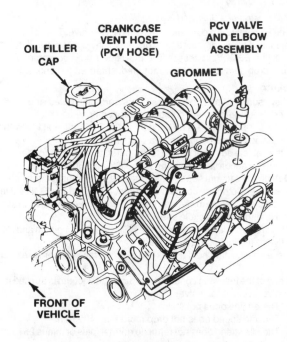

5.1b   Positive Crankcase Ventilation system – V6 models

2   The PCV system consists of a replaceable PCV valve and connecting hoses.
3   The air source for the crankcase ventilation system is in the air cleaner. Air passes through a hose connected to the air cleaner housing, into the rocker arm chamber and the crankcase, from which it circulates up into another section of the rocker arm chamber and finally enters the PCV valve (which controls the amount of flow as operating conditions vary). The vapors are routed to the intake manifold through the crankcase vent hose tube and fittings. This process goes on continuously while the engine is running.

6.1a   On four-cylinder models, the oxygen sensor (arrow) is located on the front of the engine, threaded into the exhaust manifold (turbo model shown, non-turbo similar)

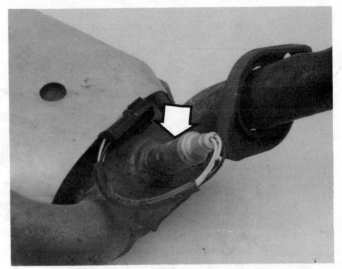

6.1b   On V6 models, the oxygen sensor (arrow) is located in the exhaust pipe upstream of the catalytic converter (pipe removed for clarity)

Checking

4   Checking procedures for the PCV system are included in Chapter 1.

Component replacement

5   Component replacement involves simply installing a new valve or hose in place of the one removed during the checking procedure.

---

6   Oxygen sensor

Refer to illustrations 6.1a and 6.1b

General description

1   The oxygen sensor, (also known as the Exhaust Gas Oxygen or EGO sensor) which is located in the exhaust manifold on four-cylinder engines and in the front exhaust pipe on V6 models **(see illustrations)**, monitors the oxygen content of the exhaust stream. The oxygen content in the exhaust reacts with the oxygen sensor to produce a voltage output which varies from 0.1-volt (high oxygen, lean mixture) to 0.9-volt (low oxygen, rich mixture). The ECA constantly monitors this variable voltage output to determine the ratio of oxygen to fuel in the mixture. The ECA alters the fuel/air mixture ratio by controlling the pulse width (open time) of the fuel injectors. A mixture ratio of 14.7 parts air to 1 part fuel is the ideal mixture ratio for minimizing exhaust emissions, thus allowing the catalytic converter to operate at maximum efficiency. It's this ratio of 14.7 to 1 which the ECA and the oxygen sensor attempt to maintain at all times.

2   The oxygen sensor produces no voltage when it's below the normal operating temperature of about 600-degrees F. During this initial period before warm-up, the ECA operates in open-loop mode.

3   If the engine reaches normal operating temperature and the oxygen sensor fails to produce a signal or produces a continuously rich or continuously lean signal, the Check Engine light will be activated.

4   When a failure is detected, the ECA operates in open loop mode – that is it controls fuel delivery in accordance with a programmed default value instead of feedback information from the oxygen sensor.

5   The proper operation of the oxygen sensor depends on four conditions:

   a) **Electrical** – The low voltages generated by the sensor depend upon good, clean connections which should be checked whenever a malfunction of the sensor is suspected or indicated.

   b) **Outside air supply** – The sensor is designed to allow air circulation to its internal areas. Whenever the sensor is removed and installed or replaced, make sure the air passages aren't restricted.

   c) **Proper operating temperature** – The ECA will not react to the sensor signal until the sensor reaches approximately 600-degrees F. This factor must be taken into consideration when evaluating the performance of the sensor.

   d) **Unleaded fuel** – The use of unleaded fuel is essential for proper operation of the sensor. Make sure the fuel you're using is this type.

6   In addition to observing the above conditions, special care must be taken whenever the sensor is serviced.

   a) The oxygen sensor has a permanently attached pigtail and connector which should not be removed from the sensor. Damage or removal of the pigtail or connector can adversely affect operation of the sensor.

   b) Grease, dirt and other contaminants should be kept away from the electrical connector and the louvered end of the sensor.

   c) Don't use cleaning solvents of any kind on the oxygen sensor.

   d) Don't drop or handle the sensor roughly.

   e) The silicone boot must be installed in the correct position to prevent the boot from being melted and allow the sensor to operate properly.

Replacement

Note: *Because it's installed in the exhaust manifold or exhaust pipe, which contracts when cool, the oxygen sensor may be very difficult to loosen when the engine is cold. Rather than risk damage to the sensor (assuming you intend to reuse it in another manifold), start and run the engine for a minute or two, then shut it off. Be careful not to burn yourself during the following procedure.*

7   Disconnect the cable from the negative terminal of the battery.

8   On V6 models, raise the vehicle and support it securely on jackstands.

9   Carefully unplug the electrical connector.

10   Note the position of the silicone boot, if equipped, and carefully unscrew the sensor from the exhaust manifold. Special deep sockets are available for EGO sensor removal. **Caution:** *Excessive force may damage the threads.*

11   Anti-seize compound must be used on the threads of the sensor to facilitate future removal. The threads of a new sensor will already be coated with it, but if an old sensor is removed and reinstalled, recoat the threads.

12   Install the sensor and tighten it securely.

13   Reconnect the electrical connector of the pigtail lead to the main engine wiring harness.

14   Lower the vehicle and reconnect the the cable to the negative terminal of the battery.

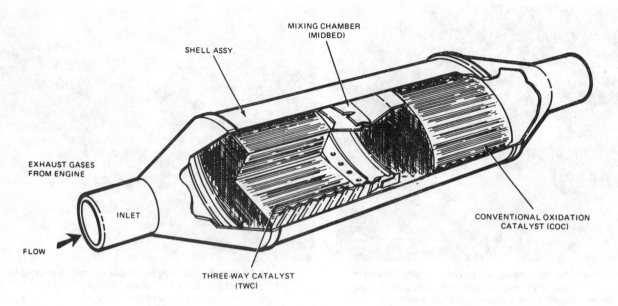

**7.1   A typical catalytic converter with a three-way catalyst (reduction of NOx) and
conventional oxidation catalyst (reduction of HC and CO)**

7   Catalytic converter

Refer to illustrations 7.1, 7.8a and 7.8b

General description

1   The three-way catalytic converter **(see illustration)** is designed to reduce hydrocarbon (HC), carbon monoxide (CO) and oxides of nitrogen
(NOx) pollutants in the exhaust. The converter "oxidizes" the hydrocarbon
and carbon monoxide components (speeds up the heat producing chemical reaction between the exhaust gas constituents) and converts them to
water and carbon dioxide. In addition, the converter "reduces" the nitrogen
oxides back to their non-photoreactive components.

2   The converter, which closely resembles a muffler, is located in the exhaust system immediately behind the front exhaust pipe. You'll need to
raise the vehicle to inspect or replace it.

3   **Warning:** *If large amounts of unburned gasoline enter the converter,
it may overheat and cause a fire. Always observe the following precautions:*

  Use only unleaded gasoline
  Avoid prolonged idling
  Do not run the engine with a nearly empty fuel tank
  Avoid coasting with the ignition turned off
  Correct engine misfiring immediately
  Do not park in tall grass or weeds

**7.8a   The rear of the front exhaust pipe connects to the front of
the catalytic converter with nuts and springs (arrows)**

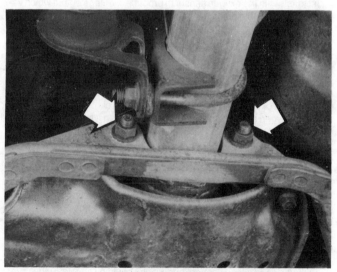

**7.8b   The rear mounting nuts of the catalytic converter
(arrows) attach the flange and support bracket
(four-cylinder shown, V6 similar)**

Checking

Note: *An infrared analyzer is required to check the actual operation of the catalytic converter. Such a device is prohibitively expensive. Take the vehicle to a dealer service department or a service station for this procedure. However, there are a few things you should check whenever the vehicle is raised for any reason.*

4   Check the nuts at the flange between the front exhaust pipe, the front end of the catalytic converter and the flange that secures the rear end of the converter to the main exhaust pipe for tightness.

5   Check the converter shell for dents (maximum 3/4-inch deep) and other damage which could affect its performance. If the converter rattles internally, the central core is adrift, replace the converter. To test for a clogged converter, temporarily unbolt the exhaust pipe between the engine and catalytic converter. If the engine now responds well to throttle opening, inspect the inside of the converter for damage and replace as necessary.

6   Inspect the heat insulator plates above and below the catalytic converter for damage and loose fasteners.

Replacement

Warning: *Don't attempt to remove the catalytic converter until the complete exhaust system is cool.*

7   Raise the vehicle and support it securely on jackstands. Apply penetrating oil to the fasteners and allow it to soak in.

8   Remove the flange nuts **(see illustrations)** from the flanges at each end of the converter. Remove the old gaskets if they are stuck to the pipes.

9   Remove the catalytic converter. **Note:** *Catalytic converters may be recycled – check with a dealer or muffler shop for details.*

10   Installation is the reverse of removal. Be sure to use new exhaust pipe gaskets at the flanges.

11   It's always a good idea to inspect and, if necessary, replace the exhaust pipe rubber hangers while the vehicle is raised (see Chapter 4).

12   Start the engine and check carefully for exhaust leaks.

Chapter 7 Part A   Manual transaxle

Contents

Specifications

Torque specifications

	Ft-lbs
Transaxle case-to-clutch housing bolts	
Non-turbo four-cylinder models	13 to 14
Turbo four-cylinder and V6 models	27 to 38
Transaxle-to-engine bolts	
Four-cylinder models	66 to 86
V6 models	47 to 66

---

1   General information

The vehicles covered by this manual are equipped with either a five-speed manual transaxle or a three-speed automatic transaxle. Information on the manual transaxle is included in this Part of Chapter 7. Service procedures for the automatic transaxle are contained in Chapter 7, Part B.

The manual transaxle is a compact, two-piece, lightweight aluminum alloy housing containing both the transmission and differential assemblies.

Because of the complexity, unavailability of replacement parts and special tools required, internal repair of the manual transaxle by the home mechanic is not recommended. For readers who wish to tackle a transaxle rebuild, exploded views and a brief Transaxle overhaul – general information Section are provided. The bulk of information in this Chapter is devoted to removal and installation procedures.

---

2   Transaxle lubricant change

Refer to illustration 2.3

1   Place the vehicle on level ground and apply the parking brake.
2   Remove the speedometer driven gear (analog instrument cluster) or vehicle speed sensor (digital instrument cluster) (see Section 23 in Chapter 1).

3   Position a container under the drain plug (see illustration) and remove the drain plug. Allow all the lubricant to drain. Watch for metal particles in the lubricant which indicate transaxle wear.

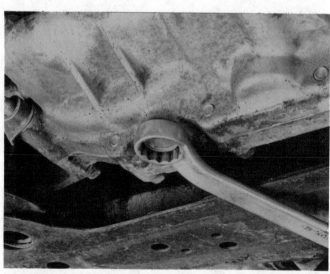

2.3 To drain the transaxle lubricant, remove the drain plug

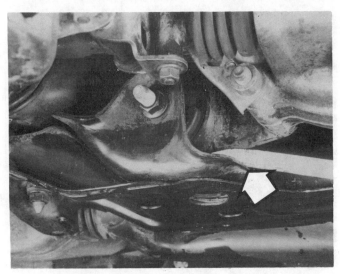

3.1   To check a transaxle mount, position a prybar or a large screwdriver as shown and try to pry the transaxle up

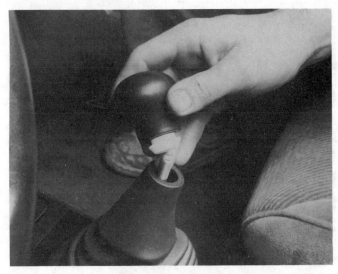

4.1   Unscrew the shift lever knob

4   Install the drain plug and tighten it securely.
5   Place a funnel into the speedometer driven gear/vehicle speed sensor mounting hole. Add the fluid listed in the Recommended lubricants and fluids chart in Chapter 1 a little at a time, checking the level between each addition. Continue adding lubricant until the "Full" level on the driven gear assembly/vehicle speed sensor is reached (see Section 23 in Chapter 1).
6   Install the speedometer driven gear/vehicle speed sensor.

3   Transaxle mounts – check and replacement

Refer to illustration 3.1

1   Insert a large screwdriver or prybar between each mount and the transaxle and pry up while watching the mount **(see illustration)**.
2   If the transaxle moves more than about 1/2-inch, or the case moves up but not down (mount bottomed out), replace the mount.

3   To replace a mount, support the transaxle with a jack, remove the nuts and bolts and detach the mount. It may be necessary to raise the transaxle slightly to provide enough clearance to remove the mount.
4   Installation is the reverse of removal.

4   Shift linkage – removal and installation

Removal

Refer to illustrations 4.1, 4.2a, 4.2b, 4.3a, 4.3b, 4.4a, 4.4b, 4.6, 4.7a, 4.7b, 4.8, 4.10a, 4.10b and 4.11

1   Unscrew and remove the shift lever knob **(see illustration)**.
2   Remove the shift lever boot and the upper trim piece from the center console **(see illustrations)**.

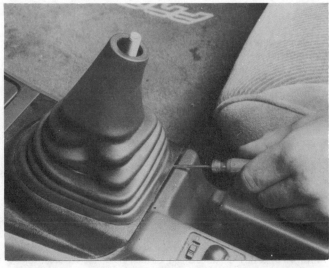

4.2a   Pry the shift lever boot and the upper trim piece loose with a small screwdriver like this . . .

4.2b   . . . and remove them as a single assembly (don't pry the boot loose from the trim piece – it's difficult to reinstall)

4.3a   Remove the mounting boot . . .

4.3b   . . . and the sound deadening material

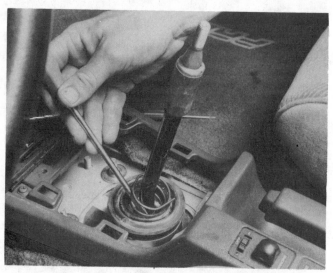

4.4a   Use a small screwdriver to pry the spring loose . . .

4.4b   . . . then remove the ball seat

4.6   Remove the screws that secure the shift rod shield (left screw shown) and remove the shield

3   Remove the mounting boot and the sound deadening material (see illustrations).

4   Use a screwdriver to pry out the spring (see illustration). Caution: Wear safety goggles while removing the spring. If it flies out, you could receive an eye injury. Remove the upper ball seat (see illustration).

5   Raise the vehicle and place it securely on jackstands.

6   From underneath the vehicle, remove the shift rod shield screws and remove the shield (see illustration).

7   Remove the bolt, nut and washer from the clevis at the rear end of the shift rod, the bolt and nut from the clevis at the front end and remove the shift rod (see illustrations).

8   Remove the shift lever assembly (see illustration).

9   Remove the center console (see Chapter 11).

10   Remove the center console bracket nuts and bracket (see illustration) and remove the four nuts and washers from the housing assembly studs (see illustration).

11   Remove the nut from the forward end of the extension bar (see illustration 4.7b), slide the extension bar off the stud on the transaxle and remove the extension bar/housing assembly from underneath the vehicle (see illustration).

4.7a To remove the shift rod, remove the bolt, nut and washer (arrows) from the rear clevis . . .

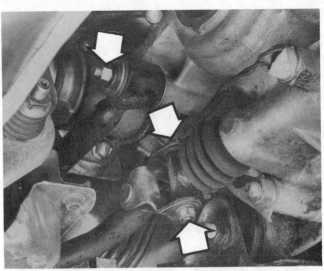

4.7b . . . then remove the bolt and nut (arrows) from the front clevis – to detach the forward end of the extension bar from the transaxle, remove the nut (arrow) and slide the extension bar off the stud

4.8 Remove the shift lever from the housing assembly

4.10a Remove the nuts that secure the center console bracket, then remove the bracket (arrows)

4.10b Remove the nuts from the four housing assembly studs . . .

4.11 . . . then remove the extension bar/housing assembly from under the vehicle

4.12   An exploded view of the shift linkage assembly

1	Shift lever knob	14	Washer
2	Nut	15	Nut
3	Washer	16	Extension bar
4	Nut	17	Boot
5	Washer	18	Retainer
6	Seal	19	Lower ball seat
7	Housing assembly	20	Bushings
8	Bolt	21	Shift lever
9	Shift rod	22	Upper ball seat
10	Bolt	23	Spring
11	Washer	24	Mounting boot
12	Bushing	25	Assist boot
13	Spacer	26	Shift lever boot

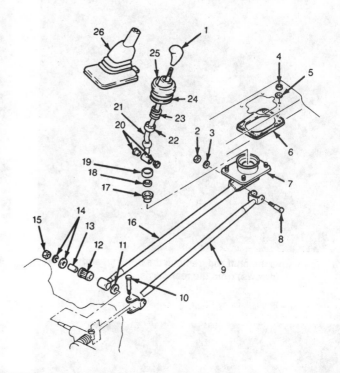

Installation

Refer to illustration 4.12

12   Place the extension bar/housing assembly in position **(see illustration)**. Have an assistant hold it in place while – from inside the vehicle – you install the four nuts and washers onto the housing assembly studs.
13   Install the center console bracket and console (see Chapter 11).
14   Place the shift lever assembly in position.
15   Place the shift rod in position. At the rear end of the shift rod, install the bolt through the clevis and the lower end of the shift lever assembly. Install the nut and washer and tighten securely.
16   At the front end of the shift rod, install the bolt through the clevis and the transaxle shift lever. Install the nut and tighten it securely.
17   Install the forward end of the extension bar onto the stud on the transaxle case, install the nut and tighten it securely.
18   Install the shift rod shield. Tighten the retaining screws securely.
19   Lower the vehicle.
20   Slide the upper ball seat onto the shift lever and push it into position.
21   Using a large screwdriver, install the spring. **Caution:** *Wear safety goggles when you install the spring to protect your eyes in case the spring flies out.*
22   Install the sound deadening material and the mounting boot.
23   Install the shift lever boot and the upper trim piece.
24   Install the shift lever knob.

5   Transaxle – removal and installation

Removal

Refer to illustrations 5.15, 5.22a, 5.22b, 5.24a, 5.24b, 5.27, 5.28, 5.30a, 5.30b, 5.31, 5.32, 5.33, 5.34a, 5.34b, 5.34c, 5.34d, 5.35, 5.36 and 5.38

1   Remove the battery and the battery carrier (see Chapter 5).
2   Disconnect the main fuse block (see Chapter 12).
3   Disconnect the coil wire from the center distributor terminal (see Chapter 5).
4   Disconnect the back-up light switch electrical connector.

5   Disconnect the airflow meter connector and remove the air cleaner assembly (see Chapter 4).
6   On non-turbo four-cylinder models, remove the resonance chamber and bracket (see Chapter 4). On turbo models, remove the throttle body-to-intercooler air hose and the air cleaner-to-turbocharger air hose (see Chapter 4).
7   Disconnect the speedometer cable (analog instrument cluster) or the vehicle speed sensor electrical connector (digital instrument cluster).
8   On V6 models, drain the cooling system (see Chapter 1).
9   On V6 models, remove the upper radiator hose.
10   Disconnect the two ground wires from the transaxle.
11   Loosen the front wheel lug nuts, raise the vehicle and support it securely on jackstands.
12   Remove the front wheels.
13   Remove the inner fender splash shields (see Chapter 11).
14   Drain the transaxle lubricant (see Chapter 1).
15   Disconnect the clutch hydraulic line **(see illustration)**.
16   Disconnect the tie-rod ends (see Chapter 10).
17   Remove the stabilizer bar link assemblies (see Chapter 10).
18   Remove the bolts and nuts from the lower arm balljoints (see Chapter 10).
19   Pull the lower arms down to separate them from the knuckles (see Chapter 10).
20   Remove the right driveaxle bracket (see Chapter 8).
21   Remove the driveaxles (see Chapter 8).
22   Install transaxle plugs (T88C-7025-AH, or equivalent) into the differential side gears **(see illustrations)**. **Caution:** *Failure to install the transaxle plugs may allow the differential side gears to become mispositioned.*
23   Remove the front exhaust pipe (see Chapter 4).
24   On four-cylinder models, remove the intake manifold brace **(see illustrations)**.
25   On four-cylinder models, remove the starter access bracket **(see illustration 5.24a)**.
26   Disconnect the extension bar and shift control rod from the transaxle (see Section 4).
27   On four-cylinder models, remove the transaxle/engine support bracket from the front of the engine **(see illustration)**.

5.15   Using a flare-nut wrench, disconnect the clutch hydraulic line fitting at the left fenderwell bracket

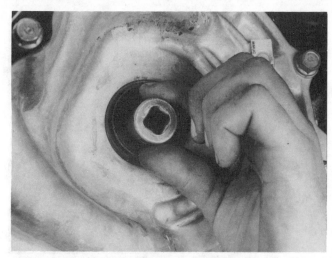

5.22a   Insert transaxle plugs or sockets (shown) into each differential side gear . . .

5.22b   . . . and tape them in place to ensure they don't fall out – if you neglect this vital protective measure, the side gears may fall out of place, necessitating disassembly of the transaxle!

5.24a   On four-cylinder models, remove the bolts (A) that secure the intake manifold brace to the block (the other two bolts (B) are for the starter access bracket, which can't be removed until you remove the intake manifold brace) . . .

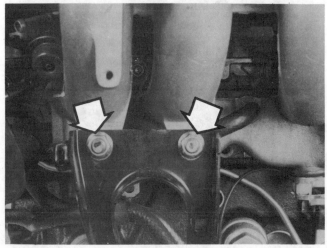

5.24b   . . . then remove the nuts and detach the intake manifold brace

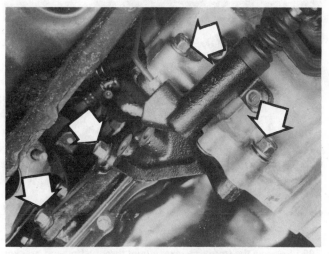

5.27   On four-cylinder models, remove the bolts (arrows) and detach the transaxle/engine support bracket

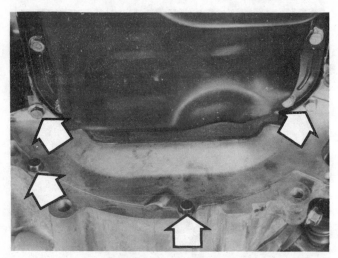

5.28   Remove the bolts (arrows) and detach the flywheel
inspection cover

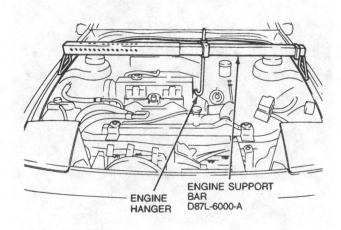

5.30a   If you don't have an engine support bar, . . .

5.30b   . . . support the engine with a hoist, hang it from a sturdy
wood beam with a chain, as shown here, or place a floor jack
under the engine oil pan (be sure to place a block of wood
under the pan to protect it)

5.31   Remove the upper transaxle mount through bolt and
bracket bolts (arrows) and remove the entire mount and
bracket as an assembly

5.32   Remove the front transaxle mount through bolt and bracket
bolts (arrows) and remove the entire mount and bracket as
an assembly

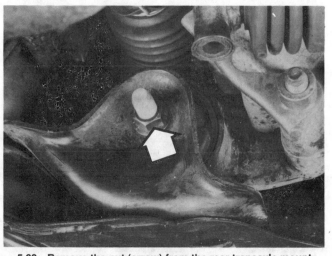

5.33   Remove the nut (arrow) from the rear transaxle mount
through bolt and remove the through bolt

5.34a   Remove the bolts and nut (arrows) from the left side
of the crossmember . . .

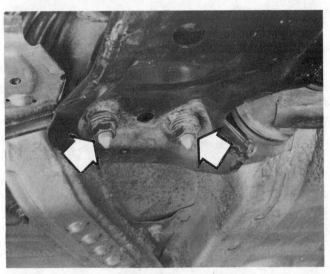

5.34b   . . . the two rear nuts (arrows) . . .

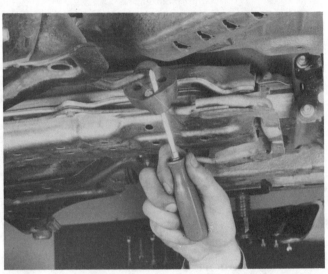

5.34c   . . . carefully pry the exhaust hanger out of the way . . .

5.34d   . . . and remove the crossmember from the vehicle

28   Remove the flywheel inspection cover **(see illustration)**.
29   Remove the starter motor (see Chapter 5).
30   Support the engine with an engine support bar (D87L-6000-A or
equivalent) **(see illustration)**. If you don't have an engine support bar, use
a heavy wooden beam **(see illustration)** or place a jack under the engine
oil pan. Use a block of wood as an insulator between the pan and the jack.
The engine must be supported while the transaxle is out of the vehicle.
31   Remove the upper transaxle mount and bracket **(see illustration)**.
32   Remove the front transaxle mount **(see illustration)**.
33   Remove the rear transaxle mount nut and through-bolt **(see illustration)**.
34   Unscrew the mounting bolts and nuts and remove the left crossmember and control arm as an assembly **(see illustrations)**.
35   Position a jack, preferably a special transaxle jack, under the transaxle and secure the transaxle to the jack **(see illustration)**.
36   Remove the transaxle-to-engine bolts **(see illustration)**.
37   Make a final check that all wires and hoses have been disconnected
from the transaxle, then carefully pull the transaxle and jack away from the
engine. If the transaxle "sticks," first check to be sure all bolts are removed,
then carefully pry it loose. **Caution:** *Do not use much force when prying or
you could crack the transaxle case!*

5.35   Position a transaxle jack under the transaxle – a floorjack
can also be used if you secure the transaxle to it and have an
assistant on hand to steady the transaxle during removal

5.36   Remove the transaxle-to-engine bolts (arrows) (one bolt, not shown, goes from the engine to the transaxle)

5.38   Once the input shaft (arrow) is clear, slide the transaxle away from the engine and rotate it slightly until it clears the stabilizer bar

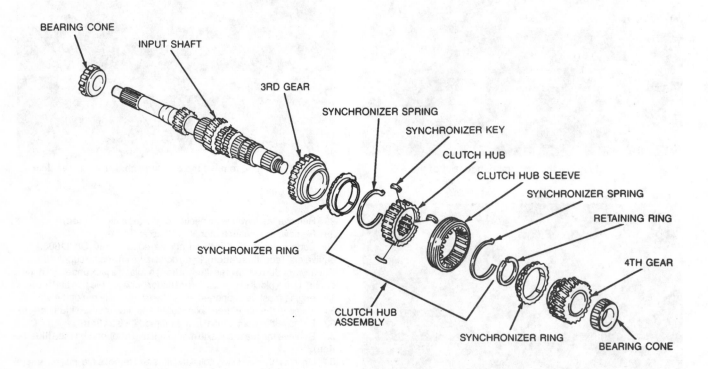

6.4a   An exploded view of the input shaft assembly (non-turbo four-cylinder models)

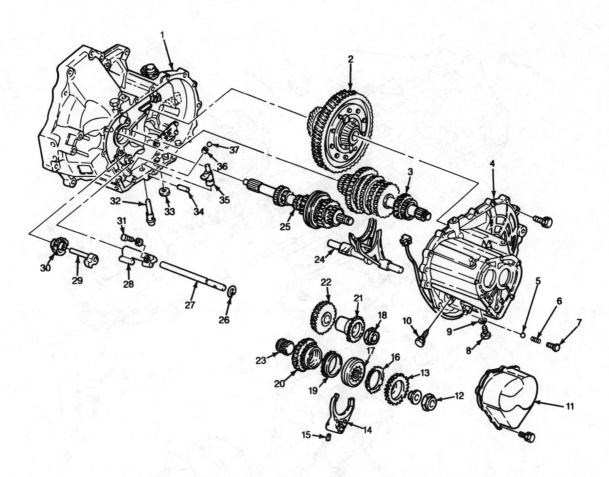

6.4b An exploded view of the transaxle assembly (non-turbo four-cylinder models)

1	Clutch housing	14	Shift fork	26	Clip
2	Differential	15	Roll pin	27	Shift rod (fifth and reverse)
3	Main shaft gear assembly	16	Synchronizer ring	28	Gate
4	Transaxle case	17	Clutch hub assembly	29	Reverse idler shaft
5	Ball	18	Locknut	30	Reverse idler gear
6	Spring	19	Synchronizer ring	31	Lock bolt
7	Lock bolt	20	Input fifth gear	32	Crank lever shaft
8	Guide bolt	21	Main reverse synchronizer gear	33	Magnet
9	Washer	22	Main fifth gear	34	Pin
10	Lock bolt	23	Gear sleeve	35	Crank lever assembly
11	Rear cover	24	Shift fork and shift rod assembly	36	Spring
12	Locknut	25	Input shaft gear assembly	37	Ball
13	Input reverse synchronizer gear				

38   Once the input shaft is clear, slide the transaxle away from the engine and rotate it slightly until it clears the stabilizer bar **(see illustration)**. Lower the transaxle and remove it from under the vehicle. **Caution:** *Do not depress the clutch pedal while the transaxle is out of the vehicle.*
39   Inspect the clutch components (see Chapter 8). It's usually a good idea to install new clutch components when the transaxle is removed.

Installation

40   Install the clutch components, if you removed them (see Chapter 8.)
41   With the transaxle secured to the jack with a chain, raise it into position behind the engine, then carefully slide it forward, engaging the input shaft with the clutch plate hub splines. Do not use excessive force to install the transaxle – if the input shaft does not slide into place, readjust the angle of the transaxle so it is level and/or turn the input shaft so the splines engage properly with the clutch plate hub.
42   Install the transaxle-to-engine bolts. Tighten the bolts to the torque listed in this Chapter's Specifications. Remove the transaxle jack.
43   The remainder of installation is the reverse of removal.
44   Refill the transaxle with lubricant (see Section 2).
45   On V6 models, refill the cooling system (see Chapter 1).
46   Bleed the clutch hydraulic system (see Chapter 8).
47   Road test the vehicle for proper operation and check for leaks.

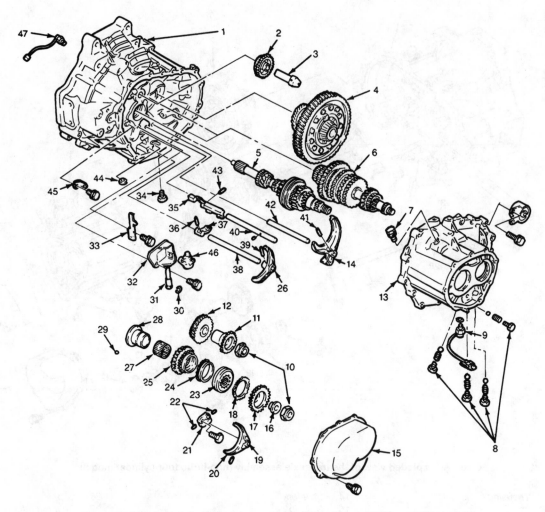

6.4c   An exploded view of the transaxle assembly (turbo four-cylinder and V6 models)

1	Clutch housing		24	Synchronizer ring
2	Reverse idler gear		25	Input fifth gear
3	Reverse idler shaft		26	Shift fork (third/fourth)
4	Differential assembly		27	Needle bearing
5	Input shaft gear assembly		28	Sleeve
6	Main shaft gear assembly		29	Ball
7	Reverse idler shaft set bolt		30	Snap-ring
8	Spring and ball bolt		31	Crank lever shaft
9	Backup light switch		32	Base plate
10	Locknuts		33	Reverse shift lever
11	Main reverse synchronizer gear		34	Drain plug
12	Main fifth gear		35	Shift rod end (fifth/reverse)
13	Transaxle case		36	Roll pin
14	Shift fork (first/second)		37	Shift rod end (third/fourth)
15	Rear cover		38	Shift rod (third/fourth)
16	Sleeve		39	Roll pin
17	Input reverse synchronizer gear		40	Roll pin
18	Synchronizer ring		41	Roll pin
19	Roll pin		42	Shift rod (first/second)
20	Shift fork (fifth and reverse)		43	Roll pin
21	Interlock plate		44	Magnet
22	Interlock pin		45	Lever set spring
23	Clutch hub assembly		46	Crank lever assembly
			47	Neutral switch

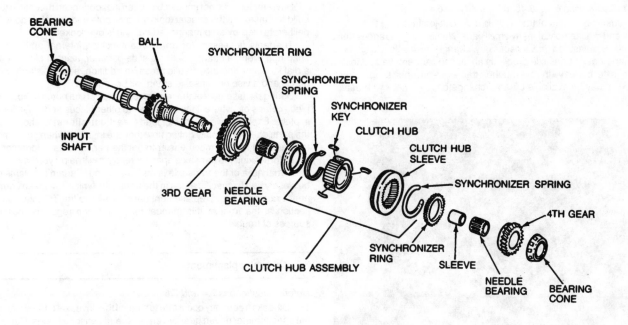

6.4d An exploded view of the input shaft assembly (turbo four-cylinder and V6 models)

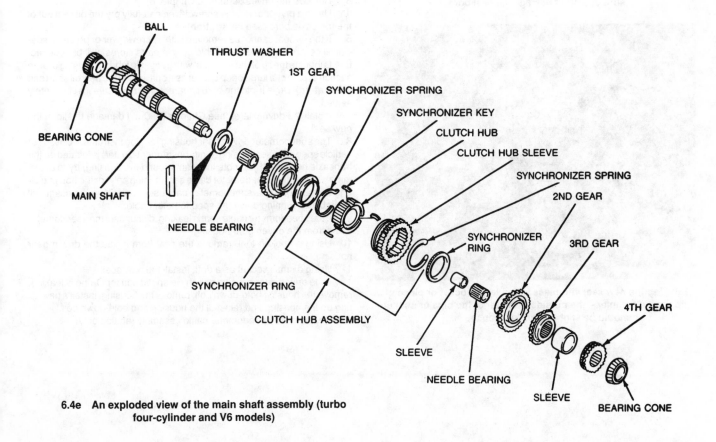

6.4e An exploded view of the main shaft assembly (turbo four-cylinder and V6 models)

6   Transaxle overhaul – general information

Refer to illustrations 6.4a, 6.4b, 6.4c, 6.4d and 6.4e

Overhauling a manual transaxle is a difficult job involving the disassembly and reassembly of many small parts. Numerous clearances must be precisely measured and, if necessary, changed with select fit spacers and snap-rings. If transaxle problems arise, you can remove and install the transaxle, but leave the overhaul to a transmission repair shop. Rebuilt transaxles may be available on an exchange basis – check with dealer parts departments and auto parts stores. If you overhaul the transaxle yourself, the time and money involved in the overhaul is almost sure to exceed the cost of a rebuilt unit.

Nevertheless, it's not impossible for an inexperienced mechanic to rebuild a transaxle if the special tools are available and the job is done in a deliberate step-by-step manner so nothing is overlooked.

The tools necessary for an overhaul include internal and external snap-ring pliers, a bearing puller, a slide hammer, a set of pin punches, a dial indicator and a hydraulic press. In addition, a large, sturdy workbench and a vise or transaxle stand will be required.

During disassembly of the transaxle, make careful notes of how each piece comes off, where it fits in relation to other pieces and what holds it in place. Exploded views are included **(see illustrations)** to show where the parts go – but actually noting how they are installed when you remove the parts will make it much easier to get the transaxle back together.

Before taking the transaxle apart for repair, it will help if you have some idea what area of the transaxle is malfunctioning. Certain problems can be closely tied to specific areas in the transaxle, which can make component examination and replacement easier. Refer to the Troubleshooting section at the front of this manual for information regarding possible sources of trouble.

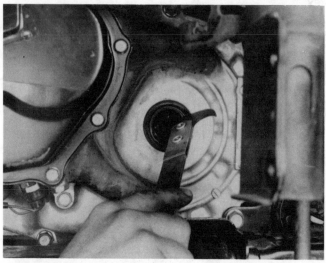

7.4   Pry the seal out of the transaxle bore with a special seal removal tool (shown) or with a prybar or large screwdriver – make sure you don't damage the seal bore

7   Oil seal replacement

Refer to illustrations 7.4 and 7.6

1   Oil leaks frequently occur due to wear of the driveaxle oil seals, and/or the speedometer driven gear or vehicle speed sensor oil seals. Replacement of these seals is relatively easy, since the repairs can usually be performed without removing the transaxle from the vehicle.

2   The driveaxle oil seals are located at the sides of the transaxle, where the driveaxles are attached. If leakage at the seal is suspected, raise the vehicle and support it securely on jackstands. If the seal is leaking, lubricant will be found on the sides of the transaxle.

3   Remove the driveaxle(s) (see Chapter 8).

4   Using a prybar or a large screwdriver, carefully pry the oil seal out of the transaxle bore **(see illustration)**.

5   If the oil seal cannot be removed with a screwdriver or prybar, a special oil seal removal tool (available at auto parts stores) will be required.

6   Lubricate the lip of the new seal with transaxle lubricant. Using a large section of pipe or a large deep socket as a drift, install the new oil seal **(see illustration)**. Drive it into the bore squarely and make sure it's completely seated.

7   Install the driveaxle(s) (see Chapter 8). Don't damage the lip of the new seal.

8   The speedometer driven gear housing (analog instrument cluster) or vehicle speed sensor housing (digital instrument cluster) is located on the transaxle housing. If you note lubricant around the housing, try to determine whether the speedometer cable seal (analog only) or the housing O-ring is leaking. If the speedometer cable seal is leaking, lubricant will probably be running down the speedometer cable.

9   If the speedometer cable seal is leaking, disconnect the speedometer cable from the driven gear housing.

10   Using a hooked tool, remove the seal from inside the driven gear housing.

11   Using a small socket as a drift, install the new seal.

12   If the driven gear housing or vehicle speed sensor O-ring is leaking, remove the housing hold-down bolt, remove the housing, install a new O-ring on the housing and reinstall the housing and hold-down bolt.

13   Reattach the speedometer cable assembly (analog only).

7.6   Tap the new seal into place with a large socket or piece of pipe and a hammer – the outside diameter of the pipe or socket should be slightly smaller than the seal

Chapter 7 Part B Automatic transaxle

Contents

Specifications

Kickdown cable adjustment pressure
(idle speed at 700 to 800 rpm) . . . .   63 to 66 psi

Torque specifications   **Ft-lbs**
Driveplate-to-torque converter nuts . . . .   27 to 38
Transaxle-to-engine bolts . . . .   66 to 86

---

1 General information

All vehicles covered in this manual come equipped with either a five-speed manual transaxle or an automatic transaxle. All information on the automatic transaxle is included in this Part of Chapter 7. Information on the manual transaxle can be found in Part A of this Chapter.

Due to the complexity of the automatic transaxles covered in this man-ual and the need for specialized equipment to perform most service opera-tions, this Chapter contains only general diagnosis, routine maintenance, adjustment and removal and installation procedures.

If the transaxle requires major repair work, it should be left to a dealer service department or an automotive or transmission repair shop. You can, however, remove and install the transaxle yourself and save the ex-pense, even if the repair work is done by a transmission shop.

2   Diagnosis – general

Note: *Automatic transaxle malfunctions may be caused by five general conditions: poor engine performance, improper adjustments, hydraulic malfunctions, mechanical malfunctions or malfunctions in the computer or its signal network. Diagnosis of these problems should always begin with a check of the easily repaired items: fluid level and condition (see Chapter 1), shift linkage adjustment and throttle linkage adjustment. Next, perform a road test to determine if the problem has been corrected or if more diagnosis is necessary. If the problem persists after the preliminary tests and corrections are completed, additional diagnosis should be done by a dealer service department or transmission repair shop. Refer to the Troubleshooting section at the front of this manual for transaxle problem diagnosis.*

Preliminary checks

1   Drive the vehicle to warm the transaxle to normal operating temperature.
2   Check the fluid level as described in Chapter 1:
   a) If the fluid level is unusually low, add enough fluid to bring the level within the designated area of the dipstick, then check for external leaks.
   b) If the fluid level is abnormally high, drain off the excess, then check the drained fluid for contamination by coolant. The presence of engine coolant in the automatic transmission fluid indicates that a failure has occurred in the internal radiator walls that separate the coolant from the transmission fluid (see Chapter 3).
   c) If the fluid is foaming, drain it and refill the transaxle, then check for coolant in the fluid or a high fluid level.
3   Check the engine idle speed. **Note:** *If the engine is malfunctioning, do not proceed with the preliminary checks until it has been repaired and runs normally.*
4   Inspect the shift cable (see Section 3). Make sure it's properly adjusted and the linkage operates smoothly.

Fluid leak diagnosis

5   Most fluid leaks are easy to locate visually. Repair usually consists of replacing a seal or gasket. If a leak is difficult to find, the following procedure may help.
6   Identify the fluid. Make sure it's transmission fluid and not engine oil or brake fluid (automatic transmission fluid is a deep red color).
7   Try to pinpoint the source of the leak. Drive the vehicle several miles, then park it over a large sheet of cardboard. After a minute or two, you should be able to locate the leak by determining the source of the fluid dripping onto the cardboard.
8   Make a careful visual inspection of the suspected component and the area immediately around it. Pay particular attention to gasket mating surfaces. A mirror is often helpful for finding leaks in areas that are hard to see.
9   If the leak still cannot be found, clean the suspected area thoroughly with a degreaser or solvent, then dry it.
10   Drive the vehicle for several miles at normal operating temperature and varying speeds. After driving the vehicle, visually inspect the suspected component again.
11   Once the leak has been located, the cause must be determined before it can be properly repaired. If a gasket is replaced but the sealing flange is bent, the new gasket will not stop the leak. The bent flange must be straightened.
12   Before attempting to repair a leak, check to make sure the following conditions are corrected or they may cause another leak. **Note:** *Some of the following conditions cannot be fixed without highly specialized tools and expertise. Such problems must be referred to a transmission shop or a dealer service department.*

Gasket leaks

13   Check the pan periodically. Make sure the bolts are tight, no bolts are missing, the gasket is in good condition and the pan is flat (dents in the pan may indicate damage to the valve body inside).
14   If the pan gasket is leaking, the fluid level or the fluid pressure may be too high, the vent may be plugged, the pan bolts may be too tight, the pan sealing flange may be warped, the sealing surface of the transaxle housing may be damaged, the gasket may be damaged or the transaxle casting may be cracked or porous. If sealant instead of gasket material has been used to form a seal between the pan and the transaxle housing, it may be the wrong sealant.

Seal leaks

15   If a transaxle seal is leaking, the fluid level or pressure may be too high, the vent may be plugged, the seal bore may be damaged, the seal itself may be damaged or improperly installed, the surface of the shaft protruding through the seal may be damaged or a loose bearing may be causing excessive shaft movement.
16   Make sure the dipstick tube seal is in good condition and the tube is properly seated. Periodically check the area around the speedometer gear or sensor for leakage. If transmission fluid is evident, check the O-ring for damage. Also inspect the side gear shaft oil seals for leakage.

Case leaks

17   If the case itself appears to be leaking, the casting is porous and will have to be repaired or replaced.
18   Make sure the oil cooler hose fittings are tight and in good condition.

Fluid comes out vent pipe or fill tube

19   If this condition occurs, the transaxle is overfilled, there is coolant in the fluid, the case is porous, the dipstick is incorrect, the vent is plugged or the drain back holes are plugged.

3   Shift cable – adjustment, removal and installation

Adjustment

Refer to illustrations 3.3, 3.4, 3.5, 3.6, 3.7 and 3.14
1   On 1990 models, detach the cable from the negative battery terminal to deactivate the shift-lock system.
2   Be sure the selector lever is in the Park position.
3   Remove the selector knob screws and pull off the knob **(see illustration)**.

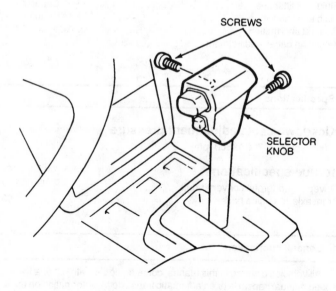

SCREWS

SELECTOR KNOB

3.3   To remove the selector knob, remove these two screws and pull it off

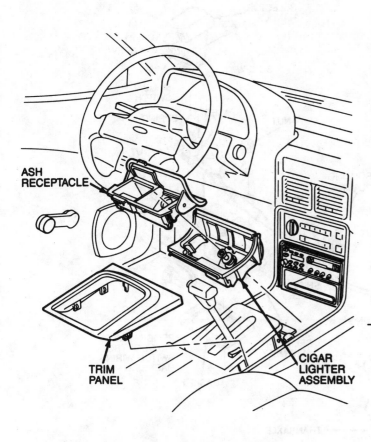

3.4   Remove the trim panel to access the shift cable for adjustment – when removing the cable, take out the ash receptacle and cigar lighter assembly

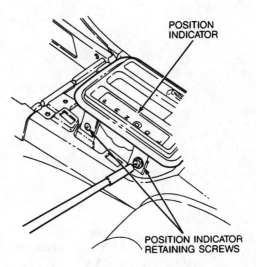

3.5   To remove the gear position indicator, remove these screws, lift up the indicator and unplug all electrical connectors

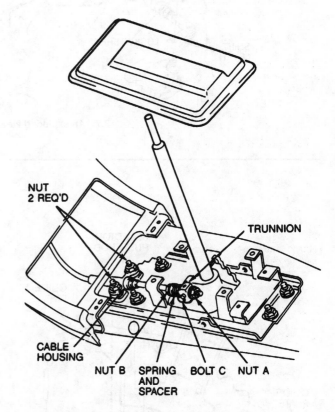

3.6   Details of the selector lever end of the shift cable

4   Detach the selector lever trim panel **(see illustration)**.

5   Remove the screws securing the gear position indicator **(see illustration)**, lift it up, unplug all electrical connectors and remove it.

6   Loosen nuts A and B and bolt C **(see illustration)**.

7   Check that the transaxle is in Park by trying to move the shift lever at the transaxle counterclockwise **(see illustration)**.

8   Make sure the selector lever is still in the Park position.

9   On 1990 models, tighten nut B by hand until it contacts the spacer, then tighten it an additional 1/2-turn.

10   Tighten bolt C securely.

11   Tighten nut A until the nut touches the trunnion.

12   Tighten nut B securely.

13   Make sure the linkage adjustment hasn't affected the operation of the neutral safety switch: With the brakes applied, try to start the engine in each selector lever position. The engine must crank only in the N (Neutral) and P (Park) positions. If it cranks in any other selector lever position, check the linkage adjustment and the operation of the neutral safety switch (see Section 6).

14   On 1990 models, lightly press the selector lever pushrod and make sure the guide plate and guide pin clearances are within the specifications shown **(see illustration)**. If the clearances are not as specified, readjust the shift cable.

15   Plug in all electrical connectors.

16   Install the gear position indicator and mounting screws.

17   Install the selector lever trim panel.

18   Install the selector lever knob and screws.

19   On 1990 models, connect the cable to the negative battery terminal.

20   Perform Steps 1 through 5.

Removal

Refer to illustrations 3.22, 3.23, 3.27 and 3.29

21   Remove the ash receptacle and cigar lighter assembly **(see illustration 3.4)**.

22   Remove the console kick panels **(see illustration)**.

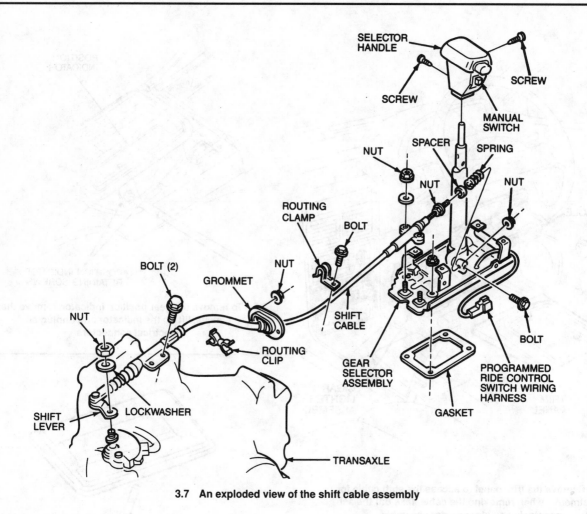

3.7   An exploded view of the shift cable assembly

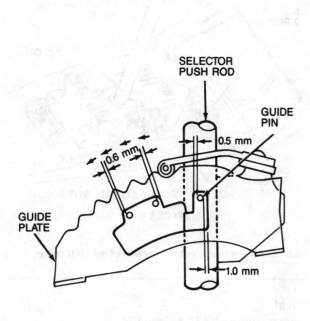

3.14   Details of the guide plate and guide pin clearances
(1990 models)

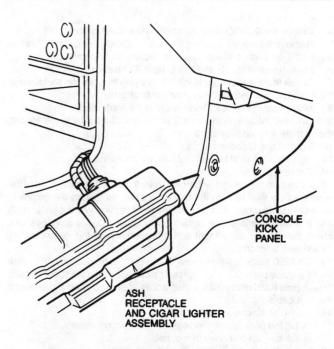

3.22   Remove the screws and pull off the console
kick panels

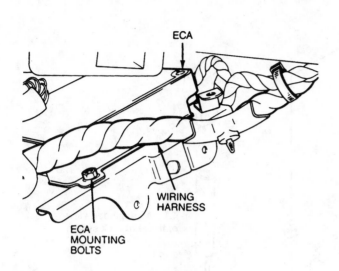

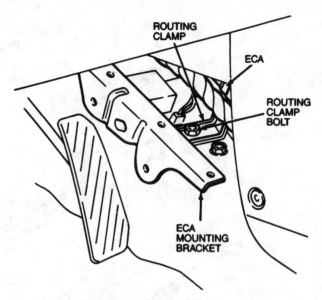

3.23   Detach the wiring harness from the right side of the ECA mounting bracket

3.27   To gain access to the wire harness routing clamp, slide the ECA to the right

23   Detach the wiring harness from the right side of the ECA mounting bracket **(see illustration)**.
24   Remove the ECA mounting bolts.
25   Remove nut A and bolt C **(see illustration 3.6)**.
26   Remove the two nuts from the cable housing bracket **(see illustration 3.7)**. Lift the cable off the studs and slide the cable out of the trunnion. Remove the spring, spacer and nut B.
27   Slide the ECA to the right, then remove the routing clamp bolt and the routing clamp **(see illustration)**.
28   Remove the two nuts securing the grommet to the firewall **(see illustration 3.7)**
29   Remove the two cable housing mounting bolts from the transaxle **(see illustration)**.
30   Remove the nut, lock washer and shift lever from the transaxle.
31   Remove the shift cable by pulling it into the engine compartment.

Installation

32   Push the shift cable into place from the engine compartment side of the firewall. Install the grommet mounting nuts and tighten them securely.
33   Install the shift lever, lock washer and nut onto the transaxle. Tighten the nut securely.
34   Install the cable housing mounting bolts on the transaxle and tighten them securely.
35   Install nut B, the spacer and the spring onto the selector lever end of the shift cable **(see illustration 3.6)**.
36   Install the shift cable into the trunnion.
37   Install the routing clamp.
38   Install the ECA mounting bolts and tighten them securely.
39   Put the wiring harness back into the ECA mounting bracket.
40   Install the console kick panels.
41   Install the ash receptacle and cigar lighter assembly.
42   Adjust the shift cable (see Steps 6 through 14).
43   Perform Steps 15 through 19.

4   Shift-lock system (1990 models) – description and check

Description

Refer to illustration 4.1
1   The shift-lock system **(see illustration)** secures the selector lever in Park unless the brake pedal is depressed when the ignition switch is in the

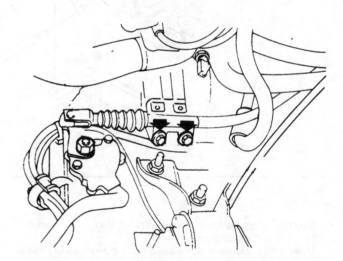

3.29   Locations of the cable housing mounting bolts (arrows)

On position. The system consists of a Park (P) range switch, a shift-lock servo, a shift-lock cable and an override switch. When the ignition switch is on and the brake pedal is depressed, the servo extracts a guide pin from the linkage and allows the selector lever to be moved. The lever can also be freed by pushing back on the override switch. Because of the shift-lock system's complexity and its relation to vehicle safety, repairing the system is beyond the scope of the home mechanic. Have the system repaired by a dealer service department.

Check

Shift-lock system
2   Put the selector lever in Park.
3   Turn the ignition switch to On, but don't start the engine.
4   Verify that the selector lever cannot be moved from Park when the brake pedal is not depressed; verify it can be moved from Park when the brake pedal is depressed.

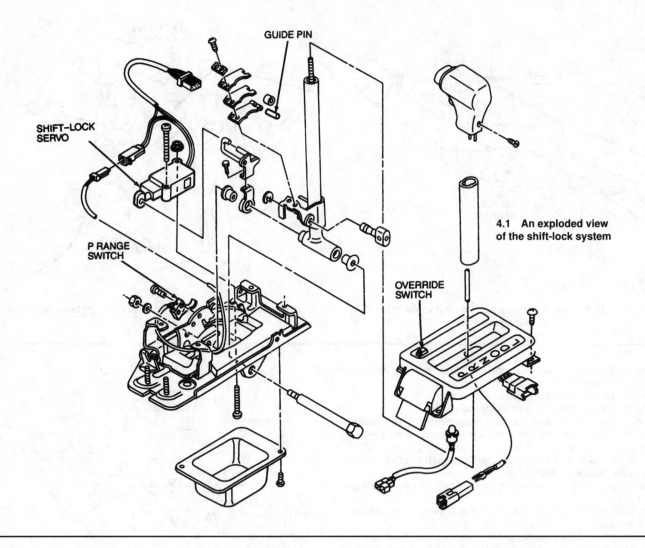

4.1   An exploded view of the shift-lock system

5   Move the selector lever to Reverse and verify the ignition switch cannot be turned to the Lock position.
6   Move the selector lever to Park and verify the ignition key can be turned to the Lock position.
7   If the shift-lock system doesn't operate as described, take the vehicle to a dealer service department for further diagnosis.

Override switch

8   Put the selector lever in Park.
9   Slide the override switch back and hold it there. Verify the selector lever can be shifted from Park.
10   If the switch doesn't operate as specified, take the vehicle to a dealer service department for further diagnosis.

5   Selector lever – removal and installation

Removal

Refer to illustrations 5.3, 5.5 and 5.7

1   On 1990 models, detach the cable from the negative battery terminal.
2   Remove the center console (see Chapter 11).
3   Unplug the electrical connector for the manual shift button wiring harness **(see illustration)**.
4   Slide the plastic sleeve and wiring harness off the selector lever.

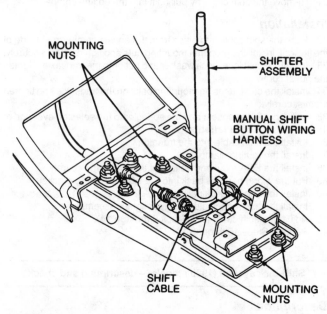

5.3   Details of the selector lever assembly on 1989 models

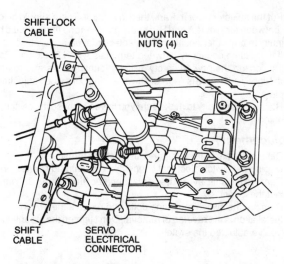

5.5 Details of the selector lever assembly on 1990 models

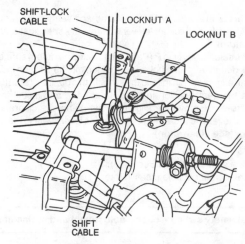

5.7 On 1990 models, loosen locknut A and disconnect the shift-lock cable from the gear selector assembly – don't loosen locknut B, which is preset at the factory

5 On 1990 models, disconnect the servo electrical connector (**see illustration**).

6 Referring to illustration 3.6, remove nut A and the two cable housing nuts and detach the shift cable from the selector lever.

7 On 1990 models, loosen locknut A, then disconnect the shift-lock cable from the gear selector assembly (**see illustration**). **Caution:** *Don't loosen locknut B. It's preset at the factory for proper shift-lock operation.*

8 Remove the four nuts securing the selector lever assembly to the floorpan.

9 Remove the selector lever assembly and gasket.

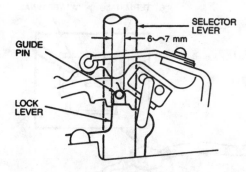

5.18 On 1990 models, lightly press the selector lever pushrod and verify that the overlap between the guide pin and lock lever is within the specification shown

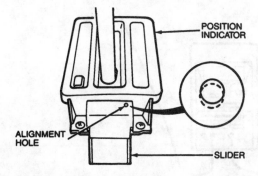

5.19a On 1990 models, move the selector lever to Park, align the holes in the slider and position indicator and install an alignment pin to hold the slider in this position

Installation

All models

10 Position the selector lever assembly and gasket onto the mounting studs.

11 Install the four mounting nuts and tighten them securely.

12 Carefully slide the plastic cover and wiring harness onto the selector lever. Make sure the wiring harness is in the channel in the plastic cover.

13 Connect the electrical connector for the manual shift button.

14 On 1990 models, position the shift-lock cable, install locknut A and tighten it securely.

15 Install the shift cable in the selector lever trunnion (see Section 3, if necessary).

16 Position the cable housing onto the studs, install the mounting nuts and tighten them securely.

1990 models only

Refer to illustrations 5.18, 5.19a and 5.19b

17 Connect the servo electrical connector.

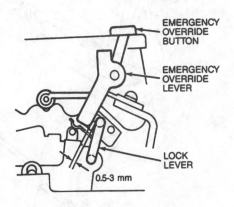

5.19b On 1990 models, after the alignment pin is in place, move the position indicator into proper alignment, install the mounting screws, remove the alignment pin and verify the clearance between the lock lever and the emergency override lever is within the specification shown

18 Lightly press the selector lever pushrod and verify the overlap between the guide pin and the lock lever is within the specification shown **(see illustration)**.
19 Move the selector lever to P (Park). Make sure the detent spring roller is in the Park detent. Align the holes in the slider and the position indicator, then install an alignment pin to hold the slider in this position **(see illustration)**. Place the gear position indicator in position and install the four mounting screws. Remove the alignment pin. Verify the clearance between the lock lever and the emergency override lever is within the specification shown **(see illustration)**.

All models
20 Adjust the shift cable (see Section 3).
21 Install the center console (see Chapter 11).

---

6   Neutral safety switch – check, adjustment and replacement

---

Check
Refer to illustration 6.2
1 Locate the three-pronged neutral safety switch electrical connector under the battery tray and unplug it.
2 Connect an ohmmeter between terminals A and B **(see illustration)**. With the selector lever in the Park or Neutral position, there should be continuity between the terminals.
3 If there is no continuity, first try adjusting the switch. If there is still not continuity after adjustment, replace the switch and adjust the new unit.

Adjustment
4 Attach an ohmmeter to terminals A and B **(see illustration 6.2)**.

5 Put the selector lever in Park, then in Neutral. There should be continuity between terminals A and B in both positions (and there should be no continuity in any other position of the selector lever).
6 If there is no continuity between terminals A and B in either Park or Neutral, loosen the neutral safety switch mounting bolts and rotate the switch slightly until there is. Tighten the mounting bolts when adjustment is complete.
7 Recheck continuity to make sure you haven't moved the switch while tightening it.

Replacement
8 Detach the cable from the negative battery terminal.
9 Unplug the switch electrical connector, if not already done.
10 Remove the shift lever nut and washer **(see illustration 3.7)** and disconnect the lever.
11 Remove the switch mounting bolts and remove the switch.
12 Installation is the reverse of removal. Don't tighten the mounting bolts until you've adjusted the switch.

---

7   Automatic transaxle – removal and installation

Removal
Refer to illustrations 7.11, 7.30, 7.31 and 7.32
1 Remove the battery and battery carrier (see Chapter 5).
2 Disconnect the main fuse block (see Chapter 12).
3 Disconnect the coil wire from the distributor cap center terminal.
4 Disconnect the airflow meter electrical connector (see Chapter 4).
5 On non-turbo four-cylinder models, disconnect the resonance chamber and bracket (see Chapter 4).

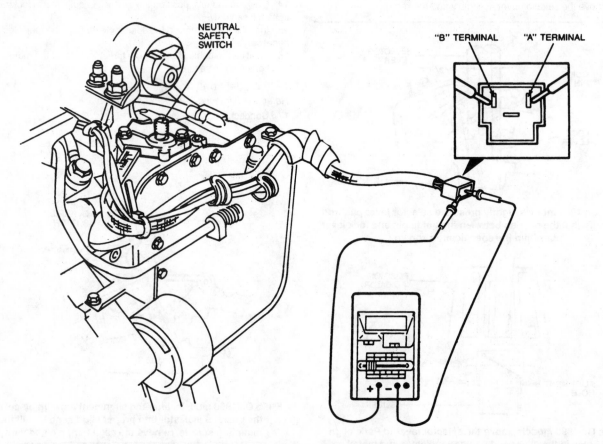

6.2   To check the neutral safety switch, unplug the three-pronged connector under the battery tray and connect an ohmmeter between terminals A and B – there should be continuity with the selector lever in Park or Neutral

6   On turbo four-cylinder models, remove the throttle body-to-intercooler air hose and the air cleaner-to-turbocharger air hose.

7   Disconnect the speedometer cable (analog instrument cluster) or unplug the vehicle speed sensor (digital instrument cluster) at the transaxle.

8   Disconnect the five 4EAT electrical connectors and separate the 4EAT harness from the transaxle clips.

9   Disconnect the two ground wires from the transaxle case.

10   Disconnect the range selector cable from the transaxle case.

11   Disconnect the kickdown cable (see illustration). If you're not planning to disassemble or replace the transaxle, carefully mark the cable housing's position on the bracket(s) so it can be reinstalled in exactly the same position.

12   Loosen the front wheel lug nuts. Raise the vehicle and support it securely on jackstands.

13   Remove the front wheels.

14   Remove the inner fender splash guards (see Chapter 11).

15   Drain the transaxle fluid (see Chapter 1).

16   Disconnect the transaxle cooler hoses from the transaxle. Insert plugs to prevent fluid leakage.

17   Remove the stabilizer bar link assemblies (see Chapter 10).

18   Disconnect the tie-rod ends (see Chapter 10).

19   Remove the nuts from the balljoints (see Chapter 10).

20   Separate the lower control arms from the knuckles (see Chapter 10).

21   Remove the right driveaxle bracket (see Chapter 8).

22   Remove the driveaxles (see Chapter 8).

23   Install plugs (the cut-off ends of broom handles work well) into the differential side gears, through the holes from which the driveaxles were removed. Caution: *Failure to install these plugs may allow the differential side gears to become mispositioned.*

24   On four-cylinder models, remove the gusset plate-to-transaxle bolts.

25   Remove the torque converter cover.

26   Mark the driveplate and one of the studs with white paint so the converter can be reinstalled in the same relative position.

27   Remove the torque converter-to-driveplate nuts. Turn the crankshaft pulley bolt for access to each nut.

28   Remove the starter motor (see Chapter 5).

29   Support the engine using a hoist from above or a jack and a block of wood under the oil pan to spread the load.

30   Remove the center transaxle mount and bracket (see illustration).

31   Remove the left transaxle mount (see illustration).

32   Remove the nut and bolt attaching the right transaxle mount to the frame (see illustration).

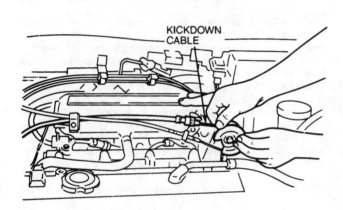

7.11   Disconnect the kickdown cable

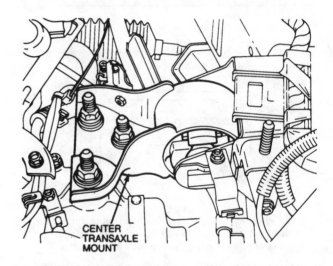

7.30   Remove the center transaxle mount and bracket

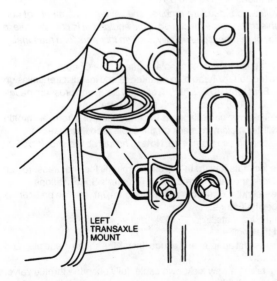

7.31   Remove the left transaxle mount

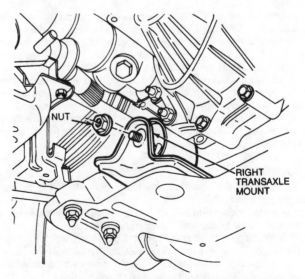

7.32   Remove the bolt and nut from the right transaxle mount

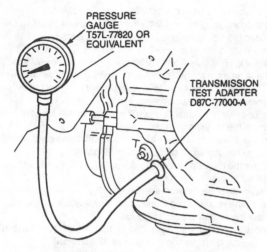

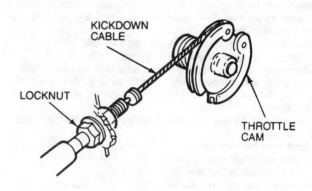

8.2   Remove the square-head plug (marked L) and install a test adapter and pressure gauge, as shown

8.3   Turn the kickdown cable locknuts to the point furthest from the throttle cam

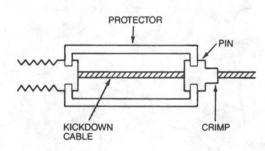

8.10   When installing a new kickdown cable, fully open the throttle valve, crimp the pin with the protector installed as shown, then remove the protector

33   Remove the crossmember and left control arm as an assembly (see Chapter 10).
34   Support the transaxle with a jack – preferably a special jack made for this purpose. Safety chains will help steady the transaxle on the jack.
35   Remove any remaining chassis or suspension components which will interfere with transaxle removal.
36   Remove the bolts securing the transaxle to the engine.
37   Move the transaxle back to disengage it from the engine block dowel pins and make sure the torque converter studs are detached from the driveplate. If necessary, insert a screwdriver between the driveplate and converter and carefully disengage the studs. Secure the torque converter to the transaxle so it will not fall out during removal. Lower the transaxle from the vehicle.

Installation

38   Prior to installation, make sure the torque converter hub is securely engaged in the pump.
39   Secure the transaxle to the jack and raise it into position. Be sure to keep it level so the torque converter does not slide out.
40   Turn the torque converter to line up the drive studs with the holes in the driveplate. The white paint marks made in Step 26 must line up.
41   Move the transaxle forward carefully until the engine block dowel pins are engaged with the holes in the transaxle mounting flange.
42   Install the transaxle-to-engine housing bolts. Tighten them to the torque listed in this Chapter's Specifications. **Caution:** *Do not use the*

bolts to pull the transaxle against the engine. The transaxle case may crack!
43   Install the center transaxle mount and bracket. Tighten the nuts and bolts securely.
44   Install the left transaxle mount. Tighten the fasteners securely.
45   Install the crossmember and left lower arm as an assembly. Tighten the bolts and nuts securely.
46   Install the right transaxle mount bolt and nut and tighten them securely.
47   The remainder of installation is the reverse of removal. If the transaxle has been disassembled or a different one is being installed, adjust the kickdown cable (see Section 8). If the same transaxle is being reinstalled and it has not been disassembled, carefully align the marks made when the cable was disconnected; kickdown cable adjustment is not usually necessary.
48   Fill the transaxle (see Chapter 1), run the vehicle and check for fluid leaks.

8   Kickdown cable – adjustment

Refer to illustrations 8.2, 8.3 and 8.10
Note: *The following procedure requires special test equipment not normally available to the home mechanic. If the equipment is not available, a dealer service department can usually perform this work for a reasonable charge.*

1   Remove the left inner fender splash guard (see Chapter 11).
2   Remove the square-head plug (marked L) and install a transmission test adapter (Ford tool D87C-77000-A or equivalent) and pressure gauge (Ford tool T57L-77820 or equivalent) **(see illustration)**.
3   Turn the kickdown cable locknuts to the furthest point from the throttle cam – this will put maximum slack on the cable **(see illustration)**.
4   Start the engine and warm it up. **Note:** *The idle speed should be 700 to 800 rpm.*
5   Turn the locknuts toward the throttle cam until the line pressure just begins to exceed the range listed in this Chapter's Specifications.
6   Turn the locknuts away from the throttle cam until the line pressure is within the specified range.
7   Tighten the locknuts.
8   Turn off the engine.
9   Remove the test adapter and gauge. Install the square head plug and tighten it securely
10   When installing a new kickdown cable, fully open the throttle valve, then crimp the pin with the protector installed as shown **(see illustration)**. Remove the protector.

Chapter 8   Clutch and driveaxles

Contents

Specifications

Torque specifications   Ft-lbs

Clutch
Master cylinder mounting nuts .... 14 to 19
Release cylinder mounting bolts
    All 1989 models and 1990 non-turbo four-cylinder models .... 14 to 19
    1990 turbo four-cylinder and V6 models .... 12 to 17
Pressure plate-to-flywheel bolts .... 13 to 20

Driveaxles
Driveaxle hub nut .... 116 to 174
Dynamic damper mounting bolts .... 31 to 46

---

1   General information

The information in this Chapter deals with the components from the left end of the engine to the front wheels, except for the transaxle, which is dealt with in the previous Chapter. For the purposes of this Chapter, these components are grouped into two categories: clutch and driveaxles. Separate Sections within this Chapter offer general descriptions and checking procedures for both groups.

Since nearly all the procedures covered in this Chapter involve working under the vehicle, make sure it's securely supported on sturdy jackstands or on a hoist where the vehicle can be easily raised and lowered.

2   Clutch – description and check

Refer to illustrations 2.1 and 2.2

1   All vehicles with a manual transaxle use a single dry-plate, diaphragm spring-type clutch **(see illustration)**. The clutch disc has a splined hub which allows it to slide along the splines of the transaxle input shaft. The clutch and pressure plate are held in contact by spring pressure exerted by the diaphragm in the pressure plate.

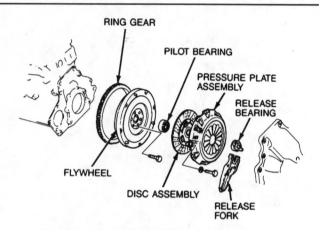

RING GEAR
PILOT BEARING
PRESSURE PLATE ASSEMBLY
RELEASE BEARING
FLYWHEEL
DISC ASSEMBLY
RELEASE FORK

2.1   An exploded view of the clutch components

2   The clutch release system **(see illustration)** is operated by hydraulic pressure. The hydraulic release system consists of the clutch pedal, a master cylinder and fluid reservoir, the hydraulic pressure line, a release (or slave) cylinder which actuates the clutch release fork and the clutch release (or throwout) bearing.

3   When pressure is applied to the clutch pedal to release the clutch, hydraulic pressure is exerted against the outer end of the clutch release fork. As the fork pivots, the shaft fingers push against the release bearing. The bearing pushes against the fingers of the diaphragm spring of the pressure plate assembly, which in turn releases the clutch plate.

4   Terminology can be a problem when discussing the clutch components because common names are in some cases different from those used by the manufacturer. For example, the driven plate is also called the clutch plate or disc, the clutch release bearing is sometimes called a throwout bearing, the release fork is also known as the release lever and the release cylinder is sometimes called the operating or slave cylinder.

5   Other than to replace components with obvious damage, some preliminary checks should be performed to diagnose clutch problems.

   a) The first check should be of the fluid level in the clutch master cylinder. If the fluid level is low, add fluid as necessary and inspect the hydraulic system for leaks. If the master cylinder reservoir has run dry, bleed the system as described in Section 8 and retest the clutch operation.

   b) To check "clutch spin-down time," run the engine at normal idle speed with the transaxle in Neutral (clutch pedal up – engaged). Disengage the clutch (pedal down), wait several seconds and shift the transaxle into Reverse. No grinding noise should be heard. A grinding noise would most likely indicate a problem in the pressure plate or the clutch disc.

   c) To check for complete clutch release, run the engine (with the parking brake applied to prevent movement) and hold the clutch pedal approximately 1/2-inch from the floor. Shift the transaxle between 1st gear and Reverse several times. If the shift is rough, component failure is indicated. Check the release cylinder pushrod travel. With the clutch pedal depressed completely, the release cylinder pushrod should extend substantially. If it doesn't, check the fluid level in the clutch master cylinder.

   d) Visually inspect the pivot bushing at the top of the clutch pedal to make sure there is no binding or excessive play.

   e) Crawl under the vehicle and make sure the clutch release fork is solidly mounted on the ball stud.

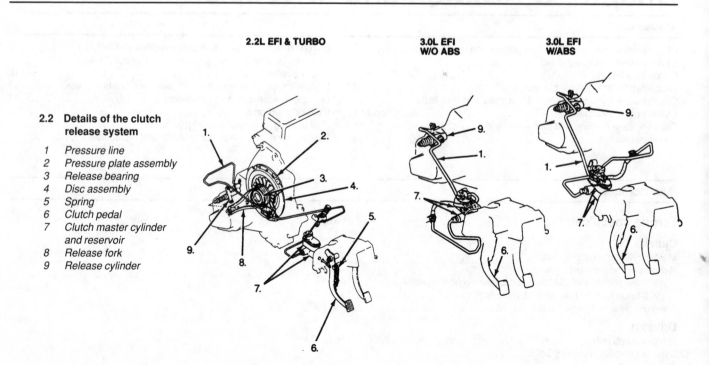

2.2L EFI & TURBO   3.0L EFI W/O ABS   3.0L EFI W/ABS

2.2   Details of the clutch release system

1   *Pressure line*
2   *Pressure plate assembly*
3   *Release bearing*
4   *Disc assembly*
5   *Spring*
6   *Clutch pedal*
7   *Clutch master cylinder and reservoir*
8   *Release fork*
9   *Release cylinder*

3   Clutch components – removal, inspection and installation

Warning: *Dust produced by clutch wear and deposited on clutch components may contain asbestos, which is hazardous to your health. DO NOT blow it out with compressed air and DO NOT inhale it. DO NOT use gasoline or petroleum-based solvents to remove the dust. Brake system cleaner should be used to flush the dust into a drain pan. After the clutch components are wiped clean with a rag, dispose of the contaminated rags and cleaner in a covered, marked container.*

Removal

Refer to illustration 3.4

1   Access to the clutch components is normally accomplished by removing the transaxle, leaving the engine in the vehicle. If, of course, the engine is being removed for major overhaul, then check the clutch for wear and replace worn components as necessary. However, the relatively low cost of the clutch components compared to the time and trouble spent gaining access to them warrants their replacement anytime the engine or transaxle is removed, unless they are new or in near-perfect condition. The following procedures are based on the assumption the engine is still installed in the vehicle.

2   Remove the transaxle from the vehicle (see Chapter 7, Part A). Support the engine while the transaxle is out. Preferably, an engine hoist should be used to support it from above. However, if a jack is used underneath the engine, make sure a piece of wood is positioned between the jack and oil pan to spread the load. **Caution:** *The pickup for the oil pump is very close to the bottom of the oil pan. If the pan is bent or distorted in any way, engine oil starvation could occur.*

3   To support the clutch disc during removal, install a clutch alignment tool through the clutch disc hub **(see illustration 3.13).**

4   Scribe or paint a mark on the pressure plate and the flywheel to align them during installation **(see illustration).**

5   Turning each bolt only 1/4-turn at a time, loosen the pressure plate-to-flywheel bolts. Work in a criss-cross pattern until all spring pressure is relieved. Then hold the pressure plate securely and completely remove the bolts, followed by the pressure plate and clutch disc.

Inspection

Refer to illustrations 3.9 and 3.11

6   Ordinarily, when a problem occurs in the clutch, it's caused by a worn clutch disc. But you should inspect all components while the clutch is apart.

7   Inspect the flywheel for cracks, heat checking, grooves and other obvious defects. If the imperfections are slight, a machine shop can machine the surface flat and smooth (highly recommended regardless of the surface appearance). Refer to Chapter 2 for the flywheel removal and installation procedure.

8   Inspect the pilot bearing (see Section 5).

9   Inspect the lining on the clutch disc. There should be at least 1/16-inch of lining above the rivet heads. Check for loose rivets, distortion, cracks, broken springs and other obvious damage **(see illustration)**. As mentioned above, ordinarily the clutch disc is routinely replaced, so if in doubt about the condition, replace it with a new one.

10   The release bearing should also be replaced along with the clutch disc (see Section 4).

11   Check the machined surfaces and the diaphragm spring fingers of the pressure plate **(see illustration)**. If the surface is grooved or otherwise damaged, replace the pressure plate. Also check for obvious damage, distortion, cracking, etc. Light glazing can be removed with medium grit emery cloth. If a new pressure plate is required, new and factory-rebuilt units are available.

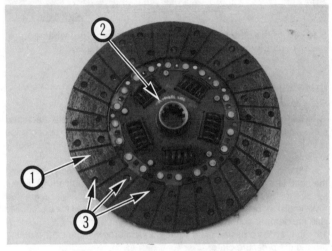

3.9   The clutch disc

1   *Lining – this will wear down in use*
2   *Marks – "Flywheel side" or something similar*
3   *Rivets – secure the lining and will damage the pressure plate if allowed to contact it*

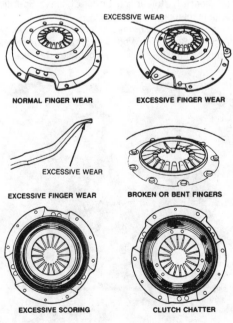

EXCESSIVE WEAR

NORMAL FINGER WEAR   **EXCESSIVE FINGER WEAR**

EXCESSIVE WEAR

EXCESSIVE FINGER WEAR   **BROKEN OR BENT FINGERS**

EXCESSIVE SCORING   **CLUTCH CHATTER**

3.11   Replace the pressure plate if the fingers are worn excessively, broken or bent

3.4   Mark the flywheel and pressure plate to ensure they're reassembled correctly

3.13   Hold the clutch in place with an alignment tool while you're tightening the pressure plate mounting bolts

4.3a   Detach the release fork from the ball stud and pull it off the release bearing

Installation

Refer to illustration 3.13

12   Before installation, clean the flywheel and pressure plate machined surfaces with lacquer thinner or acetone. It's important that no oil or grease is on these surfaces or the lining of the clutch disc. Handle the parts only with clean hands.

13   Position the clutch disc and pressure plate against the flywheel with the clutch held in place with an alignment tool **(see illustration)**. Make sure it's installed properly (most replacement clutch plates will be marked "flywheel side" or something similar – if not marked, install the clutch disc with the damper springs toward the transaxle).

14   Tighten the pressure plate-to-flywheel bolts only finger tight, working around the pressure plate.

15   Center the clutch disc by ensuring the alignment tool extends through the splined hub and into the pilot bearing in the crankshaft. Wiggle the tool up, down or side-to-side as needed to bottom the tool in the pilot bearing. Tighten the pressure plate-to-flywheel bolts a little at a time, working in a criss-cross pattern to prevent distorting the cover. After all of the bolts are snug, tighten them to the torque listed in this Chapter's Specifications. Remove the alignment tool.

16   Using high-temperature grease, lubricate the inner groove of the release bearing (see Section 4). Also place grease on the release fork contact areas and the transaxle input shaft bearing retainer.

17   Install the clutch release bearing (see Section 4).

18   Install the transaxle, release cylinder and all components removed previously. Tighten all fasteners to the proper torque specifications.

---

4   Clutch release bearing and fork – removal, inspection and installation

Warning: *Dust produced by clutch wear and deposited on clutch components may contain asbestos, which is hazardous to your health. DO NOT blow it out with compressed air and DO NOT inhale it. DO NOT use gasoline or petroleum-based solvents to remove the dust. Brake system cleaner should be used to flush the dust into a drain pan. After the clutch components are wiped clean with a rag, dispose of the contaminated rags and cleaner in a covered, marked container.*

Removal

Refer to illustrations 4.3a, 4.3b and 4.3c

1   Disconnect the negative cable from the battery.

2   Remove the transaxle (see Chapter 7).

3   Remove the clutch release fork from the ball stud, slide the bearing off the input shaft and pull the release fork through the clutch housing **(see illustrations)**.

4.3b   Slide the release bearing off the input shaft

4.3c   Pull the release fork through the access hole in the clutch housing

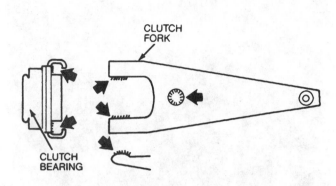

4.6 Lubricate the release fork ball socket, the fork ends and the release bearing (lubrication points indicated by arrows)

Inspection

4   Hold the center of the bearing and rotate the outer portion while applying pressure. If the bearing doesn't turn smoothly or if it's noisy, replace the bearing/hub assembly with a new one. Wipe the bearing with a clean rag and inspect it for damage, wear and cracks. Don't immerse the bearing in solvent – it's sealed for life and to do so would ruin it. Also check the release fork for cracks and distortion.

Installation
Refer to illustration 4.6

5   Fill the inner groove of the release bearing with high-temperature grease. Also apply a light coat of the same grease to the transaxle input shaft splines.

6   Lubricate the release fork ball socket, fork ends, release cylinder pushrod socket and release bearing with high-temperature grease **(see illustration)**.

7   Attach the release bearing to the release fork. Slide the release bearing onto the transaxle input shaft while passing the end of the release fork through the opening in the clutch housing. Push the release fork onto the ball stud until it's firmly seated.

8   Apply a light coat of high-temperature grease to the face of the release bearing, where it contacts the pressure plate diaphragm fingers.

9   The remainder of installation is the reverse of the removal procedure. Tighten all bolts to the correct torques.

---

5   Pilot bearing – removal and installation

Refer to illustrations 5.4 and 5.9

1   Remove the transaxle (see Chapter).

2   Remove the clutch components (see Section 3).

3   Inspect the pilot bearing for wear or scoring. As with the clutch components, the pilot bearing is normally routinely replaced, even if it appears to be in good condition.

4   The pilot bearing can be removed with a puller (T58L-101-B or equivalent) **(see illustration)**, but an alternative method also works very well.

5   Find a solid steel bar which is slightly smaller in diameter than the hole in the bearing. Alternatives to a solid bar are a wood dowel or a socket with a bolt fixed in place to make it solid.

6   Check the bar for fit – it should just slip into the bearing with very little clearance.

7   Pack the bearing and the area behind it (in the crankshaft recess) with heavy grease. Pack it tightly to eliminate as much air as possible.

8   Insert the bar into the bearing bore and strike the bar sharply with a hammer, which will force the grease to the back side of the bearing and push it out. Remove the bearing and clean all grease from the crankshaft recess.

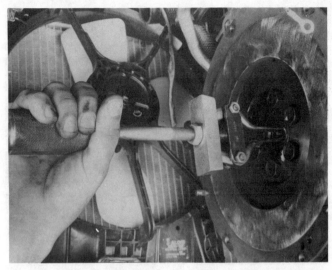

5.4 Remove the pilot bearing with a puller like this or force it out hydraulically using the procedure described in the text

5.9 Tap the pilot bearing into place with a large socket

9   Install the new pilot bearing with a pilot bearing installer (special tool number T88C-7025-EH or equivalent) or a large socket **(see illustration)**. The pilot bearing should be about 5/32-inch below the surface of the crankshaft flange.

10   Install the clutch components (see Section 3).

11   Install the transaxle (see Chapter 7).

---

6   Clutch release cylinder – removal, overhaul and installation

Note: *Before beginning this procedure, contact local parts stores and dealer service departments concerning the purchase of a rebuild kit or a new release cylinder. Availability and cost of the necessary parts will determine whether you rebuild the cylinder or replace it with a new one. If you decide to rebuild the cylinder, inspect the bore as described in Step 10 before purchasing parts.*

Removal
Refer to illustration 6.3

1   Disconnect the negative cable from the battery.

2   Raise the vehicle and support it securely on jackstands.

6.3   To remove the release cylinder, disconnect the hydraulic line with a flare-nut wrench and remove the two mounting bolts (arrows)

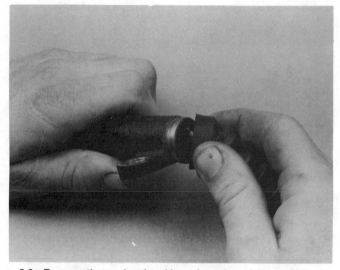

6.6   Remove the pushrod and boot from the release cylinder

3   Disconnect the hydraulic line at the release cylinder. If available, use a flare-nut wrench on the fitting, which will prevent the fitting from being rounded off **(see illustration)**. Have a small can and rags handy – some fluid usually spills when the line is removed.
4   Remove the two release cylinder mounting bolts.
5   Remove the release cylinder.

Overhaul

Refer to illustrations 6.6, 6.7 and 6.9
6   Remove the pushrod and the boot **(see illustration)**.
7   Tap the cylinder body on a block of wood to eject the piston and cup assembly from the bore **(see illustration)**. If it won't come out, gently blow compressed air through the pressure line fitting. **Caution:** *Hold a block of wood over the bore opening to prevent the piston and cup assembly from shooting out of the release cylinder when the air pressure is applied.*
8   Pull the piston and cup assembly, along with the spring, out of the cylinder bore.
9   Remove the bleeder cap, screw and ball **(see illustration)**.

10   Wash the parts in brake system cleaner and allow them to air dry. **Caution:** *Do not use gasoline, kerosene or petroleum-based cleaning solvents.* Carefully inspect the piston and the bore of the cylinder. Check for deep scratches, score marks and ridges. The piston and bore must be smooth to the touch. If you find any imperfections, replace the release cylinder.
11   Using the new parts in the rebuild kit, assemble the components using plenty of fresh brake fluid for lubrication. Note the installed direction of the spring and the cup **(see illustration 6.9).**

Installation

12   Install the release cylinder on the clutch housing. Make sure the pushrod is seated in the release fork pocket.
13   Connect the hydraulic line to the release cylinder. Tighten the fitting.
14   Fill the clutch master cylinder with brake fluid conforming to DOT 3 specifications.
15   Bleed the system (see Section 8).
16   Lower the vehicle and connect the negative battery cable.

6.7   Tap the release cylinder on a block of wood to remove the piston and cup assembly

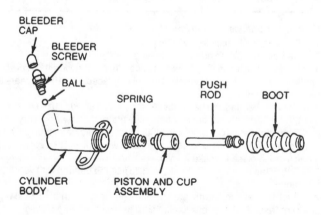

6.9   An exploded view of the release cylinder assembly

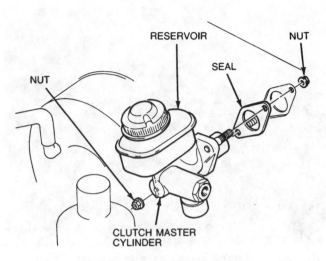

7.4   Clutch master cylinder mounting details

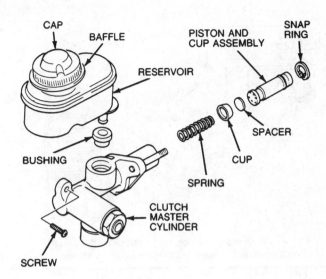

7.6a   An exploded view of the clutch master cylinder assembly

7   Clutch master cylinder – removal, overhaul and installation

Note: *Before beginning this procedure, contact local parts stores and dealer service departments concerning the purchase of a rebuild kit or a new master cylinder. Availability and cost of the necessary parts will determine whether you rebuild the cylinder or replace it. If you decide to rebuild the cylinder, inspect the bore as described in Step 12 before purchasing parts.*

Removal

Refer to illustration 7.4

1   Disconnect the negative cable from the battery.
2   Remove the Anti-lock Brake System (ABS) relay box (if equipped).
3   Disconnect the hydraulic line at the clutch master cylinder. If available, use a flare-nut wrench on the fitting, which will prevent the fitting from being rounded off. Have rags handy – some fluid will usually spill when you disconnect the line. **Caution**: *Don't allow brake fluid to come into contact with paint as it will damage the finish.*
4   Remove the two nuts which secure the master cylinder to the engine compartment firewall **(see illustration)**. Note that one of the nuts is on the dashboard side of the firewall and the other is on the engine compartment side. Remove the master cylinder and seal, again being careful not to spill any of the fluid.

Overhaul

Refer to illustrations 7.6a and 7.6b

5   Remove the reservoir cap and drain all fluid from the master cylinder.
6   Press down on the piston and cup assembly with a Phillips screwdriver and remove the snap-ring with snap-ring pliers **(see illustrations)**.
7   Tap the master cylinder on a block of wood to eject the piston assembly from inside the bore.
8   Remove the spacer, cup and spring.
9   Remove the reservoir attaching screw.
10   Remove the reservoir and bushing.
11   Remove the cap and baffle.
12   Inspect the bore of the master cylinder for deep scratches, score marks and ridges. The surface must be smooth to the touch. If the bore isn't perfectly smooth, the master cylinder must be replaced with a new or rebuilt unit.
13   If you're going to rebuild the cylinder, use the new parts contained in the rebuild kit and follow any specific instructions included with the rebuild kit. Wash all parts to be re-used with brake cleaner, denatured alcohol or clean brake fluid. DO NOT use petroleum-based solvents.
14   Apply brake fluid to the cup and cylinder bore before assembly. Make sure no foreign material is on the cup.

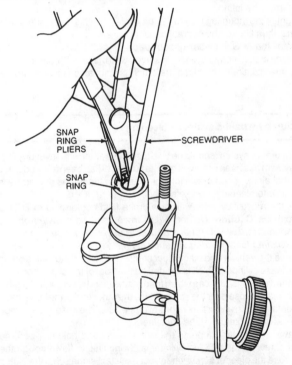

7.6b   Depress the piston and cup assembly with the tip of a Phillips screwdriver and remove the snap-ring with snap-ring pliers

15   Install a new reservoir bushing. Install the reservoir, baffle and cap.
16   Install the reservoir attaching screw.
17   Lubricate the bore of the cylinder and the cups with plenty of fresh brake fluid. Install the spring, cup and spacer.
18   Carefully guide the piston, cup and spring into the bore, being careful not to damage the cup. Make sure the spring end of the piston is installed first, with the pushrod end facing toward the open end of the bore.
19   Press the piston and cup assembly in with a phillips screwdriver and install the snap-ring.

Installation

20   Place the master cylinder in position on the firewall and install the mounting nuts finger-tight.

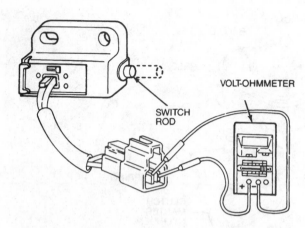

9.2   To check the starter/clutch interlock switch, hook up a continuity tester or volt-ohmmeter as shown

11.1   Raise the staked portion of the driveaxle hub nut with a cape chisel or similar tool

21   Connect the hydraulic line to the master cylinder, moving the cylinder slightly as necessary to thread the fitting properly into the bore. Don't cross-thread the fitting.

22   Tighten the mounting nuts to the torque listed in this Chapter's Specifications, then tighten the hydraulic line fitting.

23   Install the ABS relay box (if equipped).

24   Fill the clutch master cylinder reservoir with brake fluid conforming to DOT 3 specifications and bleed the clutch system as described in Section 8.

8   Clutch hydraulic system – bleeding

1 The hydraulic system should be bled to remove all air whenever any part of the system has been removed or if the fluid level has been allowed to fall so low that air has been drawn into the master cylinder. The procedure is very similar to bleeding a brake system.

2   Fill the master cylinder with new brake fluid conforming to DOT 3 specifications. **Caution:** *Do not re-use any of the fluid coming from the system during the bleeding operation or use fluid which has been inside an open container for an extended period of time.*

3   Raise the vehicle and place it securely on jackstands to gain access to the release cylinder, which is located on the front of the clutch housing.

4   Remove the bleeder cap which fits over the bleeder screw and push a length of plastic hose over the screw. Place the other end of the hose into a clear container with about two inches of brake fluid. The hose end must be in the fluid at the bottom of the container.

5   Have an assistant depress the clutch pedal and hold it. Open the bleeder screw on the release cylinder, allowing fluid to flow through the hose. Close the bleeder screw when your assistant signals that the clutch pedal is at the bottom of its travel. Once closed, have your assistant release the pedal.

6   Continue this process until all air is evacuated from the system, indicated by a solid stream of fluid being ejected from the bleeder screw each time with no air bubbles in the hose or container. Keep a close watch on the fluid level inside the clutch master cylinder reservoir – if the level drops too low, air will be sucked back into the system and the process will have to be started all over again.

7   Install the bleeder cap and lower the vehicle. Check carefully for proper operation before placing the vehicle in normal service.

9   Starter/clutch interlock switch – check and replacement

Check

Refer to illustration 9.2

1   Locate the starter/clutch interlock switch next to the clutch pedal.

2   Unplug the switch electrical connector from the wire harness. Using a volt-ohmmeter or continuity tester, check for continuity between the two connector terminals **(see illustration)**. There should be continuity when the switch rod is pushed into the switch; there should be no continuity when the switch rod is released.

3   If the switch fails this test, replace it.

Replacement

4   Unplug the switch electrical connector, if you haven't already done so.

5   Remove the mounting bolts and remove the switch.

6   Installation is the reverse of removal.

7   Check the switch as outlined above to ensure that it works properly.

10   Driveaxles, constant velocity (CV) joints and boots – check

1   The driveaxles, CV joints and boots should be inspected periodically and whenever the vehicle is raised for any reason. The most common symptom of driveaxle or CV joint failure is knocking or clicking noises when turning.

2   Raise the vehicle and support it securely on jackstands.

3   Inspect the CV joint boots for cracks, leaks and broken retaining bands. If enough lubricant leaks out through a hole or crack in the boot, the CV joint will wear prematurely and require replacement, so replace damaged boots immediately (see Section 12). It's a good idea to disassemble, clean, inspect and repack the CV joint whenever replacing a CV joint boot, to ensure that the joint is not contaminated with moisture or dirt, which would cause premature CV joint failure.

4   Check the entire length of each axle to make sure it isn't cracked, dented, twisted or bent.

5   Grasp each axle and rotate it in both directions while holding the CV joint housings to check for excessive movement, indicating worn splines or loose CV joints.

6   If a boot is damaged or loose, remove the driveaxle (see Section 11) and disassemble and inspect the CV joint (see Section 12). **Note:** *Both types of inner CV joints (Rzeppas on vehicles with manual transaxles, tripots on those with automatics) can be removed from the driveaxle, disassembled and rebuilt. The outer (Birfield type) CV joint cannot be rebuilt or removed. If an outer joint is damaged, you'll have to replace it and the driveaxle as a single assembly.*

7   Some auto parts stores carry "split" type replacement boots, which can be installed without removing the driveaxle from the vehicle. This is a convenient alternative, but we recommend that you remove the driveaxle and disassemble and clean the CV joint to ensure that the joint is free from contaminants such as moisture and dirt, which will accelerate CV joint wear.

11.5   Remove the dynamic damper mounting bolts (arrows) (two bolts not visible in this photo)

11.9   Pull the driveaxle out of the wheel hub

11   Driveaxles – removal and installation

Removal

Refer to illustrations 11.1, 11.5 and 11.9

1   Remove the wheel center cap. Carefully raise the staked portion of the driveaxle attaching nut with a small cape chisel **(see illustration)** and loosen – but don't remove – the hub nut. Also loosen – but don't remove – the wheel lug nuts.
2   Raise the front of the vehicle and support it securely on jackstands.
3   Remove the front wheel.
4   Remove the inner fender splash shield (see Chapter 11).
5   If you're removing the right driveaxle, detach the dynamic damper from the cylinder block **(see illustration)**.
6   Disconnect the tie-rod end (see Chapter 10).
7   Disconnect the strut from the steering knuckle (see Chapter 10).
8   Remove the driveaxle hub nut and discard it. Don't reuse it. To prevent the wheel from turning while you remove the nut, place a prybar between the wheel studs.
9   Pull the driveaxle out of the wheel hub **(see illustration)**. If the wheel hub binds on the driveaxle splines, loosen it with a puller (tool number D80L-1002-L or equivalent). Don't use a hammer to separate the dri-

veaxle from the hub. Hammering can damage the CV joint internal components.
10   Support the outer end of the driveaxle with a piece of wire from the underbody to prevent damage to the inner CV joint.
11   Pull the driveaxle out of the transaxle. If it is difficult to remove, use a prybar to loosen it from the differential side gear. Insert the bar between the driveaxle and the transaxle case. Lightly tap on the end of the prybar until the driveaxle loosens from the differential side gear. Make sure the prybar doesn't damage the transaxle case, oil seal, CV joint or CV joint boot.
12   Supporting both ends of the driveaxle, remove it from the vehicle.
13   Install a differential plug (tool number T87C-7025-C or equivalent) to hold the differential side gear in place. If the plug isn't available, tape a socket into the side gear **(see illustrations 5.22a and 5.22b in Chapter 7B)**.

Installation

Refer to illustrations 11.14a and 11.14b

14   Pry the old circlip from the inner end of the driveaxle **(see illustration)** and install a new one. To install the new circlip properly, start one end in the groove and work the clip over the shaft end and into the groove **(see illustration)**. Using this method will prevent over-expansion of the circlip.

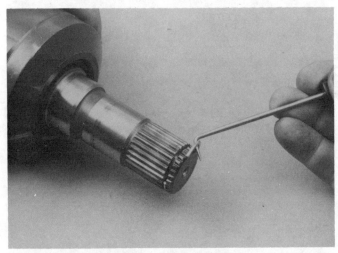

11.14a   Pry the old circlip from the inner end of the driveaxle with a small screwdriver or awl

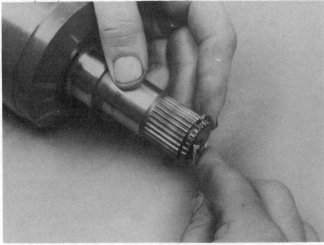

11.14b   To install the new circlip, start one end in the groove and work the clip over the shaft end into the groove

15   Remove the differential plug.
16   Inspect the transaxle oil seal. If it shows any signs of wear or damage that may cause a leak, replace it (see Chapter 7).
17   Lubricate the transaxle oil seal and the driveaxle splines with multi-purpose grease.
18   Make sure the circlip gap is facing up, then raise the driveaxle into position. While supporting the CV joints, carefully align the CV joint splines with the differential side gear splines and push the driveaxle into the differential. You can "feel" the circlip snapping into the differential side gear groove when it seats properly. If the driveaxle doesn't seat easily, insert a screwdriver into the groove in the CV joint and tap it into position with a hammer.
19   Apply a light coat of multi-purpose grease to the outer CV joint splines, pull out on the steering knuckle/hub assembly and insert the stub axle through the hub. Install a new hub nut but don't tighten it.
20   If you're installing the right driveaxle, attach the dynamic damper to the engine block and tighten the bolts securely.
21   Attach the strut to the steering knuckle (see Chapter 10).
22   Attach the tie-rod end to the steering knuckle (see Chapter 10).
23   Install the inner fender splash shield.
24   Using a prybar between the wheel studs, lock the disc so it can't turn and tighten the hub nut. Don't tighten it completely until the vehicle is on the ground.
25   Grasp the inner CV joint housing (not the driveaxle) and pull out to make sure it has seated securely in the transaxle.
26   Install the wheel and tighten the lug nuts finger tight.
27   Remove the jackstands and lower the vehicle.
28   Tighten the wheel lug nuts to the torque specified in Chapter 1.
29   Tighten the driveaxle hub nut to the torque listed in this Chapter's Specifications. Have an assistant depress the brake pedal if necessary. Using a cold chisel with the cutting edge rounded, stake the hub nut into the driveaxle.

12   Driveaxle boot replacement and constant velocity (CV) joint overhaul

Note: *If the CV joints are worn, indicating the need for an overhaul (usually due to torn boots), explore all options before beginning the job. Complete rebuilt driveaxles are available on an exchange basis, which eliminates much time and work. If you decide to rebuild a CV joint, check on the cost and availability of parts before disassembling the driveaxle.*

1   Remove the driveaxle from the vehicle (see Section 11).
2   Mount the driveaxle in a vise. The jaws of the vise should be lined with wood or rags to prevent damage to the driveaxle.

Inner CV joint and boot
Rzeppa type (manual transaxle)
Disassembly
Refer to illustrations 12.3a, 12.3b, 12.3c, 12.4, 12.5, 12.6, 12.7, 12.9, 12.10a and 12.10b

3   Cut off both boot clamps (see illustrations) and discard them. Slide the boot out of the way (see illustration).
4   Slide the boot back on the axleshaft. Mark the inner race, outer race, cage and shaft so they can be reassembled in the same way (see illustration).
5   Pry the wire ring bearing retainer from the outer race (see illustration).
6   Pull the outer race off the inner bearing assembly (see illustration).
7   Remove the snap-ring from the groove in the axleshaft with a pair of snap-ring pliers (see illustration).
8   Slide the inner bearing assembly off the axleshaft.

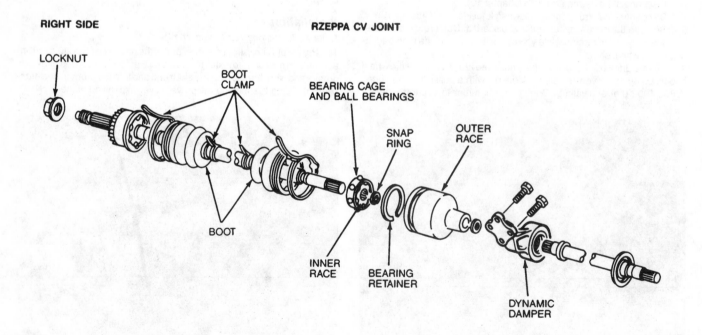

12.3a   An exploded view of the right driveaxle (manual transaxle)

12.3b Cut the boot clamps off and discard them

12.3c Slide the boot down the driveaxle, out of the way

12.4 Paint alignment marks on the outer race, cage, inner race and shaft for assembly reference

12.5 Pry out the bearing retainer with a screwdriver . . .

12.6 . . . then slide the outer race off the inner bearing assembly – the ball bearings may fall out when the race is removed, so be ready to catch them

12.7 Remove the snap-ring from the end of the axleshaft

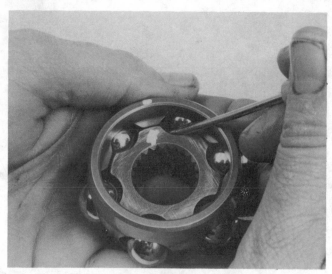

12.9   Pry the ball bearings out of the cage with a screwdriver – be careful not to nick or scratch them

12.10a   Align the lands of the inner race with the windows of the cage, . . .

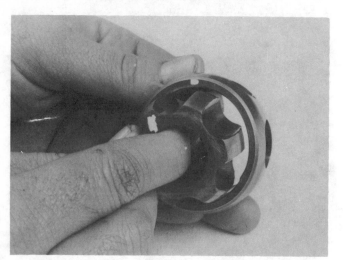

12.10b   . . . then remove the inner race from the cage

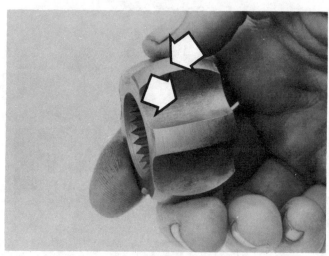

12.11a   Inspect the inner race lands and grooves for pitting and score marks

9   Using a screwdriver or piece of wood, pry the ball bearings from the cage **(see illustration)**. Be careful not to scratch the inner race, the ball bearings or the cage.

10   Align the inner race lands with the cage windows and pull the race out of the cage **(see illustrations)**.

Inspection

Refer to illustrations 12.11a and 12.11b

11   Clean the components with solvent to remove all traces of grease. Inspect the cage and races for pitting, score marks, cracks and other signs of wear and damage. Shiny, polished spots are normal and will not adversely affect CV joint performance **(see illustrations)**.

Reassembly

Refer to illustrations 12.12, 12.13, 12.14, 12.17, 12.19, 12.20 and 12.21

12   Insert the inner race into the cage with the chamfered splines on the larger diameter (bulged) side of the cage **(see illustration)**. Verify that the matchmarks are on the same side. However, it's not necessary for them to be in direct alignment with each other.

13   Press the ball bearings into the cage windows with your thumbs **(see illustration)**. If they won't stay in place, apply CV joint grease to hold them.

14   Wrap the axleshaft splines with tape to avoid damaging the boot. Slide the small boot clamp and boot onto the axleshaft, then remove the tape **(see illustration)**.

12.11b   Check the cage for cracks, pitting and score marks (shiny spots are normal and don't affect operation)

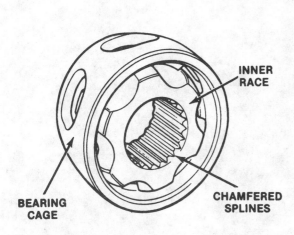

12.12 The chamfered splines on the inner race must be on the larger diameter (bulged) side of the cage

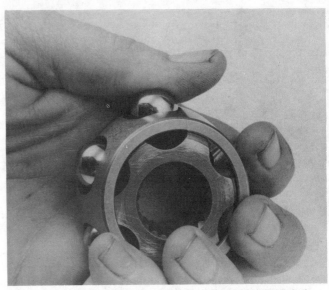

12.13 Press the ball bearings into the cage through the windows using thumb pressure only

12.14 Wrap the splined area of the axleshaft with tape to prevent damage to the boot when installing it

12.17 Pack the inner race and cage assembly full of CV joint grease (also note that the larger diameter side, or "bulge," is facing out)

15 Install the inner race and cage assembly on the axleshaft with the larger diameter side or "bulge" of the cage (and the previously applied marks) facing out.

16 Install the snap-ring in the groove. Make sure it's completely seated by pushing on the inner race and cage assembly.

17 Fill the outer race and boot with the correct type and quantity of CV joint grease (normally included with the new boot kit). Pack the inner race and cage assembly with grease, by hand, until grease is worked completely into the assembly (see illustration).

18 Slide the outer race down onto the inner race and install the wire ring bearing retainer.

19 Wipe any excess grease from the axle boot groove on the outer race. Seat the small diameter of the boot in the recessed area on the axleshaft. Push the other end of the boot onto the outer race and move the race in or out to adjust the joint to the proper length (see illustration).

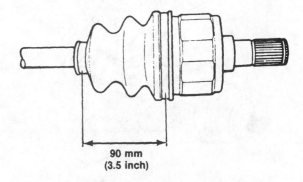

90 mm (3.5 inch)

12.19 Adjust the length of the CV joint (distance between the boot bands) before tightening the clamps

12.20   Equalize the pressure inside the boot by inserting a small, dull screwdriver between the boot and the outer race

12.21   Secure the boot clamps with a pair of special boot clamp pliers like these (available at most auto parts stores)

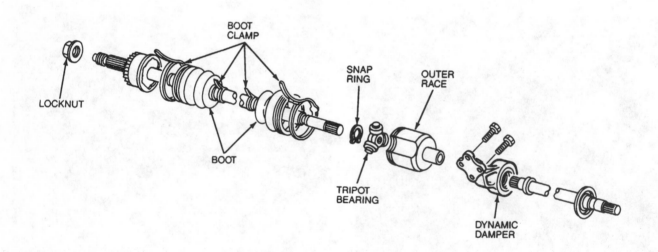

12.24   An exploded view of the right driveaxle (automatic transaxle)

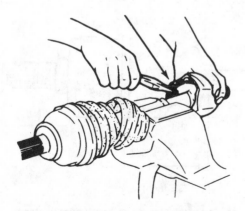

12.25   Remove the wire ring bearing retainer

20   With the axle set to the proper length, equalize the pressure in the boot by inserting a dull screwdriver between the boot and the outer race (see illustration). Don't damage the boot with the tool.

21   Install the boot clamps. A pair of special clamp-crimping pliers are used to tighten the clamp. The pliers are available at most auto parts stores (see illustration).

22   Install a new circlip on the inner CV joint stub axle (see illustrations 11.14a and 11.14b).

23   Install the driveaxle as described in Section 7.

Tripot type (automatic transaxle)
Disassembly
Refer to illustrations 12.24, 12.25, 12.26, 12.27 and 12.28

24   Cut off both boot clamps (see illustration) and slide the boot towards the center of the driveaxle.

25   Remove the wire ring bearing retainer (see illustration).

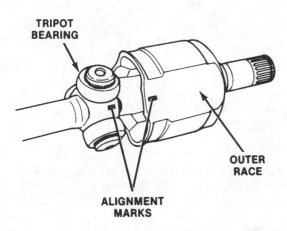

12.26 Scribe or paint alignment marks on the tripot assembly and the outer race, then slide the outer race off

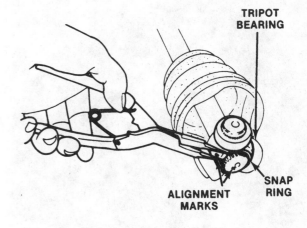

12.27 Scribe or paint alignment marks on the tripot and the driveaxle and remove the snap-ring

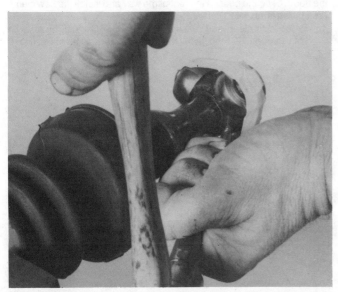

12.28 Secure the bearing rollers with tape and drive the tripot off the shaft with a hammer and a brass drift

26 Scribe or paint alignment marks on the outer race and the tripot bearing assembly **(see illustration)** so they can be returned to its original position, then slide the outer race off the tripot bearing assembly.

27 Scribe or paint alignment marks on the tripot bearing assembly and the driveaxle and remove the snap-ring **(see illustration)**.

28 Secure the bearing rollers with tape, then remove the tripot bearing assembly from the driveaxle with a brass drift and a hammer **(see illustration)**. Remove the tape.

29 Slide the old boot off the driveaxle and discard it.

Inspection

30 Clean the old grease from the outer race and the tripot bearing assembly. Carefully disassemble each section of the tripot assembly, one at a time, and clean the needle bearings with solvent. Inspect the rollers, tri-pot, bearings and outer race for scoring, pitting or other signs of abnormal wear, which will warrant the replacement of the inner CV joint.

Reassembly

31 Apply a coat of CV joint grease to the inner bearing surfaces to hold the needle bearings in place when reassembling the tripot assembly. Pack the outer race with half of the grease furnished with the new boot and place the remainder in the boot.

32 Wrap the driveaxle splines with tape to avoid damaging the boot, then slide the boot onto the axle **(see illustration 12.14).**

33 Align the match marks you made before disassembly and tap the tripot assembly onto the driveaxle with a hammer and brass drift.

34 Install the snap-ring.

35 Install the outer race over the tripot assembly and install the wire ring bearing retainer.

36 Seat the boot in the grooves in the outer race and the driveaxle, then adjust the driveaxle to the proper length **(see illustration 12.19)**.

37 With the driveaxle set to the proper length, equalize the pressure in the boot by inserting a blunt screwdriver between the boot and the outer race **(see illustration 12.20)**. Don't damage the boot with the tool.

38 Install new boot clamps. A pair of special clamp-crimping pliers are used to tighten the clamp. The pliers are available at most auto parts stores **(see illustration 12.21)**.

39 Install the driveaxle assembly **(see Section 11)**.

Outer CV joint and boot

Disassembly

40 Following Steps 1 through 10, remove the inner CV joint from the axleshaft and disassemble it.

41 Remove the outer CV joint boot clamps, using the technique described in Step 3. Slide the boot off the axleshaft.

Inspection

Refer to illustrations 12.43 and 12.44

42 Thoroughly wash the inner and outer CV joints in clean solvent and blow them dry with compressed air, if available. **Note:** *Because the outer joint cannot be disassembled, it is difficult to wash away all the old grease and to rid the bearing of solvent once it's clean. But it is imperative that the job be done thoroughly, so take your time and do it right.*

12.43   After the old grease has been rinsed away and the solvent has been blown out with compressed air, rotate the outer joint assembly through its full range of motion and inspect the bearing surfaces for wear and damage – if any of the ball bearings, the race or the cage look damaged, replace the driveaxle and outer joint assembly

43   Bend the outer CV joint housing at an angle to the driveaxle to expose the bearings, inner race and cage **(see illustration)**. Inspect the bearing surfaces for signs of wear. If the bearings are damaged or worn, replace the driveaxle.

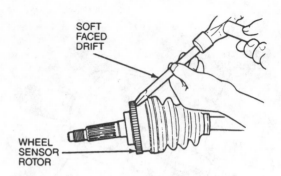

12.44   The ABS wheel sensor rotor can be tapped on and off the outer joint assembly using a soft-faced drift

44   If you replace the driveaxle on an ABS-equipped vehicle, be sure to tap the wheel sensor rotor from the old outer joint and and tap it onto the new joint with a soft-faced drift **(see illustration)**.

Reassembly

45   Slide the new outer boot onto the driveaxle. It's a good idea to wrap vinyl tape around the splines of shaft to prevent damage to the boot **(see illustration 12.14)**. When the boot is in position, add the specified amount of grease (included in the boot replacement kit) to the outer joint and the boot (pack the joint with as much grease as it will hold and put the rest into the boot). Slide the boot on the rest of the way and install the new clamps **(see illustration 12.21)**.

46   Proceed to clean and reassemble the inner CV joint by following Steps 11 through 22, then install the driveaxle as outlined in Section 11.

Chapter 9   Brakes

Contents

Specifications

General

Brake fluid type	See Chapter 1
Brake pedal height	8 1/2 to 8 3/4 in (217 to 222 mm)
Rear hub bearing endplay (maximum)	0.008 in (0.2 mm)

Disc brakes

Disc thickness	
Front	
Standard	0.94 in (24 mm)
Minimum*	0.86 in (22 mm)
Rear	
Standard	0.39 in (10 mm)
Minimum*	0.35 in (9 mm)
Disc thickness variation (parallelism)	0.0006 in (0.015 mm)
Disc runout limit	0.003 in (0.1 mm)
Pad minimum thickness	See Chapter 1

Refer to marks stamped on the disc (they supersede information printed here)

Drum brakes

Drum diameter	
Standard	9.0 in (228.6 mm)
Maximum*	9.06 in (230.1 mm)
Brake lining minimum thickness	0.04 in (1.0 mm)

Refer to marks cast into the drum (they supersede information printed here)

Torque specifications

	Ft-lbs (unless otherwise indicated)
Front caliper anchor-to-steering knuckle bolts	58 to 72
Rear caliper anchor-to-spindle bolts	33 to 49
Disc brake caliper mounting bolts	
Front	23 to 30
Rear	12 to 17
Brake hose-to-caliper banjo bolt	16 to 22
Drum brake backing plate-to-spindle	31 to 47
Wheel cylinder bolts	84 to 108 in-lbs
Rear hub nut	73 to 131
Wheel lug nuts	See Chapter 1

1   General information

The vehicles covered by this manual are equipped with hydraulically operated front and rear brake systems. The front brakes are disc type and the rear brakes are disc or drum type, depending on the model. Both the front and rear brakes are self adjusting. The disc brakes automatically compensate for pad wear, while the drum brakes incorporate an adjustment mechanism which is activated as the brakes are applied when the vehicle is driven in reverse.

Hydraulic system

The hydraulic system consists of two separate circuits. The master cylinder has separate reservoirs for the two circuits and in the event of a leak or failure in one hydraulic circuit, the other circuit will remain operative.

Proportioning valve

A proportioning valve, located on the firewall, regulates hydraulic pressure in the rear brake circuit. When the brake pedal is applied, full rear brake circuit pressure passes through the proportioning valve to the rear brake circuit until the valve reaches its split point. Above the split point, the proportioning valve begins to reduce hydraulic pressure to the rear brake circuit, creating a balanced braking condition between the front and rear wheels while maintaining balanced hydraulic pressure at each rear wheel.

Power brake booster

The power brake booster, utilizing engine manifold vacuum and atmospheric pressure to provide assistance to the hydraulically operated brakes, is mounted on the firewall in the engine compartment.

Parking brake

The parking brake operates the rear brakes only, through cable actuation. It's activated by a hand lever mounted to the left of the center console.

Service

After completing any operation involving disassembly of any part of the brake system, always test drive the vehicle to check for proper braking performance before resuming normal driving. When testing the brakes, perform the tests on a clean, dry flat surface. Conditions other than these can lead to inaccurate test results.

Test the brakes at various speeds with both light and heavy pedal pressure. The vehicle should stop evenly without pulling to one side or the other. Avoid locking the brakes because this slides the tires and diminishes braking efficiency and control of the vehicle.

Tires, vehicle load and front-end alignment are factors which also affect braking performance.

2   Disc brake pads – replacement

Refer to illustrations 2.5 and 2.6a through 2.6o

Warning: *Disc brake pads must be replaced on both front – or both rear – wheels at the same time. Never replace the pads on only one wheel. Also, the dust created by the brake system may contain asbestos, which is*
harmful to your health. Never blow it out with compressed air and don't inhale any of it. An approved filtering mask should be worn when working on the brakes. Do not, under any circumstances, use petroleum-based solvents to clean brake parts. Use brake cleaner or denatured alcohol only!

Note: *When servicing the disc brakes, use only high quality, nationally recognized name brand pads.*

1   Remove the filler cap from the brake fluid reservoir. Using a syringe, remove about two-thirds of the brake fluid from the master cylinder (this is necessary because the fluid level in the reservoir will rise when you perform Step 5).

2   Loosen the wheel lug nuts, raise the front or rear of the vehicle and support it securely on jackstands.

3   Remove the front or rear wheels. Work on one brake assembly at a time, using the assembled brake for reference if necessary.

4   Inspect the brake disc carefully as outlined in Section 4. If machining is necessary, remove the caliper (see Section 3), remove the disc (see Section 4) and have it serviced.

5   To provide sufficient clearance for the new brake pads, push the piston back into the bore with a C-clamp **(see illustration)**. As the piston is pushed into the caliper bore, the fluid in the master cylinder will rise. Make sure it doesn't overflow. If necessary, siphon off some more fluid.

6   Follow the accompanying illustrations, beginning with 2.6a, for the pad replacement procedure. Be sure to stay in order and read the caption under each illustration. Illustrations 2.6a through 2.6i are for front pad replacement; illustrations 2.6j through 2.6o are for the rear pads. Before replacing the rear pads, loosen the adjusting nut of the parking brake cable, then detach the cable housing from the bracket and the parking brake lever (see Section 13).

2.5 Install a C-clamp on the caliper like this and tighten it to push the piston into the caliper before replacing pads or removing the caliper – otherwise, you won't be able to get the caliper over the pads

2.6a   Remove the caliper mounting bolt

2.6b   Pivot the caliper up . . .

2.6c   . . . then slide the caliper off the guide pin

2.6d   Hang the caliper out of the way by tying it to the coil spring with a piece of rope or wire – don't let the caliper hang by the brake hose

2.6e   Mark the anti-rattle shim to ensure proper reassembly, then detach it from the outer pad

2.6f   Remove the outer pad from the caliper anchor

2.6g   Remove the inner pad from the caliper anchor

2.6h   Mark the first anti-rattle shim to ensure proper reassembly, then detach it from the inner pad

2.6i   Mark the second anti-rattle shim to ensure proper reassembly, then detach it from the inner pad

2.6j   Remove the caliper retaining bolt

2.6k   Pivot the caliper back to clear the brake pads, slide the caliper off its fixed guide pin and hang it out of the way with a piece of rope or wire – don't let it hang by the brake hose

2.6l   Remove the upper and lower V-springs from the pads – note how each spring is installed before you remove it

2.6m   Remove the pads

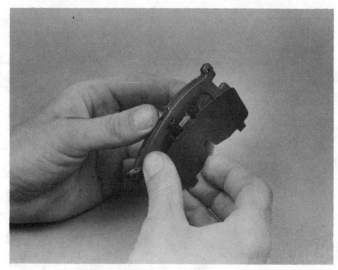

2.6n   Mark each anti-rattle shim for reassembly, then detach it from the old pad

7   Installation of the pads is the reverse of removal. When reinstalling the caliper, tighten the mounting bolt to the torque listed in this Chapter's Specifications.

8   After you've completed the installation, firmly depress the brake pedal a few times to bring the pads into contact with the disc.

9   Check for fluid leakage and make sure the brakes operate normally before driving in traffic.

---

3   Disc brake caliper – removal, overhaul and installation

Warning: *Dust created by the brake system may contain asbestos, which is harmful to your health. Never blow it out with compressed air and don't inhale any of it. An approved filtering mask should be worn when working on the brakes. Do not, under any circumstances, use petroleum-based solvents to clean brake parts. Use brake cleaner or denatured alcohol only!*

Note: *If an overhaul is indicated (usually because of fluid leakage), explore all options before beginning the job. New and factory rebuilt calipers are available on an exchange basis, which makes this job quite easy. If it's decided to rebuild the calipers, make sure a rebuild kit is available before proceeding. Always rebuild the calipers in pairs – never rebuild just one of them.*

Removal

Refer to illustration 3.5

1   Remove the cover from the brake fluid reservoir, siphon off two-thirds of the fluid into a container and discard it.

2   Loosen the wheel lug nuts, raise the front or rear of the vehicle and support it securely on jackstands. Remove the wheels.

3   If you're removing a rear caliper, loosen the parking brake cable housing adjustment nut, and remove the cable housing from the bracket and the parking brake lever (see Section 13).

4   Bottom the piston in the caliper bore **(see illustration 2.5).**

5   Remove the banjo bolt and detach the brake hose **(see illustration).**

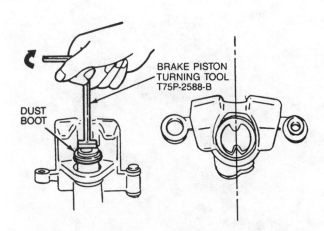

2.6o   Rotate the piston clockwise with a brake piston tool or needle-nose pliers – screw the piston in all the way and align the notches in the piston with the openings in the caliper as shown

3.5   Remove the banjo bolt attaching the brake hose to the caliper – discard the two sealing washers

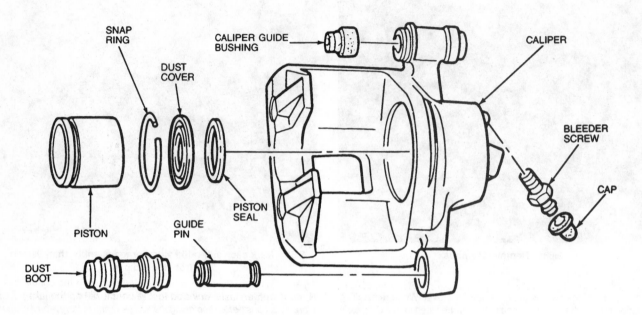

3.9   **Exploded view of the caliper assembly**

Have a rag handy to catch spilled fluid and wrap a plastic bag tightly around the end of the hose to prevent fluid loss and contamination. Remove the two copper washers that seal the banjo fitting and discard them. **Note:** *Don't detach the brake hose from the caliper if you're only removing the caliper to gain access to other components.*

6   Remove the caliper mounting bolt (see Section 2).

7   Pivot the caliper up and slide the caliper off the guide pin (see Section 2).

8   If the caliper anchor is to be removed also, remove the brake pads from the anchor (see Section 2).

Overhaul (front caliper)

Refer to illustrations 3.9, 3.11, 3.12, 3.13, 3.14, 3.21 and 3.22

9   Remove the caliper guide bushing, guide pin and dust boot (**see illustration**). Discard all rubber parts.

10   Clean the exterior of the caliper with brake cleaner or denatured alcohol. DO NOT use gasoline, kerosene or petroleum-based cleaning solvents. Place the caliper on a clean workbench.

11   Place a wood block or several shop rags in the caliper as a cushion, then use compressed air to remove the piston from the caliper (**see illustration**). Use only enough air pressure to ease the piston out of the bore. If the piston is blown out, even with the cushion in place, it may be damaged.

12   Remove the dust boot retaining ring (**see illustration**). **Warning:** *Never place your fingers in front of the piston in an attempt to catch or protect it when applying compressed air, as serious injury could occur.*

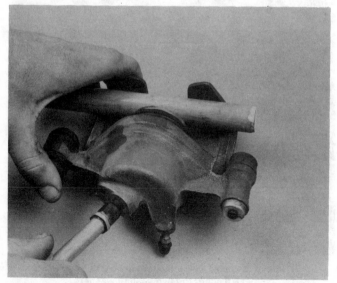

3.11   **With the caliper padded to catch the piston, use compressed air to force the piston out of the bore – make sure your fingers are out of the way**

3.12   **Remove the dust boot retaining ring**

3.13   Pull the old dust boot out of the caliper bore and discard it

3.14   Remove the piston seal from its groove in the caliper bore with a plastic or wood tool (a pencil will do the job)

13   Pull the dust boot from the caliper **(see illustration)**.

14   Using a wood or plastic pick, remove the piston seal from the groove in the caliper bore **(see illustration)**. Metal tools may cause bore damage.

15   Remove the caliper bleeder screw.

16   Clean the remaining parts with brake system cleaner or denatured alcohol, then blow them dry with compressed air.

17   Carefully examine the piston for nicks and burrs and loss of plating. If surface defects are evident, replace the caliper assembly.

18   Inspect the caliper bore and seal groove. Look for damage to similar to that described in the previous Step. Make sure the seal groove is free of scratches that would prevent the seal from working properly. You can lightly polish the bore with crocus cloth to remove light corrosion and stains. If that fails to clean up the damage, replace the caliper.

19   Inspect the mounting bolt. If it's corroded or damaged, discard it.

20   Before reassembling the caliper, lubricate the piston bore and seal with clean brake fluid. Position the seal in the groove.

21   Lubricate the piston with clean brake fluid, then install a new dust boot in the piston groove with the fold toward the open end of the piston **(see illustration)**.

22   Insert the piston squarely into the caliper bore, then apply force to bottom it **(see illustration)**.

23   Seat the dust boot in the caliper bore, then install the retaining ring.

24   Install the new dust boot for the guide pin, then install the guide pin.

25   Install the bleeder screw.

26   Install a new caliper guide bushing.

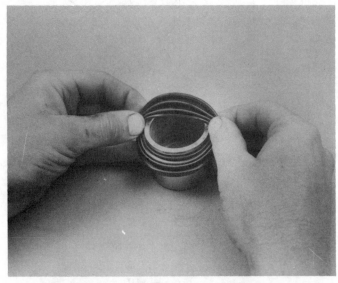

3.21   Install the new dust boot onto the piston – make sure the inner lip seats in the recessed groove in the piston

3.22   Place the piston squarely over the caliper bore, then push it into the bore with both hands

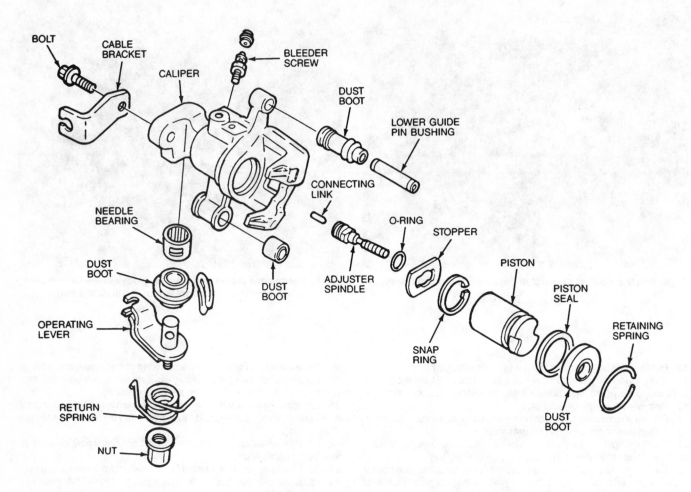

3.27   Exploded view of the rear caliper assembly

Overhaul (rear caliper)

Refer to illustrations 3.27, 3.36, 3.46, 3.47, 3.49, 3.52 and 3.61

27   Remove the caliper guide bushing and dust boots **(see illustration)**. Discard all rubber parts.

28   Clean the exterior of the caliper with brake cleaner or denatured alcohol. DO NOT use gasoline, kerosene or petroleum-based cleaning solvents. Place the caliper on a clean workbench.

29   Pry the retaining ring off the dust boot with a screwdriver. Discard the dust boot.

30   Rotate the piston counterclockwise using a brake piston turning tool (T75P-2588-B) or a pair of needle-nose pliers, and remove the piston from the adjuster spindle **(see illustration 2.6o).**

31   Using a wood or plastic pick, remove the piston seal from the groove in the caliper bore **(see illustration 3.14).** Metal tools may cause bore damage.

32   Remove the caliper bleeder screw.

33   Remove the snap-ring above the stopper **(see illustration 3.27).**

34   Remove the adjuster spindle, stopper and connecting link. Separate the adjuster spindle from the stopper.

35   Remove the O-ring from the adjuster spindle. Discard the O-ring.

36   Remove the return spring from the operating lever of the parking brake mechanism **(see illustration)**.

37   Remove the operating lever nut and lockwasher.

38   Mark the relationship between the operating lever and the shaft. Remove the operating lever from the shaft.

39   Remove the seal from the caliper housing.

40   Remove the shaft from the caliper housing.

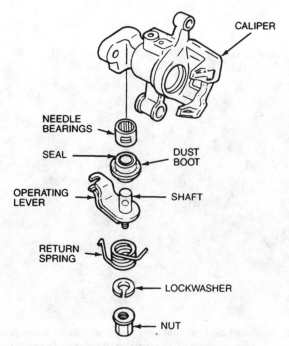

3.36   Exploded view of the parking brake lever assembly

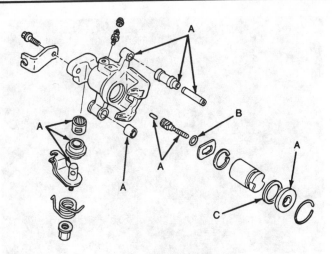

A—ORANGE COLORED GREASE
B—WHITE COLORED GREASE
C—RED COLORED GREASE

NOTE: APPLY THE GREASE
SUPPLIED IN THE SEAL KIT TO THE
POINTS SHOWN IN THE FIGURE.

3.46 Be sure to lubricate the indicated parts with the correct grease before reassembly

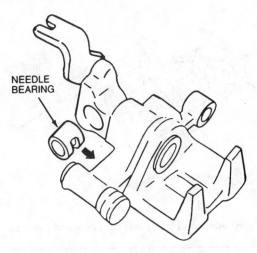

3.47 Align the opening in the needle bearings with the bore in the caliper housing

41 Remove the needle bearing from the caliper housing.

42 Carefully examine the piston for nicks and burrs and loss of plating. If surface defects are evident, replace the caliper assembly.

43 Inspect the caliper bore. Look for similar damage and wear. You can lightly polish the bore with crocus cloth to remove light corrosion and stains. If that fails to clean up the damage, replace the caliper.

44 Inspect the mounting bolt. If it's corroded or damaged, discard it.

45 Inspect the guide pin bushings for wear. If they're worn or corroded, replace them.

46 Lubricate the needle bearings with the orange grease included in the rebuilding kit **(see illustration)**.

47 Align the opening in the needle bearings with the bore in the caliper housing **(see illustration)**. Install the needle bearings.

48 Install the operating shaft into the caliper housing.

49 Install the operating lever **(see illustration)**. Align the marks made during removal.

50 Install the lockwasher nut.

51 Install the connecting link into the operating shaft.

52 Install the O-ring onto the adjuster spindle. Position the stopper onto the adjuster spindle so the pins will align with the caliper housing **(see illustration)**.

53 Install the adjuster spindle and the stopper into the caliper.

54 Install the stopper retaining snap-ring. Be sure the operating lever and adjuster spindle move freely.

55 Install the parking brake return spring.

56 Before reassembling the caliper, lubricate the piston bore and O-ring with clean brake fluid.

57 Install the O-ring into its groove in the caliper bore.

58 Lubricate the piston with clean brake fluid, then insert it into the caliper bore. Rotate the piston clockwise using a brake piston turning tool (T75P-2588-B or equivalent), or a pair of needle-nose pliers, to install it onto the adjuster spindle. Screw the piston in fully. Align the notches in the piston with the opening in the caliper **(see illustration 2.6o)**.

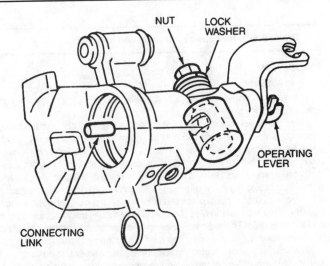

3.49 When you install the operating lever, be sure to align the marks you made before disassembly

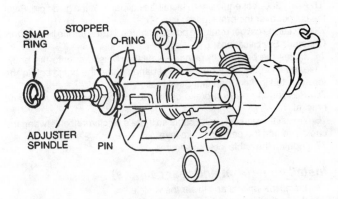

3.52 Exploded view of the adjuster spindle and stopper assembly

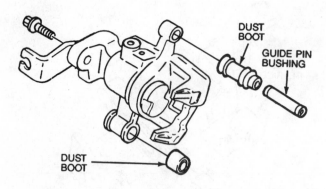

3.61   Exploded view of the caliper dust boot and guide pin

59   Install a new dust boot in the piston groove with the fold toward the open end of the piston. Seat the boot in the caliper bore.
60   Install the retaining ring.
61   Install the dust boots for the guide pin bushings **(see illustration)**.
62   Install the caliper guide pin bushing.

Installation (front caliper)

63   If the caliper hasn't been overhauled, remove the guide pin bushing dust boots and push out the caliper guide pin bushing.
64   Install the caliper anchor, if it was removed previously. Lubricate the guide pin bushings with high temperature grease (D7AZ-19590-A or equivalent) and install the caliper.
65   Install the guide pin dust boots.
66   Position the caliper onto the guide pin. Pivot the caliper over the brake pads (to provide the necessary clearance, it may be necessary to pull out slightly on the caliper).
67   Inspect the mounting bolt for excessive corrosion. If it's in bad shape, replace it. Install the caliper mounting bolt and tighten it to the torque listed in this Chapter's Specifications.
68   Using new sealing washers, position the brake hose on the caliper and install the banjo bolt. Tighten the bolt to the torque listed in this Chapter's Specifications.

Installation (rear caliper)

69   Install the anchor bracket, if it was removed previously. Tighten the bolts to the torque listed in this Chapter's Specifications.
70   Install the lower guide pin onto the anchor bracket.
71   Install the brake pads and shims (see Section 2).
72   Lubricate the guide pin bushings with high temperature grease (D7AZ-19590-A or equivalent). Install the caliper onto the guide pin. Pivot the caliper over the brake pads.
73   Install the caliper retaining bolt and tighten it to the torque listed in this Chapter's Specifications.
74   Install the banjo bolt, using new sealing washers, onto the brake hose. Position the hose on the caliper and tighten the banjo bolt to the torque listed in this Chapter's Specifications.
75   Position the parking brake cable into the parking brake lever and bracket.
76   Adjust the parking brake cable so there's no clearance between the cable end and the parking brake lever.
77   Tighten the cable locknut securely.

Installation (front and rear calipers)

78   Install the wheels and lower the vehicle.
79   If a brake line was disconnected, bleed the hydraulic system (see Section 11).
80   After the job has been completed, firmly depress the brake pedal a few times to bring the pads into contact with the disc.
81   Check brake operation before driving the vehicle in traffic.

4.3a   Check disc runout with a dial indicator positioned approximately 1/2-inch from the edge of the disc – it the reading exceeds the maximum allowable runout, the disc will have to be resurfaced or replaced

4.3b   Using a swirling motion, remove the glaze from the disc with emery cloth or sandpaper

4   Brake disc – inspection, removal and installation

Inspection

Refer to illustrations 4.3a, 4.3b, 4.4a and 4.4b

1   Loosen the wheel lug nuts, raise the vehicle and support it securely on jackstands. Remove the wheel.
2   Visually check the disc surface for score marks and other damage. Light scratches and shallow grooves are normal after use and may not always be detrimental to brake operation, but deep score marks – over 0.015-inch (0.38 mm) – require disc removal and refinishing by an automotive machine shop. Be sure to check both sides of the disc. If you have noticed pulsating during application of the brakes, suspect disc runout.
3   To check disc runout, place a dial indicator at a point about 1/2-inch from the outer edge of the disc **(see illustration)**. Set the indicator to zero and turn the disc. The indicator reading should not exceed the specified allowable runout limit. If it does, the disc should be refinished by an automotive machine shop. **Note:** *Professionals recommend resurfacing of brake discs regardless of the dial indicator reading (to produce a smooth, flat surface that will eliminate brake pedal pulsations and other undesirable symptoms related to questionable discs). At the very least, if you elect not to have the discs resurfaced, deglaze them with sandpaper or emery*

4.4a   The minimum thickness is cast into the center of the disc

4.4b   Check the disc thickness with a micrometer

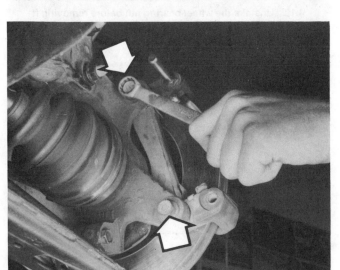

**4.6   Remove the caliper anchor bolts, then lift the anchor from
the steering knuckle**

**4.7   Remove the disc retaining screws, then slide the disc
from the hub**

cloth (use a swirling motion to ensure a nondirectional finish) **(see illustration)**.

4   The disc must not be machined to a thickness less than the specified minimum thickness. The minimum wear (or discard) thickness is cast into the center of the disc **(see illustration)**. Check the disc thickness with a micrometer **(see illustration)**.

Removal

5   Remove the brake caliper (see Section 3). It's not necessary to disconnect the brake hose. After removing the caliper bolts, suspend the caliper out of the way with a piece of rope or wire. Don't let the caliper hang by the hose and don't stretch or twist the hose.

Front

Refer to illustrations 4.6 and 4.7

6   Remove the caliper anchor bolts **(see illustration)** and remove the anchor.

7   Remove the disc retaining screws **(see illustration)** and remove the disc from the hub.

Rear

Refer to illustrations 4.8, 4.9, 4.10 and 4.12

8   Remove the caliper anchor bolts, then lift the anchor from the spindle **(see illustration)**. Check the wheel bearing endplay as described in Section 5.

4.8   Remove the bolts securing the rear caliper anchor

4.9   Tap the grease cap off using a hammer and chisel

4.10   Unstake the wheel bearing nut before removing it

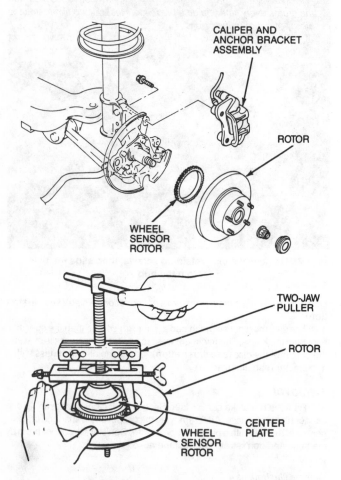

CALIPER AND
ANCHOR BRACKET
ASSEMBLY

ROTOR

WHEEL
SENSOR
ROTOR

TWO-JAW
PULLER

ROTOR

CENTER
PLATE

WHEEL
SENSOR
ROTOR

4.12   If the vehicle is equipped with ABS, remove the wheel sensor rotor from the disc using a two-jaw puller

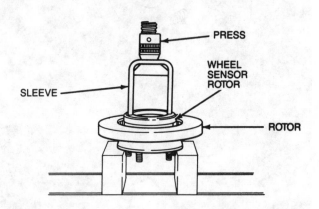

PRESS

WHEEL
SENSOR
ROTOR

SLEEVE

ROTOR

4.14   On an ABS-equipped vehicle, position the disc in a hydraulic press with the wheel studs facing down and, using a sensing ring installer (T88C-20202-AH, or equivalent) press the sensor onto the disc

12   If the vehicle is equipped with ABS, you'll need to remove the wheel sensor rotor from the disc with a two-jaw puller, if you're installing a new disc **(see illustration)**. Also, if a new disc is being installed, a new bearing must be pressed into the hub.

Installation

Front
13   Install the disc on the hub and install the disc retaining screw.

Rear
Refer to illustration 4.14

14   If the vehicle is equipped with ABS, position the disc in a hydraulic press with the wheel studs facing down **(see illustration)**. Using a sensing ring installer (T88C-20202-AH, or equivalent), press the sensor onto the disc.

15   Install the disc/hub assembly and install a new wheel bearing nut and washer. Tighten the nut to the torque listed in this Chapter's Specifications. Stake the nut to the spindle and install the grease cap.

Front and rear
16   Install the caliper anchor bracket, brake pads (see Section 2) and caliper (see Section 3). Tighten the caliper bolt to the torque listed in this Chapter's Specifications.

9   Using a hammer and chisel, remove the grease cap from the center of the disc **(see illustration)**.
10   Using a small chisel or punch, unstake the wheel bearing nut **(see illustration)**. Remove the nut and washer.
11   Remove the disc from the spindle.

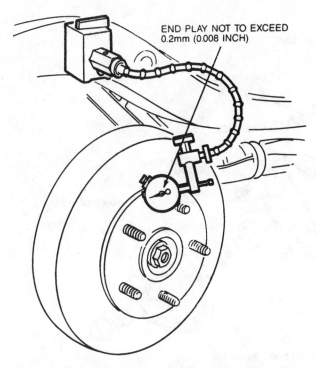

END PLAY NOT TO EXCEED
0.2mm (0.008 INCH)

5.4 Check the endplay of the rear wheel bearing with a dial indicator – push the drum (or disc) in, zero the indicator, then pull the drum (or disc) out – if the endplay exceeds the figure listed in this Chapter's Specifications, replace the wheel bearing

17 Install the wheel, then lower the vehicle to the ground. Depress the brake pedal a few times to bring the brake pads into contact with the disc. Bleeding of the system will not be necessary unless the brake hose was disconnected from the caliper. Check the operation of the brakes carefully before placing the vehicle into normal service.

5   Brake drum/wheel bearing assembly – removal, inspection and installation

Bearing endplay check

Refer to illustration 5.4

1   Loosen the rear wheel lug nuts, raise the vehicle and place it securely on jackstands.
2   Remove the rear wheels.
3   Rotate the brake drum to ensure that there's no brake drag. If the brakes drag, check the parking brake cable adjustment (see Section 12), the brake shoe assembly (see Section 6), the wheel cylinder (see Section 7), the brake pedal adjustment (see Section 15), the brake light switch (see Section 17), the power brake booster (see Section 16) and the master cylinder (see Section 8).
4   Set up a dial indicator as shown **(see illustration)**. Grasp the drum firmly and try to move it in and out. Endplay should not exceed the figure listed in the Specifications at the beginning of this Chapter.
5   The bearing is sealed and non-adjustable. If endplay exceeds the specified figure, remove the drum (see below), take the drum to a dealer or

automotive machine shop and have the bearing pressed out and a new bearing pressed in.

Removal

6   Pry off the grease cap with a small screwdriver.
7   Carefully raise the staked portion of the attaching nut with a small chisel or punch **(see illustration 4.10)**. Remove and discard the attaching nut.
8   Release the parking brake, if you haven't already done so.
9   Remove the brake drum/bearing assembly from the spindle. If you can't pull the brake drum off, loosen the parking brake cable (see Section 12) and try again.
10   If you're going to take the drum to the dealer or an automotive machine shop to have the old bearing pressed out, and a new bearing installed, pry out the grease seal with a large screwdriver.

Inspection

11   Inspect the drum for cracks, score marks, deep scratches and hard spots (which will appear as small discolored areas).
12   If the hard spots can't be removed with fine emery cloth, or if any of the above conditions are evident, take the drum must to an automotive machine shop and have it turned. **Note:** *Professionals recommend resurfacing the drums every time you do a brake job. Resurfacing eliminates the possibility of out-of-round drums.*
13   If the drums are worn so much that they can't be resurfaced without exceeding the maximum allowable diameter, replace them. **Note:** *The maximum allowable diameter is shown in cast figures on the drum.*
14   Even if you decide against having the drums resurfaced, remove the glazing from the surface with emery cloth or sandpaper, using a swirling motion.

Installation

15   If you had a new bearing pressed in, tap a new grease seal into place with a large socket having a diameter slightly smaller than that of the seal.
16   Lubricate the spindle with a thin film of wheel bearing grease. Position the brake drum on the spindle.
17   Install a new nut and tighten it to the torque listed in this Chapter's Specifications.
18   Check the bearing endplay (see above).
19   Stake the nut to the spindle. **Caution:** *If the nut splits or cracks after staking, it must be replaced with a new nut.*
20   Install the grease cap.
21   Install the wheel and lugs nuts. Lower the vehicle and tighten the lug nuts to the torque listed in the Chapter 1 Specifications section.

6   Drum brake shoes – replacement

Refer to illustrations 6.4a, 6.4b, 6.6, 6.8, 6.9 and 6.12
Warning: *Drum brake shoes must be replaced on both wheels at the same time – never replace the shoes on only one wheel. Also, the dust created by the brake system may contain asbestos, which is harmful to your health. Never blow it out with compressed air and don't inhale any of it. An approved filtering mask should be worn when working on the brakes. Do not, under any circumstances, use petroleum-based solvents to clean brake parts. Use brake cleaner or denatured alcohol only!*

Caution: *Whenever the brake shoes are replaced, the retractor and hold-down springs should also be replaced. Due to the continuous heating/cooling cycle that the springs are subjected to, they lose their tension over a period of time and may allow the shoes to drag on the drum and wear at a much faster rate than normal. When replacing the rear brake shoes, use only high quality nationally recognized brand-name parts.*

1   Loosen the wheel lug nuts, raise the rear of the vehicle and support it securely on jackstands. Block the front wheels to keep the vehicle from rolling.
2   Remove the wheel.

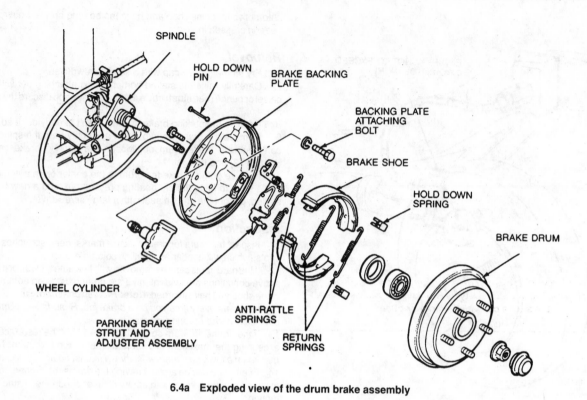

6.4a   Exploded view of the drum brake assembly

3   Remove the brake drum (see Section 5).

4   Remove the brake shoe return springs and anti-rattle springs **(see illustrations)**.

5   Using a screwdriver, push in and twist the hold-down springs to disengage them from from the hold-down pins.

6   Disconnect the rear brake shoe from the parking brake strut and remove it **(see illustration)**, then remove the front shoe. **Note:** *Unless they're broken or worn, leave the parking brake strut, adjuster mechanism and adjuster spring in place.*

7   Clean the backing plate with brake cleaner and dry it off. If you find it necessary to remove the backing plate from the spindle, detach the parking brake cable from the backing plate (see Section 14), disconnect the hydraulic line from the wheel cylinder (see Section 7), then remove the bolts that attach the backing plate to the spindle.

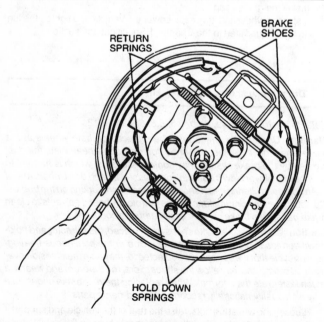

6.4b   Remove the brake shoe return springs and anti-rattle spring

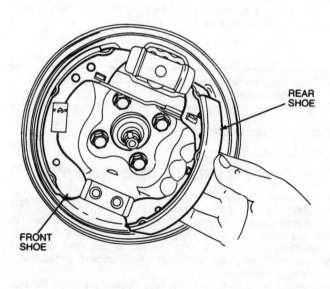

6.6   Detach the rear shoe from the parking brake strut and lift it from the backing plate

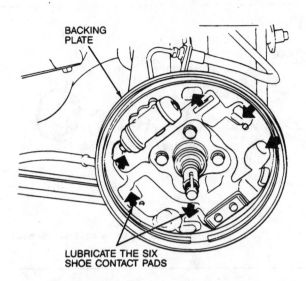

6.8   Using high-temperature grease, lubricate the shoe contact pads, the adjuster mechanism, and the points where the shoes contact the anchor plate

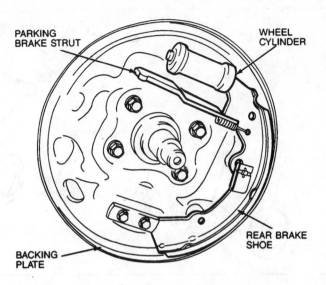

6.9   Assemble the rear shoe to the parking brake strut and install the rear hold-down pin and spring

8   Lubricate the shoe contact pads, the adjuster mechanism and the anchor plate with a thin film of high-temperature grease **(see illustration)**.
9   Position the rear brake shoe in the parking brake strut and install the rear hold-down pin and spring **(see illustration)**.
10   Position the front brake shoe against the parking brake strut and backing plate, then install the hold-down pin and spring.
11   Install the shoe return springs and the anti-rattle springs.
12   Insert a screwdriver between the quadrant and the parking brake strut, then twist the screwdriver until the quadrant just touches the backing plate **(see illustration)**.
13   Install the brake drum (see Section 5).
14   Install the wheel and lugs nuts. Lower the vehicle and tighten the lug nuts to the torque listed in the Chapter 1 Specifications section.
15   Make a number of forward and reverse stops to adjust the brakes until satisfactory pedal action is obtained.
16   Check brake operation before driving the vehicle in traffic.

7   Wheel cylinder – removal, overhaul and installation

Note: *If an overhaul is necessitated by fluid leakage or sticky operation, you have two options – new wheel cylinders or rebuilding the old ones. If you decide to rebuild the wheel cylinders, make sure that a rebuild kit is available before proceeding. Never overhaul only one wheel cylinder – always rebuild both of them at the same time.*

Removal
Refer to illustration 7.4

1   Raise the rear of the vehicle and support it securely on jackstands. Block the front wheels to keep the vehicle from rolling.
2   Remove the brake shoes (see Section 6).
3   Remove all dirt and foreign material from around the wheel cylinder.
4   Unscrew the brake line fitting **(see illustration)**. Don't pull the brake line away from the wheel cylinder.
5   Remove the wheel cylinder mounting bolts.

6.12   Pry the quadrant back until it just touches the backing plate

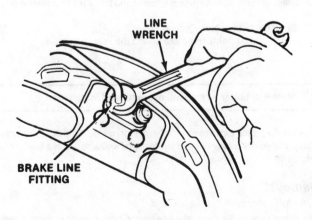

7.4   Completely loosen the brake line fitting, then remove the wheel cylinder mounting bolts

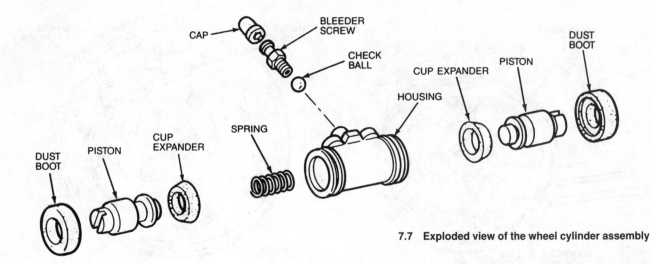

7.7   Exploded view of the wheel cylinder assembly

6   Detach the wheel cylinder from the brake backing plate and place it on a clean workbench. Immediately plug the brake line to prevent fluid loss and contamination. **Note:** *If the brake shoe linings are contaminated with brake fluid, install new brake shoes.*

Overhaul

Refer to illustration 7.7

7   Remove the bleeder screw, check ball, dust boots, pistons, cup expanders and spring from the wheel cylinder body **(see illustration)**.
8   Clean the wheel cylinder with brake fluid, denatured alcohol or brake system cleaner. **Warning:** *Do not, under any circumstances, use petroleum-based solvents to clean brake parts!*
9   Use compressed air to remove excess fluid from the wheel cylinder and to blow out the passages.
10   Check the cylinder bore for corrosion and score marks. Crocus cloth can be used to remove light corrosion and stains, but the cylinder must be replaced with a new one if the defects cannot be removed easily, or if the bore is scored.
11   Lubricate the new expander cups with brake fluid.
12   Assemble the wheel cylinder components. Make sure the cup expander lips face in **(see illustration 7.7).**

Installation

13   Place the wheel cylinder in position and install the bolts, tightening them to the torque listed in this Chapter's Specifications.
14   Connect the brake line and tighten the fitting.
15   Install the brake shoes (see Section 6) and the brake drums (see Section 5).
16   Bleed the brakes (see Section 11).
17   Check brake operation before driving the vehicle in traffic.

---

8   Master cylinder – removal, overhaul and installation

Note: *Before deciding to overhaul the master cylinder, check on the availability and cost of a new or factory rebuilt unit and also the availability of a rebuild kit.*

Removal

Refer to illustration 8.2, 8.4a and 8.4b

1   Place rags under the brake line fittings and prepare caps or plastic bags to cover the ends of the lines once they are disconnected. **Caution:** *Brake fluid will damage paint. Cover all body parts and be careful not to spill fluid during this procedure.*

8.2   Using a flare-nut wrench, unscrew the brake line fittings at the master cylinder

2   Unscrew the fittings at the ends of the brake lines where they enter the master cylinder. To prevent rounding off the flats on these nuts, a flare-nut wrench, which wraps around the fitting, should be used **(see illustration)**.
3   Pull the brake lines away from the master cylinder slightly and plug the ends to prevent contamination.
4   Unplug the electrical connector for the fluid level warning light switch **(see illustration)**, remove the two master cylinder mounting nuts and detach the master cylinder from the power brake booster **(see illustration)**.
5   Remove the reservoir cap, screen(s) and the boot for the fluid level switch, then discard any fluid remaining in the reservoir.

Overhaul

Refer to illustrations 8.6, 8.7, 8.8, 8.9, 8.10a, 8.10b and 8.10c

6   Put the master cylinder in a vise, upside down, with the jaws clamping on the mounting flange, then remove the secondary piston stop screw **(see illustration)**.
7   Depress the piston with a Phillips screwdriver and remove the snapring with a pair of snap-ring pliers **(see illustration)**.
8   Remove the primary piston assembly from the cylinder bore **(see illustration)**.
9   Remove the secondary piston assembly from the cylinder bore. It may be necessary to remove the master cylinder from the vise and invert it, carefully tapping it against a block of wood to expel the piston **(see illustration)**.

8.4a   Unplug the electrical connector for the fluid
level warning light

8.4b   Remove the two master cylinder mounting nuts (arrows)
and remove the master cylinder from the brake booster

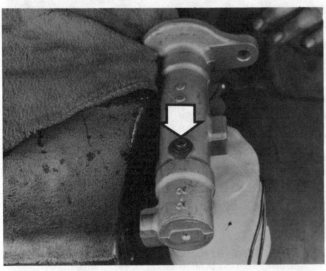

8.6   With the master cylinder flange clamped in a bench vise,
remove the secondary piston stop screw (arrow)

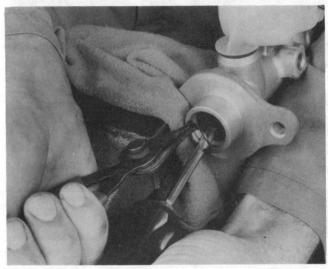

8.7   Depress the primary piston and remove the snap-ring

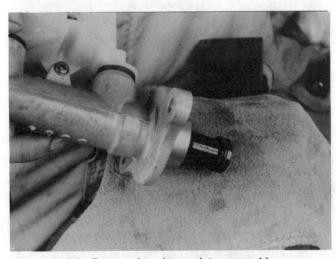

8.8   Remove the primary piston assembly

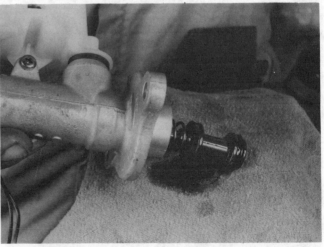

8.9   Remove the secondary piston assembly (if the secondary
piston is difficult to dislodge from the bore, gently tap the master
cylinder on a wood block)

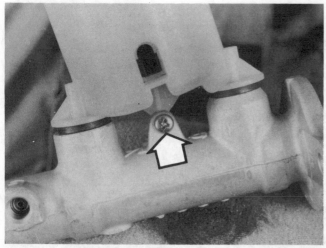

8.10a   To remove the reservoir, remove the retaining screw . . .

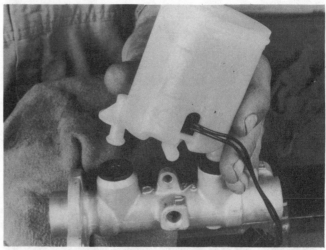

8.10b   . . . and pry the reservoir off the master cylinder

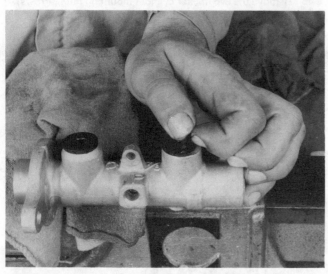

8.10c   Remove the reservoir grommets

9.2   Using a flare-nut wrench, unscrew the brake line fittings (arrows) from the proportioning valve, remove the two mounting bolts (arrows) and remove the proportioning valve

10.2   Use a flare-nut wrench to unscrew the brake line fitting from the brake hose

10.3   Use pliers to disconnect the U-clip from the brake hose bracket

10   If fluid has been leaking past the reservoir grommets, remove the reservoir retaining screw **(see illustration)** and pry the reservoir out of the cylinder body with a screwdriver **(see illustration)**. Remove and discard the old grommets **(see illustration)**.

11   Inspect the cylinder bore for corrosion and damage. If any corrosion or damage is found, replace the master cylinder body with a new one, as abrasives cannot be used on the bore.

12   Lubricate the new reservoir grommets with silicone lubricant and press them into the master cylinder body. Make sure they're properly seated.

13   Lay the reservoir on a hard surface and press the master cylinder body onto the reservoir, using a rocking motion. Install the reservoir retaining screw.

14   Lubricate the cylinder bore and primary and secondary piston assemblies with clean brake fluid. Insert the secondary piston assembly into the cylinder. Install the secondary piston stop screw and tighten securely.

15   Install the primary piston assembly in the cylinder bore, depress it and install the snap-ring.

16   Inspect the reservoir filler cap and diaphragm for cracks and deformation. Replace it if it's damaged.

17   **Note:** *Whenever the master cylinder is removed, the complete hydraulic system must be bled. The time required to bleed the system can be reduced if the master cylinder is filled with fluid and bench bled (refer to Steps 18 through 25) before the master cylinder is installed on the vehicle.*

18   Insert threaded plugs of the correct size into the cylinder outlet holes and fill the reservoir with brake fluid. The master cylinder should be supported in such a manner that brake fluid will not spill during the bench bleeding procedure.

19   Loosen one plug at a time, starting with the rear outlet ports first (closest to the booster), and push the piston assembly into the bore to force air from the master cylinder. To prevent air from being drawn back into the cylinder, the appropriate plug must be replaced before allowing the piston to return to its original position.

20   Stroke the piston three or four times for each outlet to ensure that all air has been expelled.

21   Since high pressure is not involved in the bench bleeding procedure, an alternative to the removal and replacement of the plugs with each stroke of the piston assembly is available. Before pushing in on the piston assembly, remove one of the plugs completely. Before releasing the piston, however, instead of replacing the plug, simply put your finger tightly over the hole to keep air from being drawn back into the master cylinder. Wait several seconds for the brake fluid to be drawn from the reservoir to the piston bore, then repeat the procedure. When you push down on the piston it will force your finger off the hole, allowing the air inside to be expelled. When only brake fluid is being ejected from the hole, replace the plug and go on to the other port.

22   Refill the master cylinder reservoir and install the low fluid level switch boot, screen(s) and filler cap.

Installation

23   Carefully install the master cylinder by reversing the removal steps, then bleed the brakes (see Section 11).

---

9   Proportioning valve – removal and installation

Removal

Refer to illustration 9.2

1   Remove the two bolts from the fuel filter mounting bracket (see Chapter 4). Position the fuel filter out of the way.

2   Using a flare nut wrench, unscrew all of the brake lines connected to the proportioning valve **(see illustration)**.

3   Using a flare nut wrench, loosen the brake lines at the master cylinder (see Section 8).

4   Remove the brake lines between the proportioning valve and the master cylinder.

5   Disconnect all brake lines connected to the proportioning valve.

6   Remove the proportioning valve mounting bolts and remove the proportioning valve.

Installation

7   Position the valve on the firewall and connect the brake lines to it, starting all of the fittings by hand. Connect the brake lines to the master cylinder. Don't tighten any of the fittings yet.

8   Install the mounting bolts, tightening them securely.

9   Tighten the brake line fittings securely.

10   Bleed the brake system (see Section 11).

---

10   Brake hoses and lines – inspection and replacement

Inspection

1   About every six months, with the vehicle raised and supported securely on jackstands, the rubber hoses which connect the steel brake lines with the front and rear brake assemblies should be inspected for cracks, chafing of the outer cover, leaks, blisters and other damage. These are important and vulnerable parts of the brake system and inspection should be complete. A light and mirror will be helpful for a thorough check. If a hose exhibits any of the above conditions, replace it with a new one.

Replacement

Flexible brake hose

Refer to illustrations 10.2 and 10.3

2   Disconnect the brake line from the hose fitting, being careful not to bend the frame bracket or brake line **(see illustration)**.

3   Use a pair of pliers to remove the U-clip from the female fitting at the bracket **(see illustration)**, then detach the hose from the bracket.

4   Unscrew the brake hose banjo bolt from the caliper **(see illustration 3.5)**.

5   To attach the hose, install the banjo bolt (using new sealing washers) through the banjo fitting on the end of the hose into the caliper, then tighten it securely.

6   Without twisting the hose, install the female fitting in the hose bracket.

7   Attach the brake line to the hose fitting, making sure the threads screw in easily.

8   Install the U-clip retaining the female fitting to the frame bracket, then tighten the fitting securely.

9   When the brake hose installation is completed, there should be no kinks in the hose. Make sure the hose doesn't contact any part of the suspension. On the front this can be checked by turning the wheels to the extreme left and right positions. If the hose makes contact, remove it and correct the installation as necessary.

10   Fill the master cylinder and bleed the system (see Section 11).

Metal brake lines

Note: *When replacing brake lines be sure to use the correct parts. Don't use copper tubing for any brake system components. Purchase steel brake lines from a dealer parts department or an auto parts store.*

11   Prefabricated brake line, with the tube ends already flared and fittings installed, is available at auto parts stores and dealers. These lines are also bent to the proper shapes.

12   When installing the new line make sure it's securely supported in the brackets and has plenty of clearance between moving or hot components.

13   After installation, check the master cylinder fluid level, add fluid as necessary and bleed the brake system (see Section 11).

14   Test the brakes carefully before driving the vehicle in traffic.

---

11   Brake system bleeding

Refer to illustration 11.8

Warning: *Wear eye protection when bleeding the brake system. If the fluid comes in contact with your eyes, immediately rinse them with water and seek medical attention.* **Note:** *Bleeding the hydraulic system is necessary to remove any air that manages to find its way into the system when*

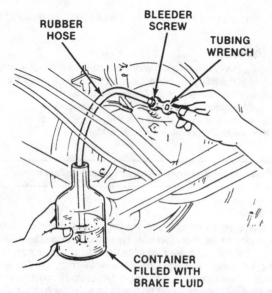

11.8 When bleeding the brakes, a clear piece of tubing is attached to the bleeder screw and submerged in brake fluid – air bubbles can be seen easily in the tube and container (when no more bubbles appear, the air has been purged from the caliper or wheel cylinder

it's been opened during removal and installation of a hose, line, caliper or master cylinder.

1   It will probably be necessary to bleed the system at all four brakes if air has entered the system due to low fluid level, or if the brake lines have been disconnected at the master cylinder.

2   If a brake line was disconnected only at a wheel, then only that caliper or wheel cylinder must be bled.

3   If a brake line is disconnected at a fitting located between the master cylinder and any of the brakes, that part of the system served by the disconnected line must be bled.

4   Remove any residual vacuum from the brake power booster by applying the brake several times with the engine off.

5   Remove the master cylinder reservoir cover and fill the reservoir with brake fluid. Reinstall the cover. **Note:** *Check the fluid level often during the bleeding operation and add fluid as necessary to prevent the fluid level from falling low enough to allow air bubbles into the master cylinder.*

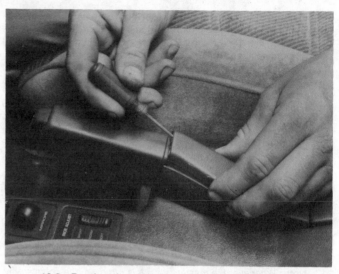

12.2   Pry the trim plate off with a small screwdriver

6   Have an assistant on hand, as well as a supply of new brake fluid, a clear container partially filled with clean brake fluid, a length of 3/16-inch clear tubing to fit over the bleeder screw and a wrench to open and close the bleeder screw.

7   Beginning at the right rear wheel, loosen the bleeder screw slightly, then tighten it to a point where it is snug but can still be loosened quickly and easily.

8   Place one end of the tubing over the bleeder screw and submerge the other end in brake fluid in the container **(see illustration)**.

9   Have the assistant pump the brakes slowly a few times to get pressure in the system, then hold the pedal firmly depressed.

10   While the pedal is held depressed, open the bleeder screw just enough to allow a flow of fluid to leave the valve. Watch for air bubbles to exit the submerged end of the tube. When the fluid flow slows after a couple of seconds, close the valve and have your assistant release the pedal.

11   Repeat Steps 9 and 10 until no more air is seen leaving the tube, then tighten the bleeder screw and proceed to the left front wheel, the left rear wheel and the right front wheel, in that order, and perform the same procedure. Be sure to check the fluid in the master cylinder reservoir frequently.

12   Never use old brake fluid. It contains moisture which will deteriorate the brake system components.

13   Refill the master cylinder with fluid at the end of the operation.

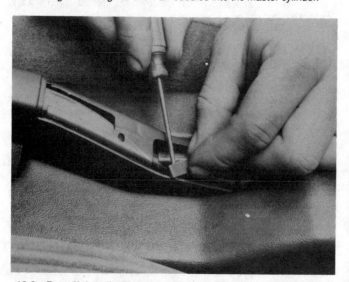

12.3   Pry off the clip that prevents the adjuster nut from turning

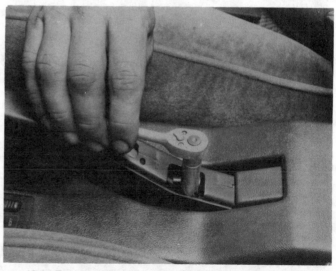

12.4   Turn the adjuster nut clockwise to tighten the cable, counterclockwise to loosen it

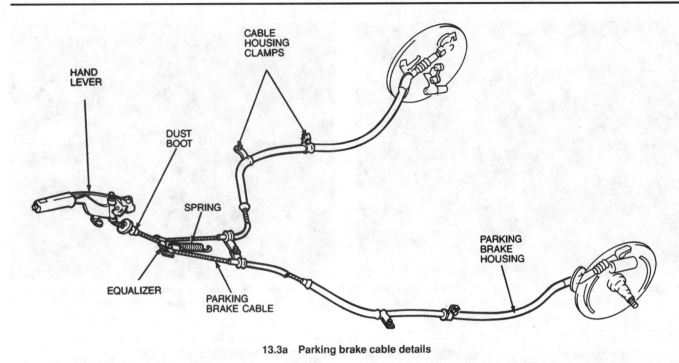

13.3a Parking brake cable details

14   Check the operation of the brakes. The pedal should feel solid when depressed, with no sponginess. If necessary, repeat the entire process. **Warning:** *Do not operate the vehicle if you are in doubt about the effectiveness of the brake system.*

12   Parking brake cable – check and adjustment

Refer to illustrations 12.2, 12.3 and 12.4

1   Operate the parking brake lever. If the cable feels like it's loose, binding or not releasing completely, check the adjustment at the lever. It should take five to seven clicks to set the parking brake.
2   Pry the trim plate off the brake lever using a small screwdriver **(see illustration)**.
3   Remove the clip that prevents the adjuster nut from turning **(see illustration)**.
4   Turn the adjuster nut clockwise to tighten the cable, counterclockwise to loosen it **(see illustration)**. Every few turns, try the lever again. When

you count five to seven notches to fully set the parking brake, it's adjusted correctly.
5   If you can't adjust the cable, it's probably binding, kinked, misrouted or broken. Raise the vehicle and place it securely on jackstands.
6   Inspect the parking brake cable for damage and proper routing.
7   If the cable is damaged, replace it (see Section 14).

13   Parking brake lever – removal and installation

Removal

Refer to illustrations 13.3a, 13.3b, 13.4, 13.5 and 13.7

1   Remove the floor console (see Chapter 11).
2   Raise the vehicle and place it securely on jackstands.
3   From under the vehicle, disconnect the parking brake return spring from the parking brake equalizer **(see illustrations)**.
4   Remove the three-piece plastic cover from the parking brake lever **(see illustration)**.

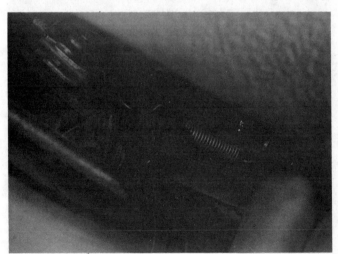

13.3b Disconnect the parking brake return spring from the equalizer – diagonal cutting pliers grip the spring well, but be careful not to cut or damage it

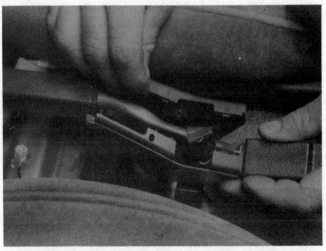

13.4 Remove the three-piece cover from the lever (the top piece pops off, the two lower halves are split vertically)

13.5   Unplug the electrical connector from the warning light
switch, then remove the screw and detach the switch

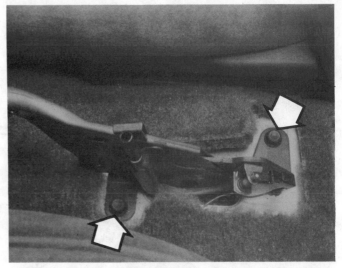

13.7   Remove the mounting bolts from the base of the parking
brake lever and remove the lever assembly

5   Unplug the warning light switch, remove the switch mounting screw
and remove the switch **(see illustration)**.
6   Remove the locknut from the parking brake adjusting nut **(see illustration 12.4)**.
7   Remove the two mounting bolts from the parking brake lever assembly **(see illustration)**.
8   Remove the parking brake lever assembly.

Installation

9   If the short parking brake cable (the one attached to the equalizer)
drops through the tunnel, have an assistant thread it back through the tunnel and hold it in place while you mount the parking brake lever and thread
the adjuster nut onto the end of the cable.
10   The remainder of installation is the reverse of removal.
11   When you're finished, adjust the parking brake cable (see Section 12).

14   Parking brake cables – replacement

Note: *The parking brake cable assembly actually consists of three cables.
The two main cables extend from the equalizer to each of the rear brakes.
These two cables are independently replaceable, so if either of them
breaks, it's not necessary to replace both. The third cable connects the
equalizer to the parking brake lever via a tunnel through the floor. This
cable is permanently affixed to the equalizer. To replace it, you'll have to
disconnect the main cables from the equalizer.*

Removal

Main cables

Models with rear drum brakes

Refer to illustrations 14.1, 14.2 and 14.3

1   Remove the parking brake return spring at each backing plate with a
pair of needle-nose pliers, remove the parking brake return spring at each
backing plate **(see illustration)**. Be careful not to overextend the spring.

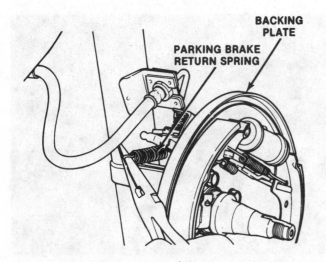

14.1   Remove the parking brake return spring at each backing
plate with a pair of needle-nose pliers (vehicles with drum brakes)

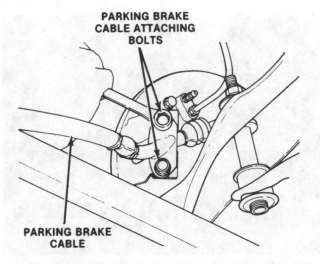

14.2   Remove the parking brake cable mounting bolts and pull it
away from the backing plate (vehicles with drum brakes)

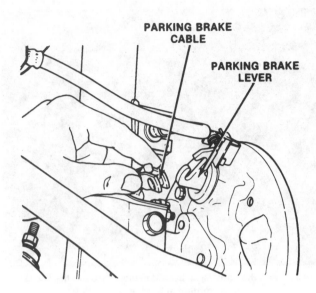

14.3   Detach the parking brake cables from the levers on the
backing plates (vehicles with drum brakes)

14.4   Loosen the locknut on the parking brake cable housing,
then detach the cable from its bracket

2   Remove the mounting bolts from the parking brake cable housing and pull it away from the backing plate (see illustration).
3   Disconnect the parking brake cables from the levers on the backing plates (see illustration).

Models with rear disc brakes
Refer to illustration 14.4

4   Loosen the locknut on the parking brake cable housing and detach the cable from the bracket (see illustration).
5   Disconnect the cable from the parking brake lever.

All models
Refer to illustrations 14.6, 14.8, 14.9 and 14.10

6   Unbolt the cable housing clamp from the rear suspension trailing arm (see illustration).
7   Follow the cable back and unbolt the cable housing clamps from the body.
8   Detach the cable clamp which secures both cables (see illustration).
9   Disconnect the cables from the bracket behind the equalizer (see illustration).

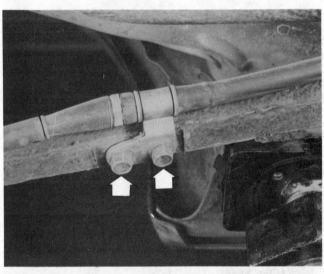

14.6   Unbolt the cable housing clamp from the trailing arm

14.8   Remove the clamp which secures both cables to the
body (arrow)

14.9   Pull the U-clip off the cable bracket with a pair of pliers,
then detach the cable from the bracket

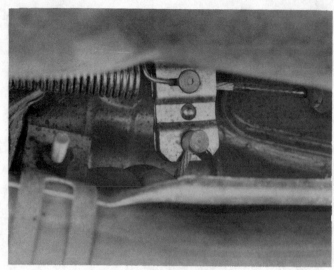

14.10   To detach the cables from the equalizer, align the cable with the slot in the equalizer, then slide the cable end out

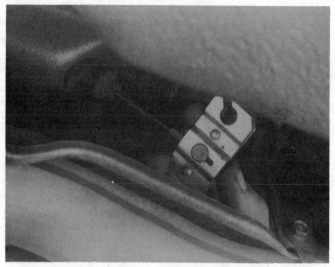

14.15   Pull the cable/equalizer assembly through the access tunnel in the floor

10   Disconnect the cables from the equalizer (see illustration).

Front cable/equalizer assembly
Refer to illustration 14.15

11   Unscrew the cable adjuster nut at the parking brake lever (see Section 13).
12   Disconnect the two main cables from the bracket behind the main equalizer (see Step 9).
13   Disconnect the parking brake return spring from the parking brake equalizer (see illustration 13.3b).
14   Disconnect the cables from the equalizer (see Step 10).
15   Pull the cable/equalizer assembly down through the access tunnel in the floor (see illustration).

Installation
16   Installation is the reverse of removal. Be sure to adjust the cables when you're done (see Section 12).

15   Brake pedal – adjustment

Brake pedal height
Refer to illustrations 15.1 and 15.2

1   Check the distance from the center of the pedal pad to the floor (see illustration). It should be as specified. If it isn't, adjust the pedal height by adjusting the brake light switch.
2   Unplug the electrical connector from the brake light switch (see illustration).
3   Loosen the brake light switch locknut.
4   Rotate the switch until the pedal height is 8 1/2 to 8 3/4-inches (217 to 222 mm).
5   Tighten the switch locknut.
6   Plug in the electrical connector.

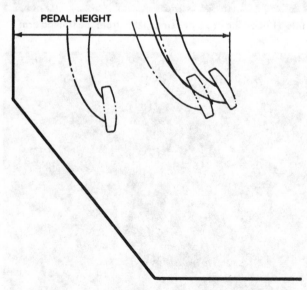

15.1   Verify that the distance from the center of the pedal pad to the floor is between 8 3/4 to 9-inches (222 to 227 mm)

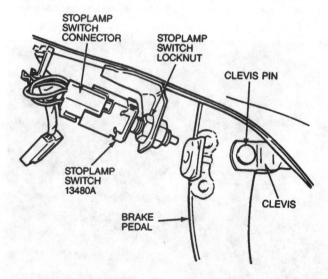

15.2   If the pedal height is incorrect, loosen the brake light switch locknut, rotate the switch until the pedal height is 8 1/2 to 8 3/4-inches (217 to 222 mm), then tighten the locknut

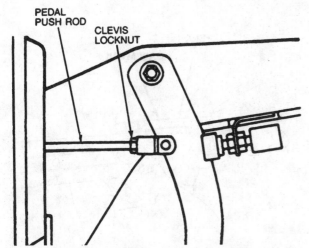

15.9   Loosen the clevis locknut on the brake pedal pushrod, then turn the clevis to adjust pedal freeplay

Brake pedal freeplay

Refer to illustration 15.9

7   If the vehicle is equipped with power brakes, depress the pedal a few times to eliminate the vacuum in the power booster.

8   Gently depress the pedal by hand and check the pedal freeplay. Freeplay is the distance between the point at which the pedal begins to move and the point at which the valve plunger contacts the stopper plate (the point at which you feel resistance).

9   If the freeplay needs adjusting, loosen the clevis locknut on the brake pedal pushrod **(see illustration)**, turn the clevis to obtain 1/8 to 1/4-inch (4 to 7 mm) and tighten the clevis locknut.

16   Power brake booster – check, removal and installation

Operating check

1   Depress the brake pedal several times with the engine off and make sure that there is no change in the pedal reserve distance.

2   Depress the pedal and start the engine. If the pedal goes down slightly, operation is normal.

Air tightness check

3   Start the engine and turn it off after one or two minutes. Depress the brake pedal several times slowly. If the pedal goes down farther the first time but gradually rises after the second or third depression, the booster is airtight.

4   Depress the brake pedal while the engine is running, then stop the engine with the pedal depressed. If there is no change in the pedal reserve travel after holding the pedal for 30 seconds, the booster is airtight.

Removal

Refer to illustration 16.10

5   Do not disassemble the power brake booster unit. You need special tools to disassemble this complex component. Because of its critical relationship to brake performance, replace a defective booster unit with a new or rebuilt unit.

6   Remove the master cylinder (see Section 8).

7   From inside the vehicle, locate the pushrod clevis connecting the booster to the brake pedal **(see illustration 15.9).**

8   Remove the clevis pin retaining clip with pliers and pull out the pin.

9   Holding the clevis with pliers, disconnect the clevis locknut with a wrench. The clevis is now loose.

10   Disconnect the hose leading from the engine to the booster **(see illustration)**. Be careful not to damage the hose when removing it from the booster fitting.

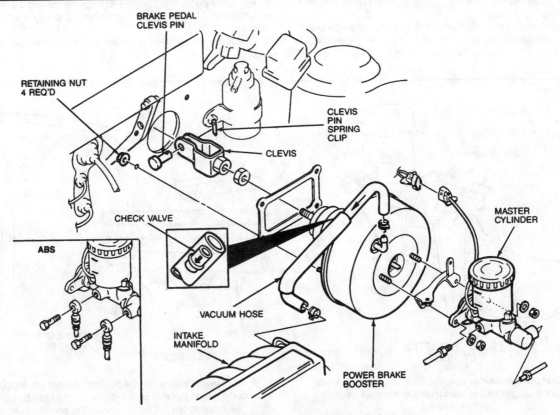

16.10   Installation details of the power brake booster

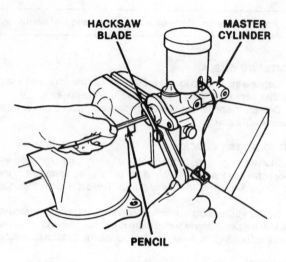

**16.15   Insert a pencil into the pushrod socket and mark it
with a hacksaw blade**

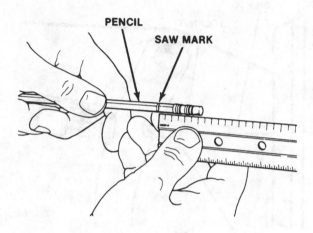

**16.16   Measure the length of the pencil to the saw mark
and write it down**

11   Remove the four nuts and washers holding the brake booster to the firewall. You may need a light to see these, as they're up under the dash area.

12   Slide the booster straight out from the firewall until the studs clear the holes and pull the booster, brackets and gaskets from the engine compartment area.

Installation

Refer to illustrations 16.15, 16.16, 16.17 and 16.18

13   Installation is the reverse of removal. Tighten the clevis locknut and booster mounting nuts securely.

14   The push rod doesn't normally require adjustment, unless the brake booster (or, in some cases, the master cylinder) has been changed. If the push rod is too long, it will cause the brakes to drag; if it's too short, it'll cause a low pedal.

15   Insert a pencil into the pushrod socket and mark it with a hacksaw blade **(see illustration)**.

16   Measure the length of the pencil to the saw mark **(see illustration)**.

17   Measure the master cylinder boss with a ruler **(see illustration)**. Subtract the length of the boss from the marked length of the pencil. The difference in length between the master cylinder pushrod and the marked pencil length, minus 0.025-inch (1 mm), is equal to the pushrod desired length.

18   Measure how far the master cylinder pushrod protrudes from the booster face **(see illustration)**.

19   Adjust the pushrod to the desired length by holding the serrated portion with a pair of pliers and turning the end of the pushrod in or out, as necessary.

20   Check the operation of the brakes carefully before driving the vehicle in traffic.

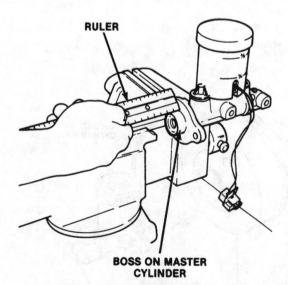

**16.17   Measure the master cylinder boss with a ruler, then
subtract the length of the boss from the marked length
of the pencil**

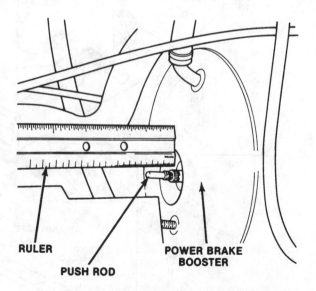

**16.18   Measure how far the pushrod protrudes from the
booster – turn the end of the pushrod in or out to obtain
the desired length calculated in the previous Step**

17.1   The brake light switch is located at the top of the brake pedal, up under the dash

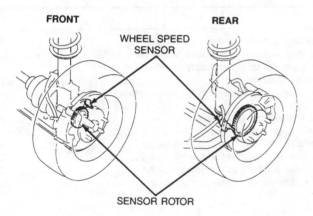

18.2   ABS wheel sensors

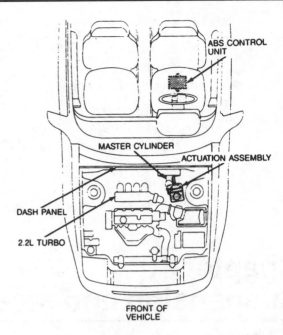

18.1   Locations of the Anti-lock Brake System (ABS) components

a) If voltage is present or the test light comes on, the switch itself is working correctly. Check the circuit between the switch and the brake lights.
b) If no voltage is present, or the test light doesn't come on, go to the next Step.

Replacement

6   Unplug the connector, loosen the locknuts and rotate the switch so that the plunger protrudes less. Tighten the locknuts, plug in the connector and repeat Step 4. If adjustment fails to activate the switch, replace it.
7   Adjust the brake pedal height (see Section 15).

---

18   Anti-lock Braking System (ABS) – general information

Refer to illustrations 18.1 and 18.2

    The ABS system **(see illustration)** includes the brake master cylinder, the actuation assembly, the accumulator, the solenoid valves, the control valves, the fluid reservoir, the control unit, the wheel sensors and the proportioning valve.
    A sensor **(see illustration)** at each wheel constantly monitors its speed of rotation and sends this data to a digital control unit which compares the input from each wheel to the input from the other three wheels. As long as the wheels all rotate at the same speed, the ABS system is inactive.
    When you depress the brake pedal, the master cylinder applies brake pressure to the wheel cylinders or brake calipers. A proportioning valve splits front-to-rear brake fluid pressure. As long as the rotational speed of all four wheels decreases at the same rate, the ABS system still remains inactive.
    When a heavy braking situation occurs – and one or more wheels starts to lock up, i.e. rotate slower than the other wheels – the control unit activates the ABS actuation assembly, which instantly relieves the hydraulic pressure at the locked wheel(s). The moment the wheel begins rolling again, the actuation assembly reapplies brake hydraulic pressure. This release-and-apply action is repeated, in rapid succession, in response to the behavior of each wheel. It has no effect on front-to-rear brake proportioning.
    Because of the complexity of the ABS system, we recommend that you take the vehicle to a dealer if a problem arises. Working on this system is generally beyond the scope of the average home mechanic.

---

17   Brake light switch – check and replacement

Check

Refer to illustration 17.1

1   The brake light switch is a simple off-on type switch located under the dash at the top of the brake pedal **(see illustration)**. Voltage is available to the brake light circuit at all times – even when the ignition is turned off – but the circuit is open at the switch until the brake pedal is applied. When you depress the pedal, it releases a plunger on the switch, which closes the circuit and turns on the brake lights.
2   If the brake lights don't come on when you apply the brake pedal, either the brake lights themselves are defective, or the switch isn't getting power, isn't adjusted correctly or isn't working.
3   First, check the fuse and the brake light bulbs (see Chapter 12).
4   If the fuse is okay and the bulbs are good, insert one probe of a voltmeter or a test light into the backside of the brake light switch connector **(see illustration 15.2)** – don't unplug it – at the hot wire (wire between the battery and the switch) and touch the other probe to a good ground. The meter should indicate 12+ volts, or the test light should come on.
    a) If voltage is present, go to the next Step.
    b) If it isn't, trace the circuit toward the battery and find the problem (refer to the Wiring Diagrams at the end of Chapter 12).
5   Insert both probes into the backside of the connector, one at the hot wire and the other at the wire to the brake lights. Apply the brake pedal. The meter should indicate 12+ volts, or the light should come on.

Chapter 10
Suspension and steering systems

Contents

Specifications

Torque specifications

Ft-lbs

Front suspension

Knuckle-to-strut bolts	69 to 86
Strut upper mounting nuts	34 to 46
Shock absorber nut	47 to 67
Balljoint clamp bolt	32 to 40
Tie-rod end-to-knuckle nut	22 to 33

Rear suspension

Strut-to-spindle bolts	69 to 86
Strut upper mounting nuts	34 to 46
Shock absorber nut	47 to 67
Lateral links-to-spindle through-bolt nut	64 to 86
Trailing arm-to-spindle bolt	64 to 86
Trailing arm front mounting bolt	46 to 69
Rear crossmember mounting bolts	27 to 40
Lateral links-to-rear crossmember bolt	64 to 86

Steering

Steering wheel retaining nut	29 to 36
Tie-rod end-to-steering knuckle nut	22 to 33
Steering gear mounting bolts	27 to 40
Intermediate shaft lower U-joint clamp bolt	13 to 20

Wheel lug nuts

Wheel lug nuts	See Chapter 1

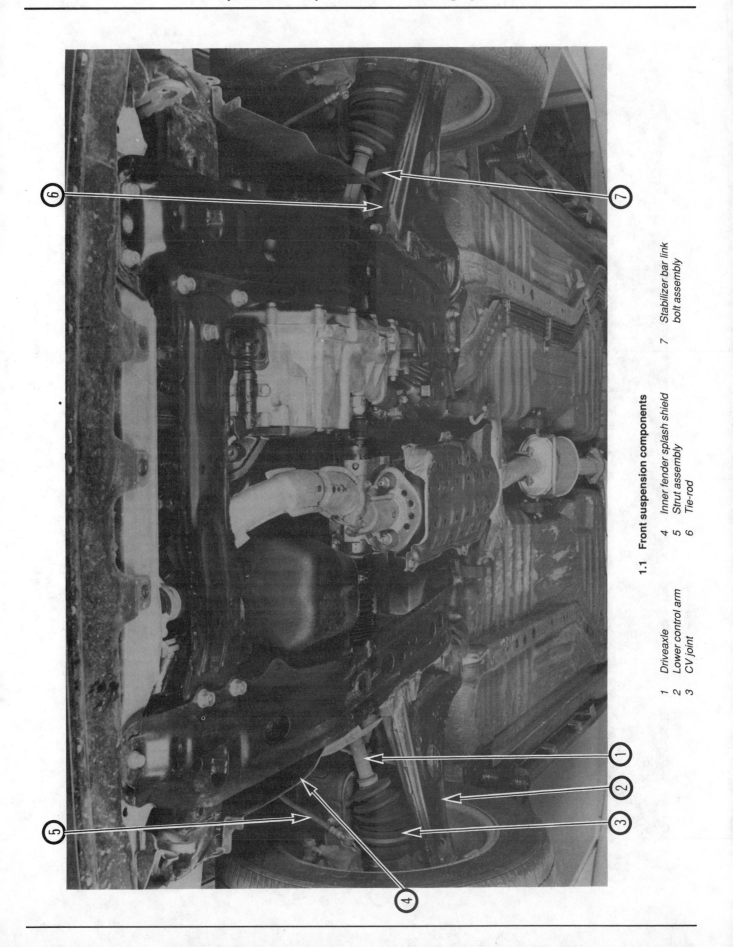

1.1 Front suspension components

1 Driveaxle
2 Lower control arm
3 CV joint

4 Inner fender splash shield
5 Strut assembly
6 Tie-rod

7 Stabilizer bar link
    bolt assembly

1.2 Rear suspension components

1   Front lateral link
2   Stabilizer bar
3   Trailing arm
4   Spindle
5   Rear lateral link
6   Crossmember

2.3   Remove the rubber cap from the strut mounting block

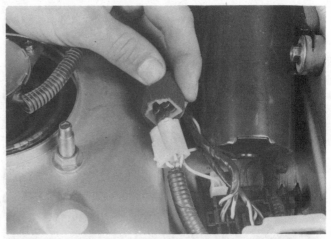

2.4   If the vehicle is equipped with Programmed Ride Control (PRC), unplug this electrical connector

1   General information

Refer to illustrations 1.1 and 1.2

The front suspension **(see illustration)** is a MacPherson strut design. The upper ends of the struts are located by strut towers in the wheel wells. The lower ends of the struts are located by steering knuckles. The lower end of each steering knuckle is located by a lower control arm. Both front control arms are connected by a stabilizer bar, which controls body lean in turns.

The rear suspension **(see illustration)** also utilizes MacPherson struts. The upper ends of the struts are located by strut towers and the lower ends are located by the spindles. Each spindle is located by a pair of lateral links and a trailing arm. Body lean is controlled by a stabilizer bar.

If the vehicle is equipped with Programmed Ride Control (PRC), the PRC actuators are located at the top of each front and rear strut. PRC struts are adjustable; non-PRC struts aren't. The two strut types cannot be interchanged.

All models covered by this manual are equipped with power steering. A power rack-and-pinion steering gear, located behind the engine/transaxle assembly on the lower firewall, actuates tie-rods attached to the steering knuckles. The steering column is connected to the steering gear through a U-joint and intermediate shaft. The steering column is designed to collapse in the event of an accident. The steering wheels on some models are equipped with air bags.

Warning: *When suspension or steering fasteners are loosened or removed, they must be inspected and, if necessary, replaced with new ones. Make sure replacement fasteners have the same part number or are of the same original equipment quality and design. Follow torque specifications for proper reassembly and component retention.*

2   Strut and coil spring assembly (front) – removal and installation

Refer to illustrations 2.3, 2.4, 2.5, 2.9, 2.10, 2.11, 2.14

1   Loosen the front wheel lug nuts.
2   Raise the front of the vehicle and place it securely on jackstands.
3   Remove the rubber cap from the strut mounting block **(see illustration)**.
4   Unplug the electrical connector for the Programmed Ride Control (PRC) control module, if equipped **(see illustration)**.
5   Paint or scribe alignment marks to ensure the strut assembly is reinstalled in the same position **(see illustration)**.
6   Remove the two screws and detach the PRC control module, if equipped.

2.5   Paint or scribe alignment marks across the top of the strut and the strut mounting block – after the strut has been disconnected from below, support the strut and remove the upper mounting nuts (arrows)

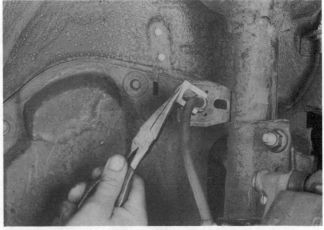

2.9   Remove the U-clip from the brake line hose and slide it out of its bracket on the strut

7   Remove the anti-lock brake system wiring harness and bracket, if equipped.
8   Remove the brake caliper (see Chapter 9).
9   Remove the U-clip from the brake hose and slide the hose out of its bracket on the strut **(see illustration)**.

2.10   Scribe or paint an alignment mark across the strut bracket and steering knuckle

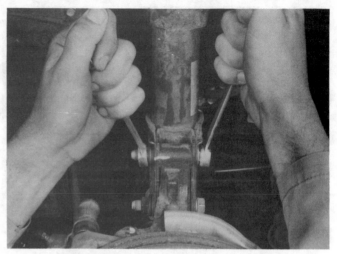

2.11   Remove the steering knuckle-to-strut bolts

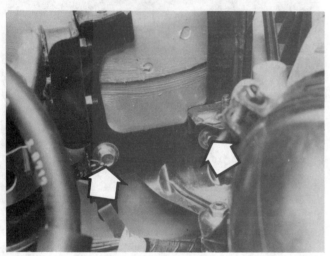

2.14   Remove these bolts and detach the ignition coil bracket (arrows)

10   Scribe or paint an alignment mark across the edge between the strut bracket and the steering knuckle **(see illustration)**.

11   Remove the steering knuckle-to-strut attaching bolts **(see illustration)**.

12   Remove the vane airflow meter assembly (see Chapter 4).

13   Remove the ignition coil (see Chapter 5).

14   Remove the ignition coil bracket **(see illustration)**.

15   While an assistant supports the strut assembly, remove the strut mounting nuts from the strut tower **(see illustration 2.5)**. DO NOT remove the shock absorber nut in the center.

16   Remove the strut assembly from the vehicle.

17   Installation is the reverse of removal.

---

3   Strut assembly – replacement

Note: *This procedure applies to both front and rear struts.*

Refer to illustration 3.5

1   If the struts exhibit the telltale signs of wear (leaking fluid, loss of dampening capability) explore all options before beginning any work. The strut assemblies are not serviceable and must be replaced if a problem develops. However, strut assemblies complete with coil springs may be available on an exchange basis, which eliminates much time and work. Whichever route you choose to take, check on the cost and availability of parts before disassembling the vehicle. **Warning:** *Disassembling a strut is*

dangerous – be very careful and follow all instructions or serious injury could result. Use only a high quality spring compressor and carefully follow the manufacturer's instructions furnished with the tool.*

Removal

2   Remove the strut and coil spring assembly (see Section 2 or 9).

3   Mount the strut assembly in a vise. Slightly loosen – DO NOT remove – the shock absorber nut.

4   Install a spring compressor (can be obtained at most auto parts stores or equipment yards on a daily rental basis) in accordance with the manufacturer's instructions.

5   Compress the spring far enough to relieve pressure from the upper spring seat, strut bearing and mounting block, then remove the shock absorber nut **(see illustration)**. **Warning:** *Keep the ends of the spring facing away from your body while the spring is compressed – the spring could fly out of the spring compressor, causing serious injury*

6   Gradually release tension on the spring. Make sure you don't strip the threads on the shock absorber as the spring extends.

7   Remove the control module bracket (if equipped), the strut mounting block, the spring seat, the dust boot, the bump stopper and the spring itself from the strut **(see illustration 3.5)**.

Installation

8   Install the spring, bump stopper, dust boot and upper spring seat on the new strut.

9   Install the strut mounting block and, if equipped, the control module bracket. Make sure the notch on the mounting block is 180-degrees from the knuckle mounting bracket on the shock absorber.

10   Compress the spring with the spring compressor. **Warning:** *Keep the ends of the spring facing away from your body while the spring is compressed – the spring could fly out of the spring compressor, causing serious injury.*

11   Install the shock absorber nut and tighten it to the torque listed in this Chapter's Specifications.

12   Gradually release the spring compressor and remove it.

13   Install the strut/coil spring assembly (see Section 2).

---

4   Stabilizer bar (front) – removal and installation

Removal

Refer to illustrations 4.2a, 4.2b and 4.3

1   Apply the parking brake. Raise the front of the vehicle and support it securely on jackstands.

2   Remove the stabilizer bar-to-lower control arm link assembly. Note how the spacers, washers and bushings are positioned **(see illustrations)**.

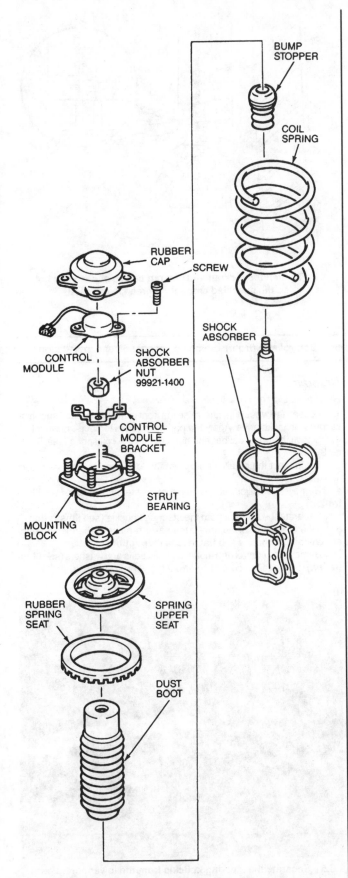

3.5   An exploded view of the strut assembly (PRC-equipped model shown)

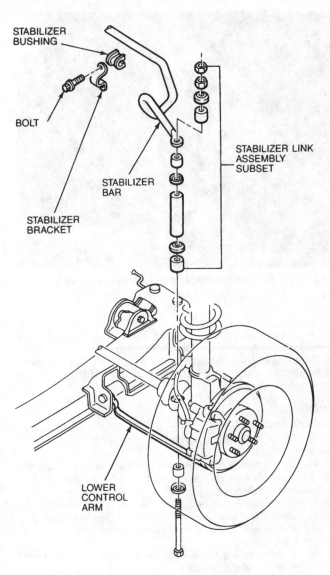

4.2a   An exploded view of the stabilizer link assembly

4.2b   Use a back-up wrench when breaking loose the jam nut at the top of the link bolt

4.3   Each of the two stabilizer bar brackets is secured by two bolts (arrows)

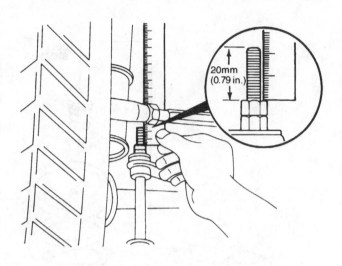

4.7   Tighten the locknut and jam nut on top of each link bolt so the specified amount of thread is exposed

3   Support the stabilizer bar, remove the stabilizer bar bracket bolts and detach the bar from the vehicle **(see illustration)**.
4   Pull the brackets off the stabilizer bar and inspect the bushings for cracks, hardness and other signs of deterioration. If the bushings are damaged, replace them.

Installation
Refer to illustration 4.7

5   Position the stabilizer bar bushings on the bar with the slits facing the front of the vehicle.
6   Push the brackets over the bushings and raise the bar up to the firewall. Install the bracket bolts but don't tighten them completely yet.
7   Install the stabilizer bar-to-lower control arm bolts, washers, spacers and rubber bushings. Install and tighten the locknut and jam nut so the specified amount of thread remains above the nut **(see illustration)**.
8   Install the wheels and hand tighten the wheel lug nuts.
9   Lower the vehicle.
10   Tighten the wheel lug nuts to the torque specified in Chapter 1, then tighten the bracket bolts completely.

5   Control arm (front) – removal, inspection and installation

Removal
Refer to illustrations 5.4, 5.5, 5.6 and 5.7

1   Loosen the wheel lug nuts, raise the front of the vehicle and support it securely on jackstands. Apply the parking brake. Remove the wheel.
2   Unbolt the brake caliper and hang it from the coil spring (see Chapter 9).
3   Disconnect the stabilizer bar from the lower control arm (see Section 4).
4   Remove the balljoint clamp bolt from the steering knuckle **(see illustration)**.
5   Separate the balljoint from the steering knuckle **(see illustration)**.
6   If the vehicle has an automatic transaxle, remove the harmonic damper from the left chassis sub-frame **(see illustration)**.
7   Remove the control arm mounting nuts, bolts and washers **(see illustration)**. Remove the control arm from the vehicle.

5.4   Remove the balljoint clamp bolt

5.5   Separate the steering knuckle from the lower control arm with a prybar positioned as shown – be careful not to damage the balljoint grease seal

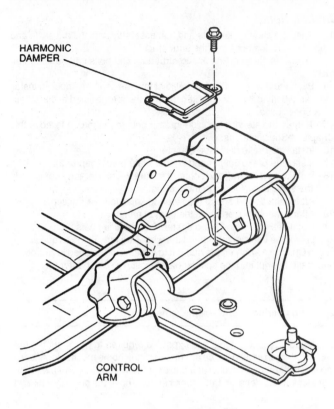

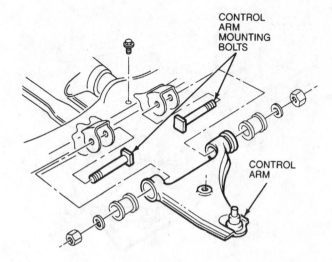

5.7 An exploded view of the lower control arm mounting nuts, washers and bolts

5.6 If the vehicle has an automatic transaxle, remove the harmonic damper

Inspection

8   Check the control arm for distortion and the bushings for wear, damage and deterioration. Replace a damaged or bent control arm with a new one. If the bushings are worn, take the control arm to a dealer service department or other repair shop. Special tools are required to replace them. If the balljoint is worn or damaged, the control arm must be replaced.

Installation

9   Place the lower control arm in position, install the mounting bolts, washers and nuts. Tighten the nuts to the torque listed in this Chapter's Specifications.
10   If the vehicle is equipped with an automatic transaxle, install the harmonic damper.
11   Insert the balljoint stud into the steering knuckle, install the balljoint clamp bolt and tighten it to the torque listed in this Chapter's Specifications.
12   Connect the stabilizer bar link assembly to the lower control arm (see Section 4).
13   Install the brake caliper (see Chapter 9).
14   Install the wheel and hand tighten the wheel lug nuts.
15   Lower the vehicle.
16   Tighten the wheel lug nuts to the torque specified in Chapter 1.

6   Balljoints – replacement

The balljoints are not replaceable. If a balljoint is worn (see *Suspension and steering check* in Chapter 1), you'll have to replace the control arm.

7   Steering knuckle and hub assembly – removal and installation

Removal

Refer to illustrations 7.1 and 7.11

1   Loosen the wheel lug nuts. Carefully raise the staked portion of the hub nut with a small cape chisel and loosen the hub nut **(see illustration)**. Raise the front of the vehicle and support it securely on jackstands. Remove the wheel.
2   Wedge a large prybar between two of the wheel studs to prevent the rotor from turning, then remove the hub nut and discard it. DO NOT reuse the nut.
3   Remove the brake caliper and anchor plate. Suspend the caliper from the coil spring with a piece of wire (see Chapter 9).
4   Remove the brake disc (see Chapter 9).
5   Detach the stabilizer bar from the control arm (see Section 4).

7.1 Raise the staked portion of the driveaxle hub nut with a small cape chisel or similar tool (wheel removed for clarity)

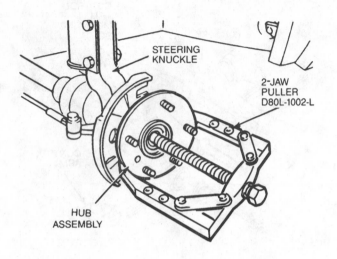

7.11   If the hub won't pull off the driveaxle splines, install a two-jaw puller as shown to pull it off

6   Separate the tie-rod end from the steering knuckle (see Section 19).
7   Remove the balljoint clamp bolt and separate the lower control arm from the steering knuckle (see Section 5).
8   Paint or scribe an alignment mark across the strut and steering knuckle, then remove the bolts that attach the strut to the steering knuckle (see Section 2).
9   Slide the front hub/steering knuckle assembly out of its bracket in the strut and off the end of the driveaxle. Use care to avoid damaging the grease seals.
10   If the wheel hub binds on the driveaxle splines, loosen it by tapping on the end of the driveaxle with a plastic mallet. DO NOT use a metal faced hammer to separate the hub from the driveaxle, or you may damage the CV joint.
11   If tapping with a plastic mallet does not loosen the hub, draw it off with a two-jaw puller (D80L-1002-L, or equivalent) **(see illustration)**.

Installation

12   Push the steering knuckle and hub assembly onto the driveaxle and guide the knuckle boss into the strut bracket.
13   Install the steering knuckle-to-strut nuts and bolts and hand tighten them.
14   Push the lower control arm balljoint into the steering knuckle, install the clamp bolt and nut and tighten them to the torque listed in this Chapter's Specifications.
15   Tighten the steering knuckle-to-strut nuts to the torque listed in this Chapter's Specifications.
16   Install the brake disc (see Chapter 9).
17   Install the brake caliper and anchor plate (see Chapter 9).
18   Install a new hub nut and tighten it securely. Don't torque it completely until the vehicle is lowered to the ground.
19   Attach the tie-rod end to the steering knuckle (see Section 19).
20   Attach the stabilizer bar to the control arm.
21   Install the wheel and hand tighten the wheel lug nuts.
22   Lower the vehicle and tighten the wheel lug nuts to the torque specified in Chapter 1. Tighten the hub nut to the torque specified in Chapter 8 and stake the nut into the spindle (see Section 11 in Chapter 8).

---

8   Hub bearing (front) – replacement

Due to the special tools and expertise required to press out the hub bearing, this job should not be attempted by the home mechanic. After removing the steering knuckle and hub assembly (see Section 7), take it to a dealer service department or repair shop to have the bearing replaced.

---

9   Strut and coil spring assembly (rear) – removal and installation

---

Refer to illustrations 9.2, 9.3, 9.9 and 9.10

1   Disconnect the negative cable from the battery. From inside the rear of the vehicle, lower the side trim to gain access to the strut upper mount.
2   Unplug the programmed ride control (PRC) module electrical connector, if equipped **(see illustration)**.
3   Remove the PRC module, if equipped **(see illustration)**.
4   Remove the ABS harness and bracket, if equipped.

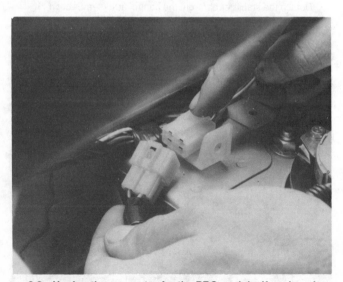

9.2   Unplug the connector for the PRC module, if equipped

9.3   Remove these screws and separate the PRC module, if equipped (arrows)

9.9   Scribe or paint alignment marks across the strut and spindle boss, then remove the strut-to-spindle nuts and bolts (arrows)

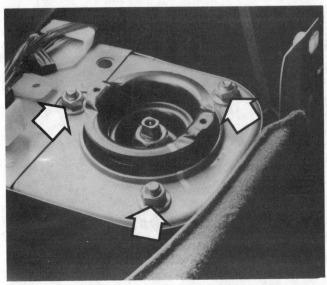

9.10   Scribe or paint alignment marks across the strut mounting block and body and remove the strut attaching nuts (arrows)

10.2a   Use a back-up wrench when removing the jam nut from the stabilizer bar mounting bolt assembly

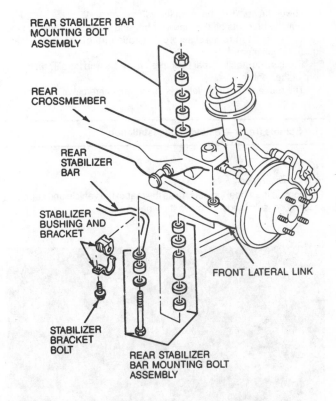

10.2b   An exploded view of the rear stabilizer bar mounting bolt assembly

5   Loosen the wheel lug nuts, raise the rear of the vehicle and support it securely on jackstands. Remove the wheel.

6   Remove the brake caliper and disc or brake drum and backing plate (see Chapter 9).

7   Remove the brake line U-clip from the strut housing **(see illustration 2.9)**.

8   Disconnect the trailing arm from the spindle **(see illustration 12.3)**.

9   Remove the spindle-to-strut nuts and bolts **(see illustration)** and pull the spindle away from the strut mounting bracket.

10   From inside the vehicle, scribe or paint an alignment mark across the strut mounting block and strut body. Have an assistant support the strut while you remove the three strut attaching nuts **(see illustration)**. DO NOT remove the shock absorber nut in the center.

11   Lower the strut assembly from the vehicle.

12   Installation is the reverse of removal. Be sure to align the marks you made during removal and tighten all fasteners to the correct torque specifications.

10   Stabilizer bar (rear) – removal and installation

Refer to illustrations 10.2a, 10.2b and 10.3

1   Loosen the wheel lug nuts, raise the rear of the vehicle and support it securely on jackstands. Remove the rear wheels.

2   Remove the mounting bolt assemblies **(see illustrations)**.

10.3   Remove the bolt from each stabilizer bar bracket (left side shown, right side similar)

11.4   Remove the nut and bolt that attaches the lateral links to the spindle (upper arrows) and the trailing arm mounting bolt (lower arrow)

3   Support the bar and remove the mounting brackets **(see illustration)**.

4   Lower the stabilizer bar from the vehicle.

5   Pull the brackets off the stabilizer bar and inspect the bushings for cracks, hardness and other signs of deterioration. If the bushings are damaged, replace them.

6   Position the stabilizer bar bushings on the bar with the slits facing the front of the vehicle.

7   The remainder of installation is the reverse of removal.

11   Spindle (rear) – removal and installation

Removal

Refer to illustration 11.4

1   Loosen the wheel lug nuts, raise the rear of the vehicle and support it securely on jackstands. Remove the wheel.

2   Remove the brake drum and backing plate assembly or the caliper and disc (see Chapter 9).

3   Loosen, but don't completely remove, the spindle-to-strut bolts (see Section 9).

4   Remove the bolt that attaches the lateral links to the spindle **(see illustration)**.

5   Remove the trailing arm mounting bolt at the spindle **(see illustration 12.3)**.

6   Support the spindle so it won't fall, then remove the spindle-to-strut bolts **(see illustration 9.9)**.

7   Remove the spindle from the strut.

Installation

8   Position the spindle on the strut mounting bracket, install the bolts, align the marks made during removal and hand tighten the nuts.

9   Attach the lateral links to the spindle, install the bolt and hand tighten the nut.

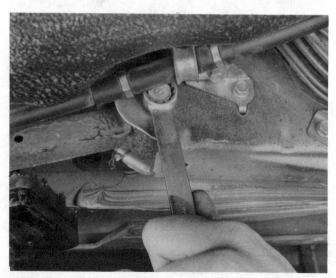

12.2   Remove the mounting bolt and nut from the front end of the trailing arm

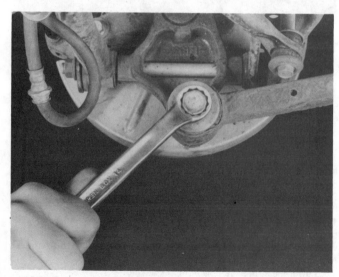

12.3   Remove the bolt from the rear end of the trailing arm, at the spindle

13.4   Remove the nut and detach the rear lateral link

10   Attach the trailing arm to the spindle and tighten the bolt to the torque listed in this Chapter's Specifications.
11   Tighten the spindle-to-strut bolts to the torque listed in this Chapter's Specifications.
12   Tighten the lateral link bolt nut to the torque listed in this Chapter's Specifications.
13   The remainder of installation is the reverse of removal.

12   Trailing arm – removal and installation

Refer to illustrations 12.2 and 12.3

1   Loosen the wheel lug nuts, raise the rear of the vehicle and support it securely on jackstands. Remove the wheel.
2   Remove the bolt and nut from the front end of the trailing arm **(see illustration)**.
3   Support the trailing arm so it won't fall, remove the bolt at the spindle **(see illustration)** and remove the trailing arm.
4   Installation is the reverse of removal.

13   Lateral links – removal and installation

Removal

Refer to illustrations 13.4, 13.9 and 13.12

1   Loosen the wheel lug nuts, raise the rear of the vehicle and support it securely on jackstands. Remove the wheel.
2   Remove the spindle (see Section 11).
3   Remove the rear stabilizer bar (see Section 10).
4   Remove the nut from the lateral link mounting bolt at the rear crossmember **(see illustration)** and remove the rear lateral link.
5   Because of the lack of clearance between the fuel tank and the lateral link mounting bolt, the bolt and the front lateral link can't be removed yet.
6   Remove the parking brake cable clamp bolts from the trailing arm (see Chapter 9).
7   Detach the trailing arm from its front mounting bracket **(see illustration 12.2)**.
8   Detach any exhaust components that would interfere with removal of the rear crossmember (see Chapter 4).
9   Detach the brake line retaining bracket from the rear crossmember **(see illustration)**.
10   Have an assistant support the crossmember while you remove the mounting bolts from the ends of the crossmember **(see illustration 13.9)**.

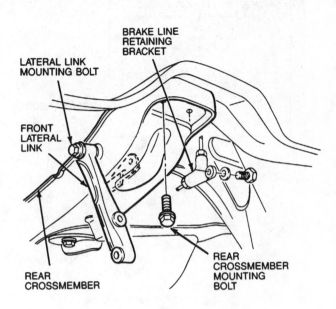

13.9   Remove the brake line retaining bracket and the mounting bolts at the ends of the crossmember

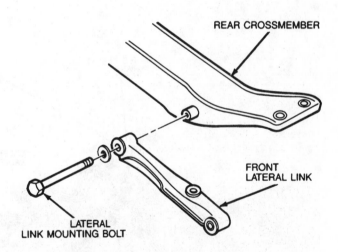

13.12   Remove the lateral link mounting bolt from the rear crossmember and remove the front lateral link

11   Lower the crossmember and front lateral link from the vehicle as an assembly.
12   Remove the lateral link mounting bolt from the rear crossmember **(see illustration)**.
13   Remove the front lateral link from the crossmember.

Installation

14   Position the front lateral link on the crossmember and install the bolt.
15   Place the crossmember in position, install the mounting bolts and tighten them to the torque listed in this Chapter's Specifications.
16   The remainder of installation is the reverse of removal. Tighten the fasteners to the correct torque specifications.

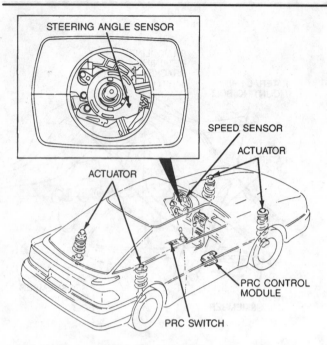

14.2   Programmed Ride Control (PRC) system components

14   Programmed Ride Control (PRC) – general information

Refer to illustration 14.2

Programmed Ride Control (PRC) allows the driver to select soft, firm or very firm damping positions for the suspension. Turning the PRC switch on the center console to the "NORM" (normal) or "SPORT" settings engages the Automatic Adjusting Suspension feature, which alters the shock absorber damping settings to control vehicle roll, pitch and dive. In the NORM and SPORT settings, the PRC system monitors vehicle speed, steering wheel angle, abrupt acceleration and hard braking to determine when to alter the amount of damping.

A PRC module **(see illustration)** located under the passenger's seat receives input from various sensors and switches the ride control mode based on input from the sensors.

The vehicle speed sensor is located inside the speedometer assembly on vehicles with an analog instrument cluster and on the transaxle on vehicles with an electronic instrument cluster.

The steering angle sensor, located inside the steering column, enables the PRC module to determine the magnitude of the lateral forces acting on the vehicle under normal driving conditions.

Four PRC actuators, located at the top of each strut, alter the damping characteristics of the shock absorber within each strut assembly. The struts themselves are a special adjustable design.

Because of the complexity of the PRC system, service and diagnosis is beyond the scope of the average home mechanic. If the PRC system develops trouble, take the vehicle to a dealer for service.

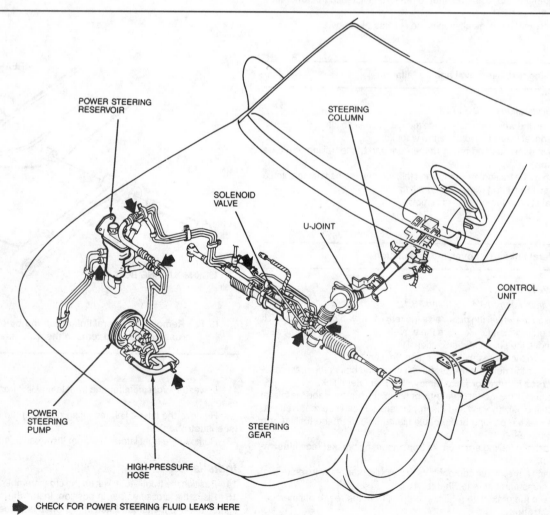

CHECK FOR POWER STEERING FLUID LEAKS HERE

15.1   The power steering system

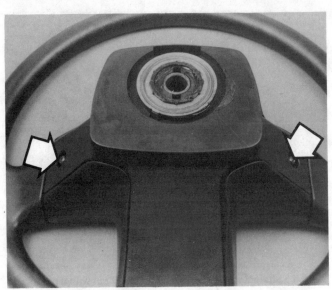

16.2 To get the horn pad off, remove these two screws at the back of the steering wheel (steering wheel removed for clarity)

16.4 Scribe or paint an alignment mark across the steering shaft and hub

15 Steering system – general information

Refer to illustration 15.1

All models are equipped with power-assisted rack-and-pinion steering **(see illustration)**. The steering gear, which is bolted to the lower firewall, operates the steering knuckles via tie-rods. The inner ends of the tie-rods are protected by rubber boots which should be inspected periodically for secure attachment, tears and leaking lubricant.

The power assist system consists of a belt-driven pump, a fluid reservoir and associated lines and hoses. The fluid level should be checked periodically (see Chapter 1).

The steering wheel operates the steering shaft, which actuates the steering gear through a U-joint and intermediate shaft. Looseness in the steering can be caused by wear in the steering shaft U-joint, the steering gear or the tie-rod ends; or by loose steering gear retaining bolts.

16 Steering wheel – removal and installation

Removal

Refer to illustrations 16.2, 16.4 and 16.5

1 Disconnect the cable from the negative terminal of the battery.
2 Remove the two horn pad screws from the back side of the steering wheel **(see illustration)**.
3 Detach the horn pad from the steering wheel and disconnect the wire to the horn switch.
4 Remove the steering wheel retaining nut, then mark the relationship of the steering shaft to the hub (if marks don't already exist or don't line up) to simplify installation and ensure steering wheel alignment **(see illustration)**.
5 Use a puller to detach the steering wheel from the shaft **(see illustration)**. Don't hammer on the shaft to dislodge the steering wheel.

Installation

6 Align the mark on the steering wheel hub with the mark on the shaft and slide the wheel onto the shaft.

7 Install the retaining nut and tighten it to the torque listed in this Chapter's Specifications.
8 Connect the horn wire, install the horn pad and install the two horn pad screws.
9 Connect the negative battery cable.

17 Power steering pump – removal and installation

Refer to illustration 17.4

1 Remove the inner fender splash shield from the right fender (see Chapter 11).
2 Remove the pump drivebelt (see Chapter 1).

16.5 Pull the steering wheel off with a steering wheel puller

17.4   To remove the power steering pump, disconnect the pressure and return hoses (lower arrows) and remove the bolts (upper arrows)

19.3   Straighten the cotter pin and pull it out with a pair of pliers or wire cutters

3   Raise the front of the vehicle and place it securely on jackstands. Place a drain pan under the pump to catch the fluid that will spill when the hoses are disconnected.

4   From underneath the vehicle, disconnect the pressure hose and return hose from the pump **(see illustration)**. Use a flare-nut wrench on the pressure hose fitting to avoid rounding off the corners of the fitting's nut. Plug the ends of the hoses to prevent excessive fluid loss.

5   Remove the three pump bracket mounting bolts and remove the pump/bracket assembly **(see illustration 17.4).**

6   If you're replacing the pump, you'll need a special spanner wrench (T70P-4067-A, or equivalent) to hold the pulley while you unscrew the center bolt.

7   After removing the pulley, detach the pump from its mounting bracket and switch the mounting bracket to the new pump.

8   Install the pulley on the new pump and tighten the bolts securely.

9   Installation is the reverse of removal.

10   After you've installed the pump, check the fluid level and bleed the power steering system (see Section 18).

19.4   Separate the tie-rod end with a two-jaw puller

---

18   Power steering system – bleeding

---

1   Following any operation in which the power steering fluid lines have been disconnected, the power steering system must be bled to remove all air and obtain proper steering performance. The following procedure will eliminate excessive steering system noise caused by air trapped in the system during servicing.

2   With the front wheels in the straight ahead position, check the power steering fluid level (see Chapter 1). If it's low, add more fluid

3   Start the engine and allow it to run at fast idle. Recheck the fluid level and add more if necessary to reach the correct level.

4   Bleed the system by turning the wheels from side-to-side, without hitting the stops. This will work the air out of the system. Keep the reservoir full of fluid as this is done.

5   When the air is worked out of the system, return the wheels to the straight ahead position and leave the vehicle running for several more minutes before shutting it off.

6   Road test the vehicle to be sure the steering system is functioning normally and noise free.

7   Recheck the fluid level to be sure it is at the correct level. Add fluid if necessary.

---

19   Tie-rod ends – removal and installation

Refer to illustrations 19.3 and 19.4

Removal

1   Loosen the wheel lug nuts. Raise the front of the vehicle, support it securely, block the rear wheels and apply the parking brake. Remove the front wheel(s).

20.3a   Remove the outer boot clamp with a pair of pliers

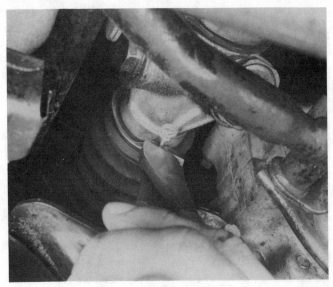

20.3b   Cut off the wire inner boot clamp

2   Hold the tie-rod with a pair of locking pliers or a wrench and loosen the jam nut enough to mark the position of the tie-rod end in relation to the threads.

3   Remove the cotter pin and loosen the nut on the tie-rod end stud **(see illustration)**.

4   Disconnect the tie-rod from the steering knuckle arm with a puller **(see illustration)**. Remove the nut and separate the tie-rod.

5   Unscrew the tie-rod end from the tie-rod.

Installation

6   Thread the tie-rod end on to the marked position and insert the tie-rod stud into the steering knuckle arm. Tighten the jam nut securely.

7   Install the castellated nut on the stud and tighten it to the torque listed in this Chapter's Specifications. Install a new cotter pin.

8   Install the wheel and lug nuts. Lower the vehicle and tighten the lug nuts to the torque specified in Chapter 1.

9   Have the alignment checked by a dealer service department or an alignment shop.

20   Steering gear boots – replacement

Refer to illustrations 20.3a and 20.3b

1   Loosen the lug nuts, raise the front of the vehicle and support it securely on jackstands. Apply the parking brake. Remove the wheel.

2   Refer to Section 19 and remove the tie-rod end and jam nut.

3   Remove the steering gear boot clamps and slide the boot off **(see illustrations)**.

4   Before installing the new boot, wrap the threads and serrations on the end of the steering rod with a layer of tape so the small end of the new boot isn't damaged.

5   Slide the new boot into position on the steering gear until it seats in the groove in the steering rod and install new clamps.

6   Remove the tape and install the tie-rod end (see Section 19).

7   Install the wheel and lug nuts. Lower the vehicle and tighten the lug nuts to the torque specified in Chapter 1.

21   Steering gear – removal and installation

Removal

Refer to illustrations 21.5 and 21.9

1   Apply the parking brake, loosen the front wheel lug nuts, raise the front of the vehicle and support it securely on jackstands.

2   Remove the front wheels.

3   Separate the tie-rod ends from the steering knuckle arms (see Section 19).

4   Remove both inner fender splash shields (see Chapter 11).

5   Place a drain pan under the steering gear. Disconnect the power steering pressure and return hoses **(see illustration)** and cap the ends to prevent excessive fluid loss and contamination.

21.5   Remove the bolts and disconnect the pressure and return hoses from the steering gear (arrows)

21.9   Remove the six steering gear mounting bolts (upper three shown, lower three not visible in this photo)

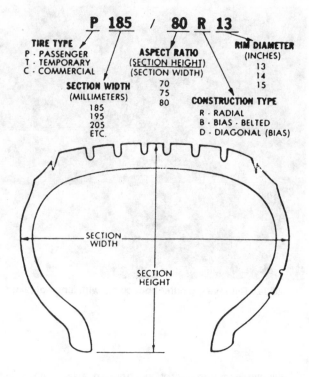

22.1   Metric tire size code

6   Pull back the dust boot covering the intermediate shaft and U-joint, have an assistant turn the steering wheel until the clamp bolt is accessible, then lock the steering column by turning the key to OFF.

7   Paint an alignment mark on the steering column pinion shaft and the intermediate shaft lower U-joint.

8   Remove the clamp bolt from from the intermediate shaft.

9   Support the steering gear and remove the six mounting bolts **(see illustration)**.

10   Lower the unit until it rests on the crossmember.

11   Carefully slide the steering gear toward the right until the left tie-rod clears the lower control arm, then slide it to the left and remove it from the vehicle.

Installation

12   Slide the steering gear into position and connect the intermediate shaft, aligning the marks.

13   Install the steering gear mounting bolts and tighten them to the torque listed in this Chapter's Specifications.

14   Install the clamp bolt in the intermediate shaft lower U-joint and tighten it to the torque listed in this Chapter's Specifications.

15   Connect the power steering pressure and return hoses.

16   Connect the tie-rod ends to the steering knuckle arms (see Section 19).

17   Install the wheels and hand tighten the wheel lug nuts.

18   Lower the vehicle.

19   Tighten the wheel lug nuts to the torque listed in this Chapter's Specifications.

20   Fill the reservoir with fluid (see Chapter 1) and bleed the system (see Section 18).

22   Wheels and tires – general information

Refer to illustration 22.1

All vehicles covered by this manual are equipped with metric-sized fiberglass or steel-belted radial tires **(see illustration)**. Use of other size or type of tires may affect the ride and handling of the vehicle. Don't mix different types of tires, such as radials and bias belted, on the same vehicle as handling may be seriously affected. It's recommended that tires

be replaced in pairs on the same axle, but if only one tire is being replaced, be sure it's the same size, structure and tread design as the other.

Because tire pressure has a substantial effect on handling and wear, the pressure on all tires should be checked at least once a month or before any extended trips (see Chapter 1).

Wheels must be replaced if they are bent, dented, leak air, have elongated bolt holes, are heavily rusted, out of vertical symmetry or if the lug nuts won't stay tight. Wheel repairs that use welding or peening are not recommended.

Tire and wheel balance is important to the overall handling, braking and performance of the vehicle. Unbalanced wheels can adversely affect handling and ride characteristics as well as tire life. Whenever a tire is installed on a wheel, the tire and wheel should be balanced by a shop with the proper equipment.

23   Wheel alignment – general information

Refer to illustration 23.1

Wheel alignment is the series of adjustments to the wheels that positions them in the correct angular relationship to the suspension and the ground. Front wheels that are out of proper alignment affect steering control. When front or rear wheels are misaligned, tire wear increases. The front end adjustments normally required are camber, caster and toe-in **(see illustration)**.

Bringing the wheels into proper alignment is a very exacting process that requires complicated and expensive machines. That's why you should have a professional alignment technician with the proper equipment perform these tasks. The following brief descriptions of camber, caster and toe-in will give you an idea of how wheels are aligned so you can understand the procedure well enough to deal intelligently with the shop that does the work.

Toe-in is the turning in of the front wheels. The purpose of a toe specification is to ensure parallel rolling of the front wheels. In a vehicle with zero toe-in, the distance between the front edges of the wheels will be the same as the distance between the rear edges of the wheels. The actual amount of toe-in is normally only a fraction of an inch. Toe-in adjustment is controlled by the tie-rod end position on the inner tie-rod. Incorrect toe-in will cause the tires to wear improperly by making them scrub against the road surface.

Camber is the tilting of the front wheels from the vertical when viewed from the front of the vehicle. When the wheels tilt out at the top, the camber is said to be positive (+). When the wheels tilt in at the top the camber is negative (-). The amount of tilt is measured in degrees from the vertical and this measurement is called the camber angle. This angle affects the amount of tire tread which contacts the road and compensates for changes in the suspension geometry when the vehicle is cornering or travelling over an undulating surface.

Caster is the tilting of the top of the front steering axis from the vertical. A tilt toward the rear is positive caster and a tilt toward the front is negative caster. Front caster is not a separate procedure on the vehicles covered by this manual – it should fall within specification when front camber is adjusted. Rear caster isn't adjustable.

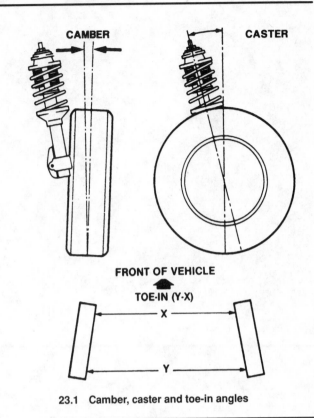

23.1   Camber, caster and toe-in angles

Chapter 11   Body

Contents

1   General information

These models feature a "unibody" layout, using a floor pan with front and rear frame side rails which support the body components, front and rear suspension systems and other mechanical components.

Certain components are particularly vulnerable to accident damage and can be unbolted and repaired or replaced. Among these parts are the body moldings, bumpers, the hood and trunk lids and all glass.

Only general body maintenance practices and body panel repair procedures within the scope of the do-it-yourselfer are included in this Chapter.

2   Body – maintenance

1   The condition of your vehicle's body is very important, because the resale value depends a great deal on it. It's much more difficult to repair a neglected or damaged body than it is to repair mechanical components. The hidden areas of the body, such as the wheel wells, the frame and the engine compartment, are equally important, although they don't require as frequent attention as the rest of the body.

2   Once a year, or every 12,000 miles, it's a good idea to have the underside of the body steam cleaned. All traces of dirt and oil will be removed and the area can then be inspected carefully for rust, damaged brake

lines, frayed electrical wires, damaged cables and other problems. The front suspension components should be greased after completion of this job.

3   At the same time, clean the engine and the engine compartment with a steam cleaner or water soluble degreaser.

4   The wheel wells should be given close attention, since undercoating can peel away and stones and dirt thrown up by the tires can cause the paint to chip and flake, allowing rust to set in. If rust is found, clean down to the bare metal and apply an anti-rust paint.

5   The body should be washed about once a week. Wet the vehicle thoroughly to soften the dirt, then wash it down with a soft sponge and plenty of clean soapy water. If the surplus dirt is not washed off very carefully, it can wear down the paint.

6   Spots of tar or asphalt thrown up from the road should be removed with a cloth soaked in solvent.

7   Once every six months, wax the body and chrome trim. If a chrome cleaner is used to remove rust from any of the vehicle's plated parts, remember that the cleaner also removes part of the chrome, so use it sparingly.

3   Vinyl trim – maintenance

Don't clean vinyl trim with detergents, caustic soap or petroleum-based cleaners. Plain soap and water works just fine, with a soft brush to clean dirt that may be ingrained. Wash the vinyl as frequently as the rest of the vehicle.

After cleaning, application of a high quality rubber and vinyl protectant will help prevent oxidation and cracks. The protectant can also be applied to weatherstripping, vacuum lines and rubber hoses, which often fail as a result of chemical degradation, and to the tires.

4   Upholstery and carpets – maintenance

1   Every three months remove the carpets or mats and clean the interior of the vehicle (more frequently if necessary). Vacuum the upholstery and carpets to remove loose dirt and dust.

2   Leather upholstery requires special care. Stains should be removed with warm water and a very mild soap solution. Use a clean, damp cloth to remove the soap, then wipe again with a dry cloth. Never use alcohol, gasoline, nail polish remover or thinner to clean leather upholstery.

3   After cleaning, regularly treat leather upholstery with a leather wax. Never use car wax on leather upholstery.

4   In areas where the interior of the vehicle is subject to bright sunlight, cover leather seats with a sheet if the vehicle is to be left out for any length of time.

5   Body repair – minor damage

See color photo sequence

Repair of minor scratches

1   If the scratch is superficial and does not penetrate to the metal of the body, repair is very simple. Lightly rub the scratched area with a fine rubbing compound to remove loose paint and built up wax. Rinse the area with clean water.

2   Apply touch-up paint to the scratch, using a small brush. Continue to apply thin layers of paint until the surface of the paint in the scratch is level with the surrounding paint. Allow the new paint at least two weeks to harden, then blend it into the surrounding paint by rubbing with a very fine rubbing compound. Finally, apply a coat of wax to the scratch area.

3   If the scratch has penetrated the paint and exposed the metal of the body, causing the metal to rust, a different repair technique is required. Remove all loose rust from the bottom of the scratch with a pocket knife, then apply rust inhibiting paint to prevent the formation of rust in the future. Using a rubber or nylon applicator, coat the scratched area with glaze-type

filler. If required, the filler can be mixed with thinner to provide a very thin paste, which is ideal for filling narrow scratches. Before the glaze filler in the scratch hardens, wrap a piece of smooth cotton cloth around the tip of a finger. Dip the cloth in thinner and then quickly wipe it along the surface of the scratch. This will ensure that the surface of the filler is slightly hollow. The scratch can now be painted over as described earlier in this section.

Repair of dents

4   When repairing dents, the first job is to pull the dent out until the affected area is as close as possible to its original shape. There is no point in trying to restore the original shape completely as the metal in the damaged area will have stretched on impact and cannot be restored to its original contours. It is better to bring the level of the dent up to a point which is about 1/8-inch below the level of the surrounding metal. In cases where the dent is very shallow, it is not worth trying to pull it out at all.

5   If the back side of the dent is accessible, it can be hammered out gently from behind using a soft-face hammer. While doing this, hold a block of wood firmly against the opposite side of the metal to absorb the hammer blows and prevent the metal from being stretched

6   If the dent is in a section of the body which has double layers, or some other factor makes it inaccessible from behind, a different technique is required. Drill several small holes through the metal inside the damaged area, particularly in the deeper sections. Screw long, self tapping screws into the holes just enough for them to get a good grip in the metal. Now the dent can be pulled out by pulling on the protruding heads of the screws with locking pliers.

7   The next stage of repair is the removal of paint from the damaged area and from an inch or so of the surrounding metal. This is easily done with a wire brush or sanding disk in a drill motor, although it can be done just as effectively by hand with sandpaper. To complete the preparation for filling, score the surface of the bare metal with a screwdriver or the tang of a file or drill small holes in the affected area. This will provide a good grip for the filler material. To complete the repair, see the Section on filling and painting.

Repair of rust holes or gashes

8   Remove all paint from the affected area and from an inch or so of the surrounding metal using a sanding disk or wire brush mounted in a drill motor. If these are not available, a few sheets of sandpaper will do the job just as effectively.

9   With the paint removed, you will be able to determine the severity of the corrosion and decide whether to replace the whole panel, if possible, or repair the affected area. New body panels are not as expensive as most people think and it is often quicker to install a new panel than to repair large areas of rust.

10   Remove all trim pieces from the affected area except those which will act as a guide to the original shape of the damaged body, such as headlight shells, etc. Using metal snips or a hacksaw blade, remove all loose metal and any other metal that is badly affected by rust. Hammer the edges of the hole inward to create a slight depression for the filler material.

11   Wire brush the affected area to remove the powdery rust from the surface of the metal. If the back of the rusted area is accessible, treat it with rust inhibiting paint.

12   Before filling is done, block the hole in some way. This can be done with sheet metal riveted or screwed into place, or by stuffing the hole with wire mesh.

13   Once the hole is blocked off, the affected area can be filled and painted. See the following subsection on filling and painting.

Filling and painting

14   Many types of body fillers are available, but generally speaking, body repair kits which contain filler paste and a tube of resin hardener are best for this type of repair work. A wide, flexible plastic or nylon applicator will be necessary for imparting a smooth and contoured finish to the surface of the filler material. Mix up a small amount of filler on a clean piece of wood or cardboard (use the hardener sparingly). Follow the manufacturer's instructions on the package, otherwise the filler will set incorrectly.

15   Using the applicator, apply the filler paste to the prepared area. Draw the applicator across the surface of the filler to achieve the desired contour

and to level the filler surface. As soon as a contour that approximates the original one is achieved, stop working the paste. If you continue, the paste will begin to stick to the applicator. Continue to add thin layers of paste at 20-minute intervals until the level of the filler is just above the surrounding metal.

16   Once the filler has hardened, the excess can be removed with a body file. From then on, progressively finer grades of sandpaper should be used, starting with a 180-grit paper and finishing with 600-grit wet-or-dry paper. Always wrap the sandpaper around a flat rubber or wooden block, otherwise the surface of the filler will not be completely flat. During the sanding of the filler surface, the wet-or-dry paper should be periodically rinsed in water. This will ensure that a very smooth finish is produced in the final stage.

17   At this point, the repair area should be surrounded by a ring of bare metal, which in turn should be encircled by the finely feathered edge of good paint. Rinse the repair area with clean water until all of the dust produced by the sanding operation is gone.

18   Spray the entire area with a light coat of primer. This will reveal any imperfections in the surface of the filler. Repair the imperfections with fresh filler paste or glaze filler and once more smooth the surface with sandpaper. Repeat this spray-and-repair procedure until you are satisfied that the surface of the filler and the feathered edge of the paint are perfect. Rinse the area with clean water and allow it to dry completely.

19   The repair area is now ready for painting. Spray painting must be carried out in a warm, dry, windless and dust free atmosphere. These condi-

tions can be created if you have access to a large indoor work area, but if you are forced to work in the open, you will have to pick the day very carefully. If you are working indoors, dousing the floor in the work area with water will help settle the dust which would otherwise be in the air. If the repair area is confined to one body panel, mask off the surrounding panels. This will help minimize the effects of a slight mismatch in paint color. Trim pieces such as chrome strips, door handles, etc., will also need to be masked off or removed. Use masking tape and several thicknesses of newspaper for the masking operations.

20   Before spraying, shake the paint can thoroughly, then spray a test area until the spray painting technique is mastered. Cover the repair area with a thick coat of primer. The thickness should be built up using several thin layers of primer rather than one thick one. Using 600-grit wet-or-dry sandpaper, rub down the surface of the primer until it is very smooth. While doing this, the work area should be thoroughly rinsed with water and the wet-or-dry sandpaper periodically rinsed as well. Allow the primer to dry before spraying additional coats.

21   Spray on the top coat, again building up the thickness by using several thin layers of paint. Begin spraying in the center of the repair area and then, using a circular motion, work out until the whole repair area and about two inches of the surrounding original paint is covered. Remove all masking material 10 to 15 minutes after spraying on the final coat of paint. Allow the new paint at least two weeks to harden, then use a very fine rubbing compound to blend the edges of the new paint into the existing paint. Finally, apply a coat of wax.

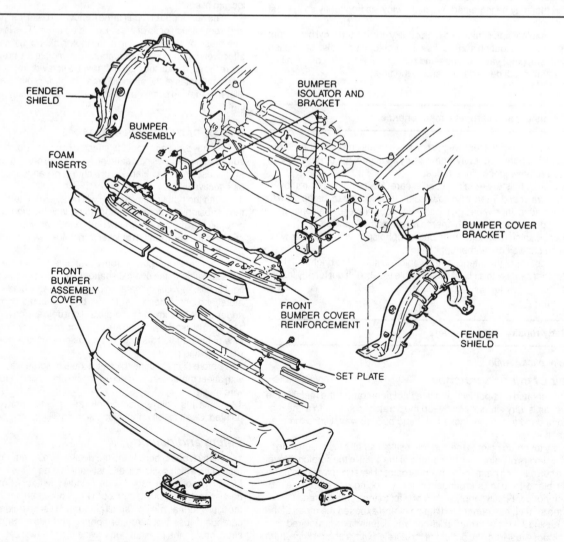

8.2a   An exploded view of the front bumper assembly

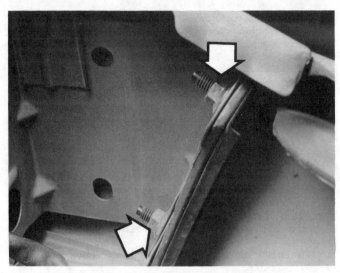

8.2b   Remove these bumper cover retaining nuts

8.3   Remove the retaining bolts from the bumper cover bracket (arrows)

6   Body repair – major damage

1   Major damage must be repaired by an auto body shop specifically equipped to perform unibody repairs. These shops have the specialized equipment required to do the job properly.

2   If the damage is extensive, the body must be checked for proper alignment or the vehicle's handling characteristics may be adversely affected and other components may wear at an accelerated rate.

3   Due to the fact that all of the major body components (hood, fenders, etc.) are separate and replaceable units, any seriously damaged components should be replaced rather than repaired. Sometimes the components can be found in a wrecking yard that specializes in used vehicle components, often at considerable savings over the cost of new parts.

7   Hinges and locks – maintenance

Once every 3000 miles, or every three months, the hinges and latch assemblies on the doors, hood and trunk should be given a few drops of light oil or lock lubricant. The door latch strikers should also be lubricated with a thin coat of grease to reduce wear and ensure free movement. Lubricate the door trunk locks with spray-on graphite lubricant.

8   Bumpers – removal and installation

Front bumper

.*Refer to illustrations 8.2a, 8.2b, 8.3, 8.4, 8.5a and 8.5b*

1   To gain access to the bumper cover attaching bolts, remove the battery (see Chapter 5) and headlight assemblies (see Chapter 12).

2   Disconnect the side marker and parking light electrical connectors **(see illustration)**. Remove the shoulder bolt from each upper corner of the bumper cover. Remove the two upper bumper cover-to-front fender retaining nuts **(see illustration)**.

3   Remove the screw from under the inside of each front fender. Remove the bolts securing both of the bumper assembly cover brackets and remove the brackets **(see illustration)**.

4   Remove the seven screws securing each fender shield and remove the shields **(see illustration 8.2a)**. Working from underneath, remove the bolts securing the bumper cover to each fender. Disconnect the five plastic retainers from the lower part of the bumper cover **(see illustration)**.

5   Remove the six bolts securing the upper part of the bumper cover **(see illustration)**. Remove the four nuts securing the bumper to each

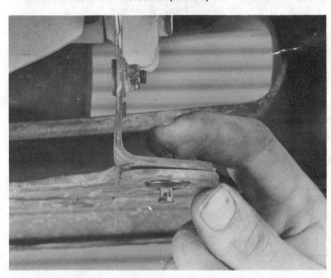

8.4   Push out the center of each plastic retainer, then pull out the retainer

8.5a   Locations of the front bumper cover upper retaining bolts (arrows)

8.5b   The front bumper is attached by two mounting brackets like this – remove the four nuts at each bracket and separate the bumper from the vehicle

mounting bracket **(see illustration)**. Remove the bumper. Installation is the reverse of removal.

Rear bumper

Refer to illustration 8.7

6   Remove the liftgate end trim. Remove the lower liftgate side trim. Remove all of the rear lights from the vehicle (see Chapter 12). Remove both license plate cover retaining screws. Remove the license plate cover.
7   Remove the nut located under the license plate cover. Working from inside the vehicle, remove the eight bumper cover retaining nuts. Remove the two screws under each side of the bumper cover **(see illustration)**.
8   Remove the eight plastic screws under the back side of the bumper. At each upper corner of the bumper cover, remove the screws in both clips that retain the bumper cover.

9   Slide the bumper cover away from the back of the vehicle and remove it. Remove the eight bumper retaining bolts and the bumper. Installation is the reverse of removal.

---

9   Hood – removal, installation and adjustment

Refer to illustration 9.2
Note: *The hood is heavy and somewhat awkward to remove and install – at least two people should perform this procedure.*

Removal and installation

1   Use blankets or pads to cover the cowl area of the body and the fenders. This will protect the body and paint as the hood is lifted off.
2   Make alignment marks around the bolt heads to insure proper alignment during installation **(see illustration)**.
3   Disconnect any cables or wire harnesses which will interfere with removal.
4   Have an assistant support the weight of the hood. Remove the hinge-to-hood nuts or bolts.
5   Lift off the hood.
6   Installation is the reverse of removal.

Adjustment

7   Fore-and-aft and side-to-side adjustment of the hood is done by moving the hood in relation to the hinge plate after loosening the bolts.
8   Scribe a line around the entire hinge plate so you can judge the amount of movement **(see illustration 9.2)**.
9   Loosen the bolts or nuts and move the hood into correct alignment. Move it only a little at a time. Tighten the hinge bolts and carefully lower the hood to check the alignment.
10   If necessary after installation, the entire hood latch assembly can be adjusted up-and-down as well as from side-to-side on the radiator support so the hood closes securely and is flush with the fenders. To do this, scribe a line around the hood latch mounting bolts to provide a reference point **(see illustration 10.1)**. Then loosen the bolts and reposition the latch assembly as necessary. Following adjustment, retighten the retaining bolts.
11   Finally, adjust the hood bumpers on the radiator support so the hood, when closed, is flush with the fenders.
12   The hood latch assembly, as well as the hinges, should be periodically lubricated with white lithium-base grease to prevent sticking and wear.

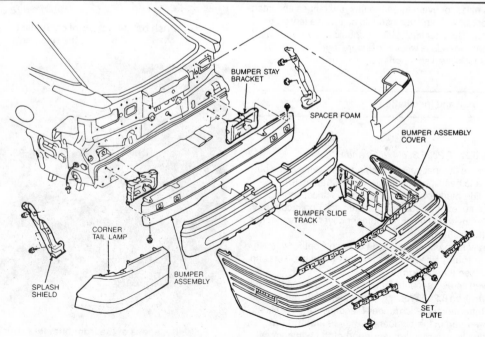

8.7   An exploded view of the rear bumper assembly

9.2   Use a felt-tip marker to make alignment marks around the hood bolts and hinge plate

10.1   Locations of the hood latch retaining bolts

10   Hood release latch and cable – removal and installation

Refer to illustration 10.1

1   Remove the two bolts attaching the upper bumper cover reinforcement (see Section 8). Remove the two bolts attaching the latch bracket to the upper bumper cover reinforcement **(see illustration)**.

2   Remove the bolt securing the release cable bracket. Remove the release cable bracket. Remove the bolts and the stud nut retaining the hood latch to the latch bracket.

3   Pull the latch bracket away and remove the latch. Disengage the cable and bushing from the hood latch lever. Installation is the reverse of removal.

11   Front fender – removal and installation

Refer to illustrations 11.1a, 11.1b and 11.1c

1   Remove the splash shield **(see illustration)**. If necessary, remove the battery (see Chapter 5), five battery tray retaining bolts and the battery tray. Remove the two retaining bolts and nuts and disconnect the retractor linkage from the retractable headlight assembly **(see illustrations)**. Remove the retractable headlight assembly

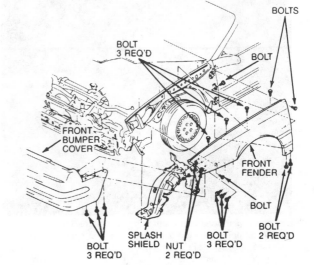

11.1a   An exploded view of the front fender assembly

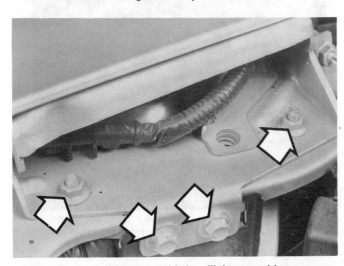

11.1b   To remove the retractable headlight assembly, unscrew these nuts and bolts (arrows). . .

11.1c   . . . then disconnect the retractor linkage ball-and-socket joint by inserting a screwdriver where indicated by the arrow and prying gently

This photo sequence illustrates the repair of a dent and damaged paintwork. The procedure for the repair of a hole is similar. Refer to the text for more complete instructions

After removing any adjacent body trim, hammer the dent out. The damaged area should then be made slightly concave

Use coarse sandpaper or a sanding disc on a drill motor to remove all paint from the damaged area. Feather the sanded area into the edges of the surrounding paint, using progressively finer grades of sandpaper

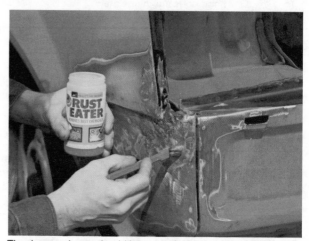

The damaged area should be treated with rust remover prior to application of the body filler. In the case of a rust hole, all rusted sheet metal should be cut away

Carefully follow manufacturer's instructions when mixing the body filler so as to have the longest possible working time during application. Rust holes should be covered with fiberglass screen held in place with dabs of body filler prior to repair

Apply the filler with a flexible applicator in thin layers at 20 minute intervals. Use an applicator such as a wood spatula for confined areas. The filler should protrude slightly above the surrounding area

Shape the filler with a surform-type plane. Then, use water and progressively finer grades of sandpaper and a sanding block to wet-sand the area until it is smooth. Feather the edges of the repair area into the surrounding paint.

Use spray or brush applied primer to cover the entire repair area so that slight imperfections in the surface will be filled in. Prime at least one inch into the area surrounding the repair. Be careful of over-spray when using spray-type primer

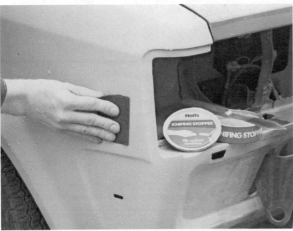

Wet-sand the primer with fine (approximately 400 grade) sandpaper until the area is smooth to the touch and blended into the surrounding paint. Use filler paste on minor imperfections

After the filler paste has dried, use rubbing compound to ensure that the surface of the primer is smooth. Prior to painting, the surface should be wiped down with a tack rag or lint-free cloth soaked in lacquer thinner

Choose a dry, warm, breeze-free area in which to paint and make sure that adjacent areas are protected from over-spray. Shake the spray paint can thoroughly and apply the top coat to the repair area, building it up by applying several coats, working from the center

After allowing at least two weeks for the paint to harden, use fine rubbing compound to blend the area into the original paint. Wax can now be applied

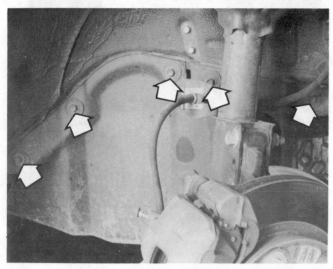

12.1   To remove the inner fender splash shield, remove these retaining bolts (arrows)

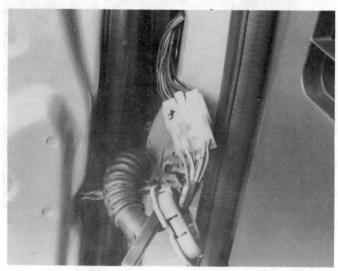

13.1   Door wiring harness details

2   Remove the retaining bolt and detach the black plastic resonance chamber. Remove the three bolts and one nut retaining the rear of the fender. Remove the four bolts from the top of the fender. Remove the bolt retaining the fender side bracket.
3   Remove the two nuts and three bolts attaching the fender to the bumper cover. Remove the three bolts retaining the fender to the bumper assembly. Remove the fender. Installation is the reverse of removal.

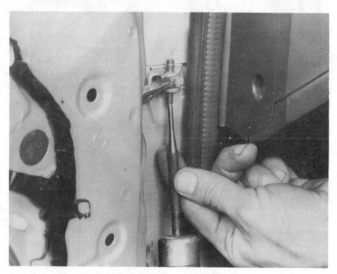

13.2   Removing the door check pin

12   Front inner fender splash shield – removal and installation

Refer to illustration 12.1

Remove the front wheel. Remove the bolts retaining the inner fender splash shield **(see illustration)**. Remove the splash shield. Installation is the reverse of removal.

13   Door – removal and installation

Refer to illustration 13.1, 13.2 and 13.5

1   Remove the door trim panel (see Section 14). Remove the electrical boot from the door **(see illustration)**. Disconnect the wire harness connector and push it through the door opening so it won't interfere with door removal.
2   Remove the door check pin **(see illustration)**. Place a jack or jackstand under the door or have an assistant on hand to support it when the hinge bolts are removed. **Note:** *If a jack or jackstand is used, place a rag between it and the door to protect the door's painted surfaces*
3   Scribe around the door hinges to create a reference for reassembly. Remove the hinge-to-door bolts and carefully lift off the door.
4   Installation is the reverse of removal.
5   Following installation of the door, check the alignment and adjust it if necessary as follows:
   a) Up-and-down and forward-and-backward adjustments are made by loosening the hinge-to-body bolts and moving the door as necessary.
   b) The door lock striker can also be adjusted both up-and-down and sideways to provide positive engagement with the lock mechanism. This is done by loosening the mounting bolts and moving the striker as necessary **(see illustration)**.

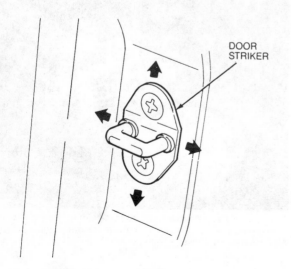

DOOR STRIKER

13.5   To adjust the door latch striker, loosen the mounting screws and gently tap it with a soft-face hammer

14.2a   Open the door and remove this screw from the upper front corner of the door trim panel (arrow)

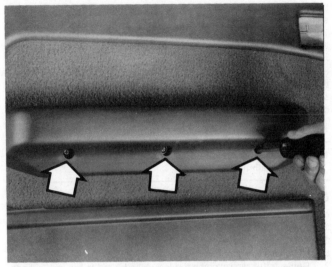

14.2b   Removing the armrest retaining screws (arrows)

14   Door trim panel – removal and installation

Refer to illustrations 14.2a, 14.2b, 14.2c, 14.3, 14.4 and 14.6

1   Disconnect the negative cable from the battery (see Chapter 5).

2   Remove all door trim panel retaining screws, armrest assemblies and interior door latch screws **(see illustrations)**.

3   On manual window regulator equipped models, remove the window crank **(see illustration)**. On power window regulator models, pry out the control switch assembly and unplug it. On power lock equipped vehicles, remove the power locking mechanism.

4   Insert a putty knife or screwdriver between the trim panel and the door and disengage the retaining clips. Work around the outer edge until the panel is free **(see illustration)**.

5   Once all of the clips are disengaged, detach the trim panel, unplug any wire harness connectors and remove the trim panel from the vehicle.

14.2c   Remove this door latch trim screw (arrow)

14.3   Remove the retaining clip from behind the regulator handle – special tools, such as the one shown here, are available from most auto parts stores – sometimes the clip can be removed by working a shop rag up between the trim panel and handle

14.4   Use a putty knife or wide-bladed screwdriver to pop loose the trim panel retaining clips

6   For access to the inner door, carefully peel back the plastic water-shield **(see illustration)**.

7   Prior to installation of the door panel, be sure to reinstall any clips in the panel which may have come out during the removal procedure and remain in the door itself.

8   Plug in the wire harness connectors and place the panel in position in the door. Press the door panel into place until the clips are seated and install the armrest. Install the manual regulator window crank or power window switch assembly.

15   Door latch, lock cylinder and handle – removal and installation

Door latch

Refer to illustrations 15.1, 15.2 and 15.3

1   Remove the door trim panel and the plastic watershield (see Section 14). Disengage the outside door handle rod and clip **(see illustration)**. Remove the door handle from the door.

2   Remove the clip retaining the lock cylinder rod to the lock cylinder **(see illustration)**. Remove the clip from the actuator motor (if equipped). Remove the clip connecting the push-button rod to the latch. Remove the clip attaching the outside door handle rod to the latch assembly.

3   Remove the three screws attaching the latch assembly to the door **(see illustration)**. It may be necessary to tap on the latch assembly to free it from inside the door. Remove the latch assembly with the remote control linkages and lock cylinder rod. Installation is the reverse of removal.

Lock cylinder

4   Remove the door trim panel and the plastic watershield (see Section 14). Remove the clip attaching the lock cylinder rod to the lock cylinder **(see illustration 15.1)**. Pry the lock cylinder from the door. Installation is the reverse of removal.

Inside handle

5   Remove the screw retaining the inside door handle. To gain access to the remote control rod clip, carefully pull the handle away from the door panel. Disengage the remote control link rod clip. Remove the handle. Installation is the reverse of removal.

Outside handle

Refer to illustration 15.6

6   Remove the door trim panel and plastic watershield (see Section 14). Remove the control rod to the latch assembly by unsnapping the clip **(see illustration 15.1)**. To gain access to the door handle nuts, remove the rubber access plugs located on the outside edge of the door **(see illustration)**. Remove the door handle retaining nuts and remove the handle. Installation is the reverse of removal.

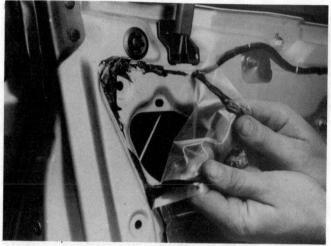

14.6   For access to the inside of the door, peel back the plastic watershield

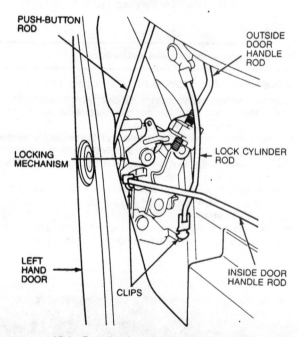

15.1   Door latch and lock cylinder details

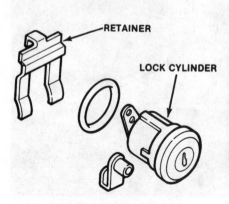

15.2   Door lock cylinder and related components

15.3   Locations of the door latch assembly retaining screws

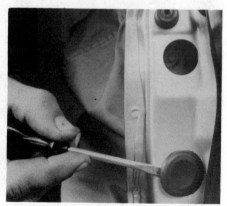

15.6   The outside door handle retaining nuts are located beneath these rubber access plugs

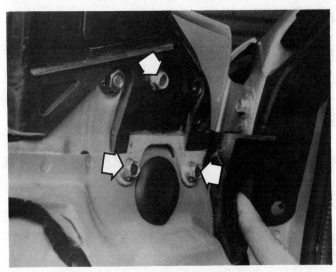

16.1   Remove the door corner bracket retaining bolts

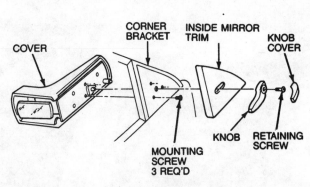

17.1   Installation details of the manual outside mirror

---

16   Door window glass – removal and installation

Refer to illustration 16.1

1   Remove the door trim panel and the plastic watershield (see Section 14). Remove the upper retaining bolts and stops. Remove the door mirror (see Section 17). Remove the three bolts retaining the door corner bracket **(see illustration)**.

2   Position the door glass so the bolts securing the window glass can be removed through the door service hole. Carefully remove the door glass by pulling it up, out of the door. Installation is the reverse of removal.

---

17   Outside mirror – removal and installation

Manual

Refer to illustration 17.1

1   Remove the mirror adjustment knob cover **(see illustration)**. Remove the retaining screw and pull off the knob. Remove the inside mirror

trim. Remove the three mirror mounting screws. Remove the mirror assembly. Installation is the reverse of removal.

Power

Refer to illustrations 17.2a and 17.2b

2   Disconnect the negative battery cable (see Chapter 5). Remove the mirror access cover **(see illustration)**. Remove the mirror mounting screws **(see illustration)**. Remove the mirror from the door. Disconnect the electrical connector. Installation is the reverse of removal.

---

18   Liftgate – removal, installation and adjustment

Refer to illustrations 18.4a and 18.4b

1   Open the liftgate and cover the upper body area around the opening with pads or cloths to protect the painted surfaces when the liftgate is removed.

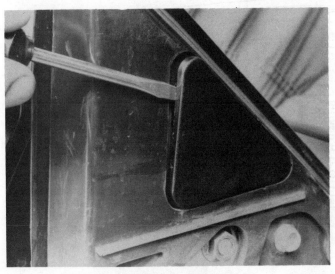

17.2a   Pry off this access cover . . .

17.2b   . . . then remove the power mirror mounting screws

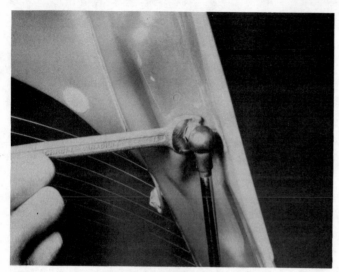

18.4a   Use a wrench to unscrew the nut at the upper end of each support strut . . .

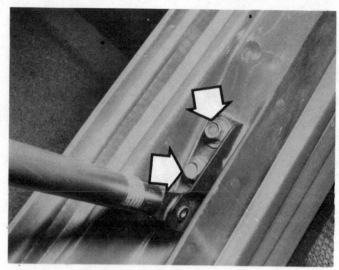

18.4b   . . . then remove the bolts at the lower end (arrows)

2   Disconnect all cables and wire harness connectors that would interfere with removal of the liftgate.
3   Paint or scribe a reference mark around the hinge flanges.
4   While an assistant supports the liftgate, detach the support struts by backing out the nuts and bolts retaining the ends of the strut to the liftgate and body **(see illustrations)**.
5   Remove the hinge bolts and detach the liftgate from the vehicle.
6   Installation is the reverse of removal.
7   After installation, close the liftgate and make sure it's in proper alignment with the surrounding body panels.
8   Adjustments are made by moving the position of the hinge bolts in the slots. To adjust it, loosen the hinge bolts and reposition the hinges either side-to-side or fore-and-aft the desired amount and retighten the bolts.
9   The engagement of the liftgate can be adjusted by loosening the latch mounting bolts, reapportioning the latch and retightening the bolts.

19   Dashboard finish panels – removal and installation

Refer to illustrations 19.2 and 19.3
1   Disconnect the negative battery cable (see Chapter 5). Remove the instrument cluster (see Chapter 12). Remove the center console (see Section 20). Remove the hood release handle.
2   Remove the ash tray and cigarette lighter assembly. Remove the left and right console kick panels. Remove the left and right dash side covers **(see illustration)**. Remove the heating/air conditioning control panel.
3   To remove the dashboard assembly, remove the radio and/or tape player (if equipped). Remove the trip computer (if equipped). Remove the access cover and mounting nut from the center dash panel **(see illustration)**.
4   Remove the remaining eight dash panel mounting bolts. Remove the dash panel assembly.

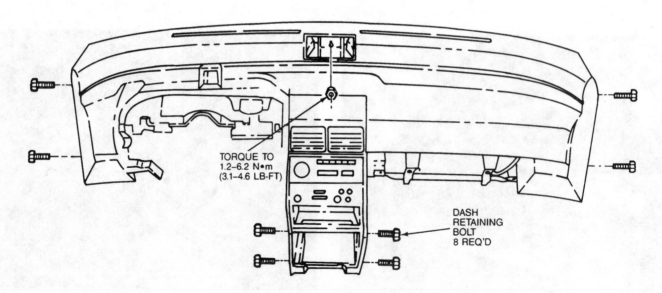

19.3   Dash-to-body mounting fasteners

TORQUE TO
1.2–6.2 N•m
(3.1–4.6 LB-FT)

DASH
RETAINING
BOLT
8 REQ'D

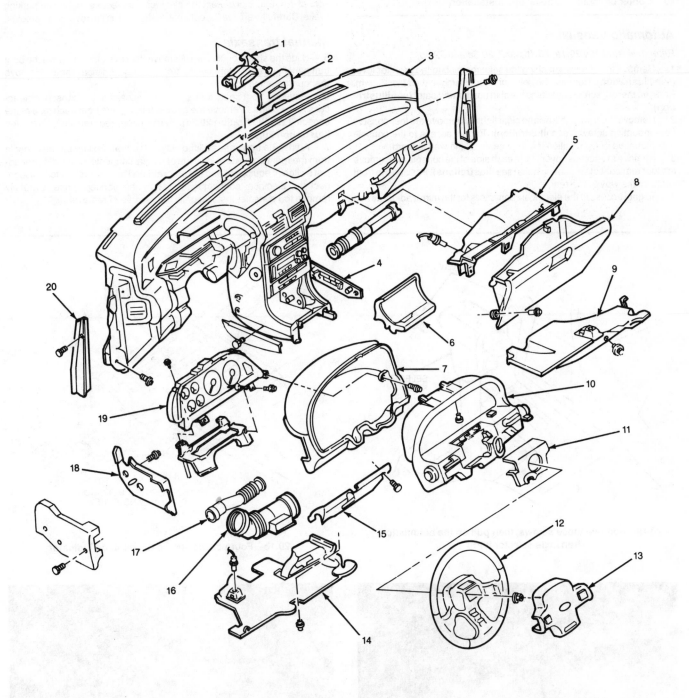

19.2   An exploded view of the dashboard assembly

1	Trip computer	11	Column cover
2	Trip computer cover	12	Steering wheel
3	Instrument panel	13	Steering wheel cover
4	Dash side cover	14	Left sound deadening panel
5	Glove compartment panel	15	Lower panel
6	Lap duct	16	Lap duct
7	Cluster cover	17	Defrost duct
8	Glove compartment	18	Dash side wall
9	Right sound deadening panel	19	Instrument cluster
10	Switch module	20	Dash side cover

20   Center console – removal and installation

Automatic transaxle

Refer to illustrations 20.1a, 20.1b, 20.2, 20.3a and 20.3b

1   Remove the screws attaching the selector knob to the selector lever **(see illustration)**. Remove the selector knob. Remove the selector trim. Remove the four screws attaching the shift position indicator **(see illustration)**.

2   Remove the front ash tray and cigar lighter. Remove the four console front mounting screws **(see illustration)**. To gain access to the console rear mounting bolts, position the front seats all the way forward.

3   Remove the access covers from each side of the console and remove the four rear console mounting bolts **(see illustrations)**. Position the front seats all the way to the rear.

4   To gain access to the electrical connectors for the mirror adjust switch (if equipped) and the programmed ride control switch, pull up on the console at the rear. Disconnect the electrical connectors. Apply the parking brake. Carefully remove the console. Installation is the reverse of removal.

Manual transaxle

5   Slide the shifter boot down. Remove the shift knob. Remove the boot trim panel and boot. Remove the front ashtray and cigar lighter. Remove the four mounting screws.

6   Move the front seats forward to gain access to the console rear access hole covers . Remove the access hole covers from each side of the console **(see illustration 20.3a)**. Remove four rear retaining bolts **(see illustration 20.3b)**.

7   Adjust the front seats all the way to the rear. Pull up on the console from the rear to gain access to the electrical connectors for the mirror adjust switch (if equipped) and the programmed ride control switch. Disconnect the electrical connector and apply the parking brake. Carefully remove the console. Installation is the reverse of removal.

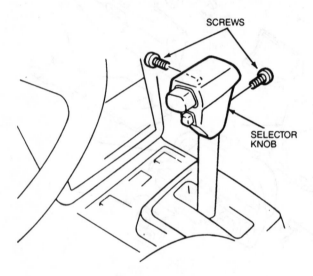

20.1a   Remove these screws, then pull off the automatic transaxle selector knob

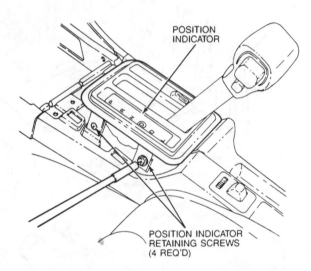

20.1b   Four screws secure the position indicator

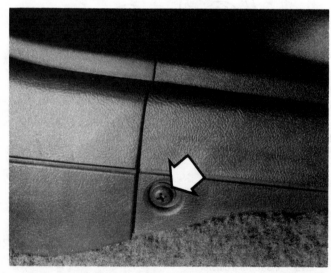

20.2   Location of a console front mounting screw (arrow)

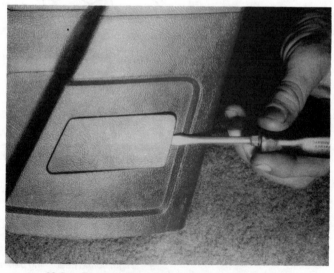

20.3a   Remove the rear console access cover . . .

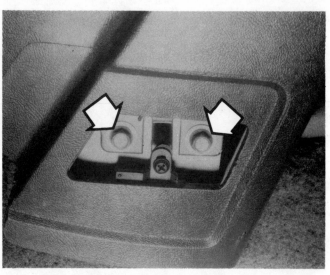

20.3b . . . then unscrew the mounting bolts (arrows)

21 Automatic shoulder harnesses – general information

Many late model vehicles are equipped with automatic front seat shoulder harnesses. They are termed automatic because you don't have to buckle them – the shoulder harness automatically positions itself when the door is closed and the key is turned on. An emergency release lever allows the harness to be manually removed for exit in an emergency. **Warning:** *Be sure to fasten the manual seatbelt as well. The automatic shoulder harness will not work properly unless the seatbelt is fastened.*

Most systems have a warning light and buzzer that indicate the emergency release lever has been pulled up, releasing the shoulder harness. Make sure the release lever is down and the light/buzzer are off to ensure proper operation of the automatic shoulder harness. Also, if you disconnect any wires or remove any automatic shoulder harness components when performing repair procedures on other vehicle components, be sure to reinstall everything and check the harness for proper operation when the repairs are complete.

Since the automatic shoulder harness is operated by several electrical switches and is computer controlled, diagnosis and repair must be done by a dealer service department. Do not jeopardize the safety of front seat occupants – if the automatic shoulder harness malfunctions, or you have questions regarding the proper use or operation of the system, contact a dealer service department.

Chapter 12   Chassis electrical system

Contents

1   General information

The electrical system is a 12-volt, negative ground type. Power for the lights and all electrical accessories is supplied by a lead/acid-type battery which is charged by the alternator.

This Chapter covers repair and service procedures for the various electrical components not associated with the engine. Information on the battery, alternator, distributor and starter motor can be found in Chapter 5.

It should be noted that when portions of the electrical system are serviced, the negative battery cable should be disconnected from the battery to prevent electrical shorts and/or fires.

2   Electrical troubleshooting – general information

A typical electrical circuit consists of an electrical component, any switches, relays, motors, fuses, fusible links or circuit breakers related to that component and the wiring and connectors that link the component to both the battery and the chassis. To help you pinpoint an electrical circuit problem, wiring diagrams are included at the end of this book.

Before tackling any troublesome electrical circuit, first study the appropriate wiring diagrams to get a complete understanding of what makes up that individual circuit. Trouble spots, for instance, can often be narrowed

down by noting if other components related to the circuit are operating properly. If several components or circuits fail at one time, chances are the problem is in a fuse or ground connection, because several circuits are often routed through the same fuse and ground connections.

Electrical problems usually stem from simple causes, such as loose or corroded connections, a blown fuse, a melted fusible link or a bad relay. Visually inspect the condition of all fuses, wires and connections in a problem circuit before troubleshooting it.

If testing instruments are going to be utilized, use the diagrams to plan ahead of time where you will make the necessary connections in order to accurately pinpoint the trouble spot.

The basic tools needed for electrical troubleshooting include a circuit tester or voltmeter (a 12-volt bulb with a set of test leads can also be used), a continuity tester, which includes a bulb, battery and set of test leads, and a jumper wire, preferably with a circuit breaker incorporated, which can be used to bypass electrical components. Before attempting to locate a problem with test instruments, use the wiring diagram(s) to decide where to make the connections.

Voltage checks

Voltage checks should be performed if a circuit is not functioning properly. Connect one lead of a circuit tester to either the negative battery terminal or a known good ground. Connect the other lead to a connector in the circuit being tested, preferably nearest to the battery or fuse. If the bulb of the tester lights, voltage is present, which means that the part of the circuit between the connector and the battery is problem free. Continue checking the rest of the circuit in the same fashion. When you reach a point at which no voltage is present, the problem lies between that point and the last test point with voltage. Most of the time the problem can be traced to a loose connection. **Note:** *Keep in mind that some circuits receive voltage only when the ignition key is in the Accessory or Run position.*

Finding a short

One method of finding shorts in a circuit is to remove the fuse and connect a test light or voltmeter in its place to the fuse terminals. There should be no voltage present in the circuit. Move the wiring harness from side-to-side while watching the test light. If the bulb goes on, there is a short to ground somewhere in that area, probably where the insulation has rubbed through. The same test can be performed on each component in the circuit, even a switch.

Ground check

Perform a ground test to check whether a component is properly grounded. Disconnect the battery and connect one lead of a selfpowered test light, known as a continuity tester, to a known good ground. Connect the other lead to the wire or ground connection being tested. If the bulb goes on, the ground is good. If the bulb does not go on, the ground is not good.

Continuity check

A continuity check is done to determine if there are any breaks in a circuit – if it is passing electricity properly. With the circuit off (no power in the circuit), a self-powered continuity tester can be used to check the circuit. Connect the test leads to both ends of the circuit (or to the "power" end and a good ground), and if the test light comes on the circuit is passing current properly. If the light doesn't come on, there is a break somewhere in the circuit. The same procedure can be used to test a switch, by connecting the continuity tester to the switch terminals. With the switch turned On, the test light should come on.

Finding an open circuit

When diagnosing for possible open circuits, it is often difficult to locate them by sight because oxidation or terminal misalignment are hidden by the connectors. Merely wiggling a connector on a sensor or in the wiring harness may correct the open circuit condition. Remember this when an open circuit is indicated when troubleshooting a circuit. Intermittent problems may also be caused by oxidized or loose connections.

Electrical troubleshooting is simple if you keep in mind that all electrical circuits are basically electricity running from the battery, through the wires, switches, relays, fuses and fusible links to each electrical component (light bulb, motor, etc.) and to ground, from which it is passed back to the battery. Any electrical problem is an interruption in the flow of electricity to and from the battery.

---

3   Electrical connectors – general information

Refer to illustrations 3.1, 3.2, and 3.3

Always release the lock tab(s) before attempting to unplug inline-type connectors. There are a variety of lock tab configurations (**see illustration**). Although nothing more than a finger is usually necessary to pry lock tabs open, a small pocket screwdriver is effective for hard to release tabs. Once the lock tabs are released, try to pull on the connectors themselves, not the wires, when unplugging two connector halves (there are times, however, when this is not possible – use good judgement).

It is sometimes necessary to know which side, male or female, of the connector you're checking. Male connectors are easily distinguished from female connectors by the shape of their internal pins (**see illustration**). When checking continuity or voltage with a circuit tester, insertion of the test probe into the receptacle may open the fitting to the connector and result in poor contact. Instead, insert the test probe from the wire harness side of the connector (**see illustration**).

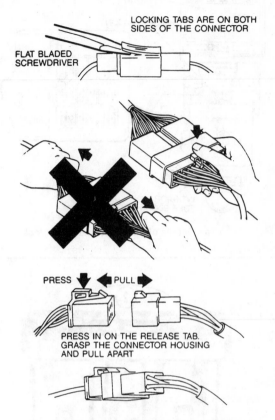

3.1   Various types of locking electrical connectors are used on these models

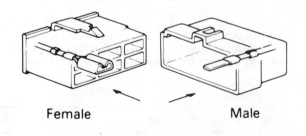

Female   Male

3.2   To distinguish between male and female halves of the connector, look at the terminal pins

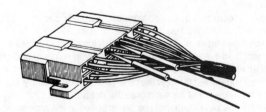

3.3   When checking for continuity or voltage with a circuit testing device, insert the test probe from the wire harness side (rear side of connector)

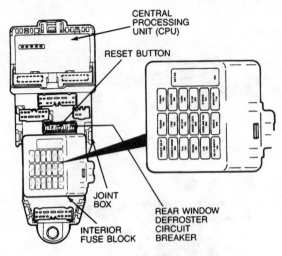

4.1a   Details of the underdash fuse block

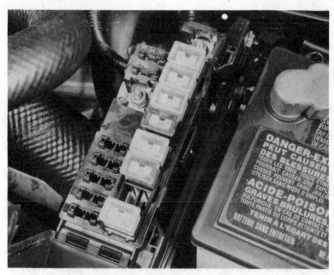

4.1b   View of the main fuse block

4.3   To check for a blown fuse, pull it out and inspect it visually for an open (1), or with the fuse installed, use a test light to check for voltage at the top of each blade (2)

6.2   The control handle for the turn signal/dimmer switch is retained with a screw

4   Fuses – general information

Refer to illustrations 4.1a, 4.1b and 4.3

The electrical circuits of the vehicle are protected by a combination of fuses, circuit breakers and fusible links. The fuse blocks are located under the left side of the dashboard and under the hood next to the battery **(see illustrations)**.

Each of the fuses is designed to protect a specific circuit, and the various circuits are identified on the fuse panel itself.

Miniaturized fuses are employed in the fuse block. These compact fuses, with blade terminal design, allow fingertip removal and replacement. If an electrical component fails, always check the fuse first. A blown fuse is easily identified through the clear plastic body. Visually inspect the element for evidence of damage **(see illustration)**. If a continuity check is called for, the blade terminal tips are exposed in the fuse body.

Be sure to replace blown fuses with the correct type. Fuses of different ratings are physically interchangeable, but only fuses of the proper rating should be used. Replacing a fuse with one of a higher or lower value than specified is not recommended. Each electrical circuit needs a specific amount of protection. The amperage value of each fuse is molded into the fuse body.

If the replacement fuse immediately fails, don't replace it again until the cause of the problem is isolated and corrected. In most cases, the cause will be a short circuit in the wiring caused by a broken or deteriorated wire.

5   Circuit breakers – general information

Circuit breakers protect components such as power windows, power door locks and headlights. Some circuit breakers are located in the fuse box.

On some models the circuit breaker resets itself automatically, so an electrical overload in a circuit breaker protected system will cause the circuit to fail momentarily, then come back on. If the circuit does not come back on, check it immediately. Once the condition is corrected, the circuit breaker will resume its normal function. Some circuit breakers must be reset manually **(see illustration 4.1a)**.

6   Multi-function (turn signal/dimmer) switch – replacement

Refer to illustrations 6.2 and 6.5
1   Disconnect the cable from the negative terminal of the battery.
2   Remove the screw from the turn signal control handle **(see illustration)**.

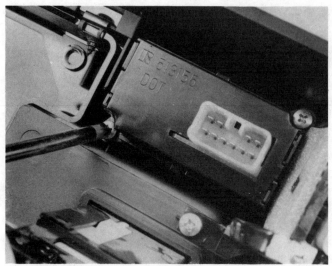

6.5   The turn signal/dimmer switch is retained by two screws

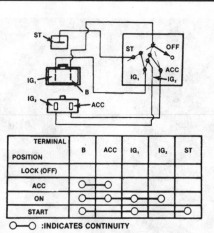

TERMINAL POSITION	B	ACC	IG₁	IG₂	ST
LOCK (OFF)					
ACC	○—○				
ON	○—○—○		○	○	
START	○—○		○		○

O—O :INDICATES CONTINUITY

7.2   Check for continuity across the indicated terminals of the ignition switch (the boxes with the connected circles should have continuity)

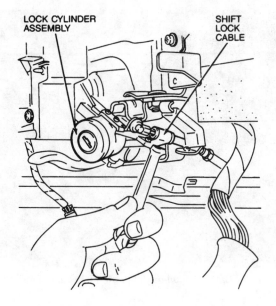

7.4   Unbolt the shift lock cable and position it out of the way

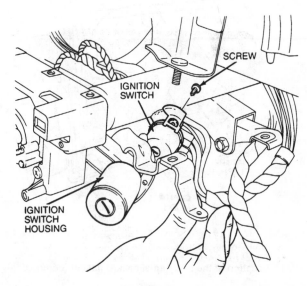

7.5   Remove the mounting screw for the ignition switch and pull the switch out of its housing

3   Remove the turn signal control handle.
4   Remove the instrument cluster (see Section 18).
5   Working from the rear of the cluster, remove the two screws retaining the switch **(see illustration)**.
6   Remove the switch from the backside of the instrument cluster.
7   Installation is the reverse of removal.

7   Ignition switch/key lock cylinder – check and replacement

Ignition switch

Refer to illustrations 7.2, 7.4 and 7.5

Check

1   Disconnect the cable from the negative terminal of the battery.
2   To check the continuity of the ignition switch, unplug the electrical connectors and, using an ohmmeter or self powered test light, check the terminals indicated in the accompanying illustration for continuity **(see illustration)**. If the ignition switch fails any one of the checks, replace it.

Replacement

3   Remove the instrument cluster cover. Lower the steering column by removing the bolts that secure it to the dash.
4   Remove the nut that retains the shift lock cable and allow the cable to hang free **(see illustration)**.
5   Remove the screw attaching the ignition switch to the ignition switch housing **(see illustration)**.
6   Follow the wires from the back of the switch and unplug the electrical connectors.
7   Remove the electrical harness protector from the ignition switch and remove the switch from the steering column.
8   Installation is the reverse of removal.

Key lock cylinder replacement

9   Follow the above procedure and remove the ignition switch.
10   Remove the two screws that secure the lock cylinder to the steering column, then remove the lock cylinder.
11   Installation is the reverse of the removal procedure.

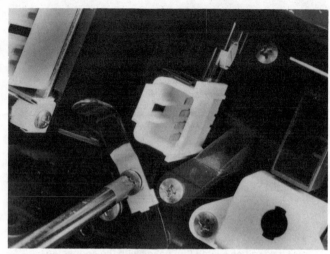

8.4   Removing the mounting screws for the hazard switch

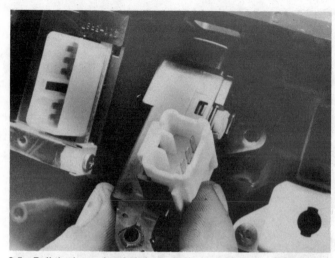

8.5   Pull the hazard switch from the rear of the instrument cluster – when installing the switch, guide the button on the top into the hole in the cluster cover

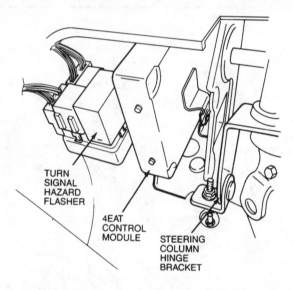

9.1   Location of the turn signal/hazard flasher (behind dash)

10.3   Carefully pull the knob off the headlight switch

8   Hazard switch – replacement

Refer to illustrations 8.4 and 8.5

1   Disconnect the cable from the negative terminal of the battery.
2   Remove the steering wheel (see Chapter 10).
3   Remove the instrument cluster (see Section 18).
4   Remove the screws mounting the hazard switch **(see illustration)**.
5   Remove the hazard switch **(see illustration)**.
6   Installation is the reverse of removal.

9   Hazard/turn signal flasher – check and replacement

Refer to illustration 9.1

Check

1   The hazard/turn signal flasher, a small cube-shaped unit located behind the dash **(see illustration)**, flashes the hazard or turn signal lights by repeatedly interrupting the circuit.
2   When the flasher unit is functioning properly, an audible click can be heard during its operation. If the hazard or turn signals fail on one side or the other and the flasher unit does not make its characteristic clicking sound, a faulty turn signal bulb is indicated.
3   If the hazard lights or the turn signals for both sides fail to blink, the problem may be due to a blown fuse, a faulty flasher unit, a broken switch or a loose or open connection. If a quick check of the fuse box indicates that the fuse has blown, check the wiring for a short before installing a new fuse.

Replacement

4   To replace the flasher, simply pull it out of it's mounting. Make sure the replacement unit is identical to the original.
5   Installation is the reverse of removal.

10   Headlight switch – replacement

Refer to illustrations 10.3 and 10.4

1   Remove the instrument cluster (see Section 18)
2   Remove the turn signal switch (see Section 6).
3   Remove the headlight switch knob by gently pulling it away from the

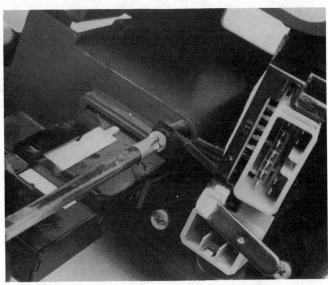

10.4   Remove the mounting screws from the light switch

11.2a   Remove the headlight bezel screws (there's one on each side)

switch (see illustration).

4   Remove the mounting screws from the switch (see illustration). Remove the switch from the instrument cluster.

5   Installation is the reverse of removal.

11   Headlights – removal and installation

Refer to illustrations 11.2a, 11.2b and 11.3

Warning: Halogen gas filled headlights are under pressure and may shatter if the surface is scratched or is dropped. Wear eye protection and handle the headlight carefully.

1   Turn the headlights on, then disconnect the cable from the negative terminal of the battery.

2   Remove the retaining screws and detach the headlight bezel (see illustrations).

3   Remove the screws from the headlight retaining ring (see illustration), taking care not to disturb the adjustment screws.

4   Remove the retainer and pull the headlight out enough to allow the electrical connector to be unplugged.

5   Remove the headlight.

6   Installation is the reverse of removal.

12   Headlight housing assembly – removal and installation

Refer to illustrations 12.2 and 12.3

1   Turn the headlight switch to the On position to raise the headlights. Disconnect the cable from the negative terminal of the battery.

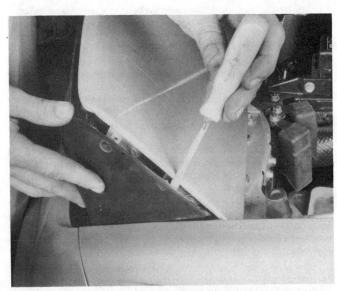

11.2b   Pry the sides of the headlight bezel out to detach the locater pins, then remove the bezel

11.3   The headlight retaining ring is secured by four screws

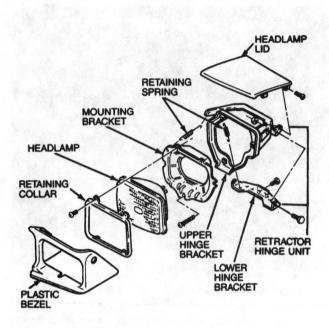

12.2   Headlight housing assembly – exploded view

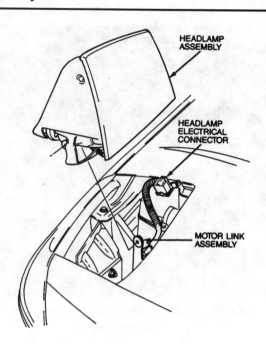

12.3   After disconnecting the electrical connector and
motor link, the headlight housing can be removed

13.2a   Using jumper wires, ground terminal BK, apply battery
voltage to terminal BK/W then momentarily apply battery voltage
to terminal BK/R – the motor should now run

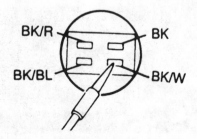

13.2b   Terminal positions in the electrical connector for
the headlight retractor motor

2   Remove the nuts that secure the retractor hinge to the vehicle **(see illustration)**.
3   Unplug the electrical connector from the headlight. Detach the motor link from the housing and remove the housing assembly from the vehicle **(see illustration)**. Be careful not to scratch the paint.
4   Installation is the reverse of the removal procedure.

---

13   Headlight retractor motor – check, removal and installation

Refer to illustrations 13.2a, 13.2b and 13.9

Check

1   The headlights should raise when the headlight switch is turned on. If they don't raise, check the fuses on the main fuse block, near the battery. If the fuses are OK, use a 12-volt test light to check for power to the motor. Probe each terminal in the electrical connector to the motor while an assistant turns the headlight switch off and on. If there is no power to the motor, either the switch, the relay or the wiring is faulty. If those items check out OK, proceed to test the motor.
2   Unplug the electrical connector to the headlight motor. Test the motor by using a jumper wire to ground the terminal "BK" **(see illustrations)**.
3   Using a second jumper wire, connect battery voltage to terminal "BK/W" of the motor connector.
4   Using a third jumper wire, momentarily apply battery voltage to the terminal "BK/R" of the motor connector. The motor should move to the Up position. If it doesn't, it may be defective. Proceed to the next Step before condemning the motor.
5   Now, momentarily apply battery voltage to the terminal "BK/BL". The motor should move to the down position. If the motor doesn't move to the down position, it can be considered defective.

Removal and installation

6   Disconnect the cable from the negative terminal of the battery.
7   Detach the lower link arm from the motor arm. **Caution:** *Do not remove the motor arm from the motor shaft, as it may cause incorrect automatic stop operation.*
8   Disconnect the retractor motor electrical connector.

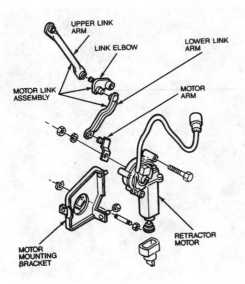

13.9   Headlight retractor motor and related hardware – exploded view

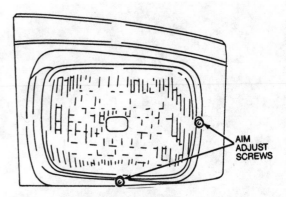

14.1   Headlight aiming screws – the lower screw controls vertical adjustment, the one on the side controls horizontal adjustment

9   Remove the attaching bolts from the retractor motor **(see illustration)**.
10   Remove the retractor motor.
11   Installation is the reverse of removal.

14   Headlights – adjustment

Note: *The headlights must be aimed correctly. If adjusted incorrectly they could blind the driver of an oncoming vehicle and cause a serious accident or seriously reduce your ability to see the road. The headlights should be checked for proper aim every 12 months and any time a new headlight is installed or front end body work is performed. It should be emphasized that the following procedure is only an interim step which will provide temporary adjustment until the headlights can be adjusted by a properly equipped shop.*
Refer to illustration 14.1

1   Headlights have two spring loaded adjusting screws, one for controlling up-and-down movement and one for controlling left-and-right movement **(see illustration)**.
2   There are several methods of adjusting the headlights. The simplest method requires a blank wall 25 feet in front of the vehicle and a level floor.
3   Position masking tape vertically on the wall in reference to the vehicle centerline and the centerlines of both headlights.
4   Position a horizontal tape line in reference to the centerline of all the headlights. **Note:** *It may be easier to position the tape on the wall with the vehicle parked only a few inches away.*
5   Adjustment should be made with the vehicle sitting level, the gas tank half-full and no unusually heavy load in the vehicle.
6   Starting with the low beam adjustment, position the high intensity zone so it is two inches below the horizontal line and two inches to the right of the headlight vertical line. Adjustment is made by turning the bottom adjusting screw clockwise to lower the beam and counterclockwise to raise the beam. The adjusting screw on the side should be used in the same manner to move the beam left or right.
7   With the high beams on, the high intensity zone should be vertically centered with the exact center just below the horizontal line. **Note:** *It may not be possible to position the headlight aim exactly for both high and low beams. If a compromise must be made, keep in mind that the low beams are the most used and have the greatest effect on driver safety.*
8   Have the headlights adjusted by a dealer service department or service station at the earliest opportunity.

15   Bulb replacement

1   The lenses of many lights are held in place by screws, which makes it a simple procedure to gain access to the bulbs.
2   On some lights the lenses are held in place by clips. The lenses can be removed either by unsnapping them or by using a small screwdriver to pry them off.
3   Several types of bulbs are used. Some are removed by pushing in and turning them counterclockwise. Others can simply be unclipped from the terminals or pulled straight out of the socket.
4   To gain access to the instrument panel lights, the instrument cluster will have to be removed first (see Section 18).

16   Radio and speakers – removal and installation

Radio
Refer to illustrations 16.4, 16.6, 16.7 and 16.8
1   Disconnect cable from the negative terminal of the battery.
2   Remove the ashtray.
3   Remove the gear selector trim panel (on automatic transaxle), or gearshift and boot trim panel (on manual transaxle).
4   Remove the cigar lighter assembly **(see illustration)**.

16.4   Removing the cigar lighter

16.6   Pry the ashtray trim out of the center console

16.7   Removing the lower mounting screws of the radio

5   Disconnect the electrical connector for the cigar lighter and detach the cigar lighter light by twisting the socket.
6   Remove the trim plate on the center console that surrounds the gearshift lever (see Section 11). Carefully pry out the trim surrounding the ashtray opening (see illustration).
7   Remove the lower mounting screws of the radio (see illustration).
8   Using a piece of coat hanger bent in a "U" shape, release the two anti-theft locking tabs on each side of the radio (see illustration).
9   Pull out the radio.
10   Disconnect the antenna cable and the electrical connectors.
11   Installation is the reverse of removal.

Speaker (door-mounted)

Refer to illustration 16.13

12   Remove the door inner trim panel (see Chapter 11).
13   Remove the speaker retaining screws (see illustration).

14   Pull out the speaker and disconnect the electrical connectors.
15   Remove the speaker.
16   Installation is the reverse of removal.

Speaker (rear seat)

Refer to illustrations 16.18a, 16.18b, 16.18c, 16.21, 16.23a and 16.23b

17   Remove the side and rear trim in the luggage compartment (see Section 17)
18   Remove the quarter panel trim (see illustrations).
19   Disconnect the electrical connector from the speaker.
20   Remove the speaker cover.
21   Remove the mounting bolts for the speaker housing (see illustration).
22   Remove the speaker and housing.
23   Remove the speaker from the housing (see illustrations).

16.8   Insert a piece of bent coat hanger into the slots on the side of the radio to release the locking tabs

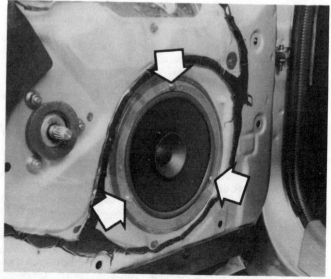

16.13   The door speakers are secured with three screws (arrows)

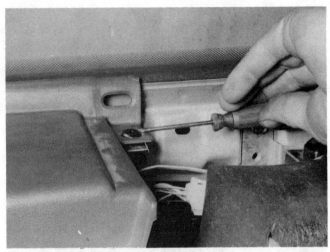

16.18a   Pry up on the plastic retainers of the quarter panel trim to remove them

16.18b   Remove the rear mounting screws of the quarter panel trim

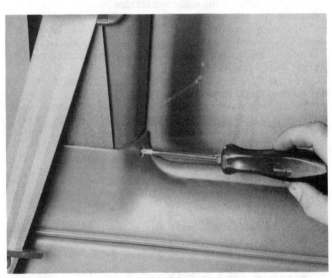

16.18c   Remove the upper mounting screw of the quarter panel trim

16.21   the rear speaker housing is retained by two mounting bolts

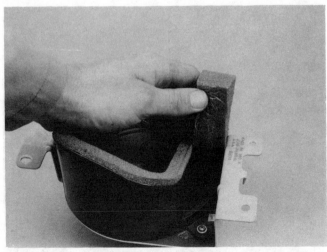

16.23a   Removing insulation to gain access to the speaker mounting screws

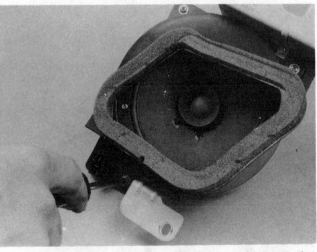

16.23b   Remove the speaker mounting screws and separate the speaker from the housing

16.25   Remove the screws and lift off the luggage compartment upper trim

16.26   Remove the sub-woofer mounting screws and lift it from its mounting bracket

24   Installation is the reverse of removal. If necessary, use a little trim adhesive to bond the insulation to the speaker housing.

Speaker (sub-woofer)

Refer to illustrations 16.25 and 16.26

25   Remove the luggage compartment upper trim **(see illustration)**.
26   Remove the sub-woofer mounting screws **(see illustration)**.
27   Disconnect the electrical connectors from the sub-woofer.
28   Remove the sub-woofer.
29   Installation is the reverse of removal.

17   Radio antenna – removal and installation

Refer to illustrations 17.1, 17.2, 17.4, 17.5, 17.6 and 17.9

1   Remove the trim from the rear of the luggage compartment **(see illustration)**.
2   Remove the lower side trim and the upper side cover from the luggage compartment **(see illustration)**.
3   On power antenna equipped models, disconnect the antenna motor electrical connector.
4   On all models, disconnect the antenna cable **(see illustration)**.

5   Unscrew and remove the bezel and the bezel mount **(see illustration)**.
6   Note the drain tube routing and remove the bolts mounting the antenna **(see illustration)**.
7   Remove the sub-woofer (see Section 16) and its mounting bracket.
8   Remove the antenna.
9   Installation is the reverse of removal. **Note:** *When installing the antenna bezel mount, line up the tab on the bezel mount with the tab slot on the support* **(see illustration)**.

18   Instrument cluster – removal and installation

Refer to illustrations 18.3, 18.5, 18.10, 18.11, 18.12 and 18.13

1   Disconnect the cable from the negative terminal of the battery.
2   Remove the steering wheel (see Chapter 10).
3   Remove the two mounting screws on the column cover **(see illustration)**.
4   Remove the cover from the steering column.
5   Remove the mounting screws from the instrument cluster module **(see illustration)**.

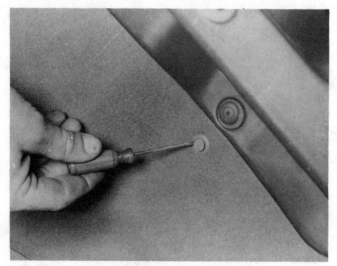

17.1   Pry the centers of the pop retainers up and remove them from the luggage compartment trim

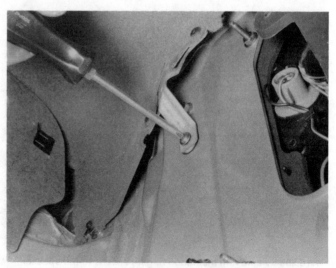

17.2   Remove the rear mounting screw for the luggage compartment side trim

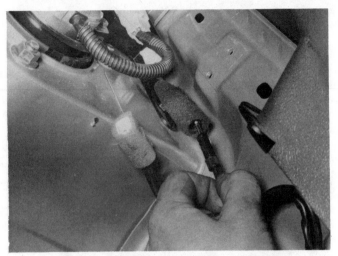

17.4   Unplug the antenna cable from the antenna

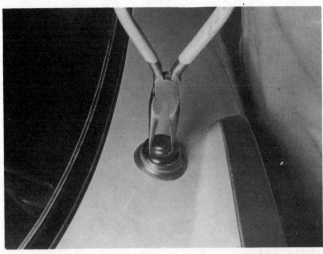

17.5   Unscrew the antenna bezel using a pair of needle-nose pliers – be careful not to let the pliers slip and scratch the paint

17.6   The lower mounting bolts for the power antenna (arrows)

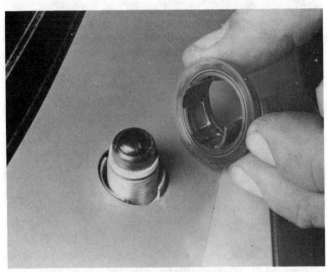

17.9   Be sure to line up the bezel mounting tabs with the slots on the antenna support

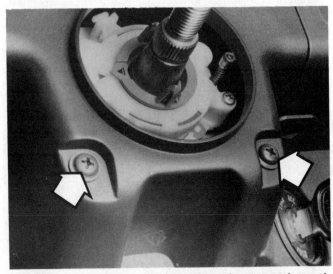

18.3   Remove the screws for the steering column cover (arrows)

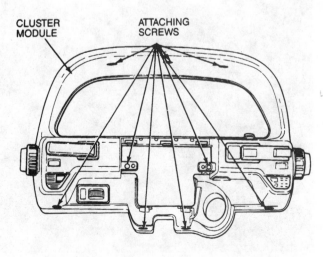

CLUSTER MODULE   ATTACHING SCREWS

18.5   Remove the screws from the cluster module

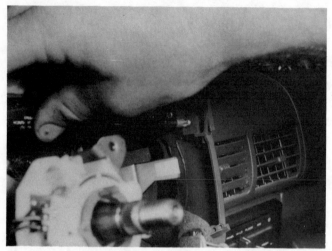

18.10   Remove the hinge screws from the cluster cover

18.11   Remove the mounting screws retaining the instrument
cluster cover

6   Carefully pull the cluster module out to access the electrical connectors.
7   Disconnect the electrical connectors from the cluster module.
8   Remove the ignition illumination bulb.
9   Remove the instrument cluster from the cluster cover.
10   Remove the screws from the cluster cover hinge (see illustration).
11   Remove the mounting screws from the instrument cluster cover (see
illustration).
12   Remove the cluster cover (see illustration). Note: During removal,
be careful not to rip the rubber seal that joins the upper and lower portions
of the cluster cover panels.
13   Remove the four mounting screws from the cluster (see illustration).
14   Disconnect the electrical connectors from the back of the cluster.
15   Disconnect speedometer cable (see Section 19).
16   Remove the instrument cluster from the vehicle.
17   Installation is the reverse of removal.

19   Speedometer cable – replacement

Refer to illustrations 19.3, 19.7, 19.8 and 19.11
1   Disconnect the battery (see Chapter 5).
2   Remove the upper and lower cover panels from the instrument cluster. Note: It is not necessary to remove the instrument cluster from the vehicle to remove the speedometer cable.
3   Reach behind the instrument cluster and depress the cable locking
tab (see illustration).

18.12   Removing the instrument cluster cover

18.13   Remove the upper mounting screws for the
instrument cluster

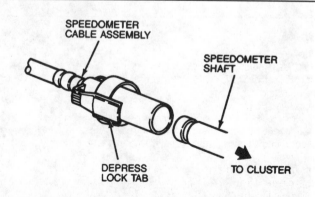

19.3   To disconnect the speedometer cable from the instrument
cluster, depress the locking tab and pull the cable off the
speedometer shaft

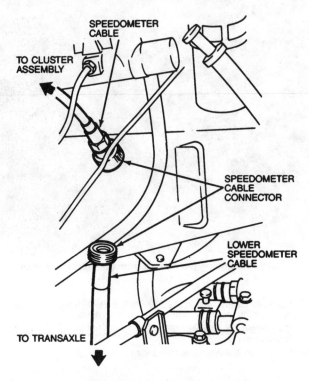

19.7   The two halves of the speedometer cable are joined by a threaded connector

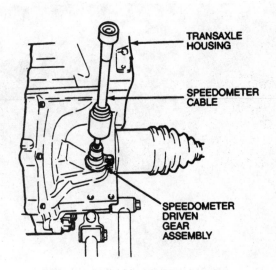

19.8   Details of the speedometer lower cable

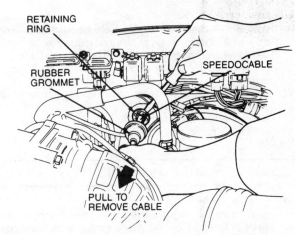

19.11   Pry the speedometer cable retaining ring out of the firewall

4   Pull the speedometer cable from the instrument cluster.
5   Open the hood and locate the speedometer cable connector.
6   Slide the rubber dust boot back from the cable connector.
7   Unscrew the speedometer cable connector and separate the cables **(see illustration)**.
8   On the transaxle, unscrew the speedometer cable connector from the speedometer driven gear **(see illustration)**.
9   Remove the lower cable from the transaxle.
10   Remove the rubber grommet from the engine compartment side of the firewall. Slide the grommet down the cable.
11   Working from the engine compartment, gently pry the retaining ring out of the firewall **(see illustration)**.
12   Pull the speedometer cable through the firewall.
13   Installation is the reverse of removal.

20   Rear window defroster and switch – check, repair and replacement

Check

Refer to illustration 20.3

1   Check the power and ground circuits of defroster (see Section 2). If there isn't any voltage available to the circuit, check the fuses, the switch, the relay and the wiring harness. If you determine the switch is defective, proceed to Step 7.
2   If the power and ground circuits are okay and voltage is available to the rear window, check the grid. Attach the negative lead of a voltmeter to a good ground. Attach the positive lead of the voltmeter to the middle of each grid wire.
3   If a grid wire is broken, voltmeter will register either zero volts or battery voltage. If a grid wire is unbroken, the voltmeter will register about six volts **(see illustration)**.
4   To locate a brake in a grid wire, move the positive lead of the voltmeter along the grid wire until the voltmeter needle moves suddenly.

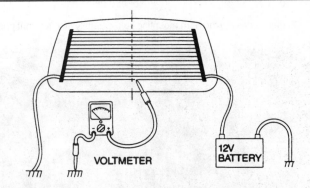

20.3   The voltmeter should read six volts in the middle of the grid

Grid wire repair

5   If any break in the grid wire is longer than 1 inch (25 mm), the rear window must be replaced.
6   With the use of a defroster grid repair kit (available at most auto parts stores), breaks less than 1 inch (25mm) can be repaired. Follow the instructions included in the repair kit.

20.9   Removing the defroster button

20.10   Removing the screws from the defroster switch

Switch replacement

Refer to illustrations 20.9 and 20.10

7   Disconnect the cable from the negative terminal of the battery.
8   Remove the instrument cluster from the vehicle (see Section 18).
9   Pull the switch button from the housing **(see illustration)**.
10 Working behind the cluster module, remove the mounting screws from the defroster switch housing **(see illustration)**.
11 To provide clearance for defroster switch removal, turn the headlights rotary switch to the On position.
12 Remove the defroster switch.
13 Installation is the reverse of removal.

---

21   Horns – removal and installation

Refer to illustration 21.4

1   Loosen the front wheel lug nuts (left or right side, depending on which horn is being dealt with). Raise the vehicle and support it securely on jackstands. Remove the left or right front wheel.
2   Remove the front bumper brace.
3   Remove the forward fasteners of the front fender liner (see Chapter 11).
4   To gain access to the horn mounting bolt, carefully flex the front portion of the fender liner out of the way **(see illustration)**.
5   Remove the mounting bolt for the horn assembly.
6   Disconnect the electrical connector from the horn.
7   Remove the horn.
8   Installation is the reverse of removal.

---

22   Windshield wiper/washer switch and motor – replacement

Front wiper/washer switch

Refer to illustration 22.4

1   Remove the instrument cluster (see Section 18).
2   Pull off the front washer/wiper control knob.
3   Remove the switch retaining screws.
4   Remove the wiper/washer switch **(see illustration)**.
5   Installation is the reverse of removal

Rear wiper/washer switch

Refer to illustrations 22.8 and 22.9

6   Remove the cluster module (see Section 18).
7   Remove the front wiper/washer switch, (see Steps 1-4 in this Section).

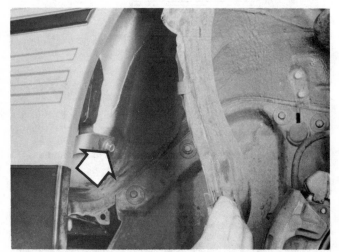

21.4   Carefully pull back the fender liner to gain access to the horn – the horn mounting bolt can now be seen (arrow)

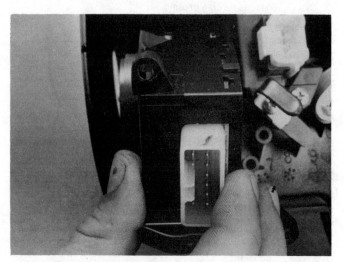

22.4   Remove the wiper/washer switch from the rear of the instrument cluster

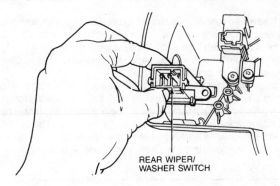

22.8   Removing the rear wiper/washer switch

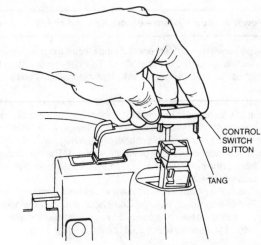

22.9   Remove the rear wiper/washer switch button

8   Remove the mounting screws for the rear wiper/washer switch (**see illustration**).
9   Release the switch button tangs and remove the switch button (**see illustration**).
10   Remove the rear wiper/washer switch.
11   Installation is the reverse of removal.

Front wiper motor

Refer to illustration 22.13
12   Disconnect the cable from the negative terminal of the battery.
13   Remove the blade and arm assembly (**see illustration**).
14   Disconnect the hose from the washer jet.
15   Remove the lower moulding.
16   Remove the wiper linkage cover.
17   Pry the wiper linkage from the wiper motor arm.
18   Disconnect the electrical connectors from the motor.
19   Remove the mounting bolts of the wiper motor.
20   Remove the wiper motor.
21   Installation is the reverse of removal.

Rear wiper motor

Refer to illustration 22.23
22   Disconnect the cable from the negative terminal of the battery.
23   Remove the arm and blade assembly (**see illustration**).
24   Remove the boot protecting the wiper motor shaft.
25   Remove the wiper motor-to-cowl nut.
26   Remove the wiper motor-to-cowl mount.
27   Pry off the interior trim panel from the liftgate.
28   Disconnect the wiper motor electrical connector.
29   Remove the bolts mounting the wiper motor.
30   Remove the wiper motor.
31   Installation is the reverse of removal.

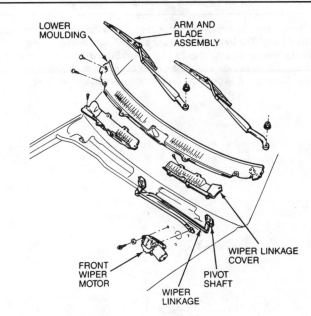

22.13   Details of the windshield wiper system

23   Cruise control system – description and check

The cruise control system maintains vehicle speed with a vacuum or electrically actuated servo motor located in the engine compartment.
Because of the complexity of the cruise control systems and the special tools and techniques required for diagnosis, repair should be left to a dealer service department or a repair shop. However, it is possible for the home mechanic to make simple checks of the wiring and vacuum connections for minor faults which can be easily repaired. These include:

a) Inspect the cruise control actuating switches for broken wires and loose connections.
b) Check the cruise control fuse.
c) If the cruise control is operated by vacuum it's critical that all vacuum switches, hoses and connections are secure. Check the hoses in the engine compartment for tight connections, cracks and obvious vacuum leaks.

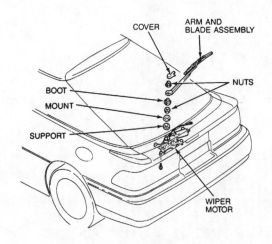

22.23   Exploded view of the rear wiper assembly

.24   Power window system – description and check

The power window system operates the electric motors mounted in the doors which lower and raise the windows. The system consists of the control switches, the motors (regulators), glass mechanisms and associated wiring.

Because of the complexity of the power window system and the special tools and techniques required for diagnosis, repair should be left to a dealer service department or a repair shop. However, it is possible for the home mechanic to make simple checks of the wiring connections and motors for minor faults which can be easily repaired. These include:

a) Inspect the power window actuating switches for broken wires and loose connections.

b) Check the power window fuse/and or circuit breaker.

c) Remove the door panel(s) and check the power window motor wires to see if they're loose or damaged. Inspect the glass mechanisms for damage which could cause binding.

25   Power door lock system – description and check

The power door lock system operates the door lock actuators mounted in each door. The system consists of the switches, actuators and associated wiring. Since special tools and techniques are required to diagnose the system, it should be left to a dealer service department or a repair shop. However, it is possible for the home mechanic to make simple checks of the wiring connections and actuators for minor faults which can be easily repaired. These include:

a) Check the system fuse and/or circuit breaker.

b) Check the switch wires for damage and loose connections. Check the switches for continuity.

c) Remove the door panel(s) and check the actuator wiring connections to see if they're loose or damaged. Inspect the actuator rods (if equipped) to make sure they aren't bent or damaged. Inspect the actuator wiring for damaged or loose connections. The actuator can be checked by applying battery power momentarily. A discernible click indicates that the solenoid is operating properly.

26   Wiring diagrams – general information

Since it isn't possible to include all wiring diagrams for every year covered by this manual, the following diagrams are those that are typical and most commonly needed.

Prior to troubleshooting any circuits, check the fuse and circuit breakers (if equipped) to make sure they're in good condition. Make sure the battery is properly charged and check the cable connections (see Chapter 1).

When checking a circuit, make sure that all connectors are clean, with no broken or loose terminals. When unplugging a connector, do not pull on the wires. Pull only on the connector housings themselves.

Refer to the accompanying table for the wire color codes applicable to your vehicle.

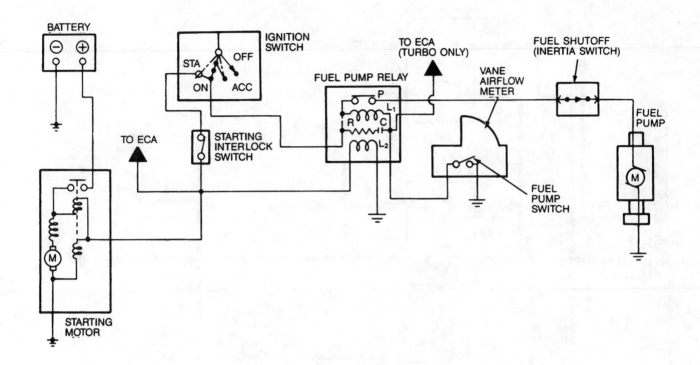

Fuel pump circuit – typical

CODE	COLOR
BK	BLACK
BR	BROWN
GN	GREEN
BL	BLUE
LB	LIGHT BLUE
LG	LIGHT GREEN
O	ORANGE
R	RED
Y	YELLOW
W	WHITE

**WIRING DIAGRAM
COLOR CODES**

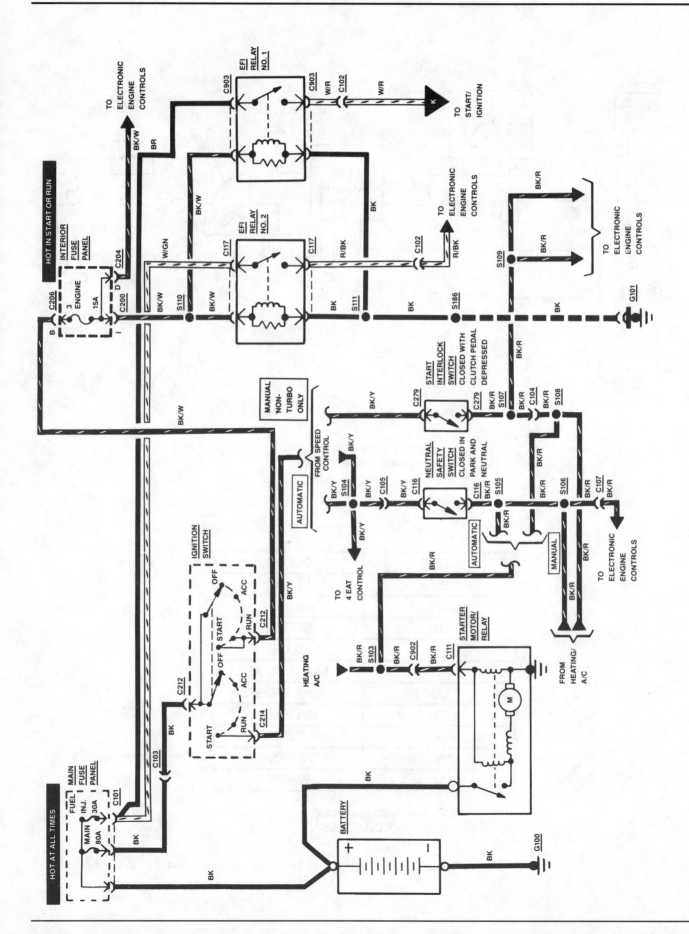

Starting/ignition circuits (part 1 of 2)

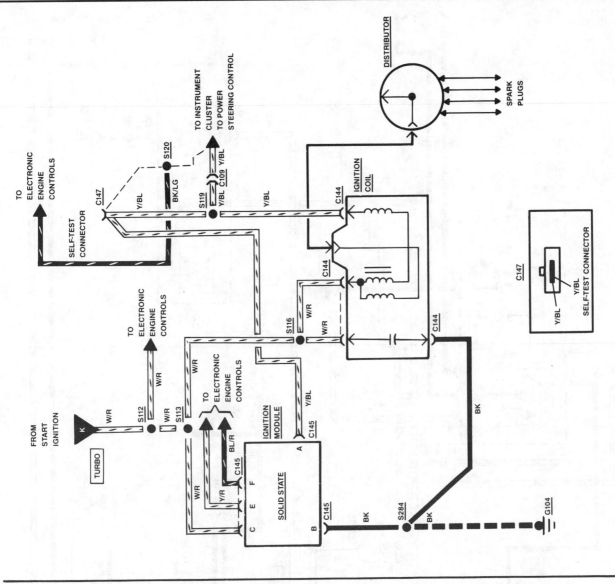

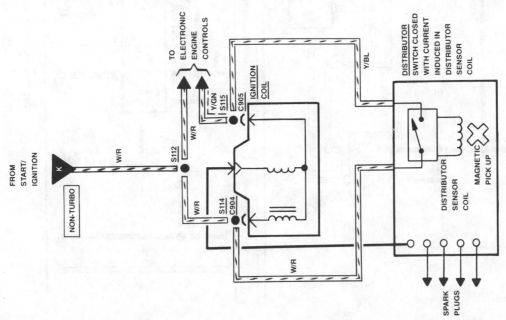

Starting/ignition circuits (part 2 of 2)

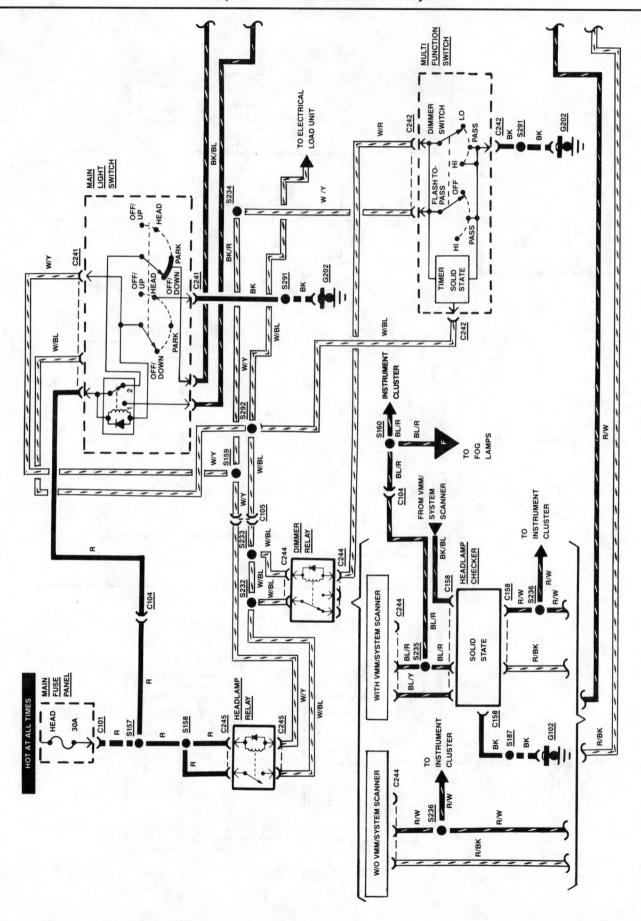

Headlight/foglight circuit (part 1 of 3)

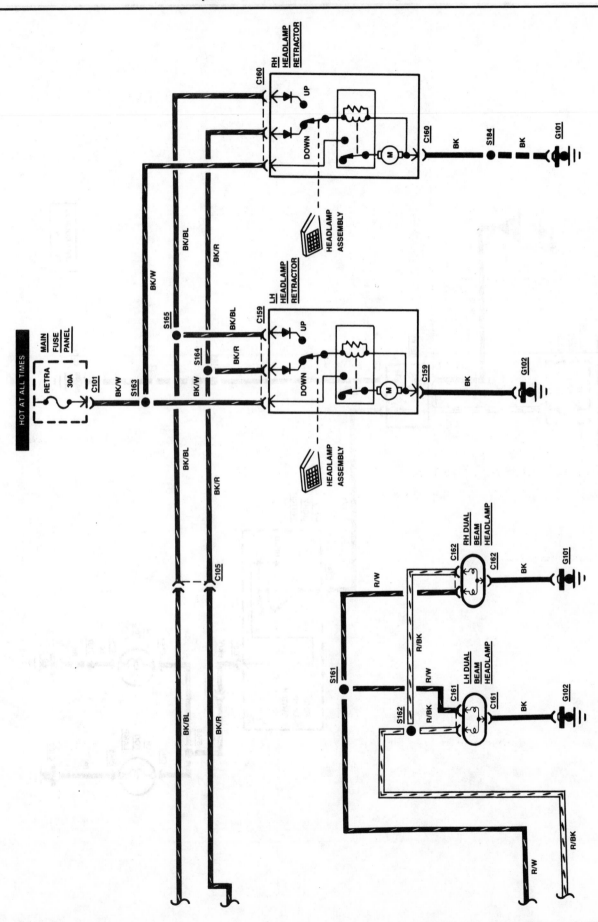

Headlight/foglight circuit (part 2 of 3)

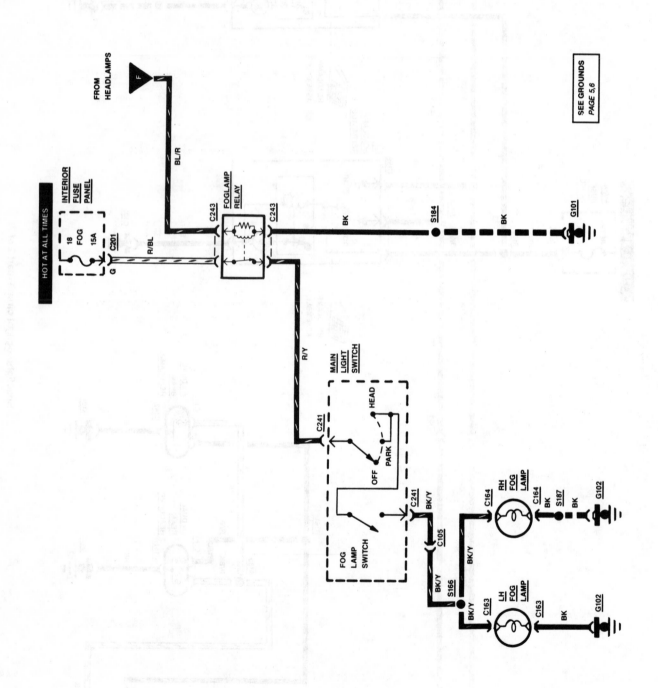

Headlight/foglight circuit (part 3 of 3)

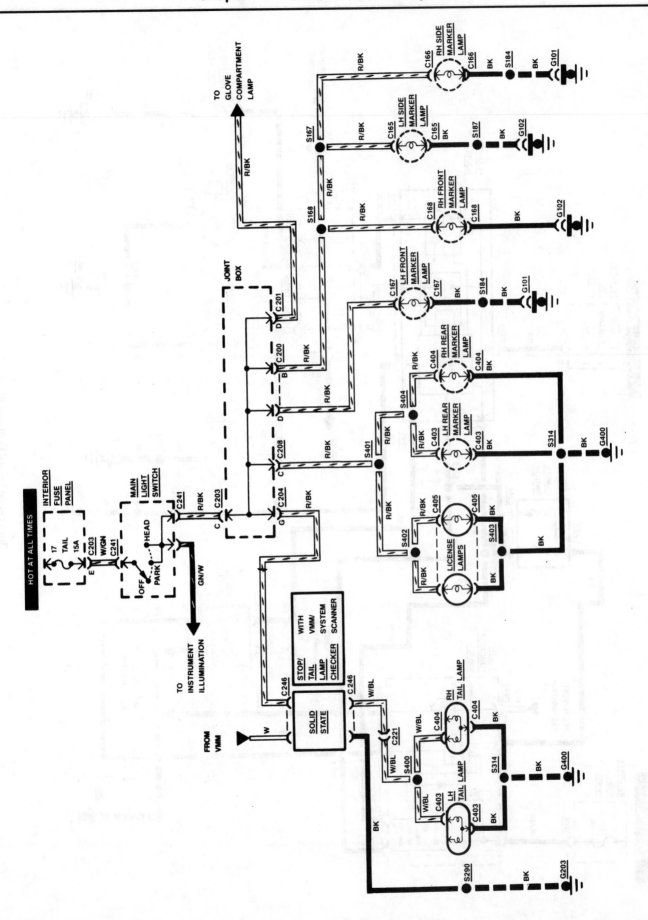

Exterior lighting circuit

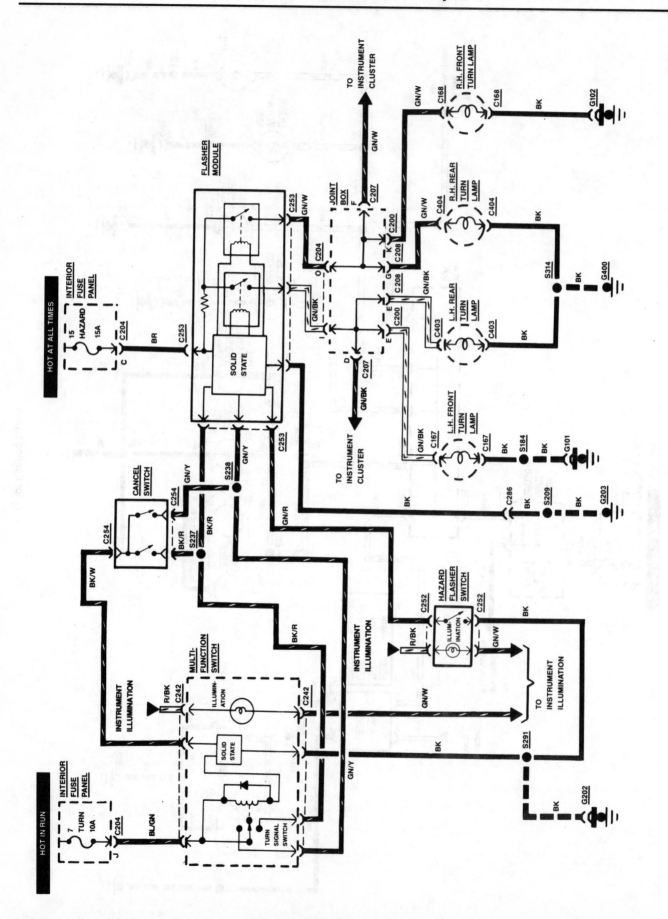

Turn signal/hazard light circuit

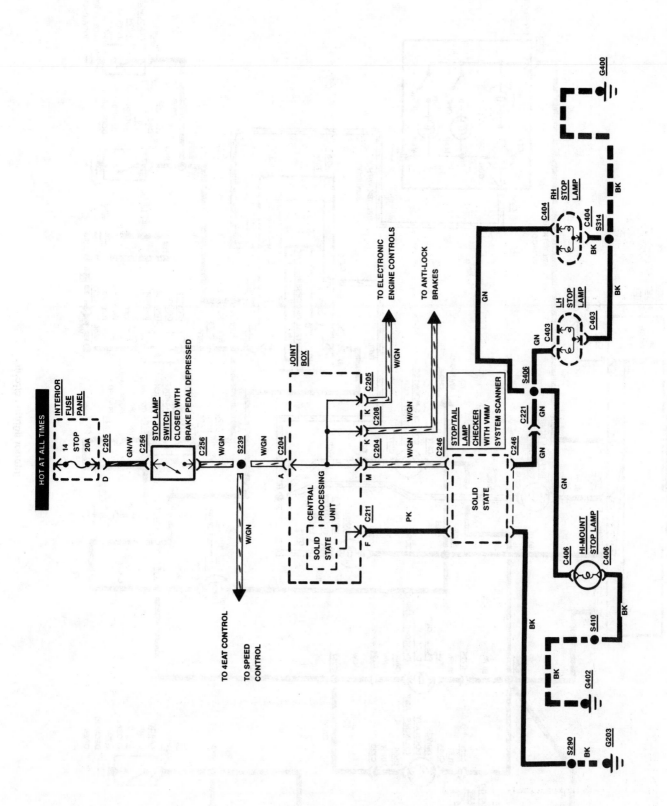

Brake light circuit

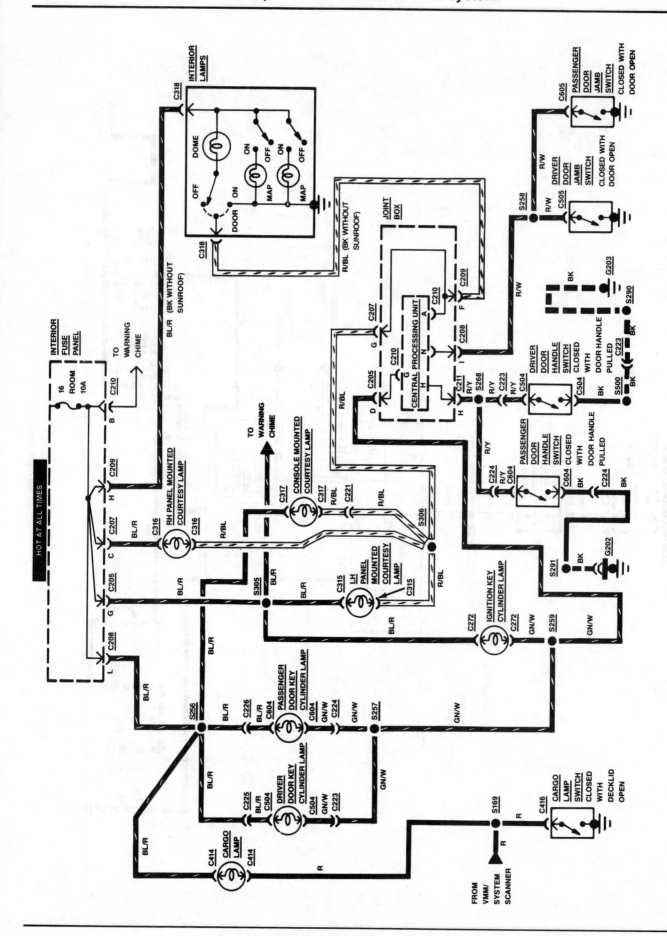

Interior lighting circuit

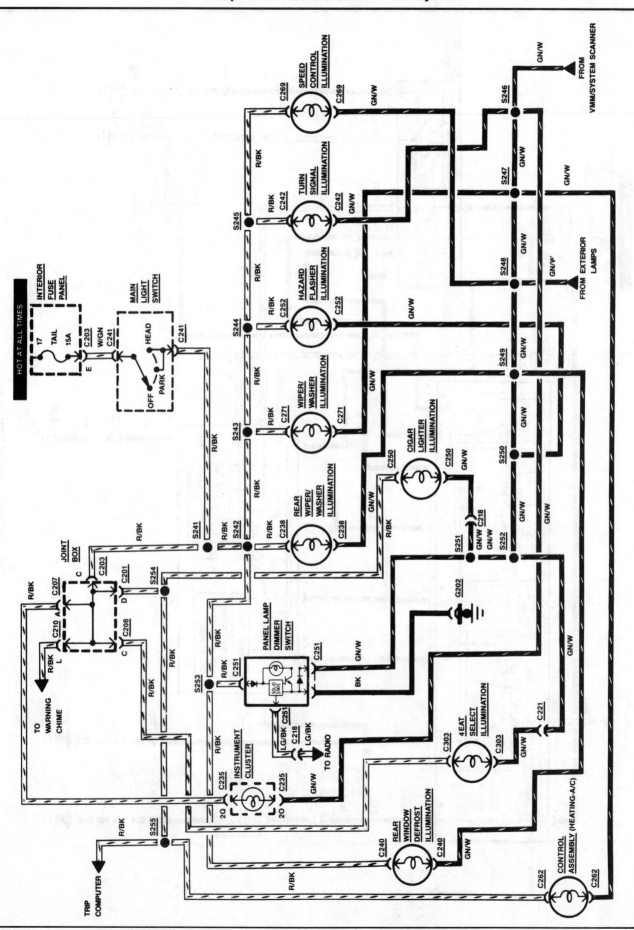

Instrument panel illumination circuit

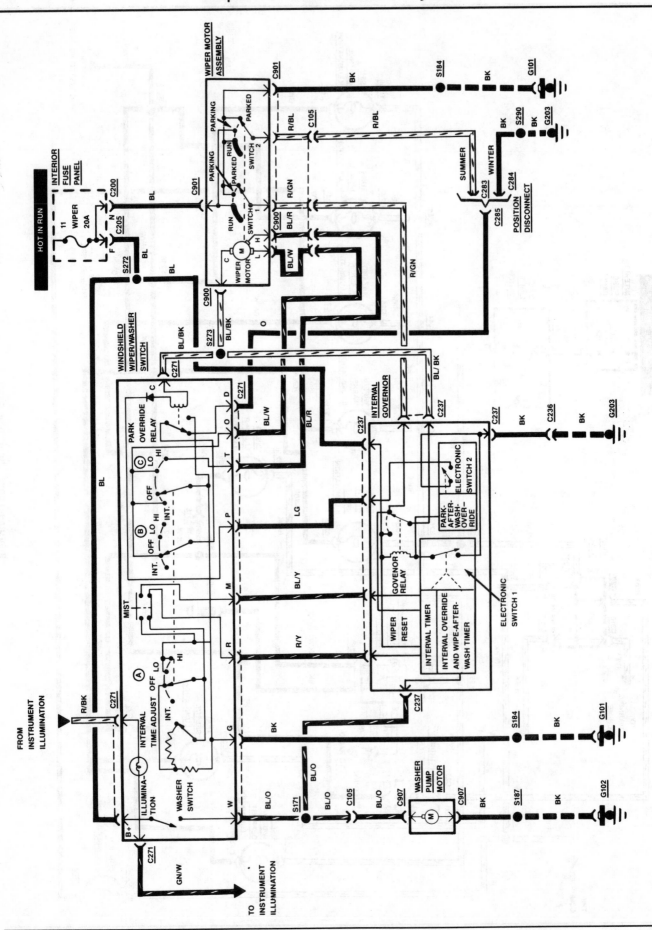

Front windshield wiper and washer circuit

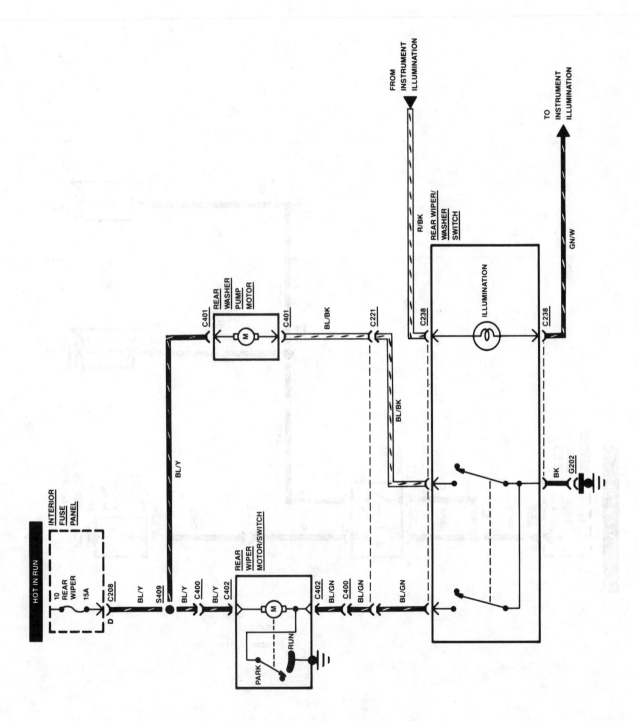

Rear wiper and washer circuit

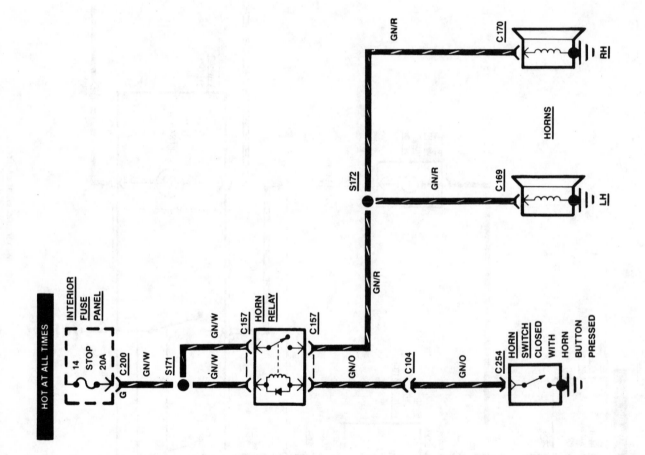

Horn circuit

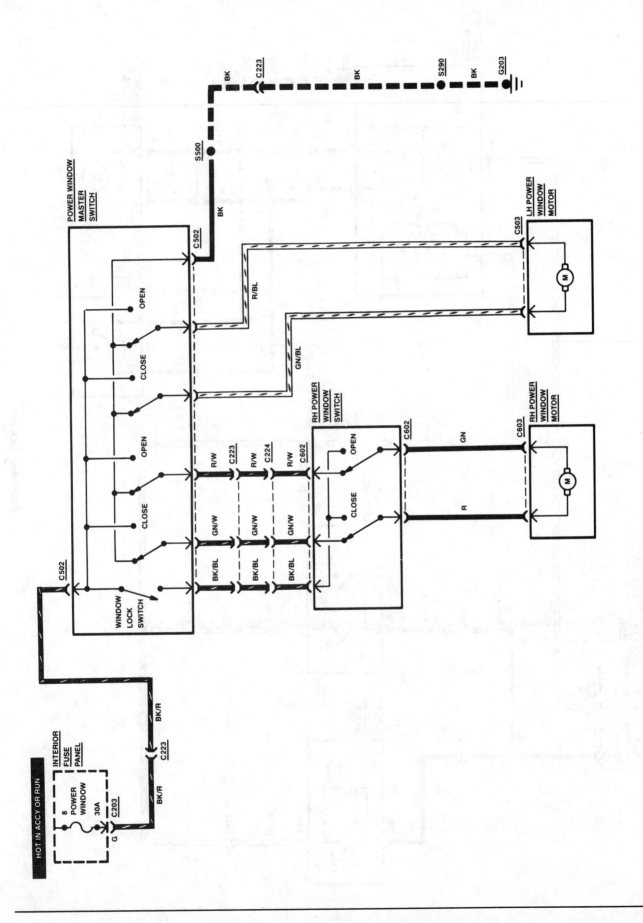

Power window circuit

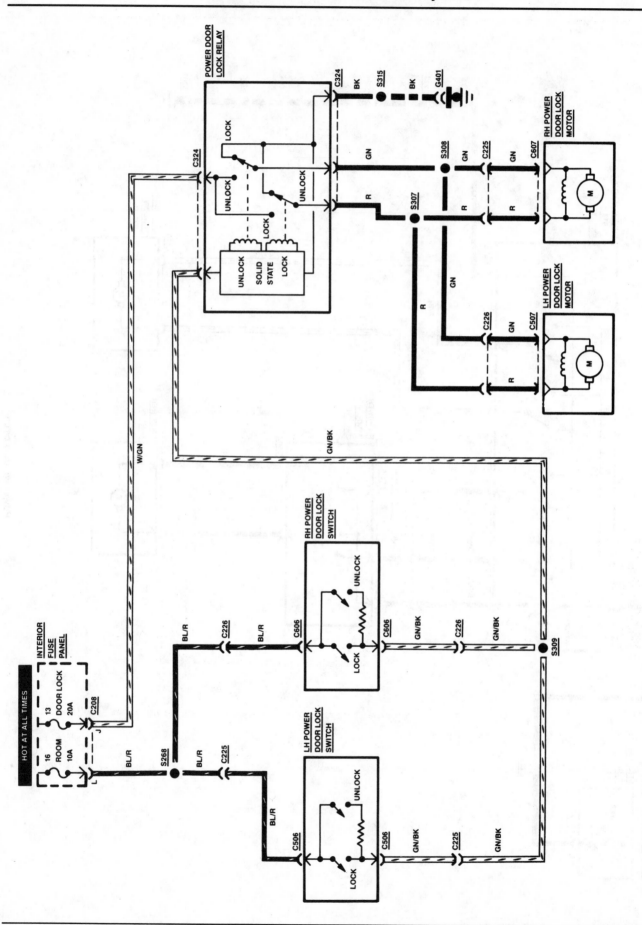

Power door lock circuit

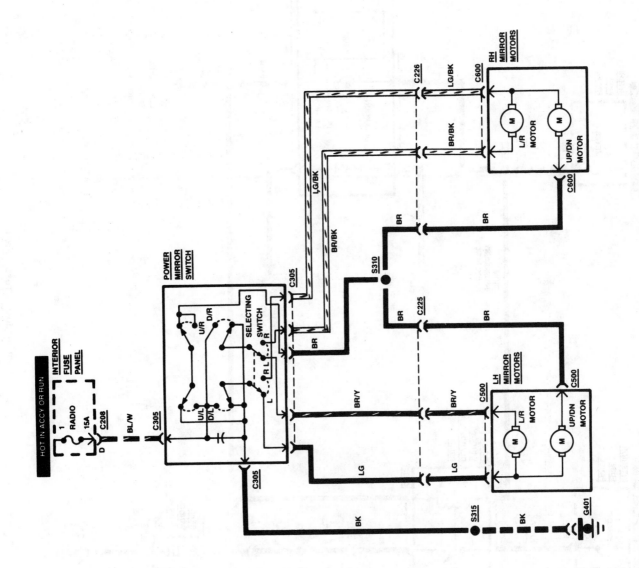

Power mirror circuit

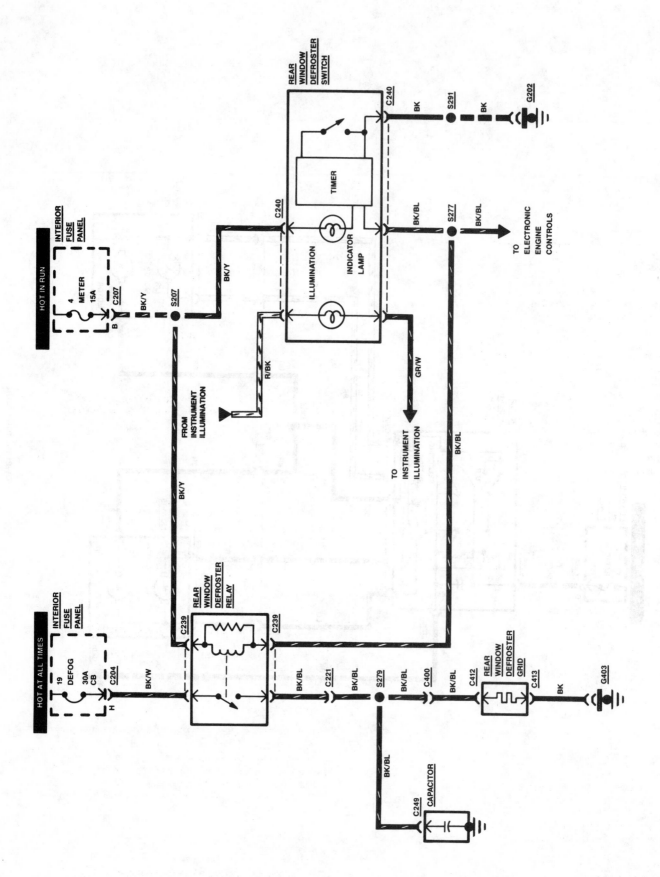

Rear window defroster circuit

Index

HAYNES AUTOMOTIVE MANUALS

NOTE: New manuals are added to this list on a periodic basis. If you do not see a listing for your vehicle, consult your local Haynes dealer for the latest product information.

ALFA-ROMEO
531 **Alfa Romeo Sedan & Coupe** '73 thru '80

AMC
Jeep CJ – see JEEP (412)
694 **Mid-size models,** Concord, Hornet, Gremlin & Spirit '70 thru '83
934 **(Renault) Alliance & Encore** all models '83 thru '87

AUDI
162 **100** all models '69 thru '77
615 **4000** all models '80 thru '87
428 **5000** all models '77 thru '83
1117 **5000** all models '84 thru '88
207 **Fox** all models '73 thru '79

AUSTIN
049 **Healey 100/6 & 3000** Roadster '56 thru '68
Healey Sprite – see MG Midget Roadster (265)

BLMC
260 **1100, 1300 & Austin America** '62 thru '74
527 **Mini** all models '59 thru '69
*646 **Mini** all models '69 thru '88

BMW
276 **320i** all 4 cyl models '75 thru '83
632 **528i & 530i** all models '75 thru '80
240 **1500 thru 2002** all models except Turbo '59 thru '77
348 **2500, 2800, 3.0 & Bavaria** '69 thru '76

BUICK
Century (front wheel drive) – see GENERAL MOTORS A-Cars (829)
*1627 **Buick, Oldsmobile & Pontiac Full-size (Front wheel drive)** all models '85 thru '90
Buick Electra, LeSabre and Park Avenue; **Oldsmobile** Delta 88 Royale, Ninety Eight and Regency; **Pontiac** Bonneville
*1551 **Buick Oldsmobile & Pontiac Full-size (Rear wheel drive)**
Buick Electra '70 thru '84, Estate '70 thru '90, LeSabre '70 thru '79
Oldsmobile Custom Cruiser '70 thru '90, Delta 88 '70 thru '85, Ninety-eight '70 thru '84
Pontiac Bonneville '70 thru '86, Catalina '70 thru '81, Grandville '70 thru '75, Parisienne '84 thu '86
627 **Mid-size** all rear-drive **Regal & Century** models with V6, V8 and Turbo '74 thru '87
Skyhawk – see GENERAL MOTORS J-Cars (766)
552 **Skylark** all X-car models '80 thru '85

CADILLAC
Cimarron – see GENERAL MOTORS J-Cars (766)

CAPRI
296 **2000 MK I Coupe** all models '71 thru '75
283 **2300 MK II Coupe** all models '74 thru '78
205 **2600 & 2800 V6 Coupe** '71 thru '75
375 **2800 Mk II V6 Coupe** '75 thru '78
Mercury in-line engines – see FORD Mustang (654)
Mercury V6 & V8 engines – see FORD Mustang (558)

CHEVROLET
*1477 **Astro & GMC Safari Mini-vans** all models '85 thru '90
554 **Camaro V8** all models '70 thru '81
*866 **Camaro** all models '82 thru '89
Cavalier – see GENERAL MOTORS J-Cars (766)
Celebrity – see GENERAL MOTORS A-Cars (829)

625 **Chevelle, Malibu & El Camino** all V6 & V8 models '69 thru '87
449 **Chevette & Pontiac T1000** all models '76 thru '87
550 **Citation** all models '80 thru '85
*1628 **Corsica/Beretta** all models '87 thru '90
274 **Corvette** all V8 models '68 thru '82
*1336 **Corvette** all models '84 thru '89
704 **Full-size Sedans** Caprice, Impala, Biscayne, Bel Air & Wagons, all V6 & V8 models '69 thru '90
319 **Luv Pick-up** all 2WD & 4WD models '72 thru '82
626 **Monte Carlo** all V6, V8 & Turbo models '70 thru '88
241 **Nova** all V8 models '69 thru '79
*1642 **Nova and Geo Prizm** all front wheel drive models, '85 thru '90
*420 **Pick-ups '67 thru '87** – Chevrolet & GMC, all V8 & in-line 6 cyl 2WD & 4WD models '67 thru '87
*1664 **Pick-ups '88 thru '90** – Chevrolet & GMC all full-size (C and K) models, '88 thru '90
*831 **S-10 & GMC S-15 Pick-ups** all models '82 thru '90
*345 **Vans** – Chevrolet & GMC, V8 & in-line 6 cyl models '68 thru '89
208 **Vega** all models except Cosworth '70 thru '77

CHRYSLER
*1337 **Chrysler & Plymouth Mid-size** front wheel drive '82 thru '88
K-Cars – see DODGE Aries (723)
Laser – see DODGE Daytona (1140)

DATSUN
402 **200SX** all models '77 thru '79
647 **200SX** all models '80 thru '83
228 **B-210** all models '73 thru '78
525 **210** all models '78 thru '82
206 **240Z, 260Z & 280Z** Coupe & 2+2 '70 thru '78
563 **280ZX** Coupe & 2+2 '79 thru '83
300ZX – see NISSAN (1137)
679 **310** all models '78 thru '82
123 **510 & PL521 Pick-up** '68 thru '73
430 **510** all models '78 thru '81
372 **610** all models '72 thru '76
277 **620 Series Pick-up** all models '73 thru '79
235 **710** all models '73 thru '77
720 Series Pick-up – see NISSAN Pick-ups (771)
376 **810/Maxima** all gasoline models '77 thru '84
124 **1200** all models '70 thru '73
368 **F10** all models '76 thru '79
Pulsar – see NISSAN (876)
Sentra – see NISSAN (982)
Stanza – see NISSAN (981)

DODGE
*723 **Aries & Plymouth Reliant** all models '81 thru '88
*1231 **Caravan & Plymouth Voyager Mini-Vans** all models '84 thru '89
699 **Challenger & Plymouth Saporro** all models '78 thru '83
236 **Colt** all models '71 thru '77
419 **Colt (rear wheel drive)** all models '77 thru '80
610 **Colt & Plymouth Champ (front wheel drive)** all models '78 thru '87
*556 **D50 & Plymouth Arrow Pick-ups** '79 thru '88
234 **Dart & Plymouth Valiant** all 6 cyl models '67 thru '76
*1140 **Daytona & Chrysler Laser** all models '84 thru '88
*545 **Omni & Plymouth Horizon** all models '78 thru '89
*912 **Pick-ups** all full-size models '74 thru '90
*349 **Vans** – Dodge & Plymouth V8 & 6 cyl models '71 thru '89

FIAT
080 **124 Sedan & Wagon** all ohv & dohc models '66 thru '75
094 **124 Sport Coupe & Spider** '68 thru '78
087 **128** all models '72 thru '79
310 **131 & Brava** all models '75 thru '81
038 **850 Sedan, Coupe & Spider** '64 thru '74
479 **Strada** all models '79 thru '82
273 **X1/9** all models '74 thru '80

FORD
*1476 **Aerostar Mini-vans** all models '86 thru '88
788 **Bronco and Pick-ups** '73 thru '79
*880 **Bronco and Pick-ups** '80 thru '90
014 **Cortina MK II** all models except Lotus '66 thru '70
295 **Cortina MK III** 1600 & 2000 ohc '70 thru '76
268 **Courier Pick-up** all models '72 thru '82
789 **Escort & Mercury Lynx** all models '81 thru '90
560 **Fairmont & Mercury Zephyr** all in-line & V8 models '78 thru '83
334 **Fiesta** all models '77 thru '80
754 **Ford & Mercury Full-size,** Ford LTD & Mercury Marquis ('75 thru '82); Ford Custom 500, Country Squire, Crown Victoria & Mercury Colony Park ('75 thru '87); Ford LTD Crown Victoria & Mercury Gran Marquis ('83 thru '87)
359 **Granada & Mercury Monarch** all in-line, 6 cyl & V8 models '75 thru '80
773 **Ford & Mercury Mid-size,** Ford Thunderbird & Mercury Cougar ('75 thru '82); Ford LTD & Mercury Marquis ('83 thru '86); Ford Torino, Gran Torino, Elite, Ranchero pick-up, LTD II, Mercury Montego, Comet, XR-7 & Lincoln Versailles ('75 thru '86)
*654 **Mustang & Mercury Capri** all in-line models & Turbo '79 thru '90
*558 **Mustang & Mercury Capri** all V6 & V8 models '79 thru '89
357 **Mustang V8** all models '64-1/2 thru '73
231 **Mustang II** all 4 cyl, V6 & V8 models '74 thru '78
204 **Pinto** all models '70 thru '74
649 **Pinto & Mercury Bobcat** all models '75 thru '80
*1026 **Ranger & Bronco II** all gasoline models '83 thru '89
*1421 **Taurus & Mercury Sable** '86 thru '90
*1418 **Tempo & Mercury Topaz** all gasoline models '84 thru '89
1338 **Thunderbird & Mercury Cougar/XR7** '83 thru '88
*344 **Vans** all V8 Econoline models '69 thru '90

GENERAL MOTORS
*829 **A-Cars** – Chevrolet Celebrity, Buick Century, Pontiac 6000 & Oldsmobile Cutlass Ciera all models '82 thru '89
*766 **J-Cars** – Chevrolet Cavalier, Pontiac J-2000, Oldsmobile Firenza, Buick Skyhawk & Cadillac Cimarron all models '82 thru '89
*1420 **N-Cars** – Pontiac Grand Am, Buick Somerset and Oldsmobile Calais '85 thru '87; Buick Skylark '86 thru '87

GEO
Tracker – see SUZUKI Samurai (1626)
Prizm – see CHEVROLET Nova (1642)

GMC
Safari – see CHEVROLET ASTRO (1477)
Vans & Pick-ups – see CHEVROLET (420, 831, 345, 1664)

---

* Listings shown with an asterisk (*) indicate model coverage as of this printing. These titles will be periodically updated to include later model years — consult your Haynes dealer for more information.

Haynes Publications Inc., P.O. Box 978, Newbury Park, CA 91320   ●   (818) 889-5400   ●   (805) 498-6703

HAYNES AUTOMOTIVE MANUALS

HONDA
138	360, 600 & Z Coupe all models '67 thru '75
351	Accord CVCC all models '76 thru '83
*1221	Accord all models '84 thru '89
160	Civic 1200 all models '73 thru '79
633	Civic 1300 & 1500 CVCC all models '80 thru '83
297	Civic 1500 CVCC all models '75 thru '79
*1227	Civic all models except 16-valve CRX & 4 WD Wagon '84 thru '86
*601	Prelude CVCC all models '79 thru '89

HYUNDAI
*1552	Excel all models '86 thru '89

ISUZU
*1641	Trooper & Pick-up, all gasoline models '81 thru '89

JAGUAR
098	MK I & II, 240 & 340 Sedans '55 thru '69
*242	XJ6 all 6 cyl models '68 thru '86
*478	XJ12 & XJS all 12 cyl models '72 thru '85
140	XK-E 3.8 & 4.2 all 6 cyl models '61 thru '72

JEEP
*1553	Cherokee, Comanche & Wagoneer Limited all models '84 thru '89
412	CJ all models '49 thru '86

LADA
*413	1200, 1300. 1500 & 1600 all models including Riva '74 thru '86

LANCIA
533	Lancia Beta Sedan, Coupe & HPE all models '76 thru '80

LAND ROVER
314	Series II, IIA & III all 4 cyl gasoline models '58 thru '86
529	Diesel all models '58 thru '80

MAZDA
648	626 Sedan & Coupe (rear wheel drive) all models '79 thru '82
*1082	626 & MX-6 (front wheel drive) all models '83 thru '90
*267	B1600, B1800 & B2000 Pick-ups '72 thru '90
370	GLC Hatchback (rear wheel drive) all models '77 thru '83
757	GLC (front wheel drive) all models '81 thru '86
109	RX2 all models '71 thru '75
096	RX3 all models '72 thru '76
460	RX-7 all models '79 thru '85
*1419	RX-7 all models '86 thru '89

MERCEDES-BENZ
*1643	190 Series all four-cylinder gasoline models, '84 thru '88
346	230, 250 & 280 Sedan, Coupe & Roadster all 6 cyl sohc models '68 thru '72
983	280 123 Series all gasoline models '77 thru '81
698	350 & 450 Sedan, Coupe & Roadster all models '71 thru '80
697	Diesel 123 Series 200D, 220D, 240D, 240TD, 300D, 300CD, 300TD, 4- & 5-cyl incl. Turbo '76 thru '85

MERCURY
See FORD Listing

MG
475	MGA all models '56 thru '62
111	MGB Roadster & GT Coupe all models '62 thru '80
265	MG Midget & Austin Healey Sprite Roadster '58 thru '80

MITSUBISHI
Pick-up – see Dodge D-50 (556)

MORRIS
074	(Austin) Marina 1.8 all models '71 thru '80
024	Minor 1000 sedan & wagon '56 thru '71

NISSAN
*1137	300ZX all Turbo & non-Turbo models '84 thru '86
*1341	Maxima all models '85 thru '89
*771	Pick-ups/Pathfinder gas models '80 thru '88
*876	Pulsar all models '83 thru '86
*982	Sentra all models '82 thru '90
*981	Stanza all models '82 thru '90

OLDSMOBILE
	Custom Cruiser – see BUICK Full-size (1551)
658	Cutlass all standard gasoline V6 & V8 models '74 thru '88
	Cutlass Ciera – see GENERAL MOTORS A-Cars (829)
	Firenza – see GENERAL MOTORS J-Cars (766)
	Ninety-eight – see BUICK Full-size (1551)
	Omega – see PONTIAC Phoenix & Omega (551)

OPEL
157	(Buick) Manta Coupe 1900 all models '70 thru '74

PEUGEOT
161	504 all gasoline models '68 thru '79
663	504 all diesel models '74 thru '83

PLYMOUTH
425	Arrow all models '76 thru '80
	For all other PLYMOUTH titles, see DODGE listing.

PONTIAC
	T1000 – see CHEVROLET Chevette (449)
	J-2000 – see GENERAL MOTORS J-Cars (766)
	6000 – see GENERAL MOTORS A-Cars (829)
1232	Fiero all models '84 thru '88
555	Firebird all V8 models except Turbo '70 thru '81
*867	Firebird all models '82 thru '89
	Full-size Rear Wheel Drive – see Buick, Oldsmobile, Pontiac Full-size (1551)
551	Phoenix & Oldsmobile Omega all X-car models '80 thru '84

PORSCHE
*264	911 all Coupe & Targa models except Turbo '65 thru '87
239	914 all 4 cyl models '69 thru '76
397	924 all models including Turbo '76 thru '82
*1027	944 all models including Turbo '83 thru '89

RENAULT
141	5 Le Car all models '76 thru '83
079	8 & 10 all models with 58.4 cu in engines '62 thru '72
097	12 Saloon & Estate all models 1289 cc engines '70 thru '80
768	15 & 17 all models '73 thru '79
081	16 all models 89.7 cu in & 95.5 cu in engines '65 thru '72
598	18i & Sportwagon all models '81 thru '86
	Alliance & Encore – see AMC (934)
984	Fuego all models '82 thru '85

ROVER
085	3500 & 3500S Sedan 215 cu in engines '68 thru '76
*365	3500 SDI V8 all models '76 thru '85

SAAB
198	95 & 96 V4 all models '66 thru '75
247	99 all models including Turbo '69 thru '80
*980	900 all models including Turbo '79 thru '88

SUBARU
237	1100, 1300, 1400 & 1600 all models '71 thru '79
*681	1600 & 1800 2WD & 4WD all models '80 thru '88

SUZUKI
*1626	Samurai/Sidekick and Geo Tracker all models '86 thru '89

TOYOTA
*1023	Camry all models '83 thru '90
150	Carina Sedan all models '71 thru '74
229	Celica ST, GT & liftback all models '71 thru '77
437	Celica all models '78 thru '81
*935	Celica all models except front-wheel drive and Supra '82 thru '85
680	Celica Supra all models '79 thru '81
1139	Celica Supra all in-line 6-cylinder models '82 thru '86
201	Corolla 1100, 1200 & 1600 all models '67 thru '74
361	Corolla all models '75 thru '79
961	Corolla all models (rear wheel drive) '80 thru '87
*1025	Corolla all models (front wheel drive) '84 thru '88
*636	Corolla Tercel all models '80 thru '82
230	Corona & MK II all 4 cyl sohc models '69 thru '74
360	Corona all models '74 thru '82
*532	Cressida all models '78 thru '82
313	Land Cruiser all models '68 thru '82
200	MK II all 6 cyl models '72 thru '76
*1339	MR2 all models '85 thru '87
304	Pick-up all models '69 thru '78
*656	Pick-up all models '79 thru '90
787	Starlet all models '81 thru '84

TRIUMPH
112	GT6 & Vitesse all models '62 thru '74
113	Spitfire all models '62 thru '81
028	TR2, 3, 3A, & 4A Roadsters '52 thru '67
031	TR250 & 6 Roadsters '67 thru '76
322	TR7 all models '75 thru '81

VW
091	411 & 412 all 103 cu in models '68 thru '73
036	Bug 1200 all models '54 thru '66
039	Bug 1300 & 1500 '65 thru '70
159	Bug 1600 all basic, sport & super (curved windshield) models '70 thru '74
110	Bug 1600 Super all models (flat windshield) '70 thru '72
238	Dasher all gasoline models '74 thru '81
*884	Rabbit, Jetta, Scirocco, & Pick-up all gasoline models '74 thru '89 & Convertible '80 thru '89
451	Rabbit, Jetta & Pick-up all diesel models '77 thru '84
082	Transporter 1600 all models '68 thru '79
226	Transporter 1700, 1800 & 2000 all models '72 thru '79
084	Type 3 1500 & 1600 all models '63 thru '73
1029	Vanagon all air-cooled models '80 thru '83

VOLVO
203	120, 130 Series & 1800 Sports '61 thru '73
129	140 Series all models '66 thru '74
244	164 all models '68 thru '75
*270	240 Series all models '74 thru '90
400	260 Series all models '75 thru '82
*1550	740 & 760 Series all models '82 thru '88

SPECIAL MANUALS
1479	Automotive Body Repair & Painting Manual
1654	Automotive Electrical Manual
1480	Automotive Heating & Air Conditioning Manual
482	Fuel Injection Manual
299	SU Carburetors thru '88
393	Weber Carburetors thru '79
300	Zenith/Stromberg CD Carburetors thru '76

See your dealer for other available titles

Over 100 Haynes motorcycle manuals also available

6-1-90

---

* Listings shown with an asterisk (*) indicate model coverage as of this printing. These titles will be periodically updated to include later model years — consult your Haynes dealer for more information.

Haynes Publications Inc., P.O. Box 978, Newbury Park, CA 91320 ● (818) 889-5400 ● (805) 498-6703